Essentials of Modern Literary Tibetan

Essentials of Modern Literary Tibetan

A Reading Course and Reference Grammar

Melvyn C. Goldstein

with
Gelek Rimpoche
and
Lobsang Phuntshog

University of California Press
Berkeley Los Angeles Oxford

University of California Press
Berkeley and Los Angeles, California

University of California Press, Ltd.
Oxford, England

Library of Congress Cataloging-in-Publication Data

Goldstein, Melvyn C.
Essentials of modern literary Tibetan: a reading course and reference grammar / Melvyn C. Goldstein with Gelek Rimpoche and Lobsang Phuntshog.
p. cm.
Includes examples of Tibetan texts with English translation.
ISBN 0-520-07622-2 (alk. paper)
1. Tibetan language—Grammar. 2. Tibetan language—Textbooks for foreign speakers. 3. Tibetan language—Readers. 4. Tibetan languages—Rhetoric. I. Rimpoche, Gelek. II. Phuntshog, Lobsang. III. Title.
PL3613.G55 1991
495'.482421—dc20
91-11882
CIP

9 8 7 6 5 4 3

The paper used in this publication meets the minimum requirements of American National Standard for Information Sciences—Permanence of Paper for Printed Library Materials, ANSI Z39.48-1984 ∞

Contents

Lesson Thirteen 329

Lesson Fourteen 347

Preface

ཡིག་ཕྱེད་གོ་བས་ཀློག

"Half of the words are read by implication"

Anon. Tibetan

This Tibetan saying pithily summarizes the main difficulty Westerners face in learning to read Tibet fluently. A knowledge of the various particles that comprise the Tibetan grammar is essential for learning how to read Tibetan, but this is not sufficient by itself. In all too many cases, the semantic context, that is to say, the meaning of what precedes and follows the clause or phrase in question, determines what the grammatical particles themselves mean.

This book, therefore, was written to assist beginners not only to master the multiplicity of Tibetan grammatical particles and markers, but also to develop the skills to cope with the semantic component of Tibetan grammar.

Lessons One and Two present the thirty letters of the Tibetan alphabet together with a description of how they are pronounced. Many instructional programs teach the pronunciation of written Tibetan by having students repeat the sounds after the instructor, and this is a good way to learn. However, for those readers who are using this book on their own, *Essentials of Modern Literary Tibetan* provides an explanation of the main rules underlying pronunciation, and provides spoken Tibetan equivalents for the first five lessons as well as a tape of these lessons (through Case Western Reserve University's Center for Research on Tibet). However, *Essentials of Modern Literary Tibetan* is not meant to be a textbook of spoken Tibetan. Spoken and written Tibetan pronunciations differ, and this book will not devote a great deal of time to these differences or on subtleties of spoken pronunciation. The aim of including pronunciation rules here is simple—to teach users how to pronounce the letters and syllables they will be reading. *Developing reading comprehension* of modern written Tibetan is the goal of this book.

Students who have studied spoken Tibetan using Goldstein and Nornang's *Modern Spoken Tibetan* will notice that the system used to transcribe the spoken language here is slightly different. The current system simplifies the more linguistically complicated system used earlier by employing symbols for the Tibetan sounds which are closer to English equivalents and thus easier to learn. For example, the system used in this book no longer employs the letter /q/ for the Tibetan letter ཀ་, but instead uses the most similar English letter—/g/—even though /g/ differs from the Tibetan sound by being voiced. The rationale for representing Tibetan sounds by a neutral letter such as /q/ was to avoid predisposing English speakers to voice the Tibetan sound, but I now believe that this approach has been counter-productive and has hampered students from readily learning how to pronounce Tibetan.

Essentials of Modern Literary Tibetan will teach reading skills in a range of genres of written Tibetan. It moves quickly to cover essential grammatical structures so that stories can be introduced. The sentences in the lessons in Part One utilize both the basic colloquial and literary written styles, but the readings reflect the neoclassical style which is the basis for both of these. This style is becoming the standard for modern literary Tibetan. The aim throughout the lessons is to accustom the reader to understand more and more complex (and, therefore, more realistic) constructions. Part One provides a solid foundation in Tibetan morphology, syntax, and vocabulary.

Part Two contains both lessons and extended reading examples taken from novels, folk tales, histories, newspapers and magazines. Throughout the book the readings are translated as close to the original Tibetan as possible, even if this results in somewhat awkward English constructions. We hope this will facilitate the rapid comprehension of the basic principles involved.

Part Three consists of an English-Tibetan Glossary, a verb declension chart listing the different stems of the verbs used in the book, and an appendix with five selections illustrating the genre of communist political essays.

A critical dimension of this book is its ability to be used as a reference grammar. The large glossary at the end of the book lists each grammatical particle or construction used in the text together with the lesson and sub-section(s) where it occurs and is explained. Consequently, whenever the user comes across an unfamiliar particle, whether one month or five years after the initial encounter in the lessons, it will be easy to find the section or sections that explain and give examples of this particle.

This text, therefore, provides a step-by-step graded introduction to basic Tibetan syntax and grammar, a solid working vocabulary, and a permanent reference grammar which can be referred to long after these lessons have been completed.

Acknowledgments

I wish to thank the many colleagues and students who have played a role in the writing and testing of this book, especially Dr. Micheal Aris for pre-testing the first part of the ms. and his student Victoria Sujata for keeping track of the numerous inconsistencies and mistakes they discovered in class. I also must express my deep gratitude to my student Kaerin Stephens, who painstakingly read through two draft manuscripts and made very useful suggestions. I am also in debt to Pierre Robillard for customizing his excellent Tibetan Macintosh font for use in the book.

And last, but certainly not least, I want to acknowledge my gratitude to the International Research and Studies Program, Center for International Education, U.S. Department of Education (G008640390-87) for funding the research and preparation of this book.

List of Abbreviations

adj.	adjective
adj. comp.	comparative adjective stem
abbr.	abbreviation
cc.	clause connective
ch.	phonetic rendering of a Chinese term in Tibetan
cf.	compare
dat. loc.	dative-locative case
eng.	phonetic rendering of an English term in Tibetan
f.	future
fut. compl.	future complements
gen.	genitive case
h.	honorific
id.	idiom
imp.	imperative
inf.	infinitive
inst.	instrumental case
lit.	literally
n.	noun
neg.	negative
nh.	non-honorific
nom.	nominalizer
p.	past
perf.	perfect
pl.	plural
pres.	present
pres. compl.	present complement
p.n.	proper name
sm.	same as
usu.	usually
usu. compl.	usual complement
va.	active verb
vi.	involuntary verb

PART ONE

Lesson One

1.1 Introduction to the Tibetan language

The written Tibetan language has 30 consonants, 4 written vowels, and 1 inherent (unwritten) vowel. *Spoken* Tibetan, however, contains at least 35 consonants and 9 spoken vowels, and the standard pronunciation of written Tibetan uses all 44 of these. Consequently, there is no simple one to one equivalence. In addition to this, however, Tibetan is not read *phonetically.* Combinations of letters in syllables are often pronounced totally differently from the inherent quality of the individual letters. For example, the seven letters *bsgrubs* are actually pronounced *drub.* This transformation is partly due to the evolution of Central Tibetan into a tonal language since many of the consonant clusters that were once pronounced (and still are in some areas) have become tonal in Central Tibetan. One of the difficult tasks facing beginners, therefore, is to learn how combinations of the written vowels and consonants are pronounced. To assist readers in this task, the first two lessons contain a set of rules, and lessons 1-5 include phonemic equivalents of the written letters (in colloquial Lhasa dialect). A cassette tape of these lessons is available from Case Western Reserve University's Center for Research on Tibet (238 Mather Memorial Building, Cleveland, Ohio 44106; ph. 216 368-2264; fax 216 368-5334). The reader is urged to use this tape regularly.

The Tibetan words used in the first part of this lesson do not have to be memorized and will not appear in the glossary unless they occur in other lessons. They are used primarily to illustrate various linguistic features such as tone and length rather than because they are common terms.

1.2 Tone

Tone is a distinctive feature of the Tibetan phonological system. It refers to the pitch of vowels. For example, whereas it makes no difference in English whether the word *dog* is pronounced in a very high pitch or a very low and deep pitch, in Tibetan such differences are critical and signal differences equivalent to those which would exist in English if different vowels were used. A line under a vowel indicates low tone and a line above, high tone. Thus, gū (high tone) means *body* while gu̲ (low tone) means *nine.*

In addition to these two tones, Tibetan also has a released glottal stop which we call a falling tone. It is marked by an oblique line over a vowel, for example, dāà ("tiger"). A lengthy set of practice drills that teach how to differentiate tones is provided in Appendix B.

1.3 Vowel Length

In English, the meaning of the word "dog" does not change if we lengthen the pronunciation of the "o" vowel so that it sounds like "doooooog." In Tibetan, however, the length of the vowel differentiates words just as different consonants do in English. There are, fortunately, only two relevant vowel lengths in Tibetan: relatively long and relatively short. Long vowels will be noted by repeating the vowel. For example, in ri ("hill") the vowel is short, but in rii ("to fall") it is long.

1.4 The thirty written letters

The 30 written letters in the Tibetan alphabet are listed below, together with their approximate pronunciations and the notational symbols I shall employ for them in this book. Two of these 30, འ་ and ཨ་, are vowels, and the remaining 28 are consonants. It should be noted that many letters such as ཀ་ and ག་ differ only in the *tone* of the accompanying vowel—not in the quality of the sound.

Written Form	Phonetic Notation	English Pronunciation Equivalent
1. ཀ་	gā[1]	similar to the "g" in gone
2. ཁ་	kā	similar to the "k" in kill
3. ག་	ga or ka	similar to the "g" in gone or the "k" in kill
4. ང་	ŋa	similar to the "ng" in sing-a-long
5. ཅ་	jā	similar to the "j" in jar
6. ཆ་	chā	similar to the "ch" in champ
7. ཇ་	ja or cha	similar to either the "j" in jar or the "ch" in champ
8. ཉ་	ña	similar to the "ny" in canyon
9. ཏ་	dā	similar to the "d" in dig
10. ཐ་	tā	similar to the "t" in tap

[1] All letters having no written vowel are considered to possess an inherent "a" vowel.

11. ད་	da̲ or ta̲	similar to the "d" in dig or the "t" in tap
12. ན་	na̲	similar to the "n" in now
13. པ་	bā	similar to the "b" in bet
14. ཕ་	pā	similar to the "p" in pat
15. བ་	ba̲ or pa̲	similar to the "b" in bet or the "p" in pet
16. མ་	ma̲	similar to the "m" in met
17. ཙ་	dzā	similar to the "dds" in adds
18. ཚ	tsā	similar to the "ts" in Patsy
19. ཛ་	dza̲	similar to the "dds" in adds
20. ཝ་	wa̲	similar to the "w" in war
21. ཞ་	sha̲	similar to the "sh" in ship
22. ཟ་	sa̲	similar to the "s" in sip
23. འ་	a̲	similar to the "a" in ah
24. ཡ་	ya̲	similar to the "y" in yet
25. ར་	ra̲	similar to the "r" in red
26. ལ་	la̲	similar to the "l" in let
27. ཤ་	shā	similar to the "sh" in ship
28. ས་	sā	similar to the "s" in sit
29. ཧ་	hā	similar to the "h" in hit
30. ཨ་	ā	similar to the "a" in ah

In addition to the above letters, there are also a number of new consonant combinations which are used to render foreign sounds such as those found in English. For example, the English sound "f" is written as ཧྥ. Other combinations will be explained as they occur.

1.4.1 Steps in writing Tibetan letters

Tibetan uses three main scripts. The one used in printed matter is called *uchen,* or literally "big head." There is also a related "headless" script known as *umay* that is often used in handwritten manuscripts, and a difficult script known as *kyu* that is used in correspondence and notes. The *uchen* script is the one used throughout this text since it is what you will encounter in books and newspapers.

In the diagram that follows, the sequence of strokes used in writing Tibetan letters is presented. You will note that they go from left to right.

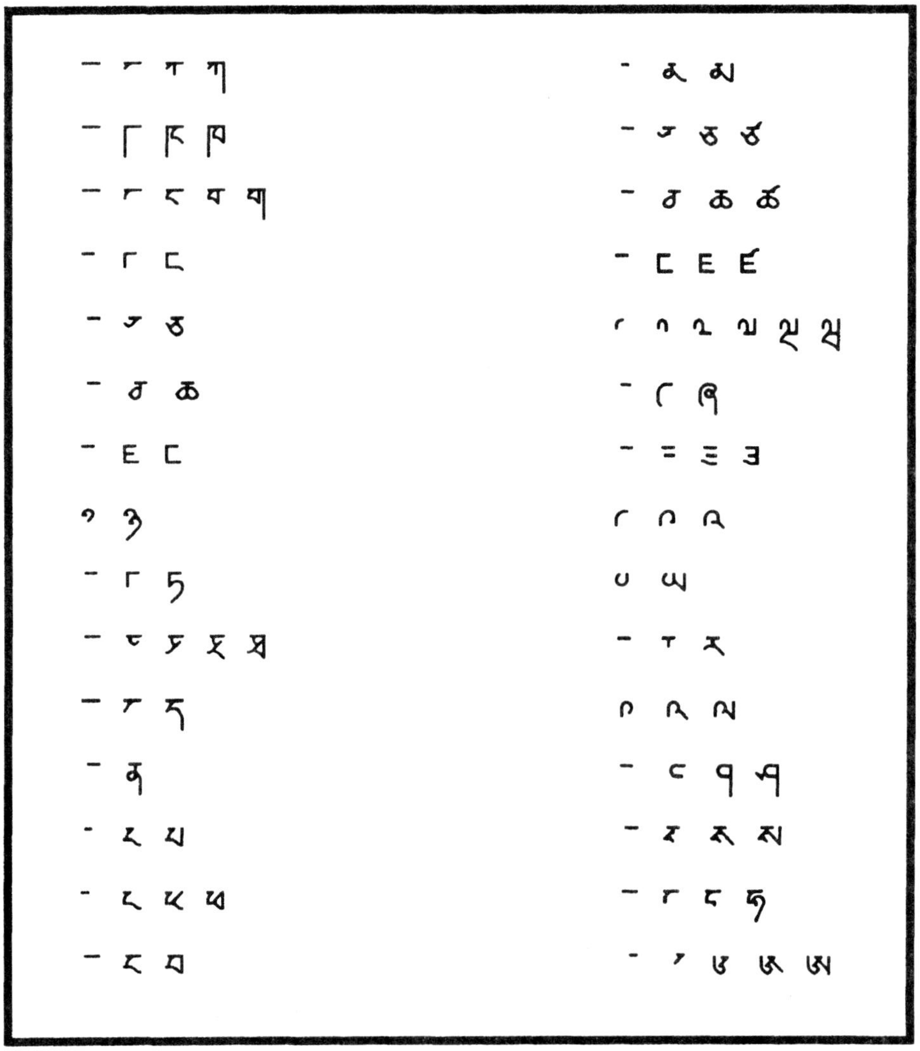

Tibetan consonants, by and large, are organized in series of four sounds on the basis of where they are pronounced in the mouth. The first consonant in such series is typically high tone and unaspirated, the second is high tone but aspirated, the third is low tone, and the fourth is nasalized. The consonants ཀ་ཁ་ག་ང་ represent this type of paradigm.

1.4.2. The consonants: ཀ་ཁ་ག་ང་

Each of these four consonants linguistically is called a velar stop because the middle part of the tongue touches the velar section of the (roof of the) mouth and "stops" the air flow momentarily. For those unfamiliar with these linguistic terms, use the rough pronunciation equivalencies provided above and listen carefully to the tape and your instructor.

ཀ་ and ཁ་ are high tone consonants made in the same part of the mouth. However, whereas the latter is pronounced with aspiration, that is, with a puff of air following the "k"sound, the former is unaspirated. The aspirated "k" sound is equivalent to the initial English consonant "k" in words such as **k**ey or **k**eep. The unaspirated "k" sound is technically an *unvoiced* velar stop and occurs in English *only* following "s" consonants, for example in the word "skip." It never occurs at the beginning of words. However, its pronunciation approximates the voiced initial "g" sound in words such as **g**oat or **g**ive, and will be transcribed in this book as "g."

The "ŋ" sound is also difficult for English speakers since it does not occur at the beginning of English words. The best one can do to approximate this sound is pronounce the phrase "sing-*nga*-long while emphasizing the second "nga." Examples of these consonants and their pronunciation are:

ཀ་	gā	(the letter ཀ་)	ག་	ga̱	(what)
ཁ་	kā	(mouth)	ང་	ŋa̱	(I)

1.4.3 The consonants: ཅ་ཆ་ཇ་ཉ་

These consonants linguistically are known as *palatal stops* because the upper front part of the tongue articulates against the palatal area on the roof of the mouth and stops the flow of air momentarily. The first of this series of sounds is high tone and unaspirated, the second is high tone and aspirated, the third is low tone but varies as to whether it is pronounced "j" or "ch." The fourth consonant is nasal.

ཅ་	jā	(the letter ཅ་)	ཇ་	cha̱	(tea)
ཆ་	chā	(a part)	ཉ་	ña̱	(fish)

1.4.4 The consonants: ཏ་ཐ་ད་ན་

These consonants are linguistically known as *alveolar stops* because the tip of the tongue articulates against the alveolar region (just behind the teeth) and stops the flow of air momentarily. Again the first of this series is high tone and unaspirated, the second is high tone and aspirated, the third is low tone but varies as to whether it is pronounced "d" or "t." The fourth consonant is nasal.

ཏ་	dā	(the letter ཏ་)	ད་	da̱	(now)
ཐ་	tā	(the letter ཐ་)	ན་	na̱	(if)

1.4.5 The consonants: པ་ཕ་བ་མ་

These consonants are known as *bilabial stops.* The lower lip articulates against the upper lip and blocks the flow of air momentarily. This series follows the same pattern as those presented above, བ་ being pronounced sometimes "b" and other times "p."

པ་	bā	(a past tense verbal particle)	བ་	pa̱	(cow)
ཕ་	pā	(father)	མ་	ma̱	(mother)

1.4.6 The consonants: ཙ་ཚ་ཛ་ཝ་

The first three consonants follow the basic pattern in that ཙ་ is high tone voiceless unaspirated, ཚ་ is high tone voiceless aspirated, and ཛ་ is low tone voiceless unaspirated.

The last consonant, ཝ་, is not a nasal consonant. It is pronounced with a "w" sound.

ཙ་	dzā	(the letter ཙ་)	ཛ་	dza̱	(the letter ཛ་)
ཚ་	tsā	(hot)	ཝ་	wa̱	(fox)

The remaining 11 consonants do not follow the above described pattern . The consonant chart presented earlier in this lesson should be consulted for their pronunciations.

1.5 Vowels

Literary Tibetan has five vowels, one of which ("a"), as mentioned above, is not written and inheres in otherwise unmarked syllables. Of the remaining four, three are written above the letter and one (the vowel "u") is written below:

Written Form	Pronunciation	Example
inherent	a (as in "father")	ཀ་ (gā)
ོ	o (as in "so")	ཀོ་ (gō)
ེ	e (as in "met")	ཀེ་ (gē)
ུ	u (as in "sue")	ཀུ་ (gū)
ི	i (as in "see")	ཀི་ (gī)

Examples of these simple syllables follow. Remember that when there is no written vowel above or below the vowel, the sound "a" is pronounced.

མི་	ཆུ་	ལོ་	ཚེ་	མེ་	བུ་	ཐོ་	ན་	ཇ་	སུ་	ཕོ་
mi	chū	lo	tsē	me	pu	tō	na	cha	sū	pō
person	water	year	life	fire	son	list	if	tea	who	male

In addition to these, there are also a several spoken vowels which have no written form. These include:

- ɛ approximately the "a" in the English "mate"
- ɔ approximately the "aw" in the English "saw"
- ə approximately the "a" in the English "alone"
- ö approximately the "eu" in the French "seul"
- ü approximately the "ü" in the German "füllen" (or the u in the French "pur")

The two "e" vowels (e and ɛ) are difficult for English speakers to hear and produce. They differ in that the "e" sound is made higher in the front of the mouth with the teeth very close together, while the teeth are wider apart for the "ɛ" sound and the tongue is also lower in the mouth.

1.6 Pronunciation drill

Sequences of words have been compiled to facilitate the development of oral/aural skills in differentiating difficult sounds and phonological features such as tone and length. These are available in Appendix B. Listen to them on the tape and try to reproduce them. Do not worry about memorizing the written Tibetan. It is included only to allow a native Tibetan speaker to identify and pronounce the words.

1.7 Structure and pronunciation of complex syllables

Tibetan orthography separates syllables by a dot (called a tsēg or tsā) immediately following each syllable (་). For example, ག་མ་ (ga ma) are two syllables whereas གམ་ (gam) is only one.

Syllables are either *simple* or *complex*. Simple syllables consist of a single consonant and vowel. They are exemplified by the examples cited above. Complex syllables consist of clusters of consonants and a vowel. All syllables have a "*root*" or "*head*" consonant to which other consonants are joined by being *prefixed, suffixed, superfixed,* and *subfixed.* We shall number the possible consonant slots surrounding the root consonant (labeled **X** in the diagram below) as follows:

	v			
	2			
1	**X**	**4**	**5**	**(v = vowel)**
	3			
	v			

1.7.1 Complex syllables

As shown above, there are five slots where consonants can be added to the head consonant. Since these slots are optional, a variety of combinations occur. However, while all thirty letters can fill the head slot, the other slots (1-5) have restricted membership. Consequently, it is necessary to learn which letters occur in which slots, as well as the changes in the form and pronunciation that these letters can undergo when added to a head consonant.

List of letters which can fill the five syllable slots

slot-1 (prefixed letters)	ག་ད་བ་མ་འ་
slot-2 (superfixed letters)	ར་ལ་ས་
slot-3 (subfixed letters)	ཡ་ར་ལ་ཝ་འ་
slot-4 (suffixed letters)	ག་ང་ད་ན་བ་མ་འ་ར་ལ་ས་
slot-5 (post-suffixed letters)	ས་

In this lesson we will examine the suffixed letters used in slots 4 and 5. The other three slots will be dealt with in Lesson 2.

1.7.2 Slot-4 (suffixed letters)

As indicated above, ten letters fill this slot: ག་ང་ད་ན་བ་འ་མ་ར་ལ་ས་. Letters in slot-4 are pronounced after the vowel.

1.7.2.1 The suffixed letter ག་

This letter adds either a final "g" sound to the initial consonant or makes the vowel falling tone (as illustrated below). Reading pronunciations typically pronounce the "g" sound whereas spoken pronunciations use the falling vowel tone, except in disyllabic compounds where the second syllable begins with a consonant.

When one encounters a complex syllable *the first step is to identify which of the letters is the root.* Because vowels are *always* written above or below the "root" letter, syllables with vowels are easy to decipher.

In situations without written vowels, identifying the root letter can be difficult at first and a process of elimination of options is useful. For example, if you encountered the syllable ནག་ you would see that it consists of the consonant "n" and the consonant "g." Since there is no written vowel, the inherent "a" vowel would be inferred. But which is the root letter? The answer is that "n" is the root letter and "g" is a slot-4 (suffixed) letter. The incorrect hypothetical alternative would have been that "g" is the root letter and "n" is a prefixed letter. We know that this hypothetical alternative is impossible because "n" *never* occurs as a slot-1 letter (see section 1.7.1). On the other hand, "g" does occur as a slot-4 consonant. The syllable is therefore pronounced na̲g.

Similarly, the syllable ངག་ must be read as ŋa̲g since ང never occurs in the 1-slot , and ག can fill the 4-slot.

Some combinations using the letter "g" in the 4-slot are:

ནག་	na̲g or nà̲à	black
ལག་	la̲g or là̲à	hand
ཐག་	tāg or tāà	rope
དུག་	tu̲g or tù̲ù	poison
འོག་	ɔ̲g or ɔ̲̀ɔ̀	under

Notice that the last example, ɔ̲g, begins with the letter vowel "a" (འ). When it functions as the root letter and has a written vowel, the vowel is pronounced low tone.

1.7.2.2 The suffixed letter ང་

This consonant usually adds the sound "ŋ" after the vowel.

རང་	སོང་	ཆང་	རིང་	ལུང་	ཡོང་	ཉུང་	མིང་
ra̲ŋ	sōŋ	chāŋ	ri̲ŋ	lu̲ŋ	yo̲ŋ	ñu̲ŋ	mi̲ŋ
self	went	beer	long	handle	come	few	name

In colloquial Tibetan, however, the "ŋ" endings are sometimes pronounced as nasalized vowels, i.e., vowels that contain an "n" sound made simultaneously with the vowel. For example, སོང་ could also be pronounced sōn and ཡོང་, yo̲n. Reading pronunciations tend to pronounce the "ŋ" sound whereas spoken pronunciations usually use the nasalized vowels. Examples of the nasalized versions of the above words are:

རང་	སོང་	ཆང་	ཡོང་	ཉུང་
ran	sōn	chān	yon	ñun

1.7.2.3 The suffixed letters ད་ and ས་

These consonants are never pronounced as a "d" or "s" sound. Instead, they:

1) make the tone of the vowel falling tone—high tone vowels become high and falling, and low tone vowels become low falling. For example, རེད་ is pronounced *not* as red but rather as reè and མེས་ is pronounced meè.

2) These suffixed consonants also change the quality of the vowel sound for some vowels. These vowel changes follow a regular pattern:

a becomes ɛ   o becomes ö   u becomes ü

"e" and "i" do not change their inherent vowel quality although the vowel becomes falling tone.

For example:

ནད་	བོད་	ལུད་	མེད་	སུས་	ལས་	གོས་	རིས་
nɛɛ̀	pöö̀	lüǜ	meè	sūǜ	lɛɛ̀	göö̀	riì
sick	Tibet	manure	none	by whom	work	clothes	design

1.7.2.4 The suffixed letter ན་

This suffixed letter lengthens and nasalizes the vowel it follows. The tone remains the same although there are a series of vowel shifts analogous to those we encountered with the suffixed letter ད་.

Vowel Shifts: a becomes ɛn   u becomes ün
o becomes ön   e becomes en
i becomes in

ལན་	ཀུན་	ཟིན་	རིན་
lɛn	gūn	sin	rin
message	all	catch	price

1.7.2.5 The suffixed letter མ་

This suffixed letter adds an "m" sound. The tone is unchanged.

ཧམ་	གམ་	ལམ་	དོམ་	ཙམ་
hām	g<u>a</u>m	l<u>a</u>m	t<u>o</u>m	dzām
lie	near	road	bear	about

1.7.2.6 The suffixed letter བ་

This suffixed letter adds a "b" sound equivalent to the final "p" in the English word "plop." It also changes the "a" vowel to an "ə" vowel. The "ə" vowel is pronounced like the "a" vowel in "alone."

ཁབ་	ནུབ་	ཧོབ་	ཡིབ་
kə̄p	n<u>u</u>p	hōp	y<u>i</u>p
needle	west	sudden	hide

1.7.2.7 The suffixed letter ར་

This letter either lengthens the vowel or adds a final "r" sound. It changes the quality of the "o" vowel to that of "ɔ" (the "aw" sound in "saw"). Other vowels are unchanged.

པར་	གསེར་	ཟུར་	ནོར་	མར་
bār	sēē (sēr)	s<u>uu</u> (s<u>u</u>r)	n<u>ɔɔ</u> (n<u>ɔ</u>r)	m<u>aa</u> (m<u>a</u>r)
photo	gold	corner	wealth	butter

1.7.2.8 The suffixed letter ལ་

This letter lengthens the vowel and alters its sound quality as follows:

a becomes ɛɛ

u becomes üü

o becomes öö

The "e" vowel is lengthened but does not change its quality.

བལ་	ཕུལ་	རིལ་	ཚོལ་	ཟེལ་
p<u>ɛɛ</u>	pǖü	r<u>ii</u>	tsȫö	s<u>ee</u>
wool	give	round	look for	shavings, chips

1.7.2.9 The suffixed letter འ་

When this letter is used in the 4-slot, it marks the root letter of certain otherwise ambiguous syllables where both letters can be used in the 1-slot and 4-slot. For example, in the syllable དགའ་, it indicates that the root letter is the "ག" and not the "ད," which is a prefixed letter. Thus it is pronounced "ga." By convention, then, དག་ without the འ་ would be read as tag or dag, the "g" being a 4-slot letter here.

This letter, however, also alters the main vowel sound if it has a vowel above it. It is frequently used in this capacity to mark changes in grammatical cases (inflections). The most common instance of this is འི, which changes the main vowel as follows:

a becomes εε —	ང་ (ŋa - "I")	becomes	ངའི་ (ŋεε -"my")
u becomes üü —	སུ་ (sū - "who")	becomes	སུའི་ (sǖü - "whose")
o becomes öö —	མོ་ (mo - "she")	becomes	མོའི་ (möö -"her")
e becomes ee —	དེ་ (de -"that")	becomes	དེའི་ (dee - "of that")

1.7.3 Slot-5 consonants

Only one consonant ས་ (s) can occur in this slot,[2] and when it does, the 4-slot must also be filled. It does not change the quality of thc vowel:[3]

སེམས་	ལངས་	ལུགས་	ཕོགས་
sēm	laŋ	lug or luù	phɔ̄ɔ̀
mind	stood up	system	salary

1.8 The syllabic nature of the Tibetan language

A difficult dimension of Tibetan for English speakers is its syllabic nature. Almost every syllable in Tibetan carries independent semantic meaning. Thus, the reader must determine whether a syllable is functioning alone with its basic meaning or as a part of a disyllabic or multisyllabic word. For example, both the English and Tibetan words for "rifle" are disyllabic (the Tibetan = མེ་མདའ་). However, unlike the English word of which neither of the two syllables (ri-fle) has independent meaning, both of the Tibetan syllables (men-da) do and can occur independently and in other compounds: མེ་ means "fire" and མདའ་ means "arrow."

To make matters more difficult, written Tibetan does not indicate the breaks between words. Rather, written Tibetan consists of a series of syllables each separated from the others by a syllable marking dot called a ཚེག་, regardless of which syllables

---

2 Ancient Tibetan, however, used other letters there.

3 It actually adds a kind of falling tone component to nasals, which we have decided to leave unmarked for simplicity's sake.

group together to form words. Consequently, the burden of grouping the syllables into words falls entirely on the reader, and it is very common for beginners to misgroup the syllables and create horrendous translations, for example, by misdividing the phrase "the teach-er's beau-ti-ful glass-es" as *theteach ersbeau ti fulglass es.* This is one of the most difficult features of literary Tibetan for beginners, and the following chapters are designed to help you develop the skill of correctly grouping syllables into words by stressing not only basic recurring vocabulary items but also important grammatical clues. Ultimately, however, only time and experience will reduce the frequency of such "grouping" errors.

From this point on, Tibetan words should be memorized. Note that colloquial pronunciations will be used throughout the book.

1.9 Sentence and verb types: introduction

There are four basic types of verbs in Tibetan (active, involuntary, linking, existential). Each defines a type of sentence and clause. "Active" verbs (and constructions) express action done by actors, e.g., "He *hit* the ball." They are, therefore, roughly equivalent to transitive sentences in English. "Involuntary" verbs (and constructions) express unintentional, non-purposive action or states, e.g., "I *got sick.*" or " I *saw* it." They are similar to intransitive verb constructions in English. Thus, in the sentence "I *looked* there and *saw* John," "looked" is an active verb since the actor purposely did the looking, and "saw" is an involuntary verb since it represents a non-purposive state, the image appearing in the subject's vision.

Whereas English uses the copula (the verb "be") both for sentences that link the subject to an object, e.g., "He *is* a boy," and for sentences that express existence, e.g., "He *is* here," Tibetan requires two separate verb classes—the former requires a linking verb and the latter an existential verb.

Simple linking constructions will be discussed in this lesson. Existential constructions will be introduced in Lesson Two, and active and involuntary constructions in Lessons Three and Five.

1.10 Linking verbs and sentences

As indicated above, Tibetan uses different verbs to express the ideas that we express in English by means of the verb "to be."

The linking sentence typically consists of a subject, an object, and a linking verb. The verb links the subject to the object so that the object is either a class to which the subject belongs or a definition of the subject. For example, in the sentence "This is a book," a linking verb is required since the verb explains or defines what "this" is.

There are two main linking verbs in Tibetan: ཡིན་ and རེད་. A third verb ཡིན་པ་རེད་ is occasionally used in modern colloquial materials.

Unlike English linking verbs (is, are, were, etc.), these verbs, as discussed below, *do not* express tense or number, both of which are conveyed in Tibetan by context or other linguistic markers.

The first of these verbs (ཡིན་) is normally used with first person subjects.

a. ང་པད་མ་ཡིན།[4]
ŋa̱ bɛ̄ɛ̄ma yi̱n
i pema is/[5]
I am Pema.

Note that པད་མ་ is not pronounced pɛ̄ɛ̄ma, as you would expect from the preceding rules, but bɛ̄ɛ̄ma. When a single syllable is part of a disyllabic compound such as Pema, a series of shifts occur. These are discussed in Lesson Two, section five. For the time being, simply pronounce the words as they appear in the pronunciation transliteration.

b. ང་ཚོང་པ་ཡིན།
ŋa̱ tsōŋba yi̱n
i trader is/
I am a trader.

The linking verbs རེད་ and ཡིན་པ་རེད་, on the other hand, are usually used with third person subjects. However, there is no fixed rule and they too occasionally occur with first person subjects, although ཡིན་ never occurs with third person subjects.

c. ཁོ་པད་མ་རེད།
kō bɛ̄ɛ̄ma re̱è

---

[4] The vertical line is called a ཤད་. It is placed after sentences and various kinds of clauses. It will be noted in the interlinear translation by a slash mark (/).

[5] Note that all sentences in the first eight lessons contain an "interlinear" translation such as that presented in this line. These translations identify the words and particles in the order they were written in Tibetan and are included to assist you to break down the sentence correctly into its meaningful parts.

he pema is/
He is Pema.

d. ནོར་བུ་དགེ་རྒན་ཡིན་པ་རེད། [རྒན་ (rgan) is a complex syllable that includes a 2-slot letter ("r") that is discussed in Lesson Two. For the time being treat it as if རྒན་ were written གན་.]

nɔɔbu gegɛn yimbəreè [ཡིན་ is pronounced yim rather than yin here because it is part of a disyllabic compound which is followed immediately by the letter པ. This is discussed in Lesson Two. Note also that the "a" vowel in པ་ is pronounced bə rather than ba. This is common after an "i" vowel and is also discussed in Lesson Two.]

norbu teacher is/
Norbu is a teacher.

ཡིན་པ་རེད་ and རེད་ actually have slightly different connotations. When a writer uses ཡིན་པ་རེད་ rather than རེད་ he conveys to the reader that he is less certain about the validity of what he is writing. Sentence d. conveys the idea that "it is said" or "it seems he is a teacher." The writer, therefore, through the use of ཡིན་པ་རེད་, is expressing some uncertainty about whether "he" (the subject) is really a teacher. However, at this stage of learning Tibetan, both of these will be translated the same.

Second person statements are constructed the same as the third person constructions cited above.

e. ཁྱེད་རང་ནོར་བུ་རེད། [ཁྱེད་ is a type of complex syllable (khyed) that will be discussed in Lesson Two. For the time being simply treat it as ཁེད་ and pronounce it kē.]

kēraŋ nɔɔbu reè
you norbu is/
You are Norbu.

Word order in linking sentences, therefore, normally follows the rule: Subject + Object + Verb.

The subject of a linking sentence is usually not marked (or identified by another particle) but it can be, as we see in the following examples where the particle ནི་ (meaning roughly "as-for") identifies the subject.

f. ཞིང་པ་ནི་བོད་པ་རེད།
shiŋbəni pöba reè

farmer as-for[6] Tibetan is/
The farmer is a Tibetan.

g. ཞྭ་མོ་ནི་སེར་པོ་རེད།
sha̲moni sēēbo [sērbo] re̲è
hat as-for yellow is/
The hat is yellow.

The subject in a linking construction can also be modified by the addition of a demonstrative such as "that" (དེ་).

h. ཚོང་པ་དེ་བོད་པ་ཡིན་པ་རེད།
tsōŋba de̲ pö̲ba yi̲mbəreè
trader that tibetan is/
That (the) trader is Tibetan.

i. བོད་པ་དེ་ཞིང་པ་རེད།
pö̲ba de̲ shi̲ŋbə re̲è
tibetan that farmer is/
That Tibetan is a farmer.

j. དེབ་དེ་ནག་པོ་རེད།
te̲p de̲ na̲go [na̲gbo] re̲è
book that black is/
That book is black.

Demonstratives are sometimes used in combination with ནི་

k. བོད་པ་དེ་ནི་ཞིང་པ་རེད།
pö̲ba de̲ni shi̲ŋbə re̲è
tibetan that as-for farmer is/
That Tibetan is a farmer.

Note that there is no change in meaning when both ནི་ and a demonstrative are used together.

1.11 Question formations

There are two ways to construct questions in Tibetan. The first is by means of question particles placed *after* the verb. The second is by placing one of a class of interrogative words *before* the verb. The former will be introduced in this lesson and the latter in Lesson Two.

---

[6]The hyphen in the interlinear translation indicates either that the two English words stand for one Tibetan syllable or that the second word is a suffix of the first.

The more colloquial (spoken) question particle is -པས་.

a. དེ་ཇ་རེད་པས།

de cha rebɛɛ̀ [Note that reè becomes re when it joins with -bɛɛ̀.]

that tea is ?/

Is that tea?

b. མོ་པད་མ་རེད་པས།

mo bɛ̄ɛma rebɛɛ̀

she pema is ?/

Is she Pema?

c. ཁྱེད་རང་ནོར་བུ་ཡིན་པས།

kēraŋ nɔɔbu yimbɛɛ̀

you norbu is ?/

Are you Norbu?

Note that ཡིན་པས is usually (but not always) used in place of རེད་པས in first and second person constructions. The answer to c. would normally be:

d. ང་ནོར་བུ་ཡིན།

ŋa nɔɔbu yin

i norbu is /

I am Norbu.

e. དགེ་རྒན་དེ་ནང་པ་རེད་པས།

gegɛn de naŋba rebɛɛ̀

teacher that buddhist is ?/

Is that teacher a Buddhist?

f. པད་མ་བུ་མོ་རེད་པས།

bɛ̄ɛma pomo rebɛɛ̀ [Note that བུ་ is pronounced *po* when joined with *mo.*]

pema girl is ?/

Is Pema a girl?

g. པད་མ་བུ་རེད།

bɛ̄ɛma pu reè

pema boy is/

Pema is a boy.

The standard literary question particle is formed by repeating the final letter of the verb and then adding the letter མ་ to it.

h. དེ་དེབ་རེད་དམ།

de̱ te̱p re̱dam
that book is ?/
Is that a book?

i. ཁྱེད་རང་ཞིང་པ་ཡིན་ནམ།
kēraŋ shi̱ŋbə yi̱nnam
you farmer is ?/
Are you a farmer?

j. ཁོང་ཞིང་པ་རེད་དམ།
kōŋ shi̱ŋbə re̱dam/
he farmer is ?/
Is he a farmer?

k. ཞྭ་[7] མོ་དེ་སེར་པོ་རེད་དམ།
sha̱mo de̱ sēēbo re̱dam
hat that yellow is ?/
Is that hat yellow?

If we now add the pronouns "your" (ཁྱེད་རང་གི་), "my" (ངའི་), and "his" (ཁོང་གི), we see that they precede the nouns they modify:

l. དེ་ཁྱེད་རང་གི་དེབ་རེད་དམ།
de̱ kēraŋki te̱p re̱dam
that your book is ?/
Is that your book?

m. དེ་ངའི་དེབ་རེད།
de̱ ŋɛ̱ɛ̱ te̱p re̱è
that my book is/
That is my book

It should be noted that the pronouns "my" (ངའི་) and "your" (ཁྱེད་རང་གི་) in the above examples are really combinations of the pronoun plus a genitive case particle. For example, "my" is really "i" (ང་) and the genitive case particle "of" (འི་)—literally "of i" or "of me." Similarly, "your" consists of "you" (ཁྱེད་རང་) plus the genitive particle "of" (གི་).

---

[7] The small triangle beneath the syllable is called a wazur. It does not change the pronunciation.

Inflection and case declensions will be discussed in later lessons and need not concern you here.

n. དེབ་དེ་ཁོང་གི་རེད་པས།

tep de kōŋki rebɛɛ̀

book that his is ?/

Is that book his?

o. ཁྱེད་རང་ཁོང་གི་བུ་ཡིན་པས།

kēraŋ kōŋki pu yimbɛɛ̀

you his son is ?/

Are you his son?

Word order between the subject and object segments of sentences can be inverted with change only in emphasis, not in referent meaning. Example o. therefore, could also have been written:

p. ཁོང་གི་བུ་ཁྱེད་རང་ཡིན་པས།

kōŋki pu kēraŋ yimbɛɛ̀

his son you is ?/

Are you his son?

1.12 Vocabulary

ཁོ་	he (kō)	ནག་པོ་	black (nago; nagbo)
ཁོང་	he (kōŋ) [polite term]	ནང་པ་	Buddhist (naŋba)
ཁོང་གི་	his (kōŋki) [polite term]	ནི་	as for (ni)
ཁྱེད་རང་	you (kēraŋ) [polite term]	ནོར་བུ་	proper noun (henceforth abbreviated as p.n.), (nɔɔbu)
ཁྱེད་རང་གི་	your (kēraŋki) [polite term]	པད་མ་	p.n. (bɛ̄ɛ̄ma)
དགེ་རྒན་	teacher (gegɛn)	པས་	question particle (bɛɛ̀)
ང་	I (ŋa)	བུ་	boy; son (pu)
ངའི་	my (ŋɛɛ)	བུ་མོ་	girl; daughter (pomo)
ཇ་	tea (cha)	བོད་པ་	Tibetan (pöba)
དམ་	question particle (dam)	ཚོང་པ་	trader (tsōŋba)
དེ་	that (de)	ཞིང་པ་	farmer (shiŋbə)
དེབ་	book (teb)		

ཞྭ་མོ་	hat (sha̱mo)
ཡིན་	the linking verb "is" (yi̱n)
རེད་	the linking verb "is" (re̱è)
ཤད་	the vertical line marking the end of clauses (shɛ̄ɛ̀)
སེར་པོ་	yellow (sēēbo; sērbo)
ཡིན་པ་རེད་	the linking verb "is" (yi̱mbəreè)

Lesson Two

2.1 The Alphabet, continued: Slot-1 (prefixed letters): ག་ད་བ་མ་འ་

In Lesson One, simple syllables consisting of a root letter and a Slot-4 suffixed letter were introduced: ཁ + ང = ཁང་ (kāŋ). In this lesson the remaining combinations and their pronunciations are presented. The diagram of syllabic structure is repeated below for your convenience.

```
          v
          2
      1   X   4   5          (v = vowel)
          3
          v
```

When this slot is filled, at least one additional slot (other than the "root") must also be filled or the root letter must have a vowel. Since you are familiar with 4-slot letters, the following examples will be restricted to them.

Each of the five consonants which fill the 1-slot occur only before certain root consonants:

- ག་ occurs before the root consonants ཅ་ཉ་ཏ་ད་ན་ཙ་ཞ་ཟ་ཡ་ཤ་ས་ and combinations of these with letters in the other slots
- ད་ occurs before the root consonants ཀ་ག་ང་པ་བ་མ་ and combinations of these with letters in the other slots
- བ་ occurs before the root consonants ཀ་ག་ང་སྔ་ཙ་ཛ་རྟ་སྟ་ཏ་ད་ཉ་སྙ་ཙ་ཛ་ཞ་ཟ་ and combinations of these with letters in other slots
- མ་ occurs before the root consonants ཁ་ག་ང་ཆ་ཇ་ཉ་ཐ་ད་ན་ཚ་ཛ་ and combinations of these with letters in other slots
- འ་ occurs before the root consonants ཁ་ག་ཆ་ཇ་ཐ་ད་ཕ་བ་ཚ་ཛ་ and combinations of these with letters in other slots

The presence of these 5 prefixed consonants does not change the sound of the syllable's vowel, but can affect its tone. When they are joined with root letters that are high tone consonants, the resultant syllable remains high tone regardless of whether the prefixed consonant is high or low tone by itself. For example the root letters ས and ཀ are high tone so in གསུམ་ /sūm/ "three," གསར་ /sāā, sār/ "new", and དཀོན་ /gōn/ "scarce, rare," the vowels remain high tone. They are pronounced the same as if they were སུམ་, སར་, and ཀོན་.

However, when prefixed consonants are joined to root letters that are *low tone* consonants, the resultant syllable may become high tone, although the pronunciation of the vowel quality is not changed. The rules for these changes are rather complex.

1. If the prefixed letter is བ་ or འ་, the resultant syllable is always low tone (if the root consonant is low tone). These letters never transform a low tone syllable to a high tone one. Thus, since ད་ is a low tone letter, use of it as the root letter with the འ་ prefixed consonant does not change the tone: འདོད་ /dö̱ö̀/ "want," is low tone.

2. If the prefixed letter is ག་, ད་, or མ་, then the resultant syllable is low tone if the root letter is a low tone consonant with the exception of ང་ཉ་ན་བ་མ་ཡ. With these, the tone changes to high tone. For example:

ངུས་ (ŋü̱ù) is low tone falling, but དངུལ་ (ŋǖǖ) is high tone
ཉིད་ (ñi̱ì) is low tone falling, but གཉིད་ (ñīì) is high tone falling
ནད་ (nɛ̱ɛ̀) is low tone falling, but གནད་ (nɛ̄ɛ̀) is high tone falling
ན་ (na̱) is low tone short, but མནའ་ (nā) is high tone short
མར་ (ma̱a̱) is low tone long, but དམར་ (māā) is high tone long
ཡུ་ (yu̱) is low tone short, but གཡུ་ (yū) is high tone short
བུས་ (pü̱ù) is low tone falling but དབུས་ (ǖù) is high tone falling

Note that another unusual feature of prefixed letters is that certain combinations of letters change the consonant sound. One such combination is དབ. When it occurs without a written vowel it is pronounced as a "w," high tone. For example, དབང་ is pronounced wāŋ. When this combination occurs with a written vowel, that vowel becomes the initial sound. The tone is always high. For example:

དབུ་	དབུས་	དབེན་	དབོར་
ū	ǖù	ēn	ɔ̄ɔ̀
head	center	deserted	transport

Let us now examine some syllables to reiterate how to apply the above rules:

འབར་ is pronounced ba̱a̱. It remains low tone because the prefixed letter is not one of those that change low tone root letters to high tone.

དམག་ is pronounced māà. Here the root letter, མ , is one of the low tone letters that become high tone when used with the prefixed letter ད་ or ག་.

གདོང་ is pronounced low tone—do̱ŋ. Although the prefixed letter ག changes some low tone root letters to high tone, ད is not one of the 6 consonants (ང་ཉ་ན་བ་མ་ཡ་) that can be altered.

2.2 Slot-3 (subfixed letters): ྱ (ཡ), ྲ (ར), ླ (ལ)

The 3 letters ཡ་, ར་, and ལ་ join beneath certain consonants in attenuated form (as indicated above).

2.2.1 The subfixed letter ཡ (ྱ)

This can be placed beneath the following consonants: ཀ་ཁ་ག་པ་ཕ་བ་མ་. The resulting combination is a palatalized version of the original consonant. Palatalization refers to the addition of a "y-like" sound to the basic consonant.

ཀྱ་	ཁྱ	གྱ་	པྱ་	ཕྱ་	བྱ་	མྱ་
gyā	kyā	gya̱	jā	chā	ja̱	ña̱

(gyu- would be similar in sound to the "gu" in regulate; kyu- would be similar to the "cu" in cute)

When a final consonant (slot-4 consonant) is present, the rules for the vowel changes discussed in Lesson One are operative. For example:

ཀྱང་	ཁྱག་	བྱས་	ཕྱིར་	མྱོང་
gyāŋ	kyāà	chɛ̱ɛ̀	chi̅r	ño̱ŋ
also	cold	did	outside	experience

When the prefixed (slot-1) letters are added, the vowels in syllables with a high tone root letter remain high tone (e.g., དཔྱད་ = jɛ̄ɛ̀-"examine"). Low tone letters such as བ and མ, however, change to high tone according to the rules presented in 2.1 above. For example, དབྱར་ yāā (summer) or དམྱལ་ ñɛ̄ɛ̀ (hell).

2.2.2 The subfixed letter ར་ (ྲ)

The subfixed letter ྲ is attached to the following letters: ཀ་ཁ་ག་ད་པ་ཕ་བ་མ་ས་ཧ་.
It does not change the tone of root letters to which it is joined but produces retroflexed consonants in the following manner:

ཀྲ་ is pronounced "dr"—this sound is similar to the "dr" in drill. To produce a more accurate reproduction of the Tibetan sound, the tip of the tongue should be bent slightly backwards so that a part of its underside articulates with the roof of the mouth.

ཀྲུང་
drūŋ
crane

པྲ་ is pronounced "dr" in reading style, but often "b" in the spoken pronunciation. Each case will have to be learned.

དཔྲང་(པོ་)	དཔྲལ་	པྲ་
pāŋgo [drāŋbo]	bɛ̄ɛ (go) [drɛ̄ɛ]	drā
beggar	forehead	type of divination

གྲ་, བྲ་ and དྲ་ are pronounced "dr" when preceded by a consonant of slot 1 or slot 2. In other situations these are pronounced "tr," i.e., similar to the "tr" in the word triumph.

གྲི་	འབྲས་	དྲིས་	ཕྲུ་(གུ་)	བྲང་	དགྲ་	འདྲ་
tri̲	drɛ̲ɛ̀	tri̲ì	trū (gu)	tra̲ŋ	dra̲	dra̲
knife	rice	asked	child	chest	enemy	similar

Note that slot 1 prefixed consonants can be used with a root letter + slot 3 (+ slot 4) combinations. In these situations they do not change either the pronunciation of the vowel or the tone of the syllable.

སྲ་ is pronounced "dr" before the letter ན་ (if there is no written vowel), but "s" elsewhere.

སྲན་	སྲིད་
drɛ̄n	sīì
lentil	politics

ཁྲ་ and ཕྲ་ are pronounced "tr."

ཁྲག་	ཕྲེང་	ཁྲི་
trāà [trāg]	trēŋ	trī
blood	a row	10,000

ཧྲ is pronounced "hr."

ཧྲེང་
hrēŋ
alone

2.2.3 The subfixed letter ལ

With one exception, compounds with the subfixed ལ are pronounced with an "l" sound. Tone becomes *high* even with low tone root consonants.

ཀླུ་	གླ་	བླ་	རླག་	སླེ་
lū	lā	lā	lāà	lē
a kind of deity (nāga)	wage	superior	destroy	weave

The exception to this is ཟླ་, which is pronounced da̲, low tone.

2.3 Slot-2 (suprafixed letters): ར་, ལ་, and ས་

These three consonants affix on top of the "root" letter and function identically. When they are joined to high tone root letters, the syllable remains high tone. When they are joined to the following 4 low tone consonants ང་ ཉ་ ན་ མ་, the low tone root letters become high tone. For example:

མ་	རྨ་	ནག་	སྣག་	ང་	ལྔ་	ཉ་	རྙིང་
ma	mā	nag	nāg	ŋa	ŋā	ña	ñiŋ
mother	sore	black	ink	I	five	fish	old

These changes take precedence over the slot 1-letters.

When these suprafixed consonants are joined with the other low tone consonants the tone does not change—it remains low. For example, སྒོ་ is pronounced low tone, go, and རྡོ་ is pronounced do.

2.4 Exercise: Write the pronunciation of the following syllables:

1	2	3	4	5	6	7	8	9
བསད་	དགུང་	མཁས་	གནང་	སྙིང་	དགེ་	མི་	སྔོན་	ཇེ་
10	11	12	13	14	15	16	17	18
ཁྲིམ་	རྩམ་	རྟ་	ཞབས་	ཟས་	གྱི་	བྱམས་	དཔོན་	ནང་

2.5 The pronunciation of disyllabic compounds

The pronunciation of a disyllabic word is not simply the sum of the pronunciation of the two syllables. One or both of the syllables are usually altered, and the manner in which these alterations occur are complicated. Although there are basic rules for these alterations, they are rather cumbersome and too complex for a textbook of this type. Moreover, there are numerous exceptions. Consequently, only the basic pronunciation rules will be included in this text. The rest will have to be learned on a word-by-word basis.

1. Tone in the first syllable of disyllabic compounds remains the same as when that syllable is pronounced alone. High tone in the second syllable, however, becomes a mid-tone—lower than high but higher than low. For example, with དམག་ས་ māgsa (a battleground), the pronunciation of the second syllable—ས་—is not written as high tone (sā), but left unmarked (sa), indicating that it is neither high tone nor low tone, but rather somewhere in between—a mid tone. Similarly, syllables following a low tone consonant

are higher than the low tone but not as high as a high tone.

2. With the exception of ཐ, consonants that are aspirated in the initial position of the second syllable, lose their aspiration in disyllabic compounds. For example:

p	changes to	b	ཚ་ཕོག་	tshā + pɔ̄ɔ̀ = tshābɔɔ̀
ch	"	j	ཁ་ཆེ་	kā + chē = kāje
ky	"	gy	སྤྱི་ཁྱབ་	jī + kyə̄b = jīgyəb
k	"	g	དཔར་ཁང་	bār + kāŋ = bārgaŋ
tr	"	dr	བཟོ་གྲྭ་	s<u>o</u> + tr<u>a</u> = s<u>o</u>dra
ts	"	dz	མི་ཚེ་	m<u>i</u> + tsē = m<u>i</u>dze (really between ts and dz)

3. Slot-4 consonants in the first of two syllables are affected differently when part of disyllabic compounds. For example, while the consonant ག normally produces a falling tone in monosyllables (ལག་ is pronounced l<u>a</u>à), in disyllabic words the "g" sound is pronounced, e.g., ལག་པ་ l<u>a</u>à + bā = l<u>a</u>gba and སྟག་པ་ dāà + bā = dāgba.

The slot-4 consonant ང་ normally appears in disyllabic words as ŋ, e.g., ཡང་སེ་ (y<u>a</u>ŋse), or ཡོངས་རྫོགས་ is pronounced y<u>o</u>ŋdzɔɔ̀.

The slot-4 consonants ད་ and ས་ typically are changed from falling tone when alone to either long or short tone when part of disyllabic compounds, e.g., རྩེད་མོ་ dzēè + m<u>o</u> = dzēēmo.

These rules, however, are not hard and fast and there are many exceptions and pronunciation differences even within Lhasa dialect. Thus, the best advice for the reader without an experienced native teacher is to listen to the tape carefully and try to reproduce its sounds.

4. Another typical feature of disyllabic compounds is what is called regressive assimilation. That is to say, when the first syllable of a disyllabic compound ends in a vowel or an unpronounced final consonant (for example, a final ད) there is a tendency for it to pick up the sound of certain slot-1 letters of the second syllable (i.e., a "m" or "n" or "b" sound). The slot 1 letters that do this are མ་, འ་, and བ་. For example,

མེ་མདའ་ m<u>e</u> + d<u>a</u> = m<u>e</u>nda (gun)	དགུ་བཅུ་ g<u>u</u> + jū = g<u>u</u>bju (90)
དགེ་འདུན་ g<u>e</u> + d<u>ü</u>n = g<u>i</u>ndün (monk)	མཆོད་མཇལ་ chȫȍ + j<u>ɛɛ</u> = chȫȫnjɛɛ (religious visit)

Similarly, disyllabic compounds in which the first syllable ends in ན་ or མ་ and the second syllable begins in a "g" or "k" (ག་ or ཁ་) typically pick up an "ŋ" sound. For example, ལམ་ཁ་ lam + kā = laŋga. And disyllabic compounds in which the first syllable ends in a ན and the second begins with a "p" or "b", typically pick up a "m" sound. For example: སྦྱིན་པ་ chīn + bā = chīmbə.

You may have noticed that occasionally the vowel in the first or second syllable of disyllabic compounds is different than when pronounced alone. For example, in the word དགེ་འདུན་ gindün (monk), the ge (དགེ་) had changed to gi. Such changes are a result of what linguistically is known as vowel harmony—i.e., a pattern wherein vowels in successive syllables should be members of the same class of vowels.

In Tibetan there are two classes of vowels: high vowels (ə, i, u, ü) and low vowels (a, o, e, ɛ, ɔ, and ö).[1]

Complete vowel harmony requires that all syllables in a word have vowels from the same class. Spoken Tibetan follows this—more or less—in disyllabic words, with the vowel in the first syllable changing to match that in the second syllable. Thus, the "ge" in the word "monk" (དགེ་འདུན་) changes to "gi" because the "u" in "dun" is a high vowel. Vowels harmony shifts generally occur as follows:

a	>	ə
e or ɛ	>	i
ö	>	ü

Vowel harmony, however, has many exceptions and cannot be applied by rote to all disyllabic words. Nevertheless, knowing that it exists will explain why Tibetans, sometimes pronounce words differently in isolation than when they are joined to other syllables.

2.6 Existential verbs and sentences

Existential verbs and sentences express existence and location ("there is," "there exists"). Like linking verbs, they do not indicate tense or number, and indicate person only somewhat equivocally. The three basic existential verbs are: ཡོད་པ་རེད་, འདུག་, and ཡོད. The latter is generally used for first person constructions as well as for dependent clauses, but can also be used with third person subjects. The other two are normally used only for third person constructions.

There are also several subtle differences between these verbs that should be

[1] High and low here refer to the relative height of the tongue.

mentioned, even though they will be translated the same.

The འདུག་ verb is generally used when one has first-hand knowledge, *but,* and this is important, it also conveys "specificity." Specificity refers to that fact that འདུག་ is used with respect to knowledge deriving from a specific situation or state in contrast to general, usual, or commonly known situations or states. For these, the ཡོད་པ་རེད་ form is used. Let us suppose that you are standing in a parking lot and want to say that there are a lot of cars there. You would have to use the འདུག་ verb since it is a specific statement based on first-hand knowledge. However, if you wanted to convey that there are lots of cars in America, you would normally use the ཡོད་པ་རེད་ form since this is a general statement of a commonly known fact.

Consequently, while ཡོད་པ་རེད་ does not imply first-hand knowledge, it is wrong to think of it as always connoting less certainty than འདུག་. In fact, in certain contexts, ཡོད་པ་རེད་ expresses more certainty than འདུག་, e.g,. if someone said "He is good," using the ཡོད་པ་རེད་ form when an actor came on the screen, it would imply that the actor probably is famous and that it is generally said that he is good. Or it could mean that the speaker has had previous experience with the actor (or person) and therefore can state that he is good. If འདུག་ was used, it would generally mean that based on seeing the actor, the speaker feels he is good.

Thus, while འདུག་ implies first-hand knowledge, the more basic differences between these two existential verbs rests on information about a specific or particular situation or state versus information or knowledge regarding a commonly accepted or generally known situation or state. We will see in later sections that when these existential verbs are used as auxiliary verbs, these basic distinctions will carry over. However, it should be noted that written Tibetan is not a highly standardized language and exceptions to almost all rules occur, particularly when the authors are not native Lhasa dialect speakers and are using distinctions and forms typical of their dialect.

The simplest existential constructions consist of a subject and an existential verb. These sentences express the existence of the subject. For example:

a. དམག་མི་ཡོད་པ་རེད།

mə̄ə̄mi yɔ̲̄ɔ̄reè [or yö̲bəreè][yö̲bəreè is the reading pronunciation and yɔ̲̄ɔ̄reè is the spoken pronunciation]

soldier exist[2] /

---

2 "Exist" will be used in the interlinear translation for all three existential verbs.

There are soldiers.

Note that this sentence has been translated as plural despite the fact that there is no plural marker. This is typical of Tibetan syntax. When no marker of "singular" is present, it is assumed that the sentence construction is plural. If one wanted to convey the meaning "There is *a* soldier" normally the subject ("soldier") would be modified by the word "one." The existential verb, however, would not change.

b. སློབ་གྲྭ་པ་གཅིག་ཡོད་པ་རེད།
lābdraà [lōbdrawa] chī[3] yɔ̱̄ɔreè
student one exist /
There is a (one) student.

Plural numbers are also used to modify the subject.

c. བོད་པ་གསུམ་འདུག།
pö̱ba sūm du̱ù
tibetan three exist/
There are three Tibetans.

d. གཞོན་ནུ་གཉིས་འདུག།
shö̱nnu ñiì du̱ù
youth two exist/
There are two youths.

As with linking verbs, one way to construct questions is by means of question particles placed *after* the verb. After ཡོད་པ་རེད་, either the particle པས་ (more colloquial) or དམ་ (more literary) is used. And after འདུག་, either གས་ or གམ་ is used.

e. བོད་པ་གསུམ་འདུག་གས།
pö̱ba sūm du̱gɛ
tibetan three exist ?/
Are there three Tibetans?

f. བོད་པ་གསུམ་འདུག་གམ།
pö̱ba sūm du̱gam
tibetan three exist ?/
Are there three Tibetans?

g. དམག་མི་ཡོད་པ་རེད་པས།
māāmi yɔ̱̄ɔrebɛ

---

[3] Chī is the colloquial pronunciation of jīg. Transcriptions in brackets represent reading pronunciations.

soldier exist ?/
Are there soldiers?

h. དམག་མི་ཡོད་པ་རེད་དམ།
mə̄ə̄mi yö̱baredam
soldier exist ?/
Are there soldiers?

2.6.1 The dative-locative case

Tibetan nouns are inflected, that is to say, most of them change in form according to their function in sentences. The different functions in Tibetan are grouped into four classes or *cases*, each with its own endings: nominative, dative-locative, genitive, instrumental. The nominative is the basic, or unaltered, case in that it is the form that occurs when the noun is used alone as in the glossary of this book. We encountered it as the subject of linking sentences. Some inflected languages such as Russian also have an "accusative" case which denotes the direct object, but in Tibetan the direct object is left unmarked (like the nominative case).

The dative-locative case is used with nouns (and adjectives) to denote the recipient of something that is sent or given (the indirect object), or the location of some action (in, at, or on something). It has a number of different forms which are used in accordance with the final letter of the syllable it follows.

Dative-locative case particles	Usage
ལ་	after any consonant or vowel (all finals)
-ར་ or རུ་	after a vowel -ར་ attaches to the preceding syllable)
དུ་	after ང་ ད་ ན་ མ་ ར་ ལ་
སུ་	after ས་
ཏུ་	after ག་ བ་

The dative-locative particles will be glossed as "to" in the interlinear translation.

In the following sentences, the dative-locative functions to mark off the place of existence or the location of something or someone. In this role it answers the question "where?"

a. བོད་ལ་ཚོང་པ་ཡོད་པ་རེད།
pö̱ö̀lə tsōŋba yɔ̱ɔ̀reè
tibet to trader exist/

There are traders *in* Tibet.

b. དགོན་པར་གྲྭ་པ་གསུམ་འདུག།
gombaa [gombar] traba sūm duù
monastery-to monk three exist/
There are three monks in the monastery.

In spoken Tibetan, final vowels become long in the dative-locative. Thus དགོན་པར་ is pronounced in spoken as gombaa rather than gombar, and ཨ་མི་རི་ཀར་ below is pronounced əmerigaa.

c. ཨ་མི་རི་ཀར་སློབ་གྲྭ་པ་ཡོད་པ་རེད།
əmerigaa [əmerigar] lābdraà [lōbdrawa] yɔ̀reè
america-to student exist/
There are students in America.

d. སློབ་གྲྭར་དགེ་རྒན་གསུམ་འདུག།
lābdraa [lōbdrar] gegen sūm duù
school-to teacher three exist/
There are three teachers in the school.

e. ཡུལ་དེར་རྒྱལ་པོ་ཡོད་པ་རེད།
yüü dee gyɛbo yɔ̀reè
place that-to king exist/
There are kings in that country.

f. ཨ་མི་རི་ཀར་ཞིང་པ་ཡོད་པ་རེད།
əmerigaa [əmerigar] shiŋbə yɔ̀reè
america-to farmers exist/
There are farmers in America.

g. བྱང་ཐང་ལ་འབྲོག་པ་འདུག།
chaŋdaŋlə drogba duù
changtang to nomad exist/
There are nomads on the Changtang.

To indicate singularity, the number "one" is usually added:

h. ལྷ་སར་ལྷ་ཁང་ཞིག་འདུག།
lhɛ̄ɛsaa lhāgan chī duù [ལྷ་ས་ is pronounced lhɛ̄ɛsa rather than lhāsa in colloquial Lhasa dialect. With the dative-locative, this becomes lhɛ̄ɛsaa.]
lhasa-to temple one exist/
There is a (one) temple in Lhasa.

This could also have been written as:

i. ལྷ་སར་ལྷ་ཁང་གཅིག་འདུག།

lhɛ̄ɛsaa lhāgan chī du̱ù [In spoken Tibetan "one" is pronounced chi or jīì.]
lhasa-to temple one exist/
There is a (one) temple in Lhasa.

The number "one," therefore, has several forms: ཞིག་ occurs after ང་, ན་, འ་, མ་, ར་, ལ་, and vowels, ཤིག་ occurs after final ས་, and ཅིག་ after ག་, ད་, and བ་. གཅིག་ is used after any final. Thus:

j. ལྷ་སར་གཡག་ཅིག་འདུག།
lhɛ̄ɛsaa yāà chī du̱ù
lhasa-to yak one exist/
There is a (one) yak in Lhasa.

k. ལྷ་སར་གཡག་གཅིག་འདུག།
lhɛ̄ɛsaa yāà chī du̱ù
lhasa-to yak one exist/
There is a (one) yak in Lhasa.

It should be kept in mind that there is considerable variation with regard to the use of these particles and sometimes authors do not use these variant forms consistently.

2.6.2 Possessive constructions with the dative-locative case

The dative-locative particle(s) are also commonly used to indicate that the subject has or possesses something.

a. ཁོང་ལ་དེབ་ཡོད་པ་རེད།
kōŋla te̱p yɔ̱ɔ̄reè
he (h.) to book exists/
He has a book. (lit., To him a book exists.)

b. ཕུན་ཚོགས་ལ་ཁྱི་འདུག།
pūntsoòla kī du̱ù
phuntsog to dog exist/
Phuntsog has dogs.

Note that because the word dog is not modified by the number one, it is assumed to convey the plural. If a singular meaning was intended, the object would normally have been modified as follows:

c. ཕུན་ཚོགས་ལ་ཁྱི་ཞིག་འདུག།
pūntsoòla kī chī du̱ù
phuntsog to dog one exist/
Phuntsog has a dog.

d. དམག་མིར་མེ་མདའ་ཡོད་པ་རེད།
   mə̄əmee menda yɔ̄reè
   soldiers-to gun exist/
   Soldiers have guns.

First person constructions usually use ཡོད་.

e. ངར་ཁྱི་ཞིག་ཡོད།
   ŋaa kī chī yö̀ö
   i-to dog exist/
   I have a dog.

We have seen that the subject in linking sentences can be modified by a demonstrative such as དེ ("that"). When these are used with the subject of an existential sentence, the dative-locative particle is placed immediately *after* the demonstrative.

f. གྲྭ་པ་དེར་དཔེ་ཆ་འདུག།
   traba dee bēja duù
   monk that-to book exist
   That monk has (Tibetan style) books.

Another common demonstrative is འདི་ ("this").

g. གྲྭ་པ་འདིར་དཔེ་ཆ་ཞིག་འདུག།
   traba dee[4] bēja chī duù
   monk this-to book one exist
   This monk has a (Tibetan style) book.

Existential constructions can be further expanded by adding numerals and other modifiers to the object or subject, e.g.:

མང་པོ་	ཉུང་ཉུང་	ཁ་ཤས་	ཆུང་ཆུང་
məŋgu [maŋbo]	ñunñun [ñuŋñuŋ]	kāshɛɛ̀	chūnjun [chūŋjuŋ]
many	few	several	small

h. བོད་ལ་གྲྭ་པ་མང་པོ་འདུག།
   pȫlə traba məŋgu duù
   tibet to monk many exist/
   There are many monks in Tibet.

i. སློབ་གྲྭར་དགེ་རྒན་ཁ་ཤས་འདུག།
   lābdraa gegen kāsheè duù
   school to teacher several exist/

---

[4] Spoken pronunciation of འདིར་ and དེར་ are both dee.

There are several teachers in school.

j. ལྷ་སར་ཁང་པ་ཆུང་ཆུང་མང་པོ་འདུག།
lhɛ̄ɛ̄saa kāŋbə chūnjun mə̲ŋgu du̲ù
lhasa-to house small many exist
There are many small houses in Lhasa.

As example i. indicates, when two adjectives modify a noun, the second modifies the noun + first modifier [small houses] [many].

Demonstratives can also be used with adjectives. When this occurs, the demonstrative follows the adjective. In the following two examples, the demonstrative also has the dative-locative particle suffixed to it.

k. གྲྭ་པ་ཆུང་ཆུང་དེར་དགེ་རྒན་ཁ་ཤས་ཡོད་པ་རེད།
tra̲ba chūnjun te̲e̲ ge̲gɛn kāsɛɛ̀ yɔ̲̀ɔreè
monk small that-to teacher several exist
That small monk has several teachers. (lit., To that small monk, several teachers exist.)

l. གྲྭ་པ་གསར་པ་དེར་དགེ་རྒན་རྒན་ཁོག་ཁ་ཤས་ཡོད་པ་རེད།
tra̲ba sāāba [sārba] de̲e̲ ge̲gɛn gɛ̲ngɔɔ̀ kāsɛɛ̀ yɔ̲̀ɔreè
monk new that-to teacher old several exist
That new monk has several old teachers.

A noun can also be modified by two adjectives linked by the conjunction དང་ ("and").

m. ལྷ་སར་དགོན་པ་ཆེན་པོ་དང་སྐྱིད་པོ་འདུག་
lɛ̄ɛ̄saa go̲mba chēmbo da̲ŋ gyību du̲ù
lhasa-to monastery big and pleasant exist
Lhasa has big and pleasant monasteries.

Temporal words, i.e., words conveying a time component, are usually placed at the beginning of a sentence. Three common temporal words are:

ད་ལྟ་	སྔས་མ་	དེ་རིང་
ta̲nda	ŋɛ̄ɛ̄ma	te̲riŋ
now	formerly, in the past	today

n. ད་ལྟ་བྱང་ཐང་ལ་འབྲོག་པ་མང་པོ་ཡོད་པ་རེད།
ta̲nda cha̲ŋdaŋlə dro̲gba mə̲ŋgu yɔ̲̀ɔreè
now changtang to nomad many exist/
There are many nomads now on the Changtang.

o. སྔས་མ་བོད་ལ་དགོན་པ་མང་པོ་འདུག།
ŋɛ̄ɛ̄ma pö̲lə go̲mba mə̲ŋgu du̲ù
formerly tibet to monastery many exist/

Formerly there were many monasteries in Tibet.

p. དེ་རིང་སློབ་གྲྭར་སློབ་གྲྭ་བ་གསུམ་འདུག།
teriŋ lābdraa lābdraà sūm duù
today school-to student three exist/
Today there are three students in school.

2.7 Linking and existential verbs used in adjectival constructions

The distinction between existential and linking verbs often is blurred in adjectival constructions in the sense that existential verbs are used in contexts that otherwise appear to call for linking verbs. For example, in sentence a. འདུག་ is normally used rather than རེད་, although the latter can be used to convey general or comparative statements.

a.཈ོ་ཆེན་པོ་འདུག།
kō chēmbo duù
he big exist
He is big.

Similarly, the adjective "hot" normally takes the existential verb.

b. ཆུ་འདི་ཚ་པོ་འདུག།
chū di tsābo duù
water this hot exist
The water is hot.

There is no simple rule to predict this, usage generally depending on the specific adjective. For example, color adjectives such as found in sentence c. *always* take linking verbs.

c. འདི་ནི་དམར་མོ་རེད།
dini māāmo [mārmo] reè
this as-for red is
This is red.

2.8 Negation of linking and existential verbs

Negation of linking and existential sentences is expressed through the addition of the negative particles མི་ and མ་, and by negative verbs such as མེད་ and མིན་. In sentence a., for example, རེད་ becomes མ་རེད and in b., འདུག་ becomes མི་འདུག་.

a. དགོན་པར་གྲྭ་པ་ཡོད་པ་མ་རེད།
gombaa traba yɔ̀ɔmaareè [yöbamaareè]
monastery-to monk exist no/
There are no monks in the monastery.

b. ཆུ་འདི་ཚ་པོ་མི་འདུག།
chū di tsābo minduù
water this hot no exist/
This water is not hot.

མེད་པ་རེད་ in example (c.) is a variant of མི་འདུག་

c. ལྷ་ཁང་དེར་དགེ་རྒན་མང་པོ་མེད་པ་རེད།
lhāgan dee gegen məŋgu mɛ̀bəreè
temple that-to teacher many no exist/
That temple does not have many teachers.

d. དེབ་འདི་དམར་པོ་མ་རེད། དཀར་པོ་རེད།
tepdi māābo maaree, gāābo reè
book this red no is/ white is
This book is not red, (it) is white.

e. ཁོ་གྲྭ་པ་མ་རེད།
kō traba maareè
he monk not is
He is not a monk.

f. ཁྱེད་རང་བླ་མ་མ་རེད།
khēraŋ lāma maaree
you lama no is
You are not a lama.

The linking verb ཡིན་ is negated by substituting the negative linking verb མིན་ for it.

g. ང་སློབ་གྲྭ་བ་མིན།
ŋa lābdraà mɛn [min]
i student not
I am not a student.

Possessive constructions are negated similarly.

h. ངར་དེབ་མེད།
ŋaa teb mɛɛ̀
i-to book no-exist
I do not have books.

2.9 Question formation with interrogative words

Some of the main interrogatives you will encounter in literary Tibetan are presented below. The interrogatives that typically are used in the spoken language are marked by an asterisk.

གང་	what (kan; kaŋ)	གང་ཙམ་	how much (kaŋdzam)
ཅི་	what (jī)	ག་ཚད་	how much, how many* (kədzɛɛ̀)
ག་རེ་	what* (kare)	ག་ཚོད་	how much/many (kədzöö̀)
ག་ནས་	from where* (kənɛɛ̀)	ཅི་ཙམ་	how much/many (jīdzam)
གང་དུ་	where (kaŋtu)	ཇི་ཙམ་	how much/many (jedzam)
གང་ན་	where (kaŋna)	ག་དུས་	when* (kədüü)
གང་ལ་	where (kaŋla)	ག་གི་	which* (kəgi)
ག་རུ་	where (kəru)	ག་འདྲ་	how* (kəndrɛ)
གར་	where (kar)	ག་འདྲ་ཞིག་	what kind* (kəndrɛs)
ག་པར་	where* (kəbaa)	སུ་	who* (sū)
ག་ལ་	where (kala)	སུའི་	whose* (sǖǖ)
ག་ན་	where (kana)		
གང་ནས་	from where (kaŋnɛ)		

a. འདི་ག་རེ་རེད།
di kare reè
this what is
What is this?

b. དགོན་པ་འདི་ག་པར་འདུག་
gomba di kaba do[5] [duù]
monastery this where exist ?
Where is the monastery?

c. དགོན་པ་འདི་ག་པར་འདུག་གམ།
gomba di kabaa dugam
monastery this where exist ?
Where is the monastery?

Note that in example c. the question particle (གམ་) is used in conjunction with the interrogative. This does not change the meaning in any way. Its use is simply a matter of style.

d. དེབ་ག་ཚད་འདུག།
tep kədzɛɛ̀ do [duù]
book how many exist
How many books are there?

---

5 With interrogatives, འདུག་ is pronounced *do* (as in dough).

e. གཡག་ག་གི་རེད།
yāà kə̱gi re̱è
yak which is
Which (one) is a yak?

f. གཡག་འདི་སུའི་རེད།
yāà di̱ sǖü re̱è
yak this whose is
Whose yak is this?

g. སྨན་ཁང་ཆེན་པོ་ག་པར་ཡོད་པ་རེད།
mɛ̄ngan chēmbo ka̱baa yɔ̱ɔ̀reè
hospital big where exist
Where is the big hospital?

h. ཁོ་ག་ནས་རེད།
kō kə̱nɛɛ̀ re̱è
he from where is
Where is he from?

2.10 Reference section: Looking up words in the glossary and new vocabulary sections

In order to translate the readings in each lesson you will have to learn to look up words in the glossary at the end of the book. Because Tibetan syllables can have prefixed, affixed, suffixed and subfixed letters, glossary word order is somewhat confusing. In general, each syllable is listed under its root letter. Thus, for a word like ཁང་པ་ the listing will be under the letter ཁ and for a word such as དམག་མི་ the listing would be under its root letter མ. The difficulty in looking up words derives primarily from the difficulty of determining the order of words *within* a single dictionary letter. The following set of rules is used in this book and virtually every other modern dictionary. We urge that you study the discussion below together with either a dictionary or the glossary at the end of this book.

1. The alphabetical order of the 30 Tibetan letters is: ཀ་ ཁ་ ག་ ང་ ཅ་ ཆ་ ཇ་ ཉ་ ཏ་ ཐ་ ད་ ན་ པ་ ཕ་ བ་ མ་ ཙ་ ཚ་ ཛ་ ཝ་ ཞ་ ཟ་ འ་ ཡ་ ར་ ལ་ ཤ་ ས་ ཧ་ ཨ་. [The alphabetical order of vowels is: inherent a, i, u, e, o (ི ུ ེ ོ)].

2. The first entries under any letter are the simple syllables that have no prefixed or affixed letters and which have the inherent "a" vowel (that is, those with no written vowels). For example, ཀ་.

3. Then the single letter in multi-syllabic compounds, alphabetized according to the second syllable, e.g., ག་གིར་, ག་དུས་, ག་ནས, ག་ཚོད་, etc.

4. After this, syllables consisting of the root letter plus a vowel (in the above-mentioned order) are listed. Thus, first all the syllables with the letter "i" are cited. For example, གི་ before གི་གུ་ and གིན་ before གིས་. This is then repeated for each of the other vowels.

5. Up to now, we have discussed entries consisting of a root letter plus a slot-4 and possibly a slot-5 letter (for all the vowels). Following such entries are syllables beginning with the root letter and a slot-3 subfixed letter. The order of the slot-3 letters is first letters with "y" (ྱ), then "r" (ྲ), and then "l" (ླ).

In other words, first all the "y" syllables are cited in accordance with the above rules, i.e., first no vowel and only the root letter + y, then no vowel and the slot-4 and slot-5 letters. For example, གྱ་ before གྱ་ནོམ་, and གྱང་ before གྱར་. Then all the "y" syllables of this kind with the "i" vowel are listed, and then with the other vowels. After all the "y" syllables are listed, then all the "r" ones are listed. Following this, all the "l" syllables of this type are listed.

6. After this, syllables beginning not with the root letter but rather with a slot-1 (prefixed) letter are cited. The order of listing of the slot-1 letters is : ག་ ད་ བ་ མ་ འ. Thus, དགག་ before དགུ་ and དགུ་ before དགེ་ and དགྱི་ and དགྲ་. After all the ད་ prefix syllables, then the བ་ prefix ones, and so forth.

7. Following this come syllables beginning with one of the slot-2 (affixed) letters. The affix "r" is listed first, and then the affix "l" and finally the affix "s." As in the above examples, first the affix + root letter with the inherent "a" vowel occur, e,g., རྒ་. Then slot-4 and slot-5 letters are added, and then this is repeated with each of the written vowels.

After this, the affix+root letter combination adds the series of slot-3 subjoined letters beginning with "y." For example, this part would start with རྒྱ་ and then add slot-4 letters (and when they exist, slot-5 letters), for example, རྒྱབ་. After this is done for the inherent "a" vowel, it is repeated for each of the other vowels and then each of the other slot-3 subfixed letters. After the listing of the "r" slot-2 affix, then the list is repeated for ས, the other slot-2 letter.

8. Finally, the dictionary lists syllables that begin with a slot-1 prefixed letter, but which also have a slot-2 affixed letter. These are listed in the order of the slot-1, slot-2, and slot-3 letters. For example, བརྒ་ before བརྒྱ་ and བསྒ་ before བསྒྲ་.

2.11 Reading exercise

1. Q. རྡོ་རྗེ་བོད་ལ་དགོན་པ་མང་པོ་ཡོད་པ་རེད་དམ།
2. A. དགོན་པ་དང་ལྷ་ཁང་མང་པོ་ཡོད་པ་རེད།
3. Q. ཁྱེད་རང་གྲྭ་པ་ཡིན་པས།
4. A. ཡིན། ང་གྲྭ་པ་ཡིན།
5. Q. དགོན་པ་ག་ནས་རེད།
6. A. ང་འབྲས་སྤུངས་ནས་ཡིན།
7. Q. འབྲས་སྤུངས་དེ་ག་པར་འདུག།
8. A. འབྲས་སྤུངས་ལྷ་ས་ལ་འདུག།
9. Q. འབྲས་སྤུངས་ལ་གྲྭ་པ་དང་བླ་མ་ག་ཚད་ཡོད་པ་རེད།
10. A. འབྲས་སྤུངས་ལ་གྲྭ་པ་ཁྲི་གཅིག་ཡོད་པ་རེད།
11. Q. གྲྭ་པ་ཁ་ཤས་ལ་མི་མདའ་གསར་པ་ཡོད་པ་རེད་པས།
12. A. གྲྭ་པ་ཁ་ཤས་ལ་མི་མདའ་གསར་པ་ཡོད་པ་མ་རེད།

1. Q. dɔɔje pölə gomba məŋgu [maŋbo] yɔ̀redam
dorje tibet to monastery many exist ?/
Dorje, are there many monasteries in Tibet?

2. A. gomba daŋ lhāgan məŋgu [maŋbo] yɔ̀reè
monastery and temple many exist/
There are many monasteries and temples.

3. Q. kēraŋ traba yimbɛɛ̀
you monk is ?/
Are you a monk?

4. A. yin/ ŋa traba yin
is/ i monk is/
Yes, I am a monk.

5. Q. gomba kənɛɛ̀ reè
monastery from-where is/
What monastery (are you) from?

6. A. ŋa drɛɛbun nɛ yin

i drepung from is/

I am from Drepung (monastery).

[Prepositions like nɛ (or la) are slurred in normal speech and pronounced mid-tone, so are written without a tone marker. Note too that *yi̲n* not *re̲è* is used for 1st person in 6A.]

7. Q. drɛ̲ɛ̲bun ni ka̲baa do̲

drepung as-for where exist/

As for Drepung, where is it [located]?

8. A. drɛ̲ɛ̲bun lhɛ̄ɛ̄saa du̲ù

drepung lhasa-to exist/

Drepung is in Lhasa.

9. Q. drɛ̲ɛ̲bunlə tra̲ba da̲ŋ lāma kə̲dzɛ̀ɛ̀ yɔ̲ɔ̀rɛɛ

drepung to monk and lama how-many exist/

How many monks and lamas are there in Drepung?

10. A. drɛ̲ɛ̲bunlə tra̲ba trī chī yɔ̲ɔ̀reè

drepung to monk ten-thousand one exist/

There are ten thousand monks in Drepung.

11. Q. tra̲ba kāshɛɛ̀lə me̲nda sāāba yɔ̲ɔ̀rebɛɛ̀

monk several-to gun new exist ?/

Do several monks have new guns?

12. A. tra̲ba kāshɛɛ̀lə me̲nda sāāba yɔ̲ɔ̀maareè

monk several-to gun new no exist /

Several monks do not have new guns.

2.12 Vocabulary

དཀར་པོ་	white (gāābo)
སྐྱིད་པོ་	happy, glad (gyību)
ཁ་ཤས་	several, a few (kāshɛɛ̀)
ཁང་པ་	house (kāŋba)
ཁོང་	he (h.) (kōŋ)
ཁྱི་	dog (kī)
ཁྲི་གཅིག་	ten thousand (trījiì or trī chī)
ག་གི་	which (kə̲gi)
ག་དུས་	when (kə̲düǜ)
ག་འདྲ་	how (kə̲ndrɛ)
ག་འདྲ་ཞིག་	what kind (kə̲ndrɛs)
ག་ན་	where (ka̲na)
ག་ནས་	from where (kə̲nɛɛ̀)
ག་པར་	where (ka̲baa)
ག་ཚད་	how much (kə̲dzɛɛ̀)
ག་ཚོད་	how much (kə̲dzöö̀)
ག་རུ་	where (kə̲ru)
ག་རེ་	what (ka̲re)
ག་ལ་	where (ka̲la)

གང་	what (ka̲n; ka̲ŋ)
གང་དུ་	where (ka̲ŋtu)
གང་ན་	where (ka̲ŋna)
གང་ནས་	from where (ka̲ŋnɛɛ̀)
གང་ཙམ་	how much (ka̲ŋdzam)
གང་ལ་	where (ka̲ŋla)
གམ་	question particle (gam)
གར་	where (ka̲r)
གས་	question particle (gɛ)
གོང་	price (go̲n)
གྲྭ་པ་	monk (tra̲ba)
དགེ་རྒན་	teacher (ge̲gɛn)
དགོན་པ་	monastery (go̲mba, gö̲nba)
རྒན་ཁོག་	old (gɛ̲ngɔɔ̀)
རྒྱལ་པོ་	king (gyɛ̲ɛ̲bo)
སྔས་མ་	formerly, in the past (ŋɛ̄ɛ̄ma)
ཅི་	what (jī)
ཅི་ཙམ་	how much (jīdzam)
ཅིག་	one, a (chī; jīì; jīg)
གཅིག་	one, a (chī; jīg)
ཆུ་	water (chū)
ཆུང་ཆུང་	small (chūnjun)
ཆེན་པོ་	big (chēmbo)
ཇི་ཙམ་	how much (je̲dzam)
ཉུང་ཉུང་	few, small amount (ñu̲nñun)
གཉིས་	two (ñīì)
ཏུ་	dative-locative particle (du)
ད་ལྟ་	now (ta̲nda)
དུ་	dative-locative particle (tu; du)
དེ་རིང་	today (te̲riŋ)
འདི་	this (di̲)
འདུག་	existential verb (du̲ù)
རྡོ་རྗེ་	p.n. (dɔ̲ɔ̲je)
ནས་	from (nɛ; nɛ̲ɛ̀)
དཔེ་ཆ་	Tibetan style book (bēja)
ཕུན་ཚོགས་	p.n. (pū̃ndzoò)
བོད་	Tibet (pö̲ö̀)
བྱང་ཐང་	p.n., "Northern Plateau" (cha̲ŋdaŋ)
བླ་མ་	lama (lāma)
འབྲས་སྤུངས་	Drepung monastery (dre̲bun)
འབྲོག་པ་	nomad (dro̲gba)
མ་	negative particle, mother (ma̲)
མང་པོ་	many (mə̲ŋgu; ma̲ŋbo)
མི་	person, negative particle (mi̲)
མིན་	negative particle (me̲n; mi̲n)
མེ་མདའ་	gun (me̲nda)
མེད་	negative particle (me̲è)
དམག་མི་	soldier (mə̄ə̄mi)
དམར་མོ་	red (māāmo; mārmo)
སྨན་ཁང་	hospital (mɛ̄ngan)
ཚ་པོ་	hot (tsābo)
ཞིག་	one, a (chī; shi̲g)
གཞོན་ནུ་	youth (shö̲nnu)
ཡུལ་	place, area, region, country (yü̲ü̲)
ཡོད་པ་རེད་	existential verb (yɔ̲ɔ̲reè; yö̲bareè)
གཡག་	yak (yāà)
ར་ or རུ་	dative-locative particle (ra̲, ru̲)
ལ་	dative-locative particle (lə; la̲)
ཤིག་	one, a (chī; shīg)

སུ་	1. dative-locative particle; 2. who (sū)
སུའི་	whose (sūū)
སོ་	tooth (so)
སློབ་གྲྭ་	school (lāpdra)
སློབ་གྲྭ་པ་	student (lāpdraà; lōpdrawa)
གསར་པ་	new (sāāba)
གསུམ་	three (sūm)
ལྷ་ཁང་	temple (lhāgan)
ལྷ་ས་	Lhasa (lhɛ̄ɛ̄sa; lhāsa)
ཨ་མེ་རི་ཀ་	America (əmerigə)

Lesson Three

3.1 The subject of active sentences and the instrumental case

In addition to linking and existential verbs, Tibetan has two categories of verbs we shall call active and involuntary. These verbs convey intentional and unintentional action. For example, the English sentence "I went to sleep" can be constructed with either an active or involuntary verb meaning "to sleep." With the active verb "to sleep" (ཉལ་), the sentence "I went to sleep" connotes sleep resultant from an intentional act, but with the involuntary verb "to sleep" (གཉིད་ཁུག་), the same English sentence connotes unintentional sleep, i.e., falling asleep without wanting or trying to do so. In this lesson active verbs and sentences will be examined.

The main (and only obligatory) element in Tibetan *active* sentences (and clauses) is the *main active verb*, although most active sentences usually also have both a *subject* and an *object*. When these three sentence components are filled, the normal sentence order is *subject + object + main verb.*

Active sentences require that their subjects be placed in what is called the instrumental case. That is to say, one of the six instrumental case particles presented below is suffixed to or follows the subject.

Instrumental case particles indicate the agent or the means by which an action took or takes place. For example, in the sentence "He killed the yak," the agent or actor is "he" (ཁོ་). However, unlike English, Tibetan grammar requires that "he" be placed in the instrumental case so that the sentence literally means: "*By* him yak killed." Thus, as explained below, ཁོ་ becomes ཁོས་.

Although the instrumental case has several functions, for the present we need only concern ourselves with its function as marking the subject (actor) in active sentences.

The instrumental case consists of six different particles, all of which perform identical functions. Five of these particles are used in accordance with the final consonant (or vowel) of the immediately preceding syllable. One is used with all finals.

Syllable final	Instrumental particle	Example
ག་ or ང་	གིས་	གཡག་གིས (by a yak)
ད་ or བ་ or ས་	ཀྱིས་	ཕུན་ཚོགས་ཀྱིས་ (by Phuntsog)
ན་ or མ་ or ར་ or ལ་	གྱིས་	དགེ་རྒན་གྱིས་ (by the teacher)
vowels	-ས་ (is suffixed to preceding syllable)	ངས་ (by me)

	ཡིས་	ང་ཡིས་ (by me)
all final letters	ནས་	གཡག་ནས་, ཕུན་ཚོགས་ནས་, དགེ་རྒན་ནས་

For a short period of time written materials in Tibet simplified this pattern by using the གིས་ form exclusively with all finals. This, however, has gone out of favor, and the traditional pattern presented above is again followed nowadays.

Because the instrumental particle occurs after the noun or noun phrase that is the subject of active verbs, finding the instrumental case particle is the simplest way to identify the subject. Sentences a., b., and c. below illustrate the basic structure. In example a., "tiger" is the subject and "yak" is the object. In examples b., and c. "yak" is the subject and "tiger" is the object.

a. སྟག་གིས་གཡག་བསད་པ་རེད།
dāà ki yāà sɛ̃ɛ̀bəreè
tiger by yak killed past compl./
The tiger killed yaks.

གིས་ here marks the actor, the tiger. The direct object, the yak, is left unmarked. The main verb, བསད་ (killed), is followed by the standard third person past tense verb complement པ་རེད[1] ("bəreè"). Thus, བསད་པ་རེད means: "(An actor: he, she, it, they) killed (it)." In this sentence, the actor is the tiger.

Sentence b. reverses the subject and object.

b. གཡག་གིས་སྟག་བསད་པ་རེད།
yāà ki dāà sɛ̃ɛ̀bəreè
yak by tiger killed past compl./
The yaks killed tigers.

Sentence c. changes the normal word order shown in b. by placing the object *before* the subject. This causes no ambiguity in Tibet because the subject (actor)—the yak—is marked by the presence of the instrumental particle གིས་. Therefore, unlike English where changes in word order in active sentences change the referent meaning (Jim hit John—John hit Jim), in Tibetan they affect only emphasis.

c. སྟག་གཡག་གིས་བསད་པ་རེད།
dāà yāà ki sɛ̃ɛ̀bəreè
tiger yak by killed past compl./

---

[1] Although this complement itself can be broken down into the linking verb རེད་ and the particle པ་, at this stage it is better treated as an indivisable unit conveying past tense.

The yaks killed tigers. (emphasis on tiger)

The direct object (the person or thing directly affected by the verbal action) is *not* marked by any grammatical particle in Tibetan. It can be filled by a noun (or noun phrase) or an adjective (or adjective phrase) or both. In examples a., b., and c. a single noun ("yak" or "tiger") served as the object of the verb "killed."

Sentences d.-f. illustrate the above rules using several new active verbs and nouns: ཟས་ ("ate"), ཉོས་ ("bought"), and ཤ་ ("meat"):

d. སྟག་གིས་ཤ་ཟས་པ་རེད།

dāà ki shā sɛ̱ɛ̀bəreè

tiger by meat ate past compl./

(The) tigers ate meat.

e. ཁོས་ཤ་ཟས་པ་རེད།

kȫö shā sɛ̱ɛ̀bəreè

he-by meat ate past compl./

He ate meat.

f. འབྲོག་པས་མེ་མདའ་ཉོས་པ་རེད།

dro̱gbɛɛ̀ me̱nda ño̱öbəreè

nomad-by gun bought past compl./

(The) nomads bought guns.

3.2 Plurality and singularity

In English, nouns change their form to indicate plurality. Tibetan nouns do not do this. They may connote either singularity or plurality depending on the context, although as indicated earlier, unmarked nouns normally convey the plural. Ultimately, plurality and singularity are determined by *semantic context* and by one of a variety of *semantically plural or singular modifiers and postpositions.*

3.2.1 Singularity

Singularity is indicated by modifying nouns with a *determinative* such as འདི་ ("this") or དེ་ ("that"), or by the number "one" (གཅིག་ or ཅིག་ or ཞིག་ or ཤིག་).

Nouns modified by the above determinatives will often be translated in English as articles, but it is important for the reader to remember that Tibetan has no articles per se. Thus, although གཡག་འདི་ ("this yak") will often be translated as "the yak," technically it means "this yak." Similarly, the word "one" will typically be translated as "a" or "an"—

for example, གཡག་ཞིག་ as "a yak" rather than "one yak." The use of modifiers such as these eliminates ambiguity with regard to number. Such modifiers always *follow* the noun or noun phrase they modify, but *precede* the instrumental particle. For example, "by a tiger" would be སྟག་གཅིག་གིས་, *not* སྟག་གིས་གཅིག་.

a. སྟག་གཅིག་གིས་ཁྱི་འདི་བསད་པ་རེད།
dāà chī ki kī d̲i sɛ̄ɛ̀bəreè
tiger one by dog this killed past compl./
A tiger killed the (this) dog.

b. དམག་མི་ཞིག་གིས་གཡག་ཅིག་བསད་པ་རེད།
mə̄ə̄mi chī ki yāà chī sɛ̄ɛ̀bəreè
soldier one by yak one killed past compl./
A soldier killed a yak.

3.2.2 Plural words and postpositions

As seen in Lesson Two, unmarked nouns generally convey plurality. However, plural number in Tibetan is explicitly expressed by a number of plural modifiers and pluralizing postpositions, some of the most common of which are:

མང་པོ་	ཁ་ཤས་	གཉིས་
mə̱ŋgu*	kāshɛɛ̀*	ñīì*
many, much	several	two
ཚང་མ་	འགའ་ཤས་	གསུམ་
tsāŋma*	g̲ashɛɛ̀	sūm*
all	several	three
ཐམས་ཅད་	འགའ་ཞིག་	དུ་མ་
tāmjɛɛ̀	g̲ashig	d̲uma
all	several	many
ཏོག་ཙམ་	ཞེ་དྲགས་	
dōgdzam	sh̲edraà*	
a little	lots	

[The asterisk indicates that the term is currently used in colloquial Tibetan.]

Each of these words *follows* the noun or noun phrase it modifies, but *precedes* the instrumental particle, for example, དམག་མི་ཁ་ཤས་ཀྱིས་ ("by several soldiers"), not དམག་མི་ཀྱིས་ཁ་ཤས་.

In addition to these *plural words*, there are two common pluralizing postpositions (རྣམས་ and ཚོ་) that are placed after count nouns (nouns such as "house" that can be counted) and demonstratives ("this" and "that") to express plurality.[2] These postpositions pluralize the words and phrases they follow. For example, when these are joined to the demonstratives "this" and "that" (འདི་ཚོ་ and དེ་ཚོ་) the meaning "these" and "those" is conveyed.

a. གཡག་འདི་ཚོས་སྟག་ཅིག་བསད་པ་རེད།

yāà di̲ndzöö dāà chī sɛ̄ɛ̀bəreè

yak this pl.-by tiger one killed past compl./

These (the) yaks killed a (one) tiger.

Note again that the instrumental particle follows the pluralizer.

b. སྟག་ཁ་ཤས་ཀྱིས་གཡག་གཅིག་བསད་པ་རེད།

dāà kāshɛ̀ɛ̀ ki yāà chī sɛ̄ɛ̀bəreè

tiger several by yak one killed past compl./

Several tigers killed a (one) yak.

c. གྲྭ་པ་གཅིག་གིས་དེབ་གཉིས་ཉོས་པ་རེད།

tra̲pa chī ki te̲p ñīì ño̲öbəreè

monk one by book two bought past compl./

A monk bought two books.

Other examples are:

d. སློབ་གྲྭ་བ་མང་པོས་ཤ་ཟས་པ་རེད།

lābdrāà ma̲ŋböö shā sɛ̲ɛ̀bəreè

student many-by meat ate past compl./

Many students ate meat.

e. མོས་སོན་ཞེ་དྲགས་ཉོས་པ་རེད།

mo̲ö sōn she̲traà ño̲öbəreè

she-by seed lots bought past compl./

She bought lots of seed.

f. སྔས་མ་ནོར་བུས་ཁྱི་གསུམ་ཉོས་པ་རེད།

ŋɛ̄ɛ̄ma nɔ̲ɔ̲büù kī sūm ño̲öbəreè

formerly norbu-by dog three bought past compl./

Formerly, Norbu bought three dogs.

---

[2] There is also one less common pluralizer that is used after all nouns: དག་.

Sentence f. illustrates how temporal words such as སྔས་མ་ normally occur at the very beginning of Tibetan sentences and clauses.

g. ཁ་སང་ཞིང་པ་ཞིག་གིས་ཤ་ཏོག་ཙམ་ཟས་པ་རེད།

kɛ̄ɛ̄sa shi̱ŋbə chī ki shā dōgdzam sɛ̱ɛ̀bəreè

yesterday farmer one by meat little ate past compl./

A farmer ate a little meat yesterday.

3.3 Complex subject and object constructions

3.3.1 Complex subjects

The subjects of active sentences can be modified by demonstratives, pluralizers (including numbers), and adjectives. Using the symbols "+" (mandatory presence) and ">" (optional) we can express the format of the subject of active sentences as a formula:

+ noun > determinative > pluralizer/singularizer + instrumental.

This produces the following possibilities:

1. + n. + inst.
དམག་མིས་
mə̄ə̄miì
soldier-by
by (the) soldier(s)

2. + n. + det. + inst.
དམག་མི་འདིས་
mə̄ə̄mi di̱ì
soldier + this-by
by this soldier

3. + n. + pl. + inst.
དམག་མི་རྣམས་ཀྱིས་
mə̄ə̄mi nām ki
soldier + pl. +by
by (the) soldiers

4. + n. + det. + pl. + inst.
དམག་མི་འདི་རྣམས་ཀྱིས་
mə̄ə̄mi di̱ nām ki
soldier + this + pl. + by
by the (these) soldiers

The subject can be expanded further by the addition of an adjective. Adjectives *follow* the noun or noun phrase they modify but occur *before* the determinatives, pluralizers, and instrumentals. In terms of the formula: + n > adj. > det. > pl. + inst. For example:

> དམག་མི་ཡག་པོ་འདི་ཚོས་
> soldier good this plural-by
> by these good soldiers

a. དམག་མི་ཡག་པོ་འདི་ཚོས་བཟོས་པ་རེད།
mə̄əmi yago [yagbo] dendzöö sööbəreè
soldier good this +pl.-by made past compl./
These good soldiers made (it).

b. ཞིང་པ་དབུལ་པོ་ཚོས་ལུག་ཞིག་ཉོས་པ་རེད།
shiŋbə üübotsöö luù chī ñööbəreè
farmer poor pl.-by sheep one bought past compl./
The poor farmers bought a sheep.

c. བཟོ་པ་དབུལ་པོ་རྣམས་ཀྱིས་ལྷ་ཁང་གཅིག་བཟོས་པ་རེད།
soba üübo nām ki lhāgan chī sööbəreè
worker poor pl.-by temple one made past compl./
The poor workers made (built) a temple.

d. བཟོ་པ་གསར་པ་འདིས་འཕྲུལ་འཁོར་ཚང་མ་བཟོས་པ་རེད།
soba sāāba diì trüügɔɔ tsāŋma sööbəreè
worker new this-by machine all made past compl./
This new worker made all the machines.

e. ལུག་ཆེན་པོས་རྩྭ་ཟས་པ་རེད།
luù chēmböö dzā sɛ̀ɛbəreè
sheep big-by grass ate past compl./
The big sheep ate grass.

f. སྟག་ཆེན་པོ་གཅིག་གིས་ཁྱི་ཞིག་བསད་པ་རེད།
dāà chēmbo chī ki kī chī sɛ̀ɛbəreè
tiger big one by dog one killed past compl./
A (one) big tiger killed a dog.

g. བཟོ་པ་ཞིག་གིས་བཏང་པ་རེད།
soba chī ki dāmbəreè
worker one by sent past compl./
A worker sent (it).

3.3.2 The complex object

The object slot of active sentences can be similarly expanded by the addition of adjectives, pluralizers, and determinatives. For example:

a. བཟོ་པ་ཚོས་འཕྲུལ་འཁོར་ཡག་པོ་ཞིག་བཟོས་པ་རེད།

sobadzöö trüügɔɔ yago chī sööbəreè

worker pl.-by machine good one made past compl./

The workers made a good machine.

b. ཞིང་པ་ཚོས་ལག་ཆ་མང་པོ་བཟོས་པ་རེད།

shiŋbətsöö lagja məŋgu sööbəreè

farmer pl.-by tool many made past compl./

The farmers made many tools.

c. དམག་མི་རྣམས་ཀྱིས་ཚ་ལུ་མ་ཆེན་པོ་ཁ་ཤས་ཟས་པ་རེད།

mə̄əmi nāmki tsə̄lumə chēmbo kāshɛɛ̀ sɛɛ̀bəreè

soldier pl.-by orange big several ate past compl./

The soldiers ate several big oranges.

The object can also be modified by two adjectives linked by the conjunctive particle དང་ ("and").

d. དམག་མི་རྣམས་ཀྱིས་ལུག་དཀར་པོ་དང་ཆེན་པོ་ཁ་ཤས་ཟས་པ་རེད།

mə̄əmi nāmki luù gāābo daŋ chēmbo kāshɛɛ̀ sɛɛ̀bəreè

soldier pl.-by sheep white and big several ate past compl./

The soldiers ate several big white sheep (sheep that were both big and white).

3.3.3 The active verb

Verbs change their form (or stem) in different tenses and can have up to four stems. The verb "to kill" is an example of a 4-stem verb.

I	II	III	IV
present	*future*	*past*	*imperative*
གསོད་	གསད་	བསད་	སོད་

In modern literary Tibetan, some 3- and 4-stem verbs have been collapsed into 2-stem verbs—i.e., verbs with only a past and a non-past stem. In these cases the present tense stem is used for the future. The verbs introduced in this lesson up to this point have the following stems:

present (non-past)	*future*	*past*	*imperative*	
ཉོ་	ཉོ་	ཉོས་	ཉོས་	buy
བཟོ་	བཟོ་	བཟོས་	བཟོས་	make
འདེབས་	གདབ་	བཏབ་	ཐོབས་	plant, sow
ཟ་ (or བཟའ་)	ཟ་ (or བཟའ་)	ཟས་ (or བཟས་)	ཟས་ (or བཟས་)	eat
གསོད་	གསད་	བསད་	སོད་	kill
གཏོང་	གཏོང་/གཏང་	བཏང་	ཐོང་	send

[A complete alphabetical list of all verb stems is presented in Appendix A.]

Tibetan verbs themselves do not indicate gender, number or person. "I buy," "He buys," and "They buy" all use the same stem of the verb "to buy." Person, however, can be expressed through the modern *verb complement,* although traditionally it was dertermined solely though context.

There are two kinds of verbal complements: 1) *final complement* and 2) *connective complement.* The former functions to complete a sentence, while the latter is used to connect dependent clauses. In this section only the final complement will be discussed.

The final verbal complement is the vehicle through which tense and person are conveyed. For example, the third person narrative past tense complement is པ་རེད་ and the first person past complement is པ་ཡིན་. However, these forms derive from spoken Lhasa Tibetan and do not appear in classical Tibetan or in the many contemporary works that use the more literary modern genre. In these only the main verb is used (e.g., ཉོས་ rather than ཉོས་པ་རེད་). In this more classical style, context conveys person while context and the verb stem determines tense. This textbook will use a variety of alternative verb complements including the neo-classical style.

3.4 Simple past tense

All of the active verb examples presented in the above sections of this lesson illustrate the simple or narrative past tense. This tense expresses an action completed in the past. These constructions consist of the *past stem* of an active verb and the *simple past complement* (the linking verb རེད་ and a particle པ་). Together they express the *simple past tense, second and third person.*

a. བསད་པ་རེད། (He, she, they, you) killed (it).
sɛ̃ɛ̀bəreè

b. ཉོས་པ་རེད། (He, she, they, you) bought (it).

ñö̱ö̀bəreè

c. བཟོས་པ་རེད། (He, she, they, you) made (it).

sö̱ö̀bəreè

Person is conveyed through the verb complement. For example, by substituting the linking verb ཡིན་ for རེད་, the verb complement changes from third person to *first person.*

d. (ངས་) ཟས་པ་ཡིན་

(ŋɛ̱ɛ̀) sɛ̱ɛ̀bəyin

(i-by) ate past compl.

(I) ate (it).

These rules, however, are not hard and fast, and the reader will sometimes encounter the པ་རེད་ complement used with first person subjects, e.g., (ངས་) ཟས་པ་རེད་.

It should be noted that sometimes བ་རེད་ is used in place of པ་རེད་. This change is governed by the final letter of the preceding verb and does not affect the meaning:

པ་ is used with final: ག་, ད་, ན་, བ་, མ་, and ས་

བ་ is used with final: ང་, ར་, ལ་, and vowels

Thus, གཞས་བཏང་བ་རེད་ ("sang a song") but ཤ་ཟས་པ་རེད་ ("ate meat").

Second person past tense constructions, as indicated above, use the same complements as third person. For example:

ཁྱོད་རང་གིས་གཡག་ཅིག་བསད་པ་རེད། You killed a yak.

In addition to the པ་རེད་ (third person) past complement, another commonly used simple past complement consists of the verb སོང་ (which means "went" when used alone) used directly with the past tense stem of an active verb.

e. སྟག་གིས་ལུག་གཅིག་ཟས་སོང་།

dāà ki lu̱g chi̅ sɛ̱ɛ̀soŋ

tiger by sheep one ate past compl./

A tiger(s) ate a sheep.

Finally, as indicated above, classical Tibetan does not use the པ་རེད་, and པ་ཡིན་ complements at all. The past tense stem of the verb suffices. Thus, sentence e. above would be written: སྟག་གིས་ལུག་གཅིག་ཟས།

3.5 Present tense

Present tense constructions are formed by joining the present (or non-past) form of active verbs to one of the present tense verbal complements listed below. These constructions express both action currently going on and action that was currently going on at some point in the past. For example, in the sentence "Last year, when I came to Tibet he was building a house," the present would be used to convey that the building of a house was going on when "I" was in Tibet.

The present complement consists of several particles and either a linking or existential verb in the combinations listed below. Second and first person endings typically do not differ from third person endings (although they do in spoken Tibetan). Context—for example, pronouns—normally makes it clear which person is intended.

ALTERNATIVE PRESENT TENSE COMPLEMENTS

1. vb. + ཀྱི་ཡོད་(པ་) (རེད་)	7. vb. + བཞིན་ཡོད་(པ་) (རེད་)	13. vb. + མུས་ཡོད་པ་རེད་
2. vb. + ཀྱི་འདུག་	8. vb. + བཞིན་འདུག་	14. vb. + མུས་ཡོད་
3. vb. + ཀྱིན་ཡོད་(པ་) (རེད་)	9. vb. + བཞིན་དུ་ཡོད་(པ་) (རེད་)	15. vb. + མུས་ཡིན་
4. vb. + ཀྱིན་འདུག་	10. vb. + བཞིན་པ་རེད་	16. vb. + མུས་ཡིན་འདུག་
5. vb. + གྱི་ཡོད་(པ་) (རེད་)	11. vb. + བཞིན་པ་ཡིན་པ་རེད་	17. vb. + མུས་རེད་
6. vb. + གྱི་འདུག་	12. vb. + བཞིན་པར་	

The overall present-time meaning of these complements derives not from the inherent meaning of the constituent parts (ཀྱི་, for example, is simply the genitive case particle "of"), but rather from the particular concatenation of them. Thus, while ཀྱི་ + ཡོད་པ་ རེད་ expresses present time, the same particle with the linking verb རེད་ (ཀྱི་+རེད་) expresses future time.

Before examining some examples of present tense sentences, note should be made of the different forms that some of the present particles manifest. Like the instrumental case particles discussed above, these particles change form in accordance with the final letter of the immediately preceding syllable:

གི་ and གིན་ occur after ག་, ང་ and vowels (e.g., གཏོང་གི་ཡོད་པ་རེད་)
ཀྱི and ཀྱིན་ occur after ད་, བ་ and ས་ (e.g., གསོད་ཀྱི་ཡོད་པ་རེད་)
གྱི་ and གྱིན་ occur after ན་, མ་, ར་ and ལ་ (e.g., གཡར་གྱི་ཡོད་པ་རེད་)

Now let us examine some examples:

a. སྟག་གཅིག་གིས་ལུག་གཅིག་གསོད་བཞིན་ཡོད་པ་རེད།
" གསོད་བཞིན་དུ་ཡོད་པ་རེད།
" གསོད་མུས་རེད།
" གསོད་ཀྱི་ཡོད་པ་རེད།

dāà chi̅ ki lu̲g chi̅ sȫöshi̲n yɔ̲ɔ̀reè
" shi̲ntu yɔ̲ɔ̀reè

" müüreè

" giyɔ̀ɔreè

tiger one by sheep one kill pres. compl./

A tiger is killing a sheep.

b. བཟོ་པ་ཚོས་གནམ་གྲུ་གཅིག་བཟོ་བཞིན་དུ་ཡོད་པ་རེད།

sobətsöö nə̄mdru chī soshintu yɔɔ̀reè

worker pl.-by airplane one make pres. compl./

The workers are making an airplane.

c. གཞོན་ནུ་གསུམ་གྱིས་ཁང་པ་གཅིག་རྒྱག་བཞིན་ཡོད་པ་རེད།

shönu sūm ki kāŋbə chī gyəbshinyɔɔ̀reè

youth 3 by house one make pres. compl./

Three youths are building a house.

d. ཞིང་པ་རྣམས་ཀྱིས་ཞིང་ཁ་ལ་སོན་འདེབས་ཀྱི་ཡོད་པ་རེད།

shiŋbə nām ki shiŋga lə sōn debgiyɔɔ̀reè

farmer pl.-by field to seed plant pres. compl./

The farmers are planting (seeds) on the fields.

e. མི་མང་པོས་ལྟད་མོ་བལྟ་མུས་རེད།

mi maŋböö dɛ̄ɛ̄mo dāmüüreè

person many-by show look pres. compl./

Many people are watching the show.

f. རྡོ་རྗེས་ཁང་པ་ཉམས་གསོ་བྱེད་བཞིན་ཡོད།

dɔɔjeè kāŋba ñamso cheshinyöö

dorje-by house repair do pres. compl./

Dorje is repairing the house.

g. གྲྭ་པ་གཅིག་གིས་དཔེ་ཆ་ཀློག་བཞིན་པ་རེད།

traba chī ki bēja lɔ̄ɔ̀shinbəreè

monk one by book read pres. compl./

A monk is reading (a) book.

h. དམག་མི་འདིས་སྔོ་ཚལ་སོས་པ་ཟ་གི་ཡོད་པ་རེད།

mə̄ə̄mi diì ŋōtsɛɛ sööba səgiyɔɔ̀reè

soldier this-by vegetable fresh eat pres. compl./

The soldier is eating fresh vegetables.

i. ཕུན་ཚོགས་ཀྱིས་དགོན་པར་མཆོད་མཇལ་ཞུ་བཞིན་ཡོད།

pǖndzo ki gombar chönjɛɛ shushinyöö

phuntso by monastery-to religious visit do pres. compl./

Phuntso is making a religious visit to the monastery.

Present constructions are often used together with a temporal term such as ད་ལྟ་ ("now").

j. བླ་མ་འདིས་ད་ལྟ་ཆོས་གསུང་བཞིན་པ་རེད།

lāma di̱ì ta̱ndə chö̀ö sūŋshinbəreè

lama this-by now religion say pres. compl./

This lama is giving (saying) religious teachings now.

k. ད་ལྟ་ཁོས་སློབ་གྲྭར་གཞས་གཏོང་བཞིན་པ་རེད།

ta̱nda kö̀ö lāpdraa shɛ̱è dōŋshimbareè

now he-by school-to song sing pres. compl./

He is singing a song at school now.

3.6 Usual constructions

The first six present tense complements listed in section 3.5 above are also used to express usual or general actions. Context indicates which meaning is intended. For example:

a. ཞིང་པ་ཚོས་དཔྱིད་དུས་སོན་འདེབས་ཀྱི་ཡོད་པ་རེད།

shi̱ŋbətsö̀ö ji̇dǜü sön de̱bgiyɔ̱̀reè

farmer pl.-by spring-time seed plant pres. compl./

Farmers plant seeds in the springtime.

Tibetan also uses a number of words such as ནམ་རྒྱུན་ ("usually") and རྟག་པར་ ("always") to clarify meaning.

b. དམག་མི་འདིས་ནམ་རྒྱུན་ཤ་སོས་པ་ཟ་གི་ཡོད་པ་རེད།

mɔ̄ɔ̀mi di̱ì nə̱mgyün shā sōba sə̱gyɔ̱̀reè

soldier this-by usually meat fresh eat pres. compl./

This soldier usually eats fresh meat.

The usual tense is also conveyed by the pattern: *present* (non-past) stem of a verb + པ་རེད་ or བ་རེད་.

Since the པ་རེད་ part of this ending is normally the past complement, context or some modifying word like "usually" will differentiate between usual and past when the verb in question *does not have* different stems for past and present tense.

c. ཁོས་འཕྲུལ་འཁོར་བཟོ་བ་རེད།

kö̀ö trǖügɔɔ so̱wareè

he-by machine make usual compl./

He makes machines.

Because the verbs "to make" and "to sow" in c. and d. have a present tense stem, the usual meaning is easy to identify.

d. དབྱིད་དུས་ཞིང་པ་རྣམས་ཀྱིས་སོན་འདེབས་པ་རེད།

jīdüü shiŋbə nāmki sȫn debəreè

spring time farmer pl. by seed plant usual compl./

In spring, farmers plant seeds.

Note again that if past tense were intended the sentence would have been written using the past tense stem, e.g.,

e. དབྱིད་དུས་ཞིང་པ་རྣམས་ཀྱིས་སོན་བཏབ་པ་རེད།

jīdüü shiŋbə nām ki sȫn dābəreè

spring time farmer pl. by seed plant past compl./

In spring, farmers planted seeds.

However, with a one stem verb such as the verb "to come" (ཡོང་), only context differentiates between past and usual tenses.

f. དབྱིད་དུས་ཁོ་འདིར་ཡོང་བ་རེད།

jīdüü kō dee yombareè

spring time he here come past compl./

In spring he came here.

g. དབྱིད་དུས་ཁོ་འདིར་རྣམ་རྒྱུན་ཡོང་བ་རེད།

jīdüü kō dee namgyün yoŋwareè

spring time he here usually come usual compl./

In spring he usually comes here.

3.7 Future tense

The future tense is formed by using the future stem of the verb alone or by joining the future or non-past stem of active verbs to one of the following complements:

Third person	*Second person*	*First person*
vb. + གི་རེད་	vb. + གི་རེད་	vb. + གི་ཡིན་

The future complement consists of the genitive particle (གྱི་, ཀྱི་, etc.) with a linking verb. As with the past tense, however, note should be taken that the classical style omits the verbal complement (as in examples c.-e. below).

a. ཁོས་དེབ་ཞིག་ཉོ་གི་རེད།

kȫö teb chī ñugireè

he-by book one buy fut.-compl./

He will buy a book.

b. ངས་དེབ་གཅིག་ཉོ་གི་ཡིན།

ŋɛɛ̀ teb chī ñugiyin

i-by book one buy fut.-compl./

I will buy a book.

c. དགུན་དུས་གྲྭ་པ་གསུམ་གྱིས་གཡག་གཅིག་ཉོ།

gündüǜ traba sūm ki yāà chī ño

winter time monk three by yak one buy

In winter time, three monks will buy a yak.

d. གྲོགས་པོ་རྒན་ཁོག་དེ་ཚོས་གཡག་གཅིག་གསད།

trogo gɛngɔɔ̀ dendzöö̀ yāà chī sɛ̄ɛ̀

friend old that pl.-by yak one kill

Those elderly friends will kill a yak.

e. ཁོས་ངར་དེབ་གཅིག་གཡར།

kȫö̀ ŋaa teb chī yāā

he-by i-to book one lend

He will lend me a book.

3.8 Active verbs in interrogative constructions

Questions can be constructed with active verbs by (1) adding a question particle, (2) by adding an interrogative word, or (3) adding both an interrogative word and a question particle. The same set of interrogatives listed in Lessons One and Two apply here.

a. ཁོས་ག་རེ་བྱས་པ་རེད།

kȫö̀ kare chɛɛ̀bəreè

he-by what did past compl./

What did he do?

b. ཁོས་ཅི་བྱས་པ་རེད།

kȫö̀ jī chɛɛ̀bəreè

he-by what did past.compl./

What did he do?

c. ཁོས་ལས་ཀ་བྱས་པ་རེད་པས།

kȫö̀ lɛɛga chɛɛ̀bərebɛɛ̀

he-by work did past compl. ?/

Did he (do) work?

Did he (do) work?

d. ཁོས་ཤ་ཉོས་པ་རེད་དམ།

kȫö̀ shā ñöbəredam

he-by meat bought past compl. ?/

Did he buy meat?

e. ཁོས་ལས་ཀ་ག་པར་བྱས་པ་རེད།

kȫö̀ lɛɛga kabaa chɛɛ̀bəreè

he-by work where did past compl./

Where did he work?

f. མོས་དེབ་ག་ཚད་ཉོ་བཞིན་འདུག

möö̀ tep kədzɛɛ̀ ñoshinduù

she-by book how-many buy pres. compl./

How many books is she buying?

g. ཆོས་སུས་གསུངས་པ་རེད།

chȫö̀ sṻǜ sūmbəreè

religion who-by say past compl./

Who gave religious teachings?

h. བླ་མས་ཆོས་གསུངས་པ་རེད་དམ།

lāmɛɛ̀ chȫö̀ sūmbəredam

lama-by religion say past compl. ?/

Did the lama give religious teachings?

i. བླ་མས་ཆོས་ག་པར་གསུངས་པ་རེད་དམ།

lāmɛɛ̀ chȫö̀ kabaa sūmbəredam

lama-by religion where say past compl. ?/

Where did the lama give religious teachings?

j. ཁོ་ཚོས་དགོན་པ་ཆེན་པོ་དེ་ག་དུས་རྒྱབ་སོང་།

kōndzöö̀ gomba chēmbo de kədüǜ gyəbsoŋ

he pl.-by monastery big that when built past compl./

When did they build that big monastery?

k. དགོན་པ་ཆེན་པོ་དེ་གྲྭ་པས་རྒྱབ་པ་རེད་པས།

gomba chēmbo de trabɛɛ̀ gyəbərebeè

monastery big that monk-by built past compl. ?/

Was that big monastery built by monks?

l. གྲྭ་པས་དགོན་པ་ག་གི་རྒྱབ་པ་རེད།

trabɛɛ̀ gomba kəgi gyəbəreè

monks-by monastery which built past compl./

Which monastery was built by the monks?

First and second person constructions observe the following patterns:

m. ཁྱེད་རང་གིས་ཆོས་གསུངས་བས།

kēraŋki chȫö̀ sūmbɛɛ̀

you-by religion say (h.) past compl.?/

Did you give religious teachings?

n. ངས་ཆོས་བཤད་པ་ཡིན།

ŋɛ̱ɛ̀ chȫö̀ shɛ̄ɛ̀bəyin

i-by religion say past compl./

I gave religious teachings.

o. ཁྱེད་རང་གིས་ཤ་ཉོས་སམ།

kēraŋki shā ñö̱ö̀sam

you-by meat bought past compl.?/

Did you buy meat?

p. ངས་ཤ་ཉོས་པ་ཡིན།

ŋɛ̱ɛ̀ shā ñö̱ö̀bəyin

i-by meat bought past compl./

I bought meat.

q. ཁྱེད་རང་གིས་ག་རེ་ཉོས་པ་ཡིན་ནམ།

kēraŋki ka̱re ñö̱ö̀bəyinam [Standard spoken would simply be: ñö̱ö̀baa.]

you-by what bought past compl. ?/

What did you buy?

r. ཁྱེད་རང་གིས་ག་རེ་ཉོས་སམ།

kēraŋki ka̱re ñö̱ö̀sam

you-by what bought ?/

What did you buy?

3.9 Sentence final marker

Literary Tibetan denotes the end of a sentence by reduplicating the final letter of the verb and adding the vowel "o." For example, ཐུབ་བོ་ would be written in place of ཐུབ་པ་རེད. When verbs end in a vowel, the particle འོ་ is added to the stem, e.g., ཉོའོ་.

3.10 Reading exercise

The following exercise is a conversation between an American student and a Tibetan friend named Pema. When new words are used they should be looked up in the lesson vocabulary or the glossary.

1. Q. པད་མ་ལགས་སྐུ་གཟུགས་བདེ་པོ་ཡིན་པས།
2. A. ང་གཟུགས་པོ་བདེ་པོ་ཡིན།
3. Q. པད་མ་ལགས་བོད་ལ་ཞིང་པ་ག་ཚད་ཡོད་པ་རེད།
4. A. བོད་ལ་ཞིང་པ་མང་པོ་ཡོད་པ་རེད།
5. Q. ཞིང་པས་ལས་ཀ་ག་རེ་བྱེད་ཀྱི་ཡོད་པ་རེད།
6. A. ཞིང་པས་ཞིང་ཁ་འདེབས་ཀྱི་ཡོད་པ་རེད།
7. Q. ཁོ་ཚོར་ལུག་དང་ར་ཡོད་པ་རེད་པས།
8. A. ཞིང་པ་ཁ་ཤས་ལ་ཡོད་པ་རེད། ཁ་ཤས་ལ་ཡོད་པ་མ་རེད།
9. Q. སོན་ག་རེ་འདེབས་ཀྱི་ཡོད་པ་རེད།
10. A. དཔྱིད་དུས་འབྲུ་འདེབས་ཀྱི་ཡོད་པ་རེད། དགུན་དུས་གྲོ་འདེབས་ཀྱི་ཡོད་པ་རེད།
11. Q. འབྲས་འདེབས་ཀྱི་ཡོད་པ་རེད་དམ།
12. A. ཞིང་པ་ཚང་མས་འདེབས་ཀྱི་ཡོད་པ་མ་རེད། འགའ་ཤས་འདེབས་ཀྱི་ཡོད་པ་རེད།
13. Q. གྲྭ་པས་ཞིང་ཁར་སོན་འདེབས་ཀྱི་ཡོད་པ་རེད་པས།
14. A. ནམ་རྒྱུན་འདེབས་ཀྱི་ཡོད་པ་མ་རེད། གྲྭ་པས་དགོན་པར་དེབ་སློག་གི་ཡོད་པ་རེད།
15. Q. དགོན་པར་དགེ་རྒན་ག་ཚོད་ཡོད་པ་རེད།
16. A. དགེ་རྒན་བཅུ་ཡོད་པ་རེད།
17. Q. ཁྱེད་རང་གྲྭ་པ་ཡིན་པས།
18. A. ང་གྲྭ་པ་མིན། ང་སློབ་གྲྭ་བ་ཡིན།
19. Q. ཁྱེད་རང་གི་སློབ་གྲྭ་ག་པར་ཡོད་པ་རེད།
20. A. ལྷ་སར་ཡོད་པ་རེད།

1. bɛ̄malaà,[3] gūsuù de̱bo yi̱mbɛɛ̀
   pema la body (h.) well is ?/
   Pemala, how are you?
2. ŋa̱ su̱gu de̱bo yi̱n[4]

---

[3] The ɛ in bɛ̄malaà is short here (whereas in Lesson One it was long) because it is joined with the polite particle laà.

[4] Tibetan culture actually has no greeting that is equivalent to "hello." The phrase "How are you" usually is used for somebody whom you haven't seen for some time. In India,

i body well is/

I am well.

3. bēmalaà, pö̱ö̀ la shi̱ŋbə kə̱dzɛɛ̀ yɔ̱ɔ̀reè

pema la tibet to farm how many exist/

Pemala, in Tibet how many farmers are there?

4. pö̱ö̀ la shi̱ŋbə mə̱ŋgu yɔ̱ɔ̀reè

tibet to farmer many exist/

In Tibet there are many farmers.

5. shi̱ŋbɛɛ̀ lɛ̱ɛ̱ga ka̱re chi̱giyɔɔ̀reè

farmer-by work what do pres./usu. compl./

What work do farmers do?

6. shi̱ŋbɛɛ̀ shi̱ŋgə de̱bgiyɔɔ̀reè

farmer-by farm plant pres./usu. compl./

The farmers plant fields.

7. kōndzɔɔ lu̱ù da̱ŋ ra̱ yɔ̱ɔ̀rebɛɛ̀

he pl.-to sheep and goat exist ?/

Do they have sheep and goats?

8. shi̱ŋbə kāshɛɛ̀la yɔ̱ɔ̀reè kāshɛɛ̀la yɔ̱ɔ̀maareè

farmer several to exist/ several to exist no/

Some farmers have them. Some do not.

9. sȭn ka̱re de̱bgiyɔɔ̀reè

seed what plant pres./usu. compl./

What seeds are (usually) planted?

10. jīdüù dru̱ de̱bgiyɔɔ̀reè gü̱ndüù tro̱ də̱bgiyɔɔ̀reè

spring barley plant pres./usu. compl./ wintertime wheat plant pres./usu. compl./

In spring (they) plant barley. In winter, (they) plant wheat.

11. drɛ̱ɛ̀ de̱bgiyöbaredam

rice plant pres./usu. compl.?/

Is rice (usually) planted?

12. shi̱ŋbə tsāŋmɛɛ̀ de̱bgiyɔɔ̀maareè. ga̱shɛɛ̀ de̱bgiyɔɔ̀reè

---

the phrase "Tashidele" is commonly used for "hello," and in some groups such as the nomads of W.Tibet, "Did you have a good sleep?" is used. Other villagers simply ask, "Where are you going?" or something similar.

farmer all-by plant pres./usu. compl. no/ several plant pres./usu. compl./
All the farmers do not plant (it). Several plant it.

13. trabεὲ shiŋgaa sȭn debgiyɔɔ̀rebεὲ
monk-by field to seed plant pres./usu. compl?/
Do monks plant seed in the fields?

14. nə̄mgyün debgiyɔɔ̀maareè. trabεὲ gombaa teb lōgiyɔɔ̀reè
usually plant pres./usu. compl. no/ monk-by monastery-to book read pres./usu. compl./
Usually, (they) do not plant. Monks read books in the monastery.

15. gombaa gegεn kədzöö̀ yɔɔ̀reè
monastery-to teacher how many exist/
How many teachers are there in the monastery?

16. gegεn jū yɔɔ̀reè
teacher ten exist/
There are ten teachers.

17. kēraŋ traba yimbεὲ
you monk is ?/
Are you a monk?

18. ŋa traba mεn. ŋa lābdraà yin/
i monk no-is/ i student is/
I am not a monk. I am a student.

19. kēraŋki lābdra kabaa yɔɔ̀reè
your school where exist?/
Where is your school?

20. lε̄ε̄saa yɔɔ̀reè
lhasa-to exist/
(It) is in Lhasa.

3.11 Vocabulary

ཀྱི་འདུག་	present tense complement (giduù)
ཀྱི་ཡོད་(པ་) རེད་	present tense complement (gi yɔɔ̀reè)
ཀྱིན་འདུག་	present tense complement (ginduù)
ཀྱིན་ཡོད་(པ་) རེད་	present tense complement (gin yɔɔ̀reè)
ཀྱིས་	instrumental particle (ki)
ཀློག་	va. to read (lɔ̄ɔ̀)

སྐུ་གཟུགས་ body (h.) (gūsuù)

སྐུ་གཟུགས་བདེ་པོ་ཡིན་པས་ idiom. How are you? (h.) (gūsuù de̱bo yi̱mbɛɛ̀)

ཁ་སང་ yesterday (kɛ̄ɛ̄sa)

ཁང་པ་རྒྱག་ va. to build a house (kāŋba gya̱à)

ཁོས་ he + instrumental (kȫȍ)

གི་ཡིན་ future tense complement (giyin)

གི་རེད་ future tense complement (gireè)

གིས་ instrumental particle (ki)

གྲོ་ wheat (tro̱)

གྲོགས་པོ་ friend (tro̱go)

བཀྱི་འདུག་ present tense complement (giduù)

བཀྱི་ཡོད་(པ) རེད་ present tense complement (gi yɔ̱ɔ̀reè)

འགའ་ཤིག་ several (ga̱shig)

འགའ་ཤས་ several (ga̱shɛɛ̀)

རྒྱག་ va. 1. verbalizer for nouns; 2. to build; 3. to shoot (gya̱à)

རྒྱབ་ va. p. of རྒྱག་

སྔོ་ཚལ་ vegetable (ŋōtsɛɛ)

ཅིག་ a, one (ji̱g, chi̱)

ཆོས་ religion, dharma (chȫȍ)

ཆོས་གསུང་ va. to teach religion (h.) (chȫȍ sūŋ)

མཆོད་མཇལ་ religious visit (chȫnjɛɛ)

ཉམས་གསོ་ repair; va. — བྱེད་ to repair, restore (ña̱mso)

ཉལ་ va. to sleep (ñɛ̱ɛ̱)

ཉོ་ va. to buy (ño̱)

ཉོས་ va. p. of ཉོ་ (ñȫȍ)

གཉིད་ཁུག་ vi. to fall asleep (ñīì kūù)

གཉིས་ two (ñīì)

ཏོག་ཙམ་ a little (dōgdzam, dɛ̄ɛ̄tsə)

གཏོང་ va. to send (dōŋ)

བཏང་ va. p. of གཏོང་ (dāŋ)

བཏབ་ va. p. of འདེབས་ (dāb)

རྟག་པར་ always (dāgbar)

ལྟད་མོ་ a show (dɛ̄ɛ̄mo)

སྟག་ tiger (dāà)

ཐམས་ཅད་ all (tāmjɛɛ̀)

ཐོབས་ va. imp. of འདེབས་ (tōb)

ད་ལྟ་ now (ta̱ndə)

དག་ plural (da̱à)

དུ་མ་ many (tu̱mə)

དེ་ཚོ་ those (de̱ndzo)

གདབ་ va. f. of འདེབས་ (də̱b)

འདི་ཚོ་ these (di̱ndzo)

འདིས་ by this (di̱ì)

འདེབས་ va. to plant, sow (de̱b)

ནམ་རྒྱུན་ usually (nə̄mgyu)

གནམ་གྲུ་ airplane (nə̄mdru)

རྣམས་ plural (nām)

པ་རེད་ past compl. (bəreè)

པས་ question particle (bɛɛ̀)

དཔྱིད་དུས་ spring, springtime (ji̱düù)

འཕྲུལ་འཁོར་ machine (trǖügɔɔ)

བྱས་ va. p. of བྱེད་ (che̱ɛ̀)

བྱེད་ va. to do (che̱è)

དབུལ་པོ་ poor (üübo)

འབྲས་ rice (drɛ̱ɛ̀)

འབྲུ་ barley; grain (dru̱)

མུས་ present tense particle (mü̱)

མུས་ཡིན་ present tense complement (mü̱yin)

མུས་ཡིན་འདུག་	present tense complement (müyinduù)
མུས་ཡོད་	present tense complement (müyöö̀)
མུས་ཡོད་(པ) རེད་	present tense complement (müyɔɔ̀reè)
མུས་རེད་	present tense complement (müreè)
རྩྭ	grass (dzā)
ཚ་ལུ་མ་	orange (fruit) (tsə̄lumə)
ཚང་མ་	all (tsāŋma)
ཚོ	plural (tsō)
ཞིང་ཁ་	field, farm (shiŋga)
ཞུ་	va. to say, request, ask (h.) (shu)
ཞེ་དྲགས	a lot (shedraà)
གཞས་	song (shɛɛ̀)
གཞས་བཏང་	va. p. of གཞས་གཏོང་: sang song (shɛɛ̀ dāŋ)
བཞིན་དུ་ཡོད་པ་རེད་	present tense complement (shintu yɔ̀ɔreè)
བཞིན་འདུག་	present tense complement (shinduù)
བཞིན་པ་ཡིན་པ་རེད་	present tense complement (shimbə yimbəreè)
བཞིན་པར་	present tense complement (shimbar)
བཞིན་པ་རེད་	present tense complement (shimbəreè)
བཞིན་ཡོད་(པ)རེད་	present tense complement (shin yɔ̀ɔreè)
ཟ་	va. to eat (sa)
ཟས་	va. p. of ཟ་ (sɛɛ̀)
གཟུགས་པོ་	body (sūgu)
གཟུགས་པོ་བདེ་པོ་ཡིན་	idiom. I am fine. (sūgu debo yin)
བཟོ་	va. to make (so)
བཟོས་	va. p of བཟོ་ (söö̀)
ཡག་པོ་	good (yago)
ཡོང་	va. to come
གཡར་	va. to lend, to borrow (yāā)
ར་	1. dative-locative particle; 2. goat (ra)
ལག་ཆ་	tool (lagja)
ལགས་	particle used after personal names to convey politeness (laà)
ལས་ཀ་	work; va. — བྱེད་ to work (lɛɛga)
ལུག་	sheep (luù)
ཤ་	meat (shā)
སོང་	past complement (sōŋ)
སོད་	va. imp. of གསོད་ (sȫö̀)
སོན་	seed (sön)
སོས་པ་	fresh (sȫöba)
གསད་	va. f. of གསོད་ (sɛ̄ɛ̀)
གསུངས་	va. to say (h.) (sūŋ)
གསོད་	va. to kill (sȫö̀)
བསད་	va. p. of གསོད་ (sɛ̄ɛ̀)

Lesson Four

4.1 Clause construction: introduction

Tibetan sentences normally contain two or more clauses serially linked by a class of verbal postpositions called clause connectives (cc.) These clause connectors link the various clauses in different ways, e.g., *because Clause A, Clause B*, or *as soon as Clause A, Clause B.* This lesson will introduce two of the most common of these clause connectives.

Unfortunately for beginners, many of these clause connectives are multifunctional, that is to say, single particles often link clauses in more than one way. Which of the different functions of a single particle is intended in any given instance can usually only be discerned by the context of the clauses in question (i.e., with respect to the meaning of the clauses that precede and follow it). The applicability of each of the alternative uses of a multi-functional clause connective will have to considered when it is encountered in a sentence to determine which function is intended in that instance. One of the main goals of this book is to teach readers this skill.

4.2 The པ་དང་ connective

དང་ normally means *and* and is used to join nouns, e.g. Dorje *and* Tsering is written རྡོ་རྗེ་དང་ཚེ་རིང་. དང་, however, is also used with verbs and verbal phrases to connect clauses. When used in this manner, it also acts as a simple conjunction linking two clauses in the manner of Clause A *and* Clause B. In example a. the two clauses (in this case, sentences) are ཁ་སང་མོས་དེབ་བཀླགས་པ་རེད་ (Yesterday she read a book) and དེ་རིང་ཁྲོམ་ལ་ཕྱིན་པ་རེད་ (Today (she) went to the market).

a. མོས་ཁ་སང་དེབ་བཀླགས་པ་དང་དེ་རིང་ཁྲོམ་ལ་ཕྱིན་པ་རེད།
   mö̱ö kɛ̄ɛ̄sa te̱p lɔ̄ɔ̄ba da̱ŋ te̱riŋ trōmlə chīmbəreè [1]
   she-by yesterday book read and today market went past compl./
   Yesterday she read a book and today (she) went to the market.

b. དབྱིད་དུས་ཁོས་དགོན་པར་དངུལ་སྤྲད་པ་དང་དབྱར་དུས་མོས་མཆོད་མཇལ་ལ་ཕྱིན་སོང་།
   jīdüü köö go̱mbaa ŋüü drɛ̄ɛ̄ba da̱ŋ yərdüü mö̱ö chōnjɛɛlə chīnsu (soŋ)

---

[1] Recall that a final "n" is pronounced as "m" when immediately followed by a bilabial consonant such as "p." Thus ཕྱིན་པ་ is pronounced chīmbə, not chīnbə.

spring time he-by monastery-to money gave and summer time she-by religious-visit
went past compl./
In spring he gave the monastery money, and in summer she went for a religious visit.

c. གཟའ་སྤེན་པར་མོས་ཟ་ཁང་ལ་ལས་ཀ་བྱས་པ་དང་། ཁོས་ནང་ལ་བསྡད་པ་རེད།
s̱a bēmbaa mö̱ö̀ s̱aganlə lɛ̱ɛga chɛ̱ba da̱ŋ kȫö̀ na̱nlə dɛ̱ɛ̀bəreè
Saturday-to she-by restaurant to work did and/ he-by home to stayed past compl./
On Saturday, she worked at the restaurant and he stayed home.

The word "Saturday" occupies the normal time slot in Tibetan sentences, i.e., the beginning of the sentence. Other time words and phrases such as སྔོན་མར་ ([ŋōnmaa] in the past, formerly) and གནའ་རབས་སུ་ ([nārəbsu] in ancient times) could be substituted for "Saturday" here. Time slot words normally require the dative-locative particle (lə/la), here conveying "at" or "on".

d. བུ་འདི་རྒྱལ་པོའི་སྲས་མོར་དགའ་པོ་ཡོད་པ་དང་རྒྱལ་པོའི་སྲས་མོས་ཁོ་ལ་དགའ་པོ་ཡོད།
pu̱di gyɛ̱ɛ̱böö sɛ̄ɛ̄mɔɔ ga̱bo yö̱ba da̱ŋ gyɛ̱ɛ̱böö sɛ̄ɛ̄möö̀ kōlə (kɔ̄ɔ̄) ga̱bo yö̱ö̀
child-boy this princess-to like/love exist and princess-by he to like/love exist/
This boy likes/loves the princess and the princess likes/loves him.

The clause connective པ་དང་ can also convey the meaning of "as soon as" the verbal action occurred or occurs, but this aspect will be discussed later in Lesson 6.2.

4.3 The temporal connectives: རྗེས་ and པའི་/བའི་རྗེས་སུ་

These clause connectives have only one function: they link two clauses so that the latter occurs *after* the action stated in the former. They require the verb to be in the past stem.

a. ཁོས་ལས་ཀ་བྱས་པ་རེད།
kȫö̀ lɛ̱ɛga chɛ̱ɛ̀bəreè
he-by work did past compl./
He worked.

b. ཁོས་ཟ་ཁང་ལ་ཁ་ལག་ཟས་སོང་།
kȫö̀ s̱aganlə kālaà s̱ɛ̱ɛ̀soŋ
he-by restaurant to food ate past compl./
He ate at the restaurant.

If one wanted to express these two actions so that the subject ("He") did the second action *after* doing the first, the temporal clause connective could be used.

c. ཁོས་ལས་ཀ་བྱས་རྗེས་ཟ་ཁང་ལ་ཁ་ལག་ཟས་སོང་།

kō̈ö lɛɛga chɛɛ̀jeè saganlə kālaà sɛɛ̀su [su is the spoken form of soŋ]

he-by work did after, restaurant to food ate past compl./

After he worked (he) ate at a restaurant.

The other temporal connective—པའི་/བའི་རྗེས་སུ་—can be substituted without any change in meaning.

d. ཁོས་ལས་ཀ་བྱས་པའི་རྗེས་སུ་ཟ་ཁང་ལ་ཁ་ལག་ཟས་སོང་།

same as c. except for pronunciation

The relationship between the clauses in sentences a. and b. can be reversed.

e. ཁོས་ཟ་ཁང་ལ་ཁ་ལག་ཟས་རྗེས་ལས་ཀ་བྱས་པ་རེད།

he-by restaurant to food ate after, work did past compl./

kō̈ö saganla kālaà sɛɛ̀jeè lɛɛga chɛɛ̀bareè

After he ate at the restaurant, (he) worked.

Whether པའི་ or བའི་ is used with རྗེས་སུ་ depends on the final letter of the preceding verb:

པའི་ is used with final ག་, ད་, ན་, བ་, མ་ and ས་

བའི་ is used with final ང་, ར་, ལ་, and vowels

4.4 Marking quotations and naming names

Quotations in Tibetan traditionally were not marked by quotation marks, although a few modern works now employ them. Traditionally, quotes were indicated by a quotation marking particle placed immediately *after* the quote. This particle has several forms:

ཅེས་ occurs after final ག་, ད་ and བ་

ཤེས་ occurs usually after final ས་

ཞེས་ occurs after all other finals including vowels

For example, in example a. below, the direct statement ང་འགྲོ་གི་ཡིན་ ("I am going") is not formally identified as a quote until ཞེས་.

a. ཁོས་ང་འགྲོ་གི་ཡིན་ཞེས་ལབ་པ་རེད།

kō̈ö ŋa drugiyin sheè ləbəreè

he-by i go fut. compl. quote say past compl./

He said, "I will go."

b. བླ་མས་གྲྭ་པར་ངས་ཁ་སང་ཆོས་བཤད་ཅེས་གསུངས།

lāmɛɛ̀ trabaa ŋɛɛ̀ kɛɛ̄sa chō̈ö shɛɛ̀jeè sūŋ

lama-by monk-to i-by yesterday religion taught quote say past compl./

The lama said to (told) the monk, "I taught religion yesterday."

When one wants to specify a name within a sentence, either ཟེར་བ་ or ཞེས་བྱ་བ་ ("the one called/named") is normally used.

c. བླ་མ་རྡོ་རྗེ་ཟེར་བ་དེས་གྲྭ་པར་ངས་ཁ་སང་ཆོས་བཤད་ཅེས་གསུངས་པ་རེད་
lāma dɔɔje sewa deè trabar ŋɛè kɛɛsa chöö shɛɛ jēè sūŋbəreè
lama dorje called that-by monk-to i-by yesterday religion taught quote say past compl./
The lama named Dorje said to (told) the monk, "I taught religion yesterday."

Note that the subject is: "by that lama called dorje."

d. འབྲས་སྤུངས་ཞེས་བྱ་བ་དེ་དགོན་པ་རེད།
drɛbuŋ shechawa de gomba reè
drepung called that monastery is/
That which is called Drepung is a monastery.

4.5 Review of the declension of pronouns

	I	he	she	you	he/she (honorific)
nominative	ང་ (ŋa)	ཁོ་ (kō)	མོ་ (mo)	ཁྱེད་རང་ (kēraŋ)	ཁོང་ (kōŋ)
instrumental	ངས་ (ŋɛè)	ཁོས་ (köö)	མོས་ (möö)	ཁྱེད་རང་གིས་ (kēraŋki)	ཁོང་གིས་ (kōŋki)
dative-locative	ངར་ (ŋaa)	ཁོར་ (kɔɔ)	མོར་ (mɔɔ)	ཁྱེད་རང་ལ་ (kēraŋla)	ཁོང་ལ་ (kōŋlə)

4.6 Reading Exercise:

Reading extensively is the best way to learn how to group syllables correctly into words and how to decode the often complex sentence/clause constructions of literary Tibetan. From this point on, therefore, each lesson will present one or more reading selections which will use the basic grammar covered up to that point (with occasional new features). The reader should:

(1) first try to translate the reading by looking up new (and forgotten) words in the glossary and vocabulary sections;

(2) use the interlinear translation when problems of word division arise; and

(3) only after this, consult the English translation and the grammatical notes.

4.6.1 Tibetan text

༄༅ གནའ་རབས་སུ་ཡུལ་ཞིག་ཏུ་རྒྱལ་པོ་ཞིག་ཡོད། ཁོང་ལོ་བཞི་བཅུ་རེད། ཁོང་ལ་བུ་མོ་མཛེས་པོ་ཞིག་ཡོད། ཡུལ་དེར་རྡོན་པ་
སྐྱོ་པོ་ཞིག་འདུག། ཁོར་བུ་གསུམ་ཡོད། བུ་ཆུང་པ་འདི་ལོ་ཉི་ཤུ་རེད། བུ་དེས་རྒྱལ་པོའི་སྲས་མོར་སྙིང་ནས་བརྩེ་གི་ཡོད་པ་དང་།

རྒྱལ་པོའི་སྲས་མོས་ཀྱང་ཁོ་པར་སྙིང་ནས་བརྩེ་གི་ཡོད། སྐབས་གཅིག་ལ་རྔོན་པ་དང་བུ་གཉིས་ཀས་རི་ལ་རི་དྭགས་རྒྱབ་བཞིན་པར་ དུད་འགྲོ་དཀར་པོ་ཞིག་ལ་རྙི་རྒྱབ་རྗེས་པ་ཕས་བུར་འདི་དུད་འགྲོ་དངོས་གནས་རེད་དམ་ཞེས་དྲིས་པའི་རྗེས་སུ་ལམ་སང་དུད་འགྲོ་ དེས་རྔོན་པར་ང་དུད་འགྲོ་མིན་ང་ལྷ་མོ་ཡིན་ཞེས་ལན་བཏབ་པ་རེད། རྔོན་པ་དང་བུ་གཉིས་ཀར་ཆོས་ལ་དད་པ་འདུག། བྱས་ཙང་ ཁོ་གཉིས་ཀྱིས་དུད་འགྲོ་དེ་སྲོད་རྗེས། དུད་འགྲོ་དཀར་པོ་དེས་ཁོ་གཉིས་ལ་ཐུགས་རྗེ་ཆེ་ཞེས་ཟེར་བའི་རྗེས་སུ་ལམ་སང་ཕ་ལམ་ འོད་ཆེམ་ཆེམ་ཞིག་སྤྲད་པ་དང་། ང་དུང་ཐུགས་རྗེ་ཆེ་ཞེས་བཤད་པ་རེད། དེ་ནས་དུད་འགྲོ་དཀར་པོ་དེས་གནམ་ལ་འཕུར། པ་ཕས་ དགའ་རྗེས་མཆི་མ་གཏོང་བཞིན་པར་ད་ང་ཚོ་ཕྱུག་པོ་རེད་ཅེས་ལབ་རྗེས་ཕྱིར་ལོག་བྱས། རྔོན་པས་ཕ་ལམ་དེ་ཚོང་པར་བཙོང་རྗེས་ ཞིང་ཁ་མང་པོ་ཉོས་པ་དང་། ཁང་པ་གསར་པ་ཡང་རྒྱབ་སོང་། དེ་ནས་བུ་དེས་རྒྱལ་པོའི་སྲས་མོ་དེ་མནའ་མར་བླངས་པ་རེད།།

4.6.2 Interlinear translation/pronunciation

1. nārəbsu y<u>üü</u> sh<u>i</u>gtu gy<u>εε</u>bo chī y<u>öö</u>/ kōŋ l<u>o</u> sh<u>i</u>bju r<u>eè</u>/ kōŋlə p<u>o</u>mo dz<u>e</u>bo chī yöö/ y<u>üü</u> d<u>ee</u> ŋōmba

ancient-time to place one king one exist/ he year 40 is/ he to daughter beautiful one exist/ country that-to hunter

2. gyōbo chī d<u>u</u>ù/ kɔ̄ɔ p<u>u</u> sūm y<u>ö</u>ò/ p<u>u</u> g<u>ε</u>mbadi l<u>o</u> ñīshu r<u>e</u>è/ p<u>u</u> t<u>e</u>è gy<u>εε</u>böö sε̄εmor ñīŋnεὲ dzēgiyöbə d<u>a</u>ŋ/

poor one exist/ he-to son three exist/ son older this year 20 is/ child that-by princess-to heart from love usual compl. and/

3. gy<u>εε</u>böö sε̄εmöö gyāŋ kōbar ñīŋnεὲ dzēgiyöò/ gəb chīlə ŋōmba d<u>a</u>ŋ p<u>u</u> ñīigεὲ [see 4.6.4.8] r<u>i</u>lə r<u>i</u>daà gy<u>ə</u>b sh<u>i</u>mbar

princess-by also he-to heart from love usual compl./ time one to hunter and son both-by hill to hunt while-doing

4. d<u>ü</u>ndro gāābo chīlə ñī gy<u>ə</u>bjeè bābeè p<u>oo</u> [or p<u>u</u>r] d<u>i</u> d<u>ü</u>ndro ŋōnnεὲ r<u>e</u>dam sh<u>e</u>è trīibεjesu l<u>a</u>msan d<u>ü</u>ndro

[Note that p<u>u</u> becomes p<u>oo</u> (or p<u>u</u>la) in spoken. Also the "n" in d<u>ü</u>ndro appears because the 2nd syllable begins with འ.]

animal white one to snared after/ father-by son-to this animal really is ? quote asked after at-once animal

5. teè ŋōmbar ŋ<u>a</u> d<u>ü</u>ndro m<u>ε</u>n ŋ<u>a</u> lhāmo y<u>i</u>n sh<u>e</u>è l<u>ε</u>n dəbəreè/ ŋōmba d<u>a</u>ŋ p<u>u</u> ñīigar chöölə t<u>ε</u>ba d<u>u</u>ù/ ch<u>ε</u>èdzaŋ

that-by hunter-to i animal no is i goddess is quote answer made past compl./
hunter and son both-to religion belief exist/ therefore

6. kūñīìki [Note: kō becomes kū when linked with ñīì] dü̲ndrode lȫò je̲è/ dü̲ndro gāābo deè kūñiìlə tūjeche she̲è se̲rwεε je̲èsu la̲msan pālam

he two by animal that released after./ animal white that-by he both to thank
you quote say after at-once diamond

7. ö̲ò chēmjem chī drε̄ὲbəda̲ŋ/ tə̲duŋ tūjeche she̲è shε̄ὲbareè/ te̲nεὲ dü̲ndro gāābo deè nāmlə pīr/ bābεὲ

glittering one gave and/ once-again thank you quote say past compl./ that
from animal white that-by sky to fly past compl./ father-by

8. ga̲jeè chīmə dōŋ shi̲nbar ta̲ ŋa̲ndzo chūgbo re̲è jēè lə̲bjeè chīlɔɔ̀ chε̲ὲ/ ŋȫmbεὲ pālamte tsōŋbaa dzōŋjeè

happy after cry while-doing now we rich are quote say after return did/
hunter-by diamond trader-to sold after

9. shi̲ŋgə mə̲ŋgu ñö̲ö̀bə da̲ŋ/ kāŋba sāāba ya̲ŋ gyə̲bsoŋ/ te̲nεὲ pu̲deè gyε̲ε̲böö sε̄ὲmote nāmaa lēmbəreè/

field many bought and/ house new also built past compl./ then son
that-by princess that bride-to took past compl.//

4.6.3 Translation

In ancient time, in a country, there lived a king. He was 40 years old. He had a beautiful daughter. In that country there was a poor hunter. He had three sons. The eldest son was 20 years old. That son loved the princess with all his heart and the princess also loved him with all her heart. One time while the hunter and his son both were hunting in the mountains they snared a white animal, after which the father asked his son, "Is this really an animal?" Immediately the animal replied to the hunter, "I am not an animal. I am a goddess." The hunter and the son both had faith in religion. Therefore, they released the animal. Afterwards, the white animal said, "Thank you," to the two of them and after this immediately gave them a glittering diamond and again said "Thank you," and then flew off into the sky. The father got happy and after that started to cry and while crying said, "Now we are rich," and then returned (home.) After this, the hunter sold that diamond to a trader and then bought many fields and also built a new house. After that, the son took the princess as (his) bride.

4.6.4 Grammatical notes

1. The first segment consists of: གནའ་རབས་སུ་ཡུལ་ཞིག་ཏུ་རྒྱལ་པོ་ཞིག་ཡོད་.

It begins with a typical time-slot phrase (that is, with a phrase indicating when the action took place). In this instance, the time-slot phrase is གནའ་རབས་སུ་. It consists of the word "ancient time" (གནའ་རབས་) and the dative-locative particle སུ་ (in/at). This is followed by a clause specifying the location of the action that consists of a noun (ཡུལ་— place, country), the indefinite article "a" (ཞིག་), and the dative-locative (ཏུ་). Together these convey the meaning: "in a place/country" (ཡུལ་ཞིག་ཏུ་).

After this we finally get to the heart of the first clause, namely: "a king existed" (རྒྱལ་པོ་ཞིག་ཡོད་). This construction is, therefore, basically a simple existential sentence ("There existed a king") with two sets of modifiers explaining *when* and *where* the king existed.

2. The next segment consists of: ཁོང་ལོ་བཞི་བཅུ་རེད་

It is a simple linking verb construction: "He *is* 40 years old". The subject is "he (honorific)" (ཁོང་), the object is "year/age (ལོ་) + 40 (བཞི་བཅུ་), and the linking verb is རེད .

3. The next clause consists of: ཁོང་ལ་བུ་མོ་མཛེས་པོ་ཞིག་ཡོད།.

This is a simple existential construction expressing possession: "to the king there was a daughter." The object in this clause, "daughter" (བུ་མོ་), is modified by the adjective "beautiful" (མཛེས་པོ་), which follows it. The subject + dative-locative segment, ཁོང་ལ་("he-to"), alternatively could have been expressed as "to the king" (རྒྱལ་པོར་) or "to that king" (རྒྱལ་པོ་དེར).

4. The next segment consists of: ཡུལ་དེར་རྗོན་པ་སྐྱོ་པོ་ཞིག་འདུག.

This is still another simple existential construction that begins with a location slot phrase ཡུལ་དེར་ ("place + that-to" or "in that place"). It is followed by a simple subject ("hunter"—རྗོན་པ་) modified by the adjective "poor" (སྐྱོ་པོ་). Thus, this existential construction conveys the meaning: "there was a poor hunter in that place." The word order can be reversed with no basic change in meaning: རྗོན་པ་སྐྱོ་པོ་ཞིག་ཡུལ་དེར་འདུག.

5. The next segment consists of: ཁོར་བུ་གསུམ་ཡོད།.

This existential sentence conveys possession: "to him (ཁོར་) there existed (ཡོད་) three (གསུམ་) sons (བུ་) (i.e., he had three sons)."

6. The next segment consists of: བུ་ཆེན་པ་འདི་ལོ་ཉི་ཤུ་རེད་.

This linking sentence tells something about the subject, "the eldest son" (བུ་ཆེན་པ་). The linking verb in this sentence, རེད་, links the subject with an attribute: "twenty years old" (ལོ་ཉི་ཤུ་), making the sentence mean "the eldest son was twenty years old." Note that this use of a linking verb to convey age is arbitrary—a matter dictated by Tibetan semantics. From our point of view an existential construction would have been just as logical.

7. The next segment consists of two clauses: 1. བུ་དེས་རྒྱལ་པོའི་སྲས་མོར་སྙིང་ནས་བརྩེ་གི་ཡོད་པ་དང་། 2. རྒྱལ་པོའི་སྲས་མོས་ཀྱང་ཁོ་པར་སྙིང་ནས་བརྩེ་གི་ཡོད།.

Clause one begins with a subject in the instrumental ("by that son"—བུ་དེས་), this indicating that either all or part of this segment is an active verb construction. The subject (the son) is marked by "that" + the instrumental case (དེ་ + ས་). The object, "the princess," is marked by the dative-locative particle which is suffixed to the last syllable in "princess" (མོ་ + ར་), becoming "to that princess." The verb phrase in this construction centers on the 4-stem verb བརྩེ་ ("love") with the present-future stem being used here. This verb is modified by the phrase "from the heart" (སྙིང་ནས་), which acts as an adverb - conveying the *manner* in which the verbal action occurred. Thus, the overall active verb sentence conveys the *usual* mode--"the son loved the princess deeply."

Although this could be a complete sentence if it had a final verb complement (for example: བུ་དེས་རྒྱལ་པོའི་སྲས་མོར་སྙིང་ནས་བརྩེ་གི་ཡོད་), it does not. Instead it ends with the clause connective པ་དང་ which indicates a simple conjunction of the action in two clauses—"he loved her deeply and. . . ."

The second clause conveys that "the princess also loved him deeply." As in the previous clause, the subject, "the princess," is marked by the instrumental case (the -ས་) in རྒྱལ་པོའི་སྲས་མོས་. It is followed by the word ཀྱང་ ("also, even"), and then the object in the dative-locative (he+ to = him [ཁོ་པ་ + ར་]), conveying that the love is going *from* her *to* him.

8. The next segment consists of four clauses: 1. སྐབས་གཅིག་ལ་རྔོན་པ་དང་བུ་གཉིས་ཀས་རི་ལ་རི་དྭགས་རྒྱབ་བཞིན་པར 2. དུད་འགྲོ་དཀར་པོ་ཞིག་ལ་རྡ་རྒྱབ་རྗེས་ 3 པ་ཕས་བུར་འདི་དུད་འགྲོ་དངོས་གནས་རེད་དམ་ཞེས་དྲིས་པའི་རྗེས་སུ་ 4. ལམ་སེང་དུད་འགྲོ་དེས་རྔོན་པར་ང་དུད་འགྲོ་མིན་ང་ལྷ་མོ་ཡིན་ཞེས་ལན་བཏབ་པ་རེད།.

This clause starts with a time-slot word, "at (ལ་) one (གཅིག་) time (སྐབས་)." It is followed by a joint subject—the hunter *and* the son (རྔོན་པ་དང་བུ་). With joint subjects such as this it is customary to add the phrase "both" or "the two together" (གཉིས་ཀ་). The instrumental particle is added to this, making it གཉིས་ཀས་ ("by the two together").

The next phrase indicates the location of the verbal action (i.e., in the mountains), which breaks down into "mountain" (རི་) + "to" (ལ་).

The verbal clause follows this. The verb in this clause is a compound verb consisting of the noun "herbivorous wild animal" (རི་དྭགས་) + རྒྱག་, an auxiliary verb that typically verbalizes nouns (makes nouns into verbs or creates verbal phrases out of nouns). This combination produces the standard Tibetan phrase "to hunt."

It, in turn, is modified by བཞིན་པར་, one of the present tense complements which conveys the idea that the subjects were *in the process* of doing the verbal action, "hunting." However, the sentence is not a complete sentence as would have been the case if the verb complement had been བཞིན་ཡོད་ or བཞིན་ཡོད་པ་རེད. Instead, it conveys the idea that while in the state of doing the hunting, something else occurred. That something else is explained in the next clause, which continues until the verb རྒྱག་ in clause two.

The subject of clause two is not overtly specified, but is the same as that in the preceding clause, i.e., the hunter and the son. The object of this clause is "the white animal," which breaks down into "animal" (དུད་འགྲོ་) modified by the adjective "white" (དཀར་པོ་). In turn, it is modified by an indefinite article and the dative-locative (ཞིག་ལ་), conveying "to a (white animal)."

This is followed by a compound verb phrase consisting of the verb རྙི་རྒྱག་, "to snare/trap."

This clause does not contain a final sentence complement. Instead the temporal connector རྗེས་ conveys the idea that *after* snaring the completely white animal, something happened. Thus, the two clauses preceding the clause connector could be glossed as: "*after* snaring the completely white animal *while* (being in the state of) hunting in the mountains." This stringing together of clauses where English would use separate sentences is typical of literary Tibetan style. As the reading selections in this book become more difficult, you will encounter whole pages which consist of clauses strung together without any final sentence break. Thus, a goal of this book is to familiarize you with this style and teach you how to make the appropriate breaks yourself.

The third clause (པ་ཕས་བུ་ར་འདི་དུད་འགྲོ་དངོས་གནས་རེད་དམ་ཞེས་དྲིས་པའི་རྗེས་སུ་) begins with the subject "father" in the instrumental (པ་ཕས་), immediately followed by the object, "the son," in the dative-locative (བུ་ར་). This literally translates as: "by the father to the son."

It is followed by a direct quote from the father. As was explained earlier, such quotes are *only* marked at their conclusion, so that the reader must discern this by the meaning of the words and by the quotation particle- ཞེས་. The quote itself is a complete linking verb sentence, "Is this really an animal?" (འདི་དུད་འགྲོ་དངོས་གནས་རེད་དམ་), followed by the quote particle (ཞེས་) and then by the verb དྲིས་ ("ask") in the past tense stem. This active verb goes with the earlier subject, "by the father," making the overall structure: *by* the father *to* the son, *asked.* The quote conveys what was asked.

Here again, Tibetan syntax does not use a complete sentence ending (for example, a sentence such as: "The father asked the son, 'It this really an animal?'"). Instead, this clause is linked to the next one by the temporal clause connective- པའི་རྗེས་སུ་. Thus, *after* asking . . ., something happened.

The fourth clause begins with another time word, "immediately" (ལམ་སེང་). It is followed by the subject, "that animal" (དུད་འགྲོ་དེས་) in the instrumental case, and then the object, "the hunter" (རྔོན་པ) in the dative-locative case (རྔོན་པར་).

These are followed by another direct speech quotation, made "by the animal," which itself consists of two sentences. The first sentence is the simple linking verb sentence, "I am not an animal (ང་དུད་འགྲོ་མིན་)." The second sentence is another linking verb sentence, "I am a goddess (ང་ལྷ་མོ་ཡིན)." This direct speech is followed by the quotation marker (ཞེས་) and the noun-active verb combination ལན་བཏབ་, meaning "to answer." This verbal phrase consists of the noun "answer" (ལན་) plus the past tense stem of the verb "throw" or "cast" (འདེབས་). This verbal phrase ("answered") goes with the subject "by that animal (དུད་འགྲོ་དེས་)." Thus, the clause means, "That animal answered (to) the hunter, 'I am not an animal. I am a goddess.'"

This is followed by the final past tense complement (པ་རེད་). The entire segment reads: "*After* snaring the animal *while* (being in the state of) hunting in the mountains, the father said to his son, 'Is this really an animal?' and *after* saying this, immediately the animal replied, 'I am not an animal. I am a goddess.'"

The structure of this segment is: . . . རི་དྭགས་རྒྱབ་བཞིན་པར་ [while hunting wild animals] . . . རྙི་རྒྱབ་རྗེས་ [after snaring] . . . དྲིས་པའི་རྗེས་སུ་ [after asking] . . . ལན་བཏབ་པ་རེད [answered].

9. The next segment consists of five clauses: 1. རྔོན་པ་དང་བུ་གཉིས་ཀར་ཆོས་ལ་དད་པ་འདུག། 2. ཕྱས་ཙང་ཕོ་གཉིས་ཀྱིས་དུད་འགྲོ་དེ་སློད་རྗེས། 3. དུད་འགྲོ་དཀར་པོ་དེས་ཕོ་གཉིས་ལ་ཐུགས་རྗེ་ཆེ་ཞེས་ཟེར་པའི་རྗེས་སུ་ 4. ལམ་སེང་ཕ་ལམ་འོད་ཆེམ་ཆེམ་ཞིག་སྒྲད་པ་དང་། 5. ད་དུང་ཐུགས་རྗེ་ཆེ་ཞེས་བཤད་པ་རེད།.

The first clause is a simple existential sentence conveying that the subject possessed something, in this case "faith in religion." As usual in such constructions, the compound subject (hunter and son) is placed in the dative-locative case: "to the hunter and the son both" (རྔོན་པ་དང་བུ་གཉིས་ཀར་). It is followed by the indirect object "religion" (ཆོས་ལ་). and the direct object "faith" (དད་པ་). Finally, the existential verb འདུག་ occurs. Together they convey: "to both the hunter and son, there existed faith in religion."

The second clause begins with a clause connector (ཐུས་ཚང་ - "because" or "consequently.") placed at the start of the second clause rather than at the end of the first clause. Other common clause connectors used in this manner (i.e., that go in this slot) are: ལྷག་པར་ ("moreover" or "in particular"), འོན་ཀྱང་ ("nevertheless"), དེས་མ་ཚད་ ("not only that"), དེས་ན་ ("therefore"), དེ་མིན་ ("besides that"), ད་དུང་ ("still," "furthermore," "once again"), དེ་ནས་ (after that, then) and དེ་བཞིན་ ("similarly").

This phrase is followed by the subject (ཁོ་གཉིས་) + the instrumental case particle (ཀྱིས་), conveying "he two + by" or "by those two". Immediately, therefore, one looks for an active verb, which in this clause is the verb སློད་ ("to release, let go"). The object here is དུད་འགྲོ་དེ་ ("that animal"), so that the sentence reads, "Consequently, those two released the animal." This is followed by the temporal clause connective རྗེས་ ("after")

Clause three begins with the subject (དུད་འགྲོ་), but this time it is modified by the adjective "white" (དཀར་པོ་), the demonstrative "that" (དེ), and the instrumental particle (ས་). Together these mean "by that white animal."

This is followed by the indirect object "those two" together with the dative-locative particle, i.e., "to those two" (ཁོ་གཉིས་ལ་). The direct object comes next in the form of a direct quote: "thank you" (ཐུགས་རྗེ་ཆེ་). This is followed by the quote marking particle (ཞེས་) and the active verb "to say" (ཟེར་). ཟེར་ is a one stem verb with no special past tense form. Together these componments convey: "By that white animal, said "Thank you" to the two of them." It is followed by the temporal clause connective པའི་རྗེས་སུ་ ("after"), so that the entire unit means: "after the white animal said, . . . "

The fourth clause indicates what happened after the white animal spoke. It has no overt subject, the subject being implicit, i.e., being carried over from the previous clause (དུད་འགྲོ་དཀར་པོ་དེས་). There is no simple way to ascertain this other than context.

The main verb in this clause is the past tense stem of the active verb "give" (སྤྲད་), so one would expect a subject in the instrumental. Since there is none, one immediately backtracks to think which of the previous subjects seem appropriate. Here it obviously is "the white animal."

The fourth clause has no subject. It starts with the time-slot word "at once" (ལམ་སེང་), followed by the object, "a diamond" (ཕ་ལམ་), modified by the adjective phrase "glittering" (འོད་ཆེམ་ཆེམ་). The past tense stem of the active verb "give" (སྤྲད་) follows these. Thus, an unnamed subject gave a glittering diamond to an unnamed indirect object, or: "At once (he) gave a glittering diamond." This clause is then linked to clause five by the connective particle "and" (པ་དང་).

Clause five starts with "once again" (ད་དུང་), one of the clause connectives that occur at the start of the second of two clauses. It is followed by a direct quote and the quote marker (ཐུགས་རྗེ་ཆེ་ཞེས); the subject and object are again left implicit. This clause ends with the past tense stem (བཤད་) of the active verb"say" (ཤོད་) , and the པ་རེད་ verbal complement . The structure of this long segment, therefore, is:

. . . འདུག་ [exists] . . . བྱས་ཙང་ [consequently] . . . གློད་རྗེས་ [after releasing] . . . ཞེས་ཟེར་པའི་རྗེས་སུ་ [after saying] . . . སྤྲད་པ་དང་ [gave and] . . . བཤད་པ་རེད། [said]

10. The next segment consists of a single active sentence: དེ་ནས་དུད་འགྲོ་དཀར་པོ་དེས་གནམ་ལ་འཕུར་.

It begins with the time-slot phrase "after that" (དེ་ནས་), followed by the subject in the instrumental, "by that white animal" (དུད་འགྲོ་དཀར་པོ་དེས་).

Then the location of the verbal action, "to/in the sky" (གནམ་ལ་), is encountered. And finally, there is the active verb "fly" (འཕུར་). Thus, "after that, by that white animal, flew to the sky."

11. The next segment consists of four clauses: 1. པ་ཕས་དགའ་རྗེས་ 2. མཆི་མ་གཏོང་བཞིན་པར་ 3. ད་ང་ཚོ་ཕྱུག་པོ་རེད་ཅེས་ལབ་རྗེས་ 4. ཕྱིར་ལོག་བྱས་.

The first clause begins with the subject in the instrumental case, "by the father" (པ་ཕས་) . It is followed by the verb "be happy" or "to like something" (དགའ་) and the temporal connective རྗེས་ ("afterwards"). It conveys that the father became happy at this, and after that, something happened.

Clause two explains what he did. He cried, literally "shed tears" (མཆི་མ་གཏོང་). The present complement བཞིན་པར་ following གཏོང་ indicates that *while* being in the state of "crying," something else happened.

Clause three is a direct quote in the form of a linking verb construction meaning "Now we are rich" (ད་ང་ཚོ་ཕྱུག་པོ་རེད་). This clause begins with a time-slot word "now" (ད་), followed by the subject, "we/us" (ང་ཚོ་), the object "rich" (ཕྱུག་པོ་), and the linking verb "is" (རེད་).

The quote is followed by the quote marker (ཅེས་) and one of the verbs that means "to say" (ལབ་), followed by the temporal clause connector རྗེས་ ("after"). Note that the quote marker here is ཅེས་ rather than ཞེས་, because the last letter of the word it follows is

ད. The rule for this is given in section 4.4. Thus the construction now means, "...after he said, 'Now we are rich.'"

This and the two prior clauses jointly convey that: the father, getting happy, cried, and while doing this said, "Now we are rich." And after that, . . . (པ་ཕས་དགའ་རྗེས་མཆིལ་མ་གཏོང་བཞིན་པར་ང་ཚོ་ཕྱུག་པོ་རེད་ཅེས་ལབ་རྗེས་).

Clause four consists of the verbal phrase "returned (home)" (ཕྱིར་ལོག་བྱས་), with the subject, "they" being implicit. Note that although there is no verb complement because the verb is in the past tense stem, the construction is clearly past tense.

12. The next segment consists of three clauses: 1. རྔོན་པས་ཕ་ལམ་དེ་ཚོང་པར་བཙོང་རྗེས་ 2. ཞིང་ཁ་མང་པོ་ཉོས་པ་དང་། 3. ཁང་པ་གསར་པ་ཡང་རྒྱབ་སོང་།.

The first clause begins with the subject ,"by the hunter" (རྔོན་པས་), followed by the object ,"that diamond" (ཕ་ལམ་དེ་), followed by the indirect object "to a trader" (ཚོང་པར་), and the active verb "sold" (བཙོང་). Together they mean, "The hunter sold that diamond to a trader." This clause (a sentence in English) is linked to the next clause once again by the temporal clause connector "after."

The subject of the second clause is carried over from the previous clause (i.e., "by the hunter"). The clause actually starts with the direct object "field" (ཞིང་ཁ་), followed by the adjective "many" (མང་པོ་) and the past stem of the active verb "buy" (ཉོ་ > ཉོས་). Thus, "after the hunter sold the diamond to a trader (he) bought many fields." This clause is linked to the next one by the conjunctive connector "and" (པ་དང་).

The third clause again takes the subject ("by the hunter") as given. It begins with the object, i.e., "house," modified by the adjective "new" (གསར་པ་). Note also that ཡང་ ("also") follows the adjective. This segment therefore means, "After the hunter sold that diamond to a trader, (he) bought many fields and also built a new house."

13. The next segment consists of a single active sentence: དེ་ནས་བུ་དེས་རྒྱལ་པོའི་སྲས་མོ་དེ་མནའ་མར་བླངས་པ་རེད།.

The sentence starts with the time-slot term "after that" (དེ་ནས་). Then comes the subject in the instrumental, "by the son" (བུ་དེས་), followed by the object, "that princess" (རྒྱལ་པོའི་སྲས་མོ་དེ་), and finally the active verb, "took as a bride" and the པ་རེད་ verbal complement (མནའ་མར་བླངས་ + པ་རེད་). Note that "bride" is required to to be in the dative-locative (མནའ་མ་ + ར་). This is really an adverbial construction, but for the time being it should be simply considered an idiom. Thus the story concludes, "After that, the boy took that princess as (his) bride."

4.7 Vocabulary

ཀྱང་	even though; also (gyāŋ)
བཀླགས་	va. p. of ཀློག་: read (lɔ̄ɔ̀; lāà)
སྐབས་ཅིག་	one time (gābjig)
སྐྱོ་པོ་	poor (gyōbo)
ཁ་ལག་	food (kālaà)
ཁོ་གཉིས་	those two (kūñiì)
ཁོར་	he + dat.-loc. (kɔ̄ɔ̄)
ཁྲོམ་	market (trōm)
གི་ཡིན་	future tense complement (giyin)
གློད་	va. to release (lö̀ö̀)
དགའ་	vi. to like (g̱a)
དགའ་པོ་	like (g̱abo)
རྒན་པ་	elder (gɛ̱mba)
རྒྱལ་པོའི་སྲས་མོ་	princess (lit., daughter of king) (gyɛ̱ɛ̱böö sɛ̄ɛ̄mo)
ང་ཚོ་	we (ŋa̱ndzo)
དངུལ་	silver; money (ŋǖǖ)
དངོས་གནས་	really (ŋōnɛɛ̀)
རྔོན་པ་	hunter (ŋōmba)
ཅེས་	quotation marker (jēè)
ཆོས་བཤད་	va. to give religious teaching (chö̀ö̀ shɛ̄ɛ̀)
མཆི་མ་	tears; va. — གཏོང་ to cry, shed tears (chi̅mə dōŋ)
རྗེས་	temporal connective (je̱è)
ཉི་ཤུ་	twenty (ñi̱shu)
གཉིས་ཀ་	two together (ñi̅igə)
རྙི་རྒྱབ་	va. to trap, snare (ñi̅ gyə̱b)
གཏོང་	va. to send (dōŋ)
བཏང་	va. p. of གཏོང་ (dān)
བཏབ་	va. p. of འདེབས་ (dāp)
ཐུགས་རྗེ་ཆེ་	thank you (tōjeche)
ད་དུང་	still (tə̱duŋ)
དད་པ་	faith (tɛ̱ba)
དུད་འགྲོ་	animal (tü̱ndro)
དེ་ནས་	then (te̱nɛɛ̀)
དེ་རིང་	today (te̱riŋ)
དེས་	by that (te̱è)
དྲིས་	va. p. of འདྲི་ (tri̱ì)
འདེབས་	va. to throw, cast out, fling (de̱b)
འདྲི་	va. to ask (tri̱)
སྡོད་	va. to sit, stay, live (dö̱ö̀)
བསྡད་	va. p. of སྡོད་ (dɛ̱ɛ̀)
ནང་	inside, in; home (na̱ŋ)
གནམ་	sky (nām)
གནའ་རབས་	in ancient times, long ago (nārəb)
མནའ་མ་	bride (nāma)
མནའ་མ་ལེན་	va. to take a bride (nāmaa le̱n)
པ་དང་	conjunctive verbal connective (badaŋ)
པ་ཕ་	father (bāba)
པའི་རྗེས་སུ་	temporal connective (bɛje̱su)
སྤྲད་	va. p. of སྤྲོད་ (drɛ̄ɛ̀)
སྤྲོད་	va. to give (drȫö̀)
ཕ་ལམ་	diamond (pālam)
ཕྱུག་པོ་	rich (chūgbu)
ཕྱིན་	va. p. of འགྲོ་: went (chi̅n)
ཕྱིར་ལོག་	returning; va. — བྱེད་ to return (chi̅lɔ̀ɔ̀ che̱è)
འཕུར་	va. to fly (pi̅r; pūr)
བུ་	son; young boy (pu̱)
བུ་མོ་	daughter; young girl (po̱mo)
བྱས་ཙང་	because, therefore (che̱dzaŋ)

བླངས་	va. p. of ལེན་: took (lāŋ)
དབྱར་དུས་	va. summertime (yə̄rdü)
མོས་	she + by (mö̱ö̀)
བཙོང་	va. to sell (dzōn)
བརྩེ་	va. to love (dzē)
ཚང་མ་	all (tsāŋma)
ཚེ་རིང་	p.n. (tsēriŋ)
མཛེས་པོ་	pretty, beautiful (dze̱ebo)
ཞེས་	quotation marker (she̱è)
ཞེས་བྱ་བ་	that called (she̱chawa)
བཞི་བཅུ་	forty (shi̱bju)
ཟ་ཁང་	restaurant (sa̱gan)
ཟེར་བ་	that called (se̱rwa)
གཟའ་སྤེན་པ་	Saturday (sa̱ bēmba)
བཟོ་	va. to make (so̱)
འོད་ཆེམ་ཆེམ་	glittering (ö̱ö̀ chēmjem)
ཡང་	also; even (ya̱ŋ)
རི་	hill, mountain (ri̱)
རི་དྭགས་	herbivorous wild animal; va. — རྒྱག་ (p . རྒྱབ་) to hunt (ri̱daà gyə̱b)
ལན་	answer, reply; va. — འདེབས་ to answer, reply (le̱n)
ལབ་	va. to say (lə̱b)
ལམ་སེང་	at once, immediately (la̱msan; la̱mseŋ)
ལོ་	year (lo̱)
ཤེས་	question marker (shēè)
སྲས་མོ་	daughter (h) (sɛ̄ɛmo)
ལྷ་མོ་	goddess (lhāmo)

Lesson Five

5.1 Involuntary verbs and sentences

Involuntary verbs and sentences express an action or state which is not the result of intentional action by a subject. The semantic difference between involuntary verbs and active verbs can be seen from the following sentences:

a. [ཨ་མི་རི་ཀས་] དམག་འཁྲུག་བསླང་པ་རེད།
[əmerikɛɛ̀] mə̄gdruù lāmbəreè
[America-by] war started past compl./
[America] started a/the war.

b. [ཨ་མི་རི་ཀར་] དམག་འཁྲུག་ལངས་པ་རེད།
[əmerikaa] mə̄gdruù la̲mbəreè
[America-to] war started past compl./
A war started [in America].

The difference between these sentences is the difference between the verbs བསླངས་ and ལངས་. While both could be translated as "started" in English, the first is an active verb and the second is an involuntary verb. The first sentence therefore conveys the idea that a subject (he, they, America, etc.) intentionally started or incited a war while the second merely expresses the idea that a war started. The writer did not want to indicate an actor in the second. This difference would be more accurately expressed if the above sentences were translated as "[America] caused a war to start" and "A war broke out [in America]." Note that America, the subject of the first sentence, is in the instrumental case, whereas in the second sentence America is in the dative-locative case since it is the recipient or site of the action—the war broke out *in* America.

Involuntary actions or states, of course, are often caused by something or someone, for example, "Because the soldiers shot at the crowd, a war broke out." A key factor in Tibetan semantics, therefore, again is whether the causal element is intentional or unintentional. In the sentence cited above, the cause of the war is the shooting, but since the shooting was *not intended* by the actors to cause a war, the involuntary verb "broke out" was used. The active verb would have been used if the meaning to be conveyed was that the soldiers shot at the crowd so as to cause a war. In the first case, the disturbance was an unintended consequence. In the second, it was the intent of the shooting.

c. ཁོས་ཉལ་པ་རེད།

kȫö̀ ñɛ̲ɛ̲bəreè

he-by slept past compl./

He slept (actively went to sleep).

d. ཁོ་གཉིད་ཁུག་པ་རེད།

kō ñi̅ì kūbəreè

he slept past compl./

He slept (fell asleep).

The difference between c. and d. parallel that between a. and b. The subject of c. intentionally went to sleep whereas the subject of d. unintentionally fell asleep.

The སོང་ past complement is often used with involuntary verbs.

e. ཁོ་གཉིད་ཁུག་སོང་།

kō ñi̅ì kūùsoŋ

he slept past compl./

He slept (fell asleep).

Note that involuntary constructions do *not* require the subject phrase to be in the instrumental case.[1]

f. སློབ་ཕྲུག་ཚང་མ་ན་བ་རེད།

lāpdra tsāŋma na̲bəreè

student all sick past compl./

All the students got sick.

Example g. illustrates the more classical style (i.e., the style without verbal complements such as པ་རེད).

g. ཆུ་འཁོལ་།

chū kȫö̀

water boiled/

The water boiled.

h. མི་འདི་གྲག་རྗེས་།

mi̲ di̲ kyāàje

person this cold after/

After the person (man) got cold, . . .

i. ཉི་མ་ཆུ་ཚོད་བརྒྱད་པར་ཤར་བ་རེད།

ñi̲mə chūdzȫö̀ gyɛ̲èbar shāābəreè

---

[1] A small group of involuntary verbs such as མཐོང་ ("to see") and ཤེས་ ("to know") are exceptions to this rule in that they require the subject to have the instrumental particle.

sun o-clock eight-to rose past compl./

The sun rose at eight o'clock.

In constructions such as i., the time number requires the dative-locative (བརྒྱད་པར་ - "at" eight o'clock).

First person involuntary past tense constructions commonly add the irregular verb ཕྱུང་ ("got") after the involuntary verb stem. ཕྱུང་ will be indicated in the interlinear translation by "got."

j. ངས་ཟ་ཁང་དེར་ཁ་ལག་ཟས་རྗེས་ན་ཕྱུང་།

ŋɛ̱ɛ̀ sa̱gan de̱e̱ kālaà sɛ̱ɛ̀jeè na̱chu

i-by restaurant that-to food ate after sick got/

(I) got sick after eating at that restaurant.

k. ངས་དེབ་བཀླགས་རྗེས་གཉིད་ཁུག་ཕྱུང་།

ŋɛ̱ɛ̀ te̱p lɔ̄ɔ̀jeè ñīì kūùchu

i-by book read after slept got/

I fell asleep after reading a book.

l. ངས་དེབ་ཀློག་བཞིན་པར་གཉིད་ཁུག་ཕྱུང་།

ŋɛ̱ɛ̀ te̱p lɔ̄ɔ̀shinbar ñīì kūùchu

i-by book read while slept got/

I fell asleep while reading a book.

m. ཁ་སང་ང་ཚོ་ཁྱག་ཕྱུང་།

kɛ̄ɛ̄sa ŋa̱ndzo kyāàchu

yesterday i pl. cold got/

We got cold yesterday.

The present-usual complement in involuntary constructions can be any of the present-usual forms such as གི་ཡོད་པ་རེད་ or གི་འདུག་ or just the verb itself. The future complement for both first and third person is either གི་རེད་ or the verb stem alone.

n. གྲྭ་པ་མང་པོ་ན་གི་འདུག།

tra̱ba mə̱ŋgu nə̱giì [Note that in spoken Tibetan the verb complement གི་ འདུག (du̱ù) becomes giì.]

monk many sick pres. compl./

Many monks are sick.

o. བཟོ་པ་འདི་ཚོ་མཁས་པ་ཆགས་ཀྱི་ཡོད་པ་རེད།

so̱ba di̱ndzo kɛ̄ɛ̄ba chə̄ə̄giyɔɔ̀reè

worker these expert become pres. compl./

These workers are becoming expert.

p. དགུན་ཁར་གངས་ཞེ་དྲགས་འབབ་ཀྱི་ཡོད་པ་རེད།
güngaa kan shedraà pəbgiyɔ̀ɔreè
winter-to snow lots falls pres. compl./
It snows a lot in winter.

q. ང་ན་གི་འདུག།
ŋa nəgiì
i sick pres. compl./
I am sick.

r. ཚོང་ཁང་འདི་ཆེན་པོ་ཆགས་ཀྱི་རེད།
tsōŋgan di chēmbo chə̄ə̄giréè
store this big become fut. compl./
This store will become big.

s. . . . ང་ན་གི་རེད།
. . . ŋa nəgireè
. . . i sick fut. compl./
. . . I will get sick.

5.2 Location and indirect objects in active and involuntary constructions

Location—the place where the action occurs—is expressed through the dative-locative case particles. The location element is usually placed between the object and the verb (see example a. below), or between the subject and object (see example b. below), but sometimes also occurs before the subject.

a. ཁོ་ཚོས་དེབ་འདི་བོད་ལ་ཉོས་པ་རེད།
kōndzöö tep di pööla ñööbəreè
he pl.-by book this tibet to bought past compl./
They bought the book in Tibet.

b. ཞིང་པ་ཚོས་ཟ་ཁང་དུ་ཤ་ཟས་པ་རེད།
shiŋbədzöö sagantu shā sɛ̀ɛbəreè
farmer pl.-by restaurant to meat ate past compl./
The farmers ate meat in the restaurant.

c. ཟ་ཁང་དེར་ཞིང་པ་ཚོས་ཤ་ཟས་པ་རེད།
sagandee shiŋbədzöö shā sɛ̀ɛbəreè
restaurant to farmer pl.-by meat ate past compl./
The farmers ate meat in the restaurant.

d. བོད་ལ་གངས་ཞེ་དྲགས་འབབ་ཀྱི་ཡོད་པ་རེད།

pö̲ö̀la ka̲ǹ she̲draà pə̲bgiyɔɔ̀reè

tibet to snow lots fall pres. compl./

Lots of snow falls in Tibet (It snows a lot in Tibet).

Like the location of verbal actions, indirect objects are also marked by the dative-locative particle in active constructions.

e. ཞིང་པས་བླ་མ་ཚོར་དངུལ་སྤྲད་པ་རེད།

shi̲ŋbɛɛ̀ lāmatsɔr ŋǖǖ drɛ̄ɛ̀bəreè

farmer-by lama pl.-to money gave past compl./

The farmers gave money to the lamas.

f. དམག་མི་འདིས་ལས་བྱེད་པར་དེབ་གཅིག་སྐྱེལ་གྱི་རེད།

mə̄ə̄mi di̲ì lɛ̲ɛ̲jebaa te̲p chī gyēēgireè

soldier this-by official-to book one deliver fut. compl./

This soldier will deliver a book to the official.

5.3 བྱུང་ constructions

བྱུང་ is a commonly used involuntary verb that means "got" (past tense). It requires the recipient of the action (the person or thing that "got" something) to take the dative-locative particle.

a. མོར་དངུལ་བྱུང་བ་རེད།

mɔ̲ɔ̲ ŋǖǖ chu̲mbəreè

she-to money got past compl./

She got money.

b. ཞིང་པ་རྣམས་སུ་སོན་གསར་པ་བྱུང་སོང་།

shi̲ŋbə nāmsu sȫn sāāba chu̲nsu (chu̲nsoŋ)

farmer pl. to seed new got past compl./

The farmers got new seed.

The subject in the next example is implicit.

c. འདི་ལོ་ཐོན་སྐྱེད་ཡག་པོ་བྱུང་སོང་།

di̲lo tȫngyeè ya̲go chu̲nsu (chu̲nsoŋ)

this year production good got past-compl./

This year (they) got good production (got a good yield).

The long version of this would be:

d. འདི་ལོ་ཁོ་ཚོར་ཐོན་སྐྱེད་ཡག་པོ་བྱུང་སོང་།

di̲lo kōndzɔɔ tȫngyeè ya̲go chu̲nsu (chu̲nsoŋ)

this year he pl.-to production good got past compl./

This year they got good production (got a good yield).

བྱུང་ is also used as an auxiliary verb in active constructions. Here it indicates that the action goes from a third person actor to a first person recipient [from he/she to me]. The actor is placed in the instrumental and the recipient in the dative-locative.

e. ཁོས་ང་ལ་དངུལ་བཏང་བྱུང་།
   kȫȫ ŋa̱a̱ ŋǖǖ dānchu (dānchuŋ)
   he-by i to money sent got/
   He sent money to me.

f. ལས་བྱེད་པ་འདིས་ང་ལ་ཁ་ལག་སྤྲད་བྱུང་།
   lɛ̱ɛ̱jeba di̱ì ŋa̱a̱ kālaà drɛ̄ɛ̀chu (drɛ̄ɛ̀chuŋ)
   official this-by i to food gave got/
   This official gave me food.

Another function of བྱུང་ is the one we saw in section 5.1 (j., k., l. and m.) where it joined with involuntary verbs to form first person past constructions. Sentence g. illustrates this use.

g. ངར་ན་བྱུང་།
   ŋa̱a̱ na̱chu (na̱chuŋ)
   i-to got sick/
   I got sick.

Since བྱུང་ is used only for past actions, the verb "to come" (ཡོང་) is required in equivalent future constructions.

h. མོར་དངུལ་ཡོང་གི་རེད།
   mɔ̱ɔ̱ ŋǖǖ yu̱ŋgireè
   she-to money come fut.compl./
   She will get money.

i. ཞིང་པ་ཚོར་སོན་གསར་པ་ཡོང་གི་རེད།
   shi̱ŋbədzɔɔ sȭn sāāba yu̱ŋgireè
   farmer pl.-to seed new come fut. compl./
   Farmers will get new seed.

5.4 Tense and temporals in existential and linking constructions

As indicated earlier, existential and linking verbs do not inflect to indicate tense. Just as number is specified through context or modifying particles, so too is tense delimited through context or one of a class of words expressing time, called temporals.

a. དེང་སང་བོད་ལ་རྒྱ་རིགས་འདུག།

te̱ŋsaŋ pö̱ö̀la gyə̱ri du̱ù
these days tibet to chinese exist/
These days there are Chinese in Tibet.

b. སྔོན་མ་བོད་ལ་རྒྱ་མི་འདུག།
ŋȫnma pö̱ö̀la gyə̱mi du̱ù
formerly tibet to chinese exist/
Formerly, there were Chinese in Tibet.

Note that only the "temporal" word changed in examples a. and b.

c. དེ་རིང་ཁོ་ཟ་ཁང་ལ་འདུག།
te̱riŋ kō sa̱ganla du̱ù
today he restaurant to exists/
Today he is at the restaurant.

Temporal words function the same way in linking constructions.

d. སྔར་ཁོ་དམག་མི་རེད།
ŋār kō mə̄ə̄mi re̱è
formerly he soldier is/
Formerly he was a soldier.

e. དེང་སྐབས་ཁོ་དམག་མི་རེད།
te̱ŋgəb kō mə̄ə̄mi re̱è
nowadays he soldier is/
Nowadays he is a soldier.

5.5 Temporals in active and involuntary constructions

Temporal words are also placed at the beginning of active and involuntary sentences and clauses.

a. སྔར་ཞིང་པས་སོན་ཡག་པོ་བཏབ་པ་རེད།
ŋār shi̱ŋbɛɛ̀ sȭn ya̱go də̄bbəreè
formerly farmer-by seed good planted past compl./
Formerly, farmers planted good seed.

b. ད་ལྟ་གྲྭ་པ་ཚོས་དེབ་གསར་པ་བཟོ་བཞིན་ཡོད་པ་རེད།
ta̱nda tra̱badzöö̀ te̱p sāāba so̱shinyɔ̱ɔ̀reè
now monk pl.-by book new make pres. compl./
Now monks are making new books.

c. ན་ཉིང་བཟོ་པ་ཚང་མས་མི་མདའ་བཟོས་སོང་།
nə̱niŋ so̱ba tsāŋmɛɛ̀ me̱nda sö̱ö̀soŋ

last year worker all-by gun made went compl./

Last year all the workers made guns.

d. གཞེས་ཉིང་སྨན་ཁང་འདིར་ནད་པ་མང་པོ་ཤི་བ་རེད།

shi̱ñiŋ mēngan de̱e nɛ̱ba mə̱ŋgu shībəreè [Note that འདིར་ is pronounced de̱e.]

year-before-last hospital this-to patient many die past compl./

The year before last many patients died at this hospital.

e. ལོ་གསུམ་གྱི་སྔོན་དུ་ཁོས་ཟ་ཁང་ཆེན་པོ་གཅིག་ཉོས་པ་རེད།

lo̱ sūmgi ŋöntu kȫö̀ sa̱gan chēmbo chī ñö̱ö̀bəreè

year three of before to he-by restaurant big one bought past compl./

Three years ago he bought a big restaurant.

f. 1967 ལོར་སྐྱེ་དམན་འདི་ཚོས་འཛིན་ཆས་མང་པོ་ཉོས།

1967 lo̱r gyīmɛn di̱ndzöö̀ dzi̱njɛɛ̀ mə̱ŋgu ñö̱ö̀

1967 year women this pl.-by furniture many bought/

In 1967, these women bought much furniture.

The present/usual complement expresses usual past action when used with past temporals.

g. སྔོན་མ་མི་དེ་ཚོས་ཞྭ་མོ་བཟོ་གི་ཡོད་པ་རེད།

ŋönma mi̱ de̱ndzöö̀ sha̱mo su̱giyɔɔ̀reè

formerly people pl.-by hat make pres. compl./

Formerly, those people used to make hats.

5.6 Verbalizers: object-verb compounds

Many concepts that are expressed in English through verbs, e.g., "to shoot," are expressed in Tibetan through noun-verb compounds. In these constructions the verb verbalizes the meaning of the noun, e.g., གནམ་གྲུ་གཏོང་ ("to fly a plane") consists of the noun གནམ་གྲུ་ ("plane") and the verb གཏོང་ ("to send"). There are three main verbalizers:

Present (non-past)	Past	Future	
རྒྱབ་/རྒྱག་ (gyə̱b; gya̱à)	(བ) རྒྱབ་ (བརྒྱབས་) (gyə̱b)	རྒྱག་ (gya̱à)	"to do
གཏོང་ (dōŋ)	བཏང་ (dāŋ)	གཏོང་/གཏང་ (dōŋ)	"to send"
བྱེད་ (che̱è)	བྱས་ (chɛ̱ɛ̀)	བྱ་ (cha̱)	"to do"

While each of these verbs has independent meaning, in some instances the connection between the noun and the verb is arbitrary. Let us now examine some commonly used compounds.

ལས་ཀ་བྱེད་	to work	ཁང་པ་རྒྱག་	to build a house
work		house	

མེ་མདའ་རྒྱག་	to shoot (a gun)	དམག་རྒྱག་	to war, to fight
gun		war	
ཁ་པར་གཏོང་	to phone	ཚོན་གཏོང་	to paint
phone		paint	

The direct object slot can also be filled by derived nouns (nominals) consisting of N+Vb. or Vb.+Vb. compounds. This is one of the most common ways that new lexical items are created. For example, བཅིངས་འགྲོལ་གཏོང་ ("to liberate"), consists of the two verbs བཅིངས་ ("to bind") and འགྲོལ་ ("to release, untie"), which together express the sum of their independent meanings: "releasing a bond," or the modern political concept of "liberation." This compound can be used as a noun, e.g., བཅིངས་འགྲོལ་དམག་མི་ ("liberation army soldier") or with a verbalizer as a verb, བཅིངས་འགྲོལ་གཏོང་ ("to liberate"). Word formation is discussed in detail in section 11.7, and for the time being you should treat these compounds as verbal units.

Other common examples are:.

བཙན་འཛུལ་བྱེད། — to invade, to commit aggression
[བཙན་འཛུལ་ = invasion, aggression]

བཅིངས་འགྲོལ་གཏོང་། — to liberate
[བཅིངས་འགྲོལ་ = liberation]

ངོ་ལོག་རྒྱག། — to revolt, to rebel
[ངོ་ལོག་ = revolt, rebellion]

རྩ་མེད་གཏོང་། — to annihilate
[རྩ་མེད་ = annihilation]

སློབ་སྦྱོང་བྱེད། — to study
[སློབ་སྦྱོང་ = studying]

དམག་འཁྲུག་བྱེད་ — to war, to make war
[དམག་འཁྲུག་ = war, warfare]

ངོ་སྤྲོད་བྱེད། — to aquaint, to introduce
[ངོ་སྤྲོད་ = introduction]

ངོ་རྒོལ་བྱེད། — to oppose, to struggle against
[ངོ་རྒོལ་ = opposition, struggle]

ཐོན་སྐྱེད་བྱེད། — to produce
[ཐོན་སྐྱེད་ = production]

སྦྱོང་བརྡར་བྱེད། — to train
[སྦྱོང་བརྡར་ = training]

ངལ་རྩོལ་བྱེད། — to labor, to do manual work, to do hard work

[ངལ་རྩོལ་ = hard work]

ལྟ་སྐོར་བྱེད། to tour (sightseeing), to make an inspection visit

[ལྟ་སྐོར་ = tour]

སློབ་གསོ་བྱེད to educate

[སློབ་གསོ་ = education]

These are used in sentences as follows:

a. 1949 ལོར་མི་དམངས་ཀྱིས་ངོ་ལོག་བརྒྱབ་པ་རེད།
1949 lo̱r mi̱maŋki ŋo̱loò gyə̱bəreè
1949 year-to people by revolt acted past compl./
In 1949, the people revolted.

b. ད་ལོ་བཟོ་པ་ཚོས་གནམ་གྲུ་མང་པོ་ཐོན་སྐྱེད་བྱེད་ཀྱི་རེད།
ta̱lo so̱badzöö nə̄mdru mə̱ŋgu tȭngyeè chi̱gireè
now year worker pl.-by airplane many produce do fut. compl./
This year the workers will produce many airplanes.

c. ཁོས་ཟ་ཁང་ལ་ལས་ཀ་བྱེད་ཀྱི་འདུག།
kȫö sa̱ganla lɛ̱ɛ̱ga chi̱giì
he-by restaurant to work do pres. compl./
He is working in the restaurant.

d. དམག་མི་ཚོས་མི་དམངས་བཅིངས་འགྲོལ་བཏང་།
mə̄ə̄midzöö mi̱maŋ jīŋdröö dāŋ
soldier pl.-by people liberation sent/
The soldiers liberated the people.

e. ལོ་གསུམ་གྱི་སྔོན་དུ་ཁོ་ཚོས་མི་གོ་ལ་སློབ་སྦྱོང་བྱས་པ་རེད།
lo̱ sūmgi ŋȭntu kōndzöö me̱gola lōbjoǹ chɛ̱ɛ̀bəreè
year three of before to he pl.-by U.S.-to study did went-compl./
Three years ago they studied in America.

f. དེང་སང་ཧྲེ་ཡོན་ཚོས་བཟོ་གྲྭ་གསར་པ་རྣམས་ལ་ལྟ་སྐོར་བྱེད་མུས་རེད།
te̱ŋsaŋ hrēyöndzöö so̱dra sāāba nāmlə dāgɔɔ che̱müreè
these days commune member pl.-by factory new pl. to visit do pres. compl./
These days, commune members are visiting the new factories.

g. དེ་རིང་སློབ་ཕྲུག་ཚང་མས་ངལ་རྩོལ་བྱེད་བཞིན་དུ་ཡོད་པ་རེད།
te̱rin lāpdra tsāŋmɛɛ̀ ŋɛ̱ɛ̱dzöö che̱shinduyɔɔ̀reè
today student all-by manual labor do pres. compl./
All the students are doing manual labor today.

The object of such sentences can be modified by adjectives:

h. ཁོས་ཁང་པ་གསར་པ་ཞིག་རྒྱག་གི་ཡོད་པ་རེད།

kȫȍ kāŋba sāāba chī gyəgiyɔ̄ɔ̀reè

he-by house new act pres. compl./

He is building a new house.

5.7 Verbs of motion

5.7.1 Active verbs

There are several very common active verbs of motion:

Non-past	Past	
འགྲོ་	ཕྱིན་	"to go"
བསྐྱོད་	བསྐྱོད་	"to go"
ཡོང་	ཡོང་	"to come"
ཕེབས	ཕེབས་	"to go" or "to come"

These verbs are somewhat irregular in that their subjects *often do not* take the instrumental particle as do active verbs. Nevertheless, since Tibetans perceive them as "intentional," and since grammatically their first person past complement is active (པ་ཡིན), they are classified as active verbs.

a. ཁོ་སྨན་ཁང་ལ་ཕྱིན་པ་རེད།

kō mēnganla chīmbəreè

he hospital to went past compl./

He went to a (the) hospital.

b. ཁོང་ཚོ་བོད་ལ་བསྐྱོད་སོང་།

kōndzo pȫȍla gyȫȍsoŋ

he pl. tibet to went past compl./

They went to Tibet.

c. དེང་སྐབས་ཞིང་པ་ཚོ་གྲོང་ཁྱེར་ལ་འགྲོ་བ་རེད།

teŋgəb shiŋbədzo troŋkyeela drowareè

these days farmer pl. city to go usual compl./

These days, farmers are going to the city.

d. ང་ཟ་ཁང་ནས་ཡོང་བ་ཡིན།

ŋa sagan nɛ yombəyin

i restaurant from came past compl./

I came from the restaurant.

e. བླ་མ་ཆེན་པོ་ལྷ་ཁང་གསར་པ་དེར་ཕེབས་ཀྱི་རེད།

lāma chēmbo lhāgan sāāba dee pīgireè

lama big temple new that-to go fut. compl./

The important (lit., big) lama will go to the new temple.

f. རྒྱ་མི་མང་པོ་འདིར་ཡོང་གི་རེད།

gyəmi məŋgu dee yuŋgireè

chinese many that-to come fut. compl./

Many Chinese will come here.

5.7.2 Involuntary verbs of motion

Three of the most common involuntary verbs of motion are:

Non-past	Past	
སླེབས་	སླེབས་	"to arrive"
འབྱོར་	འབྱོར་	"to arrive"
ཕེབས་	ཕེབས་	"to arrive" (h.)

Note that the verb ཕེབས་ functions as both an active and involuntary verb and can mean "come," "go," and "arrive."

The involuntary verbs of motion require that the object (or the location of their "arrival") takes the dative-locative particle. They also use the involuntary complement (e.g., བྱུང་) for first person subjects (see b.).

a. ཁོ་བོད་ལ་འབྱོར་པ་རེད།

kō pö̀la jɔɔbəreè

he tibet to arrived past compl./

He arrived in Tibet.

b. ང་ཁ་སང་ལྷ་སར་སླེབས་བྱུང་།

ŋa kɛ̄ɛsa lhɛ̄ɛsaa lēèchu

i yesterday lhasa-to arrive past compl./

I arrived in Lhasa yesterday.

c. འབྲོག་པ་དང་ཞིང་པ་རྣམས་དེ་རིང་ཚོགས་འདུ་ལ་སླེབས་པ་རེད།

drogba daŋ shiŋbə nām terin tsōndoo lēèbəreè

nomad and farmer pl. today meeting to arrived past compl./

The nomads and farmers arrived today at the meeting.

d. སང་ཉིན་ང་ཚོ་གཞིས་ཀ་རྩེར་འབྱོར་གྱི་རེད།

sə̄ñiì ŋandzo shigədzee jɔɔgireè

tomorrow i pl. shigatse-to arrive fut. compl./

We will arrive in Shigatse tomorrow.

5.8 Honorific language

Words are selected in Tibetan with regard not only to their referent meaning, but also to the relative social status of the person(s) being spoken or written about. Although spoken Tibetan has several honorific levels, written Tibetan can be conceived of as using just two levels: an honorific (h.) and non-honorific (nh.). Until now only non-honorific forms have been used, with the exception of ཞབས་ and ཁོང་.

Honorific language refers to words that are synonyms with respect to their referent meaning, but which differ with regards to the respect they convey to the subject. For example, the third person pronoun "he" has two forms, one of which, ཁོ་ (or ཁོ་པ་), is non-honorific and the other, ཁོང་, is honorific. The latter is used when the referent is a person of high social status.

Nominals may, as with "he," have two separate forms, or they may use one of a small number of honorificizing words together with the non-honorific form. Two of the most common of these honorificizers are ཕྱག་ (the h. of ལག་པ་ "hand") and སྐུ་ (the h. of གཟུགས་པོ་ "body"). For example, དེབ་ ("book, nh.") becomes ཕྱག་དེབ་ ("book, h."); ལས་ཀ་ ("work, nh.") becomes ཕྱག་ལས་ ("work, h.").

Verbs also have honorific forms. Like nominals, some verbs have completely different honorifics, e.g., བྱེད་ > གནང་ or མཛད་ and རྒྱབ་ > སྐྱོན་. Others use གནང་ or བ་གནང་ after the nh. form to form honorifics, e.g., གཏོང་ > གཏོང་བ་གནང་.

a. ཁོས་ལས་ཀ་བྱས།

kȫȫ lεεga chεὲ

he-by work did/

He worked.

b. ཁོང་གིས་ཕྱག་ལས་གནང་།

kōŋki chāālεὲ nān

he (h.) by work (h.) did (h.)/

He worked (h.). Or., He will work (h).

c. ཁོས་གནམ་གྲུ་གཅིག་བཏང་སོང་།

kȫȫ nəmdru chī dānsu

he-by plane one send past compl./

He flew a plane.

d. ཁོང་གིས་ཁ་སང་གནམ་གྲུ་གཅིག་གཏོང་བ་གནང་།

kōŋgi kεεsa nəmdru chī dān nān

he (h.) by yesterday plane one send did (h.) past compl./

He flew a plane yesterday.

Note that the word for "airplane" has no honorific form and that the entire phrase is made honorific by making the verb honorific: "send" becomes གཏོང་པ་གནང་.

Earlier we saw that Tibetan uses different verbs to express "coming" (ཡོང་) and "going" (འགྲོ). As indicated earlier, the honorific of both of these is ཕེབས་.

e. ཁོང་ལྷ་ས་ནས་ཕེབས་པ་རེད།

kōŋ lɛ̄ɛ̄sa nɛ pēèbəreè

he (h.) lhasa from come (h.) past compl./

He came from Lhasa. (h.)

f. ཁོང་ལྷ་སར་ཕེབས་པ་རེད།

kōŋ lɛ̄ɛ̄sar pēèbəreè

he (h.) lhasa-to come (h.) past compl./

He went to Lhasa. (h.)

Note that the use of ནས་ and the dative-locative particle -ར་ indicate clearly which meaning is intended in sentences e. and f.

Most of the verbs already introduced add གནང་ to make them honorific but some have separate honorific forms, e.g.:

nh.	h.	
ཉོ་	གཟིགས་	"to buy"
ཉལ་	གཟིམ་	"to sleep"
གཉིད་ཁུག་	མནལ་ཁུག་	"to fall asleep"
ན་	སྙུང་	"to get sick"
ཟ་	མཆོད་	"to eat"
སྤྲོད་ (སྤྲད་)	འབུལ་ (ཕུལ་)	"to give"
རྒྱབ་ or རྒྱག་	སྐྱོན་	"to act"
བྱེད་	གནང་ or མཛད་	"to do"
འགྲོ་; ཡོང་	ཕེབས་	"to go, to come"

5.9 The "causal" connectives: བར་/པར་བརྟེན་, སྟབས་, ཙང་, རྐྱེན་(གྱིས་), ཙ་ན་, པས་/བས་, གཤིས་, and (པའི་/བའི་) དབང་གིས་

These clause connectives express the idea of "because" in the sense that because of the action in clause X, clause Y occurs. They are used not only with active and passive verbs, but also with linking and existential verbs. They sometimes also convey the meaning of "by (means of)" or "according to" or "by the force of."

a. ཁོང་གྲྭ་པ་ཡིན་པར་བརྟེན་ཚོགས་འདུ་ལ་ཞུགས་པ་རེད།

kōŋ tra̲ba yi̲mbarden tsōndulə shu̲bəreè

he monk is because, meeting to participated past compl./

Because he is a monk, (he) participated in the meeting.

b. རྐྱང་མང་པོ་ཡོད་སྟབས་གཞུང་གིས་ཁ་ཤས་གསོད་ཀྱི་ཡོད་པ་རེད།

gyāŋ mə̲ŋgu yö̲dəb shu̲ŋki kāshɛɛ̀ sɛ̄ɛ̄giyɔɔ̀reè

wild-ass many exist because, government by some kill pres. compl./

Because there are many wild asses, the government is killing some.

c. སློབ་ཕྲུག་ཚོས་བོད་ལ་ཕྱིན་ཙང་། དགོན་པ་མང་པོ་མཐོང་པ་རེད།

lāpdradzöö̀ pö̲ö̀lə chi̅ndzaŋ/ go̲mba mə̲ŋgu tōmbareè

student pl.-by tibet to went because/ monasteries many saw past compl./

Because the students went to Tibet, (they) saw many monasteries.

d. ངས་གྲོད་ཁོག་ལྟོགས་ཙ་ན་ལུག་གཅིག་བསད་པ་ཡིན།

ŋɛ̲è tro̲gɔɔ̀ dɔ̄ɔ̀dzāna lu̲ù chi̅ sɛ̄ɛ̀bəyin

i-by hungry because, sheep one killed past compl./

Because I was hungry, I killed a sheep.

e. ངས་གྲོད་ཁོག་ལྟོགས་པའི་རྐྱེན་གྱིས་ལུག་གཅིག་བསད་པ་ཡིན།

ŋɛ̲è tro̲gɔɔ̀ dɔ̄ɔ̀bɛgye̲nki lu̲ù chi̅ sɛ̄ɛ̀bəyin

i-by hungry because, sheep one killed past compl./

Because I was hungry, I killed a sheep.

f. འདི་ནི་སློབ་ཕྲུག་གིས་བྱས་པའི་རྐྱེན་གྱིས་རེད།

di̲ni lāpdraà ki chɛ̲ɛ̀bɛgyēnki rɛ̲è

this as-for student older-of did because is/

As for this, it is because the students did it.

g. ང་ལ་དད་པ་ཡོད་པས་མཆོད་མཇལ་ཞུས་པ་ཡིན།

ŋa̲a̲ tɛ̲ɛ̀ba yö̲ö̀bɛɛ chȫnjɛɛ shü̲bəyin

i to faith exist-by religious visit did past compl./

Because I have faith, (I) made a religious visit [to a temple, etc.]

h. ད་ལོ་ཆར་པ་མང་པོ་འབབས་པའི་དབང་གིས་ལོ་ཏོག་ཡག་པོ་བྱུང་བ་རེད།

ta̲lo chāāba mə̲ŋgu bə̲bbɛwaŋki lo̲doò ya̲go chu̲mbəreè

this-year rain much fell by crop good got past compl./

Because there was a lot of rain this year, (they, he, etc.) got a good crop.

Sometimes, however, as seen in sentence i., དབང་གིས་ is best translated as "according to."

i. གཞིས་ཀ་ཡག་ཉེས་ཡོད་པའི་དབང་གིས་ཁྲལ་སྣ་ཚོགས་བྱུང་བ་རེད།

shi̅gə ya̲ñeè yö̲bɛwaŋki trɛ̄ɛ̄ nātsoò chu̲mbəreè

estate quality exist by tax various got past compl./

They got various taxes according to the quality of the estate.

5.10 The "when" connectives: དུས་, སྐབས་, བའི་/པའི་སྐབས་སུ་(ལ་), བའི་/པའི་དུས་སུ་, རིང་, མཚམས་སུ་, ཚེ་, མཚམས་, བ་/པ་ན་, and བའི་/པའི་སྐང་ལ་

These clause connectives translate as "when" or "at the time of," and link two clauses so that the latter occurs at the time of the former. The verb in the first clause is put in the non-past (present or future).

a. ཁོ་བོད་ལ་འགྲོ་སྐབས་དེབ་མང་པོ་ཉོས་པ་རེད།

kō pö̱ö̀lə dro̱gəb te̱p mə̱ŋgu ñö̱ö̀bəreè

he tibet to go when, book many bought past compl./

When he went to Tibet, (he) bought many books.

The reader should take note that although this connective requires the first clause verb to be in the non-past stem (འགྲོ་), the overall tense of the sentence is controlled by the verb and verb complement of the latter clause.

b. ཁོང་བོད་ལ་ཕེབས་དུས་ཕྱག་དེབ་རྙིང་པ་གཟིགས་ཀྱི་རེད།

kōŋ pö̱ö̀lə pēèdü chāādep ñīŋbə si̱ìgireè

he (h.) tibet to go (h.) when, book (h.) old buy (h.) fut. compl./

When he goes to Tibet, (he) will buy old books.

c. ཞིང་པ་ཚོས་པེ་ཅིང་ལ་སྡོད་སྐབས་རྒྱ་མི་མང་པོ་མཐོང་བ་རེད།

shi̱ŋbədzöö̀ bējiŋlə dö̱ö̀gəb gya̱mi mə̱ŋgu tōmbareè

farmer this pl.-by Beijing to stay when, Chinese many saw past compl./

When the farmers stayed (lived) in Beijing, (they) saw many Chinese.

d. ངས་སློབ་གྲྭར་སློབ་སྦྱོང་བྱེད་ཚེ་ངར་བསོད་ནམས་ཐུག་བྱུང་།

ŋɛ̱ɛ̀ lāpdraa lōbjoŋ che̱tse ŋa̱a̱ sönam trɛ̄ɛ̀chu

i-by school-to study do when, i-to sonam met past compl./

When I was studying at school, I met Sonam.

Note that the verb ཐུག་ ("meet") requires the subject (ང་) to be in the dative-locative(ངར་) case.

e. མོ་སླེབས་པ་ན་ཁོ་ཕྱིན་སོང་།

mo̱ lēèbana kō chīnsu

she arrive when he went past compl./

When she arrived, he went.

f. རི་བོང་དེ་སླེབས་པ་ན་འདམ་སེང་ཞིག་གིས་བསད་པ་རེད།

re̱gon de̱ lēbana da̱mseŋ chīki sɛ̄ɛ̀bəreè

rabbit that arrive when lion one by killed past compl./

When that rabbit arrived, a lion killed (him).

Sometimes སྐང་ or པའི་སྐང་ལ་ conveys a similar meaning: "at the point or time of." For example:

g. ངས་སློབ་གྲྭར་སློབ་སྦྱོང་བྱེད་པའི་སྐང་ལ་ངར་བསོད་ནམས་ཕྲད་བྱུང་།

ŋɛ̱ɛ̀ lāpdraa lōpjon che̱bɛganlə ŋa̱a̱ sõnam trɛ̃ɛ̀chu

i-by school-to study do when, i-to sonam met past compl./

When (I) was studying, I met Sonam.

This would differ from ངས་སློབ་གྲྭར་སློབ་སྦྱོང་བྱེད་པའི་དུས་ལ་ངར་བསོད་ནམས་ཕྲད་པ་རེད་ in the sense that སྐང་ implies that a specific instance is indicated whereas when དུས and རིང་ are used, a longer period is conveyed. It should be noted that སྐང་ can also be used at the end of a sentence.

h. ཁོ་འགྲོ་དུས་ཁོང་ཚོ་ཟ་ཁང་ལ་ཁ་ལག་ཟ་པའི་སྐང་རེད།

kō dru̱düǜ kōndzo sa̱ganlə kālaà sa̱beganrèe

he go when he pl. restaurant to food eat when be/

When he went, they were (in the act of) eating at the restaurant.

i. ཁོས་སློབ་གྲྭར་སློབ་སྦྱོང་བྱེད་པའི་རིང་ལ་དེབ་གསུམ་བཀླགས་པ་རེད།

kö̃ö̀ lāpdraa lōpjoŋ che̱bɛriŋlə te̱p sūm lɔ̃ɔ̀bəreè

he-by school-to study when book three read past compl./

He read three books when he studied in school.

This use of རིང་ here conveys that the action (the "reading") took place "during" the period from when he began school to when he finished it.

5.11 The "gerundive" connectives: དེ་, ཏེ་, སྟེ་, and ནས་

These clause connectives have multiple functions. They are used according to the following rules:

དེ་	occurs after words ending in	ད་
ཏེ་	occurs after words ending in	ན་ར་ལ་ས་
སྟེ་	occurs after words ending in	ག་ང་བ་མ་ (and vowels)
ནས་	occurs after all finals	

They relate or link clauses in three basic ways.

5.11.1 The temporal-causal function

This function has a range of meaning that encompasses both རྗེས་ and སྐབས་. That is to say, it conveys the idea that "a verbal action having been done, something else occurred," or "as a result of" or "because of" one action, another occurred. Unfortunately, there is no simple way to know whether the first or second of these meanings is intended. Only context and experience provide the answer.

a. ཁོས་ལས་ཀ་བྱས་ཏེ་ཟ་ཁང་ལ་ཕྱིན་པ་རེད།

kö̀ö lɛɛga chɛɛde saganla chīmbəreè

he-by work did having restaurant to went past compl./

Having worked, (he) went to a restaurant.

or

After he worked (he) went to a restaurant.

b. ཁོས་ལྟོ་ཆས་ཟས་ནས་བུ་བཙོལ་ཁང་ལ་འགྲོ་བཞིན་པ་རེད།

kö̀ö dōpjɛɛ̀ sɛɛ̀nɛ pujöganlə droshimbəreè

he-by food ate having, nursery to go pres. compl./

Having eaten, he is going (now) to the nursery.

c. མི་དེ་ཚོས་དགོན་པར་ཕྱིན་ནས་མཆོད་མཇལ་ཞུས་པ་རེད།

mi dendzö̀ö gombaa chīnnɛ chōnjɛɛ shübəreè

person that-by monastery-to went having, religious-visit did past compl./

After going (having gone) to the monastery, they made a religious visit (e.g., gave offerings).

d. བཟོ་པ་གཅིག་ལས་ཀ་ཤོར་ཏེ་དཔྲང་པོ་ཆགས་པ་རེད།

soba chī lɛɛga shɔ̄ɔ̄de bāŋgo chāàbəreè

worker one work lost having, beggar became past compl./

A worker became a beggar after [as a result of] losing (his) job.

e. ཁོས་ཞིང་ཁ་བཏབ་སྟེ་རྒྱ་མ་ ༡༠༠༠ [ཆིག་སྟོང་] ཐོན་པ་རེད།

kö̀ö shiŋgə dəbde gyama chīgdoŋ tōmbəreè

he-by field planted having, jin[2] 1000 produced past compl./

He planted the field and (as a result of this) got 1,000 jin (in yield).

f. ཁོས་སོན་གསར་པ་བཏབ་སྟེ་སྟོན་ཐོག་ཡག་པོ་བྱུང་བ་རེད།

kö̀ö sōn sāāba dəbde dōndoò yago chumbəreè

he-by seed new sow having crop good got past compl./

Because he planted a new seed, (he) got a good crop.

5.11.2 The adverbial or simultaneous function

These same clause connectives can also link two clauses so that the former explains the manner in which (or how or by doing what) the latter occurs. For example,

---

[2] A *jin* is a Chinese weight measure equalling 0.5 kilograms.

a. ཁོས་སྔོ་ཚལ་འཁྱེར་ཏེ་ཕྱིན་པ་རེད།

kȫö̀ ŋōtsɛɛ kērde chi̅mbəreè

he-by vegetable carry having went past compl.

He went carrying vegetables. (How did he go? Carrying vegetables, he went.)

b. ཁོས་སྐད་རྒྱབ་སྟེ་ལན་བསྐྱལ་བ་རེད།

kȫö̀ gɛ̄ɛ̀ gy<u>ə</u>bde l<u>ɛ</u>n gyɛ̄ɛ̄bəreè

he-by shout having message delivered past compl./

He delivered the message (in a) shouting or yelling (manner).

c. ཁོས་རྟ་བཞོན་ཏེ་ནང་ལ་ལོག་སོང་།

kȫö̀ dā sh<u>ö</u>nde n<u>a</u>nlə l<u>ɔ</u>ɔ̀soŋ

he-by horse rode having home to returned past compl./

He returned home on horseback (How did he return? Riding a horse, he returned.)

d. རྔོན་པས་མེ་མདའ་རྒྱབ་སྟེ་བསྡད་པ་རེད།

ŋȫmbɛɛ̀ m<u>e</u>nda gy<u>ə</u>bde d<u>ɛ</u>ɛ̀bəreè

hunter-by gun shoot having stayed past compl./

The hunter stayed (there) shooting a gun.

e. ཁོས་སྐད་རྒྱབ་སྟེ་མེ་མདའ་རྒྱབ་པ་རེད།

kȫö̀ gɛ̄ɛ̀ gy<u>ə</u>bde m<u>e</u>nda gy<u>a</u>bəreè

he-by shout having gun shot past compl./

Shouting, he shot the gun.

Example e. represents a type of construction that is somewhat ambiguous in that it could convey the idea that he shouted and then immedately shot the gun. In other words, the two actions would be almost, but not completely, simultaneous. Only context will determine which is the appropriate interpretation.

5.11.3 The defining function

In this role these connectives link two clauses so that the latter clause defines or tells something specific about the former. It can also give the reason for the former clause (see example c. below). These connectives are used with both linking and existential verbs and in place of them (as in example a.).

a. སྟག་འཚེར་ནི་གྲོང་གསེབ་ཞིག་སྟེ།   ཟ་ཆས་གཙོ་བོ་འབྲུ་རིགས་རེད།

dāgdzeni tr<u>o</u>ŋse chi̅gde/ s<u>a</u>pjɛɛ̀ dzōwo dr<u>u</u>rig r<u>e</u>è

taktser as-for village one having/ foodstuff main grains is/

Taktser is a village (whose) main foodstuff is grain.

b. སྟག་འཚེར་ནི་གྲོང་གསེབ་ཞིག་ཡིན་ཏེ།   ཟ་ཆས་གཙོ་བོ་འབྲུ་རིགས་རེད།

dāgdzeni tro̱ŋse chī yi̱nde/ sa̱bjɛɛ̀ dzōwo dru̱rig re̱è

taktser as-for village one is having/ foodstuff main grains is/

Taktser is a village (whose) main foodstuff is (various kinds of) grain.

c. ལྷ་ས་ནི་གྲང་སྐྱེ་ས་མཐོ་པོ་རེད།

lhɛ̄ɛ̄sani tra̱ŋde sā tōbo re̱è

lhasa as-for cold having/ area high is/

(The reason why) Lhasa is cold, is because it is high.

5.12 The "conjunctive" connectives: ཅིང་, ཞིང་, and ཤིང་

These connectives function in a manner equivalent to the དང་ connective encountered in Lesson Three, and can be translated as "and." They link clauses with different subjects and different tenses.

These are used according to the following rule:

ཅིང་ occurs after words ending in ག་བ་ད་

ཞིང་ occurs after words ending in ང་ན་མ་འ་ར་ལ་ and vowels

ཤིང་ occurs after words ending in ས་

a. ཁོས་ལས་ཀ་བྱས་ཤིང་། མོ་སྨན་ཁང་ལ་ཕྱིན་པ་རེད།

kȫö lɛ̱ɛ̱ga chɛ̱ɛ̀shiŋ/ mo̱ mɛ̄nganlə chīmbəreè

he-by work did and/ she hospital to went past compl./

He worked and she went to the hospital.

Different tenses are expressed by changing the verb stems and the verb complements.

b. ཁོས་ལས་ཀ་བྱས་ཤིང་། མོ་སྨན་ཁང་ལ་འགྲོ་བ་རེད།

kȫö lɛ̱ɛ̱ga chɛ̱ɛ̀shiŋ/ mo̱ mɛ̄nganlə dro̱wareè

he-by work did and/ she hospital to go usual compl./

He worked and she goes to the hospital.

c. ཁོས་ལས་ཀ་བྱེད་ཅིང་། མོས་སྨན་ཁང་ལ་འགྲོ་གི་ཡོད་རེད།

kȫö lɛ̱ɛ̱ga che̱èjiŋ/ mȫö mɛ̄nganlə dru̱giyɔɔ̀reè

he-by work do and/ she hospital to go pres. compl./

He is working and she is going to the hospital.

d. ཁོས་ལས་ཀ་བྱེད་ཀྱི་ཡོད་ཅིང་། མོ་སྨན་ཁང་ལ་འགྲོ་གི་ཡོད་པ་རེད།

kȫö lɛ̱ɛ̱ga chi̱giyööshiŋ/ mo̱ mɛ̄nganlə dru̱giyɔɔ̀reè

he-by work do pres. compl. and/ she hospital to go pres. compl./

He is working and she is going to the hospital.

e. རྡོ་རྗེ་སློབ་གྲྭ་འགྲིང་བར་འགྲོ་ཞིང་། བཀྲ་ཤིས་སློབ་གྲྭ་ཆུང་བར་འགྲོ་བ་རེད།

dɔ̱ɔ̱je lāpdra dri̱ŋwaa dro̱shiŋ/ trāshiì lāpdra chūŋwaa dro̱wareè

dorje school middle-to go and/ tashi school lower-to go usual compl./
Dorje goes to secondary school and Tashi goes to primary school.

5.13 The "purposive" connectives: ཆེད་, སླད་, པའི་/བའི་ཆེད་དུ་, རྒྱུའི་ཆེད་དུ་, ཆེད་དུ་, དོན་དུ་, and ཕྱིར་

These clause connectives follow the non-past (present or future) stem of verbs and link two clauses so that the latter occurs (or will occur) "for the purpose of" or "in order to" or "on behalf of" the former.

a. ངས་ཁ་ལག་བཟོ་ཆེད་ཤ་དང་ཚལ་ཉོས་པ་ཡིན།
ŋɛɛ̀ kālaà socheè shā daŋ tsɛ̄ɛ ñö̀öbəyin
i-by food make for meat and vegetable bought past compl./
I bought meat and vegetables for the purpose of making a meal.

b. གཞུང་ལ་ངོ་ལོག་རྒྱག་སླད་ཚོགས་པ་གཅིག་འཛུགས་བཞིན་པ་རེད།
shuŋlə ŋoloò gyalɛɛ̀ tsɔ̄gba chi̅ dzuù shimbəreè
government to rebel for party one establish do pres. compl./
(They) are establishing an organization for the purpose of rebelling against the government.

c. ཁང་པ་གསར་པ་གཅིག་ཉོ་བའི་དོན་དུ་ཁོས་དངུལ་ཁང་ནས་དངུལ་གཡར་གྱི་རེད།
kāŋba sāāba chi̅ ñowɛɛtöntu kö̀ö ŋüüganne ŋüü yɔ̄ɔgireè
house new one buy for he-by bank from money borrow fut. compl./
He will borrow money from the bank in order to buy a new house.

d. ཁོ་ཚོས་ཁང་པ་གསར་པ་རྒྱག་རྒྱུའི་ཆེད་དུ་ལག་ཆ་གསར་པ་ཉོས་པ་རེད།
kōndzö̀ö kāŋba sāāba gyə gyüchetu lagja sāāba ñö̀öbəreè
he pl.-by house new build for tool new bought past compl.
They bought new tools for the purpose of building a new house.

e. ཐོན་སྐྱེད་ཆེན་པོ་ཡོང་ཕྱིར་འཕྲུལ་འཁོར་མང་པོ་གཡར་པ་རེད།
tōngyeè chēmbo yonchi̅r trüügoo məŋgu yāābareè
production big come for machine many borrowed/
In order to obtain large production, (they) borrowed many machines.

f. སློབ་སྦྱོང་ཆེད་ཨ་མེ་རི་ཀར་ཕྱིན།
lōpjon cheē əmerigar chi̅n
study for america-to went/
(He) went to America to study (for studies).

g. ཁྱོད་ཀྱི་དོན་དུ་ངས་ཁྱི་འདི་ཉོ་གི་ཡིན།
kyö̀öki dontu ŋɛɛ̀ ki̅ di ñugiyin

you of for i-by dog this buy fut. compl./

I will buy this dog for you.

The infinitive particle also sometimes conveys this meaning. It is discussed below in section 5.15.

5.14 The genitive case

We have already encountered the genitive particles through some of the clause connectives and verb complements, e.g., the འི in པའི་སྐབས་ and the གི in གི་རེད་. Like the instrumental (3.1) and dative-locative (2.6.1) cases, the genitive case has a number of particles whose use is governed by the final letter of the preceding word.

གི་	after final ག་ and ང་
ཀྱི་	after final ད་, བ་, and ས་
གྱི་	after final ན་, མ་, ར་, and ལ་
-འི་ or ཡི་	after vowel finals

The genitive corresponds in a number of ways to the English preposition "of" and is used, as in English, to express *ownership* and *possession*, for example, "the book of he = his book."

a. ཁོའི་དེབ་འདིར་འདུག།

kö̈ö tep dee duù

he-of book this-to exist/

His book is here.

b. དེབ་འདི་ཁོའི་རེད།

tep di kö̈ö reè

book this he-of is/

This book is his.

The genitive is also used for descriptive modification. In this role it joins a noun or noun phrase with another noun or noun phrase so that the former modifies the latter. In many instances the modifier is translated in English simply as an adjective. For example:

c. བོད་པའི་ཁ་ལག་

pö̈öbɛ kālaà

tibetan-of food

Tibetan food (What kind of food?—Tibetan food.)

d. རྒྱ་གར་གྱི་ས་མཚམས་

gyagarki sāndzam

india of border

Indian border

e. བྱང་ཐང་གི་རི་དྭགས་
chaŋdaŋki ridaà
changtang of animals
Changtang animals

f. གསར་བརྗེའི་དམག་འཁྲུག་
sārjee mәgdruù
revolution-of war
revolutionary war

Genitive particles also often join a series of three or more nouns and noun phrases. Determination of the relationship between the elements in such a series is often problematic since it is not unusual for two or more sets of nouns linked by a genitive to modify a common third noun. Let us examine some examples of this:

g. གསར་བརྗེའི་དམག་འཁྲུག་གི་ལྟ་ཚུལ་
sārjee mәgdruùki dәdzüü
revolution-of war of viewpoint
revolutionary war viewpoint (the viewpoint of revoluntary war)

In example g. we see that just as "revolution" modifies "war" (What kind of war—revolutionary war), the unit "revolutionary war" in turn modifies "viewpoint" (What kind of viewpoint—revolutionary war viewpoint).

h. རྒྱ་གར་གྱི་རང་བཙན་གྱི་ལས་འགུལ་
gyagarki raŋdzɛnki lɛngüü
india of independence of movement
India's independence movement (the independence movement of India)

i. གསར་བརྗེའི་དམག་འཁྲུག་གི་ཁྱོན་ཡོངས་ཀྱི་ལྟ་ཚུལ་
sārjee mәgdruùki kyōnyoŋki dәdzüü
revolution-of war of overall of viewpoint
revolutionary war overall viewpoint (the overall viewpoint of revoluntary war)

In example i., the unit "revolutionary war" is not linked with the next unit, "overall," but rather with "viewpoint," the head noun of the entire phrase. The phrase breaks down into two units: "revolutionary war" and "overall viewpoint," with the former modifying the latter (What kind of "overall viewpoint"?—"revolutionary war"). Unfortunately, it is not possible to determine by grammar whether a given phrase is of the sequential type illustrated by g. or of that illustrated by i. Semantic considerations will determine which is intended and this will be one of the more difficult tasks facing the reader.

As the following sentence illustrates, the genitive case can be used in both the subject (by a lama *of* Drepung) and object (to the people *of* Lhasa) slots:

j. འབྲས་སྤུངས་ཀྱི་བླ་མ་ཞིག་གིས་ལྷ་སའི་མི་དམངས་ལ་ཆོས་གསུང་པ་རེད།

drḛbuŋki lāma chi̅kiì lɛ̄ɛ̄sɛɛ mi̱maŋlə chȫö̀ sūm̀bəreè

drepung of lama one by lhasa-of people to religion said past compl./

A lama of Drepung monastery gave religious teachings to the people of Lhasa.

5.15 Infinitive usage: vb. + བར་ or པར་

Infinitive constructions convey the idea that one action occurs "in order to" do a second one. They attach to the non-past stem of verbs.

a. ཁོས་ཚོང་ཁང་ལ་དེབ་ཉོ་བར་ཕྱིན།

kȫö̀ tsōŋganlə tḛp ño̱war chi̅n

he store to book buy inf. went/

He went to the store to buy a book.

b. ཁོ་གཉིས་དགེ་ལུགས་པའི་བླ་མ་ཞིག་སང་ཉིན་མཇལ་བར་འགྲོ་གི་རེད།

kūñiì gḛlugbɛɛ lāma chi̅ sə̄ñii jɛ̰ɛ̰war dru̱gireè

he two gelugpa-of lama one tomorrow meet inf. go fut. compl./

(The two of them) will go to meet a Gelugpa lama tomorrow.

These particles can also convey the "purposive" connective meanings discussed in section 5.13.

c. ཁོས་ཡིག་ཚད་ཡག་པོ་ཡོང་བར་སློབ་སྦྱོང་བྱེད་བཞིན་པ་རེད།

kȫö̀ yi̱gdzɛɛ̀ ya̱go yo̱ŋwar lōpjon chḛshimbəreè

he-by exam good come inf. study do pres.compl./

He is studying in order to do well on the exam.

d. ཁོས་གནམ་གྲུ་གཏོང་བར་སྦྱོང་བརྡར་བྱེད་བཞིན་དུ་ཡོད་པ་རེད།

kȫö̀ nə̄mdru dōŋwar jo̱ŋdar chḛshinduyɔ̄ɔ̀reè

he-by plane send inf. practice do pres. compl./

He is practicing in order to fly a plane.

Note that the infinitive is actually comprised of the dative-locative case suffixed to nominalized verb stems. Nominalization of verbs is discussed below. These two functions of the infinitive particle can be joined in one sentence.

e. ཁོ་ཡིག་ཚད་ཡག་པོ་ཡོང་བར་སློབ་སྦྱོང་བྱེད་པར་དཔེ་མཛོད་ཁང་ལ་འགྲོ་བ་རེད།

kō yi̱gdzɛɛ̀ ya̱go yo̱ŋwar lōpjon chḛbar bēndzökaŋ la dro̱wareè

he exam good come inf. study do inf. library to go usual compl./

He goes to the library to study in order to do well on the exam.

Or alternatively:

f. ཁོ་དཔེ་མཛོད་ཁང་ལ་ཡིག་ཚད་ཡག་པོ་ཡོང་ཆེད་སློབ་སྦྱོང་བྱེད་པར་འགྲོ་བ་རེད།

kō bēndzöganlə yigdzɛɛ̀ yago yoŋche lōpjon chebar drowareè

he library to exam good come for study do inf. go usual compl./

He goes to the library to study in order to do well on the exam

In colloqual Tibetan the infinitive is pronounced "ga." This is sometimes written as ཀ་ or ག་. For example:

g. ཁོས་དངུལ་ཁང་ལ་དངུལ་ལེན་ཀ་ཕྱིན་པ་རེད།

kō ŋüüganlə ŋüü lenga chi̅mbəreè

he bank to money take inf. went past compl./

He went to the bank to get money.

h. ཁོ་ཚོ་བོད་པའི་ཁ་ལག་ཟ་ག་འགྲོ་གི་རེད།

kōndzo pööbɛ kālaà saga drugireè

he pl. tibet-of food eat inf. go fut. compl./

They will go to eat Tibetan food.

5.16 The "agentive" verbal particles: མཁན་, མི་, and པ་/བ་

The agentive verbal particles are used with the non-past stem of verbs to express the idea of "the one who does" the verbal action. Note that it converts the verb into a verbal noun phrase which can then stand as the subject of linking, existential and active constructions. It is something like the "-er" in the English "baker" or "skater."

a. འདིར་སྡོད་མཁན་སུ་རེད་དམ།

dee döñɛn sū redam

here stay doer who is ?/

Who is the person staying here? (lit., The one who is staying here--who is it?)

b. འདིར་སྡོད་མཁན་དེ་ང་ཚོའི་དགེ་རྒན་རེད།

dee döñɛn de ŋandzöö gegɛn reè

here stay doer that i pl.-of teacher is

That person staying here is our teacher.

c. ལས་ཀ་བྱེད་མི་ཁ་ཤས་འདུག།

lɛɛga chemi kāshɛɛ̀ duù

work do doer several exist/

There are several workers (people doing work).

In the next example, the agentive verbal noun phrase ("the one who came from Lhasa") modifies a noun (via the genitive particle) so that it functions as a relative clause in English: the father *of* the one who came from Lhasa.

d. ལྷ་ས་ནས་ཡོང་མིའི་པ་ཕ་དེས་ཅ་ལག་མང་པོ་ཉོས་པ་རེད།

lhɛ̄ɛ̄sanɛ yo̲ŋmii bāba de̲è jālaà mə̲ŋgu ñö̲öbareè

lhasa from come person-of father that-by things many bought past compl./

The father of the person who came from Lhasa bought many things.

The agentive idea is also conveyed by the nominalizing particles པ་ and བ་. We have already encountered this in words such as ཞིང་པ་ ("farmer"). Thus, whereas ངོ་ལོག་རྒྱག་/རྒྱབ་ means "to rebel," ངོ་ལོག་པ་ (ŋo̲logba) means a person who rebels. And while སློབ་གྲྭ་ means "school," སློབ་གྲྭ་བ་ (lāpdraà or lāpdrawa) means "student."

In example e. the agentive verbal noun phrase ("that one who came from Lhasa") is linked to the instrumental particle and acts as the subject of an active sentence.

e. ལྷ་ས་ནས་ཡོང་མཁན་དེས་ཅ་ལག་མང་པོ་ཉོས།

lhɛ̄ɛ̄sanɛ yo̲ŋɛn de̲è jālaà mə̲ŋgu ñö̲ö

lhasa from come doer that-by things many bought/

The person who came from Lhasa bought many things.

Sentences such as d. can be constructed also with མཁན་.

f. ལྷ་ས་ནས་ཡོང་མཁན་གྱི་པ་ཕ་དེས་ཅ་ལག་མང་པོ་ཉོས་པ་རེད།

lhɛ̄ɛ̄sanɛ yo̲ŋɛnki bāba de̲è jālaà mə̲ŋgu ñö̲öbəreè

lhasa from come doer -of father that-by things many bought past compl./

The father of the person who came from Lhasa bought many things.

When མཁན་ is immediately followed by a linking verb, it expresses future time:

g. ཁོ་རྒྱ་ནག་ལ་འགྲོ་མཁན་རེད།

kō gya̲naàla dro̲ŋɛn re̲è

he china to go doer is/

He is going to China. (lit., "He is someone who is going to China.")

5.17 Reading exercise: "The Rabbit Takes Revenge"

5.17.1 Tibetan text

རི་བོང་གིས་དགྲ་ཤ་ལེན་པ་

༄༅ གནའ་རབས་སུ་རི་བོང་དང་འདམ་སེང་དཀར་པོ་ཞིག་ནགས་ཚལ་སྟུག་པོ་ཞིག་གི་ནང་གནས་ཏེ་འཚོ་བ་སྐྱེལ་བཞིན་ཡོད་པ་རེད། རི་བོང་དང་འདམ་སེང་གཉིས་ཁྱིམ་མཚེས་རེད། ཡིན་ན་ཡང་འདམ་སེང་གིས་རང་ཉིད་ཀྱི་ཤེད་ཤུགས་ངོམས་ནས་རྟག་ཏུ་རི་བོང་ལ་འཇིགས་བསྐུལ་བྱེད་ཀྱི་ཡོད་པ་རེད། རི་བོང་འདམ་སེང་དཀར་པོའི་བརྙས་བཅོས་ལ་དགའ་པོ་མེད་སྟབས་ཉིན་ལྟར་ཁོས་བྲག་ཕུག་གི་མདུན་དུ་བསྡད་ནས་དགྲ་ཤ་ག་འདྲ་ཞིག་ལེན་གྱི་རེད་བསམ་བློ་གཏོང་བཞིན་ཡོད། ཉིན་ཞིག་རི་བོང་གིས་

འདམ་སེང་ལ་ཁ་སང་ང་ལ་ཁྱེད་རང་དང་འདྲ་བའི་འདམ་སེང་སྔོན་པོ་ཞིག་ཐུག་བྱུང་། འདམ་སེང་སྔོན་པོ་དེས་ཁྱེད་དང་མཐུ་རྩལ་འགྲན་གྱི་ཡིན་ཟེར་གྱི་འདུག་ཅེས་བཤད། འདམ་སེང་དཀར་པོས་ང་རོ་སྐད་རྒྱབ་སྟེ་རི་བོང་ལ་འདམ་སེང་སྔོན་པོ་དེ་ལམ་སེང་ངའི་རྩ་ལ་སྐད་གཏོང་ཞེས་བཤད་པ་རེད། རི་བོང་གིས་འདམ་སེང་སྔོན་པོས་འདམ་སེང་ཁྱེད་ལ་འཛིན་ཐང་ཡོད་པ་མ་རེད་ཅེས་ཁྱད་ཤོབ་ཤོད་ཀྱི་འདུག་ཅེས་བཤད། འདམ་སེང་དཀར་པོ་དེ་ཁོང་ཁྲོ་ཟས་ནས་ཁོ་ད་ལྟ་ག་པར་འདུག་གམ། ང་ལམ་སེང་ཁོའི་རྩ་ལ་ཁྲིད་ཞེས་རི་བོང་ལ་ལབ་པ་རེད། རི་བོང་གིས་འདམ་སེང་དཀར་པོ་དེ་རི་ཆེན་པོ་ཞིག་གི་རྒྱབ་ཏུ་ཁྲིད་རྗེས་ཁྲོན་པ་ཞིག་ལ་མཛུབ་མོ་བཙུགས་ཏེ་སེམས་ཅན་དེ་ཕ་གིའི་ནང་ལ་འདུག་ཅེས་ལན་བཏབ་ཅིང་། འདམ་སེང་དེས་ང་རོ་སྐད་ཆེན་པོ་རྒྱབ་ནས་ཁྲོན་པའི་ཁ་ལ་ཕྱིན་ནས་ལྟ་སྐབས་ཁྲོན་པའི་ནང་ནས་འདམ་སེང་ཞིག་མཐོང་། འདམ་སེང་དཀར་པོ་དེས་ཁྲོན་པའི་ནང་དུ་ང་རོ་དྲག་པོ་ལན་འགའ་ཞིག་བསྒྲགས་པས་ཁྲོན་པའི་ནང་གི་འདམ་སེང་དེས་ཀྱང་ཚུར་ང་རོ་བསྒྲགས། སྐབས་དེར་འདམ་སེང་དཀར་པོ་དེས་མཆེ་གཙིགས་སྡེར་བགྲད་བྱས་ཏེ་ཁྲོན་པའི་ནང་ལ་མཆོངས་པ་རེད། རི་བོང་གིས་ཕུའུ་དུང་ཟེར་བའི་སྒྲ་དེ་ཐོས་སྐབས་ཨ་ཁ་ལྟ་བ་མཐོ་བའི་འདམ་སེང་ཁྲོན་པའི་ནང་ལ་ལྷུང་ནས་ཤི་སོང་ཞེས་བཤད་པ་རེད། དེ་ནས་རི་བོང་གིས་ཁོའི་ཁྱིམ་ལ་ལོག་སོང་།།

5.17.2 Interlinear translation

1. rabbit by revenge get
2. ancient-time to rabbit and lion white one forest thick one of in live having livlihood get pres. compl./
3. rabbit and lion two neighbor is/ nevertheless lion by self of strength show-offish having
4. always rabbit to intimidation do usual compl./ rabbit lion white-of bullying to like without since day
5. every he-by cave of front to sat having/ revenge how one get fut. compl. think send pres. compl./ day one rabbit by
6. lion to yesterday i to you and similar-of lion blue one met past compl./ lion blue that-by you and strength
7. contest fut. compl. say pres. compl. quote said/ lion white by roar did having rabbit to lion blue that im-
8. mediately i-of presence to call send quote said past compl./ rabbit by lion blue-by you to capable exist neg.
9. quote brag say usual compl. quote said/ lion white that angry ate having he now where exist ?/ i quick
10. he-of presence take quote rabbit to say past compl./ rabbit by lion white that mountain big one of behind to took after well one
11. to finger point having animal that there-of in to exist quote answer gave and/ lion

that-by roar big did having

12. well-of edge to went having look when well-of in from lion one saw/ lion white that-by well-of in to roar
13. powerful time several did-since well-of in of lion that-by also hither roar made/ time that-to lion white
14. that-by bare-fangs claw scratch did having well-of in to jump past compl./ rabbit by splash call-of sound that hear when oh
15. pride high-of lion well-of in to fall having die went compl. quote said past compl./ that after rabbit by he-of house to returned went compl.//

5.17.3 Translation

The Rabbit Takes Revenge

A long time ago a rabbit and a white lion lived (lit., subsisted living) in a thick forest. The lion and the rabbit were neighbors. Nevertheless, the lion always threatened the rabbit, showing off his strength. Because the rabbit did not like the bullying of the lion, he sat in front of a cave every day thinking about what kind of revenge he could take.

One day the rabbit said to the lion, "Yesterday I met a blue lion that was just like you. That blue lion says he will compete with you." The white lion roared in anger and said to the rabbit, "Bring that blue lion to me immediately!" The rabbit said, "The blue lion is saying braggingly that you are not capable." The white lion got angry and said to the rabbit, "Where is he now? Quickly take me to him (his presence)."

The rabbit took the white lion behind a large hill and (after that) pointed with his finger to a well, answering, "That animal is in that [well] over there." The lion roared and went to the edge of the well and looked in. At that time from within the well he saw a lion. The white lion roared several times inside the well and because of this the lion inside the well also roared back. At that time, the white lion, baring his fangs and claws, jumped into the well. When the rabbit heard the sound "phu-dung" (he) said, "Oh my, that conceited lion has fallen into the well and died." After that the rabbit returned to his home.

5.17.4 Grammatical notes

1. The first segment consists of: རི་བོང་གིས་དགྲ་ཤ་ལེན་པ་.

Titles in Tibetan publications typically utilize an incomplete verbal complement, i.e., rather than ལེན་པ་རེད་ only ལེན་པ is used. This title consists of a subject in the instrumental case (རི་བོང་གིས་) and an active verb, "took revenge" (དགྲ་ཤ་ལེན་). It should be noted that the rabbit is one of Tibetan folklore's famous tricksters.

2. The second segment consists of two clauses: 1. གནའ་རབས་སུ་རི་བོང་དང་འདམ་སེང་དཀར་པོ་ཞིག་ནགས་ཚལ་སྟུག་པོ་ཞིག་གི་ནང་གནས་ཏེ་ 2. འཚོ་བ་སྐྱེལ་བཞིན་ཡོད་པ་རེད།.

The first clause begins with a time slot word—"in the past" (གནའ་རབས་སུ་). It is followed by the subject of the two clauses, a rabbit and a white lion (རི་བོང་དང་འདམ་སེང་དཀར་པོ་ཞིག་). Note that there is no instrumental particle following the subject. Normally this would convey that this was not an active construction. However, in this case it is because the verbs "to live" (གནས་) and "to subsist" (འཚོ་བ་སྐྱེལ་) do not require the subject ("the rabbit and the lion") to be in the instrumental case.

Following the subject is the object phrase "in a dense forest" (ནགས་ཚལ་སྟུག་པོ་ཞིག་གི་ནང་). It consists of "forest" (ནགས་ཚལ་) modified by the adjective "dense" (སྟུག་པོ་) and the indefinite article (ཞིག་). Together these mean "a dense forest."

They are linked to the word "inside" (ནང་) by the genitive particle (གི་) so that together they convey "inside of a dense forest." It should be noted that the term "inside" almost always is linked to the phrase or word it modifies by the genitive. Thus, "inside the restaurant" would be: ཟ་ཁང་གི་ནང་ལ་.

The dative-locative particle (e.g., ལ་ in the previous example) is also often used together with ནང་ conveying "at" or "to" the inside of. The clause in the reading exercise could just as easily have been written as: ནགས་ཚལ་སྟུག་པོ་ཞིག་གི་ནང་ལ་གནས་. However, whether or not the dative-locative is present, the translation remains the same.

Following this comes the verb གནས་ which means "dwell" or "live." Together they convey, "A long time ago, a rabbit and a white lion, lived in a dense forest."

This clause is linked to the second clause by the gerundive clause connective ཏེ་, which here functions to convey to the reader that two *simultaneous* actions occurred: "(along with) living in a dense forest" (ནགས་ཚལ་སྟུག་པོ་ཞིག་གི་ནང་གནས་) something else follows.

Clause two explains what follows. It consists of a verbal phrase that conveys "being in the process of deriving their livelihood or subsisting" (འཚོ་བ་སྐྱེལ་བཞིན་ཡོད་པ་རེད). In other words, "(the rabbit and lion) were subsisting, living in a dense forest." Note also that the final verb complement (བཞིན་ཡོད་པ་རེད་) conveys that they were in the act of doing something, albeit in this case the action is in the past. This tense dimension is indicated not by the verbs which normally imply present-usual tense, but rather by གནའ་རབས་སུ་, the temporal word at the start of the story.

3. The third segment consists of a linking sentence: རི་བོང་དང་འདམ་སེང་གཉིས་ཁྱིམ་མཚེས་རེད།

This is a simple linking sentence stating that the subject, "the two of them—lion and rabbit " (རི་བོང་དང་འདམ་སེང་གཉིས་)— are or were neighbors. Again, tense is determined not by the verb (རེད), but rather by context and the temporal word (གནའ་རབས་སུ་) occurring in the previous clause.

4. The fourth segment consists of two clauses: 1. ཡིན་ན་ཡང་འདམ་སེང་གིས་རང་ཉིད་ཀྱི་ཤེད་ཤུགས་ངོམས་ནས་ 2. རྟག་ཏུ་རི་བོང་ལ་འཇིགས་བསྐུལ་བྱེད་ཀྱི་ཡོད་པ་རེད།.

The first clause begins with ཡིན་ན་ཡང་ ("nevertheless"), one of those clause connectives that are placed at the *start* of the second of two clauses rather than the *end* of the first clause.

Following this is the subject placed in the instrumental case—"by the lion" (འདམ་སེང་གིས). The presence of the instrumental particle indicates that somewhere down the line some action done by the lion will be stated through an active verb. It is common to scan a segment to find this verb, which here, is not ངོམས་("be showoffish/conceited"), the first verb encountered, but rather འཇིགས་བསྐུལ་བྱེད་("threatened/intimidated"), the second verb (in clause two). Thus, what the lion did was "frighten" somebody.

Going back to the first part of the clause, the subject is followed by: རང་ཉིད་ཀྱི་ཤེད་ཤུགས་ངོམས་ནས་. This breaks down into the phrase རང་ཉིད་ཀྱི་ཤེད་ཤུགས་, which consists of "his own" (རང་ཉིད) and "strength" (ཤེད་ཤུགས་), linked by the genitive particle (ཀྱི་) to create the meaning "his own strength." Then the verb "show off" (ངོམས་) comes, making the clause convey "he showed off of his own strength."

Clause one is linked to clause two by the clause connector ནས་, which here conveys the adverbial or simultaneous meaning—that the action in clause two occurs in the manner of clause one. In other words, "how did the lion frighten the rabbit (རི་བོང་ལ་འཇིགས་བསྐུལ་བྱེད་ཀྱི་ཡོད་པ་རེད)—he frightened him by showing off his strength." Note that the recipient of the action, "the rabbit," is placed in the dative-locative (རི་བོང་ལ་) because the the action went *to* him.

This clause also contains the commonly used adverb རྟག་ཏུ་ ("always"). It modifies the verb བྱེད་ answering the question, "How or when did he do it?—he did it always." This adverb could have been placed immediately before the verb with no change in meaning—རི་བོང་ལ་རྟག་ཏུ་འཇིགས་བསྐུལ་བྱེད་ཀྱི་ཡོད་པ་རེད. Similarly, རི་བོང་ལ་འཇིགས་བསྐུལ་རྟག་ཏུ་བྱེད་ཀྱི་ཡོད་པ་རེད would be correct.

5. The fifth segment consists of three clauses: 1. རི་བོང་འདམ་སེང་དཀར་པོའི་བརྙས་བཅོས་ལ་དགའ་པོ་མེད་སྐབས་ 2. ཉིན་ལྟར་ཁོས་བྲག་ཕུག་གི་མདུན་དུ་བསྡད་ནས་ 3. དབྱི་ཤ་ག་འདྲ་ཞིག་ཡིན་ཀྱི་རེད་བསམ་བློ་གཏོང་བཞིན་ཡོད.

The first clause is an existential sentence conveying at its core the meaning that "the rabbit did not like the bullying" (རི་བོང་བརྙས་བཅོས་ལ་དགའ་པོ་མེད་). This is a standard existential construction and is structurally identical with ང་ཤ་ལ་དགའ་པོ་མེད་("I do not like meat"—or literally, "I am without liking to/for meat.") The sentence has been expanded by phrases such as "the white lion" (འདམ་སེང་དཀར་པོ), which is linked to "abuse" by the genitive particle (འི་) so that the larger phrase means "the abuse of the white lion."

This clause is linked to clause two by the "because" clause connective (སྟབས་), thus: "because the rabbit did not like the abuse—he did something." That "something" is expressed in clause two. It begins with the time-slot phrase "every day" (ཉིན་ལྟར་). This is followed by the subject in the instrumental case (ཁོས་). This is not really necessary since the subject ("the rabbit") is the same as in the previous clause, but we added it to emphasize the carryover of subjects in multiple clauses.

Next comes the verbal phrase verb བྲག་ཕུག་གི་མདུན་དུ་བསྡད་. It consists of the active verb "sat/lived/stayed" (བསྡད་) preceeded by a phrase indicating the location of the verbal action—"in front of a cave" (བྲག་ཕུག་གི་མདུན་དུ་). Note that, like ནང་, the word མདུན་དུ་ ("in front") usually has the genitive case particle (གི་) linking it to the noun it modifies.

After the verb བསྡད་, the clause connective ནས་ occurs, linking clause two with clause three. In this instance it conveys simultaneous action: "in the manner of sitting in front of a cave, something else happened."

Clause three indicates what that "something else" is—namely, "think" (བསམ་བློ་གཏོང་). Thus, the skeletal sentence means: "sitting in front of a cave . . . he thought." The phrase immediately preceeding "thought" (དགྲ་ཤ་ག་འདྲ་ཞིག་ལེན་གྱི་རེད་) indicates what he thought. It is an interrogative active sentence asking, "How will he get revenge?" This phrase breaks down into the compound verb "revenge get" (དགྲ་ཤ་ལེན་), modified by the interrogative word "how" or "what kind of" (ག་འདྲ་ཞིག་). The verb (ལེན་) is also modified by the future tense complement (གྱི་རེད་). Together these mean: "How will (I, one) get revenge?" Actually, since the actor is thinking about himself, grammatically this would have been more correct if it had been written using the first person verb ཡིན: དགྲ་ཤ་ག་འདྲ་ཞིག་ལེན་གྱི་ཡིན་. Nevertheless, both linking verbs occur and should be expected.

This is immediately followed by the main verb compound of the two clauses, "think" (བསམ་བློ་གཏོང་). It consists of the noun "thought" (བསམ་བློ་) and the verbalizer གཏོང་. The three clauses should be read as follows: 1. *Because* the rabbit did not like the bullying of the white lion, 2. every day he sat in front of a cave, and *while* doing that, 3. he *thought* of how to get revenge *or*—སྟབས་ —ནས་—བསམ་བློ་གཏོང་བཞིན་ཡོད.

Note that the final verb complement following "think" (བཞིན་ཡོད་) conveys usual or customary action, and governs both clauses. Thus, "he *used* to sit ....

6. The sixth segment consists of two clauses (sentences): 1. ཉིན་ཞིག་རི་བོང་གིས་འདམ་སེང་ལ་ཁ་སང་ང་ལ་ཁྱོད་རང་དང་འདྲ་བའི་འདམ་སེང་སྡོན་པོ་ཞིག་ཐུག་བྱུང་། 2. འདམ་སེང་སྡོན་པོ་དེས་ཁྱོད་དང་མཐུ་རྩལ་འགྲན་གྱི་ཡིན་ཟེར་གྱི་

འདུག་ཅེས་བཤད།.

The first sentence is long and complex. It starts with the time slot word ("one day" - ཉིན་ཞིག་). This is followed by the subject, "the rabbit" (རི་བོང་), in the instrumental case (གིས). As indicated above, this tells us immediately that further on there will be an active verb that will convey what he did. That verb is actually བཤད་ ("said"), which occurs only toward the end of the second clause.

Following the subject phrase "by the rabbit" (རི་བོང་གིས་) is the phrase "to the lion" (འདམ་སེང་ལ་), which is the object of this sentence.

The heart of the construction, therefore, is: རི་བོང་གིས་འདམ་སེང་ལ་. . . བཤད་ "The rabbit said . . . to the lion." The remainder consists of the direct speech quote, which indicates what he said to the lion. Reiterating an earlier comment, quotes and direct speech are difficult to identify in Tibetan since they are only marked at their conclusions by the particle ཅེས་ or one of its variants. Thus, in this case, the direct speech quotation is: ཁ་སང་ང་ལ་འདམ་སེང་སྔོན་པོ་ཞིག་ཐུག་བྱུང་། འདམ་སེང་སྔོན་པོ་དེས་ཁྱེད་དང་མཐུ་རྩལ་འགྲན་གྱི་ཡིན་ཟེར་གྱི་འདུག—ཅེས་

This quote starts with the temporal-slot word ཁ་སང་ ("yesterday"), which is followed by the subject ("I") in the dative-locative case (ང་ལ་). This could just as easily have been written ངར་. The presence of a subject in the dative-locative immediately suggests that this is not an active construction and that something happened *to* the speaker rather than was done *by* the speaker. Looking ahead for the verb, we see ཐུག་ ("meet") which fits this assumption because it is an involuntary verb which, in fact, requires the dative-locative. Thus, the essence of this sub-unit is: ང་ལ་. . . ཐུག་ ("I met. . .").

The rest of the construction tells when he met—"yesterday" (ཁ་སང་), and who he met—"a blue lion similar to you" (ཁྱེད་རང་དང་འདྲ་བའི་འདམ་སེང་སྔོན་པོ་).

This phrase ཁྱེད་རང་དང་འདྲ་བའི་འདམ་སེང་སྔོན་པོ་ ("a blue lion similar to you") is an example of a noun modified by the adjective following it ("blue" - སྔོན་པོ་) and by a phrase before it linked by the genitive particle (ཁྱེད་རང་དང་འདྲ་བའི་). The latter consists of the term འདྲ་བ་ ("like," "similar") and the conjunction དང་ ("and"), which must be placed between འདྲ་བ་ and the word it modifies, in this case "you" (ཁྱེད་རང་). In this usage, དང་ conveys the meaning "with." Thus the phrase ཁྱེད་རང་དང་འདྲ་བ་ means "similar with (to) you." This is then joined to "lion" by the genitive particle to create a relative clause: ཁྱེད་རང་དང་འདྲ་བའི་འདམ་སེང་, which means "a lion *who* is similar to you."

Then comes the verbal phrase ཐུག་བྱུང་ ("met"). We already know from the subject having the dative-locative instead of the instrumental particle ("to me" instead of "by me"), that this clause would be either an existential or involuntary construction. Now we see that it is an involuntary construction since the verb ཐུག་ means "to meet involuntarily." Thus, the first person past tense verbal complement (as discussed in Lesson Three) བྱུང་ is used. This ends the first clause of the rabbit's direct speech: "Yesterday, I met a lion who was similar to you."

But the rabbit's direct discourse is not yet fininshed. The next segment (འདམ་སེང་སྔོན་པོ་དེས་ཁྱེད་དང་མཐུ་རྩལ་འགྲན་གྱི་ཡིན་ཟེར་གྱི་འདུག་) presents the second part of the rabbit's comment. It begins with the subject in the instrumental case—"by that blue lion" (འདམ་སེང་སྔོན་པོ་དེས་). This is followed by the object ("you") modified by the conjunctive དང་ ("and/with"), and then the verbal phrase མཐུ་རྩལ་འགྲན་གྱི་ཡིན་ ("will compete in strength").

This is followed by the verbal phrase "says" (ཟེར་གྱི་འདུག་) ending the discourse of the blue lion. This also ends the speech of the rabbit to the white lion. This finish is marked by the quote marker particle (ཅེས་) and the verb བཤད་ ("said"). These two, of course, refer back to the subject of the whole construction, the rabbit (རི་བོང་གིས་). Consequently, the Tibetan is really a sentence within a sentence: "By the rabbit . . . said," with his comment being another sentence with its own subject and verb: "I met a lion similar to you and he said that he will compete with you." The best strategy for deciphering such constructions is first to read through the entire construction and then to reread it paying careful attention to the first subject and its verb. After this, the second subject and its verb can be located and the overall structure of the construction will become clear. This is a very common Tibetan stylistic mode and we will present many other examples of it to facilitate identification and comprehension.

7. The seventh segment consists of two clauses: 1. འདམ་སེང་དཀར་པོས་ངར་སྐད་རྒྱབ་སྟེ་ 2. རི་བོང་ལ་འདམ་སེང་སྔོན་པོ་དེ་ལམ་སེང་ངའི་ཙ་ལ་སྐད་གཏོང་ཞེས་བཤད་པ་རེད།.

The first clause (འདམ་སེང་དཀར་པོས་ངར་སྐད་རྒྱབ་སྟེ་) consists of the subject (in the instrumental case—[འདམ་སེང་དཀར་པོས་] "by the white lion") followed by the verbal phrase "roared in anger" (ངར་སྐད་རྒྱབ).

This clause is linked to clause two by the simultaneous clause connector སྟེ་. However, the clause connector སྟེ་ is somewhat unclear in this context. It can be taken to convey simultaneous action—"The white lion said in a yelling or roaring manner. . . ." Or it could be take to convey two related sequential acts such that the second act is done after the first: "Having roared in anger, he said. . . ." Since the time gap of the second alternative would be so slight, the difference is moot here.

The subject of the second clause is the same as in the first clause and is not specified. Thus, the second clause starts with the object linked to the dative-locative ("to the rabbit" - རི་བོང་ལ་), followed by an active sentence that is a segment of direct discourse spoken by the white lion: འདམ་སེང་སྔོན་པོ་དེ་ལམ་སེང་ངའི་རྩ་ལ་སྐད་གཏོང་ ("Summon that blue lion to my presence at once"). The object of this sentence within a sentence is "that blue lion" (འདམ་སེང་སྔོན་པོ་དེ་), and the verb is "call/summon" (སྐད་གཏོང་). A location phrase indicating where the lion should be called to —"to my presence" (ངའི་རྩ་ལ་)—and the time-slot word "immediately" (ལམ་སེང་) follow the object phrase. It should be noted that the term "to (into) the presence" (རྩ་ལ་) requires its object to be in the genitive: ངའི་རྩ་ལ་ ("to the presence of i").

This segment concludes with the quotation marker (ཞེས་) and the verb "said" with the past complement (བཤད་པ་རེད). བཤད་ is the verb that goes with the original subject (འདམ་སེང་དཀར་པོས་). The entire section, therefore, conveys the idea that: "The white lion, in a roaring manner, said to the rabbit, "Bring that blue lion to me at once!"

8. The eighth segment consists of a single sentence: རི་བོང་གིས་འདམ་སེང་སྔོན་པོས་འདམ་སེང་ཁྱེད་ལ་འཛོན་ཐང་ཡོད་པ་མ་རེད་ཅེས་ཨུད་ཤོབ་ཤོད་ཀྱི་འདུག་ཅེས་བཤད་.

This sentence is a continuation of the rabbit's comments to the lion. It, like others, begins with the subject in the instrumental case: རི་བོང་གིས་ ("by the rabbit"). This is followed immediately by another quote, which begins with a noun (the subject of the quote) in the instrumental case འདམ་སེང་སྔོན་པོས་ ("by the blue lion"). This is followed by a simple existential construction (noun + existential verb): "you have no ability" or more literally, "to you there is no ability" (འདམ་སེང་ཁྱེད་ལ་འཛོན་ཐང་ཡོད་པ་མ་རེད).

This, in turn, is followed by the quote marker (ཅེས་) indicating the end of the direct discourse of the blue lion. It is followed by the verbal phrase ཨུད་ཤོབ་ཤོད་ཀྱི་འདུག་, which means "says it in a bragging manner," this being the rabbit's embellishment.

Since this section is an indirect quote within a direct quote ("the rabbit said the blue lion said), the next two words (ཅེས་བཤད) end the discourse of the original subject, the rabbit (རི་བོང་གིས་). The first of these two words is the quote marker, and the second is the verb "say." Thus, the entire construction means: "The rabbit said, 'That other lion is saying braggingly, that you [the original lion] are not capable.'"

9. The ninth segment consists of three clauses: 1. འདམ་སེང་དཀར་པོ་དེ་ཁོང་ཁྲོ་ཟས་ནས་ 2. ཁོ་ད་ལྟ་ག་པར་འདུག་གམ། 3. ང་ལམ་སེང་ཁོའི་རྩ་ལ་ཁྲིད་ཞེས་རི་བོང་ལ་ལབ་པ་རེད།.

This segment gives the lion's response. Normally it would start with the subject in the instrumental case འདམ་སེང་དཀར་པོ་དེས་ ("by that white lion"), but because the first clause ends in the involuntary verb ཁོང་ཁྲོ་ཟས་ ("got angry"), the subject does not require the instrumental. This clause འདམ་སེང་དཀར་པོ་དེ་ཁོང་ཁྲོ་ཟས་ ("the white lion got angry") is followed by the simultaneous clause connective ནས་ so that it means, "The lion, being or becoming angry, . . ."

After this, the lion's direct discourse segment follows. It consists of two sentences. The first is an existential construction, and the second an active verb construction: 1. ཁོ་ད་ལྟ་ག་པར་འདུག་གམ། 2. ང་ལམ་སེང་ཁོའི་རྩ་ལ་ཁྲིད་ཞིག (1."Where is he now?—2. Take me at once to him [his presence]").

Note that the adverb "at once" (ལམ་སེང་) precedes the location of the verbal action, ཁོའི་རྩ་ལ་ (to the presence of him). However, this clause could just as easily have been written: ང་ཁོའི་རྩ་ལ་ལམ་སེང་ཁྲིད་.

The end of the direct speech is marked by ཞེས་, followed by the object of the speech ("to the rabbit" - རི་བོང་ལ་) and then the verb "say" (ལབ་པ་རེད) with its past complement. Thus, the construction really breaks down into: འདམ་སེང་གིས་ (implicit subject) . . . རི་བོང་ལ་ལབ་པ་རེད ("[The lion] said . . . to the rabbit"). Note that the object, "the rabbit," could have been put at the beginning of the construction, e.g., འདམ་སེང་གིས་རི་བོང་ལ་ . . . ལབ་པ་རེད. Such alternative positionings cause no problem when careful attention is given to the markers accompanying the subject and object, such as གིས་ and ལ་.

10. The tenth segment consists of seven clauses: 1. རི་བོང་གིས་འདམ་སེང་དཀར་པོ་དེ་རི་ཆེན་པོ་ཞིག་གི་རྒྱབ་ཏུ་ཁྲིད་རྗེས་ 2. ཁྲོན་པ་ཞིག་ལ་མཛུབ་མོ་བཙུགས་ཏེ་ 3. སེམས་ཅན་དེ་ཕ་གིའི་ནང་ལ་འདུག་ཅེས་ལན་བཏབ་ཅིང་། 4. འདམ་སེང་དེས་ངར་སྐད་ཆེན་པོ་རྒྱབ་ནས་ 5. ཁྲོན་པའི་ཁ་ལ་ཕྱིན་ནས་ 6. ལྟ་སྐབས་ 7. ཁྲོན་པའི་ནང་ནས་འདམ་སེང་ཞིག་མཐོང་།.

The first of these clauses starts with the subject in the instrumental case ("by the rabbit" - རི་བོང་གིས་). This subject's action is conveyed by the active verb "take" (ཁྲིད་). Between these is the object of the taking, "the white lion," and the location of the taking, "behind a big hill" (འདམ་སེང་དཀར་པོ་རི་ཆེན་པོ་ཞིག་གི་རྒྱབ་ཏུ་). Note that the word "behind" (རྒྱབ་ཏུ་), like ནང་ and མདུན་, must be joined to its object—the big mountain—by the genitive particle. Thus, the first clause means, "The rabbit took the lion behind a big mountain."

This construction is linked to the next one by རྗེས་, the "after" clause connective, so that the translation becomes: "*After* the rabbit took the lion behind a big mountain."

The next clause consists of the verbal phrase "pointed with a finger" (མཛུབ་མོ་བཙུགས) preceded by the location of the verbal action (with the dative-locative),"to a well" (ཁྲོན་པ་ཞིག་ལ་). This clause does not contain a subject (in the instrumental); instead it assumes the same subject as the previous clause, i.e., "by the rabbit."

It is linked to the next one by the simultaneous clause connector ཏེ་. Thus the two clauses now mean: "*After* the rabbit took the lion behind a big mountain, [he] pointed to a well and simultaneously . . . ."

The next clause (སེམས་ཅན་དེ་ཕ་གིའི་ནང་ལ་འདུག་) is an existential sentence which is said by the rabbit—"That animal exists inside that over there [referring of course to the well]."

This is followed by the mandatory quote marker, and then an active verb meaning "answered" (ལན་བཏབ་). Thus, this sub-section means, "(He) answered, 'That animal is (inside that) over there.'" The three clauses would now read: "*After* the rabbit took the lion behind a big mountain, (he) pointed to a well and *simultaneously* answered, 'That animal is inside that over there.'"

This clause, in turn, is linked to the next one by the connective clause connective ཅིང་, which is commonly translated as "and."

Clause four (འདམ་སེང་དེས་ང་རོ་སྐད་ཆེན་པོ་རྒྱབ་) starts with a subject in the instrumental (འདམ་སེང་དེས་), so one knows that down the line an active verb will be encountered. That subject ("by the lion") is followed by the verbal phrase "roared in anger loudly" (ང་རོ་སྐད་ཆེན་པོ་རྒྱབ་). Thus the clause translates as: "The lion roared loudly."

It is linked to the following clause by the clause connector ནས་. Here context indicates that ནས་ means "having done the verbal act." Thus the previous clause really conveys: "The lion, *having* roared loudly, . . ."

The string of four clauses now means: "*After* the rabbit took the lion behind a big mountain, [he] pointed to a well and *simultaneously* answered, 'That animal is inside that over there', *and* the lion, *having* roared loudly, . . ."

The fifth clause starts with ཁྲོན་པའི་ཁ་ལ་ ("to the edge of the well"), the location of the verb ཕྱིན་ ("went"). The subject of this clause is unstated, but context makes it obvious that it is still "the lion." The location phrase parallels the structure encountered above in that the word "edge" is linked to "well" by the genitive (ཁྲོན་པའི་ཁ་ལ་). Thus, this clause means: "(The lion) went to the edge of the well."

This is linked to the sixth clause also by the ནས་ connective which here conveys that "Having gone to the edge of the well, . . ." something happened. All five clauses now mean: "*After* the rabbit took the lion behind a big mountain, (he) pointed to a well and *simultaneously* answered, 'That animal is inside that over there', *and* the lion, *having* roared loudly, went to the edge of the well and (*having* done that) . . . ."

The sixth clause consists of only two words: the verb "look" (ལྟ་) and the clause connective "at that time" (སྐབས་). It means "when he looked" and links with the previous clauses as follows: "*After* the rabbit took the lion behind a big mountain, (he) pointed to a well and *simultaneously* answered, 'That animal is inside that over there,' and the lion, *having* roared loudly, went to the edge of the well and (*having* done that) looked, and *when* he looked, . . ."

The final clause (ཁྲོན་པའི་ནང་ནས་འདམ་སེང་ཞིག་མཐོང་) in this section begins with the phrase ཁྲོན་པའི་ནང་ནས་, "from inside the well." Note that ནས་ here does not function as a verbal connective but rather means "from." This is followed by the phrase འདམ་སེང་ཞིག་, "a lion." This clause ends with the involuntary verb མཐོང་, "saw." Thus, this final clause means "(from) inside (of) the well (he) saw a lion." We know that འདམ་སེང་ཞིག་ is the object of the verb མཐོང་ rather than the subject because it does not contain the instrumental case particle which is required for the verb མཐོང་, even though it is involuntary.

The structure of this segment is: རི་བོང་གིས་ . . . ཁྲིད་རྗེས་, . . . བཙུགས་ཏེ་, . . . ལན་བཏབ་ཅིང་, འདམ་སེང་དེས་ . . . རྒྱབ་ནས་, . . . ཕྱིན་ནས་, . . . ལྟ་སྐབས་, . . . མཐོང་།

"*After* the rabbit took the lion behind a big mountain, (he) pointed to a well and *simultaneously* answered, 'That animal is inside that over there,' and the lion, *having* once again roared loudly, went to the edge of the well and (*having* done that) looked, and *when* he looked, *saw* a lion ."

11. The eleventh section consists of two clauses: 1. འདམ་སེང་དཀར་པོ་དེས་ཁྲོན་པའི་ནང་དུ་ང་རོ་དྲག་པོ་ལན་འགའ་ཞིག་བསྒྲགས་པས་ 2. ཁྲོན་པའི་ནང་གི་འདམ་སེང་དེས་ཀྱང་ཚུར་ང་རོ་བསྒྲགས།.

The first clause starts with the subject in the instrumental, "that white lion" (འདམ་སེང་དཀར་པོ་དེས་), indicating an active verb construction. It is followed by a phrase specifying the location of the verbal act, "inside the well" (ཁྲོན་པའི་ནང་དུ་). After this comes the verbal phrase "roared" (ང་རོ་ . . . བསྒྲགས་). It, however, is modified by two words: "loud/powerful" and "several times" (དྲག་པོ་ and ལན་འགའ་ཞིག་). Thus, this clause means: "That lion made a powerful roar several times." This clause could have been written so that the adverbial phrase did not split the verbal phrase: འདམ་སེང་དེས་ཁྲོན་པའི་ནང་དུ་ལན་འགའ་ཞིག་ང་རོ་དྲག་པོ་བསྒྲགས་.

This clause is linked to the next clause by the "because" connective (པས་), so that it means: "*Because* that lion roared loudly several times into the well, . . ."

The subsequent clause begins with a complex subject phrase in the instrumental case ཁྲོན་པའི་ནང་གི་འདམ་སེང་དེས་, which consists of the actor, "by that lion" (འདམ་སེང་དེས་), linked to a preceeding phrase by the genitive so as to create a relative clause: "who was inside of the well" (ཁྲོན་པའི་ནང་གི་). The subject, therefore, means: "by that lion who was inside of the well." This is followed by the word "also" (ཀྱང་) and then the verbal phrase ང་རོ་བསྒྲགས་ ("roared"), modified by the adverbial ཚུར་ ("hither"); that is to say, the "roar" come toward the direction of the lion outside the well. Thus the clause means: "The enemy who was in the well, also roared back (hither)." Both clauses together mean: "Because that lion roared loudly several times into the well, the lion who was in the well also roared back (hither)."

12. The twelfth segment consists of two clauses: 1. སྐབས་དེར་འདམ་སེང་དཀར་པོ་དེས་མཆེ་གཙིགས་ཕྱིར་

བསྒྲད་བྱུས་ཏེ་ 2. ཁྲོན་པའི་ནང་ལ་མཆོངས་པ་རེད.

The first clause begins with the time-slot word "at that time" (སྐབས་དེར་). It is followed by the subject in the instrumental, "by that white lion" (འདམ་སེང་དཀར་པོ་དེས་), and then what the lion did: "bared his fangs and clawed with his claws" (མཆེ་གཙིགས་སྡེར་བསྒྲད་བྱུས). It is linked to the next clause by the clause connective ཏེ་, which here conveys primarily the simultaneous meaning: "Baring his fangs and claws," he did something.

The next clause tells what was done. It starts with the location of the verbal action, "to the inside of the well" (ཁྲོན་པའི་ནང་ལ་), followed by the verb "jump" (མཆོངས་) and the past complement (པ་རེད་). Thus the two clauses together mean: "At that time, the lion, baring his fangs and claws, jumped into the well."

13. The thirteenth segment consists of three clauses: 1. རི་བོང་གིས་ཕུའུ་ཏུང་ཟེར་བའི་སྒྲ་དེ་ཐོས་སྐབས་ 2. ཨ་ཁ་ལྷ་བ་མཐོ་བའི་འདམ་སེང་ཁྲོན་པའི་ནང་ལ་ལྷུང་ནས་ 3. ཤི་སོང་ཞེས་བཤད་པ་རེད།.

The first clause begins again with the subject in the instrumental case, "by the rabbit," followed by an onomatopoetic word (ཕུའུ་ཏུང་) which in Tibetan conveys the sound "splash." Note that it is followed with the phrase ཟེར་བའི་སྒྲ་དེ་, which breaks down into སྒྲ་དེ་ ("that sound") and ཟེར་བའི་ ("which says" or "which is called") and means "that sound which is called" *puduŋ*. Following this comes the verb "heard" (ཐོས་). Thus, this clause means: "The rabbit heard the sound 'splash.'" This clause is joined to the next one by the "when" (སྐབས་) clause connective, so that the clause means: "***When*** the rabbit heard the sound 'splash', . . ."

The next clause is a direct statement made by the subject (implicitly "by the rabbit"). It starts with an exclamation meaning "Oh my" (ཨ་ཁ་) and is followed by the subject of the clause, "the lion" (འདམ་སེང་), modified by a relative clause (in the genitive), which means "who has great conceit/arrogance" (ལྷ་བ་མཐོ་བའི་), both together meaning "the lion who was conceited." The verb that goes with this is ལྷུང་ ("fall"). Thus, "that conceited lion fell." Note that this verb has only one stem so context determines that we translate it as past tense. Preceding the verb is a phrase indicating the location where he fell, namely "into the well" (ཁྲོན་པའི་ནང་ལ་). Thus, this clause means: "Oh my, that arrogant lion has fallen into the well."

This is linked to the next clause by the clause connective ནས་, which conveys the idea "that having done X, Y occurred." What occurred is conveyed by the verb "died" (ཤི་) and its past complement (སོང་). Thus, this clause means: "Oh my, that arrogant lion, having fallen into the well, has died."

14. The final segment consists of one sentence: དེ་ནས་རི་བོང་གིས་ཁོའི་ཁྱིམ་ལ་ལོག་སོང་།།.

It begins with the time-slot phrase དེ་ནས་ ("after that"), and then the subject in the instrumental: "by the rabbit." This is followed by the location of the verbal action, ཁོའི་ཁྱིམ་ལ་ ("to his house"), and the verb "returned" (ལོག་).Thus, it means: "After that, the rabbit returned home."

5.18 Vocabulary

བཀྲ་ཤིས་	p.n. (drəshi)
རྐྱང་	wild ass (gyāŋ)
རྐྱེན་	causal connective (gyēn)
སྐད	noise, a shout; va. — རྒྱག་ to shout , call, cry out, yell (gε̄ὲ gyaà)
སྐད་གཏོང་	va. to summon, to call to come (gε̄ὲ dōŋ)
སྐབས་	"when" clause connective; a time (gəp)
སྐུ་	body (h.) (gū)
སྐྱེ་དམན་	woman (gyīmεn)
སྐྱེལ་	va. to deliver (gyēē)
སྐྱོན་	va. h. of རྒྱག་/རྒྱབ་
བསྐྱལ་	va. p. of སྐྱེལ་ (gyε̄ε̄)
བསྐྱོད་	va. to go (gyȫȫ)
ཁ་པར་	telephone; va. — གཏོང་ to phone (kābaa dōŋ)
ཁ་ལ་	(on/at) edge (kāla)
ཁ་སང་	yesterday (kε̄ε̄sa; kāsaŋ)
ཁོང་ཁྲོ	anger; vi. — ཟ་ to get angry (kōndro sa)
ཁྱག་	vi. to be/get cold (kyāà)
ཁྱིམ་	home (kīm)
ཁྱིམ་མཚེས	neighbor (kīmdzeè)
ཁྱོན་	overall (kyȫn)
ཁྱོན་ཡོངས་	overall (kyȫnyoŋ)
ཁྲལ་	tax (trε̄ε̄)
ཁྲིད་	va. to bring (an animate thing) (triì)
ཁྲོན་པ་	a well (trōmba)
མཁན་	"agentive" verbal particle (ŋε̄n; gε̄n)
མཁས་པ་	experts (kε̄ba)
འཁོལ་	vi. to be/get boiled (kȫȫ)
འཁྱེར་	va. to carry, take (an inanimate object) (kīī; kēē)
གངས་	snow; vi. — འབབ་ to snow (kan bəb)
གི་	genitive case particle (gi)
གི་འདུག་	present tense complement
གི་ཡོད་པ་རེད་	present tense complement
གྲང་	cold (traŋ)
གྲོང་འཁྱེར་	city, town (troŋgyee)
གྲོང་གསེབ་	village (troŋseè)
གྲོད་ཁོག་	stomach; vi. — ལྟོགས་ to be hungry (trogɔɔ dɔ̄ɔ̀)
དགུན་ཁ་	winter (guŋga)
དགེ་ལུགས་པ་	Gelugpa (sect) (gelugba)
དགྲ་ཤ་	revenge; va. — ལེན་ to take revenge (drasha len)
འགྲན་	va. to compete (dren)
འགྲོ་	va. to go (dro)
རྒྱ་གར་	India (gyagaa)
རྒྱ་ནག་	China (gyanaà)
རྒྱ་མ་	1/2 of a kilogram (gyama)
རྒྱ་མི་	Chinese (person) [the traditional term] (gyəmi)

རྒྱ་རིགས་ Chinese (person) [the term currently used in Tibet] (gyəriì)

རྒྱབ་ཏུ་ behind (gyəbdu).

རྒྱུན་རིང་ long time; "when" connective (gyünriŋ)

རྒྱུའི་ཆེད་དུ་ "purposive" connective (gyüü chēdu)

སྒང་ "when" connective (gan)

སྒྲ་ sound (dra)

སྒྲོག་ see ང་རོ་

བརྒྱད་པ(ར)་ (at) eight o' clock (gyɛɛbar)

བརྒྱབ་ va. p. of རྒྱག (gyəb)

བསྒྲགས་ va. p. of སྒྲོག་: shouted/called out (drag)

ང་རོ་ a roar; va. — སྒྲོག་ to roar (ŋaro drɔ̀ɔ̀)

ངར་ to me (i + dative-locative) (ŋaa)

ངར་སྐད་ a shout (roar); va. — རྒྱག་ to roar, shout (ŋargɛɛ̀ gyəb)

ངལ་རྩོལ་ manual labor; va. — བྱེད་ to do manual labor (ŋɛɛdzöö cheè)

ངས་ by me (i + instrumental) (ŋɛɛ̀)

ངོ་རྒོལ་ opposition, struggling against; va. — བྱེད to oppose, struggle against (ŋogöö cheè)

ངོ་སྤྲོད་ introduction; va. — བྱེད་ to introduce someone (ŋodröö cheè)

ངོ་ལོག་ rebellion, revolt; va. — རྒྱག་ to rebel (ŋoloò gyaà)

ངོ་ལོག་པ་ rebel (ŋologba)

ངོམས་ showoff-ish; va. to show off (ŋom)

དངུལ་ཁང་ bank (ŋüügan)

སྔར་ formerly, in the past (ŋār)

སྔོན་དུ་ sm. སྔར་ (ŋōndu)

སྔོན་པོ་ blue (ŋōmbo)

ཅ་ལག་ thing(s) (jālaà)

ཅིང་ conjunctive connective (jīŋ)

བཅིངས་འགྲོལ་ liberation; va. — གཏོང་ to liberate (jīŋdrüü dōŋ)

ཆགས་ vi. to become, change into (chāà)

ཆར་པ་ rain; va. — གཏོང་ to rain (chāāba dōŋ)

ཆིག་སྟོང་ one thousand (chīgdoŋ)

ཆུ་འཁོལ་ vi. to get boiled (water) (chū kȫȫ)

ཆུ་ཚོད་ watch, clock (chōdzöò)

ཆེད་ purposive connective (chēè)

མཆེ་གཙིགས་སྡེར་བསྒྲད་ id., baring fangs and claws (chē dzīì der drɛɛ̀)

མཆོངས་ va. to jump (chōm; chōŋ)

མཆོད་ va. to eat (h.) (chȫȫ)

མཇལ་ va. to meet (h.) (jɛɛ)

འཇིགས་བསྐུལ་ intimidation, threats; va. — བྱེད་ to intimidate, threaten (jigüü cheè)

འཇོན་ཐང་ capability (jöndaŋ)

ཉལ་ va. to lie down to sleep (ñɛɛ)

ཉི་མ་ the sun; a day (ñimə)

ཉིན་	day (ñi̱n)
ཉིན་ལྟར་	every day (ñi̱ndaa)
གཉིད་ཁུག་	vi. to fall asleep (ñīì kūù)
རྙིང་པ་	old (ñīŋbə)
སྙུང་	vi. to get sick (h.) (ñūn)
བརྙས་བཅོས་	bullying; va. — གཏོང་ to bully (ñābjöò dōŋ)
དེ་	gerundive connective (de)
རྟ་	horse (dā)
རྟག་ཏུ་	always (dāgdu)
ལྟ་	va. to look (dā)
ལྟ་སྐོར་	(sightseeing) tour, visit; va. — བྱེད་ to tour, visit (dāgɔɔ chḛè)
ལྟ་བ་	conceited (dāwa)
ལྟ་ཚུལ་	viewpoint (dədzüü)
ལྟོ་ཆས་	food (dōbjɛɛ̀)
ལྟོགས་	va. to be hungry (dɔ̄ɔ̀); see གྲོད་ཁོག་
སྟག་འཚེར་	p.n. of a place in Amdo (dāgdze)
སྟབས་	causal connective (dəb)
སྟུག་པོ་	thick (dūgbu)
སྟེ་	gerundive connective
སྟོན་ཐོག་	crop (dōndoò)
ཐུག་	vi. to meet (tūù)
ཐོན་	1. vi. to be produced, get (as in a yield); 2. va. to depart (tōn)
ཐོན་སྐྱེད་	production; va. — བྱེད་ to produce (tōngyeè chḛè)
ཐོས་	vi. to hear (tōò)
མཐུ་རྩལ་	competiton of strength; va. — འགྲན་ to compete (tūdzɛɛ drḛn)
མཐོ་པོ་	high (tōbo)
མཐོང་	vi. to see (tōn)
ད་ལོ་	this year (ta̱lo)
དུས་	"when" connective (dṳṵ̀)
དེང་སྐབས་	these days, nowadays (tḛŋgəb)
དེང་སང་	these days, nowadays (tḛnsan; tḛŋsaŋ)
དོན་དུ་	purposive connective (tö̱ndu)
དྲག་པོ་	fierce, harsh (tra̱gbo)
མདུན་དུ་	in front (of) (dṳndu)
འདམ་སེང་	lion (da̱mseŋ)
འདི་ལོ་	this year (di̱lo)
འདྲ་བ་	like, similar (dra̱wa)
སྡོད་	va. to stay, live (dö̱ö̀)
བསྡད་	va. p. of སྡོད་ (dɛ̱ɛ̀)
ན་	vi. to get sick (na̱)
ན་ནིང་	last year (na̱niŋ)
ནགས་ཚལ་	forest (na̱gdzɛɛ)
ནད་པ་	sick person (nɛ̱ɛ̱ba)
གནང་	va. to do (h.) (nāŋ)
གནས་	va. to live, stay (nɛ̄ɛ̀)
མནལ་ཁུག་	vi. to fall asleep (h.) (ñɛ̄ɛ̀ kūù)
སྣ་ཚོགས་	various (na̱dzoò)
པའི་སྐབས་སུ་	"when" connective (bɛgəbsu)
པའི་དུས་སུ་	"when" connective (bɛtüsu)
པར་བརྟེན་	causal connective (bar dēn),
པས་	causal connective (bɛɛ̀)
པེ་ཅིན་	Beijing (bējiŋ)
དཔེ་མཛོད་ཁང་	library (bēndzögan)
སྤྲང་པོ་	beggar (bāŋgo; drāŋbo)
སྤྲད་	va. p. of སྤྲོད་ (drɛ̄ɛ̀)

ཕ་གི་	over there (pə̄gi)
ཕུའུ་དུང་	the noise of a sound (pūduŋ)
ཕུལ་	va. p. of འབུལ་ (pūū)
ཕེབས་	va. to go, come (h.)(pēè; pēb)
ཕྱག་	hand (h.) (chāà)
ཕྱག་དེབ་	book (h.) (chāādeb)
ཕྱག་ལས་	work (h.); va. — གནང་ to work (h.) (chāālɛɛ̀ nāŋ)
ཕྱིན་	va. p. of འགྲོ་ (chīn)
ཕྱིར་	purposive connective (chīr)
ཕྲད་	va. p. of འཕྲད་ (trɛ̄ɛ̀)
བབས་	va. p. of འབབ (pə̱b)
བའི་ཆེད་དུ་	purposive connective (bɛ chētu)
བར་	infinitive usage particle (pa̱r)
བས་	causal connective (bɛ)
བུ་བཙོལ་ཁང	nursery (pu̱jögan)
བྱ་	va. f. of བྱེད་ (cha̱)
བྱུང་	vi. got (chu̱n; chu̱ŋ)
བྲག་ཕུག་	cave (trə̱buù)
དབང་གིས་	causal connective (wāŋki)
འབབ་	va. to fall (rain, snow), to land, to come down; to dismount (pə̱b)
འབུལ་:	va. to give (h.) (bu̱u̱u̱)
འབྱོར་	vi. to arrive (jɔ̱ɔ̱)
འབྲིང་པ་	middle, secondary (dri̱ŋə)
འབྲུ་རིགས་	grain (dru̱riì)
སྦྱོང་བརྡར་	training; va. — བྱེད་ to train (jo̱ŋdaa che̱è)
མི་	agentive particle (mi̱)
མི་དམངས་	the people (mi̱maŋ)
མི་གོ་	ch. America (me̱gɔɔ)
དམག་འཁྲུག་	war (mə̄gdruù)
ཙ་ན	causal connective (dzāna)
ཙང་	causal connective (dzāŋ)
གཙོ་བོ་	main (dzōwo)
བཙན་འཛུལ་	invasion; va. — བྱེད་ to invade (dzɛ̄ndzüü che̱è)
བཙུགས་	va. p. of འཛུགས་ (dzūù)
ཙ་མེད་	annihilation; va. — གཏོང་ to annihilate (dzāmeè dōŋ)
ཙ་ལ་	to the presence (of) (dzā la)
ཚལ་	vegetable (tsɛ̄ɛ̄)
ཚུར་	hither, toward this side (tsūū)
ཚེ་	life; "when" connective (tsē)
ཚོགས་འདུ་	meeting; va. — ཚོགས་ to hold a meeting (tsōndu tsɔ̄ɔ̀)
ཚོགས་	va. to assemble, convene (tsɔ̄ɔ̀)
ཚོང་ཁང་	store (tsōngan)
ཚོན་	paint; va. — གཏོང་ to paint (tsōn dōŋ)
མཚམས་ (སུ་)	when connective (tsām)
འཚོ་བ་	livelihood, subsistence; va. — སྐྱེལ to earn livelihood, subsistence (tsōwa gyēē)
མཛད་	va. to do (h.) (dzɛ̱ɛ̀)
འཛིན་ཆས་	furniture (dzi̱njɛɛ̀)
འཛུགས་	va. to start, found, establish (dzu̱ù)
ཞིང་	conjunctive connective (shi̱ŋ)
ཞུགས་	va. to participate in, attend

	(shuù)
གཞིས་ཀ་	estate (shiigə)
གཞིས་ཀ་རྩེ་	p.n. Shigatse (shigədze)
གཞུང་	government (shuŋ)
གཞིས་ནིང་	the year before last (sheñin)
བཞོན་	va. to ride (animal); to mount (an animal) (shön)
ཟ་ཆས་	foodstuffs (sapjɛɛ̀)
ཟེར་	1.va. to say; 2. vi. to be called (se)
གཟིགས་	va. look (h.) (sii)
གཟིམ་	va. to sleep (h.) (sim)
བཟོ་གྲྭ་	factory (sodra)
འུད་ཤོབ་	bragging (üshüb)
ཡག་ཉེས་	quality (yañeè)
ཡི་	genitive particle (yi)
ཡིག་ཚད་	exam (yigdzɛɛ̀)
ཡིན་ན་ཡང་	nevertheless (yinayaŋ)
ཡོངས་	all; overall (yoŋ)
གཡར་	va. to loan, lend; borrow (yāā)
རང་ཉིད་	oneself, itself (rəŋñiì)
རང་བཙན་	independence (raŋdzɛn)
རི་བོང་	rabbit (regon)
རིང་	"when" connective (riŋ)
ལངས་	vi. to get up, rise/stand up; to start (lan)
ལན་	1. times (lɛn); 2. reply, answer; 3. message
ལས་འགུལ་	campaign, movement (lɛngüü)
ལས་བྱེད་པ་	official, cadre (lɛɛjeba)
ལེན་	va. to take (len)
ལོ་ཏོག་	crop (lodoò)
ལོག་	va. to return (lɔɔ̀)
ཤར་	vi. to arise (shāā)
ཤི་	vi. to die (shī)
ཤིང་	conjunctive connective (shīŋ)
ཤེད་ཤུགས་	strength (shīshuù)
ཤོད་	va. imp. of (བཤད་) (shȫȍ)
ཤོར་	va. to lose (shɔ̄ɔ̄)
གཤིས་	causal connective (shīì)
ས་མཚམས་	border, frontier (sāndzam)
སང་ཉིན་	tomorrow (sə̄ñiì)
སེམས་ཅན་	sentient being, animal (sēmjɛn)
སླད་	purposive connective (lɛ̄ɛ̀)
སླེབས་	vi. to arrive (lēè)
སློང་	1. va. to cause to start, incite; 2. to beg; 3. to cause or make stand up (lōŋ)
སློབ་སྦྱོང་	studying; va. — བྱེད་ to study (lōpjon cheè)
སློབ་ཕྲུག་	student (lāpdraà; lōpdruù)
སློབ་གསོ་	education (lōbso)
གསར་བརྗེ་	revolution (sārje)
བསམ་བློ་	thinking; va. — གཏོང་ to think (sāmlo dōŋ)
བསོད་ནམས་	p.n. (sōnam)
བསླངས་	p. of སློང་: made start
ཧྲི་ཡོན་	commune member (hriyün)
ལྷུང་	vi. to fall (lhūŋ)
ཨ་ཁ་	"oh my," "too bad" (ākaa)

Lesson Six

6.1 The conditional ("if") clause connectives: ན་, ཚེ་, གལ་ཏེ་...ན་, གལ་ཏེ་...ཚེ་, གལ་སྲིད་...ན་, གལ་སྲིད་....ཚེ་, and པ་ན་/བ་ན་

These clause connectives link clauses so that the latter clause occurs *if* the former clause does. They require the verb they modify (follow) to be in the past tense stem.

a. ངོ་ལོག་བརྒྱབ་ན་མི་མང་པོ་ཤི་གི་རེད།
rebel acted if people many die fut. compl./
If (he, she, you, they) rebel, many people will die.

b. ཤ་རྙིང་པ་ཟས་ཚེ་ན་གི་རེད།
meat old ate if sick fut. compl./
If (he, she, you, they) eat old meat, (he, she, you, they) will get sick.

Note that ན་ in example b. is the involuntary verb "to be ill," not the conditional particle "if." Note also that ཚེ་ in other contexts can function as a noun meaning "life," e.g., ཚེ་རིང་པོ་ means "long life."

c. གལ་ཏེ་སོན་ཡག་པོ་ཉོས་ན་སྟོན་ཐོག་ཡག་པོ་ཡོང་གི་རེད།
if seed good bought if harvest good come fut. compl./
If (one) buys good seed, (one) will get a good harvest.

d. གལ་ཏེ་བོད་ལ་སླེབས་ཚེ་ཁྱེད་རང་མཇལ་གྱི་ཡིན།
if tibet to arrive if you meet fut. compl./
If (I) arrive in Tibet (get to Tibet), (I) will meet you.

In example d., the presence of ཡིན་ in the verbal complement indicates clearly that the subject is first person.

e. བླ་མ་མགྱོགས་པོ་ཕེབས་པ་ན་ཁོ་ཚོས་མཇལ་གྱི་རེད།
lama quick/soon come if he pl.-by meet fut.comp./
If the lama comes soon, they will meet (him).

f. གལ་སྲིད་ངས་ཟ་ཁང་དེར་ཁ་ལག་ཟས་ན་[ང་]ན་གི་རེད།
if i-by restaurant that-to food ate if (i) sick fut. compl/
If I eat at that restaurant, (I) will get sick..

g. གལ་སྲིད་ངས་ཟ་ཁང་དེར་སྔོ་ཚལ་ཟས་ཚེ་[ང་] ན་གི་རེད།
if i-by restaurant that-to vegetables ate if (i) sick fut. compl/
If I eat vegetables at that restaurant, (I) will get sick.

6.2 The "as soon as" clause connectives: འཕྲལ་, པ་དག་, མ་ཐག་, ཉིད་དུ་, པ་དེ་མ་ཐག་(ཏུ་), པ་དང་, པ/བ་ཙམ་ན་, and པ་/བ་ཙམ་ནས་

These clause connectives are used with the past tense stem of verbs to convey that the action in the second clause occurs "as soon as" the action in the first clause does.

a. ལྷ་སར་སླེབས་པ་ད་ག་དོན་གཅོད་ཁང་ལ་ཕྱིན་སོང་།
   lhasa-to arrive soon-as office to went went compl./
   As soon as (he, she, etc.) arrived in Lhasa, (he, she, etc.) went to the bureau office.
b. ཁོས་འབྲོག་པའི་ལྟོ་ཆས་ཟས་མ་ཐག་ན་སོང་།
   he-by nomad-of food ate soon-as sick went compl./
   As soon as he ate the nomad food, (he) got sick.
c. སྟོན་ཐོག་བསྡུས་འཕྲལ་གཞུང་ལ་ཁྲལ་སྤྲོད་ཀྱི་རེད།
   harvest collected soon-as government to tax give fut. compl./
   As soon as (he, she, etc.) collect(s) the harvest, (he, she, etc.) will pay taxes to the government.
d. རྒྱལ་རྩེར་སླེབས་པ་དེ་མ་ཐག་ཏུ་མགྲོན་ཁང་ལ་ཕྱིན་པ་རེད།
   gyantse-to arrive soon-as hotel to went compl./
   As soon as (he, she, etc.) arrived in Gyantse, (he, she, etc.) went to the hotel.
e. ཕྱི་རྒྱལ་བ་དེས་རྒྱལ་རྩེར་སླེབས་ཉིད་དུ་ལྷ་སར་ལན་བཏང་སོང་།
   foreigner that-by gyantse-to arrive soon-as lhasa-to message sent past compl./
   As soon as (he, she, etc.) arrived in Gyantse, (he, she, etc.) sent a message to Lhasa.

It should be remembered that པ་དང་ functions to convey both "and" (see 4.2) and "as soon as." Only context and experience will allow one to ascertain which meaning is intended.

f. ཁོས་མིག་བལྟས་པ་དང་ཡལ་སོང་།
   he-by looked-soon-as vanished went compl./
   As soon as he looked, (it) vanished.
g. ཁོས་ལྷ་ཁང་ནང་ལ་འཛུལ་བ་ཙམ་ནས་བླ་མ་ཞིག་མཐོང་སོང་།
   he-by temple in to entered soon-as lama one saw went compl./
   As soon as he entered (into) the temple, (he) saw a lama.
h. མོས་ལབ་པ་དང་ངས་ཧ་གོ་བྱུང་།
   she-by speak and i-by understood got./
   As soon as she spoke, I understood.

Note that ཧ་གོ་ is one of the involuntary verbs that require their subjects to be in the instrumental case.

6.3 Negation of active and involuntary verbs

Active verbs are negated by the same particles and negatives verbs that are used in linking and existential constructions, i.e.: མ་, མི་, མིན་, ཡོད་པ་མ་རེད་, and མེད་.

Present, usual, and future tenses

Usual, present, and future actions are expressed in the negative by the present/ non-past stem of the verb plus the negativized verbal complement. For example, the negation of དེ་རིང་ཁོས་ལས་ཀ་བྱེད་ཀྱི་འདུག། ("Today he is working.") is illustrated in a. below.

a. དེ་རིང་ཁོས་ལས་ཀ་བྱེད་ཀྱི་མི་འདུག།
today he-by work do pres. compl. no/
Today he is not working.

b. ད་ལྟ་མོས་ལྟོ་ཆས་བཟོ་བཞིན་དུ་ཡོད་པ་མ་རེད།
now she-by food make pres. compl. no/
She is not making food now.

c. མོ་ལ་དངུལ་མེད་སྐབས་གློག་བརྙན་ལ་འགྲོ་གི་མ་རེད།
she to money without since movie to go fut. compl. no./
Because she has no money, (she) will not go to the movie.

More literary genre generally dispense with the verb complement and simply put the negative མི་ before the future or non-past stem of verbs. For example,

d. ཁོའི་དངུལ་ཛོགས་ཙང་རྟ་དེ་མི་ཉོ།
he-of money exhausted since horse that no buy/
Because his money is exhausted, (he) will not buy that horse.

The difference between usual and present tense constructions is generally a result of context and auxilliary words such as those used in sentences e. and f. ("now" and "often").

e. འབྲོག་པས་ལྷ་སར་ཡང་སེ་འགྲོ་གི་ཡོད་པ་མ་རེད།
nomad-by lhasa-to often go usual compl. no/
Nomads do not often go to Lhasa.

f. འབྲོག་པས་ལྷ་སར་ད་ལྟ་འགྲོ་གི་ཡོད་པ་མ་རེད།
nomad-by lhasa-to now go usual pres. compl. no/
Nomads are not going to Lhasa now.

Other typical constructions are:

g. ཁོས་བོད་པའི་ཁ་ལག་ཞེ་དྲགས་ཟ་གི་མི་འདུག།
he-by tibet-of food a-lot eat usual compl. no/
He doesn't eat Tibetan food a lot.

h. ཁོས་བོད་པའི་ཁ་ལག་ད་ལྟ་ཟ་གི་མི་འདུག།
he-by tibet-of food now eat usual pres. compl. no/
He isn't eating Tibetan food now.

i. མོས་ཞིང་ལས་ཡག་པོ་བྱེད་ཀྱི་མེད་པ་རེད།
she-by farm-work good do usual compl. no/
She does not do farm work well.

The vb.+ པ་རེད་ form of the "usual" becomes: vb.+ པ་མ་རེད་

j. ཆོས་ལྡན་ལགས་ཨ་རི་ར་སྡོད་དུས་སློབ་གྲྭར་ཕེབས་པ་མ་རེད།
chunden-la america-to stay when school-to go (h.) usual compl. no/
When Chöndenla stayed in America, (she) didn't (usually) go to school.

Past tense

Although one would have expected that the negation of the པ་རེད་ past complement would be པ་མ་རེད་, this is not the case. Instead, as example k. illustrates, the negative particle མ་ is placed before the past tense stem of the verb: (མ་ + vb. + པ་རེད).

k. ཁ་སང་ཁོས་ལས་ཀ་མ་བྱས་པ་རེད།
yesterday he-by work no did past compl./
He did not work yesterday.

As was the case for the future tense, in the more literary genre the པ་རེད་ past complement is simply dropped and just a negative particle (མ་) + verb suffices. For example,

l. ཁ་སང་ཁོས་ལས་ཀ་མ་བྱས།
yesterday he-by work no did/
He did not work yesterday.

When the སོང་ past complement is used, the negative particle follows the main verb and precedes སོང་. For example,

m. ཁ་སང་ཁོས་ལས་ཀ་བྱས་མ་སོང་།
yesterday he-by work did no went compl./
He did not work yesterday.

Negation of dependent clauses follows the same patterns that were described above. For example,

n. སང་ཉིན་ཁོ་ནང་ལ་ཁ་ལག་མི་ཟ་ན་ཟ་ཁང་ལ་ཁ་ལག་ཟ་བར་འགྲོ་གི་རེད།
tomorrow he home to food no eat if/ restaurant to food eat inf. go fut. compl./
If he does not eat at home tomorrow, (he) will go to eat at the restaurant.

o. ཁ་སང་ཁོས་རྒྱལ་པོའི་རྩ་ལ་མ་ཕྱིན་ན་དེ་རིང་འགྲོ་གི་རེད།
yesterday he-by king-of presence to no went if/ today go fut. compl./
If he did not go to the presence of the king yesterday, (he) will go today.

p. ཁ་ས་ཕྲུ་གུ་དེས་ལས་ཀ་མ་བྱས་སྐབས་ཟ་ཁང་གི་བདག་པོས་ཁོར་གླ་ཆ་མ་སྤྲད་པ་རེད།
yesterday child that-by work no did since restaurant of owner-by he-to wage no gave past compl./
Since that child did not work yesterday, the owner of the restaurant did not pay him wages.

q. སང་ཉིན་ཕྲུ་གུ་དེས་ལས་ཀ་མི་བྱ་སྐབས་ཟ་ཁང་གི་བདག་པོས་ཁོར་གླ་ཆ་སྤྲོད་ཀྱི་མ་རེད།

tomorrow child that-by work no do since restaurant of owner-by he-to wage give past compl. neg./

Because that child will not work tomorrow, the owner of the restaurant will not pay him wages.

r. ཁོས་ཆང་ཁང་ལ་འགྲོ་གི་མེད་ཅིང་། ཐ་མག་ཀྱང་འཐེན་གྱི་ཡོད་པ་མ་རེད།

he-by bar to go usual neg. and/ cigarette also smoke usual compl. neg/

He does not go to the bar and also does not smoke cigarettes.

s ཁོ་འདིར་ཡོང་གི་མིན་པར་བརྟེན། ང་ཚོ་ཟ་ཁང་ལ་འགྲོ་གི་ཡིན།

he-by here come fut. compl. neg. since/ i pl. restaurant to go fut. compl./

Because he will not come here, we will go to the restaurant.

The negation of involuntary verbs follows the same pattern as active verbs.

t. ངའི་གྲོགས་པོའི་ན་ཚ་མ་དྲག་ཙང་སྨན་ཁང་ལ་ཨེམ་ཆི་ཐུག་པར་ཕྱིན་པ་རེད།

i-of friend-of illness no recover since hospital doctor meet inf. went compl./

Because my friend's illness did not get better, (he) went to the hospital to meet (see) a doctor.

u. ཆུ་མི་འཁོལ་ཚེ་ཇ་ཞིམ་པོ་མི་འདུག།

water no boil if tea taste-good no exist /

If the water does not boil, the tea is not tasty.

v. སློབ་གྲྭ་བ་དེ་ཚོ་མཁས་པར་མི་འགྱུར་ན་ལས་ཀ་ཡག་པོ་རག་གི་མ་རེད།

student that pl. expert no become if work good obtain fut. compl. neg/

If those students do not become experts, (they) will not obtain a good jobs.

w. ཉེས་པ་དེ་ཡང་པོར་མི་འགྱུར་ན་ཁོ་ཤི་གི་རེད།

punishment that light-to no become if he die fut. compl./

If the punishment does not become lessened, he will die.

Note that འགྱུར་ typically requires the dative-locative (པར་, པོར་) to indicate change *into* something.

6.4 The enumerative particles: སོགས་ and བཅས་

While two items can be listed or enumerated by means of the connective particle དང་ ("and"), three or more items require one of the above particles. The standard practice is for དང་ to be placed after the first item mentioned followed by a "།" and a space. All subsequent items are separated by "།" until the final item, after which one of the enumerative particles is placed. The first of these, སོགས་, indicates that the list is incomplete and is generally translated as "such as" or "so forth," or "etc."

a. ཡུལ་དེར་སྟག་དང་། འདམ་སེང་། རི་བོང་སོགས་ཡོད་པ་རེད།

country that-to tiger and/ lion/ rabbit etc. exist/

There are tigers, lions, rabbits, and so forth in that country.

When བཅས་ is used after the final item in a list, it indicates that the preceding items form a complete set and are not merely illustrative of a larger set. For example, if we replace the སོགས་ in example a. with བཅས་, the meaning changes:

b. ཡུལ་དེར་སྟག་དང་། འདམ་སེང་། རི་བོང་བཅས་ཡོད་པ་རེད།
country that-to tiger and/ lion/ rabbit i.e. exist/
There are tigers, lions, and rabbits in that country.

These particles have other related, but slightly different, uses. For example, སོགས་ can be used without a list of items to convey the meaning "and so forth" or "such as."

c. ཨ་མི་རི་ཀ་སོགས་རྒྱལ་ཁབ་མང་པོས་ཀྲུང་གོར་རོགས་རམ་བྱེད་ཀྱི་ཡོད་པ་རེད།
america etc. nation many-by china-to help do present compl./
Many nations such as America are helping (assisting) China.

If བཅས་པའི་ is substituted for སོགས་, it conveys the meaning of "including." For example,

d. ཨ་མི་རི་ཀ་བཅས་པའི་རྒྱལ་ཁབ་མང་པོས་ཀྲུང་གོར་རོགས་རམ་བྱེད་ཀྱི་ཡོད་པ་རེད།
america i.e. nation many-by china-to help do present compl./
Many nations, including America, are helping (assisting) China.

བཅས་ is also used in the pattern པ་/བ་དང་བཅས་(ཏེ་), where it has a completely different meaning. Here it functions to create an adverbial phrase explaining *how* the action in the second clause occurred. In the first example below (e.), it explains *how the lion answered*—in the manner of roaring. In the second (f.), it explains *how he arrived* —in the manner of jumping/hopping. This is also sometimes translated as "together with" or "along with."

e. འདམ་སེང་གིས་ང་རོ་སྒྲོག་པ་དང་བཅས་ཏེ་རི་བོང་ལ་ལན་བཏབས་པ་རེད།
lion by roar and i.e. rabbit to answered past compl./
Roaring, the lion answered the rabbit.

f. རི་བོང་ཞིག་གློ་བུར་དུ་མཆོངས་པ་དང་བཅས་ཏེ་འདམ་སེང་གི་མདུན་དུ་སླེབས་བྱུང་།
rabbit one suddenly jump and i.e. lion of front to arrived got/
Jumping suddenly, the rabbit arrived in front of the lion.

This usage also occurs without the ཏེ་, that is to say as དང་བཅས་. For example,

g. དགའ་སྤྲོ་ཚད་མེད་དང་བཅས་ཁོང་ལ་དགའ་བསུ་ཞུས་པ་རེད།
joy boundless i.e. he to welcomed past compl./
(They) welcomed him with boundless joy.

The next example illustrates how དང་བཅས་ཏེ་ can be used with nominals. It conveys the adverbial function (*How did he go?*—She went with the monks) and would normally be translated as "along with."

h. བླ་མ་དེ་གྲྭ་པ་དང་བཅས་ལྷ་སར་ཕེབས་པ་རེད།
lama that monk i.e. lhasa-to came past compl./

That lama went to Lhasa along with the monks.

6.5 Adverbials

Adverbial constructions are generally expressed in Tibetan by means of: 1) a class of adverbializing particles which transform substantives into adverbs (see 6.5.1-4), and 2) a small class of words we can categorize as adverbs (see 6.5.5).

6.5.1 The adverbializing particles: [genitive particle] + ངང་ or ངང་ནས་ or སྒོ་ནས་

These two particles express "how" or "in what manner" or "by what means" a verbal action occurs. The are linked to substantives by the genitive particles.

a. ཁོས་དགའ་སྤྲོ་ཚད་མེད་ཀྱི་ངང་ཁོང་ལ་དགའ་བསུ་ཞུས་པ་རེད།
he-by joy boundless of manner he to welcomed past compl./
(He) welcomed him with boundless joy.

b. ཁོས་དགའ་སྤྲོ་ཚད་མེད་ཀྱི་སྒོ་ནས་ཁོང་ལ་དགའ་བསུ་ཞུས་པ་རེད།
he-by joy boundless of manner he to welcomed past compl./
(He) welcomed him with boundless joy.

6.5.2 The instrumental particles as adverbializers

The instrumental particles encountered earlier with the subject of active sentences can also function to adverbialize nominals. They are usually translated by "with," "by," or simply the "-ly" ending of English adverbs.

a. ཁོས་དགའ་སྤྲོ་ཚད་མེད་ཀྱིས་ཁོང་ལ་དགའ་བསུ་ཞུས་པ་རེད།
he joy boundless by he to welcomed past compl./
(He) welcomed him with boundless joy.

b. ལོ་མ་འདི་རླུང་གིས་འཁྱེར་སོང་།
leaf this wind by carry past compl./
This leaf was carried by the wind.

c. ཁོས་ཧུར་བརྩོན་གྱིས་ལས་ཀ་བྱེད་པ་རེད།
he-by diligence by work do past compl./
He worked diligently.

6.5.3 The dative-locative particles as adverbializers

The dative-locative particles can also be used to adverbialize adjectives.

a. ཁོས་དར་ཆ་ཞིག་བརྟན་པོར་བཙུགས་པ་རེད།
he by flag one firm to planted past compl./

He planted (put up) a flag firmly.

b. མོས་ལྟད་མོ་གསལ་པོར་མཐོང་སོང་།

she-by show clear-to see past compl./

She saw the show clearly.

The dative-locative is also used to link nominals to the various verbs meaning "to go" and to the verb "become/change" (འགྱུར་) creating constructions which are adverbials in Tibetan. For example, "improve" (ཡར་རྒྱས་) + dative-locative (སུ་) + "went" (ཕྱིན་) = "went in the manner of improving." These constructions, however, are normally translated as verbs in English, for example, this example would be translated simply as "improved."

c. ད་ལོ་བོད་ཀྱི་དཔལ་འབྱོར་ཡར་རྒྱས་སུ་ཕྱིན་པ་རེད།

this year tibet of economy improve to went compl./

This year Tibet's economy improved. [*How did it go?* It went in the manner of improving.]

d. ཕྱི་ལོ་བོད་ཀྱི་དཔལ་འབྱོར་ཡར་རྒྱས་སུ་འགྱུར་གྱི་རེད།

next year tibet of economy improve to become fut. compl./

Next year Tibet's economy will improve. [*How will it become/change?* It will become/change in the manner of improving.]

6.5.4 The particles བཞིན་པར་ and བཞིན་དུ་ as adverbializers

When used with verbs, བཞིན་པར་ and བཞིན་དུ་ typically convey the idea that "in the manner of" or "while" the first action is in the process of going on, a second verbal action occurs.

a. ཁོ་སེམས་སྐྱོ་བཞིན་དུ་ནང་ལ་ལོག་པ་རེད།

he mind sad manner in to return past compl./

He returned home sadly. (While in the state of being sad, he returned home.)

b. ཁོས་སྐད་བརྒྱབ་བཞིན་དུ་ཕྱིན་སོང་།

he-by yell manner went compl./

He went yelling. (While yelling, he went.)

c. ལྷ་སར་སྡོད་བཞིན་པར་འབྲས་སྤུངས་ལ་ཕྱིན་སོང་།

lhasa-to stay manner drepung to go went compl./

While staying in Lhasa, (he, she, they) went to Drepung (monastery).

d. ང་ན་བཞིན་དུ་དེབ་མང་པོ་བཀླགས།

i sick manner book many read/

While I was ill, (I) read many books.

བཞིན་དུ་ can also be translated by the English meaning "likewise" or "just as." In this role it functions like ནང་བཞིན་ "like."

e. མེ་ཏོག་དཀར་པོ་དེ་ལ་དགའ་པོ་ཡོད་པ་བཞིན་དུ་དམར་པོ་ལ་དགའ་པོ་ཡོད།
flower white that to like exist manner red to like exist/
Just as (I) like that white flower, (I) like red ones. (lit., in the manner of liking white flowers, I like red ones.)

f. མེ་ཏོག་དམར་པོ་དེ་ལ་དགའ་པོ་ཡོད་པ་ནང་བཞིན་སེར་པོ་ལ་དགའ་པོ་ཡོད།
flower red that to like exist manner yellow like exist/
Just as (I) like that red flower, (I) like yellow ones.

6.5.5 Adverbs

There is a small class of adverbial words that modify verbs. The most common of these are:

ནན་ཏན་	ཐད་དེ་	ཧུར་ཐག་	ཚད་མེད་
emphatically	completely	energetically	limitlessly
རྒྱུ་མཐུད་(ནས་)	ལྷག་པར་དུ་	ལམ་སེང་	གློ་བུར་དུ་
continuously	particularly	immediately	suddenly

a. ཁོས་ནན་ཏན་བཤད་པ་རེད།
he-by emphatic spoke past compl./
He spoke emphatically.

b. ཁོའི་གྲོགས་པོའི་པ་ཕས་ཁ་ལག་ཐད་དེ་ཟས་སོང་།
he-of friend-of father-by food completely ate went compl./
His friend's father (lit., by the father of his friend) ate the food completely.

c. བོད་པའི་གྲྭ་པ་ཚོས་སློབ་སྦྱོང་ཧུར་ཐག་བྱེད་ཀྱི་ཡོད་པ་རེད།
tibet-of monk pl.-by study energetically do usual compl./
The Tibetan monks are studying energetically.

d. ལྷ་ས་ནས་ཡོང་མཁན་དེ་རྒྱ་མིའི་ཟ་ཁང་ལ་ཁ་ལག་ཟས་ནས་གློ་བུར་དུ་ན།
lhasa from come doer that chinese-of restaurant to food eat having suddenly sick/
That person who came from Lhasa suddenly got sick after eating food in a Chinese restaurant.

e. བོད་པའི་གྲྭ་པ་ཚོས་སློབ་སྦྱོང་རྒྱུ་མཐུད་བྱས་པ་རེད།
tibet-of monk pl.-by study continuously did past compl./
The Tibetan monks studied continuously.

f. མོ་ལམ་སེང་ཕྱིན་སོང་།
she immediately went compl./
She went immediately.

g. ཁོ་པ་གློ་བུར་དུ་ནང་ལ་ལོག་སོང་།
he suddenly home to returned went compl./

He suddenly returned home.

6.6 Nominalization with པ་/བ་

6.6.1 Positive constructions

Nominalization is another difficult feature of Tibetan. It refers to the transformation of verbs and verbal phrases into nouns or noun phrases which are then treated as nouns in larger constructions.

One of the most common of the nominalizing particles is པ་(བ་). This has already been encountered as an untranslated component of a number of final verb complements (པ་རེད་) as well as in clause connectives (པ་དང་, པ་མ་ཟད་). However, do not worry about trying to break these into their constituent parts at this time. Continue to view them as units.

a. ཁོས་གནོད་སྐྱོན་བྱས་པ་རེད།

he-by harm did past compl./

He harmed (it). (or, He caused harm.)

This is a simple active sentence in the past tense. If we now nominalize it, we get:

b. ཁོས་གནོད་སྐྱོན་བྱས་པ་

he-by harm did nom.

This can be translated roughly as "his doing harm in the past," or "the harm done by him." In any event, this nominalized clause can now enter into larger constructions as a noun or noun phrase. In example c., it is the object of the verb "to correct."

c. ཁོས་གནོད་སྐྱོན་བྱས་པ་འདི་ཁོ་ཚོས་བཟོ་བཅོས་བྱེད་ཀྱི་ཡོད་པ་རེད།

he-by harm did nom. this he pl.-by repair do pres. compl./

They are correcting the harm done by him. (As for this harm done by him, they are correcting/repairing it.)

This could also be written with the subject ཁོ་ཚོས་ at the beginning of the sentence.

d. ཁོ་ཚོས་ཁོས་གནོད་སྐྱོན་བྱས་པ་འདི་བཟོ་བཅོས་བྱེད་ཀྱི་ཡོད་པ་རེད།

he pl.-by he-by harm did nom. this he pl.-by repair do pres. compl./

They are correcting the harm done by him. (They, as for the harm done by him, are correcting/ repairing it.)

Any semantically appropriate noun (whether nominalized or not) can be substituted for a nominalized clause. For example, in sentence e., the noun phrase ཟ་ཁང་འདི་ ("this restaurant") is substituted for གནོད་སྐྱོན་བྱས་པ་འདི་ ("this harm done by him").

e. ཟ་ཁང་འདི་ཁོ་ཚོས་བཟོ་བཅོས་བྱེད་ཀྱི་ཡོད་པ་རེད།

restaurant this he pl.-by repair do pres. compl./

They are repairing this restaurant. (as for this restaurant, they are repairing it.)

When the verb in a nominalized phrase is in the present (non-past) tense stem, the meaning of the nominalized phrase is also present (non-past).

f. ཁོས་གནོད་སྐྱོན་བྱེད་པ་འདི་ཁོ་ཚོས་བཟོ་བཅོས་བྱེད་ཀྱི་ཡོད་པ་རེད།

he-by harm do nom. this he pl.-by repair do pres. compl./

They are correcting the harm he is doing. (As for the harm he is doing, they are correcting it.)

g. རྒྱ་ནག་ལ་བཏང་ཡིག་གཏོང་བ་ཁག་པོ་རེད།

china to letter send nom. difficult is/

Sending letters (the sending of letters) to China is difficult.

However, in some contexts, e.g., the presence of a temporal word, the tense of the verb is overriden. Thus the presence of the temporal word "formerly" (སྔོན་མ་) in examples h. and i. dictates a past tense meaning for both, despite the different tense of the verb stem (བཏང་བ་ and གཏོང་བ་).

h. སྔོན་མ་རྒྱ་ནག་ལ་བཏང་ཡིག་བཏང་བ་ཁག་པོ་རེད།

formerly china to letter send nom. difficult is/

Formerly, sending letters to China was difficult.

i. སྔོན་མ་རྒྱ་ནག་ལ་བཏང་ཡིག་གཏོང་བ་ཁག་པོ་རེད།

formerly china to letter send nom. difficult is/

Formerly, sending letters to China was difficult.

Sometimes the addition of a determinative will produce something similar to a relative construction in English (e.g., a clause introduced by "which").

j. བཏང་ཡིག་བཏང་བ་འདི་ནི་འབྱོར་བྱུང་།

letter sent nom. this as-for arrived got/

As for this letter which was sent, (it) arrived. (or: (I) received the letter which was sent.)

Nominalized phrases not only take determinatives but also take many of the pluralizers encountered earlier. For example, ཚང་མ་ ("all") in sentence k., ཚོ་ in l. and རྣམས་ in m.:

k. ལས་ཀ་བྱས་པ་ཚང་མ་ཡག་པོ་འདུག།

work did nom. all good exist./

All the work that was done was good.

The genitive is commonly used before a nominalized phrase or noun phrase so that the former (the nominalized phrase) modifies the latter. These constructions will often be translated as relative constructions in English.

l. པེ་ཅིང་ལ་འགྲོ་བའི་ལས་བྱེད་པ་ཚོ་ . . . .

Beijing to go nom.-of official pl.
(the) officials (who are) going to Beijing . . . .

In the above example, the entire phrase "the going to Beijing" (པེ་ཅིང་ལ་འགྲོ་བའི་) modifies "officials" (ལས་བྱེད་པ་ཚོ) explaining what kind of officials they were. A simple adjective such as "new" (ལས་བྱེད་པ་གསར་པ་) functions identically. The next example illustrates the importance of the tense of the verb (འགྲོ་བའི་ versus ཕྱིན་པའི་):

m. པེ་ཅིང་ལ་ཕྱིན་པའི་ལས་བྱེད་པ་རྣམས་
Beijing to went nom.-of official
(the) officials who went (or have gone) to Beijing

These nominalized relative constructions can be used in sentences in either the subject or object slots. In the next three examples the nominalized construction པེ་ཅིང་ལ་འགྲོ་བའི་ལས་བྱེད་པ་ཚོ་ acts as the subject of an active verb and so is placed in the instrumental case.

n. པེ་ཅིང་ལ་འགྲོ་བའི་ལས་བྱེད་པ་ཚོས་ཀྲའོ་ཙི་དབྱང་མཇལ་གྱི་རེད།
beijing to go nom. of official pl.-by chao-jiyang meet (h.) fut. compl./
The officials who are going to Beijing will meet Zhao Ziyang.

o. པེ་ཅིང་ལ་འགྲོ་བའི་ལས་བྱེད་པ་ཚོས་ཀྲའོ་ཙི་དབྱང་མཇལ་བ་རེད།
Beijing to go nom.-of officials pl.-by chao-jiyang meet (h.) past compl./
The officials who went to Beijing met Zhao Ziyang.

Note that although the verb "go" is in the present tense stem, it is translated as a past tense verb because of the final verb complement (མཇལ་བ་རེད).

In the next example, the location of the verbal action is also a nominalized phrase.

p. པེ་ཅིང་ལ་ཕྱིན་པའི་ལས་བྱེད་པ་ཚོས་ཕྱི་རྒྱལ་གྱིས་བཟོས་པའི་མགྲོན་ཁང་ལ་བཞུགས་པ་རེད།
Beijing to went nom.-of officials pl.-by foreign by made nom.-of hotel to stayed (h.) past compl./
The officials who went to Beijing stayed in a hotel which was built by foreigners.

q. དམག་མིས་མེ་མདའ་བརྒྱབ་པའི་སློབ་གྲྭ་བ་དེ་ཕྱི་རྒྱལ་གྱིས་བཟོས་པའི་སྨན་ཁང་དེར་ཤི་པ་རེད།
soldier-by shoot-of student that foreign by made hospital that-to die past compl./
The student who was shot by the soldiers died in the hospital that was built by the foreigners.

The core of this construction (in q.) is:

སློབ་གྲྭ་བ་དེ་སྨན་ཁང་དེར་ཤི་པ་རེད།
student that hospital that-to dies past compl./
That student died in that hospital.

The addition of the nominalizing phrase དམག་མིས་མེ་མདའ་བརྒྱབ་པ་ linked by the genitive explains *what kind of a student?*—one shot by soldiers. Similarly, the nominalized phrase modifying "hospital" (ཕྱི་རྒྱལ་གྱིས་བཟོས་པའི་) conveys *what kind of a hospital?*—foreign-made.

r. རང་རྒྱལ་གྱིས་བཟོས་པའི་གནམ་གྲུ་མང་པོ་ཤར་གླིང་དབུས་མར་དམག་བརྒྱབ་པའི་རྒྱལ་ཁབ་གྱིས་ཉོས་པ་རེད།
rangyeekii söөbee nəmdru məngu shārlin üümar mää gyəbee gyeegəbki ñööbəreè
our country by made nom.-of airplanes many middle east-to war fight-of country by bought past compl./
Many airplanes which were made by our country were bought by countries fighting a war in the Middle East.

The core of example r. is རྒྱལ་ཁབ་གྱིས་གནམ་གྲུ་ཉོས་པ་རེད་, "countries bought airplanes." It is elaborated by means of a complex nominalized verb construction. In the above example, the first segment—རང་རྒྱལ་གྱིས་བཟོས་པའི་གནམ་གྲུ་མང་པོ་—is the object (*what did they buy?*). The second segment—ཤར་གླིང་དབུས་མར་དམག་བརྒྱབ་པའི་རྒྱལ་ཁབ་གྱིས་—is the subject. It breaks down into the main subject, "by countries" (རྒྱལ་ཁབ་གྱིས) modified by a long nominalized verbal phrase "who are fighting a war in the Middle East" (ཤར་གླིང་དབུས་མར་དམག་བརྒྱབ་པའི་). The order of the subject and object phrases could be reversed:

s. ཤར་གླིང་དབུས་མར་དམག་བརྒྱབ་པའི་རྒྱལ་ཁབ་གྱིས་རང་རྒྱལ་གྱིས་བཟོས་པའི་གནམ་གྲུ་མང་པོ་ཉོས་པ་རེད།
shārlin üümar mää gyəbee gyeegəbki rangyeekii söөbee nəmdru məngu ñööbəreè
middle east-to war fight-of country by our country by made nom.-of airplanes many bought past compl./
Many airplanes which were made by our country were bought by countries fighting a war in the Middle East.

6.6.2 Negative nominalized constructions with པ་/བ་

Negative nominalized constructions parallel earlier forms, མ་ being used with past verbs and མི་ with non-past verbs.

a. ཡུལ་དེར་ཡར་རྒྱས་མི་གཏོང་བ་ནི་ནོར་འཁྲུལ་ཆེན་པོ་རེད།
place that-to improve no send nom. as-for mistake big is/
Not improving that place (in the future or present) is a big mistake. Or,
Not making improvements to that place is a big mistake.

b. ཡུལ་དེར་ཡར་རྒྱས་མ་བཏང་བ་ནི་ནོར་འཁྲུལ་ཆེན་པོ་རེད།
place that-to improve no sent nom. as-for mistake big is/
Not improving the area (in the past) was a big mistake. Or,
Not having made improvements to that place was a big mistake.

c. སོན་གསར་པ་མ་བཏབ་པའི་གྲོང་གསེབ་དེ་ཚོ་སྐྱོ་པོ་ཞེ་དྲགས་འདུག།
seed new no plant nom.-of village that pl. poor very exist/
Those villages which did not plant the new seeds are very poor.

Note that changing the tense of the verb བཏབ་ to present tense (འདེབས་) in sentence d. changes the tense of that part of the sentence:

d. སོན་གསར་པ་མི་འདེབས་པའི་གྲོང་གསེབ་དེ་ཚོ་སྐྱོ་པོ་ཞི་དྭགས་འདུག།

seed new no plant nom.-of village that pl. poor very exist/

Those villages that are not planting the new seeds are very poor.

Nominalized verb phrases are frequently used with other verbs such as "know" and "see" to convey the idea that the nominal action was "known" or "seen." For example:

e. ཁོས་མོ་སོ་པ་ཡིན་པ་ཤེས་པ་རེད།

he-by she spy is nom.know past compl./

He knew that she was a spy. (lit., He—her being a spy—knew.)

f. ངས་ཆོས་རར་གྲྭ་པ་རྣམས་ཀྱིས་ཞལ་འདོན་གནང་བཞིན་པ་མཐོང་བྱུང་།

i-by religious class monk pl. by pray (h.) do (h.) pres. compl. saw got/

I saw the monks praying in the study area.

Note that both these verbs (མཐོང་ and ཤེས་) require their subjects to be in the instrumental case.

6.6.3 Nominalized constructions with the dative-locative

When the dative-locative is used in conjunction with a nominalized verb a variety of functions are expressed. We have already seen how this is used to express the infinitive.

a. ཁོས་ཚོང་ཁང་ནས་དེབ་ཅིག་ཉོ་བར་ཕྱིན་པ་རེད།

he-by store from book one buy nom.-to went compl./

He went to buy a book from the (a) store.

A second very important use of the dative-locative is to express the idea of "to" or "concerning" the verbal action. It typically becomes the object of the verbal action.

b. ཁོས་མེ་མདའ་ཉོ་བར་ཁོ་ཚོས་སྐྱོན་བརྗོད་བྱས་པ་རེད།

he-by gun bought nom.-to he pl.-by criticism did past compl./

They criticized his buying guns.

This phrase literally translates as: "To/concerning his buying guns, they criticized."

c. ཁོས་ཕྱི་རྒྱལ་ནས་ཉོས་པའི་སོན་དེ་བཏབ་པར་མི་ཁ་ཤས་ཀྱིས་ངོ་རྒོལ་བྱས་པ་རེད།

he-by foreign country from bought nom.-of seed that people several by opposition did past compl./

Several people opposed his planting seeds that had been bought from abroad. (concerning planting that seed that was bought from abroad, . . .)

In b., the dative-locative marks "what was criticized" and in c., "what was opposed."

d. ཁོས་ཧུར་བརྩོན་གྱིས་ལས་ཀ་བྱེད་པར་བྱ་དགའ་ཞིག་ཐོབ་ཀྱི་རེད།

he-by diligence by work do nom.-to prize gain fut. compl./

He will get a prize for working diligently.

The entire first clause (ཁོས་ཧུར་བརྩོན་གྱིས་ལས་ཀ་བྱེད་པར་) literally would be translated as: "to/concerning his doing work diligently, . . ."

The dative-locative particle may be preceded by a determinative.

e. ཁོས་ཧུར་བརྩོན་གྱིས་ལས་ཀ་བྱེད་པ་དེར་བྱ་དགའ་ཞིག་ཐོབ་ཀྱི་རེད།

he-by diligence by work do nom. that-to prize one win fut. compl./

He will get a prize for working diligently. (The work is being done in the present.)

This could also be written:

f. ཁོས་ཧུར་བརྩོན་གྱིས་ལས་ཀ་བྱེད་པ་དེ་ལ་བྱ་དགའ་ཞིག་ཐོབ་ཀྱི་རེད།

he-by diligence by work do nom. that to prize one gain fut. compl./

He will get a prize for working diligently.

If the present tense stem of the verb "do" (བྱེད་) is replaced by its past tense stem (བྱས་), the tense of the nominalized phrase becomes past:

g. ཁོས་ཧུར་བརྩོན་གྱིས་ལས་ཀ་བྱས་པ་དེ་ལ་བྱ་དགའ་ཞིག་ཐོབ་ཀྱི་རེད།

he-by diligence by work do nom. that to prize one gain fut. compl./

He will get a prize for having worked diligently.

6.6.4 Negative constructions with the dative-locative

a. ཁོས་ཧུར་བརྩོན་གྱིས་ལས་ཀ་མ་བྱས་པ་དེ་ལ་གཞུང་གྱིས་ཉེས་པ་བཏང་བ་རེད།

he-by diligence by work no did nom. that to government by punishment gave past compl./

The government punished his not having worked diligently. (. . . punished him for not having worked diligently.)

If the present tense stem of the verb "do" (བྱེད་) is used (as in example b.), it conveys that the work was done in the present or recent past, rather than in the more distant past.

b. ཁོས་ཧུར་བརྩོན་གྱིས་ལས་ཀ་མ་བྱེད་པ་དེ་ལ་གཞུང་གྱིས་ཉེས་པ་བཏང་བ་རེད།

he-by diligence by work no do nom. that to government by punishment gave past compl./

The government punished his not working diligently.

If the main verb is placed in the future tense, for example གཏོང་གི་རེད in example c., then the overall meaning of the sentence changes to future tense.

c. ཁོས་ཧུར་བརྩོན་གྱིས་ལས་ཀ་མ་བྱེད་པ་དེ་ལ་གཞུང་གྱིས་ཉེས་པ་གཏོང་གི་རེད།

he-by diligence by work no do nom. that to government by punishment gave fut. compl./

The government will punish him for not working diligently.

For the entire meaning to be future tense, the subordinate clause must have a conditional clause connective such as ན་. This is seen in example d.

d. ཁོས་ཧུར་བརྩོན་གྱིས་ལས་ཀ་མ་བྱེད་ན་གཞུང་གྱིས་ཉེས་པ་གཏོང་གི་རེད།

he-by diligence by work no do if government by punishment give fut. compl./

The government will punish him if (he) does not work diligently.

This type of sentence can be further complicated by nesting two nominalized phrases one within the other, for example, compare e. and f.

e. ཁོས་ཕྱི་རྒྱལ་གྱི་སོན་མི་འདེབས་པ་དེར་ཞིང་པ་ཁ་ཤས་ཀྱིས་སྐྱོན་བརྗོད་བྱེད་ཀྱི་ཡོད་པ་རེད།

he-by foreign country of seed no plant nom. that-to that farmer several by criticize do present compl./

Several farmers are criticizing his not planting the foreign seeds.

f. ཁོས་ཕྱི་རྒྱལ་ནས་ཉོས་པའི་སོན་མི་འདེབས་པ་དེར་ཞིང་པ་ཁ་ཤས་ཀྱིས་སྐྱོན་བརྗོད་བྱེད་ཀྱི་ཡོད་པ་རེད།

he-by foreign country from bought nom.-of of seed no plant nom. that-to that people several by criticize do present compl./

Several farmers are criticizing his not planting the seeds bought from abroad.

In example f. the core phrase is ཁོས་སོན་མི་འདེབས་པ་དེར་. Within that, another nominalized phrase has been inserted to modify "seed": ཕྱི་རྒྱལ་ནས་ཉོས་པའི་. We could further expand on this by inserting a time slot word or phrase such as "this year" (ད་ལོ་), altering the meaning considerably depending where it is inserted. In sentence g. below, the *criticism* is occurring this year. In sentence h. they are criticizing his not planting the seed *bought this year* from abroad, and in sentence i. they are criticizing his not *planting this year* the seed bought from abroad.

g. ཁོས་ཕྱི་རྒྱལ་ནས་ཉོས་པའི་སོན་མི་འདེབས་པ་དེར་ཞིང་པ་ཁ་ཤས་ཀྱིས་ད་ལོ་སྐྱོན་བརྗོད་བྱེད་ཀྱི་ཡོད་པ་རེད།

he-by foreign from bought nom.-gen. seed no plant nom. that-to farmer several by this-year criticize pres. compl./

This year several farmers are criticizing his not planting the seeds bought abroad.

h. ཁོས་ད་ལོ་ཕྱི་རྒྱལ་ནས་ཉོས་པའི་སོན་མི་འདེབས་པ་དེར་ཞིང་པ་ཁ་ཤས་ཀྱིས་སྐྱོན་བརྗོད་བྱེད་ཀྱི་ཡོད་པ་རེད།

he-by this-year foreign from bought nom.-gen. seed no plant nom. that-to farmer several by criticize pres. compl./

Several farmers are criticizing his not planting the seed bought from abroad this year.

i. ཁོས་ཕྱི་རྒྱལ་ནས་ཉོས་པའི་སོན་ད་ལོ་མི་འདེབས་པ་དེར་ཞིང་པ་ཁ་ཤས་ཀྱིས་སྐྱོན་བརྗོད་བྱེད་ཀྱི་ཡོད་པ་རེད།

he-by foreign from bought nom.-gen. seed this-year no plant that-to farmer several by criticize pres. compl./

Several farmers are criticizing his not planting this year the seed bought from abroad.

Note that མི་འདེབས་པ་དེར་ could also be written མི་འདེབས་པར་.

j. ཁོས་ཕྱི་རྒྱལ་ནས་ཉོས་པའི་སོན་ད་ལོ་མི་འདེབས་པར་ཞིང་པ་ཁ་ཤས་ཀྱིས་སྐྱོན་བརྗོད་བྱེད་ཀྱི་ཡོད་པ་རེད།

he-by foreign from bought nom.-gen. seed this-year no plant nom.-to farmer several by criticize pres. compl./

Several farmers are criticizing him for not planting the seed bought from abroad this year .

Sometimes, however, it is more appropriate to use the English "without" for negative nominalized constructions with the dative-locative.

k. རྒྱུ་མཚན་མེད་པར་ཁོ་ཁོང་ཁྲོ་ཟ་བ་རེད།
reason not-exist nom.-to he angry past compl./
He got angry without reason (for no reason).

Note that the subject of the above example (ཁོ་) does not have to be accompanied by the instrumental case since the verb ཁོང་ཁྲོ་ཟ་ is involuntary.

l. བོད་ནས་རྒྱ་གར་ལ་མ་ཕྱིན་པར་འདིར་ཡོང་བ་རེད།
tibet from india to no went nom.-to this-to come past compl./
(He, she, they) came here from Tibet without going to India.

The above sentence could be translated literally as: "In the manner of not having gone to India, (he, she, they) came here from Tibet ."

6.7 The use of རྒྱུ་ and ཡས་ or ཡག་

རྒྱུ་, ཡས་ and ཡག་ are important multi-functional particles.

6.7.1 Future constructions

In future contexts (indicated by a future temporal word such as སང་ཉིན་ or ཕྱི་ལོ་ or དོ་དགོང་) the particles ཡས་ or རྒྱུ་, when followed by a linking verb, express simple future action.

a. ཁོ་སང་ཉིན་འགྲོ་རྒྱུ་རེད།
he tomorrow go gyu-fut./
He will go (be going) tomorrow.

b. ཁོ་སང་ཉིན་འགྲོ་ཡས་རེད།
he tomorrow go ya-fut./
He will go (be going) tomorrow.

c. ཁོ་ཚོས་ཕྱི་ལོ་དགོན་པ་གསར་པ་ཞིག་རྒྱག་རྒྱུ་མ་རེད།
he pl.-by next year monastery new build gyu-fut. neg./
They will not build a new monastery next year.

d. དོ་དགོང་ཁོང་རྣམས་གཞིས་ཀ་རྩེར་ཕེབས་ཡས་མ་རེད།
tonight he (h.) pl. shigatse to go ya-fut. neg./
They (h.) will not go to Shigatse tonight.

e. ཁོས་དོ་དགོང་འདིར་ཁ་ལག་ཟ་རྒྱུ་རེད།
he-by tonight here food eat gyu fut./

He is going to eat here tonight.

རྒྱུ་ can also convey the substantially different meaning of "has not been done yet" or "has yet to be done," regarding the verbal action. Generally it functions this way following a question that asks whether the verbal action has been done. For example,

f. (ཁོས་ཁ་ལག་ཟས་པས?) ཁོས་ཁ་ལག་ཟ་རྒྱུ་རེད།
he-by food eat gyu-fut./
(Did he eat?) He has yet to eat.

g. ཁོས་དོ་དགོང་གི་ཁ་ལག་ཟ་རྒྱུ་རེད།
he-by tonight of food eat gyu-fut./
He has yet to eat dinner.

h. ཁོས་རྡོ་རྗེ་ལགས་ལ་ཡི་གེ་ཞིག་གཏོང་རྒྱུ་རེད།
he-by dorje to letter send gyu is/
He has yet to write Dorje (send Dorje a letter).

In the above types of sentence, ཡས་ cannot be substituted for རྒྱུ་ to convey the "has yet to do" meaning. It always conveys the simple future tense.

i. ཁོས་རྡོ་རྗེ་ལགས་ལ་ཡི་གེ་ཞིག་གཏོང་ཡས་རེད།
he-by dorje to letter send ya-fut./
He will write Dorje (send Dorje a letter).

6.7.2 Past constructions

རྒྱུ་ and ཡས་ are also used together with the verb བྱུང་ ("got") to express the idea that "someone got or did not get a chance or opportunity or possibility" to do the verbal action. For example,

a. ཁོ་ཁྲོམ་ལ་འགྲོ་རྒྱུ་བྱུང་སོང་།
he market to go gyu got went compl./
He got a chance to go to the market.

b. ཁོས་ཁང་པ་རྒྱག་ཡས་བྱུང་བ་རེད།
he-by house build ya got past compl./
He got an opportunity to build a house.

c. མོས་ཁང་པ་རྒྱག་ཡས་མ་བྱུང་བ་རེད།
she-by house build ya neg. got past compl./
She did not get a chance to build a house.

d. ང་སློབ་གྲྭར་འགྲོ་རྒྱུ་མ་བྱུང་བ་རེད།
i school-to go gyu no got/
I did not get a chance to go to school.

6.7.3 Existential constructions

རྒྱུ་ conveys the idea of "shouldn't do the verbal action" when used in the following pattern: vb. + རྒྱུ་ + negative existential verb.

a. ཐེངས་གཅིག་ལ་ཁ་ལག་ཞེ་དྲགས་ཟ་རྒྱུ་མི་འདུག
time one to food a lot eat gyu no-exist/
(One) should not eat a lot of food at one time.

b. དེབ་འདི་ཀློག་རྒྱུ་ཡོད་པ་མ་རེད།
book this read gyu no-exist/
(One) should not read this book.

c. ཁྱོད་ན་གྱི་ཡོད་ཚེ་ལས་ཀ་བྱེད་རྒྱུ་མི་འདུག
you sick pres. if/ work do gyu no-exist/
If you are sick, (you) should not work.

ཡས་ is also used in this type of construction but conveys the totally different meaning of "there is not."

d. ཁ་ལག་ཞེ་དྲགས་ཟ་ཡས་མི་འདུག
food a lot eat ya no-exist/
There is not a lot of food to eat (for eating).

e. ལས་ཀ་བྱེད་ཡས་མེད་ཙང་། ཁོ་ཚོ་ཟ་ཁང་གསར་པ་ལ་ཁ་ལག་ཟ་བར་ཕྱིན་པ་རེད།
work do ya no-exist because/ restaurant new to food eat inf.went compl./
Because there was no work, (they) went to the new restaurant to eat.

Unfortunately, the complexity of these two particles does not end here because རྒྱུ་ can also convey the above meaning of ཡས་. For example,

f. མི་དམངས་ཀྱི་ཡོང་འབབ་ཞེ་དྲགས་འཕར་ཙང་། ཁྲོམ་ལ་དཔྲང་པོ་མཐོང་རྒྱུ་ཡོད་པ་མ་རེད།
people of income a lot increase because/ market-to beggar see gyu no-exist/
Because the income of the people increased a lot, (one) does not see any beggars in the market.

g. དེང་སང་ཁོ་པ་ཚོར་འབྲས་དང་གྲོ་ཞིབ་ཟ་རྒྱུ་ཡོད་པ་མ་རེད།
these days he pl.-to rice and flour eat gyu no exist/
These days they do not have rice and flour to eat (for eating).

Semantic context will ultimately determine which of these རྒྱུ་ meanings is intended in any particular case.

6.7.4 Other constructions

རྒྱུ་ and ཡས་ also nominalize verbs in the manner of པ་/བ་, but only for present or future time. For example, ཚོང་ཁང་འཛུགས་རྒྱུ་ can mean "the future establishing of a store."

In the first two examples below, the nominalized constructions (with རྒྱུ་ and ཡས་)

occur with existential constructions.

a. མོར་ཡི་གེ་གཏོང་རྒྱུ་ཁ་ཤས་འདུག།

he-to letter send gyu several exist/

She has several letters to mail. (To her there exist several letters *for* mailing in the future.)

b. མོར་ཡི་གེ་གཏོང་ཡས་ཁ་ཤས་འདུག།

she-to letter send ya several exist/

She has several letters to mail.

In the next series of examples, རྒྱུ་ and ཡས་ occur with active and involuntary verbs, functioning as the object.

c. ཁང་པ་གསར་པ་ཞིག་རྒྱག་རྒྱུ་གཏན་འཁེལ་བ་རེད།

house new one build gyu decide past compl./

(He, she, etc.) decided to build a new house. (*What was decided?*--the building of a new house was decided.)

d. ཁོས་དེབ་ཉོ་ཡས་ཀྱི་དངུལ་བརླགས་པ་རེད།

he-by book buy ya of money lost past compl./

He lost the money (which was) for buying books. (*What did he lose?*— the money for buying books.

e. ཁང་པ་རྒྱག་རྒྱུའི་གྲ་སྒྲིག་བྱས་པ་རེད།

house build gyu-of preparation did past compl./

(He, she, etc.) made preparations for building a house. (*What did they make preparations for?*—the building of a house.)

f. ཁོ་པ་རྒྱ་ནག་ལ་འགྲོ་རྒྱུའི་འཆར་གཞི་དེ་གཏན་འཁེལ་མ་སོང་།

he china to go gyu-of plan that decided no went compl./

The plan for his going to China was not decided. (*What was not decided?*—the plan for him to go to China.)

g. ཕྱི་རྒྱལ་ལ་གཏོང་ཡས་ཀྱི་སློབ་ཕྲུག་ཚོས་དབྱིན་ཇི་སྐད་ཡིག་སློབ་སྦྱོང་བྱེད་བཞིན་དུ་ཡོད་པ་རེད།

abroad to send ya-of student pl.-by english language study do pres. compl./

The students who are going to be sent abroad are studying (spoken and written) English. (*What students are studying English?*—those who are being sent abroad.)

h. རྒྱ་གར་ནས་འབྱོར་རྒྱུའི་བླ་མ་རྣམས་འབྲས་སྤུངས་ལ་བཞུགས་ཀྱི་རེད།

india from arrive gyu-of lama pl. drepung to stay fut. compl./

The lamas who are arriving from India will stay in Drepung (monastery). (*What lamas will stay in Drepung?*—those who will arrive from India.)

A somewhat idiomatic pattern consists of verb. (non-past)+ རྒྱུ་ + བྱེད་. Together they convey the meaning that someone has "settled or decided" to do the verbal action.

i. ཁོ་ཚོས་བོད་ལ་འགྲོ་རྒྱུ་བྱས་པ་རེད།

he pl.-by tibet to go gyu did past compl./

They decided to go to Tibet.

An important distinction between genitive (ཡས་ཀྱི་) and dative-locative (ཡས་ལ་) constructions emerges in constructions ending in existential verbs. For example, in j., the nominalized phrase plus the genitive modifies the subject, the "book," describing *what kind of a book it is* (it is a book for studying Tibetan). In example k., the same nominalized phrase, this time with the dative-locative, conveys *what the "book" is good for* (it is good for studying Tibetan).

j. བོད་སྐད་སློབ་སྦྱོང་བྱེད་ཡས་ཀྱི་དེབ་འདི་ཡག་པོ་འདུག།

tibetan study do ya of book this good exist/

This book for studying Tibetan is good.

k. བོད་སྐད་སློབ་སྦྱོང་བྱེད་ཡས་ལ་དེབ་འདི་ཡག་པོ་འདུག།

tibetan language study do ya to book this good exist/

This book is good for studying Tibetan.

This sentence could also have been written:

l. དེབ་འདི་བོད་སྐད་སློབ་སྦྱོང་བྱེད་ཡས་ལ་ཡག་པོ་འདུག།

book this tibetan study do ya to good exist/

This book is good for studying Tibetan.

m. ཁ་ལག་བཟོ་རྒྱུའི་ཚལ་འདི་ཡག་པོ་འདུག།

food make gyu-of vegetable this good exist/

This vegetable for making food is good. (This *vegetable*, which is for making food, is good.)

n. ཁ་ལག་བཟོ་རྒྱུ་ལ་ཚལ་འདི་ཡག་པོ་འདུག།

food make gyu-to vegetable this good exist/

This vegetable is good *for* making food (cooking). (For making food—this vegetable is good.)

The dative-locative is also used with རྒྱུ་ and ཡས་ + active verbs (as in example o.), creating indirect objects that convey the notion of "to" or "concerning" or "for."

o. གཞུང་གིས་ཁོ་ཚོར་རོགས་རམ་བྱེད་རྒྱུར་དངུལ་གཡར་གྱི་རེད།

government by he pl.-to help do gyu-to money lend fut. compl./

The government will lend money to help them.

p. ཁོ་ཚོས་མེ་མདའ་རྙིང་པ་ཉོ་རྒྱུར་ལས་བྱེད་པ་ཚོས་སྐྱོན་བརྗོད་བྱས་པ་རེད།

he pl.-by gun old buy gyu-to official pl.-by criticism did past compl./

The officials criticized their buying old guns.

6.8 The "pretend" particles: ཁུལ་, མདོག་, མདོག་བདོག་, ཟོལ་, and ཚུལ་

The "pretend to" connectives are used with verbs to convey the idea that the subject is pretending to do the verbal action. They are commonly followed by the verb "to do."

In the first three examples the genitive particle links ཁུལ་ with the verb. This is a very common pattern.

a. ཁོས་གྲོགས་པོ་ཡིན་པའི་ཁུལ་བྱས་ནས་མགོ་སྐོར་བཏང་བ་རེད།
he-by friend is nom.-gen. pretend did having trick send past compl./
Pretending he was a friend, (he) tricked (him/her/them).

b. སྟག་དེས་ཉིད་ཁུག་པའི་ཚུལ་བྱས་ཏེ་ཉལ་བཞིན་ཡོད།
tiger that-by fall asleep nom.-gen. pretend did having lied down pres. compl./
That tiger is lying there pretending to have fallen asleep.

c. ཚོང་པས་འཛིན་ཆས་རྙིང་མ་ཡིན་པའི་ཟོལ་བྱས་ནས་ཕྱི་རྒྱལ་གྱི་མི་ཞིག་ལ་བཙོང་པ་རེད།
trader-by furniture antique is nom.-gen. pretend did having foreign of person one to sold past compl./
The trader, pretending the furniture was antique, sold it to a foreigner.

d. ཁོས་གྲོགས་པོ་ཡིན་མདོག་མདོག་བྱས་ནས་མགོ་སྐོར་བཏང་བ་རེད།
he-by friend is nom.-gen. pretend did having trick send past compl./
Pretending he was a friend, (he/she) tricked (him/her/them).

e. ཧ་མ་གོ་ན་ཧ་གོ་མདོག་མ་བྱེད།
understand if understand pretend no do/
If (you) don't understand, don't pretend to understand.

f. ཁོས་གྲོགས་པོ་ཡིན་ཁུལ་གྱིས་མགོ་སྐོར་བཏང་བ་རེད།
he-by friend is pretend by trick send past compl./
Pretending he was a friend, (he) tricked (him/them).

g. ཚོང་པས་ཆུ་ཚོད་རྙིང་མ་ཡིན་ཟོལ་གྱིས་ཕྱི་རྒྱལ་གྱི་མི་ཞིག་ལ་བཙོང་པ་རེད།
trader-by clock old is by foreigner one to sold past compl./
The trader, pretending the clock was old (antique), sold it to the foreigner.

A related but not identical usage conveys a negative connotation but not quite "pretending."

h. ཁོ་སློབ་གྲྭ་ཐོན་པའི་ཁུལ་རེད།
he school graduated nom.-gen. pretend is/
He has graduated (from) school (but (I) don't think he knows much).

i. པད་མ་ཨ་མེ་རི་ཀ་ནས་ཚུར་ལོག་ཕེབས་ནས་ཨིན་སྐད་ཤེས་པའི་ཁུལ་རེད།
pema america from hither return come (h.) having english know pretend is/
Pema has returned (hither) from America, but (I) don't think she knows English well.

In still other contexts this clause connective conveys not the pejorative meaning of "pretend to," or "doubt," but rather Tibetan politeness. If someone offers a compliment, Tibetan custom holds that one should deny it, even if it is obviously true. Thus, if someone says you know Tibetan well, even if you are completely fluent, you are expected to disagree and say you know only a little. The particle ཁུལ་ is sometimes used for this function when, for example, someone says, "Dorje is now a great scholar and you were his teacher," and the person does not want to say "Yes, I was." Tibetans sometimes use ཁུལ་ in this context to convey politely something less than a straight affirmative, for example, "I am sort of his teacher" or " I suppose I am his teacher." Basically, it means I am his teacher, but it is a modest and polite mode of expressing this.

j. ང་ཁོའི་དགེ་རྒན་ཡིན་པའི་ཁུལ་རེད།
   i he-of teacher is nom.-of pretend is/
   I am supposed to be his teacher.

This "distancing" can also be used when the "student" is a bad person, in which case it dissociates him from the student. It can also be used to modestly avoid taking credit for something.

k. (ཁྱེད་རང་གིས་ཕྱག་ལས་གནང་ཚར་སོང་ངམ་) ངའི་ལས་ཀ་བྱས་ཚར་བའི་ཁུལ་ཡིན།
   (you by work (h.) finish do past compl. ?) i-of work finish nom. gen. pretend is/
   (Is your work finished?) My work is supposed to be finished [Actually he doesn't want to take credit for it, but it is finished].

6.9 The auxiliary verb ཐུབ་ ("to be able")

This verb has only only one stem and occurs immediately after the verb it modifies. It conveys the idea of "to be able" to do the action of the verb it modifies. ཐུབ་ takes the various verb complements (both positive and negative) the same as any other verb.

a. རྒྱ་གར་ལ་བཞུགས་པའི་གྲྭ་པ་ཚོ་བོད་ལ་གཟིགས་སྐོར་ལ་ཕེབས་ཐུབ་པ་རེད།
   india to live (h.) nom.-of monk pl. tibet to tour to go (h.) able past compl./
   The monks who live in India were able to go to Tibet on a ("sightseeing") tour.
b. རྒྱ་གར་ལ་བཞུགས་པའི་གྲྭ་པ་ཚོ་བོད་ལ་གནས་སྐོར་ལ་ཕེབས་ཐུབ་ཀྱི་རེད།
   india to live (h.) nom.-of monk pl. tibet to pilgrimage to go (h.) able fut. compl./
   The monks who live in India will be able to go to Tibet on a pilgrimage.
c. སློབ་ཕྲུག་དེ་ལ་དངུལ་མང་པོ་མེད་སྟབས་འཛོན་ཆས་ཉོ་ཐུབ་མ་སོང་།
   student that to money much no exist because furniture buy able not went compl./
   Because that student hasn't got much money, (he) was unable to buy furniture.
d. ད་ལོ་ཞིང་ཁ་མང་པོ་བཏབ་ཐུབ་ཙང་ཞིང་པ་ཚོས་ཅ་ལག་ཞེ་དྲགས་ཉོ་ཐུབ་པ་བྱུང་བ་རེད།

this year field many planted able because farmer pl.-by thing very much buy able past compl./

Because they were able to plant many fields this year, farmers were able to buy many things.

e. མོ་དོ་དགོང་ཁྲོམ་ལ་འགྲོ་ཐུབ་ན་ཤ་དང་ཚལ་ཉོ་གི་རེད།

she tonight market to go able if meat and vegetable buy fut. compl./

If she is able to go to the market tonight, (she) will buy meat and vegetables.

f. འདམ་སེང་དེས་མཆོངས་མ་ཐུབ་ཙང་རི་བོང་ཐར་པ་རེད།

lion that by jump no able because rabbit escape past compl./

Because the lion was unable to jump, the rabbit escaped.

6.10 Reading exercise: "A Wolf Has Arrived"

6.10.1 Tibetan text

སྤྱང་ཀི་སླེབས་བྱུང་།

གཙང་རྒྱལ་རྩེ་རྫོང་ཁོངས་སུ་ཕྲུ་གུ་ཞིག་གིས་ཉིན་ལྟར་ལུག་ཁྱུ་གཅིག་དེད་ནས་རི་སྐྱེད་དུ་འཚོ་བར་འགྲོ་ཡི་ཡོད། ཉིན་ཞིག་ཕྲུ་གུ་དེས་བློ་ཕྱུར་དུ་སྤྱང་ཀི་སླེབས་བྱུང་ཞེས་སྐད་ཐེངས་ཁ་ཤས་བརྒྱབ། རི་ལྡེབས་སུ་ཞིང་ཁ་འདེབས་མཁན་དང་། མི་ཤིང་འཐུ་མཁན་ཚོས་སྤྱང་ཀི་སླེབས་བྱུང་ཞེས་པའི་འབོད་སྒྲ་ཐོས་མ་ཐག་ཚང་མས་ལས་ཀ་བཞག་ནས་ཟོར་ར་དང་ཏོ་མ་བཅས་འཁྱེར་ཏེ་ལུག་སྐྱོབ་པར་ཡོང་། མི་རྣམས་ཕྲུ་གུའི་འགྲམ་དུ་སླེབས་སྐབས་ལུག་རྣམས་རྩ་ཟ་བཞིན་ཡོད་པ་མཐོང་ནས་ཚང་མས་ཕྲུ་གུ་དེར་སྤྱང་ཀི་ག་པར་འདུག་གམ་ཞེས་སྐད་ཆ་འདྲི་སྐབས་ཁོ་པས་ཧ་ཧ་ཞེས་གད་མོ་དགོད་ཀྱི་ཡོད། དེ་ནི་ཕྲུ་གུ་དེས་རྩེད་མོ་རྩེ་ཀྱི་ཡོད་པ་ཤེས་སྐབས་ཚང་མ་ཁོང་ཁྲོ་ཟས་ནས་ཕྲུ་གུ་དེར་སྐྱོན་བརྗོད་བྱས་རྗེས་ལས་ཀ་བྱེད་པར་ལོག་ཕྱིན། ཉིན་ཤས་སོང་རྗེས་མི་རྣམས་ཀྱིས་ལས་ཀ་བྱེད་པའི་སྐབས་སུ་སླར་ཡང་ལུག་རྫི་ཆུང་ཆུང་དེས་སྤྱང་ཀི་སླེབས་བྱུང་། སྤྱང་ཀི་སླེབས་བྱུང་། ཞེས་སྐད་བརྒྱབ་པ་ཐོས་ཏེ་ཚང་མས་སྔར་བཞིན་ལས་ཀ་བཞག་ནས་ཟོར་ར་དང་། ཏོ་མ་འཁྱེར་ནས་ལུག་སྐྱོབ་པར་ཡོང་། ཡིན་ན་ཡང་མི་རྣམས་ལུག་རྫི་དེའི་རྩ་ལ་སླེབས་དུས་སྤྱང་ཀི་མིང་ཙམ་སླར་ཡང་ཕྲུ་གུ་དེས་མགོ་སྐོར་བཏང་བ་མི་རྣམས་ཀྱིས་ཤེས་ནས་ཕྲུ་གུ་དེར་གཤེ་གཤེ་བཏང་བ་དང་ནང་ལ་ལོག་ཕྱིན་པ་རེད། དེ་ནས་སླར་ཡང་ཉིན་ཁ་ཤས་སོང་རྗེས་ཕྲུ་གུ་དེས་སྤྱང་ཀི་སླེབས་བྱུང་། སྤྱང་ཀི་སླེབས་བྱུང་། མགྱོགས་པོ་སྤྱང་ཀི་གསོད་པར་ཤོག་ཅེས་སྐད་ཆེན་པོ་བརྒྱབ། ཡིན་ནའང་རོགས་རམ་བྱེད་མཁན་མ་སླེབས། འོན་ཀྱང་ད་རེས་ནི་སྤྱང་ཀི་དངོས་འབྲེལ་སླེབས་ཤིང་། སྤྱང་གིས་ཁ་ཆེན་པོ་གདང་བཞིན་པར་ལུག་ལ་སོ་བརྒྱབ་པ་དང་། ཕྲུ་གུ་ཆུང་ཆུང་དེར་ཡང་སོ་རྒྱག་པར་ཡོང་། ཕྲུ་གུ་དེས་སྤྱང་ཀི་སླེབས་བྱུང་། སྤྱང་ཀི་སླེབས་བྱུང་། མགྱོགས་པོ་སྤྱང་ཀི་གསོད་པར་ཤོག་ཞེས་སྐད་རྒྱག་བཞིན་དུ་བྲོས་ཕྱིན། འོན་ཀྱང་ཁོ་པར་སྐྱོབ་པར་ཡོང་མཁན་གཅིག་ཀྱང་མ་བྱུང་། སྐབས་ལེགས་པ་ཞིག་ལ་ཕྲུ་གུ་དེ་རི་ལྡེབས་ནས་མར་རིལ་སྐབས་ཁོ་པའི་སྲོག་ཐར་ཐུབ་པ་རེད། འོན་ཀྱང་ཁོ་པའི་ལུག་ཁྱུ་རྣམས་སྤྱང་ཀིས་ཚང་མ་བཟོས་སོ།།

6.10.2 Interlinear translation

wolf arrive past

1. tsang gyantse district belong to child one by day every sheep herd one herd having hill on to look-after inf. go usu. compl./ one day child
2. that-by suddenly wolf arrive past quote voice times several did/ hill side to field plant agentive and/ firewood collect
3. agentive pl.-by wolf arrive past quote-gen. cry heard as-soon all-by work leave having sickle and axe etc. carry having sheep
4. save-inf. come/ person plural child-of side to arrive time sheep plural grass eat pres. compl. see having all-by child that-to wolf
5. where exist ?/ quote ask when he-by ha ha quote laugh pres. compl./ that as-for child that-by play pres. compl. nom.
6. know because all angry having child that-to criticize did after work do infinitive return went/ day few went after people plural by
7. work do when to again shepherd small that-by wolf arrive past/ wolf arrive past/ quote yelled nom. heard
8. having all-by before like work leave having sickle and/ axe carry having sheep save infinitive come/ nevertheless person plural shepherd
9. that-of presence to arrive when wolf no-exist because again child that-by trick nom. people plural by know having child that-to scold did
10. and home to return went compl./ that after (from) again day several went after child that-by wolf arrive past/ wolf arrive past/
11. quick wolf kill infinitivecome quote say loud did/ however help do agentive no arrive/ however this-time
12. as-for wolf really arrive having/ wolf-by mouth big open manner-to sheep to bite and/ child small that-to
13. even bite infinitive come/ child that-by wolf arrive past/ wolf arrive past/ quick wolf kill infinitive come quote
14. yell manner fled went/ however, he-to save infinitive come agentive one even no got/ fortunately child that-to hill
15. side from downward fall because he-of life escape able past compl./ however he-of sheep herd plural wolf-by all ate sentence-final

6.10.3 Translation

A Wolf Has Arrived

In Tsang's Gyantse district, every day a child would herd a flock of sheep, going to look after them in the mountains. One day, that child suddenly shouted several times, "A wolf has arrived." As soon as those who were collecting firewood and farming on the side of the mountain heard the shout "A wolf has arrived," everyone left their work and came carrying sickles and pickaxes to protect the sheep. When they arrived in the presence of the child, (they) saw the sheep grazing on grass and when all asked the boy, "Where is the wolf?" he laughed, "ha ha." As for that, they knew then the boy was playing a trick on them and got angry and criticized the boy. Then they returned to work. A few days after that when the people were working, once again (they) heard that small shepherd yell out, "A wolf has arrived. A wolf has arrived." As before, (when) they heard (this), all left their work carrying sickles and pickaxes and came to protect the sheep. However, when the people arrived in the presence of the shepherd, because there was no wolf, the people again knew that the child had tricked them. (They) scolded the child and (then) returned home. After that, after a few days had passed, once again the child cried out loudly, "A wolf has arrived. A wolf has arrived. Come quickly to kill the wolf." Nevertheless, no helpers came. However, that day a wolf really arrived. The wolf opening his mouth wide, bit (the) sheep and came to bite that child. The child fled shouting, "A wolf has arrived. A wolf has arrived. Come quickly to kill the wolf." Nevertheless, not even one person came to save him. Fortunately, because that child fell down the side of the mountain, he escaped (death). However, the wolf ate his entire herd of sheep.

6.10.4 Grammatical notes

1. The first segment consists of the title: སྤྱང་ཀི་སླེབས་བྱུང་.

The title is a quotation from the story. It is a simple involuntary verb construction so the subject, wolf (སྤྱང་ཀི་), is not placed in the instrumental case. The verb སླེབས་ is a one stem verb whose tense is determined by the verbal complement བྱུང་.

One might expect that the སོང་ third person past complement would have been used with སླེབས་ instead of the བྱུང་ first person past complement. However, བྱུང་ is used here to convey that the wolf arrived at the location where the speaker is. This is a common rule. For example, while སོང་ is used in ཁོ་བོད་ལ་སླེབས་སོང་ ("He arrived in Tibet"), བྱུང་ is used in ཁོ་འདིར་སླེབས་བྱུང་ ("He arrived here"). Similarly, the sentence ཁོ་ཁ་སང་སླེབས་བྱུང་ ("He arrived yesterday") conveys that "he" came to the place where the speaker is.

2. The second segment consists of two clauses: 1. གཙང་རྒྱལ་རྩེ་རྫོང་ཁོངས་སུ་ཕྲུ་གུ་ཞིག་གིས་ཉིན་ལྟར་ལུག་ཁྱུ་གཅིག་དེད་ནས་ 2. རི་སྐྱེད་དུ་འཚོ་བར་འགྲོ་ཡི་ཡོད་.

The first clause states where the action occurred—in an unnamed place that belongs to or is a part of (ཁོངས་སུ་) Tsang (province)'s Gyantse district (རྫོང་). It is followed by the subject marked by the instrumental case particle (ཕྲུ་གུ་ཞིག་གིས་ - "by a child"). Because of the instrumental particle, we know that an active verb will appear somewhere down the line. But first a time-slot phrase is used: ཉིན་ལྟར་ ("every day"). This is followed by the object (ལུག་ཁྱུ་གཅིག་ - "a flock of sheep") and then the active verb (དེད་ - "herded").

Together they convey the meaning: "In (a place) belonging to Tsang's Gyantse district, a child herded a flock of sheep every day."

This is linked to the second clause by the ནས་ clause connective which here conveys: 1) that the second clause occurred simultaneously with the first clause, and 2) clarifies *how* the first clause occurred: he herded them in the manner of going to look after them in the mountains.

The second clause implicitly continues the subject ("the child") from the first clause, elaborating on what he did and where. It begins with a location phrase telling where the main verb (འགྲོ་ - "go") occurred, i.e., "on (or in) the mountain" (རི་སྟེང་དུ་). This is followed by the infinitive phrase "goes *to* look after/ take care of" (འཚོ་བར་འགྲོ་ཡི་ཡོད), which breaks down into the main verb འགྲོ་ ("to go") and the infintivized verb འཚོ་བར་ ("to take care of/ look after"). The object, the sheep flock, is implicit.

The second clause ends with the usual verb complement ཡི་ཡོད་, the clause thus meaning, "goes to look after in the mountains." Both clauses together mean, "A child was herding a flock of sheep every day by going to look after (them) in the mountains."

3. The third segment consists of one sentence that contains a quotation: ཉིན་ཞིག་ཕྲུ་གུ་དེས་གློ་བུར་དུ་སྤྱང་ཀི་སླེབས་བྱུང་ཞེས་སྐད་ཐེངས་ཁ་ཤས་བརྒྱབ།.

It begins with the time-slot term ཉིན་ཞིག་ ("one day"), followed by the subject modified by a demonstrative in the instrumental case (ཕྲུ་གུ་དེས་ - "by that child"). This is followed by the adverbial phrase གློ་བུར་དུ་ ("suddenly"), which modifies the main active verb སྐད་བརྒྱབ་ ("shouted"). Thus, the subject "suddenly shouted."

What he shouted follows in the form of a simple involuntary sentence meaning "A wolf has arrived" (སྤྱང་ཀི་སླེབས་བྱུང་). It is immediately followed by the quotation marking particle and the main active verb. However, the main verb phrase is split by another adverbial phrase meaning "several times" (ཐེངས་ཁ་ཤས་). Thus, "That child suddenly shouted several times."

4. The fourth segment consists of 4 clauses: 1.རི་ཕྱིབས་སུ་ཞིང་ཁ་འདེབས་མཁན་དང་། མེ་ཤིང་འཐུ་མཁན་ཚོས་སྤྱང་ཀི་སླེབས་བྱུང་ཞེས་པའི་འབོད་སྒྲ་ཐོས་མ་ཐག 2. ཚང་མས་ལས་ཀ་བཞག་ནས་ 3. ཟོར་ར་དང་ཏྲེ་མ་བཅས་འཁྱེར་ཏེ་ 4. ལུག་སྐྱོབ་པར་ཡོང་.

The long first clause has as its core a simple involuntary verb construction: subject ("the planters and firewood collectors") + verb ("heard" - ཐོས་) + object ("a cry/shout" - འབོད་སྒྲ་). The rest of the clause elaborates this event.

The clause begins with a phrase telling the location of the action: "on the face/side of the mountain" (རི་ཕྱིབས་སུ་). It is followed by a compound subject (x+y), each half of which is a nominalized phrase. The first half of the subject is ཞིང་ཁ་འདེབས་མཁན་("persons who were planting fields"). This phrase has been nominalized by the agentive particle མཁན་, which was discussed in 5.16.

This is linked to the other half of the subject by the conjunctive particle དང་ ("and"). It is also a verbal phrase that has been nominalized by the agentive particle མཁན་ ("persons who were collecting firewood"). It is followed by ཚོས་, which consists of a pluralizing particle (ཚོ་) and the instrumental particle ས་. This conveys that there were a number of "firewood collectors" and "sowers," and that they did something, i.e., that they are the subject of an active sentence.

This is followed by a quotation of what the child said ("A wolf has arrived" - སྤྱང་ཀི་སླེབས་བྱུང་), followed in turn by the quotation particle ཞེས་. However, the quotation particle is part of a nominalized construction ཞེས་པའི་འབོད་སྒྲ་ ("a cry which said . . ."). Finally we get the involuntary verb ཐོས་, which means "to hear." Thus the subject heard the boy crying out, "A wolf has arrived." Note that we know this is a subordinate verb since it is involuntary—it cannot convey the action of the subject in the instrumental case.

This clause is linked to the next by the "immediate" clause connective མ་ཐག་ ("as soon as"—see 6.2). Thus the clause finally says, "As soon as the sowers and collectors heard the cry which said . . . ."

The second clause (ཚང་མས་ལས་ཀ་བཞག་ནས་) starts to explain what action they took when they heard this. It begins with a subject in the instrumental case ("by everyone" - ཚང་མས་) followed by the verbal phrase ལས་ཀ་བཞག་. This breaks down into the noun "work" (ལས་ཀ་) and the verb "to leave" (བཞག་), so that the clause means "everyone left (his) work." This is linked to the next clause by the ནས་ clause connective which here conveys a temporal relationship: having done A, B took place.

Clause three (ཟོར་ར་དང་ཏོག་མ་བཅས་འཁྱེར་ཏེ་) explains what took place. It has an implicit subject from clause two (i.e., ཚང་མས་). It begins with a compound object phrase, "sickle and pickaxe" (ཟོར་ར་དང་ཏོག་མ་), followed by the inclusive particle བཅས་, which indicates that this listing of the two items is exhaustive (see 6.4). This is followed by the verb "carry" (འཁྱེར་) and the clause connective ཏེ་, which indicates simultaneous action with the next clause. Thus this clause means that while someone was "carrying pickaxes and sickles," simultaneously something happened.

Clause four (ལུག་སྐྱོབ་པར་ཡོང་) indicates what was done simultaneous with carrying the implements. It consists of a noun ("sheep") serving as the object of the infinitivized verb phrase "came *to* protect" (སྐྱོབ་པར་ཡོང་). Thus, clauses three and four convey, "carrying sickles and pickaxes, (everyone) came to protect (or save) the sheep."

The structure of the entire segment is: — ཚོས་ — ཐོས་མ་ཐག་ — བཞག་ནས་ — འཁྱེར་ཏེ་

—ལུག་སྐྱོབ་པར་ཡོང་.

5. The fifth segment consists of four clauses: 1. མི་རྣམས་ཕྲུ་གུའི་འགྲམ་དུ་སླེབས་སྐབས་ 2. ལུག་རྣམས་རྩྭ་ཟ་བཞིན་ཡོད་པ་མཐོང་ནས་ 3. ཚང་མས་ཕྲུ་གུ་དེར་སྤྱང་ཀི་ག་པར་འདུག་གམ་ཞེས་སྐད་ཆ་འདྲི་སྐབས་ 4. ཁོ་པས་ཧ་ཧ་ཞེས་གད་མོ་དགོད་ཀྱི་ཡོད།.

The first clause is an involuntary sentence, so the subject, "people" (མི་རྣམས་), is not in the instrumental case. Note that རྣམས་ is a pluralizing particle that is equivalent to ཚོ་ encountered above. This is followed by the object phrase ཕྲུ་གུའི་འགྲམ་དུ་, which means "to the side of the child," and explains where the people "arrived" (སླེབས་). The སྐབས་ clause connective links this clause to clause two, indicating that "when" the first clause took place, the second occurred.

The second clause (ལུག་རྣམས་རྩྭ་ཟ་བཞིན་ཡོད་པ་མཐོང་ནས་) is an involuntary construction conveying that an unspecified subject ("the people" from the previous clause) saw (མཐོང་) something. What they saw was: རྩྭ་ཟ་བཞིན་ཡོད་པ་ ("sheep eating grass"). Note that the use of པ་ converts the present tense phrase "eating grass" (རྩྭ་ཟ་བཞིན་ཡོད་) into a nominalized phrase that we can translate as "the eating of grass." This then functions as the object of the verb "saw." What did they see?—they saw "the eating of grass by the sheep." The clause connective ནས་ conveys that the first clause having occurred, the next clause took place.

The third clause (ཚང་མས་ཕྲུ་གུ་དེར་སྤྱང་ཀི་ག་པར་འདུག་གམ་ཞེས་སྐད་ཆ་འདྲི་སྐབས་) begins with a subject in the instrumental case (ཚང་མས་ - "by everyone") followed by the object ཕྲུ་གུ་དེར་ ("to that child"). Next comes the direct quote, "Where is the wolf?" (སྤྱང་ཀི་ག་པར་འདུག་གམ་), followed by the quotation marker ཞེས་. The clause ends with the active verb "asked" (སྐད་ཆ་འདྲི་). Thus the clause says, "Everyone asked the child, 'Where is the wolf?'" The "when" clause connective (སྐབས་) links this clause with the next one.

The fourth clause (ཁོ་པས་ཧ་ཧ་ཞེས་གད་མོ་དགོད་ཀྱི་ཡོད་) starts with a pronoun ("he") in the instrumental case (ཁོ་པས་). This is followed by a quote "ha ha" (ཧ་ཧ་) and the quotation particle. Next comes the active verb phrase "laughing" (གད་མོ་དགོད་ཀྱི་ཡོད་). Together these mean, "He was laughing 'ha ha.'"

6. The sixth segment consists of four clauses: 1. དེ་ནི་ཕྲུ་གུ་དེས་རྩེད་མོ་རྩེ་ཀྱི་ཡོད་པ་ཤེས་སྐབས་ 2. ཚང་མ་ཁོང་ཁྲོ་ཟས་ནས་ 3. ཕྲུ་གུ་དེར་སྐྱོན་བརྗོད་བྱས་རྗེས་ 4. ལས་ཀ་བྱེད་པར་ལོག་ཕྱིན་.

The first clause parallels the structure of the second clause discussed immediately above in that it contains a direct object construction that is a nominalized verb phrase created by པ་. The subject of this clause is implicit, i.e., it continues to be "everyone" (ཚང་མས་). The verb is "knew" (ཤེས་). What everyone knew, the direct object, is a nominalized verb phrase: "the joking around by that child" (ཕྲུ་གུ་དེས་རྩེད་མོ་རྩེ་ཀྱི་ཡོད་པ་). In other words, the simple active sentence, "The child was joking around" (ཕྲུ་གུ་དེས་ཅེད་མོ་ཅེ་ཀྱི་ཡོད་), was nominalized by པ་ to become "the joking around by that child." The "because" clause connective (སྐབས་) links this to the next clause.

Clause two is an involuntary sentence whose subject is everyone (ཚང་མ་) without the instrumental particle. It is followed by the involuntary verb "got angry" (ཁོང་ཁྲོ་ཟས་). The clause connective ནས་ again conveys *X having happened, Y occurred.*.

The subject in clause three is again implicit (i.e., "by everyone"). In this clause we first encounter the object phrase "to that child" (ཕྲུ་གུ་དེར་), followed by the verb phrase "scolded" (སྐྱོན་བརྗོད་བྱས་). The clause ends with the "after" clause connective (རྗེས་).

The final clause is an infinitive construction. The verbal phrase "work" is infinitivized by the dative-locative particle (ལས་ཀ་བྱེད་པར་), and is followed by a compound verb of motion (ལོག་ཕྱིན་), which means "returned." Thus the subject (again "everyone") "returned *to* do work."

Note that ལོག་ཕྱིན་ consists of two verbs, "return" and "went," which together convey, "returning went." This is a common pattern used to convey two simultaneous actions, one of which (the second verb) is "going" or "coming." For example, ཁོས་དེབ་གཅིག་འཁྱེར་ཡོང་བ་རེད་ means, "He came carrying a book."

Thus the core structure of this segment is —ཤེས་སྐབས་, —ཁོང་ཁྲོ་ཟས་ནས་, —སྐྱོན་བརྗོད་བྱས་རྗེས་, — ལོག་ཕྱིན་.

7. The seventh segment consists of five clauses: 1. ཉིན་ཤས་སོང་རྗེས་མི་རྣམས་ཀྱིས་ལས་ཀ་བྱེད་པའི་སྐབས་སུ་ 2. སླར་ཡང་ལུག་རྫི་ཆུང་ཆུང་དེས་སྤྱང་ཀི་སླེབས་བྱུང་། སྤྱང་ཀི་སླེབས་བྱུང་། ཞེས་སྐད་བརྒྱབ་པ་གོས་ཏེ་ 3. ཚང་མས་སྔར་བཞིན་ལས་ཀ་བཞག་ནས་ 4. ཟོར་ར་དང་། ཀོ་མ་འཁྱེར་ནས་ 5. ལུག་སྐྱོབ་པར་ཡོང་།.

The first clause begins with the short phrase ཉིན་ཤས་སོང་རྗེས་. It is a standard construction meaning "after several days" and can be treated simply as another time-slot phrase. It is followed by a subject in the instrumental case (མི་རྣམས་ཀྱིས་ - "by people") and then an active verb "working" (ལས་ཀ་བྱེད་). The clause ends with the "when" clause connective (པའི་སྐབས་སུ་). Thus together they mean, "After several days, when the people were working."

The second clause begins with an adverbial term meaning "once again" (སླར་ཡང་), followed by an active sentence whose core is ལུག་རྫི་ཆུང་ཆུང་དེས་ . . . སྐད་བརྒྱབ་ ("by that small herder . . . cried out"). Between these is what the small herder called out—སྤྱང་ཀི་སླེབས་བྱུང་། སྤྱང་ཀི་སླེབས་བྱུང་ ("a wolf has arrived, a wolf has arrived") plus the quotation particle (ཞེས་). This active sentence is then nominalized by པ་, becoming "the shouting 'a wolf has come, a wolf has come,' by the small herder"). This acts as the object of the verb "heard" (གོས་). He heard what?—"He heard the shouting 'a wolf has come, a wolf has come' by the small herder." The clause ends with the ཏེ་ clause connective which here conveys "after."

Clause three begins with a subject in the instrumental case ("by everyone" - ཚང་མས་) followed by the term "like before" (སྔར་བཞིན་). Then comes the active verb phrase and clause connective "having left (their) work" (ལས་ཀ་བཞག་ནས་).

Clause four uses "by everyone" as its implicit subject, and begins with the object phrase "sickles and pickaxes" (ཟོར་ར་དང་། ཏོག་མ་). Then the active verb "take/carry" (འཁྱེར་ནས་) appears with the ནས་ clause connective, conveying, "having taken (their) sickles and pickaxes."

Clause five is the infinitivized verb phrase encountered earlier, meaning "came to protect the sheep" (ལུག་སྐྱོབ་པར་ཡོང་).

8. The eighth segment consists of five clauses: 1. ཡིན་ན་ཡང་མི་རྣམས་ལུག་རྫི་དེའི་རྩ་ལ་སླེབས་དུས་ 2. སྤྱང་ཀི་མེད་ཙང་ 3. སླར་ཡང་ཕྲུ་གུ་དེས་མགོ་སྐོར་བཏང་བ་མི་རྣམས་ཀྱིས་ཤེས་ནས་ 4. ཕྲུ་གུ་དེར་གཤེ་གཤེ་བཏང་བ་དང་ 5. ནང་ལ་ལོག་ཕྱིན་པ་རེད།.

The first clause is a simple involuntary construction: "The people arrived" (མི་རྣམས་སླེབས). Between the subject and the verb is a phrase telling where they arrived: "in the presence of that herder" (ལུག་རྫི་དེའི་རྩ་ལ་). The "when" connective (དུས་) links this to the next clause.

Clause two is a simple negative existential sentence with the "because" clause connective: "because there was no wolf" (སྤྱང་ཀི་མེད་ཙང་).

Clause three begins with "once again" (སླར་ཡང་), followed by a nominalized phrase that acts as the object: "the tricking [in past tense] by that child" (ཕྲུ་གུ་དེས་མགོ་སྐོར་བཏང་བ་). This is followed by the subject in the instrumental (མི་རྣམས་ཀྱིས་) and the verb "knew" (ཤེས་). Thus clauses two and three convey, "Because there was no wolf, the people once again knew that the child had tricked (them)."

Clause four begins with the object (ཕྲུ་གུ་དེར་ - "to that child") followed by the active verb "scolded" (གཤེ་གཤེ་བཏང་). The subject is implicit ("by the people"). This clause is connected to the next clause of the segment by the conjunctive clause connective "and" (བ་དང་).

Clause five is the same verbal phrase we encountered earlier: "returned home" (ནང་ལ་ལོག་ཕྱིན་པ་རེད). Thus clauses four and five convey, "The people scolded the child and returned home."

9. The ninth segment consists of two clauses: 1. དེ་ནས་སླར་ཡང་ཉིན་ཁ་ཤས་སོང་རྗེས་ 2. ཕྲུ་གུ་དེས་སྤྱང་ཀི་སླེབས་བྱུང་། སྤྱང་ཀི་སླེབས་བྱུང་། མགྱོགས་པོ་སྤྱང་ཀི་གསོད་པར་ཤོག་ཅེས་སྐད་ཆེན་པོ་བརྒྱབ།

The first clause functions primarily to set the time, conveying "after that" (དེ་ནས་), "once again" (སླར་ཡང་), and "after several days passed" (ཉིན་ཁ་ཤས་སོང་རྗེས་).

The second clause is the same as encountered earlier except that an added infinitivized phrase occurs that means "come to kill the wolf quickly" (མགྱོགས་པོ་སྤྱང་ཀི་གསོད་པར་ཤོག). This is followed by a quotation marker (ཅེས་) and the verbal phrase "cried/ called out loudly" (སྐད་ཆེན་པོ་བརྒྱབ). Note that the adjective "big" (ཆེན་པོ་) here functions as an adverb and is translated as "loudly."

10. The tenth segment consists of a single sentence: ཡིན་ནའང་རོགས་རམ་བྱེད་མཁན་མ་སླེབས་.

It begins with "nevertheless" (ཡིན་ནའང་), followed by a phrase nominalized by the "agentive particle" (རོགས་རམ་བྱེད་མཁན་ - "ones who help"). It ends with the negative verb: "not arrived" (མ་སླེབས་). Thus, "Nevertheless, helpers did not arrive."

11. The eleventh segment consists of three clauses: 1. འོན་ཀྱང་ད་རེས་ནི་སྤྱང་ཀི་དངོས་འབྱོལ་སླེབས་ཤིང། 2. སྤྱང་ཀིས་ཁ་ཆེན་པོ་གདང་བཞིན་པར་ལུག་ལ་སོ་བརྒྱབ་པ་དང་། 3. ཕྲུ་གུ་ཆུང་ཆུང་དེ་ར་ཡང་སོ་རྒྱག་པར་ཡོང་།.

This clause begins with another word that conveys "nevertheless" (འོན་ཀྱང་), followed by the time-slot word "as for this time" (ད་རེས་ནི་). This is followed by the subject of an involuntary sentence, "the wolf," and then an adverb meaning "really" (དངོས་འབྱོལ་) and the verb "arrived." Together these convey, "Nevertheless, this time a wolf really arrived."

12. The twelfth segment consists of a single sentence: ཕྲུ་གུ་དེས་སྤྱང་ཀི་སླེབས་བྱུང་། སྤྱང་ཀི་སླེབས་བྱུང་། མགྱོགས་པོ་སྤྱང་ཀི་གསོད་པར་ཤོག་ཞེས་སྐད་རྒྱག་བཞིན་དུ་བྲོས་ཕྱིན།.

This segment is the same as earlier ones with the exception of the verb phrase སྐད་རྒྱག་བཞིན་དུ་བྲོས་ཕྱིན་. In this phrase བཞིན་དུ་ adverbializes "to shout" so that it modifies the compound verb construction "fled went" (བྲོས་ཕྱིན་), conveying how he "fled," i.e., he "fled shouting."

13. The thirteenth segment consists of a single sentence: འོན་ཀྱང་ཁོ་པར་སྐྱོབ་པར་ཡོང་མཁན་གཅིག་ཀྱང་མ་རྙེད་།.

This involuntary sentence again begins with "nevertheless." Then comes the subject in the dative-locative ("to him" - ཁོ་པར་), followed by a nominalized infinitive verb phrase ("ones who come to protect" - སྐྱོབ་པར་ཡོང་མཁན་). The negativized verb that goes with this means "not got" (མ་རྙེད་). Thus, literally, "he (to him) did not get anyone coming to help." The term གཅིག་ཀྱང་ ("even one") modifies the verb, conveying that he got "not even one person coming to help."

14. The fourteenth segment consists of two clauses: 1. སྐབས་ལེགས་པ་ཞིག་ལ་ཕྲུ་གུ་དེ་རི་ཕྲིབས་ནས་མར་རིལ་སྐབས་ 2. ཁོ་པའི་སྲོག་ཐར་ཐུབ་པ་རེད།.

The first clause is an involuntary sentence whose core is ཕྲུ་གུ་དེ་ . . . རིལ་ ("that child . . . fell"). It starts with a standard term meaning "fortunately" or "luckily" (སྐབས་ལེགས་པ་ཞིག་ལ་). This is followed by the subject, and then a phrase telling the location of the verbal action, i.e., where he fell—"from the side of the mountain" (རི་ལྡེབས་ནས་). The word མར་ means downward and modifies the verb "to fall." This clause is linked to the next by a "because" clause connective (སྟབས་).

The second clause is also an involuntary sentence. It begins with a subject consisting of the possessive phrase "his life" (ཁོ་པའི་སྲོག་) and then the involuntary verb "escaped" (ཐར་), followed by the verb "to be able" (ཐུབ་). Together these convey, "His life was able to escape," or in better English, "He escaped with his life."

15. The last segment consists of a single sentence: འོན་ཀྱང་ཁོ་པའི་ལུག་ཁྱུ་རྣམས་སྤྱང་ཀིས་ཚང་མ་བཟོས་སོ།།.

It starts with "nevertheless," and then the object phrase "his sheep flock" (ཁོ་པའི་ལུག་ཁྱུ་རྣམས་). This is followed by the subject marked by the instrumental case particle ("by the wolf" - སྤྱང་ཀིས་). Then comes the adverbial "all" or "completely" (ཚང་མ་) and the final verb "ate" (བཟོས་) with the sentence final particle སོ. Thus, "Nevertheless, the wolf ate his sheep flock completely."

6.11 Vocabulary

ཀྲུང་གོ་ ch. China (drūŋgo)

ཀྲའོ་ཙི་དབྱང་ p.n. Zhao Ziyang (drāo dzīyaŋ)

ཀོ་མ་ pick axe (gōma)

སྐད་ཆ་ conversation, speech; va. — འདྲི་ to ask (gɛ̄ja tri̱)

སྐད་ཡིག་ spoken and written language, speech and writing (gɛ̄yiì)

སྐྱོན་བརྗོད་ criticism, criticizing; va. — བྱེད to criticize (gyōnjöö che̱è)

སྐྱོ་པོ་ with སེམས་ = sad (sēm gyōbo)

སྐྱོབ་ va. to save, to protect (gyōb)

ཁ་ mouth; va. — གདང་ to open one's mouth (kā da̱ŋ)

ཁག་པོ་ difficult (kāgo)

ཁུལ་ "pretend" clause connective, (kūū)

ཁུལ་བྱས་ "pretend" clause connective, (kūū che̱ɛ̀)

ཁོ་པ་ he (kōba)

ཁོངས་(སུ་) part of, belonging to (kōŋsu)

ཁོས་ he (by) (kȫȫ)

ཁྱུ་ herd, flock (kyū)

ཁྱོད་ you (nh.) (kyȫȫ)

གད་མོ་ laugh, laughter; vi. — དགོད་ to laugh (ge̱e̱mo ge̱ɛ̀)

གལ་ཏེ་ "if" clause connective (ke̱e̱de)

གལ་སྲིད་ "if" clause connective (ke̱e̱siì)

གྲ་སྒྲིག་ preparation; va. — བྱེད to prepare (tra̱dri che̱è)

གྲོ་ཞིབ་ flour (tru̱shi)

གླ་ཆ་ wages (lāja)

གློ་བུར་ (དུ་) sudden(ly) (lōburtu)

གློག་བརྙན་ movie (lɔ̄ɔ̄ñɛn)

དགའ་སྤྲོ་ happiness, joy (ga̱dro)

དགའ་བསུ་ welcoming; va. — ཞུ་ to

	welcome (gəsu shu)
དགོད་	va. laugh (göö)
མགོ་བསྐོར་	trick, trickery; va. — གཏོང་ to trick (go gɔ̄ɔ or gogɔɔ dōŋ)
མགྱོགས་པོ་	quick, quickly (gyogo)
འགྱུར་	vi. to become, to change into (gyur)
མགྲོན་ཁང་	hotel, guest house (dröngan)
འགྲམ་དུ་	to/at the side, near to (dramdu)
རྒྱལ་ཁབ་	nation (gyɛɛgəb)
རྒྱལ་རྩེ་	name of a town in Tsang area (gyandze)
རྒྱུ་	see 6.7 (gyu)
རྒྱུ་མཚན་	reason (gyumdzɛn)
སྒོ་ནས་	adverbializer (in the manner of) (gonɛ)
ངང་ནས་	adverbializer (in the manner of) (ŋaŋnɛ)
དངོས་འབྲེལ་	really (ŋõnɛɛ̀)
སྔོན་མ་	formerly, in the past (ŋõnma)
བཅས་	enumerative particle (jɛ̄ɛ̀)
བཅས་པའི་	including (jɛ̄bee)
ཆང་ཁང་	bar, tavern (chāŋgan)
ཆོས་ལྡན་	p.n. Chunden (chõnden)
ཆོས་ར་	the study and debating area in a monastery (chõra)
འཆར་གཞི་	plan (chə̃əshi)
ཇ་	tea (cha)
ཉིད་དུ་	"as soon as" clause connective (ñiitu)
ཉིན་ཤས་	several days (ñinshɛɛ̀)
ཉེས་པ་	punishment; va. — གཏོང་ to punish (ñēba dōŋ)
རྙིང་མ་	old (antique) (ñiŋmə)
གཏན་འཁེལ་	va. to decide (dɛ̄n kēē)
བཏང་ཡིག་	letter (correspondence) (dəŋyig)
བརྟན་པོ་	firm (dɛ̄mbo)
བརྟེན་	because (dēn)
བལྟས་	va. p. of ལྟ་ (dɛ̄ɛ̀)
སྐབས་ལེགས་པ་ཞིག་ལ་	id. fortunately (dəb legbəshiglə)
སྟེང་	on, on top of; the upper part (dēŋ)
ཐ་མག་	cigarette; va. — འཐེན་ to smoke (tāmaà tēn)
ཐར་	vi. to escape, to get free (tār)
ཐུབ་	vi. to be able (tūb)
ཐེངས་གཅིག་	one time (tēŋ jig)
ཐོན་	va. to leave, to depart (tõn)
ཐོབ་	vi. to win (tōb)
འཐུ་	va. to collect (tū)
འཐེན་	see ཐ་མག་
དང་བཅས་	see 6.4. e-g
དར་ཆ་	flag (tarja)
ད་རེས་	this time (tarɛɛ̀)
དེད་	va. to drive a flock, herd (teè)
དོ་དགོང་	tonight (togon)
དོ་དགོང་གི་ཁ་ལག་	dinner (togon ki kālaà)
དོན་གཅོད་ཁང་	bureau office (tönjögan)
དྲག་	vi. to recover (from an illness) (traà)
གདང་	see ཁ
བདག་པོ་	owner (daggo)
མདོག་མདོག་	"pretend" clause connective (dondoò)
འདིར་	here (dee)
འདྲི་	va. to ask (tri)

ལྡེབས་ side of (deb)
བསྡུས་ va. to collect (dǖü)
ན་ཚ illness; vi. — དྲག་ to recover from an illness (nadza traà)
ནན་ཏན་ emphatically (nɛ̄ndɛn)
ནོར་འཁྲུལ་ mistake; va. — བྱེད་ to make a mistake (nondru cheè)
གནས་སྐོར་ pilgrimage (nɛ̄ɛ̄gɔɔ)
གནོད་སྐྱོན་ harm, damage; va. — གཏོང་ to harm, damage (nöögyön dōŋ)
པ་མ་ཟད་ "not only" clause connective (bə masɛɛ̀)
པ་དག་ "as soon as" clause connective (bə daga)
པ་དེ་མ་ཐག་(ཏུ) "as soon as" clause connective (bə te matag
པ་ཙམ་ན་ "as soon as" clause connective (bə dzāmna)
པ་ཙམ་ནས་ "as soon as" clause connective (bə dzāmnɛ)
དཔལ་འབྱོར་ economy (bɛ̄njɔɔ)
འཕར་ vi. to increase (pār)
སྤྱང་ཀི་ wolf (jāŋgi, jāŋgu)
ཕྱི་རྒྱལ་ foreign, foreigner (chīgyɛɛ̀)
ཕྱི་ལོ་ next year (chīlo)
ཕྲུ་གུ་ child (trūgu, būgu)
འཕྲལ་ "as soon as" clause connective (trɛ̄ɛ)
བ་ཙམ་ན་ "as soon as" clause connective (bə dzāmna)
བ་ཙམ་ནས་ "as soon as" clause connective (bə dzāmnɛ)
བྱ་དགའ་ prize (chaga)
དབྱིན་ཇི་ English (īnji)
བྲོས་ va. p. of འབྲོས་ fled, ran away (tröö)
དབུས་མ་ middle, see བར་གླིང་
འབོད་ va. to call out (böö)
འབྲས་ rice (drɛɛ̀)
ཐད་དེ་ completely (bɛ̄t)
མ་ཐག་ "as soon as" clause connective (mataà)
མར་ down, downwards (maa)
མུ་མཐུད་ continuously, without a break or interruption (mutüü)
མེ་ཏོག་ flower (medoò)
མེ་ཤིང་ firewood (meshiŋ)
དམག་ war; va. — རྒྱག་ to make war (māà gyəb)
ཙམ་ན་ "as soon as" clause connective (dzāmna)
གཙང་ region in southwest Tibet (dzāŋ)
རྩྭ་ grass (dzā)
རྩེད་མོ་ playing, a game; va. — རྩེ་ to play (tsēēmo tsē)
རྩེས་ va. p. of རྩེ་ (see རྩེད་མོ་) (dzēè)
ཚད་མེད་ boundless (tsɛ̄mɛɛ̀)
ཚུལ་བྱས་ "pretend" clause connective (tsüü chɛɛ̀)
འཚོ་ va. to look after, to take care of (tsō)
འཛོགས་ vi. to be/get exhausted, to be out of (dzɔɔ̀)
རྫོང་ district (dzoŋ)
ཞལ་འདོན་ praying; va. — བྱེད་ or གནང་ to pray (shɛndön cheè or nāŋ)

ཞིང་ལས་	farm work (shi̱ŋlɛɛ̀)
ཞིམ་པོ་	delicious (shi̱mbu)
བཞག་	va. p. of འཇོག་: left (something) (sha̱à)
བཞུགས་	va. to sit (h.) (shu̱ù)
ཟ་	va. to eat (sa̱)
ཟོར་ར་	sickle (so̱ra)
ཟོལ་	"pretend" clause connective (sö̱ö)
གཟིགས་བསྐོར་	tour (h.) (sīīgɔɔ)
བཟོ་བཅོས་	correcting, repairing; va. — རྒྱག་ or བྱེད་ to repair (so̱bjöö gyə̱b or che̱è)
ཡག་	nominalizing particle (ya̱)
ཡག་པོ་	good (ya̱go)
ཡང་པོ་	light (not heavy) (ya̱ŋbo, ya̱ŋgo)
ཡང་སེ་	often (frequent) (ya̱ŋse)
ཡར་རྒྱས་	development, progress; va. — གཏོང་ to develop, to improve (ya̱rgyɛɛ̀ dōŋ)
ཡལ་	vi. to vanish (yɛ̱ɛ)
ཡས་	nominalizing particle (ya̱)
ཡི་གེ་	a letter in the alphabet (yi̱gi)
ཡིན་ནའང་	but, nevertheless (yi̱nayaŋ)
ཡོང་འབབ་	income (yo̱ŋbəb)
རག་	vi. to obtain, to get (ra̱à)
རང་རྒྱལ་	our country, one's own country (ra̱ŋgyɛɛ̀)
རིལ་	vi. to fall (ri̱i)
རོགས་རམ་	help, assistance; va. — བྱེད་ to help (rɔ̱ɔram che̱è)
རླུང་	wind (lūŋ)
བརླགས་	vi. p. of རླག་: lost (lāà)
ལགས་	honorific word used after names and titles (la̱à)
ལུག་ཁྱུ་	herd/ flock of sheep (lu̱gkyu)
ལུག་རྫི་	shepherd (lu̱gdzi)
ལོ་མ་	leaf (lo̱ma)
ཤར་གླིང་དབུས་མ་	Middle East (shārliŋ ǖǖmə)
ཤས་	several (abbr. of ཁ་ཤས་) (shɛ̄ɛ̀)
ཤེས་	vi. to know (shēè)
ཤོག་	vi. imp., come! (shōò)
གཤེ་གཤེ་	scolding; va. — གཏོང་.to scold (shēshe dōŋ)
སེམས་	mind (sēm)
སོ་	teeth; va. — རྒྱག་ (བརྒྱབ་) to bite (sō gyə̱b)
སོ་པ་	spy (sōba)
སོགས་	enumerative particle (sɔ̄ɔ̀)
གསལ་པོ་	clear (sɛ̄ɛ̄bo)
སླར་ཡང་	again (lāryaŋ)
སྲོག་	life (sɔ̄ɔ̀)
ཧ་གོ་	vi . to understand (hā ko̱)
ཧ་ཧ་	he he; ha ha (hāha)
ཧུར་ཐག་	diligent, energetically (hūrdaà)
ཧུར་བརྩོན་	diligent, energetically (hūrdzȍn)
ཨ་རི་	abbr. America (ə̄ri)
ཨེམ་ཆི་	doctor (ə̄mji)

Lesson Seven

7.1 The "not-only" clause connectives: མ་ཟད་, མ་ཚད་ and མི་ཚད་

These two clause connectives express the idea that "not only" did the action of the first clause occur, but also something else happened (as explained in the next clause). They are used with both past and non-past verb stems that have been nominalized by པ་/བ་ and རྒྱུ་. These nominalized verb stems sometimes occur with the dative-locative particles, e.g., པར་/བར་, or with the instrumental particles, e.g., པས་/བས་.

a. ཁོ་ཚོ་རྒྱ་ནག་ལ་ཕྱིན་པ་མ་ཟད། རི་པིན་ལ་ཕྱིན་སོང་།
 they china to went not-only/ japan to went compl./
 Not only did they go to China, (they) went to Japan.

b. ཁོ་ཚོ་རྒྱ་གར་ལ་ཕྱིན་པ་མ་ཟད། རི་པིན་ལ་འགྲོ་གི་རེད།
 they india to went not-only/ japan to go fut. compl./
 Not only did they go to India, (they) will go to Japan.

c. ཁོ་ཚོ་རྒྱ་ནག་ལ་འགྲོ་རྒྱུ་མི་ཚད། རི་པིན་ལ་འགྲོ་རྒྱུ་རེད།
 they china to go gyu not-only/ japan to go gyu fut. compl./
 Not only will they go to China, (they) will go to Japan.

Very often one of the "also/even" words such as ཡང་ and ཀྱང་ will be used in the second clause.

d. གྲྭ་པ་དང་བླ་མ་རྣམས་རྒྱ་གར་ལ་ཕེབས་པ་མ་ཟད། འབྲུག་ཡུལ་ལ་ཡང་ཕེབས་པ་རེད།
 monk and lama pl. india to go not-only/ bhutan to also go past compl./
 The monks and lamas not only went to India, (they) also went to Bhutan.

These clause connectives are also used in negative constructions.

e. ཞིང་པ་དང་འབྲོག་པར་རོགས་རམ་མ་བྱས་པ་མ་ཟད། བཟོ་པ་ལའང་བྱས་མ་སོང་།
 farmer and nomad-to help neg. did not-only/ workers to-even did neg. went compl./
 Not only did (he, she, etc.) not help the farmers and nomads, (he, she, etc.) didn't even help the workers.

f. ཁོ་ཚོས་དགོན་པ་དང་ལྷ་ཁང་གསར་པ་རྒྱག་གི་མེད་པ་མ་ཚད། དགོན་པ་རྙིང་པ་ལ་ཡང་ཉམས་གསོ་བྱེད་ཀྱི་ཡོད་པ་མ་རེད།
 he pl.-by monastery and temple new build neg. pres. compl. not-only/ monastery old to even repair do neg. pres. compl./
 Not only are they not building new monasteries and temples, (they) are not even repairing the old monasteries.

The "not-only" connectives are also used with the subjects of sentences to convey the idea of "not-only the subject, but. . . ." Subjects in such constructions are required to be in the instrumental case.

g. ཞིང་པས་མ་ཚད་འབྲོག་པ་ཡང་འདུག།

farmer-by not-only nomad also exist/

Not only are there farmers, (there are) also nomads.

7.2 The "even though" clause connectives: ཀྱང་, ཡང་, འང་, རུང་, ནའང་, ན་ཡང་, མོད་, and དེ་ (དེའི་)

These clause connectives link clauses to convey the idea that "even though" the former happened or exists, the latter occurs or exists. "But" can also be used here. The various particles are used in accordance with the final letter of the verb as shown below. Recall also that ཀྱང་, ཡང་, and འང་ are used in other contexts to convey "also" and "even."

ཀྱང་ after final ག་, ད་, བ་, and ས་ (and other words that in ancient Tibetan had a final (5-slot ད་)

ཡང་ after final ང་, ན་, མ་, ར་, and ལ་

འང་ after final འ and vowel finals

རུང་, ནའང་, མོད, དེ (དེའི་), and ན་ཡང་ after vowel finals

a. ས་ཆ་འདི་མཐོ་པོ་ཡིན་ཡང་། དགུན་ཁ་གྲང་མོ་ཞེ་དྲགས་མི་འདུག།

place this high is though/ winter cold very neg. exist/

Even though this place is high [in altitude], it is not very cold in winter.

b. མོ་ར་ཕྲུ་གུ་བཞི་ཡོད་ཀྱང་། ཉིན་ལྟར་དངུལ་ཁང་ལ་ལས་ཀ་བྱེད་པར་འགྲོ་བཞིན་ཡོད།

she-to child four exist though/ day every bank to work do inf. go usual compl./

Even though she has four children, (she) goes to work at the bank every day.

c. བོད་པའི་བཙན་བྱོལ་པ་དེས་རྒྱ་གར་ལ་ལོ་ཤས་བསྡད་རུང་། རྒྱ་གར་གྱི་སྐད་ཡིག་སློབ་སྦྱོང་མ་བྱས་པ་རེད།

tibet-of refugee that-by india year several lived though/ india of language study neg. did past compl./

Even though that Tibetan refugee lived in India for several years, (he) did not study Hindi (lit., Indian language).

d. ཕྱི་ལོ་རྒྱ་གར་ལ་སྡོད་ན་ཡང་། རྒྱ་གར་གྱི་སྐད་ཡིག་སློབ་སྦྱོང་བྱེད་ཀྱི་མ་རེད།

next year india to live though/ india of language study do neg. fut. compl./

Even though (he, she, etc.) will live in India next year, (he, she, etc.) will not study Hindi (lit., Indian language).

The particle མོད་ conveys the idea of "even though" but normally occurs with འོན་ཀྱང་ ("nevertheless") at the beginning of the next clause.

e. ཕྱི་ལོ་རྒྱ་གར་ལ་སྡོད་མོད། འོན་ཀྱང་རྒྱ་གར་གྱི་སྐད་ཡིག་སློབ་སྦྱོང་བྱེད་ཀྱི་མ་རེད།

next year india to live though/ nevertheless india of language study do neg. fut. compl./

Even though (he) will live in India next year, nevertheless (he) will not study Hindi (lit., Indian language).

These particles are also used with negative verbal constructions.

f. ཁོ་ཚོར་མེ་མདའ་མང་པོ་མེད་ཀྱང་། གཞུང་ལ་ངོ་ལོག་བྱེད་ཀྱི་རེད།

he pl.-to gun many no-exist though/ government to rebel do fut. compl./

Even though they do not have many guns, (they) will rebel against the government.

g. མོས་ཁ་འདོན་ཞི་དྲགས་བྱེད་ཀྱི་ཡོད་པ་རེད་དེའི། ནང་པ་མ་རེད།

she-by prayer lots do pres. compl. though/ buddhist no is/

Even though she prays a lot, (she) is not a Buddhist.

7.3 The "plan/intend to" clause connective: རྩིས་

This clause connective usually takes the non-past stem of verbs and conveys that an actor plans or intends doing the verbal action.

a. ཕྱི་ལོ་མོ་བལ་ཡུལ་ལ་འགྲོ་རྩིས་ཡོད་པ་རེད།

next-year she nepal to go plan exist/

She plans to go to Nepal next year.

b. ངས་སྔོ་ལོ་ལྷ་ས་ནས་ཡོང་བའི་རྒན་གོག་དེ་གཉིས་ལ་རོགས་རམ་བྱེད་རྩིས་ཡོད།

i-by last-year lhasa from come nom.-of old-people that two to help do plan exist/

I plan to help those two old people who came from Lhasa last year.

Past tense is commonly conveyed by adding the past tense stem of the verb "to do" to རྩིས་ (as in example c.).

c. གྲྭ་པ་ཚང་མས་ཁང་པ་རྒྱག་རྩིས་བྱས་མ་སོང་།

monk all-by house build plan did neg. past compl./

All the monks did not plan to build a house.

7.4 The "before" clause connective: མ་ + vb. (past stem) + གོང་ + dative-locative (ལ་, etc.)

This clause connective conveys the idea that "before" the main verbal action, another took place or will take place.

a. རྡོ་རྗེས་དོ་ནུབ་ནང་ལ་མ་ལོག་གོང་ལ་ཏང་གི་ཚོགས་འདུར་འགྲོ་རྩིས་འདུག།

dorje-by tonight home to before return party of meeting-to go plan exist/

Before (he) returns home tonight, Dorje plans to go to the party meeting.

b. མོས་མ་ཉལ་གོང་དུ་ཁ་འདོན་བྱེད་ཀྱི་ཡོད་པ་རེད།

she-by before sleep pray do pres. compl./

She prays before (she) goes to sleep.

c. སློབ་གྲྭ་ཚོས་བོད་ལ་མ་ཕྱིན་གོང་ལ་བོད་སྐད་སློབ་སྦྱོང་བྱས་པ་རེད།
student pl.-by tibet to before went tibetan language study did past compl.
The students studied (spoken) Tibetan before (they) went to Tibet.

7.5 The verb དགོས་ ("to have to, to want")

This verb has only one stem but occurs both separately and together with other active verbs. When used as the main verb, it conveys the meaning of "want" or "need." When it accompanies an active verb, it immediately follows this verb (which is placed in the non-past) and conveys the meaning of "have to do" or "must do" the verbal action.

7.5.1 དགོས་ used alone as a main verb

In these constructions དགོས་ conveys the meaning of "wanting" or "needing" something. The subject of this verb normally requires the dative-locative case particle.

a. ཁྱེད་རང་ལ་ག་རེ་དགོས་སམ།
you to what want ?
What do you want?

b. ང་ལ་ཇ་མངར་མོ་དགོས།
i to tea sweet want
I want sweet tea.

c. ཁོ་ལ་ཇ་མངར་མོ་དགོས་པ་རེད།
he to tea sweet want
He wants sweet tea.

d. མོར་ཇ་མངར་མོ་དངོས་གནས་དགོས་ཀྱི་འདུག་གས།
she-to tea sweet really want pres. compl.?
Does she really want sweet tea?

e. མོར་ཇ་མངར་མོ་དངོས་གནས་མི་དགོས་། ཇ་བསྲུས་མ་དགོས།[1]
she-to tea sweet really neg. want/ tea tibetan want/
She really does not want sweet tea. (She) wants Tibetan style tea.

The following two sentences convey the "need" meaning of དགོས་. Context indicates which meaning is intended.

f. ཁོ་ཚོ་ན་ནིང་རྟ་གསར་པ་ཞིག་དགོས་པ་བྱུང་བ་རེད།
he pl. last-year horse new one have got past compl./
Last year they needed a new horse.

---

[1]Note that མ་ in the second clause does not convey the negative but rather is a part of the word བསྲུས་མ་ ("Tibetan style tea").

g. གནམ་གྲུ་གཏོང་སྐབས་ལག་ཁྱེར་དགོས་པ་རེད།

airplane fly when permit have/

When (one) pilots an airplane, a permit (license) is needed.

7.5.2 དགོས་ used in conjunction with active verbs

In this role དགོས་ occurs with the full range of verbal complements.

Past constructions

Each of the following complements expresses completed past action.

Vb. (non-past)	+	དགོས་	+	བྱུང་བ་རེད།
"	+	"	+	བྱུང་སོང་།
"	+	"	+	བྱུང་ཡོད་པ་རེད།
"	+	"	+	བྱུང་འདུག།
"	+	"	+	བྱུང་ (for 1st person subjects)
"	+	"	+	པ་ བྱུང་བ་རེད།
"	+	"	+	པ་ བྱུང་ཡོད་པ་རེད།
"	+	"	+	པ་ བྱུང་འདུག།

a. བྱ་བཙོལ་ཁང་ལ་ཕྲུ་གུ་མང་པོ་ན་ཙང་ཨེམ་ཆི་སྐད་གཏོང་བར་འགྲོ་དགོས་བྱུང་བ་རེད།

nursery to children many sick because, doctor call inf. go have got past compl./

Because many children in the nursery were sick, (they) had to go to call the doctor.

b. ཁོ་ཚོས་ངོ་ལོག་རྒྱག་དགོས་བྱུང་བ་རེད།

he pl.-by rebel act have got past compl./

They had to rebel.

Negative past constructions take one of the following forms:

Vb. (non-past)	+	དགོས་	+	མ་བྱུང་བ་རེད།
"	+	"	+	བྱུང་མ་སོང་།
"	+	"	+	བྱུང་ཡོད་པ་མ་རེད
"	+	"	+	བྱུང་མེད།
"	+	"	+	མ་བྱུང་།
"	+	"	+	པ་བྱུང་ཡོད་པ་མ་རེད།'
"	+	"	+	པ་མ་བྱུང་བ་རེད།
"	+	"	+	པ་བྱུང་མི་འདུག།
"	+	"	+	པ་བྱུང་བ་མ་རེད།
"	+	"	+	པ་བྱུང་མི་འདུག།
"	+	"	+	པ་བྱུང་མེད་པ་རེད་

c. ན་ནིང་ཆར་པ་ཞི་དྲགས་བབས་ཙང་ཞིང་ཁར་ཆུ་གཏོང་དགོས་མ་བྱུང་བ་རེད།
last year rain lots fell because field-to water send have no got past compl./
Because it rained a lot last year, (they) didn't have to irrigate the fields.

d. ན་ཉིན་དམག་རྒྱག་-སྐབས་ཕྲུ་གུ་ཚོ་སློབ་གྲྭར་འགྲོ་དགོས་བྱུང་མ་སོང་།
last year war do when, child pl. school-to go have got perf. neg./
Last year, when (they were) at war, the children didn't have to go to school.

དགོས་ occurs in dependent clauses with the following forms:

Vb. (non-past)	+	དགོས་	+ བྱུང་	+ clause connective (cc)
"	+	"	+ ཡོད་	+ cc
"	+	"	+ བྱུང་ཡོད་	+ cc
"	+	"	+ པ་ + བྱུང་	+ cc
"	+	"	+ པ་ + བྱུང་ཡོད་	+ cc
"	+	"	+ པ་ + མ་ + བྱུང་	+ cc
"	+	"	+ མེད་	+ cc
"	+	"	+ བྱུང་མེད་	+ cc
"	+	"	+ པ་ + མ་ + བྱུང་	+ cc
"	+	"	+ པ་ + བྱུང་མེད་	+ cc
"	+	"	+ cc	

e. ཁོ་ཚོས་གཞུང་ལ་དངུལ་སྤྲོད་དགོས་བྱུང་བ་མ་ཟད་འབྲུ་རིགས་ཀྱང་སྤྲོད་དགོས་བྱུང་བ་རེད།
he pl.-by government to money give have got perf. not only/ grain also give have got past compl./
They not only had to give money to the government, (they) also had to give grain.

f. ཁོ་ཚོས་གཞུང་ལ་ཁྲལ་ཆེན་པོ་སྤྲོད་དགོས་མ་བྱུང་ཡང་། ཡུལ་ལ་ཡར་རྒྱས་ཆེན་པོ་ཕྱིན་པ་རེད།
he pl.-by government to tax big give have no got though/ country to improve big went past compl./
Even though they didn't have to give large taxes to the government, the country has improved a great deal.

g. ཁོ་ཚོས་ཐོན་སྐྱེད་ཆེ་རུ་གཏོང་དགོས་སྐབས། ལག་ཆ་གསར་པ་བེད་སྤྱོད་བྱེད་དགོས་བྱུང་བ་རེད།
he pl.-by production big to send have because/tools new use did have got past compl./
Because they had to increase (make bigger) production, (they) had to use new tools.

Note that the tense of the dependent clause (ཐོན་སྐྱེད་ཆེ་རུ་གཏོང་དགོས་སྐབས་) is governed by the tense of the final verb (. . . བྱུང་བ་རེད་).

7.5.3 Non-past constructions

The following forms are commonly used to express present, usual-general, and future actions.

Vb. (non-past)	+	དགོས་	+	རེད།	(1st and 3rd person)
"	+	"	+	ཡོད་པ་རེད།	(3rd person)
"	+	"	+	ཡོད།	(1st person)
"	+	"	+	ཀྱི་ཡོད་པ་རེད།	(3rd person)
"	+	"	+	ཀྱི་འདུག།	(3rd person)
"	+	"	+	ཀྱི་ཡོད།	(1st person)
"	+	"	+	ཀྱི་རེད།	(3rd person)

The negative forms of the above follow the same pattern as presented earlier.

ཡོད་པ་རེད།	becomes	ཡོད་པ་མ་རེད།
འདུག།	becomes	མི་འདུག།
རེད།	becomes	མ་རེད།
ཡོད།	becomes	མེད།

a. ད་ལྟ་ཁོ་ཚོ་སློབ་གྲྭ་ལ་འགྲོ་དགོས་རེད།
now he pl. school to go have is/
They have to go to school now.

b. ཞིང་ལས་ཡར་རྒྱས་གཏོང་དགོས།
agriculture work improve do have/
(We, you, etc.) have to improve agricultural work.

c. ད་ལྟ་ང་དངུལ་ཁང་ལ་འགྲོ་དགོས་ཡོད།
now i bank to go have exist/
I have to go to the bank now.

d. དཔྱིད་དུས་ཞིང་པས་རྨོན་པ་རྒྱག་དགོས་ཀྱི་ཡོད་པ་རེད།
springtime farmer-by plow have usu. compl./
Farmers have to plow in the springtime.

e. དགུན་དུས་ཞིང་པས་རྨོན་པ་རྒྱག་དགོས་ཀྱི་མེད་པ་རེད།
wintertime farmer-by plow do have neg. usu.-compl./
Farmers do not have to plow in the wintertime.

This could also have been written:

f. དགུན་དུས་ཞིང་པས་རྨོན་པ་རྒྱག་དགོས་མ་རེད།
wintertime farmer-by plowing do have no.-is/
Farmers do not have to plow in the wintertime.

g. ང་ཚོ་སློབ་ཕྲུག་ཡིན་སྟབས་ང་ཚོས་ཞིང་ལས་བྱེད་དགོས་མེད།
i pl. student is since i-by agricultural work do have no-exist/
Because we are students, (we) do not have to do agricultural work.

h. ཁོས་ཨ་མེ་རི་ཀར་ལོ་ཤས་སྡོད་དགོས་ཀྱི་རེད།

he-by america-to year several live have fut. compl./

He will have to live in America for several years.

i. ཁོ་ཁམས་ལ་འགྲོ་དགོས་ཀྱང་། ལོ་མང་པོ་སྡོད་དགོས་ཀྱི་མ་རེད།

he kham to go have though/ year many live have neg. fut. compl./

Even though he has to go to Kham, (he) will not have to live (there for) many years.

7.5.4 The དགོས་ + པ་རེད་ usual complement

This construction usually conveys usual or general statements. Note how the time-context words སྔོན་མ་, དེང་སང་, and ནམ་རྒྱུན་ affect the meaning of examples a., b., and c.

a. སྔོན་མ་རྒྱ་ནག་ལ་ཞིང་འབྲོག་ཚོས་ཁྲལ་ཆེན་པོ་སྤྲོད་དགོས་པ་རེད།

formerly china to farmers-nomads pl.-by tax big give have usual compl./

In the past, farmers and nomads in China had to pay (give) big taxes.

b. དེང་སང་རྒྱ་ནག་ལ་ཞིང་འབྲོག་ཚོས་ཁྲལ་ཆེན་པོ་སྤྲོད་དགོས་པ་རེད།

these days china to farmers nomads pl.-by tax big give have usual compl./

These days, farmers and nomads in China have to pay (give) big taxes.

c. ནམ་རྒྱུན་གྲོང་གསེབ་ཀྱི་གཞོན་པ་ཚོ་སློབ་གྲྭར་འགྲོ་དགོས་པ་མ་རེད།

usually village of youths pl. school to go have usual compl. neg./

Usually village youths do not have to go to school.

7.5.5 དགོས་ constructions in the past conveying completed action

Tibetan distinguishes between past obligatory action that has been completed or carried out and general obligations or duties in the past. In English when we say, "He had to pay taxes," it could mean either that he actually paid them, or that he should have or was supposed to pay them (e.g., "He had to pay taxes but didn't"). Tibetan uses the བྱུང་ forms to convey the idea that not only did they "have to" do something — they did it!

a. སྔོན་མ་རྒྱ་གར་ལ་ཞིང་འབྲོག་ཚོས་ཁྲལ་ཆེན་པོ་སྤྲོད་དགོས་པ་རེད།

formerly india to farmers nomads pl.-by tax big give have usual compl./

In the past, farmers and nomads in India had to pay (give) big taxes.

If the writer wanted to convey that not only was there an obligation, but that the obligation had been completed, he would have used one of the བྱུང་ forms.

b. སྔོན་མ་རྒྱ་གར་ལ་ཞིང་འབྲོག་ཚོས་ཁྲལ་ཆེན་པོ་སྤྲོད་དགོས་བྱུང་བ་རེད།

formerly india to farmers nomads pl.-by tax big give have usual compl./

In the past, farmers and nomads in India had to pay (give) big taxes.

The negative forms parallel those encountered earlier.

c. སྔོན་མ་རྒྱ་གར་ལ་ཞིང་འབྲོག་ཚོས་ཁྲལ་ཆེན་པོ་སྤྲོད་དགོས་པ་མ་རེད།

formerly india to farmers nomads pl.-by tax big give have neg. usual compl./

In the past, farmers and nomads in India did not have to pay (give) big taxes.

d. སྔོན་མ་རྒྱ་གར་ལ་ཞིང་འབྲོག་ཚོས་ཁྲལ་ཆེན་པོ་སྤྲོད་དགོས་མ་བྱུང་བ་རེད།

formerly india to farmers nomads pl.-by tax big give have neg. usual compl./

In the past, farmers and nomads in India did not have to pay (give) big taxes.

7.5.6 The use of དགོས་ in two-verb constructions

The following examples of དགོས་ function to convey the need either: 1. to make someone or something do a verbal action, or 2. to do something so as to make a verbal action come about.

a. ང་ཚོས་ཁོ་སང་ཉིན་འགྲོ་ཐུབ་པ་བྱེད་དགོས།

i pl.-by he tomorrow go able do have

We have to do something so that he will be able to go tomorrow.

b. ང་ཚོས་ཁོ་སང་ཉིན་འགྲོ་ཐབས་བྱེད་དགོས།[2]

i pl.-by he tomorrow go means do have

We have to do something so that he will (have the means to) go tomorrow.

c. ང་ཚོས་ཁོ་སང་ཉིན་འགྲོ་རྒྱུ་བྱེད་དགོས།

i pl.-by he tomorrow go means do have

We have to do something so that he will go tomorrow.

These three constructions are similiar in the sense that they convey that the actor has to do something so that something else will occur, but differ in terms of the degree of strength associated with what will be done. The first example normally conveys the strongest action, meaning you will go all out to create a situation so that he will be able to go. The second example is less strong, and the third is the weakest, conveying more that the actors will go to try to persuade him to go. These differences are not hard and fast, and the third pattern can also convey taking actions as well as just speech.

7.5.7 Further examples of དགོས་ with connectives in dependent clauses

In this position there are a number of very common patterns:

Vb.	+	དགོས་ + cc
"	+	དགོས་ + ཀྱི་ཡོད་ + cc
"	+	དགོས་ + ཀྱི་འདུག་ + cc
"	+	དགོས་ + ཡོད་ + cc

---

[2]Note that ཐབས་ conveys "means" or "methods."

" + དགོས་ + མེད + cc

" + མི + དགོས་ + cc

" + དགོས་ + ཀྱི་མེད་ + cc

" + དགོས་ + བྱུང་ +cc

a. སྔོན་མ་རྒྱ་གར་ལ་ཞིང་འབྲོག་ཚོས་ཁྲལ་ཆེན་པོ་སྤྲོད་དགོས་བྱུང་སྐབས། ཁོ་ཚོར་འཚོ་བ་སྐྱོ་པོ་ཞི་དྲགས་འདུག།
formerly india to farmers nomads pl.-by tax big give have usual compl./ he pl.-to livelihood nom. poor very exist/
In the past, because farmers and nomads in India had to pay (give) big taxes, they were very poor.

b. མོ་སློབ་གྲྭར་འགྲོ་དགོས་པ་མ་ཟད། ཟ་ཁང་ལའང་ལས་ཀ་བྱས་དགོས་བྱུང་སོང་།
she school-to go have not-only/ restaurant to-also work did have got past compl./
Not only did she have to go to school, (she) also had to work in a restaurant.

c. མོ་སློབ་གྲྭར་འགྲོ་མི་དགོས་པ་མ་ཟད། ལས་ཀ་ཡང་བྱས་དགོས་བྱུང་མ་སོང་།
she school-to go no have not-only/ work also did have got neg. past compl./
Not only did she not have to go to school, (she) also did not have to work.

7.6 Constructions using ཐག་ཆོད་

ཐག་ཆོད་ is used with the stem of adjectives to convey the meaning of "very" or "extremely." Thus ཡག་པོ་ becomes ཡག་ཐག་ཆོད་ ("extremely good"), and ཆེན་པོ་ becomes ཆེ་ཐག་ཆོད་ ("very big").

a. སྙན་ཞུ་འདི་གསལ་ཐག་ཆོད་རེད།
report this clear very is/
This report is very clear.

b. གསར་འགྱུར་འདི་ནི་གསལ་ཐག་ཆོད་རེད།
news this as for clear very is/
This news is very clear.

c. ཁོ་ཚོས་ལས་ཀ་ཡག་ཐག་ཆོད་བྱས་པ་རེད།
he pl.-by work good very did past compl./
They did the work very well.

ཐག་ཆོད་ is also used with existential verbs. The pattern is: existential verb + ཐག་ཆོད་ + a linking verb. In these constructions it conveys the meaning of "certain."

d. མོ་དེང་སང་རྒྱ་ནག་ལ་ཡོད་ཐག་ཆོད་རེད།
she these days china to exist certain is/
It is certain (that) she is in China these days.

e. ཤིང་ནགས་འདིའི་ནང་འདམ་སེང་མེད་ཐག་ཆོད་རེད།

forest this-of in lion neg.-exist certain is/

It is certain that there are no lions in this forest.

f. ང་ཚོའི་གོ་ཁྲིད་སོ་པ་མིན་ཐག་ཆོད་རེད།

i pl.-of leader spy neg.-is certain is/

It is certain that our leader is not a spy.

ཐག་ཆོད་ can also be used with active and involuntary verbs:

g. ཁོ་བོད་ལ་མ་ཕྱིན་ཐག་ཆོད་རེད།

he tibet to no went certain is/

It is certain that he did not go to Tibet.

h. ཁོ་པ་དེ་རིང་འབྱོར་གྱི་ཡོད་ཐག་ཆོད་རེད།

he today arrive pres. compl. certain is/

It is certain that he is arriving today.

ཐག་ཆོད་ can also be used as a noun where it means "settlement" (of a dispute). For example:

i. ཁ་མཆུ་དེ་ཐག་ཆོད་བྱུང་བ་རེད།

dispute that settlement got past compl./

A settlement was reached for that dispute.

7.7 Constructions with the verb ཞུ་ (ཞུས་)

When ཞུ་ is used as a verb it conveys the meaning "to say" or "to tell" or "to ask/request" something to or from a superior.

a. ངས་རྡོ་རྗེ་ལགས་ལ་གནས་ཚུལ་ཚང་མ་ཞུས་པ་ཡིན།

i-by dorje la to situation all told past compl./

I told Dorje all about the situation.

b. ཞིང་པ་ཚོས་རྫོང་གི་འགོ་ཁྲིད་རྣམས་ལ་བཀའ་མོལ་ཞུས་པ་རེད།

farmer pl.-by district of leader pl. to discuss (h.) past compl./

The farmers discussed (it) [or held a discussion] with the leaders of the district.

The honorific noun-verb compound (བཀའ་མོལ་ཞུས་) here conveys that the actors were lower in status and shows respect for the leader. If one wanted to convey respect to both the subject and object, གནང་ would be substituted for ཞུས་.

c. ཁོང་ཚོས་རྫོང་གི་འགོ་ཁྲིད་རྣམས་ལ་བཀའ་མོལ་གནང་བ་རེད།

he (h.) pl.-by district of leader pl. to talk (h.) did (h.) past compl./

They talked with the leaders of the district.

Some common compounds that use ཞུ་ are:

བཀའ་དྲི་ཞུ་	དགའ་བསུ་ཞུ་	ཞབས་འདེགས་ཞུ་
to ask	to welcome	to serve

7.8 Constructions expressing "certainty": ངེས་, ལོས་, and ཤག་

Like ཐག་ཆོད་, ངེས་ is used with active and involuntary verbs (the non-past stem) and linking/existential verbs to express the idea that it is "certain" that the verbal action will occur or that something certainly exists.

a. ལས་ཀ་འདི་ཁོས་བྱེད་ཐུབ་ངེས་རེད།
   work this he-by do able certain is/
   It is certain that he will be able to do this work.

b. གཞུང་གིས་ཕྲུ་གུ་མེད་པའི་རྒན་ཁོག་རྣམས་ལ་སྐྱིབ་གསོ་སྤྲོད་དགོས་ངེས་རེད།
   government by child without nom.-of elderly pl. to welfare give need certain is/
   It is certain that the government will have to give welfare to the elderly without
   children.

ལོས་ also conveys certainty.

c. ལས་ཀ་འདི་ཁོས་ལོས་བྱེད་ཐུབ།
   work this he-by do able certain is/
   It is certain that he will be able to do this work.

d. འདི་འདྲ་བྱས་ན་ཕན་ཐོགས་ལོས་ཡོད།
   this like did if benefit certain exist/
   If (one) does like this, there will certainly be a benefit.

ཤག་ conveys certainty but with the connotation of I "presume" or I "trust" or I "take it that":

e. ཁྱེད་རང་གིས་གནས་ཚུལ་དེ་ཤེས་ཡོད་ཤག་རེད།
   you by news that know exist certain is/
   (I) presume that you definitely know that news.

f. ཁྱེད་རང་གིས་དེབ་རྙིང་པ་དེ་ཀློག་ཡོད་ཤག་རེད།
   you by book old that read certain is/
   (I) trust that you certainly have read that old book.

g. ཁྱེད་རང་གིས་དེང་སང་སློབ་སྦྱོང་ཡག་པོ་བྱེད་ཀྱི་ཡོད་ཤག་རེད།
   you by these days study good do pres. compl. definitely is
   (I) take it that you are studying well these days.

Note should be taken that when ཤག་ is used directly after past verb stems, it conveys the perfect tense. This will be examined fully in a later lesson.

h. ཁོ་པས་དེབ་རྙིང་པ་དེ་བཀླགས་ཤག།
   he-by book old that read perf./
   He has read that old book.

7.9 The "together with" clause connectives: པ་དང་སྦྲགས་, པ་དང་ཆབས་ཅིག་, པ་དང་སྟབས་བསྟུན་, པ་དང་བསྟུན་, དང་ཆབས་ཅིག་, དང་མཉམ་དུ་, བསྟུན་, བསྟུན་ནས་, དང་འབྲེལ་, and ཆབས་སྦྲགས་

These constructions convey several different meanings depending on context. First they convey the idea of a secondary act occurring together with or at the same time as a primary act. The latter action is somewhat incidental to the former — i.e., together with but secondary to A, B was done or took place.

a. པད་མ་ལགས་གཞིས་ཀ་རྩེར་ཕེབས་པ་དང་སྦྲགས་ཇ་གཟིགས་ཀྱི་རེད།
pema la shigatse-to go together tea buy (h.) fut. compl./
Pema will buy tea together with going to Shigatse. [Together with or incidental to going to Shigatse,. . . —the buying of tea is the secondary action.]

b. རྒྱ་གར་ལ་མོ་གྲོགས་པོ་ཐུག་པ་དང་འབྲེལ་གནས་སྐོར་འགྲོ་གི་རེད།
india to she friend meet together pilgrimage go fut. compl./
Together with meeting a friend in India, she will go on pilgrimage. [Here the secondary action is the going on pilgrimage.]

c. ཁོ་གྲོགས་པོ་ཐུག་པ་དང་ཆབས་ཅིག་ཉོ་ཆ་རྒྱག་གི་རེད།
he friend meet together shop fut. compl./
Together with meeting a friend, (he) will go shopping.

d. ཕྲུ་གུ་ཚོས་དགོན་པར་སླེབས་པ་དང་སྟབས་བསྟུན་མཆོད་མཇལ་ཞུས་སོང་།
child pl.-by monastery-to arrive together religious-visit did went compl./
Together with arriving at the monastery, the children did a religious visit.

e. ང་རྒྱལ་རྩེ་སླེབས་བསྟུན་འབྲོག་པ་ཁ་ཤས་ཕྲད་བྱུང་།
i gyantse arrive together nomad several met got/
Together with arriving in Gyantse, I met several nomads.

f. ཁོས་མཆོད་མཇལ་ཞུ་བ་དང་བསྟུན་ལྷད་མོ་བལྟས་སོང་།
he-by religious visit do together with show watch went compl./
Together with doing a religious visit, he watched a show.

g. ཁོས་མཆོད་མཇལ་ཞུ་བ་དང་མཉམ་དུ་ལྷད་མོ་བལྟས་སོང་།
he-by religious visit do together with show watch went compl./
Together with doing a religious visit, he watched a show.

The use of དང་མཉམ་དུ་ in example g. conveys greater equality in the importance of the two actions.

h. ང་ཚོས་ཤ་ཉོས་པ་དང་ཆབས་ཅིག་སྔོ་ཚལ་ཉོས་པ་རེད།
i pl.-by mean bought together with vegetables bought/
Together with buying meat, we bought vegetables.

Many of these same particles are used adverbially to convey the meaning "together" or "together with."

j. ཁོ་ཚོ་ཚང་མ་ཆབས་ཅིག་ཡོང་བ་རེད།
he pl. all together came past compl./
All of them came together. (Or, They all came together.)

The following substitution produces no change in meaning:

k. ཁོ་ཚོ་ཚང་མ་མཉམ་དུ་ཡོང་བ་རེད།
he pl. all together came past compl./
All of them came together.

7.10 The "according to" clause connectives: (པ)་དང་སྟབས་བསྟུན་, (པ)་དང་བསྟུན་, བསྟུན་, བསྟུན་ནས་, དང་འབྲེལ་, and གཞི་བཟུང་

Many of the clause connectives discussed in 7.9 convey a second major meaning — "according to" or "in keeping with" or "based on." Context determines which meaning is intended.

a. འཆར་གཞི་དང་སྟབས་བསྟུན་ལས་ཀ་བྱེད་དགོས་རེད།
plan accordance work do have/
(He, we, one, etc.) has to work in accordance with the plan.

b. རྩ་ཁྲིམས་གཞི་བཟུང་འཆར་གཞི་བཟོས་པ་རེད།
constitution accordance plan made past compl./
(He, she, etc.) made a plan in accordance with the constitution.

c. ཁོ་ཚོས་ཏང་གི་རྩ་ཁྲིམས་དང་འབྲེལ་འཆར་གཞི་གསར་པ་བཟོ་གི་རེད།
he pl.-by party of constitution accordance plan new make fut. compl./
They will make a new plan in accordance with the party's constitution

7.11 The "about to" clause connectives: གྲབས་, ལ་ཁད་ལ་, ཁ་ལ་ཁར་, ལ་ཁར་, ཁར་, གྲབས་བྱེད་, ཉེ་, and ཉེར་

These clause connectives convey the idea that when the action in the first clause was "about to" occur, or "just before" it occurred, something else happened. They are used in two types of constructions: 1. in dependent clauses following a verb (non-past) and 2. following a verb and immediately followed by an existential, active or involuntary verb.

a. གནམ་གྲུ་འཕུར་ལ་ཁར་སྐྱོན་ཤོར་སོང་།
airplane fly just before damage went compl./
Just before the airplane took off, (it) got damaged.

b. ཁོ་མགྲོན་ཁང་ནས་ཐོན་ལ་ཁད་ལ་ཁ་པར་འབྱོར་སོང་།
he hotel from depart about phone arrive went compl./

When he was about to depart from the hotel, (he) received a phone call.

c. ཁོ་ཚོས་ལྷོ་ཟ་གྲབས་འདུག།
he pl.-by food eat about exist/
They are about to eat food.

d. ཁོ་གཉིས་ནང་ལ་ལོག་གྲབས་ཡོད་པ་རེད
he two home to return about exist/
Those two are about to return home.

When the verb "to do" follows གྲབས་, the meaning conveyed is that the actor is getting ready to do the verbal action. For example,

e. ཁོ་ནང་ལ་ལོག་གྲབས་བྱེད་དུས་ཆར་པ་བཏང་སོང་།
he home to return about do when rain fell went compl./
When he was getting ready to return home, it rained.

f. ཁོ་པ་ཚོས་ཁ་ལག་བཟོ་གྲབས་བྱེད་ཀྱི་ཡོད་པ་རེད།
he pl.-by food make about do pres. compl./
They are getting ready to make food (a meal).

If the verb in such constructions is in the past tense, the overall meaning changes to "almost did" the verbal action. For example,

g. ཁོས་ཁ་སང་གློག་བརྙན་ལ་འགྲོ་གྲབས་བྱས་པ་རེད།
he-by movie to go about did past compl./
He almost went to the movie yesterday.

h. ཁོ་ན་ནས་ཤི་གྲབས་བྱས་པ་རེད།
he sick having die about did past compl./
Having gotten sick, he almost died.

ཉེ་ and ཉེར་ are used with verb stems to convey the meaning of "about to" or "close to" the verbal action.

i. ཁོ་བོད་ལ་འགྲོ་ཉེར་རེད།
he tibet to go about is/
He is about to go to Tibet.

j. ནང་པ་དེ་ཚོ་ལྷ་སར་ཐོན་ཉེར་སླེབས་པ་རེད།
buddhist that pl. lhasa-to depart about arrive past compl./
Those Buddhists are about to depart for Lhasa (lit., "it has arrived near to departure").

7.12 The polite imperative: vb. + དང་

དང་ is added to verbs when one wants to ask someone to do something in a polite way.

a. ཞོགས་པ་སྔ་པོ་ལངས་ནས་དེབ་ཀློག་དང་།

morning early get up having book read please/
(Please) get up early and read books.

b. མོར་རོགས་གནང་དང་།
she-to help please/
Please help her.

c. བོད་ལ་འགྲོ་དུས་མཆོད་མཇལ་ཞུས་དང་།
tibet to go when religious visit do please/
When you go to Tibet please make a religious visit.

d. ལྷ་སར་ཕེབས་དང་། ཇོ་བོ་རིན་པོ་ཆེ་མཇལ་གྱི་རེད།
lhasa-to go (h.) please/ jo rimpoche meet (h.) fut. compl.
Go to Lhasa. (You) will meet (encounter) the Jo Rimpoche (statue).

The negative of these would be:

e. ཞོགས་པ་སྔ་པོར་དེབ་མ་ཀློག་དང་།
morning early-to book no read please/
(Please) do not read books in the early morning.

f. མོར་རོགས་མ་གནང་དང་།
she-to help please/
Please do not help her.

7.13 "Help" constructions: རོགས་གནང་ and རོགས་བྱེད་

རོགས་གནང་ and རོགས་བྱེད་ ("help") are used with the non-past stems of verbs to convey "please do" the verbal action.

a. རྒྱ་གར་ལ་ཕེབས་པ་དང་ཕྱག་བྲིས་གཏོང་རོགས་གནང་།
india to arrived (h.) letter (h.) send please/
Please send a letter as soon as (you) arrive in India.

b. བོད་ཀྱི་གནས་ཚུལ་གསལ་པོ་གཅིག་ཤོད་རོགས་བྱེད།
tibet of condition clear one tell please/
Please tell clearly (about) conditions in Tibet.

c. དོ་དགོང་ཆུ་ཚོད་བརྒྱད་པར་ངའི་ནང་ལ་ཡོང་རོགས་བྱེད།
tonight o'clock eight-to i-of home at come/
Please come to my home at eight o'clock tonight.

d. སྨན་ཁང་འདི་ལ་ཉམས་གསོ་གནང་རོགས་གནང་།
hospital this repair do (h.)/
Please repair this hospital.

e. ཡི་གེ་འདི་རྡོ་རྗེ་ལགས་སུ་ཕུལ་རོགས་གནང་།
letter this dorje la (h.) to give (h.) please/

Please give this letter to Dorje.

7.14. Reading exercises

7.14.1 Reading number one: "Agu dönba and a Rich Man"

7.14.1.1 Tibetan text

ཨ་ཁུ་སྟོན་པ་དང་མི་ཕྱུག་པོ།

ཨ་ཁུ་སྟོན་པའི་ཁྱིམ་གྱི་རྩམ་པ་རྫོགས་རྗེས་ཁོས་ཡུལ་དེར་དུད་ཚང་ཕྱུག་པོ་ཞིག་ཡོད་པ་དེའི་སར་རྩམ་པ་གཡར་དུ་སོང་། འོན་ཀྱང་ཕྱུག་པོ་དེ་སེར་སྣ་ཆེན་པོ་ཡིན་ཙང་དེས་ཨ་ཁུར་རྩམ་པ་སྤར་མོ་གང་ཙམ་ཡང་གཡར་པོ་མ་བྱས། དེ་ནས་ཉིན་ཤས་སོང་རྗེས་ཨ་ཁུས་སླར་ཡང་ཕྱུག་པོ་དེའི་ཁྱིམ་དུ་ཕྱིན་ནས་སླང་ཆེན་པོ་ཞིག་གཡར་བ་དང་སྦྲགས་དེང་སང་ལྷ་སར་རྩམ་པ་གོང་ཆེན་པོ་ཡོད་ཙང་ང་སང་ཉིན་རྩམ་པ་བཙོང་བར་འགྲོ་རྩིས་ཡོད་ཅེས་བཤད། སྐད་ཆ་དེ་ཕྱུག་པོས་ཐོས་མ་ཐག་ཞུམ་བྱས་ཙི་ཙི་མཐོང་བ་ལྟར་དགའ་སྣང་ཚད་མེད་བྱུང་སྟེ་དེ་ནི་ཁ་བཟང་ཆེན་པོ་ཞིག་ཐོབ་པ་བྱེད་དགོས་བསམས་ཏེ་ཁོས་ཨ་ཁུར་ལྷ་སའི་ཁྱིམ་རའི་ཐེམ་སྒང་དང་། བྲིན་ཚོང་གི་སྐོར་སོགས་ཞིབ་པར་དྲིས་རྗེས་ཁོ་དགའ་ཐག་ཆོད་ནས་བྱས་ན་སང་ཉིན་ང་ཡང་ཁྱོད་མཉམ་དུ་ལྷ་སར་རྩམ་པ་བཙོང་བར་འགྲོ་ཡི་ཡིན་ཞེས་བཤད། ཕྱི་ཉིན་ཕྱུག་པོ་དེས་ཞོགས་པ་སྔ་པོ་ནས་ལངས་ཏེ་ཁལ་གཡག་ལ་རྩམ་པ་ཁལ་རྒྱབ་གཅིག་བཀལ་ནས་ལྷ་སར་ཐོན་རྒྱུའི་གྲ་སྒྲིག་བྱས་ཚར་ནས་ཨ་ཁུ་བསྒུགས་ནས་བསྡད། ཨ་ཁུ་སྟོན་པས་རྩམ་སྒྱེ་སྟོང་པ་གཉིས་ཀྱི་ནང་གཟན་རྩ་བཅུགས་ཏེ་རྩམ་པ་ཡིན་ཁུལ་བྱས་བོང་བུར་བཀལ་ནས་དེ་གར་སླེབས་རྗེས་ཁོང་གཉིས་མཉམ་དུ་ལྷ་སར་ཐོན། དེ་ཉིན་ཨ་ཁུ་སྟོན་པ་དང་ཕྱུག་པོ་ཁོང་གཉིས་ཉིན་གང་བསྐྱོད་ནས་དགོན་ཧྲུལ་ཆུང་ཆུང་ཞིག་གི་འགྲམ་དུ་སླེབས་པས་ཁོང་གཉིས་དོ་ནུབ་དགོན་པ་དེའི་ནང་ཞག་སྡོད་བྱ་རྒྱུར་ཁ་འཆམ། ཉིན་གང་བསྐྱོད་པའི་ངལ་དུབ་ཀྱིས་ཕྱུག་པོ་ནི་ཉལ་མ་ཐག་གཉིད་ལ་ཤོར་ནས་ཤི་བ་ལྟར་དུ་གྱུར། ནམ་ཕྱེད་ཙམ་ལ་ཨ་ཁུ་སྟོན་པས་ཁ་ཁར་ཡར་ལངས་ཏེ་རང་གི་རྩམ་སྒྱེའི་ནང་གི་གཟན་རྩ་རྣམས་བོང་བུར་སྟེར་བ་དང་ཕྱུག་པའི་རྩམ་པ་ཁལ་རྒྱབ་གཅིག་པོ་དེ་རང་གི་སྒྱེ་མོའི་ནང་དུ་བཅུགས། དེ་ནས་ཨ་ཁུས་ཕྱུག་པོ་དེའི་རྩམ་སྒྱེ་སྟོང་པ་དེ་ལྷ་སྐུའི་ལག་ཏུ་བཞག་པ་དང་ཡང་རྩམ་པ་སྤར་མོ་གང་ཁྱེར་ནས་ལྷ་སྐུ་དེའི་ཁ་ལ་བྱུགས་རྗེས་གཞི་ནས་སྔར་བཞིན་གཉིད་ཉལ། ནམ་ལངས་རྗེས་ཕྱུག་པོ་དེས་རང་ཉིད་ཀྱི་རྩམ་པ་དོ་པོ་བསྡད་མེད་པ་མཐོང་འཕྲལ་ཨ་ཁུ་བོས་ཏེ་གཉིད་ལས་སད། ཁོང་གཉིས་པོས་རྩམ་སྒྱེ་སྟོང་པ་ལྷ་སྐུའི་ལག་ཏུ་ཡོད་པ་མཐོང་། ཨ་ཁུ་སྟོན་པས་འཇིག་རྟེན་མི་རྣམས་ཀྱིས་དུས་ཡུན་རིང་པོ་ལྷ་མ་གསོལ་བར་བརྟེན་ལྷ་ཞལ་ཆེར་ལྟོགས་ནས་ཐབས་ཤེས་མ་བྱུང་སྐབས་ཁྱོད་ཀྱི་ཙམ་པ་འགམས་པ་རེད་ཅེས་བཤད། ཕྱུག་པོ་དེས་ལྷ་འདིས་ངའི་རྩམ་པ་ཁོ་ན་བཟས་པ་ལས་ཁྱོད་ཀྱི་རྩམ་པ་དེ་མི་ཟ་བ་གང་ཡིན་ནམ་ཞེས་དྲིས་པར། ཨ་ཁུས་ལྷ་ཁྱོད་ལ་མཉེས་པོ་ཡོད་པས་རེད་ཅེས་ལན་བཏབ། དེས་ན་ཕྱུག་པོ་དེས་དབུགས་རིང་གཏོང་བཞིན་པར་ང་ལྷ་སར་འགྲོ་ཡི་མིན། ཁྱོད་རང་གཅིག་པུར་རྒྱུགས་ཤིག་ཅེས་བཤད། ཨ་ཁུ་སྟོན་པས་ང་གཅིག་པུར་འགྲོ་གི་མིན་ཅེས་བཤད་ནས་ཁོང་གཉིས་མཉམ་དུ་སླར་ཡང་ཁྱིམ་ལ་ཕྱིར་ལོག་སོང་།

7.14.1.2 Interlinear translation

Agu dönba and person rich

1. Agu dönba-of house of tsamba exhausted because he-by country that-to household
rich one exist that-of place-to tsamba borrow to went/ nevertheless
2. rich that avarice great is because that-by agu-to tsamba handful full about even borrow
no send/ that from day several went after
3. agu once-again rich that-of house to went having pan big one borrow together-with
these days lhasa-to tsamba price big exist because
4. i tomorrow tsamba sell to go plan exist quote said/ talk that rich-by heard as-soon-as
cat mouse see like hap-
5. py limitless got having now as-for profit big one obtain do need thought having he-by
agu-to lhasa-of market-of goods price and/
6. selling of about etc. detail-to ask after he happy extremely having did if tomorrow i
also you together lhasa-to tsamba sell to
7. go of is quote said/ the next day rich that-by morning early from arose having
carrying yak to tsamba load one load having lha-
8. sa-to depart gyu-of prepare do finish agu wait having stayed/ agu dönba-by tsamba
bag empty two of in straw stuff having
9. tsamba is pretend by donkey-to load having there arrive after he two together lhasa-to
depart/ that day agu dönba and rich
10. he two day all go having monastery rubble small one of near to arrive because he two
this-evening monastery that-of in stop overnight
11. do gyu-to agree/ all day go-of tired by rich as-for lie down as soon as fall asleep
having death like to become/ mid-
12. night about to agu dönba-by quietly up arose having own of tsamba bag-of in of straw
pl. donkey-to gave and rich-of tsamba
13. load single that itself of bag-of in to stuff/ then agu-by rich that-of tsamba bag empty
that god statue-of hand to left and
14. also tsamba handful one carry having god statue that-of mouth to smear after only-
then before like sleep lie-down/ dawn arose after rich that-by
15. oneself of tsamba load stayed without saw at-once agu called having sleep woke/ he
two-by tsamba bag empty god statue-of hand to
16. exist saw/ agu dönba-by world people pl. by time long god no offering because god
probably hungry having
17. means no got because you of tsamba ate past compl. quote said/ rich that-by god

this-by i-of tsamba only ate than

18. you to tsamba that no eat why quote asked to/ agu-by god you to like exist-by is
quote answer give/ therefore

18. rich that-by sigh send manner i lhasa-to go neg.fut. compl./ you self alone go! quote
said/ agu dönba-

19. by i alone go neg. fut. compl. quote said having he two together once-again house to
return past compl./

7.14.1.3 Translation

Agu dönba and a Rich Man[3]

Because all of Agu dönba's family's tsamba was exhausted, he went to the house of a rich person in that area to borrow grain. However, because that man was very avaricious, he did not lend even a handful to Agu. Several days after that, Agu again went to that rich man's house and together with borrowing a (tsamba) roasting pan (from him), said, "These days because the price of tsamba is high in Lhasa, I plan to go to sell tsamba." As soon as the rich man heard that, like a cat spotting a mouse, he got very happy and thinking, "Now I have to do something so as to make a big profit," asked Agu in detail about prices and sales in the Lhasa market. After this, he got very happy and said, "Well then, tomorrow I also will go together with you to Lhasa to sell tsamba."

The next day, that rich man got up early and loaded a load of tsamba on his carrying yak and waited for Agu, all prepared to depart for Lhasa. Agu dönba stuffed two empty sacks with hay and straw and, pretending they were tsamba, loaded them on donkeys. After he arrived there (at the rich man's house), they left for Lhasa together. That day Agu dönba and the rich man went all day and, having arrived by a ruined small monastery, agreed to stay there that night.

The rich man, tired from traveling all day, lay down and immediately fell asleep (becoming) as if he were dead. At about midnight, Agu dönba quietly arose and gave the straw and hay from his sacks to the donkeys, filling his sacks with the tsamba from the rich man's load. After that, Agu put the rich man's empty tsamba bag in the hand of a statue of a deity and also carried a handful of tsamba, smearing it in the mouth of the statue. Then he slept like before. After dawn, as soon as the rich man saw that his load of tsamba was not there, he called Agu, waking him up. The two of them saw with certainty

---

[3] Agu dönba is Tibet's most famous folklore trickster. Poking fun at the rich, the hypocritical and the greedy, his stories are known and relished throughout Tibet.

the empty bags in the hand of the statue. Agu dönba said, "Because humans have not given offerings to the god for a long time, probably the god was hungry and had no means to get food so he ate your tsamba." The rich man asked, "How come the god ate only my tsamba and not yours?" Agu replied, "It is because the god likes you." Therefore, that rich man, sighingly said, "I am not going to Lhasa. You go alone!" Agu dönba said, "I will not go alone," and the two of them together again returned home.

7.14.1.4 Grammatical notes

1. The first segment consists of two clauses: 1. ཨ་ཁུ་བསྟན་པའི་ཁྱིམ་གྱི་རྩམ་པ་རྫོགས་ཀྱིན་ 2. ཁོས་ཡུལ་དེར་དུད་ཚང་ཕྱུག་པོ་ཞིག་ཡོད་པ་དེའི་སར་རྩམ་པ་གཡར་དུ་སོང་.

The core of the first clause is the noun རྩམ་པ་ ("tsamba") and the involuntary verb རྫོགས་ ("got exhausted/finished"), with the remaining component ཨ་ཁུ་བསྟན་པའི་ཁྱིམ་གྱི་ ("Agudönba's house's/family's") modifying tsamba. Thus, what was exhausted was "Agudönba's family's tsamba." The clause connective ཀྱིན་ ("because"— see 5.9) links this with the second clause.

Clause two starts with the subject in the instrumental (ཁོས་). This is followed by a nominalized existential phrase (ཡུལ་དེར་དུད་ཚང་ཕྱུག་པོ་ཞིག་ཡོད་པ་) that modifies "place" (ས་), explaining what kind of a place it is: "a place where there existed a rich family in that area." The genitive particle attached to the demonstrative "that" (དེའི་) links this modifying phrase to the noun "place" (ས་). If the demonstrative had been omitted (ཡོད་པའི་སར་), the phrase would have simply conveyed "a place where there existed. . . ." The addition of the demonstrative gives added emphasis to the specific place where that rich family lived. It is not translatable into English.

"Place," in turn, is joined with the dative-locative particle so that it conveys the location of the verbal action: "in/at a place."

The rest of this clause begins with the direct object "tsamba" (རྩམ་པ་). This is followed by an infinitive construction consisting of the first verb (གཡར) + dative-locative particle (དུ་) + main verb (སོང་): "went to borrow."

2. The second segment consists of two clauses: 1. འོན་ཀྱང་ཕྱུག་པོ་དེ་སེར་སྣ་ཆེན་པོ་ཡིན་ཙང་ 2. དེས་ཨ་ཁུར་རྩམ་པ་སྤར་མོ་གང་ཙམ་ཡང་གཡར་པོ་མ་བྱས་.

The first clause is a simple linking verb construction describing the rich man. The second clause's subject དེས་ ("by that one") refers to the rich man. The active verb is "did not lend" (གཡར་པོ་མ་བྱས་), and the remainder modifies this verb. It consists of a "handful" (སྤར་མོ་), plus གང་, which here functions as "one," and ཙམ་, which means "approximately" or "about as much." These together (སྤར་མོ་གང་ཙམ་) convey "as much as one handful." "Even" (ཡང་), which is joined to this, is commonly used with negative verbs to convey "even as much as X, did not. . . ," or here, སྤར་མོ་གང་ཙམ་ཡང་གཡར་པོ་མ་བྱས་: "did not lend even as much as a handful." Another example of this use of ཡང་ and ཀྱང་ is: ཁོས་ང་ར་སྒོར་མོ་གཅིག་ཀྱང་སྤྲད་མ་སོང་ ("He did not give me even one dollar").

The above use of གང་ to convey "one" in measurements is common. For example, ང་ར་ཇ་དཀར་ཡོལ་གང་སྤྲོད་རོགས་གནང་ ("Please give me one cup of tea").

3. The third segment consists of four clauses: 1. དེ་ནས་ཉིན་ཤས་སོང་རྗེས་ཨ་ཁུས་སླར་ཡང་ཕྱུག་པོ་དེའི་ཁྱིམ་དུ་ཕྱིན་ནས་ 2. སླང་ཆེན་པོ་ཞིག་གཡར་བ་དང་སྦྲགས་ 3. དིང་སང་ལྷ་སར་རྩམ་པ་གོང་ཆེན་པོ་ཡོད་ཙང་ 4. ང་སང་ཉིན་རྩམ་པ་བཙོང་བར་འགྲོ་རྩིས་ཡོད་ཅེས་བཤད་.

The first clause is a simple active construction beginning with the time-slot phrase (དེ་ནས་+ ཉིན་ཤས་སོང་རྗེས་ - "after that + after a few days passed"). The remainder is the verb "went" (ཕྱིན་), the location of his going (ཕྱུག་པོ་དེའི་ཁྱིམ་དུ་ - "to the house of that rich man"), an adverbial word meaning "once again" (སླར་ཡང་), and the subject in the instrumental. The connective ནས་ links this to clause two.

The second clause consists of an implict subject (by Agu), the verb "to borrow" (གཡར་) and the object phrase "a big pan" (སླང་ཆེན་པོ་ཞིག་). Note that གཡར་ can mean both "borrow" and "lend." It is linked by the "together with" clause connector (see 7.9), which here conveys the idea that together with going to borrow a pan, he said.. . .

The third clause is a simple existential sentence, "the price of tsamba is high in Lhasa," linked to clause four by the "because" connective.

The final clause centers around an infinitive construction ("go to sell" - བཙོང་བར་འགྲོ་), which in turn is modified by the "plan to" particle (རྩིས་), so that it means "plan to go to sell tsamba." The rest consists of the subject ("I") and the time of the verbal action, "tomorrow."

4. The fourth segment consists of six clauses: 1. སྐད་ཆ་དེ་ཕྱུག་པོས་ཐོས་མ་ཐག 2. ཞུམ་བྱུས་ཙི་ཙི་མཐོང་བ་ལྟར་དགའ་སྣང་ཚད་མེད་བྱུང་སྟེ་ 3. ད་ནི་ཁེ་བཟང་ཆེན་པོ་ཞིག་ཐོབ་པ་བྱེད་དགོས་བསམས་ཏེ་ 4. ཁོས་ཨ་ཁུར་ལྷ་སའི་ཁྲོམ་རའི་ཟོག་གོང་དང་། བྲིན་ཚོང་གི་སྐོར་སོགས་ཞིབ་པར་དྲིས་རྗེས་ 5. ཁོ་དགའ་ཐག་ཆོད་ནས་ 6. བྱས་ན་སང་ཉིན་ང་ཡང་ཁྱོད་མཉམ་དུ་ལྷ་སར་རྩམ་པ་བཙོང་བར་འགྲོ་ཡི་ཡིན་ཞེས་བཤད་.

The first clause is a simple involuntary verb construction. The object comes first ("that speech"), followed by the subject ("by that rich man") and then the verb ("to hear") and the "as soon as" clause connective. Thus, "as soon as that rich man heard the speech."

The second clause begins with ལྟར་ ("like/as"), a common construction used to construct similes. In this case the phrase is: "like a cat seeing a mouse" (ཞུམ་བྱུས་ཙི་ཙི་མཐོང་བ་ལྟར་). Note that ལྟ་བུ་ could have been substituted for ལྟར་.

The second part of this clause means "got joy/happiness" (དགའ་སྣང་. . . བྱུང་). It consists of "joy/happiness" and the modifying adverbial ཚད་མེད་ ("boundless" or "limitless"). Thus, "(He) got extremely happy like a cat seeing a mouse."

Clause three explains what the implicit subject (the rich man) "thought" (བསམས་). It utilizes the དགོས་ pattern explained in 7.5.6, which here conveys: "(I) *have* to do something so that (I) will get a big profit."

Clause four is an active sentence whose core structure is: ཁོས་ཨ་ཁུར་. . . དྲིས་ (by him to Agu . . . asked). The verb "asked" is modified by the adverb ཞིབ་པར་, which means "in detail."

What he asked is: ཟོག་གོང་དང་། ཉིན་ཚོང་གི་སྐོར་སོགས་. ཟོག་གོང and ཉིན་ཚོང་ are unproblematic, conveying "prices" and "sales." སྐོར་ is a common term used for "about" or "concerning" something. It is normally accompanied by the genitive particle. Thus, "he asked *about* prices. . . ." The remainder of the clause consists of two location phrases linked by the genitive: Lhasa's market's (ལྷ་སའི་ཁྲོམ་རའི་ - lit., "of the market of Lhasa"). Thus, "he asked about prices and sales in Lhasa's market." One last element remains to be discussed: སོགས་. It was discussed in 5.4 where it was explained that with lists of enumerations it conveys the meaning of "et cetera" or "such as." Thus, "he asked about *such things* as the price. . . . "

The next two clauses describe how he felt (ཁོ་དགའ་ཐག་ཆོད་ནས་-"he, having felt very happy") and what he said (བྱས་ན་སང་ཉིན་ང་ཡང་. . . འགྲོ་ཡི་ཡིན་ - "well then, tomorrow I also. . . will go"). There is also the infinitive phrase ལྷ་སར་རྩམ་པ་བཙོང་བར་ ("to sell tsamba in Lhasa").

5. The fifth segment consists of four clauses : 1. ཕྱི་ཉིན་ཕྱུག་པོ་དེས་ཞོགས་པ་སྔ་པོ་ནས་ལངས་ཏེ་ 2. ཁལ་གཡག་ལ་རྩམ་པ་ཁལ་རྒྱབ་གཅིག་བཀལ་ནས་ 3. ལྷ་སར་ཐོན་རྒྱུའི་གྲ་སྒྲིག་བྱས་ཚར་ནས་ 4. ཨ་ཁུ་བསྒུགས་ནས་བསྐྱོད་.

The first clause is straightforward: a temporal (ཕྱི་ཉིན་) + subject (ཕྱུག་པོ་དེས་) + adverb (སྔ་པོ་ནས་) + verb (ལངས་) + clause connector (ཏེ་). The second clause is also simple. Its subject is continued from clause one ("by that rich man"), and it consists of the indirect object (ཁལ་གཡག་ལ་) + the direct object (རྩམ་པ་ཁལ་རྒྱབ་གཅིག་) + verb (བཀལ་) + clause connector (ནས་).

Clause three starts with a nominalized phrase meaning "the departure for Lhasa" (ལྷ་སར་ཐོན་རྒྱུའི་). It is linked to "preparations" (གྲ་སྒྲིག་) by the genitive, so that together they convey the meaning, "preparations for departing to Lhasa." The verbal phrase གྲ་སྒྲིག་བྱས་ ("to make preparations") in turn is modified by the verb ཚར་, which conveys the meaning of "finished" and is used with verbs by being placed immediately after their stem, for example: ཁོ་ཚོས་ཁ་ལག་ཟས་ཚར་སྐབས་ ("when they finished eating"). The final clause consists of a common construction (see 5.11.2) wherein two verbs linked by ནས་ convey simultaneous action : ཨ་ཁུ་བསྒུགས་ནས་ + བསྡད་ "waiting for Agu, he stayed (there)."

6. The sixth segment consists of: 1. ཨ་ཁུ་བསྟན་པས་རྩམ་སྒྲོ་སྡོང་པ་གཉིས་ཀྱི་ནང་གཟན་ཙ་བརྒྱངས་ཏེ་ 2. རྩམ་པ་ཡིན་ཁུལ་གྱིས་པོང་བུར་བཀལ་ནས་ 3. དེ་གར་སླེབས་རྗེས་ 4. ཁོང་གཉིས་མཉམ་དུ་ལྷ་སར་ཐོན་.

The first clause is a simple active verb sentence. Beginning with the subject in the instrumental (ཨ་ཁུ་བསྟན་པས་), it is followed by the indirect object (རྩམ་སྒྲོ་སྡོང་པ་གཉིས་ཀྱི་ནང་), the direct object (གཟན་ཙ་), and the verb (བརྒྱངས་).

The second clause is a bit tricky. It begins with a verb phrase that has been first modified by the "pretend" particle (ཁུལ་) (see 6.8) and then adverbialized by the instrumental particle (གྱིས་) (see 6.5.2). Thus, the linking verb construction "it is/was tsamba" (རྩམ་པ་ཡིན་) becomes "pretending it was tsamba" (རྩམ་པ་ཡིན་ཁུལ་) and then "in the manner of pretending it was tsamba" (རྩམ་པ་ཡིན་ཁུལ་གྱིས་). Clauses three and four are unproblematic.

7. The seventh segment consists of three clauses: 1. དེ་ཉིན་ཨ་ཁུ་བསྟན་པ་དང་ཕྱུག་པོ་ཁོང་གཉིས་ཉིན་གང་བསྐྱོད་ནས་ 2. དགོན་རྡུལ་ཆུང་ཆུང་ཞིག་གི་འགྲམ་དུ་སླེབས་པས་ 3. ཁོང་གཉིས་དོ་ནུབ་དགོན་པ་དེའི་ནང་ཞག་སྡོད་བྱ་རྒྱུར་ཁ་འཆམ་.

The first clause consists of the time-slot phrase "that day" (དེ་ཉིན་), a complex subject, "the two of them, Agu and the rich man" (ཨ་ཁུ་བསྟན་པ་དང་ཕྱུག་པོ་ཁོང་གཉིས་), the adverbial phrase "all day" (ཉིན་གང་), and the verb "went" (བསྐྱོད་). The second clause does not require comment.

The third clause contains a future nominalized verb phrase ཞག་སྡོད་བྱ་རྒྱུར་ ("the stopping overnight on a trip"), which functions as the object of the verb "agree" (ཁ་འཆམ་). Thus, what did they agree to? — to making an overnight stop.

8. The eighth segment consists of three clauses: 1. ཉིན་གང་བསྐྱོད་པའི་ངལ་དུབ་ཀྱིས་ཕྱུག་པོ་དེ་ཉལ་མ་ཐག་ 2. གཉིད་ལ་ཤོར་ནས་ 3. ཤི་བ་ལྟར་དུ་གྱུར་.

The first clause starts with an adverbialized phrase ཉིན་གང་བསྐྱོད་པའི་ངལ་དུབ་ཀྱིས་ ("in the manner of being tired from going all day"). This modifies the verb "to lie down" (ཉལ), explaining that "being tired from going all day, (someone) lay down." The subject, i.e., the one who lay down, is "the rich man" (ཕྱུག་པོ་དེ་), and the clause connector is the "as soon as" particle (མ་ཐག་). Thus together these mean, "Being tired from going all day, the rich man lay down, and as soon as he did so. . . ."

The second clause is the standard verb phrase conveying involuntarily falling asleep. The "having" clause connector links it to the third clause, which begins with another metaphorical phrase marked by ལྟར་-"like being dead" (ཤི་བ་ལྟར). It ends in with the past tense verb གྱུར་ "became" or "changed into." This verb requires use of the dative-locative so that the preceeding phrase is written ཤི་བ་ལྟར་དུ་. Together they mean, "came to be as if he were dead."

9. The ninth segment consists of three clauses: 1. ནམ་ཕྱེད་ཙམ་ལ་ཨ་ཁུ་བསྟན་པས་ཁ་ཁར་ཡར་ལངས་ཏེ་ 2. རང་གི་རྩམ་སྒྱེའི་ནང་གི་གཟན་རྩ་རྣམས་བོང་བུར་སྦྱེར་བ་དང་ 3. ཕྱུག་པའི་རྩམ་པ་ཁལ་རྒྱབ་གཅིག་པོ་དེ་རང་གི་སྒྱེ་མོའི་ནང་དུ་བརྒྱངས་.

The first clause begins with a time phrase meaning "at about midnight" (ནམ་ཕྱེད་ཙམ་ལ). ཙམ་ here modifies ནམ་ཕྱེད་ to convey the idea of "about" or "approximately." This is followed by the subject in the instrumental case (ཨ་ཁུ་བསྟན་པས་) and the verb "got up/arose" (ལངས་), here modified by the adverbial ཁ་ཁར་ ("quietly/silently/secretly"). Thus, "at about midnight, Agu quietly arose."

The subject of the next clause, Agu, is implicit. Clause two, therefore, begins with a long direct object phrase: རང་གི་རྩམ་སྒྱེའི་ནང་གི་གཟན་རྩ་རྣམས་ ("the hay and grass inside his own tsamba bag"). This is followed by the indirect object, "to the donkey" (བོང་བུར་), and then the active verb "give" (སྦྱེར་).

Clause three starts with the direct object phrase "that single load of tsamba of the rich man" (ཕྱུག་པའི་རྩམ་པ་ཁལ་རྒྱབ་གཅིག་པོ་དེ་). Next comes the indirect object phrase: "to the inside of (his) own tsamba bag" (རང་གི་སྒྱེ་མོའི་ནང་དུ་). Finally the active verb "stuffed" (བརྒྱངས་). Thus, "(Agu) stuffed the single load of the rich man into his own tsamba bag."

10. The tenth segment consists of four clauses: 1. དེ་ནས་ཨ་ཁུས་ཕྱུག་པོ་དེའི་རྩམ་སྒྱེ་སྟོང་པ་དེ་ལྷ་སྐུའི་ལག་ཏུ་བཞག་པ་དང་ 2. ཡང་རྩམ་པ་སྤར་མོ་གང་ཁྱེར་ནས་ 3. ལྷ་སྐུ་དེའི་ཁ་ལ་བྱུགས་རྗེས་ 4. གཞི་ནས་ཐུར་བཞིན་གཉིད་ཉལ་.

The first clause begins with the time-slot word "after that," and then the subject in the instrumental case (ཨ་ཁུས་). The object phrase ཕྱུག་པོ་དེའི་རྩམ་སྒྱེ་སྟོང་པ་དེ་ ("that empty bag of that rich man") occurs next. Following this is the verb "leave" (བཞག་) and the indirect object "in the hand of a statue of a god" (ལྷ་སྐུའི་ལག་ཏུ་). Thus, "after that, Agu left the empty tsamba bag of that rich man in the hand of a statue of a god, and. . . ."

The second clause begins with the word ཡང་ ("also" or "again"), followed by the object phrase རྩམ་པ་སྤར་མོ་གང་ ("one handful of tsamba"), and the active verb in the past tense ཁྱེར་ ("carried/took"). The subject continues to be Agu. Thus together they mean, "also, having taken a handful of tsamba."

Clause three again does not mention the subject. It consists only of an active verb "smear" (བྱུགས་), and the location of the verbal action, "in/to the mouth of that statue of the god" (ལྷ་སྐུ་དེའི་ཁ་ལ་). Clauses two and three therefore translate as, "Also, having taken a handful of tsamba, (he) smeared it on the mouth of the statue of the god." The clause connector here is "after" (རྗེས་), so "Also, *after* having taken a handful of tsamba, (he) smeared it on the mouth of the statue of the god."

The fourth clause begins with གཞི་ནས་, a term which means "only then." It is followed by the time phrase སྔར་བཞིན་("like before") and the active verb གཉིད་ཉལ་ ("lie down to sleep"). བཞིན་ here functions as "as" or "like." Agu continues to be the implicit subject.

11. The eleventh segment consists of three clauses: 1. ནམ་ལངས་རྗེས་ 2. ཕྱུག་པོ་དེས་རང་ཉིད་ཀྱི་རྩམ་པ་དོ་པོ་བསྡད་མེད་པ་མཐོང་འཕྲལ་ 3. ཨ་ཁུ་བོས་ཏེ་གཉིད་ལས་སད་.

The first clause "after dawn arose" (ནམ་ལངས་རྗེས་) functions as a time-slot phrase. Clause two consists of a subject (ཕྱུག་པོ་དེས་) and a nominalized verb phrase (རང་ཉིད་ཀྱི་རྩམ་པ་དོ་པོ་བསྡད་མེད་པ་), which serves as the object of the verb "see" (མཐོང་). This nominalized verb phrase breaks down into: "his own tsamba load" (རང་ཉིད་ཀྱི་རྩམ་པ་དོ་པོ་) and the negative verbal phrase "not sitting there (lit., sitting there did not exist)" (བསྡད་མེད་). རང་ཉིད་ཀྱི་རྩམ་པ་དོ་པོ་ could have been written: རང་ཉིད་ཀྱི་རྩམ་པའི་དོ་པོ་. The particle པ་ converts this into the nominalized phrase: "the not sitting there of the load of his own tsamba." Thus, the rich man saw what?—"He saw that his load of tsamba was not sitting there."

The "at once" clause connector links this to clause three which carries over implicitly the subject of clause two (the rich man). Clause three consists of the active verb "to call" (བོས་) and the object of the calling, Agu. Thus, "(the rich man) called Agu." The ཏེ་ clause connector here conveys that the "calling" woke him up (གཉིད་ལས་སད་). The phrase གཉིད་ལས་སད་ breaks down into "sleep" (གཉིད་), "from, than" (ལས་), and "awoke" (སད་).

12. The twelfth segment consists of one clause: ཁོང་གཉིས་པོས་རྩམ་སྒྲེ་སྟོང་པ་ལྷ་སྐུའི་ལག་ཏུ་ཡོད་པ་མཐོང་.

The subject of this phrase (ཁོང་གཉིས་པོས་) goes with the verb "see" (མཐོང་) — thus, "the two of them saw. . ." The object phrase (what they saw) consists again of a nominalized verb construction རྩམ་སྒྲེ་སྟོང་པ་ལྷ་སྐུའི་ལག་ཏུ་ཡོད་པ་ ("the empty tsamba bag existing in the hand of the deity").

13. The thirteenth segment consists of four clauses: 1. ཨ་ཁུ་བསྟན་པས་འཛིག་རྟེན་མི་རྣམས་ཀྱིས་དུས་ཡུན་རིང་པོ་ལྷ་མ་གསོལ་བར་བརྟེན་ 2. ལྷ་ཕལ་ཆེར་ལྟོགས་ནས་ 3. ཐབས་ཤེས་མ་བྱུང་སྐབས་ 4. ཁྱེད་ཀྱི་ཙམ་པ་འགམས་པ་རེད་ཅེས་བཤད་.

These clauses convey Agu's explanation of where the tsamba went. The subject (ཨ་ཁུ་བསྟན་པས་) goes with the final verb "said" (བཤད་), the rest conveying what he said. His comment begins with an active verb sentence whose subject is "humans" (འཛིག་རྟེན་མི་རྣམས་ཀྱིས་). The verbal action is "not make offerings" (མ་གསོལ་), and the object is "god" (ལྷ་). Modifying this is the phrase "for a long time" (དུས་ཡུན་རིང་པོ་). With the "because" connector, this means, "because humans have not made offerings to the god for a long time."

The next clause completes this stating that "the god was probably hungry "(ལྷ་ལྟོགས་ཆེར་ལྟོགས་). The "having" clause connective conveys that "having been hungry, . . ."

Clause three omits the subject and begins with the object "method" (ཐབས་ཤེས་) and the verb "get" (བྱུང་), made negative by མ་. Together they convey "having not got any means [for alleviating the hunger]." The final clause concludes that the implied subject (the god) "ate your tsamba" (ཁྱེད་ཀྱི་ཙམ་པ་འགམས་པ་རེད). འགམས་ is a special verb used for "eating tsamba."

14. The fourteenth segment consists of one clause: ཕྱུག་པོ་དེས་ལྷ་འདིས་ངའི་རྩམ་པ་ཁོ་ན་བཟས་པ་ལས་ཁྱོད་ཀྱི་རྩམ་པ་དེ་མི་ཟ་བ་གང་ཡིན་ནམ་ཞེས་དྲིས་པར.

The overall structure is ཕྱུག་པོ་དེས་. . . དྲིས་ ("by the rich man . . . asked"). What the rich man asked, however, is a bit complicated. In essence it is an active verb construction with two sub-clauses within it that have been nominalized.

The subject of the first clause within a clause is ལྷ་འདིས་ ("by this god"). The object is ངའི་རྩམ་པ་ (my tsamba), the active verb is བཟས་ ("ate"), and there is an adverb ཁོ་ན་ ("only"). It is nominalized by པ་ and then linked to the next sub-clause by ལས་, which here means "than" rather than "from." Together they mean, "Than that god eating only my tsamba, . . ." Other examples of this common use of ལས་ are ཚལ་ལས་ཤ་གོང་ཆེ་: ("Meat is more expensive than vegetables") and འདིར་ཡོང་བ་ལས་ལྷ་སར་ཕྱིན་ན་ཡག་གི་རེད་ ("Rather than coming here, if (you) go to Lhasa it will be better").

The second sub-clause begins with the phrase ཁྱོད་ཀྱི་རྩམ་པ་ ("your tsamba") and is followed by མི་ཟ་བ་ ("not eating"). This in turn is followed by the interrogative phrase གང་ཡིན་ནམ་, which means "why." Together the two sub-clauses convey: "Than that god eating only my tsamba, your tsamba not eating, why?" Or in normal English, "Why did that god eat only my tsamba and not yours?"

Finally, note that the verb "asked" (དྲིས་པར་) is nominalized with the dative-locative. This construction conveys "to or concerning the asking," indicating that what follows is the answer to that question (see 6.6.3).

15. The fifteenth segment consists of one sentence: ཨ་ཁུས་ལྷ་ཁྱེད་ལ་མཉེས་པོ་ཡོད་པས་རེད་ཅེས་ལན་བཏབ.

The main structure of this is: ཨ་ཁུས་. . . ལན་བཏབ་ ("Agu replied. . ."). What he replied was: ལྷ་ཁྱེད་ལ་མཉེས་པོ་ཡོད་པས་རེད་. This is a simple existential construction consisting of subject (ལྷ་) + object (ཁྱེད་) + dative-locative (ལ་) + adjective (མཉེས་པོ་) + existential verb (ཡོད་པས་རེད་). Together these mean, "The god likes you."

Note that the existential verb ཡོད་པས་རེད་ is a new construction that conveys "it is because. . . ." This, therefore, would be translated as "it is because the god likes you."

This construction is equivalent to: ཡོད་པ་ཡིན་ཙང་་རེད་. Several other ways to express this are: (a) ཡོད་པ་ཡིན་པས་ན་རེད་, (b) ཡོད་པ་ཡིན་པས་ནའོ་, (c) ཡོད་པས་སོ་, (d) ཡིན་པས་སོ་, (e) ཡོད་པས་དབང་གིས་རེད, or negative existential verbs such as (f) མེད་པས་སོ་ or (g) མིན་པས་སོ་.

16. The sixteenth segment consists of three clauses: 1. དེས་ན་ཕྲུག་པོ་དེས་དབུགས་རིང་གཏོང་བཞིན་པར་ 2. ང་ལྟ་སར་འགྲོ་ཡི་མིན། 3. ཁྱེད་རང་གཅིག་པུར་རྒྱུགས་ཤིག་ཅེས་བཤད་.

The first clause begins with དེས་ན་ ("therefore"), another in the class of words that function as clause connectors but are placed at the head of the second of two clauses. Others in that class that occurred in earlier lessons are: འོན་ཀྱང་, བྱས་ཙང་, and ཡིན་ན་ཡང་. The remainder of the clause is a simple active construction consisting of a subject in the instrumental case, and the active verb ("sighed" - དབུགས་རིང་གཏོང་). It is modified by བཞིན་པར་, which here conveys the meaning that "while in the process of X, something else was done." In this case the second action is conveyed by the final verb, "said" (བཤད་). Thus, something was said in the manner of or while sighing. Note that "sigh" in Tibet is considered an active verb.

Clause two is a simple negative construction. Clause three is another simple construction consisting of the subject ("you"), an adverb ("alone" - གཅིག་པུར་), and a verb ("go away" - རྒྱུགས་).

The particle ཤིག་ is a common form used with verbs ending in ས་ to convey the imperative.

17. The seventeenth segment consist of two clauses: 1. ཨ་ཁུ་བསྟན་པས་ང་གཅིག་པུར་འགྲོ་གི་མིན་ཅེས་བཤད་ནས་ 2. ཁོང་གཉིས་མཉམ་དུ་སླར་ཡང་ཁྱིམ་ལ་ཕྱིར་ལོག་སོང་.

The first clause consists of a direct speech segment, "Agu said, "I will not go alone." It is linked to clause two by the "having" clause connective, constructing the phrase "having said, . . ." Clause two ends the story with a simple descriptive active sentence: "The two of them together, once again, returned to (their) house."

7.14. 2. Reading number two: "Coming from Afghanistan to Pakistan"

7.14.2.1 Tibetan text

ཨབ་གྷ་ནི་སི་ཐན་ནས་པ་ཀི་སི་ཐན་བར་དུ་ཡོང་བ་[4]

འདི་གར་ཚགས་པར་ཁང་དུ་ཁ་ར་ཆི་ནས་གློག་འཕྲིན་འབྱོར་གསལ།   ཕྱི་ལོ་ 1978 ལོ་ཨབ་གྷ་ནི་སི་ཐན་ལ་ཟིང་འབྲུག་ལངས་རྗེས་ང་ཚོ་པ་ཀི་སི་ཐན་བར་བྲོས་བྱོལ་དུ་ཡོང་ཅིང་།   ལམ་ཁ་ལ་ཉི་མ་མང་པོ་གོམ་པ་བརྒྱབ་པའི་དུས་ལ་སྐབས་རེ་

[4]This reading selection is a simplified newspaper article.

ལྟོ་ཆས་ཆད་དེ་རྒན་རྒོག་ན་ནས་ཤི་བ་མ་ཚད། མཚམས་མཚམས་གནམ་གྲུས་མེ་མདའ་བརྒྱབ་ནས་མི་མང་པོ་བསད་པ་རེད། འོན་ཀྱང་པ་ཀི་སི་ཐན་གྱི་ས་མཚམས་སུ་སླེབས་ཚེ་པ་ཀི་སི་ཐན་གྱི་གཞུང་དང་། རོགས་རམ་ཚོགས་པ་རྣམས་ཀྱིས་ང་ཚོར་སྙིང་རྗེ་ཆེན་པོའི་སྒོ་ནས་ལྟོ་ཆས་དང་། གོས་ལོག། སྨན་སོགས་སྐྱོབ་གསོ་གནང་བས་ང་ཚོར་ཕན་ཐོག་ཆེན་པོ་བྱུང་།

ས་མཚམས་དེར་ཟླ་བ་ཁ་ཤས་བསྡད་རྗེས་ང་ཚོ་ཚང་མ་གཞིས་ཆགས་བྱེད་ཆེད་པ་ཀི་སི་ཐན་གྱི་ལྷོ་ཕྱོགས་སུ་བཏང་ཞིང་། སྔོན་མར་གཞིས་ཆགས་འདིར་སླེབས་ནས་ད་བར་ང་ཚོས་ཧུར་བརྩོན་གྱིས་ཤིང་ནགས་སྟུག་པོ་བཅད་པ་མ་ཟད། ས་ཞིང་གསར་པ་མང་པོ་བཟོས་པ་དང་། ཁང་པ་དང་། སློབ་གྲྭ། ལག་ཤེས་བཟོ་གྲྭ། ཚོང་ཁང་བཅས་གསར་པ་བརྒྱབ་པས་མ་ཚད། ཕྱི་ལོ་ཡང་ང་ཚོས་སྨན་ཁང་ཞིག་རྒྱག་རྩིས་ཡོད། ད་ཆ་པ་ཀི་སི་ཐན་གྱི་ལྷོ་ཕྱོགས་ཀྱི་གཞིས་ཆགས་འདིར་ཨབ་ག་ནི་སི་ཐན་གྱི་མི་ཁྲི་གཅིག་ཙམ་ཡོད་པ་རེད།

7.14.2.2 Interlinear translation

afghanistan from pakistan up-to come

1. here newspaper house to karachi from telegram arrived clear/ year 1978 year afghanistan to disturbance
2. arose after i pl. pakistan up-to refugee to come having/ road today many walk when sometimes
3. food exhausted having old sick having die not only/ sometimes airplane-by gun fire having people many kill past compl./
4. nevertheless pakistan of boundary to arrived when pakistan of government and/ help association pl. by i pl.-to compassion
5. great-of door from food and/ clothes/ medicine etc. relief do (h.) because i pl.-to benefit great got/
6. border that-to month several stayed after i pl. all settle do for pakistan of south side to sent having/
7. formerly settlement this-to arrive having now until i pl.-by diligence by forest dense cut not only/ fields new
8. many made and/ house and/ school/ handicraft factory/ store etc. new built because not only/ year
9. also i pl.-by hospital one built plan exist/ now pakistan of settlement this-to afghanistan of person 10,000
10. one about exist/

7.14.2.3 Translation

Coming from Afghanistan to Pakistan

(What follows is according to) a cable that arrived at this newspaper office from Karachi. In 1978, after disturbances arose in Afghanistan, we came seeking refuge in Pakistan. When we were walking on the road for many days, sometimes we were out of food and the elderly got sick and died. Not only that, but sometimes airplanes shot (at us) and killed many people. Nevertheless, when we arrived at the Pakistan border, the Pakistan government and relief agencies compassionately gave us aid in the form of food, clothes, medicines, etc. Because of this, we benefited greatly.

After we stayed at the border for several months, we were sent to southern Pakistan for the purpose of resettling all of us. From the time (lit., "when") we arrived initially at the resettlement camp until now, we not only energetically cut down a dense forest, but we made many new fields and newly built such things as houses, stores, schools, and handicraft centers. Not only that, but next year we even plan to build a hospital. There are now about 10,000 Afghanistan refugees in this resettlement camp in the south of Pakistan.

7.14.2.4. Grammatical notes

1. The first segment consists of the title: ཨཕ་གྷ་ནི་སི་ཐན་ནས་པ་ཀི་སི་ཐན་བར་དུ་ཡོང་བ་.

བར་དུ་ usually means "up to" or "until," and here it is used with ནས་ (in its prepositional function of "from") to convey: "from" X "up to" Y. The subject is implicit here so that this translates as "the coming from X to Y."

2. The second segment consists of the sentence: འདི་གར་ཚགས་པར་ཁང་དུ་ཁ་ར་ཆི་ནས་གློག་འཕྲིན་འབྱོར་གསལ།.

This sentence is one of a number of standard ways that newspaper articles begin by indicating the source of the story. In this case it informs us that the story derives from a telegram from Karachi. The first part འདི་གར་ཚགས་པར་ཁང་དུ་ conveys the location of the verb འབྱོར་ ("to arrive") — "(it arrived) in the newspaper office here." The rest of this segment is straightforward until the final word གསལ་ ("clear"). In newspapers this has come to mean "as was stated in" or "according to" rather than "clear." Other parallel phrases used equivalently in newspapers are: གསལ་ལྟར, དོན་, དོན་དུ་, བརྗོད་ན་, ལྟར་, and དོན་ལྟར་ན་.

3. The third segment consists of two clauses: 1. ཕྱི་ལོ་ 1978 ལོ་ཨཕ་གྷ་ནི་སི་ཐན་ལ་ཟིང་འཁྲུག་ལངས་རྗེས་ 2. ང་ཚོ་པ་ཀི་སི་ཐན་བར་བྲོས་བྱོལ་དུ་ཡོང་ཅིང་.

བར་ in clause two is a variant of བར་དུ་ in clause one above, conveying the meaning "up to." Therefore, "they fled (up) to Pakistan."

The construction སྐྱབས་འཚོལ་དུ་ functions here as an adverbial conveying in what manner they came—they came seeking refuge.

4. The fourth segment consists of five clauses: 1. ལམ་ཁ་ལ་ཉི་མ་མང་པོ་གོམ་པ་བརྒྱབ་པའི་དུས་ལ་ 2. སྐབས་རེ་ལྟོ་ཆས་ཆད་དེ་ 3. རྒན་གོག་ན་ནས་ཤི་བ་མ་ཚད། 4. མཚམས་མཚམས་གནམ་གྲུས་མེ་མདའ་བརྒྱབ་ནས་ 5. མི་མང་པོ་བསད་པ་རེད.

Clause one begins by specifying the location of the verbal action, namely, "on the road" (ལམ་ཁ་ལ་). It is followed by the main verb ("walked") and a phrase meaning "many days." Together these mean "(they) walked many days on the road." Note that the clause connective དུས་ལ་ is identical with the more common སྐབས་ (སུ་).

Clause two is a sentence based on the involuntary verb ཆད་ ("to be short of, missing"). ལྟོ་ཆས་ ("food") conveys what is in short supply—food—and སྐབས་རེ་ ("sometimes") conveys when this occurs.

Clause three is another involuntary sentence that begins with the subject — "old people" (རྒན་གོག་)—followed by the involuntary verb "to be sick" (ན་). It is linked to the verb ཤི་ ("to die") by the ནས་ connective so that together they convey, "old people having become ill, died." The clause ends with the "not only" clause connective (མ་ཚད), so that, "not only did old people get sick and die."

The fourth clause begins with the adverb of time "sometimes" (མཚམས་མཚམས་), followed by the subject in the instrumental case: "by planes" (གནམ་གྲུས་). The clause ends with the verbal phrase "fired guns" (མེ་མདའ་བརྒྱབ་)

The fifth clause continues the subject of the previous clause ("by planes"). It begins with the object phrase མི་མང་པོ་ ("many people"), followed by the active verb "killed" (བསད་པ་རེད). Together these convey, "Planes fired guns and killed many people."

5. The fifth segment consists of three clauses: 1. འོན་ཀྱང་པ་ཀི་སི་ཐན་གྱི་ས་མཚམས་སུ་སླེབས་ཚེ་ 2. པ་ཀི་སི་ཐན་གྱི་གཞུང་དང་། རོགས་རམ་ཚོགས་པ་རྣམས་ཀྱིས་ང་ཚོར་སྙིང་རྗེ་ཆེན་པོའི་སྒོ་ནས་ལྟོ་ཆས་དང་། གོས་ལོག། སྨན་སོགས་སྐྱོབ་གསོ་གནང་བས་ 3. ང་ཚོར་ཕན་ཐོག་ཆེན་པོ་བྱུང་།.

འོན་ཀྱང་ ("nevertheless") in clause one is one of the clause connectives that occur at the beginning of the second clause rather than at the end of the first. It is followed by a phrase that specifies the location (པ་ཀི་སི་ཐན་གྱི་ས་མཚམས་སུ་-at/on the border of Pakistan) of the verb "to arrive." The "when" clause connective links this with clause two.

The second clause begins with a long subject in the instrumental case that consists of two elements joined by the conjunction "and" (དང་): པ་ཀི་སི་ཐན་གྱི་གཞུང་ ("Pakistan's government") and རོགས་རམ་ཚོགས་པ་ ("aid agencies"). Both of these are modified by the pluralizer རྣམས་ and the instrumental ཀྱིས་. The subject's action is "gave relief aid" (སྐྱོབ་གསོ་གནང་).

The rest of the segment consists of the indirect object ང་ཚོར་ ("to us"), the adverbial phrase སྙིང་རྗེ་ཆེན་པོའི་སྒོ་ནས་ ("in the manner of great compassion"), and the direct object—what was given as relief aid, namely, ལྟོ་ཆས་དང་། གོས་ལོག། སྨན་སོགས་ ("foodstuffs, clothes, medicines, and so forth"). Note again that the use of སོགས་ conveys that this list is incomplete, in other words, it means "etc." or "and so forth." Thus, together these mean, "Pakistan's government and Relief Agencies compasionately gave us relief aid of foodstuffs, clothes, medicines, etc."

6. The sixth segment consists of three clauses : 1. ས་མཚམས་དེར་ཟླ་བ་ཁ་ཤས་བསྡད་རྗེས་ 2. ང་ཚོ་ཚང་མ་གཞིས་ཆགས་བྱེད་ཆེད་ 3. པ་ཀི་སི་ཐན་གྱི་ལྷོ་ཕྱོགས་སུ་བཏང་ཞིང་.

The first has "we" as its implicit subject. It begins with the location of the action, "on that border" (ས་མཚམས་དེར་), followed by a time phrase meaning "several months" (ཟླ་བ་ཁ་ཤས་), and then the verb "to sit, stay, live" (བསྡད་). Thus, "(we) stayed on that border for several months."

The second clause consists of an object phrase, "all of us" (ང་ཚོ་ཚང་མ་), an active verb, "to settle permanently" (གཞིས་ཆགས་བྱེད་), and the "for the purpose of" particle (ཆེད་), so that together the clause conveys, "for the purpose of settling all of us." The article does not specify who wanted to do that.

The third clause says what was done to accomplish this. An unnamed subject "sent" (བཏང་) an unnamed object ("us") to the south of Pakistan (པ་ཀི་སི་ཐན་གྱི་ལྷོ་ཕྱོགས་སུ་).

7. The seventh segment consists of five clauses: 1. ཐོག་མར་གཞིས་ཆགས་འདིར་སླེབས་ནས་ 2. ད་བར་ང་ཚོས་ཧུར་བརྩོན་གྱིས་ཤིང་ནགས་སྟུག་པོ་བཅད་པ་མ་ཟད། 3. ས་ཞིང་གསར་པ་མང་པོ་བཟོས་པ་དང་། 4. ཁང་པ་དང་། སློབ་གྲྭ། ལག་ཤེས་བཟོ་གྲྭ། ཚོང་ཁང་བཅས་གསར་པ་བརྒྱབ་པས་མ་ཆད། 5. ཕྱི་ལོ་ཡང་ང་ཚོས་སྨན་ཁང་ཞིག་རྒྱག་རྩིས་ཡོད་.

The first clause is an involuntary sentence with the implicit subject "we" and the core verb "to arrive" (སླེབས་). The location of the arriving is གཞིས་ཆགས་འདིར་ ("in this settlement"). The clause begins with the term ཐོག་མར་ ("at first"). Together these convey, "At first, having arrived in this settlement."

The second clause is linked to clause one by ད་བར་, which means "up to now." Thus, it conveys that "from having arrived in the settlement up to now. . . ." The clause, however, is basically an active sentence with the subject ང་ཚོས་ ("by us") doing "cutting" (བཅད་) of dense forests (ཤིང་ནགས་སྟུག་པོ་). The adverbial phrase ཧུར་བརྩོན་གྱིས་ ("energetically") modifies the active verb. The "not-only" clause connective (མ་ཟད) is joined to these, conveying: "Not only did we energetically cut dense forests. . . ."

The third clause continues what the subject ("we") did, namely, "made" (བཟོས་)

"many new fields" (ས་ཞིང་གསར་པ་མང་པོ་).

The fourth clause continues this by listing other things the subjects did, namely, ཁང་པ་དང་། སློབ་གྲྭ། ལག་ཤེས་བཟོ་གྲྭ། ཚོང་ཁང་བཅས་གསར་པ་བརྒྱབ་ ("built newly houses, schools, handicraft centers, and stores"). Whether each of these is plural or singular is a matter of context. This ends with a "not-only" (པས་མ་ཚད་) clause connective linking this to clause five.

The fifth clause states what the same subject plans to build (རྒྱག་ཙིས་ཡོད་) next year (ཕྱི་ལོ་): a hospital (སྨན་ཁང་).

8. The eighth segment consists of a single sentence: ད་ཆ་པ་ཀི་སི་ཐན་གྱི་ལྷོ་ཕྱོགས་ཀྱི་གཞིས་ཆགས་འདིར་ ཨབ་ལྷ་ནི་སི་ཐན་གྱི་མི་ཁྲི་གཅིག་ཙམ་ཡོད་པ་རེད་.

This clause is an existential sentence whose basic structure is "in this settlement in the southern part of Pakistan (པ་ཀི་སི་ཐན་གྱི་ལྷོ་ཕྱོགས་ཀྱི་གཞིས་ཆགས་འདིར་) there exist (ཡོད་པ་རེད་) about 10,000 Afghanis (ཨབ་ལྷ་ནི་སི་ཐན་གྱི་མི་ཁྲི་གཅིག་ཙམ་)." The clause starts with the time-slot word "now" (ད་ཆ་).

7.15 Vocabulary

བཀའ་དྲི་	asking (h.); va. — ཞུ་ (gəndri shu)
བཀའ་མོལ་	talk, discussion, conversation (h.); va. — གནང་ (h.) (gāmöö nān)
བཀལ་	va. p. of འགེལ་: loaded (gɛ̄ɛ)
སྐད་གཏོང་	va. to call, invite (gɛ̄ɛ dōŋ)
སྐབས་རེ་	sometimes (gəbre)
སྐོར་	about, concerning (gɔ̄ɔ)
སྐྱོན་ཤོར་	vi. to get damaged, hurt (gyȫn shɔ̄ɔ)
སྐྱོབ་གསོ་	welfare (gyōbso)
ཁ་ཁར་	quietly (kāga)
ཁ་འཆམ་	vi. to agree (kā chām)
ཁ་འདོན་	prayers, praying; va. — བྱེད་ (kāndön cheè)
ཁ་ར་ཆི་	Karachi (kāraji)
ཁ་ལ་ཁར་	"about to" clause connective (kāla kār)
ཁམས་	Kham (eastern area of Tibet) (kām)
ཁར་	"about to" clause connective (kār)
ཁལ་	a volume measure (kɛ̄ɛ)
ཁལ་རྒྱབ་	a load (kɛ̄ɛgyəb)
ཁལ་གཡག་	a carrying/ transportation yak (kɛ̄ɛyaà)
ཁེ་བཟང་	profit (kēbsaŋ)
ཁོ་ན་	only (kōna)
ཁོང་གཉིས་པོ་	the two together (kōŋ ñ̄ibo) (h.)
ཁྱེར་	va. p. of འཁྱེར་ took, carried (kēr)
ཁྲི་གཅིག་	10,000 (tr̄ijig)
གོ་ཁྲིད་	leader, boss (gudri)
གོང་	"before" clause connective གོང་ + dative-locative (ལ་ etc.) (gən)

གོམ་པ་	walking, steps, va. — རྒྱག་ (gomba gyaà)
གོས་ལོག་	clothing (gölɔɔ̀)
གྱུར་	vi. p. of འགྱུར་ became (gyur)
གྲ་སྒྲིག་	preparation; va. — བྱེད (trədriì)
གྲབས་	"about to "clause connective (drəb)
གྲབས་བྱེད་དུས་	"about to" clause connective (drəb chedüü)
གློག་འཕྲིན་	cable, telegram, telex (lɔ̄gdrin)
དགའ་སྣང་	happiness (ganaŋ)
དགའ་བསུ་	welcome, va. — ཞུ་ (gəsu shu)
དགོན་རྡུལ་	ruined monastery (gönhrü)
དགོས་	have to; want to (göö)
འགམས་	va. to eat tsamba (gam)
འགོ་འཁྲིད་	leader (gudri)
རྒྱག་	va. auxiliary verb used with nouns: to build, shoot , etc., pres./fut. of རྒྱབ་ (gyaà)
རྒྱུགས་	va. to go (gyuù)
སྒྲེ་མོ་	bag, sack (gyemo)
བརྒྱངས་	va. p. of རྒྱོང་: stuffed (gyaŋ)
བརྒྱད་པ	8th (gyɛba)
བསྒུགས་	va. p. of སྒུག་: waited (guù)
ངལ་དུབ་	tired (ŋeedub)
ངེས་	certainty particle
དངོས་གནས་	really (ŋɔ̄nɛɛ̀)
མངར་མོ་	sweet (ŋāāmo)

སྔ་ལོ་	last year (ŋālo)
གཅིག་པུ་	alone (jīgu; jīgbu)
གཅིག་པོ་	a single item, one alone (jīgbu)
བཅད་	va. p. of གཅོད་: cut (jɛ̄ɛ̀)
ཆད་	vi. to be missing, short of (chɛ̄ɛ̀)
ཆབས་སྒྲགས་	"together with" clause connective (chə̄bdraà)
ཆུ་གཏོང་	va. to irrigate (chū dōŋ)
ཆུ་ཚོད་	o'clock; hour (chōdzöö̀)
ཆེ་རུ་	increasing, bigger; va. — གཏོང་ (to make bigger, larger); vi. — ཕྱིན་ (to become bigger, larger) (chēru)
འཇིག་རྟེན་མི་རྣམས་	human beings (jigden minə)
བརྟེན་ན་	see གསལ་
ཉིན་གང་	all day (ñingaŋ)
ཉེ་	"about to" particle (ñe)
ཉེར་	sm. ཉེ་ (ñer)
ཉོ་ཆ་	shopping (ñobja)
གཉིད་	sleep (ñiì)
གཉིད་སད་	vi. and va. to be awoken or awake from sleep (ñīì sɛ̄ɛ̀)
གཉིད་ལས་སད་	sm. གཉིད་སད་ (ñiì lɛɛ̀ sɛ̄ɛ̀)
མཉམ་དུ་	together (ñəmdu)
མཉེས་པོ་	like (h.) (ñēēbo)
སྙན་ཞུ་	report (ñɛ̄shu)
སྙིང་རྗེ་	compassion (ñīŋje)
ཏང་	political party (dāŋ)
ལྟ་བུ་	similar, like, as (dābu)
ལྟར་	similar, like, as (dār)

ལྟོ་ food (dō)
སྟེར་ va. to give (dēē)
སྟོང་པ་ empty (dōŋba)
བསྟུན་ "according to," "together with" clause connective (dūn)
བསྟུན་ནས་ sm. བསྟུན་ (dūnnɛ)
ཐག་ཆོད་ "very" or "extremely" (tāgjöö)
ཐབས་ means, methods (tāb)
ཐབས་ཤེས་ means, methods (tābshɛɛ̀)
ཐོག་མར་ initially (tɔ̄ɔmaa)
ད་ཆ་ now (ta̲cha)
ད་བར་ until now (ta̲bar)
དང་ཆབས་ཅིག་ "together with" clause connective (da̲ŋ chābji)
དང་མཉམ་དུ་ "together with" clause connective (da̲ŋ ñāmdo)
དུད་ཚང་ household, family (du̲dzan)
དེ་གར་ there (te̲gar)
དོ་དགོང་ tonight (to̲goŋ)
དོ་ནུབ་ tonight (to̲nub)
དོ་པོ་ a load (do̲bo)
དོན་ see གསལ་ (tö̲n)
དོན་ལྟར་ན་ see གསལ་ (tö̲ndarna)
དོན་དུ་ see གསལ་ (tö̲ndu)
དྲིས་ va. p. of འདྲི་: asked (tri̲ì)
འདི་གར་ here (di̲gar)
ནའང་ even though (na̲ aŋ)
ན་ཡང་ even though (na̲ yaŋ)
ནམ་ཕྱེད་ midnight (na̲mjeè)
གནས་ཚུལ་ situation; news, events, conditions (nɛ̄ɛ̄dzüü)
པ་ཀི་སི་ཐན་ Pakistan (bāgisidan)
པ་དང་ཆབས་ཅིག་ "together with" clause connective (bədaŋ chābji)
པ་དང་ཐབས་བསྟུན་ "together with" clause connective, "according to" clause connective (bədaŋ tāb dūn)
པ་དང་བསྟུན་ "together with" clause connective, "according to" clause connective (bədaŋ dūn)
པ་དང་སྦྲགས་ "together with" clause connective (bədaŋ dra̲à)
ཕན་ཐོགས་ benefit (pɛ̄ndoò)
ཕལ་ཆེར་ probably (pɛ̄ɛ̄jee)
བར་དུ་ up to (ba̲do; pa̲rtu)
ཕོང་བུ་ donkey (phu̲ŋgu)
བོས་ va p. of འབོད་: called, shouted (bö̲ö̀)
བྱས་ན་ well then (che̲na)
བྱུགས་ va. to smear (ju̲ù)
བྲིན་ཚོང་ sales, marketing (dri̲ndzoŋ)
བྲོས་བྱོལ་ seeking refuge, fleeing (drö̲jöö)
དབུགས་རིང་ sighing, a sigh; va. — གཏོང་ (ūriŋ dōŋ)
འབྲུག་ཡུལ་ Bhutan (dru̲gyüü)
འབྲེལ་ "together with" clause connective (dre̲)
འབྲེལ་ "according to" clause connective (dre̲)
སྦར་མོ་གང་ a handful (ba̲rmo ga̲n)
མ་ + vb. གོང "before" clause connective མ + vb. གོང་ (ma̲ . . . go̲ŋ)

མ་ཚད་ "not only" clause connective (matsɛɛ̀)

མ་ཟད་ sm. མ་ཚད་ (masɛɛ̀)

མོད་ "even though" clause connective (mö̈ö)

རྨོན་པ་རྒྱག་ va. to plow (mõnba gyaà)

སྨན་ medicine (mɛ̃n)

ཙམ་ about, approximately (dzām)

ཙི་ཙི་ mouse (dzīdzi)

བཙན་བྱོལ་པ་ refugee (dzɛ̃njöba)

རྩ་ཁྲིམས་ constitution (dzə̄drim)

རྩམ་སྒྲི་ small bag for carrying tsamba

རྩམ་པ་ tsamba (roasted barley flour) (dzāmba)

རྩིས་ "plan/intend to" clause connective (dzī)

ཚགས་པར་ཁང་ newspaper office (tsāgbar kāŋ)

ཚར་ vi. to be finished (tsār)

མཚམས་མཚམས་ sometimes (tsāmtsām)

ཞག་སྡོད་ an overnight stop on a trip (shagdöö)

ཞབས་འདེགས་ serving, service; va. — ཞུ་ (h.) to serve (shəbdeg shu)

ཞིབ་པ་ detailed, in detail (shibə)

ཞུ་ va. to say, ask or tell (to someone of equal or higher status) (shu)

ཞུས་ va. p. of ཞུ་ (shüü)

ཞུམ་བུ་ cat (shimi; shumbu)

ཞོགས་པ་ morning (shɔɔgɛ; shɔgba)

གཞི་ནས་ only then (shinɛɛ̀)

གཞི་བཟུང་ "according to" clause connective (shisuŋ)

གཞིས་ཆགས་ resettlement, resettling (shijaà)

གཞོན་པ་ youth (shönnu)

བཞིན་ as, like (shin)

ཟིང་འཁྲུག་ disturbance, riot; uprising; vi. — ལངས་ (siŋdru laŋ)

ཟོག་གོང་ price of goods (sɔɔ̀goṅ)

གཟན་རྩྭ་ hay and straw (sɛndzə)

བཟས་ va. p. of ཟ་: ate (sɛɛ̀)

ན་ནིང་ last year (dəñin)

ཟླ་བ་ month (dawa)

འང་ "even though" clause connective (aŋ)

ཡོད་པས་རེད་ it is because (yöbɛreè)

རང་ self (raŋ)

རང་ཉིད་ one's own (raŋñiì)

རི་པིན་ Japan (ribin)

རིང་པོ་ long (riŋgu)

རུང་ "even though" clause connective (ruŋ)

རོགས་རམ་ཚོགས་པ་ relief/ aid agency (rɔram tsɔ̄gba)

ལ་ཁད་ལ་ "about to" clause connective (la khɛla)

ལག་ hand (lag)

ལག་ཁྱེར་ permit (laggye)

ལག་ཤེས་བཟོ་གྲྭ་ handicraft workshop (lagsheè sodra)

ལམ་ཁ་ road (laŋga)

ལའང་ even (ləaŋ)

ལས་ than; from (lɛɛ̀)

ལོ་གསར་ new year (losar)

ལོས་ certainty particle (lö̈ö)

ཤག་	certainty particle (shaà)
ཤས་	several (shɛ̄ɛ̀)
ཤིག་	imperative particle after final ས (shīg)
ཤིང་ནགས་	forest (shīŋnaà)
ས་ཆ་	place (sāja)
སམ་	question particle used after final "s"
སེར་སྣ་	avaricious (sērna)
གསར་འགྱུར་	news (sə̄ngyuu)
གསལ་	used in newspapers to convey source: "as was stated in" (sɛ̄l)
གསལ་ལྟར	see གསལ་
གསོལ་	va. to make offerings (sȫȍ)
བསྲུས་མ་	Tibetan style tea (sǖmə)
སླང་	roasting pan (lāŋa)
ལྷ་	a god (lhā)
ལྷ་སྐུ་	statue of a god (lhə̄gu)
ལྷོ་ཕྱོགས་	southern direction (lhōjoò)
ཨ་ཁུ་བསྟན་པ་	p.n. (ə̄gu dȭmba)
ཨབ་ག་ནི་སི་ཐན་	Afghanistan (āb ghānisitɛ̄n)

Lesson Eight

8.1 Cardinal numbers

གཅིག་	one	བཅོ་ལྔ་	fifteen
གཉིས་	two	བཅུ་དྲུག་	sixteen
གསུམ་	three	བཅུ་བདུན་	seventeen
བཞི་	four	བཅོ་བརྒྱད་	eighteen
ལྔ་	five	བཅུ་དགུ་	nineteen
དྲུག་	six	ཉི་ཤུ་	twenty
བདུན་	seven	སུམ་ཅུ་	thirty
བརྒྱད་	eight	བཞི་ཅུ་	forty
དགུ་	nine	ལྔ་ཅུ་	fifty
བཅུ་	ten	དྲུག་ཅུ་	sixty
བཅུ་གཅིག་	eleven	བདུན་ཅུ་	seventy
བཅུ་གཉིས་	twelve	བརྒྱད་ཅུ་	eighty
བཅུ་གསུམ་	thirteen	དགུ་ཅུ་	ninety
བཅུ་བཞི་	fourteen	བརྒྱ་ (ཐམ་པ་)	one hundred

As is evident from the above list, the numbers eleven through nineteen are constructed by adding the number ten (བཅུ་) before the numbers one to nine. Thirteen is, therefore, "ten" (བཅུ་) + "three" (གསུམ་). Note that with the numbers fifteen and eighteen, བཅུ་ changes to བཅོ་.

The numbers twenty to ninety are constructed the opposite way: by adding "ten" (བཅུ་ or ཅུ་) after the numbers three through nine. Thus thirty is "three" (སུམ་) + "ten" (ཅུ་). Note, however, that the number "three" changes its form slightly, being written སུམ་ rather than གསུམ་. The number "two" in "twenty" does likewise. The number "ten" is also sometimes written without the prefixed "བ་," i.e., as ཅུ་.

Counting within each of the sets of ten (e.g., 20s, 30s) is somewhat complicated by the fact that each set of ten requires a separate particle.

ཙ་	for the twenties	རེ་	for the sixties
སོ་	for the thirties	དོན་	for the seventies
ཞེ་	for the forties	གྱ་	for the eighties
ང་	for the fifties	གོ་	for the nineties

For example:

ཉིས་ཤུ་ཙ་གཉིས་	22	དྲུག་ཅུ་རེ་བདུན་	67
སུམ་ཅུ་སོ་བཞི་	34	བརྒྱད་ཅུ་གྱ་བརྒྱད་	88

བཞི་ཅུ་ཞེ་ལྔ་	45	དགུ་ཅུ་གོ་གསུམ་	93
ལྔ་ཅུ་ང་དྲུག་	56	བདུན་ཅུ་དོན་བདུན་	77

The hundreds are written as follows:

བརྒྱ་ (ཐམ་པ་)	100	དྲུག་བརྒྱ་	600
ཉིས་བརྒྱ་	200	བདུན་བརྒྱ་	700
གསུམ་བརྒྱ་	300	བརྒྱད་བརྒྱ་	800
བཞི་བརྒྱ་	400	དགུ་བརྒྱ་	900
ལྔ་བརྒྱ་	500	སྟོང་ཕྲག་གཅིག་ or ཆིག་སྟོང་	1,000

Counting in the hundreds = the hundred number + དང་ + the remaining number. For example:

བརྒྱ་དང་བརྒྱད་	108	གསུམ་བརྒྱ་དང་བཞི་ཅུ་ཞེ་དགུ་	349
ཉིས་བརྒྱ་དང་ལྔ་ཅུ་ང་དྲུག་	256	དགུ་བརྒྱ་དང་བརྒྱད་ཅུ་གྱ་བདུན་	987

For numbers with zeros such as 108, an alternative way to express them is by the term བཅུ་མེད་ ("without ten"), which really means the "ten's place" in arithmetic. For example, the number 108 could be written: བརྒྱ་དང་བཅུ་མེད་བརྒྱད་. Sometimes even the དང་ is omitted and 108 would be written: བརྒྱ་བཅུ་མེད་བརྒྱད་ .

Counting in thousands:

1,000	སྟོང་ཕྲག་གཅིག་ or གཅིག་སྟོང་	6,000	སྟོང་ཕྲག་དྲུག་ or དྲུག་སྟོང་
2,000	སྟོང་ཕྲག་གཉིས་ or ཉིས་སྟོང་	7,000	སྟོང་ཕྲག་བདུན་ or བདུན་སྟོང་
3,000	སྟོང་ཕྲག་གསུམ་ or གསུམ་སྟོང་	8,000	སྟོང་ཕྲག་བརྒྱད་ or བརྒྱད་སྟོང་
4,000	སྟོང་ཕྲག་བཞི་ or བཞི་སྟོང་	9,000	སྟོང་ཕྲག་དགུ་ or དགུ་སྟོང་
5,000	སྟོང་ཕྲག་ལྔ་ or ལྔ་སྟོང་	7,520	བདུན་སྟོང་ལྔ་བརྒྱ་ཉི་ཤུ་

Counting in ten thousands:

10,000	ཁྲི་གཅིག་ or གཅིག་ཁྲི་	70,000	ཁྲི་བདུན་ or བདུན་ཁྲི་
20,000	ཁྲི་གཉིས་ or ཉིས་ཁྲི་	80,000	ཁྲི་བརྒྱད་ or བརྒྱད་ཁྲི་
30,000	ཁྲི་གསུམ་ or གསུམ་ཁྲི་	90,000	ཁྲི་དགུ་ or དགུ་ཁྲི་
40,000	ཁྲི་བཞི་ or བཞི་ཁྲི་	96,000	ཁྲི་དགུ་དང་སྟོང་ཕྲག་དྲུག་ or དགུ་ཁྲི་དྲུག་སྟོང་
50,000	ཁྲི་ལྔ་ or ལྔ་ཁྲི་	85,695	བརྒྱད་ཁྲི་ལྔ་སྟོང་དྲུག་བརྒྱ་དགུ་ཅུ་གོ་ལྔ་
60,000	ཁྲི་དྲུག་ or དྲུག་ཁྲི་		

Counting in hundreds of thousands:

100,000	འབུམ་གཅིག་	or	ཆིག་འབུམ་
200,000	འབུམ་གཉིས་	or	ཉིས་འབུམ་
300,000	འབུམ་གསུམ་	or	(ག)སུམ་འབུམ་
400,000	འབུམ་བཞི་	or	བཞི་འབུམ་
500,000	འབུམ་ལྔ་	or	ལྔ་འབུམ་
600,000	འབུམ་དྲུག་	or	དྲུག་འབུམ་

700,000	འབུམ་བདུན་	or	བདུན་འབུམ་
800,000	འབུམ་བརྒྱད་	or	བརྒྱད་འབུམ་
900,000	འབུམ་དགུ་	or	དགུ་འབུམ་

Tibetans in Tibet, however, nowadays typically use ཁྲི་ ("ten thousand") to express larger numbers, for example, 100,000 would be ཁྲི་བཅུ་ ("ten ten thousands").

For millions and higher:

1,000,000	ས་ཡ་གཅིག་
10,000,000	བྱེ་བ་གཅིག་
100,000,000	དུང་ཕྱུར་གཅིག་
1,000,000,000	དུང་ཕྱུར་བཅུ་

Millions can also be conveyed using ཁྲི་ (10,000). For example, 1,000,000 could be written ཁྲི་བརྒྱ་ ("one hundred ten thousands").

8.2 Ordinal numbers

Ordinal numbers with the exception of "first" are expressed by placing the particle པ་ after the cardinal number.

first	དང་པོ་	fifth	ལྔ་པ་	ninth	དགུ་པ་
second	གཉིས་པ་	sixth	དྲུག་པ	tenth	བཅུ་པ
third	གསུམ་པ	seventh	བདུན་པ	eleventh	བཅུ་གཅིག་པ་
fourth	བཞི་པ་	eighth	བརྒྱད་པ་	twelfth	བཅུ་གཉིས་པ་

8.3 Percentages

The most common way to express percentages in Tibetan is to place cardinal numbers after བརྒྱ་ཆ་, the word for percent.

one percent	བརྒྱ་ཆ་གཅིག་	ten percent	བརྒྱ་ཆ་བཅུ་
two percent	བརྒྱ་ཆ་གཉིས་	fifty percent	བརྒྱ་ཆ་ལྔ་བཅུ་

seventy-five percent བརྒྱ་ཆ་བདུན་བཅུ་དོན་ལྔ་

Another way to express percentage is through fractions. This is done by placing a number (1-10) before ཆ་ and then another number after it. The first number indicates whether it is fourths, fifths, etc., while the second number indicates how many fourths, fifths, etc.

one quarter	བཞི་ཆ་གཅིག་	four fifths	ལྔ་ཆ་བཞི་
three quarters	བཞི་ཆ་གསུམ་	one sixth	དྲུག་ཆ་གཅིག་
two fifths	ལྔ་ཆ་གཉིས་	five eighths	བརྒྱད་ཆ་ལྔ་
two thirds	གསུམ་ཆ་གཉིས་		

8.4 Months

Tibetans use three terms for month. ཟླ་བ་ is a neutral word that can refer to either Western months or months in the Tibetan lunar calendar.

First month	ཟླ་བ་དང་པོ་	Seventh month	ཟླ་བ་བདུན་པ་
Second month	ཟླ་བ་གཉིས་པ་	Eighth month	ཟླ་བ་བརྒྱད་པ་
Third month	ཟླ་བ་གསུམ་པ་	Ninth month	ཟླ་བ་དགུ་པ་
Fourth month	ཟླ་བ་བཞི་པ་	Ten month	ཟླ་བ་བཅུ་པ་
Fifth month	ཟླ་བ་ལྔ་པ་	Eleventh month	ཟླ་བ་བཅུ་གཅིག་པ་
Sixth month	ཟླ་བ་དྲུག་པ་	Twelfth month	ཟླ་བ་བཅུ་གཉིས་པ

བོད་ཟླ་ is used exclusively for "Tibetan (lunar) month" and ཕྱི་ཟླ་ is used exclusively for "Western month." For example, ཕྱི་ཟླ་ལྔ་པ་ would be the fifth Western month or "May." Similarly, བོད་ཟླ་ལྔ་པ་would be the fifth Tibetan month (roughly mid-June to mid-July).

When only ཟླ་བ་ is used, context will indicate which calendar is meant, e.g., if the sentence starts with ཕྱི་ལོ་ ("Western year") 1959 then the Western month is obviously intended.

8.5 Tibetan numerals

You will have noticed that each page in this book presents both the English and Tibetan written numerals. The latter are listed below.

1	2	3	4	5	6	7	8	9	10
༡	༢	༣	༤	༥	༦	༧	༨	༩	༡༠
གཅིག་	གཉིས་	གསུམ་	བཞི་	ལྔ་	དྲུག་	བདུན་	བརྒྱད་	དགུ་	བཅུ་

In written materials, numbers (particularly the larger ones) are usually expressed by written numerals rather that by spelling them out.

For example:

1971	༡༩༧༡	1883	༡༨༨༣
1967	༡༩༦༧	1926	༡༩༢༦
1954	༡༩༥༤	1989	༡༩༨༩

8.6 "Or" and "whether or not" constructions

"Or" constructions parallel the question particles discussed in 1.11 in that the last letter of the first element is attached to the letter "m" (མ་); e.g., in (a.) below, ག་ becomes གམ་.

a. ལུག་གམ་ར

sheep or goats

b. ཁྱེད་རང་གིས་ལུག་གམ་ར་ཉོས་སམ།

you by sheep or goat bought ?/

Did you buy a sheep or a goat?

If the final of the first syllable is a vowel, འམ་ is attached.

c. ར་འམ་ལུག་

goats or sheep

d. སློབ་གྲྭ་བ་ཚོས་ཞིང་ལས་བྱེད་པའམ། ཚོང་བརྒྱབ་པ་རེད།

student pl.-by farming did or/ trade did past compl./

The students farmed or traded.

"Whether or not" constructions are similarly formed.

e. ཁོས་རྒྱ་གར་ལ་འགྲོ་གི་ཡོད་དམ་མེད་ངར་བཤད་མ་སོང་།

he-by india to go pres. compl. or no-exist i-to said neg. went compl./

He didn't tell me whether or not he is going to India.

This, of course, literally means, "He didn't tell me whether he is going to India or not going to India."

f. ཁོ་ཚོས་ཁོ་བོད་ལ་སྡོད་དུས་གྲྭ་པ་ཡིན་ནམ་མིན་འདྲི་གི་འདུག།

he pl. by he tibet to live when monk is or no-is ask pres. compl./

They are asking whether or not he was a monk when he lived in Tibet.

g. ཁོས་འདིར་ཉི་མ་ཁ་ཤས་སྡོད་དམ་སང་ཉིན་འགྲོ་རྒྱུ་ཡིན་པ་ང་ལ་མ་བཤད།

he-by here day several live whether-or-not tomorrow go fut. compl. i to no said/

He didn't tell me whether he will stay here for several days or go tomorrow.

The more usual manner of forming "whether or not" constructions consists of joining positive and negative linking or existential verbs without any intervening particles. Thus ཡིན་མིན་ conveys "whether it is or is not" (in the linking verb sense) and ཡོད་མེད་ "whether there is or is not" (in the existential verb sense). In essence, wherever a linking verb would be used, ཡིན་མིན་ is used, and wherever an existential verb would be used, ཡོད་མེད་ is used. Thus, in example h., the sentence "He is Chinese" requires a linking verb, so ཡིན་མིན་ is used.

h. ཁོ་རྒྱ་མི་ཡིན་མིན་ངས་ཤེས་ཀྱི་མེད།

he chinese is no-is i-by know neg./

I do not know whether or not he is Chinese.

i. ཁོ་བོད་ལ་སྡོད་དུས་གྲྭ་པ་ཡིན་མིན་འདྲི་གི་འདུག།

he tibet to live when monk is no-is ask pres. compl./

(They, he, etc.) are asking whether or not he was a monk when he lived in Tibet.

j. ཁོ་ཚོས་ཁོ་ཁ་ལག་ཟ་རྒྱུ་ཡིན་མིན་འདྲི་གི་འདུག།

he pl.-by he food eat fut. is no-is ask pres. compl./

They are asking whether or not he will eat.

Examples k. and l. illustrate how the tense of such constructions is altered by changing the stem of the verb and the verb complement.

k. ཁོས་ཁ་ལག་ཟས་ཡོད་མེད་འདྲི་གི་འདུག།

he food ate is no-is ask pres. compl./

(They, he, etc.) are asking whether or not he has eaten.

l. ཁོས་ཁ་ལག་ཟ་གི་ཡོད་མེད་འདྲི་གི་འདུག།

he food eat pres.-compl. is no-is ask pres. compl./

(They, he, etc.) are asking whether or not he is eating.

Abbreviated forms are also commonly used with active or involuntary verbs to convey this. For example:

ཟ་རྒྱུ་ཡིན་མིན་ > ཟ་མིན་ ཟས་ཡོད་མེད་ > ཟས་མེད་ ཟ་གི་ཡོད་མེད > ཟ་མེད་

m. ཁོས་ཁ་ལག་ཟས་མེད་འདྲི་གི་འདུག།

he food ate no-is ask pres. compl./

(They, he, etc.) are asking whether or not he ate.

When ཡིན་མིན་ and ཡོད་མེད་ constructions are used with interrogatives such as གང་, སུ་, ཅི་, ཇི་, and ག་ they convey not the idea of "whether or not," but rather a simple interrogative meaning.

n. འདི་གང་ཡིན་མིན་བཤད་མ་སོང་།

this what is is-not said no went compl./

(They, he, etc.) didn't say what this is. (What this is, or what this is not, (they, he, etc.) did not say.

o. ཁོ་གང་དུ་འགྲོ་གི་ཡོད་མེད་སུས་ཀྱང་ཤེས་ཀྱི་མེད་པ་རེད།

he where go pres.compl. no-exist who-by even know pres. compl. neg./

Nobody knows where he is going (or not going).

p. ཞྭ་མོ་འདི་ག་ནས་ཉོས་མེད་དྲན་གྱི་མི་འདུག།

hat this where from bought no-exist remember pres. compl. neg./

(I) don't remember where (I) bought the hat from.

q. གང་གིས་ཁོ་ན་བ་ཡིན་མིན་ཁོས་ཨེམ་ཆི་ར་བཤད་སོང་ངམ།

what by he sick nom. is is-not he-by doctor -to said past compl. ?/

Did he tell the doctor what made him sick?

r. ཁོ་ལ་དངུལ་གང་ཙམ་བྱུང་ཡོད་མེད་མོས་ཤེས་པ་རེད།

he to money how much got exist no-exist she-by knew past compl./

She knew how much money he got.

s. ཁོ་ཚོས་ཁོས་ཉི་མ་ག་ཚོད་ལས་ཀ་བྱས་ཡོད་མོད་ཐོ་རྒྱབ་པ་རེད།

he pl-by he-by days how many work did exist no-exist list acted past compl./

They recorded how many days he worked.

t. ཁོ་ཚོ་ག་དུས་ནང་ལ་འགྲོ་གི་ཡོད་མེད་དོ་སྣང་མ་བྱུང་།

he pl. when home to go pres. compl. no-exist notice no got/

(I) didn't notice when they go home.

u. ཁོའི་ཁང་པ་ག་གི་ཡིན་མིན་ངས་ཤེས་ཀྱི་ཡོད།

he-of house which is is-not i-by know pres. compl./

I know which is his house.

v. མི་འདི་སུ་ཡིན་མིན་སུས་ཀྱང་ཤེས་མེད་པ་རེད།

person this who is is-not who-by even knew perf. compl.neg./

No one at all knew who the man was.

w. དེབ་འདི་སུའི་ཡིན་མིན་འདྲི་གི་འདུག།

book this who-of is-not ask pres. compl./

(They, he etc.) are asking whose book this is.

x. སུས་དེབ་འདི་ཉོས་མེད་བཀའ་འདྲི་གནང་སོང་།

who-by book this bought no-exist question (h.) did (h.) went compl./

(They, he etc.) asked who bought the book.

8.7 "With" constructions using དང་

We have already encountered དང་ as the conjunction "and," e.g., ནོར་བུ་དང་པད་མ་— "Norbu and Pema." However, it also can convey the meaning "with."

a. ཁོས་པད་མ་དང་ཁ་ལག་ཟས་པ་རེད།

he-by pema with food ate past compl./

He ate with Pema.

b. ཨ་མི་རི་ཀས་རྒྱ་གར་དང་དམག་རྒྱབ་སོང་།

america-by india with war made went compl./

America made war with India.

There are a number of standard compounds that use དང་ with this meaning. Some of these have already been discussed in 7.9 and 7.10:

དང་མཉམ་དུ་	དང་ལྷན་རྒྱས་	དང་འདྲ་བ་	དང་ལྡན་པ་
together with	together with (h.)	similar to (with)	possessing, having
དང་མཐུན་པ་	དང་འབྲེལ་	དང་མི་འདྲ་བ་	དང་བསྟུན་
compatible with/ in accordance with	related to/with	dissimilar to/with	in accordance with

c. མི་འདི་དང་མཉམ་དུ་ཕྱིན་པ་ཡིན།

man this together with went past compl./

I went (together) with this man.

d. ཆོས་དང་མཐུན་པའི་སློབ་དེབ་ཅིག་རྩོམ་པ་ཡིན།

religion compatible with-of textbook a wrote past compl./

I wrote a textbook that is compatible with religion.

e. མོས་ཁྲིམས་དང་མཐུན་པའི་ལས་ཀ་བྱས་པ་རེད།

she-by law in accordance with work did past compl./

She worked in accordance with the law.

8.8 "Coincidental" constructions: དང་སྐབས་བསྟུན་ and ཞོར་ + dative-locative

There are two common ways to convey that an action occurred secondarily or coincidentally with or to another action.

a. རི་པིན་ལ་འགྲོ་དགོས་པ་དང་སྐབས་བསྟུན་ངས་ཀྲུང་གོར་ཕྱིན་པ་ཡིན།
japan to go have nom. and coincidental i-by china-to went past compl./
(I) had to go to Japan, so coincidental with that, I went to China.

b. ཁོང་བོད་ལ་ཕེབས་ཞོར་ལ་བལ་ཡུལ་ལ་ཕེབས་སོང་།
he tibet to go incidental to nepal to go went compl./
He (h.) went (h.) to Tibet and incidental to that went to Nepal.

c. ཁྱེད་རང་ལས་ཀ་ནས་ལོག་པའི་ཞོར་དུ་ངའི་ནང་ལ་ཕེབས་རོགས་གནང་།
you work from return incidental to i-of home to go help do/
On your way home from work, please come to my house.

This particle can also be used with nouns:

d. ཁོས་ལས་ཀའི་ཞོར་ལ་སློབ་སྦྱོང་བྱས་པ་རེད།
he-by work-of incidental to study did past compl./
Incidental to his work, he studied. (i.e., during his spare time)

8.9 Constructions using སྒང་: "on top of," "on," and "in addition to"

The term སྒང་ was encountered in 5.10 where it conveyed "at the time of." It is also used to convey the physical meaning of "on" or "on top of." It commonly requires addition of the genitive particle.

a. རིའི་སྒང་ལ་ར་དང་གཡག་མང་པོ་འདུག།
mountain on to goat and yak many exist/
There are many goats and yaks on top of the mountain.

b. ཡར་ཀླུང་གཙང་པོའི་སྒང་ལ་ཆུ་གློག་ས་ཚིགས་ཤིག་བཙུགས་པ་རེད།
yarlung river on to hydroelectric station one established past compl./
(They, he, etc.) established a hydroelectric station on the Yarlung Tsangpo (river.)

སྒང་ is also used as a verbal connective to convey the meaning of "on top of" or "in addition to" in verbal clauses. In such constructions the pattern is: པའི་/བའི་སྒང་ལ་. These constructions also require ཀྱང་/ཡང་ ("also") in the second clause.

c. མོས་ཚལ་ཉོས་པའི་སྒང་ལ་ཤིང་ཏོག་ཀྱང་ཉོས་པ་རེད།
she-by vegetables bought on fruit also bought past compl./
On top of buying vegetables, she also bought fruit.

d. ཚོང་ཁང་དེར་ཅ་ལག་སྣ་ཚོགས་ཡོད་པའི་སྒང་ལ་གོང་ཡང་ཁེ་པོ་འདུག།
store that-to things various exist on price also cheap exist/
In addition to having various things, that store also has cheap prices.

The meaning of "in addition to" can also be conveyed in conjunction with nouns and noun phrases.

e. བོད་ལ་སྐྱོར་མོ་ལུང་པའི་སྣང་ལ་ལྷ་མོ་ཚོགས་པ་གཞན་དག་ཀྱང་ཡོད་པ་རེད།
   tibet to kyomolungga on opera group other also exist/
   In Tibet, in addition to Gyomo lunga, there are also other opera troupes.

f. ཁོས་བོད་སྐད་ཤེས་པའི་སྣང་ལ་སྐད་ཡིག་གཞན་དག་ཀྱང་ཤེས་ཀྱི་ཡོད་པ་རེད།
   he-by tibetan know on language other also know usu. compl./
   In addition to knowing Tibetan language, he also knows other languages.

Another meaning conveyed by སྣང་ is "at the time of" or "in the midst of doing" or "while." It was encountered earlier in Lesson Five (5.10). It should be noted that this meaning can usually be differentiated from the above meanings partly because it is not accompanied by ཀྱང་/ཡང་ in the second clause, but mainly from semantic context.

g. མོས་ཁ་པར་གཏོང་བའི་སྣང་ལ་ཁོ་ཚོ་སླེབས་པ་རེད།
   she-by telephone send on he pl. arrived past compl./
   While she was phoning, they arrived.

h. མི་དམངས་རྣམས་སོན་འདེབས་པའི་སྣང་ལ་ཆར་པ་བབས་པ་རེད།
   people pl. seed plant on rain descend past compl./
   While the people were planting, it rained.

i. ཁོང་ཚོ་ལས་ཀ་བྱེད་པའི་སྣང་རེད།
   he pl. work do on is/
   They are in the midst of working.

8.10 Reading exercise: "The Golden Axe"

The rest of this lesson consists of a lengthy reading selection containing new words but no new major grammatical constructions. Its aim is to reinforce and solidify previously encountered patterns and skills by providing a coherent segment of modern literary Tibetan in a familiar style. To make this reading more realistic, no interlinear translation will be included.

8.10.1 Tibetan text

གསེར་གྱི་སྟ་རེ་

སྔར་ལྷག་བསམ་ཟེར་བའི་ཕྲུ་གུ་ཆུང་ཆུང་ཞིག་ཡོད།1 ཁོ་པའི་ཁྱིམ་གྱི་འཚོ་བ་ཧ་ཅང་སྐྱོ་པོ་ཡིན་ཙང་ཕ་མ་གཉིས་ཀས་ཁོ་པ་ས་བདག་གི་ཁྱིམ་དུ་ལས་ཀ་བྱེད་པར་བཏང་།2 ཁོ་པས་ཉིན་ལྟར་ཞོགས་པ་ནས་དགོང་མོ་བར་ལས་ཀ་ཧ་ཅང་མང་པོ་བྱེད་ཀྱི་ཡོད་པ་རེད།3 འོན་ཀྱང་ས་བདག་གིས་ཁོང་ལ་ཁྱོད་ར་སྒྲིད་ལུག་བྱེད་ཀྱི་འདུག་ཅེས་སྐྱོན་བརྗོད་བྱས།4 ཉིན་ཞིག་ལྷག་བསམ་རི་ལ་མེ་ཤིང་འཐུ་བར་འགྲོ་བའི་ལམ་གར་ཟམ་པ་ཞིག་གི་ཐོག་ནས་འགྲོ་སྐབས་གཟབ་གཟབ་མ་བྱས་སྟབས་སྟ་རེ་ཆུ་ནང་དུ་ལྷུང་ཞིང་།5 ཆུ་

དེ་ནས་ལེན་མ་ཐུབ་ཙང་ལྷག་བསམ་སེམས་ཁྲལ་བྱུང་སྟེ་སྟ་རེ་མེད་ན་མེ་ཤིང་འཐུ་མི་ཐུབ་པ་དང་། མེ་ཤིང་མེད་ན་ས་བདག་གིས་གཤེ་གཤེ་དང་ཉེས་རྡུང་གཏོང་གི་རེད་བསམ་སྟབས་ལྷག་བསམ་དངངས་སྐྲག་གི་ངང་ནས་མཆི་མ་བཏང་།6

གློ་བུར་སྨ་ར་དུང་ལས་དཀར་བའི་རྒན་པོ་ཞིག་དེ་གར་ཡོང་ནས་ལྷག་བསམ་ལ། བུ་ཁྱོད་ཅི་ཕྱིར་མཆི་མ་གཏོང་གི་འདུག་ཞེས་དྲིས།7 ལྷག་བསམ་གྱིས་སྟ་རེ་ཆུ་ནང་དུ་ལྷུང་བའི་གནས་ཚུལ་རྣམས་རྒན་པོར་བཤད།8 རྒན་པོས་ངས་དེ་ལྟ་ཆུ་ནང་ནས་སྟ་རེ་ལེན་གྱི་ཡིན་ཅེས་བཤད་དེ་ཆུ་ནང་དུ་མཆོངས།9 ཡུད་ཙམ་སོང་རྗེས་རྒན་པོས་ཆུ་ནང་ནས་གསེར་གྱི་སྟ་རེ་ཞིག་བླངས་ཏེ་ལྷག་བསམ་ལ། བུ་སྟ་རེ་འདི་རེད་དམ་ཞེས་དྲིས་10 ལྷག་བསམ་གྱིས་མིག་ལྟས་རྗེས་དེ་ནི་གསེར་གྱི་སྟ་རེ་ཞིག་ཡིན་པ་མཐོང་བས་མགྱོགས་མྱུར་མགོ་བོ་གཡུག་གཡུག་བྱས་ནས་སྒོ་བོ་ལགས་ཐུགས་རྗེ་ཆེ་འདི་ངའི་སྟ་རེ་མ་རེད་ཅེས་ལན་བཏབ།11 དེ་ནས་རྒན་པོས་སླར་ཡང་ཆུའི་ནང་དུ་མཆོངས་ནས་དངུལ་གྱི་སྟ་རེ་ཞིག་བླངས་ཏེ་བུ་སྟ་རེ་འདི་ཁྱེད་ཀྱི་རེད་དམ་ཞེས་དྲིས།12 དངུལ་གྱི་སྟ་རེ་འདི་ཡང་ལྟས་ནས་ལྷག་བསམ་གྱིས་སླར་ཡང་མགོ་བོ་གཡུག་གཡུག་བྱས་ནས་སྒོ་བོ་ལགས་ཐུགས་རྗེ་ཆེ་སྟ་རེ་དེ་ཡང་ངའི་མ་རེད་ཅེས་ལན་བཏབ།13 རྒན་པོས་སླར་ཡང་ཆུ་ནང་དུ་མཆོངས་ནས་ལྕགས་ཀྱི་སྟ་རེ་ནག་ཐིང་ཐིང་ཞིག་བླངས་ཏེ་བུ་སྟ་རེ་འདི་ཁྱེད་ཀྱི་རེད་དམ་ཞེས་དྲིས།14 ལྷག་བསམ་གྱིས་ལྟ་སྐབས་དེ་ནི་དངོས་གནས་རང་ཉིད་ཀྱི་སྟ་རེ་ཡིན་པས་དགའ་མཆོངས་རྒྱག་བཞིན་པར་སྟ་རེ་ཚུར་བླངས་པ་དང་སྨྲགས་སྒོ་བོ་ལགས་ཐུགས་རྗེ་ཆེ་ཞེས་ཡང་ཡང་ཞུས།15 རྒན་པོ་དེས་ལྷག་བསམ་གྱི་མགོ་ལ་བྱིལ་བྱིལ་བྱེད་བཞིན་པར་ཁྱེད་ནི་དངོས་འབྲེལ་ཕྲུ་གུ་ཡག་པོ་ཞིག་རེད་ཁྱེད་མི་ཚེ་སྐྱིད་པོ་ཡོང་གི་རེད་ཅེས་བཤད་རྗེས་རྒན་པོ་གློ་བུར་དུ་ཡལ་ནས་མཐོང་རྒྱུ་མེད་པར་གྱུར།16

ལྷག་བསམ་གྱིས་སྐབས་དེར་རྒན་པོ་དེ་ནི་བླ་མའི་དྲང་སྲོང་ཡིན་པ་གཞི་ནས་ཤེས་པ་དང་མུ་མཐུད་མེ་ཤིང་འཐུ་བར་སོང་།17 ཕོ་པའི་སྟ་རེར་དྲང་སྲོང་གིས་བྱིལ་བའི་དབང་གིས་སྟ་རེ་རྣོ་པོ་ཞེ་དྲགས་ཆགས་ཏེ་ཤིང་མགྱོགས་པོ་བཅད་ནས་ཁྱིམ་ལ་ལོག་པ་རེད།18 ས་བདག་གིས་ཕོ་པ་སྡུ་པོ་དེ་འདྲ་ལོག་ཡོང་བ་མཐོང་སྐབས་ཁོས་སྐྱིད་ལུག་བྱེད་ཀྱི་འདུག་ཅེས་གཤེ་གཤེ་བཏང་བས་ལྷག་བསམ་གྱིས་གནས་ཚུལ་རྣམས་ཚང་མ་གསལ་པོ་བཤད་སྟབས་ས་བདག་ཁོང་ཁྲོ་ཟ་བཞིན་པར་ཁྱོད་ཀྱིས་གསེར་དང་དངུལ་གྱི་སྟ་རེ་མ་བླངས་པར་ལྕགས་ཀྱི་སྟ་རེ་དེ་ཁྱེར་བ་ནི་དངོས་གནས་མི་ལྐུགས་པ་ཞིག་རེད་ཅེས་ཁ་རྡུང་བཏང་།19

ཕྱི་ཉིན་ཞོགས་པ་སྔ་པོ་ནས་ས་བདག་གིས་ལྷག་བསམ་ལས་ཀ་གཞན་བྱེད་པར་བཏང་བ་དང་། ཕོ་པ་རང་ཉིད་མེ་ཤིང་འཐུ་མཁན་དབུལ་པོ་ཞིག་ཏུ་བརྫུས་ཏེ་སྟ་རེ་གོག་པོ་ཞིག་ཁྱེར་ནས་རི་ལ་མེ་ཤིང་གཅོད་པར་འགྲོ་ཁུལ་བྱས།20 ཕོ་པས་ཟམ་པའི་ཐོག་ལ་སླེབས་སྐབས་སྟ་རེ་དེ་ཆུའི་ནང་ཀང་བཙུགས་ནས་དབྱུགས་ཏེ་སྐད་ཤུགས་ཆེན་པོས་ངུས་པ་རེད།21 སྐབས་དེར་དྲང་སྲོང་སླར་ཡང་དེ་གར་ཡོང་།22 ས་བདག་གིས་མིག་ཆུ་ཕྱིས་བཞིན་པར་ངའི་སྟ་རེ་ཆུའི་ནང་དུ་ལྷུང་སོང་བས་ཁྱིམ་དུ་ལོག་ན་ངའི་དཔོན་པས་ཉེས་ཀྱི་རེད་ཞེས་བཤད་མ་ཐག་དྲང་སྲོང་གིས་སྔར་བཞིན་ཆུའི་ནང་དུ་མཆོངས་ཏེ་ལམ་སེང་ཕོ་པའི་ལྕགས་ཀྱི་སྟ་རེ་ཕོ་པར་སྤྲད།23 ས་བདག་གིས་འཕྲལ་དུ་མགོ་བོ་གཡུག་གཡུག་བྱས་ཏེ་འདི་ངའི་མ་རེད་ཅེས་བཤད།24 དྲང་སྲོང་གིས་ཡང་བསྐྱར་ཆུའི་ནང་དུ་མཆོངས་ནས་དངུལ་གྱི་སྟ་རེ་ཞིག་བླངས་བས་ས་བདག་གིས་མིག་ཆེན་པོ་གདངས་ནས་ལམ་སེང་དངུལ་གྱི་སྟ་རེ་འདི་ཡག་པོ་འདུག། འོན་ཀྱང་གསེར་གྱི་སྟ་རེ་ཞིག་བྱུང་ན་ཡག་ཤོས་རེད་ཅེས་བཤད།25 དྲང་སྲོང་གིས་དངུལ་གྱི་སྟ་རེ་དེ་ས་བདག་གི་ཁང་

པའི་འགྲམ་དུ་དབྱུགས་ཏེ་སླར་ཡང་ཆུའི་ནང་དུ་འཛུལ་ནས་གསེར་གྱི་སྟ་རེ་ཞིག་ལྡངས་པ་རེད།26 ས་བདག་གིས་གསེར་གྱི་སྟ་རེ་དེ་ཡག་པོ་ཞི་དྭགས་འདུག་ཞིས་ཡང་ཡང་བཤད་ནས་དྲང་སྲོང་གི་ལག་པ་ནས་གསེར་གྱི་སྟ་རེ་ཚུར་ལྡངས་པ་དང་ས་སྙིང་ནས་དངུལ་གྱི་སྟ་རེ་དེ་ཡར་བསྐྱུགས་ཏེ་ལག་པ་རེ་རེར་ཁྱེར་ནས་དགའ་ཐག་ཆོད་པ་རེད།27 སྐབས་དེར་དྲང་སྲོང་ནི་ཡང་སྐྱུར་ཡལ་སྟབས་ས་བདག་གིས་སྟ་རེ་གཉིས་ཀ་ཁྱེར་ན་ཡག་པོ་འདུག་བསམ་ནས་མགྱོགས་པོ་ཕྱིན་འཕྱལ་ཕོ་པ་ཆུའི་ནང་དུ་ལྷུང་སྟེ་ཤི་བ་རེད།28

8.10.2 Translation

The Golden Axe

Formerly, there was a small boy named Lhaksam. Because he (his family's livelihood) was very poor, his parents sent him to work in the house of a lord. That boy Lhaksam used to work very hard every day from morning to night. Nevertheless, the lord criticized him, saying, "You are acting lazy." One day, Lhaksam went to the hills to collect firewood and was not careful when he was going on top of a bridge along the road so the axe fell into the water. He was unable to get it from the water. He thought, therefore, that without the axe he would be unable to collect firewood, and without firewood, the lord would scold and beat him. He cried from fright.

Suddenly, an old man with a beard whiter than a conch shell came there and asked Lhaksam, "Boy, why are you crying?" Lhaksam told the old man the events of the axe falling into the river. The old man said, "I will get the axe from the water," and jumped into the river. After a moment, he emerged from the water carrying a golden axe and asked Lhaksam, "Boy, is this your axe?" Lhaksam looked and seeing that it was a golden axe, quickly shook his head and answered, "Old man, thank you, but this is not my axe." After that the old man again jumped into the water and emerged bringing a silver axe. He asked the child, "Boy, is this your axe?" Even though this axe was good, Lhaksam once again shook his head and replied, "Old man, thank you. This axe also is not mine." The old man again jumped into the river and (this time) brought a completely black iron axe. He asked the child, "Boy, is this axe yours?" Lhaksam looked at it and because it was really his own axe, jumped for joy, took the axe, and said over and over, "Old man, thank you." The old man stroking Lhaksam's head said, "You really seem a good boy. You will have a happy life." After saying that, the old man suddenly vanished from sight.

Lhaksam then (lit., at that time) knew that he (the old man) must be an ascetic lama and continued to collect firewood. Because the ascetic lama stroked his axe, the axe had become very sharp and he cut the wood quickly and returned home. Because the lord saw that he had come home so early he (thought), "He is being lazy," and scolded him. Lhaksam explained all the events to him. Because of this the lord got angry and verbally abused him, "You are really an idiot for taking the iron axe instead of (lit., rather than) the gold and silver axes."

The next day, early in the morning, the lord sent Lhaksam to do different work.

(Then), pretending he was a poor firewood collector, he himself took an old beat up axe and acted as if he was going to cut wood in the mountains. When he arrived on top of the bridge, he purposely threw the axe into the water, and (started) crying loudly. At that time, the ascetic once again come to that place. The lord, while wiping the tears from his eyes, said, "My axe fell into the water. If I return home my lord will beat me." As soon as he said that the ascetic, as before, jumped into the water and immediately gave him his iron axe. The lord shook his head and said, "This is not my axe." The ascetic again jumped into the water and brought out a silver axe. The lord stared at it wide-eyed and immediately said, "This silver axe is good, but if I get a golden axe it will be best." The ascetic threw the silver axe by the feet of the lord and again entered the water and brought a golden axe. The lord said over and over again, "That gold axe is very good," and took the gold axe from the ascetic's hands. He (also) picked up the silver axe from the ground and, carrying one in each hand, was extraordinarily happy. At that time the ascetic again disappeared. Because of that the lord thought, "If (I) take the two axes it will be good," and went quickly (home). (However), as soon as (he went), he fell in the water and died.

8.10.3 Grammatical notes

1. The first segment consists of a single sentence: སྔར་ལྷག་བསམ་ཟེར་བའི་ཕྲུ་གུ་ཆུང་ཆུང་ཞིག་ཡོད་.

The first word of this sentence is another of the temporal terms meaning "formerly" or "in the past." The remainder of the clause is a simple existential sentence —"there was a small child." The phrase ལྷག་བསམ་ཟེར་བའི་ཕྲུ་གུ་ illustrates a common way in which names are expressed: *name* + ཟེར་བ་ + *gen.* + *noun.* This glosses as, "A child who was called Lhaksam."

2. The second segment consists of two clauses: 1. ཁོ་པའི་ཁྱིམ་གྱི་འཚོ་བ་ཧ་ཅང་སྐྱོ་པོ་ཡིན་ཙང་ 2. ཕ་མ་གཉིས་ཀས་ཁོ་པ་ས་བདག་གི་ཁྱིམ་དུ་ལས་ཀ་བྱེད་པར་བཏང་.

The first clause is a linking verb construction that begins with the possessive subject: "his family's livelihood" - ཁོ་པའི་ཁྱིམ་གྱི་འཚོ་བ. It breaks down into the head word "he" + gen. + "family" (ཁྱིམ་) + gen. + "livelihood." This clause is linked by the "because" clause connective.

The second clause is typical of active sentences in that it begins with the subject in the instrumental (ཕ་མ་གཉིས་ཀས་). The main verbal phrase consists of the infinitive construction: sent to work (ལས་ཀ་བྱེད་པར་བཏང་). The remainder explains who was sent to work (he - ཁོ་པ་), and where he was sent to work ("to the landlord's house" - ས་བདག་གི་ཁྱིམ་དུ་).

3. The third segment is a simple active verb sentence conveying the usual mode: ཁོ་པས་ཉིན་ལྟར་ཞོགས་པ་ནས་དགོང་མོ་བར་ལས་ཀ་ཧ་ཅང་མང་པོ་བྱེད་ཀྱི་ཡོད་པ་རེད་.

It contains the common pattern "from X up to Y" (X ནས་ Y བར་(དུ་)), or in this case "from morning until (up to) evening." Note that "very" (ད་ཅང་) must come before the adjective it modifies.

4. The fourth segment consists of a single sentence: འོན་ཀྱང་ས་བདག་གིས་ཁོང་ལ་ཁྱོད་ར་སྐྱིད་ལུག་ཅིག་ཀྱི་འདུག་ཅེས་སྐྱོན་བརྗོད་བྱས་.

It is linked to the previous segment by "nevertheless" (འོན་ཀྱང་). This is followed by the subject ("by the lord" - ས་བདག་གིས་), the object ("to him" - ཁོང་ལ་), the main verb ("scolded" - སྐྱོན་བརྗོད་བྱས་), and a quotation of the scolding (ཁྱོད་ར་སྐྱིད་ལུག་ཅིག་ཀྱི་འདུག་ཅེས་).

5. The fifth segment consists of three clauses: 1. ཉིན་ཞིག་ལྷག་བསམ་རི་ལ་མེ་ཤིང་འཐུ་བར་འགྲོ་བའི་ལམ་གར་ཟམ་པ་ཞིག་གི་ཐོག་ནས་འགྲོ་སྐབས་ 2. གཟབ་གཟབ་མ་བྱས་སྟབས་ 3. སྟ་རེ་ཆུ་ནང་དུ་ལྷུང་ཞིང་.

The first clause is difficult since it consists of sub-clauses nestled within sub-clauses. The essence of the clause is "when Lhaksam was going" (ལྷག་བསམ་. . .འགྲོ་སྐབས་). Then there are two location modifying units: "on a bridge"—literally, from on top of a bridge" (ཟམ་པ་ཞིག་གི་ཐོག་ནས་) and "on a road" (ལམ་གར་). Note that སྟེང་ནས་ could be substituted for ཐོག་ནས་.

Modifying "road" is the nominalized verbal phrase རི་ལ་མེ་ཤིང་འཐུ་བར་འགྲོ་བའི་, which explains what kind of a road it was—"it was a road on which Lhaksam was going to collect firewood in the mountains." Thus, this clause means, "One day when Lhaksam was going on a bridge on the road to collect firewood in the mountains, . . ."

The second clause consists of only a negative verb ("was not careful" - གཟབ་གཟབ་མ་བྱས་) and the "because" clause connective སྟབས་.

The third clause is a simple involuntary verb construction: སྟ་རེ་ཆུ་ནང་དུ་ལྷུང་, "the axe fell into the water." The Tibetan term ཆུ་ conveys not only water, but in cases like this also "river." This could also have been written with the genitive: སྟ་རེ་ཆུའི་ནང་དུ་ལྷུང་. This clause is joined with the next segment by the conjunctive clause connector ཞིང་.

6. The sixth segment consists of five clauses: 1. ཆུ་དེ་ནས་ལེན་མ་ཐུབ་ཙང་ 2. ལྷག་བསམ་སེམས་ཁྲལ་བྱུང་སྟེ་ 3. སྟ་རེ་མེད་ན་མེ་ཤིང་འཐུ་མི་ཐུབ་པ་དང་། 4. མེ་ཤིང་མེད་ན་ས་བདག་གིས་གཤེ་གཤེ་དང་ཉེས་རྡུང་གཏོང་གི་རེད་བསམ་སྟབས་ 5. ལྷག་བསམ་དངངས་སྐྲག་གི་ངང་ནས་མཆི་མ་བཏང་.

The first clause consists of the active verb "to take" (ལེན་), a negative particle, and the auxiliary verb "be able" and conveys "not being able to take (the axe) from that water." Note that the subject is omitted and has to be inferred.

The second clause consists of the subject Lhagsam and the involuntary verb "worried" (སེམས་ཁྲལ་). Thus, "because (he) was unable to take (the axe) from the water, Lhagsam was worried." The clause ends with the "having" connective (སྟེ་). What follows in clauses three, four, and five is what Lhaksam was worried about.

Clause three reveals a very common structure that consists of two sub-parts: 1) "if (I) do not have the axe" (སྟ་རེ་མེད་ན་), and 2) "(I) will not be able to collect firewood" (མེ་ཤིང་འཐུ་མི་ཐུབ་). The difference between the negative particle here (མི་) and that in clause one

(མ་) is due to tense: མི་ normally is used in present-future constructions. These thoughts are incomplete, however, and པ་དང་ connects them to the rest of what Lhaksam was worried about.

Clause four begins with the sub-clause, "if (I) do not have firewood" (མེ་ཤིང་མེད་ན་), and then the main subject of Lhaksam's thought, "the lord will scold and beat (me)" (ས་བདག་གིས་གཤེ་གཤེ་དང་ཉེས་རྡུང་གཏོང་གི་རེད་). Note that the Tibetan does not specify the object ("me"), and abbreviates གཤེ་གཤེ་གཏོང་ and ཉེས་རྡུང་གཏོང་ into གཤེ་གཤེ་དང་ཉེས་རྡུང་གཏོང་. Thus, once again, we see a single construction that in English would be sentences within sentences: སྟ་རེ་མེད་ན་མེ་ཤིང་འཐུ་མི་ཐུབ་པ་དང་། མེ་ཤིང་མེད་ན་ས་བདག་གིས་གཤེ་གཤེ་དང་ཉེས་རྡུང་གཏོང་གི་རེད་ within ཆུ་དེ་ནས་ལེན་མ་ཐུབ་ཙང་། ལྷག་བསམ་གྱིས་སེམས་ཁྲལ་བྱུང་སྟེ་ . . . བསམ.

The "because" clause connective (སྟབས་) links this to the last clause. It consists of the subject followed by a གི་ངང་ནས་ type adverbial phrase meaning "in the manner of being frightened" (དངངས་སྐྲག་གི་ངང་ནས་). Then this section ends with the active verb "cried" or "shed tears" (མཆི་མ་བཏང་). Note that the syllable མ་ is not the negative particle but a part of the word for tears (མཆི་མ་).

7. The seventh segment consists of two clauses: 1. གློ་བུར་སྨ་ར་དུང་ལས་དཀར་བའི་རྒན་པོ་ཞིག་དེ་གར་ཡོང་ནས་ 2. ལྷག་བསམ་ལ། བུ་ཁྱོད་ཅི་ཕྱིར་མཆི་མ་གཏོང་གི་འདུག་ཞེས་དྲིས་.

The subject of the first clause is "an old man" (རྒན་པོ་ཞིག་) and the verb is "to come" (ཡོང་). The clause begins with the adverbial "suddenly" (གློ་བུར་) and is followed by a typical "X *than* Y" comparative phrase—དུང་ལས་དཀར་བའི་ "conch than white" (whiter than conch). This phrase is then joined to the subject by the genitive so that it describes him—"an old man with a beard whiter than a conch shell." The last element in this clause is the term དེ་གར་ ("there"), which explains where the old man came to. Thus, the entire clause means, "Suddenly, an old man with a beard whiter than a conch shell came there."

The "having" connective links this to the next clause, which contains no explicit subject. Context, however, indicates clearly that the subject of this active construction is the "old man." The main verb of the clause is "asked" (དྲིས་) and everything else indicates what was asked and to whom it was asked. The old man's question is a straightforward interrogative construction: "you why crying" or "why are you crying" (ཁྱོད་ཅི་ཕྱིར་མཆི་མ་གཏོང་གི་འདུག་). Note that use of the non-past tense stem of the verb (གཏོང་) conveys the present tense here. If past tense were to be conveyed this would have been written: ཁྱོད་ཅི་ཕྱིར་མཆི་མ་བཏང་ཞེས་དྲིས་.

8. The eighth segment consists of the sentence: ལྷག་བསམ་གྱིས་སྟ་རེ་ཆུ་ནང་དུ་ལྷུང་བའི་གནས་ཚུལ་རྣམས་རྒན་པོར་བཤད་.

This is a simple active verb sentence: "by Lhaksam—to the old man—told" (ལྷག་བསམ་གྱིས་རྒན་པོར་བཤད་). The remainder explains what he told him. As is so common, this is accomplished by means of a nominalized phrase: "the events of the axe falling into the river" (སྟ་རེ་ཆུ་ནང་དུ་ལྷུང་བའི་གནས་ཚུལ་རྣམས་).

9. The ninth segment consists of two clauses: 1. རྒན་པོས་ངས་ད་ལྟ་ཆུ་ནང་ནས་སྟ་རེ་ལེན་གྱི་ཡིན་ཅེས་བཤད་དེ་ 2. ཆུ་ནང་དུ་མཆོངས་.

The first clause conveys what the old man said: "I will get the axe from the river" (ངས་ད་ལྟ་ཆུ་ནང་ནས་སྟ་རེ་ལེན་གྱི་ཡིན་ཅེས་), and the second, what he did: "jumped in the river" (ཆུ་ནང་དུ་མཆོངས་).

10. The tenth segment consists of two clauses: 1. ཡུད་ཙམ་སོང་རྗེས་རྒན་པོས་ཆུ་ནང་ནས་གསེར་གྱི་སྟ་རེ་ཞིག་བླངས་ཏེ་ 2. ལྷག་བསམ་ལ། བུ་སྟ་རེ་འདི་རེད་དམ་ཞེས་དྲིས་.

The first clause begins with ཡུད་ཙམ་སོང་རྗེས་ ("after a moment passed"), a time-slot phrase that is similar to the one encountered in Lesson Five (ཉིན་ཤས་སོང་རྗེས་ - "after several days passed"). The first clause is straightforward, although note should be taken that the past tense stem of the verb "to take/get" (ལེན་) is བླངས་.

The second clause contains a question (བུ་སྟ་རེ་འདི་རེད་དམ་ - "Son, is this your axe?") asked by the old man (the implicit subject). The word བུ་ is a common term of address for young boys. It does not here convey a real son, although in other contexts it does, for example, ངའི་བུ་རྡོ་རྗེ་ཟེར་བ་དེ་རེད་ ("My son is the one called Dorje").

11. The eleventh segment consists of four clauses: 1. ལྷག་བསམ་གྱིས་མིག་ལྟས་རྗེས་ 2. དེ་ནི་གསེར་གྱི་སྟ་རེ་ཞིག་ཡིན་པ་མཐོང་བས་ 3. མགྱོགས་མྱུར་མགོ་བོ་གཡུག་གཡུག་བྱས་ནས་ 4. སྤོ་བོ་ལགས་ཐུགས་རྗེ་ཆེ་འདི་ངའི་སྟ་རེ་མ་རེད་ཅེས་ལན་བཏབ་.

The first clause is unproblematic. The second clause contains a nominalized linking verb phrase (གསེར་གྱི་སྟ་རེ་ཞིག་ཡིན་པ་ - (it) being a golden axe), which functions as the object of the verb "see." Thus, *what did he see?*—he saw that it was a golden axe. The "because" connective (བས་) links this clause so that "because he saw that it was a golden axe, . . ."

Clause three is also straightforward, although it should be noted that while མགོ་བོ་གཡུག་གཡུག་བྱས་ means only "shake one's head," Tibetans use this for shaking one's head to say no.

Clause four contains a direct quote (སྤོ་བོ་ལགས་ཐུགས་རྗེ་ཆེ་འདི་ངའི་སྟ་རེ་མ་རེད་ཅེས་) and the final verb "answered" (ལན་བཏབ་).

12. The twelfth segment consists of three clauses: 1. དེ་ནས་རྒན་པོས་སླར་ཡང་ཆུའི་ནང་དུ་མཆོངས་ནས་ 2. དངུལ་གྱི་སྟ་རེ་ཞིག་བླངས་ཏེ་ 3. བུ་སྟ་རེ་འདི་ཁྱེད་ཀྱི་རེད་དམ་ཞེས་དྲིས་.

The first two clauses describe what the old man did ("having jumped . . . and having taken the silver axe"), and the third clause states what he asked.

13. The thirteenth segment consists of three clauses: 1. དངུལ་གྱི་སྟ་རེ་འདི་ཡང་ལྟས་ནས་ 2. ལྷག་བསམ་གྱིས་སླར་ཡང་མགོ་བོ་གཡུག་གཡུག་བྱས་ནས་ 3. སྤོ་བོ་ལགས་ཐུགས་རྗེ་ཆེ་སྟ་རེ་དེ་ཡང་ངའི་མ་རེད་ཅེས་ལན་བཏབ་.

The first clause is the same as earlier ones with the addition of འདི་ཡང་ ("this also, this even"). Thus, he looked at "this also." Note that མིག་ལྟས་ and ལྟས་ are equivalent. The second and third clauses have also been encountered earlier with the addition of "once again" (སླར་ཡང་) in clause two and "that also" (དེ་ཡང་) in clause three.

14. The fourteenth segment consists of three clauses: 1. རྒན་པོས་སླར་ཡང་ཆུ་ནང་དུ་མཆོངས་ནས་ 2. ལྕགས་ཀྱི་སྟ་རེ་ནག་ཐིང་ཐིང་ཞིག་བླངས་ཏེ་ 3. བུ་སྟ་རེ་འདི་ཁྱོད་ཀྱི་རེད་དམ་ཞེས་དྲིས.

A new element in clause two is ཐིང་ཐིང་. When it is added to a color word it conveys "completely that color." Thus སྔོ་ཐིང་ཐིང་ is "completely blue" and སེར་ཐིང་ཐིང་ is "completely yellow."

15. The fifteenth segment consists of five clauses: 1. ལྷག་བསམ་གྱིས་ལྟ་སྐབས་ 2. དེ་ནི་དངོས་གནས་རང་ཉིད་ཀྱི་སྟ་རེ་ཡིན་པས་ 3. དགའ་མཆོངས་རྒྱག་བཞིན་པར་ 4. སྟ་རེ་ཚུར་བླངས་པ་དང་སྦྲགས་ 5. རྒན་པོ་ལགས་ཐུགས་རྗེ་ཆེ་ཞེས་ཡང་ཡང་ཞུས.

The first and second clauses are straightforward, although རང་ཉིད་ in the second clause is a typical word that conveys "oneself." It can also convey "himself" or "herself" depending on context. Here one would translate it as "my own."

The third clause consists of a verb (དགའ་མཆོངས་རྒྱག་-"jumping joyfully") with the "while in the act" particle བཞིན་པར་, together conveying "while in the process of joyfully jumping . . ." This is followed by another short clause: "(he) took the axe hither (towards him)." It, in turn, is linked to what follows by པ་དང་སྦྲགས་, the "together with" clause connective, conveying that "together with" taking the axe, something else happened. That something else is stated in clause five.

It is a direct speech clause, "Old man, thank you" (རྒན་པོ་ལགས་ཐུགས་རྗེ་ཆེ་ཞེས་). The use of the verb ཞུས་ ("said," "asked") conveys respect to the person being addressed, i.e., that the speech is going from a person of lower status to one of higher status. If this respect dimension had been ignored, the verb བཤད་ could have been used with no change in referent meaning. ཡང་ཡང་ is an adverb meaning "over and over again."

16. The sixteenth segment consists of five clauses: 1. རྒན་པོ་དེས་ལྷག་བསམ་གྱི་མགོ་ལ་བྱིལ་བྱིལ་བྱེད་བཞིན་པར་ 2. ཁྱོད་ནི་དངོས་འབྲེལ་ཕྲུ་གུ་ཡག་པོ་ཞིག་རེད་ 3. ཁྱོད་མི་ཚེ་སྐྱིད་པོ་ཡོང་གི་རེད་ཅེས་བཤད་རྗེས་ 4. རྒན་པོ་གློ་བུར་དུ་ཡལ་ནས་ 5. མཐོང་རྒྱུ་མེད་པར་གྱུར.

The first clause consists of a noun + a declarative in the instrumental (རྒན་པོ་+ དེས་). The object with the dative-locative particle follows this (ལྷག་བསམ་གྱི་མགོ་ལ་). Then comes the verb (བྱིལ་བྱིལ་བྱེད་) and བཞིན་པར་, which conveys "while in the act of doing the verbal action." Together these mean "while that old man was (in the process of) stroking Lhaksam's head, . . ."

This is followed by the old man's speech which consists of two sentences. The first is a linking construction conveying that "you" (ཁྱོད་ནི་) "are" (རེད་) "really a good boy" (དངོས་འབྲེལ་ཕྲུ་གུ་ཡག་པོ་ཞིག་). This is followed by another sentence conveying that "a happy life" (མི་ཚེ་སྐྱིད་པོ་) "will come" (ཡོང་གི་རེད་) "to you" (ཁྱོད་). The sentence ends with the direct quote marker ཅེས་, the verb "said" (བཤད་), and the temporal ("after") clause connective

(རྗེས་).

The fourth clause consists of an involuntary verb construction. The subject is "old man" (རྒན་པོ་) and the verb is "vanished (ཡལ་), modified by the adverb "suddenly" (གློ་བུར་དུ་). It conveys that "the old man vanished suddenly."

The last clause consists of the verbal phrase མེད་པར་གྱུར་. This is a common construction meaning "came into the (or a) state of not being or not existing." It is preceded by what came into this state: "the seeing (of him)" (མཐོང་རྒྱུ་). Note that རྒྱུ་ here nominalizes the verb མཐོང་. This may seem a rather strange way to convey this meaning, but it is very typical of Tibetan.

17. The seventeenth segment consists of two clauses: 1. ལྷག་བསམ་གྱིས་སྐབས་དེར་རྒན་པོ་དེ་ནི་བླ་མའི་དྲང་སྲོང་ཡིན་པ་གཞི་ནས་ཤེས་པ་དང་ 2. མུ་མཐུད་མེ་ཤིང་འཐུ་བར་སོང་.

The first clause inverts the usual sentence order by placing the time slot term (at that time - སྐབས་དེར་) after the subject (ལྷག་བསམ་གྱིས་). The clause ends with the verb "knew" (ཤེས་). It is modified by the adverbial term གཞི་ནས་, which conveys "only then." Thus, "Lhaksam, at that time, only then knew. . . ." What he knew is conveyed by the nominalized linking verb construction རྒན་པོ་དེ་ནི་བླ་མའི་དྲང་སྲོང་ཡིན་པ་ ("the old man being an ascetic lama"), so that together they translate as, "Lhaksam knew that the old man was an ascetic lama."

This clause is linked with the next by the "and" connective (པ་དང་). The final clause is a simple infinitive construction with the implicit subject "he," the verb "went" (སོང་), and the infinitivized verbal phrase "to collect firewood" (མེ་ཤིང་འཐུ་བར་). མུ་མཐུད་ is an adverbial meaning "continuing without a break." It conveys here that the boy continued on his original task, collecting firewood. སོང་ in the phrase འཐུ་བར་སོང་ functions not as a past tense marker but as the past tense stem of the verb "to go" (འགྲོ་). It is the equivalent of ཕྱིན་.

18. The eighteenth segment consists of four clauses: 1. ཁོ་པའི་སྟ་རེར་དྲང་སྲོང་གིས་བྱིལ་བའི་དབང་གིས་ 2. སྟ་རེ་རྣོ་པོ་ཞི་དྲགས་ཆགས་ཏེ་ 3. ཤིང་མགྱོགས་པོ་བཅད་ནས་ 4. ཁྱིམ་ལ་ལོག་པ་རེད་.

The first clause starts with an object phrase "to his axe" (ཁོ་པའི་སྟ་རེར་). It is followed by the subject in the instrumental (དྲང་སྲོང་གིས་) and then the verb "stroked" (བྱིལ་). "Thus, the ascetic stroked his axe. . . ." This clause is linked to the next clause by the "because" verbal clause connective (པའི་དབང་གིས་). Thus, "because the ascetic stroked his axe. . . ."

The second clause is an involuntary construction based on the verb "became" (ཆགས་). The subject of the sentence is "the axe," and what the axe became is "very sharp" (རྣོ་པོ་ཞི་དྲགས་).

This is linked to the third clause by the gerundive verbal clause connective (ཏེ་). Clause three has an implicit subject (by him) and consists only of the verb "cut" (བཅད་), the adverb "quickly" (མགྱོགས་པོ་), and the object "wood" (ཤིང་). Thus, "because the ascetic stroked his axe, the axe became very sharp and cut the wood quickly."

This is linked to clause four by the verbal clause connective (ནས་), to make "*having* cut the wood quickly. . . ." Clause four begins with the object ཁྱིམ་ལ་ (to the house), followed by the verb "returned" (ལོག་+ པ་རེད་). Thus, "having cut the wood quickly, he returned home."

19. The nineteenth segment consists of five clauses: 1. ས་བདག་གིས་ཁོ་པ་སྔ་པོ་དེ་འདྲ་ལོག་ཡོང་བ་མཐོང་སྐབས་ 2. ཁོས་སྒྱིད་ལུག་བྱེད་ཀྱི་འདུག་ཅེས་གཤེ་གཤེ་བཏང་བས་ 3. ལྷག་བསམ་གྱིས་གནས་ཚུལ་རྣམས་ཚང་མ་གསལ་པོ་བཤད་སྟབས་ 4. ས་བདག་ཁོང་ཁྲོ་ཟ་བཞིན་པར་ 5. ཁྱོད་ཀྱིས་གསེར་དང་དངུལ་གྱི་སྟ་རེ་མ་བླངས་པར་ལྕགས་ཀྱི་སྟ་རེ་དེ་ཁྱེར་བ་ནི་དངོས་གནས་མི་ལྷུགས་པ་ཞིག་རེད་ཅེས་ཁ་རྡུང་བཏང་.

The first clause begins with the subject in the instrumental case ("by the landlord" - ས་བདག་གིས་). The verb that goes with this is མཐོང་ ("see"). Thus, "the lord saw" something.

What he saw is presented as a nominalized verb phrase: ཁོ་པ་སྔ་པོ་དེ་འདྲ་ལོག་ཡོང་བ་ ("his returning early like that"). This is structurally identical with a clause encountered earlier: རྒན་པོ་དེ་ནི་བླ་མའི་དྲང་སྲོང་ཡིན་པ་ཤེས་ ("that old man being an ascetic lama, (he) knew").

Note that དེ་འདྲ་ is commonly used with adjectives to convey "like that" or "so." In this case ཆེན་པོ་དེ་འདྲ་ means "big like that" or "so big."

The "when" clause connective (སྐབས་) links this clause to clause two, which begins with the pronoun "he" in the instrumental (ཁོས་). This pronoun refers to the lord and goes with the subsequent active verb "scold" (གཤེ་གཤེ་བཏང་). Thus, what he did was to scold someone, here the boy. However, in typical literary Tibetan style, the object, the boy, is left implicit, context conveying this. The remainder of the clause is the content of what he said or scolded, སྒྱིད་ལུག་བྱེད་ཀྱི་འདུག་ ("[you] are acting lazy"). In English we would to translate this as, "He scolded him saying, "You are lazy."

The "because" clause connective (བས་) links this to clause three which consists of the simple active verb construction, "Lhaksam said/told. . . " (ལྷག་བསམ་གྱིས་. . .བཤད་). In this clause the object, ("to the lord"), is implicit.

What Lhaksam told the lord was: གནས་ཚུལ་རྣམས་ཚང་མ་ (news + plural + all — i.e., "all the news, events, or situation"). The redundancy of using the plural marker རྣམས་ plus ཚང་མ་ ("all") is typical. Either one could have been left out with no change in meaning. Note also that the adverb "clearly" (གསལ་པོ་) modifies the verb བཤད་. It could have been placed in the dative-locative (གསལ་པོར་).

This clause is linked to clause four by another of the "because" clause connectives, སྟབས་. Like English, good style in Tibetan requires avoiding repetition of words.

Clause four is an involuntary verb construction conveying that the subject experienced something—"got angry" (ཁོང་ཁྲོ་ཟ་). Since the verbal action is involuntary, the subject is not placed in the instrumental case. The verbal complement (བཞིན་པར་) here conveys not "while," but "in the manner of," and the clause is a derived adverbial meaning "angrily"—"in the manner of being angry." It modifies the final verb ཁ་རྡུང་བཏང་ ("verbally abuse"). Thus, "angrily, (he) verbally abused (him)."

The rest of this segment expresses what he said in his verbal abuse. It begins with a long nominalized verb phrase: ཁྱོད་ཀྱིས་གསེར་དང་དངུལ་གྱི་སྟ་རེ་མ་བླངས་པར་ལྕགས་ཀྱི་སྟ་རེ་དེ་ཁྱེར་བ་ནི་, which means, "as for your (by you) bringing that iron axe in the manner of not taking the gold and silver axes." Note that མ་བླངས་པར་ would normally be translated here as "without taking."

This section is followed by དངོས་གནས་མི་སྐྱུགས་པ་ཞིག་རེད་, which means (you) "are really an idiotic person."

20. The twentieth segment consists of four clauses: 1. ཕྱི་ཉིན་ཞོགས་པ་སྔ་པོ་ནས་ས་བདག་གིས་ལྷག་བསམ་ལས་ཀ་གཞན་བྱེད་པར་བཏང་བ་དང་། 2. ཁོ་པ་རང་ཉིད་མི་ཤིང་འཐུ་མཁན་དབུལ་པོ་ཞིག་ཏུ་བརྫུས་ཏེ་ 3. སྟ་རེ་གོག་པོ་ཞིག་ཁྱེར་ནས་ 4. རི་ལ་མི་ཤིང་གཅོད་པར་འགྲོ་ཁུལ་བྱས་.

The first clause begins with a long time-slot statement: ཕྱི་ཉིན་ཞོགས་པ་སྔ་པོ་ནས་ ("the next day day, from early morning"). This is followed by the subject in the instrumental (ས་བདག་གིས). The subject's action is contained in the verb བཏང་ ("sent"), which is part of an infinitive construction meaning "sent to do other (གཞན་) work" (ལས་ཀ་གཞན་བྱེད་པར་བཏང་).

The conjunctive connective བ་དང་ links this clause to the next which begins with a reflexive subject "he himself" (ཁོ་པ་+ རང་ཉིད་). The verb associated with this is བརྫུས་ which means "pretended," and the long phrase immediately preceding བརྫུས་ (མི་ཤིང་འཐུ་མཁན་དབུལ་པོ་ཞིག་ཏུ་) indicates what was pretended — "to be a poor firewood collector." Note that the object (མི་ཤིང་འཐུ་མཁན་དབུལ་པོ་ཞིག་ཏུ་) ends, as usual, with the dative-locative particle (ཏུ་). This phrase contains a shorter verb phrase converted to the agentive by means of མཁན་— མི་ཤིང་འཐུ་མཁན་ ("a person who collects firewood"). དབུལ་པོ་ then functions as an adjective modifying the previous phrase (མི་ཤིང་འཐུ་མཁན་) so that it conveys: "a poor person who collects firewood."

The particle ཏེ་ (the gerundive clause connective) links this to clause three, conveying simultaneous action: "pretending to be . . ., (he) did something."

Clause three tells what he simultaneously did: he took an old beat-up axe. It is linked to the next clause by the gerundive clause connective. Thus, clauses two and three translate: "pretending to be a poor firewood collector, he took an old axe."

The fourth clause is another infinitive clause conveying that he went to cut wood in the mountains. However, by inclusion of the "pretend"particle ཁུལ་ (འགྲོ་ཁུལ་བྱས), the clause conveys that "he pretended to go to. . . ."

21. The twenty-first segment consists of three clauses: 1. ཁོ་པས་ཟམ་པའི་ཐོག་ལ་སླེབས་སྐབས་ 2. སྟ་རེ་དེ་ཆུའི་ནང་ཀང་བཙུགས་ནས་དབྱུགས་ཏེ་ 3. སྐད་ཤུགས་ཆེན་པོས་ངུས་པ་རེད་.

The first clause begins with the subject in the instrumental (ཁོ་པས་). This, however, relates not to the involuntary verb སླེབས་ ("arrive") in this clause but rather to the active verbs དབྱུགས་ ("threw") in clause two and ངུས་ "cry" in clause three.

Clause two introduces a new adverb, ཁང་བཙུགས་ནས་ ("intentionally, purposely"), so that "at the time (he) arrived on the bridge, he intentionally threw that axe into the river." This is linked by the gerundive clause connective to the third clause.

Clause three consists of the active verb "cry" (ངུས་), modified by the adverbial phrase "loudly" or "in a loud voice" (སྐད་ཤུགས་ཆེན་པོས་). Note that this is an example of the instrumental functioning to create an adverbial (see 5.5.2). Together they convey, "When he arrived on the bridge, (he) intentionally threw the axe into the river and cried loudly . . . ."

22. The twenty second segment consists of the simple sentence: སྐབས་དེར་དྲང་སྲོང་སླར་ཡང་དེ་གར་ཡོང་.

The sentence begins with the time-slot term "at that time" (སྐབས་དེར་). This is followed by the subject, "the ascetic" (དྲང་སྲོང་), and the verb "to come" (ཡོང་). Between these is the location of the verbal action—"there-to that place" (དེ་གར་). The verb ཡོང་ is also modified by the adverbial "once again" (སླར་ཡང་). Together they convey, "At that time, the ascetic once again came there."

23. The twenty third segment consists of six clauses: 1. ས་བདག་གིས་མིག་ཆུ་ཕྱིས་བཞིན་པར་ 2. ངའི་སྟ་རེ་ཆུའི་ནང་དུ་ལྷུང་སོང་བས་ 3. ཁྱིམ་དུ་ལོག་ན་ 4. ངའི་དཔོན་པོས་རྡེས་ཀྱི་རེད་ཞེས་བཤད་མ་ཐག་ 5. དྲང་སྲོང་གིས་སྟེར་བཞིན་ཆུའི་ནང་དུ་མཆོངས་ཏེ་ 6. ལམ་སེང་ཁོ་པའི་ལྕགས་ཀྱི་སྟ་རེ་ཁོ་པར་སྤྲད་.

The first clause is a simple active construction with its subject in the instrumental (ས་བདག་གིས་). The active verb is "wiped" (ཕྱིས་) and the object is "tears" (མིག་ཆུ་). Together they mean, "The landlord wiped (his) tears." The clause connector is (བཞིན་པར་ - "while") Thus, "the lord, while wiping (his) tears, . . . "

The second clause is one half of the landlord's statement that ends in clause four with the verb བཤད་. It is an involuntary sentence construction whose subject is "my axe" (ངའི་སྟ་རེ་). The involuntary verb here is "fell" (ལྷུང་), and the location of the involuntary falling is "in the river/water" (ཆུའི་ནང་དུ་). The past complement སོང་ completes this construction. This clause is linked by the "because" connective (བས་), so that it means, "Because my axe fell into the water . . ."

The third clause continues the landlord's speech with a short conditional phrase, "if I return home" (ཁྱིམ་དུ་ལོག་ན་). The fourth clause ends the speech with an active construction consisting of the subject "by my lord" (ངའི་དཔོན་པོས་) and the verb "beat" (རྡེས་), accompanied by a future complement (ཀྱི་རེད་). Clauses three and four, therefore, conveys: "If I return home my lord will beat (me)." The "as soon as" clause connective (མ་ཐག་) links this with clause five.

Clause five narrates an action: "by the ascetic (དྲང་སྲོང་གིས་), like before (སྔར་བཞིན་), jumped into the river" (དྲང་སྲོང་གིས་སྔར་བཞིན་ཆུའི་ནང་དུ་མཆོངས་).

This is linked to clause six by the "having connective" so that "having jumped in the river," the subject in clause five (དྲང་སྲོང་གིས་) "gave" (སྤྲད་) something. The direct object phrase consists of a phrase with two genitives ཁོ་པའི་ལྕགས་ཀྱི་སྟ་རེ་—he of iron of axe, in which "he-of (his)" modifies "iron of axe (iron axe)" so that it is "his iron axe." This is followed by the indirect object "to him." Thus, "immediately (the old man) gave his (the lord's) axe to him (the lord)."

24. The twenty fourth segment consists of two clauses: 1. ས་བདག་གིས་འཕྲལ་དུ་མགོ་བོ་གཡུག་གཡུག་བྱས་ཏེ་ 2. འདི་ངའི་མ་རེད་ཅེས་བཤད་.

The subject in the first clause is in the instrumental and the active verb is "shook (head)" ([མགོ་བོ་] གཡུག་གཡུག་བྱས་).

The second clause contains a linking verb statement , "this is not mine," with the following main active verb: "said" (བཤད་). These two convey that "the lord immediately shook his head no and said, This is not mine.

25. The twenty fifth segment consists of six clauses: 1. དྲང་སྲོང་གིས་ཡང་བསྐྱར་ཆུའི་ནང་དུ་མཆོངས་ནས་ 2. དངུལ་གྱི་སྟ་རེ་ཞིག་བླངས་བས་ 3. ས་བདག་གིས་མིག་ཆེན་པོ་གདངས་ནས་ 4. ལམ་སང་དངུལ་གྱི་སྟ་རེ་འདི་ཡག་པོ་འདུག། 5. འོན་ཀྱང་གསེར་གྱི་སྟ་རེ་ཞིག་བྱུང་ན་ 6. ཡག་གྲོས་རེད་ཅེས་བཤད་.

The first two clauses parallel ones previously encountered. The third clause is an active verb construction linked to what follows by the "having" connective. However, the third clause really functions as an adverb modifying the verb བཤད་ ("said") in clause six, answering the question, "*the lord said how?*—in the manner of opening his eyes wide."

Clause four begins with another adverb (ལམ་སང་ - "at once"), which modifies "said." It is followed by what was said, namely that "this is good."

Clause five starts with "even though" (འོན་ཀྱང་). The rest of this segment is straightforward. This could have been written ཡག་པོ་འདུག་ཀྱང་.

26. The twenty sixth segment consists of three clauses: 1. དྲང་སྲོང་གིས་དངུལ་གྱི་སྟ་རེ་དེ་ས་བདག་གི་རྐང་པའི་འགྲམ་དུ་དབྱུགས་ཏེ་ 2. སླར་ཡང་ཆུའི་ནང་དུ་འཛུལ་ནས་ 3. གསེར་གྱི་སྟ་རེ་ཞིག་བླངས་པ་རེད་.

The first clause is another simple active construction: དྲང་སྲོང་གིས་ . . . དབྱུགས་. The direct object is "that axe" (སྟ་རེ་དེ་) and the location of the verbal action (where he threw it) is ས་བདག་གི་རྐང་པའི་འགྲམ་དུ་. The second and third phrases parallel those encountered earlier.

27. The twenty seventh segment consists of five clauses: 1. ས་བདག་གིས་གསེར་གྱི་སྟ་རེ་དེ་ཡག་པོ་ཞེ་དྲགས་འདུག་ཞེས་ཡང་ཡང་བཤད་ནས་ 2. དྲང་སྲོང་གི་ལག་པ་ནས་གསེར་གྱི་སྟ་རེ་ཚུར་བླངས་པ་དང་ 3. ས་སྟེང་ནས་དངུལ་གྱི་སྟ་རེ་དེ་ཡར་བསྡུགས་ཏེ་ 4. ལག་པ་རེ་རེར་ཁྱེར་ནས་ 5. དགའ་ཐག་ཆོད་པ་རེད་.

The first clause is a typical active construction presenting direct speech (ས་བདག་གིས་ . . .བཤད). The second clause is another standard type construction describing an activity with the subject ("by the lord") implicit. Note again that the verb "take" (བླངས་) often is preceded by ཚུར་ a term meaning "hither" or "toward oneself."

The third clause describes an activity, "picking up the silver axe from the ground." Note that ཡར་ ("upwards") is commonly used with the verb བསྒྲུགས་ ("pick up").

28. The final segment consists of six clauses: 1. སྐབས་དེ་ར་དྭང་སྔོང་ཉེ་ཡང་སྐྱུར་ཡལ་སྐབས་ 2. ས་བདག་གིས་སྟ་རེ་གཉིས་ཀ་ཁྱེར་ན་ 3. ཡག་པོ་འདུག་བསམ་ནས་ 4. མགྱོགས་པོ་ཕྱིན་འཕྲལ་ 5. ཕོ་པ་ཆུའི་ནང་དུ་ལྷུང་སྟེ་ 6. ཤི་བ་རེད་.

It follows the standard pattern of actions linked by clause connectives: ...སྐབས་...ན་ ...ནས་ ...འཕྲལ་ ...སྟེ་.

8.11 Vocabulary (Beginning with this lesson, pronunciation notation will not be included)

བཀའ་འདྲི་	asking; va.— ཞུ་ (h.)
རྐང་པ་	foot
རྐང་བཙུགས་ནས་	purposely
ལྐུགས་པ་	idiot
སྐད་	voice
ཁ་བརྡུང་	verbally abuse; va. — གཏོང་
ཁྱོད་རང་	you
ཁྲི་	10,000
ཁྲི་དགུ་	90,000
ཁྲི་དགུ་དང་སྟོང་ཕྲག་དྲུག་	96,000
ཁྲི་བརྒྱད་	80,000
ཁྲི་ལྔ་	50,000
ཁྲི་གཅིག་	10,000
ཁྲི་གཉིས་	20,000
ཁྲི་དྲུག་	60,000
ཁྲི་བདུན་	70,000
ཁྲི་བཞི་	40,000
ཁྲི་གསུམ་	30,000
ཁྲིམས་	law
གོ་	nineties
གོག་པོ་	old, beat up
གྱ་	eighties
གྱུར་	vi. p. of འགྱུར་
དགའ་མཆོངས་	jumping for joy; va. — རྒྱག་
དགའ་ཐག་ཆོད་	vi. to be or become very happy
དགུ་	nine
དགུ་བརྒྱ་	900
དགུ་བརྒྱ་དང་བརྒྱད་ཅུ་གྱ་བདུན་	987
དགུ་ཁྲི་	90,000
དགུ་བཅུ་	90
དགུ་སྟོང་	9,000
དགུ་པ་	ninth
དགུ་འབུམ་	900,000
དགོང་མོ་	night
མགོ་	head
མགྱོགས་མྱུར་	quickly
རྒད་པོ་	old man
བརྒྱ་ཆ་	percent
བརྒྱ་ཆ་གཅིག་	one percent
བརྒྱ་ཆ་གཉིས་	two percent
བརྒྱ་ཆ་བཅུ་	ten percent
བརྒྱ་ཆ་ལྔ་བཅུ་	fifty percent
བརྒྱ་ཆ་བདུན་ཅུ་དོན་ལྔ་	seventy-five percent
བརྒྱ་(ཐམ་པ་)	100
བརྒྱ་དང་བརྒྱད་	108
སྒྱིད་ལུག་	lazy
བརྒྱད་	eight
བརྒྱད་ཁྲི་	80,000

བརྒྱད་ཁྲི་ལྔ་སྟོང་དྲུག་ བརྒྱ་དགུ་བཅུ་ གོ་ལྔ་	85,695
བརྒྱད་བརྒྱ་	800
བརྒྱད་ཅུ་	80
བརྒྱད་ཆ་ལྔ་	five eighths
བརྒྱད་སྟོང་	8,000
བརྒྱད་པ་	eighth
བརྒྱད་འབུམ་	800,000
བསྒྲུག་	va. to pick up
བསྒྲུགས་	va. p. of བསྒྲུག་
ང་	fifties
ངའི་	my
ངུས་	va. to cry
དངངས་སྐྲག་	fright
དངུལ་	silver
ལྔ་	five
ལྔ་ཁྲི་	50,000
ལྔ་བརྒྱ་	500
ལྔ་བཅུ་	50
ལྔ་ཆ་གཉིས་	two fifths
ལྔ་ཆ་བཞི་	four fifths
ལྔ་སྟོང་	5,000
ལྔ་པ་	fifth
ལྔ་འབུམ་	500,000
སྔ་པོ་	early
སྔར་བཞིན་	like/as before
ཅི་ཕྱིར་	why
གཅིག་ཁྲི་	10,000
གཅིག་སྟོང་	1,000
གཅོད་	va. to cut
བཅད་	va. p. of གཅོད་
བཅུ་	ten
བཅུ་དགུ་	nineteen
བཅུ་གཅིག་	eleven
བཅུ་གཅིག་པ་	eleventh
བཅུ་གཉིས་	twelve
བཅུ་གཉིས་པ་	twelfth
བཅུ་དྲུག་	sixteen
བཅུ་བདུན་	seventeen
བཅུ་པ་	tenth
བཅུ་མིད་	the ten's place in a number
བཅུ་བཞི་	fourteen
བཅུ་གསུམ་	thirteen
བཅོ་ལྔ་	fifteen
བཅོ་བརྒྱད་	eighteen
ལྕགས་	iron
ཆིག་སྟོང་	1,000
ཆིག་འབུམ་	100,000
ཆུ་གློག་ས་ཚིགས་	hydroelectric station
ཆོས་	religion, dharma
ཉི་ཤུ་	twenty
ཉིས་ཁྲི་	20,000
ཉིས་བརྒྱ་	200
ཉིས་བརྒྱ་དང་ལྔ་བཅུ་ ང་དྲུག་	256
ཉིས་སྟོང་	2,000
ཉིས་འབུམ་	200,000
ཉེས་	va. to beat, hit
ཉེས་བརྡུང་བྱེད་	va. to beat
གཉིས་པ་	second
སྟ་རེ་	axe
སྟོང་ཕྲག་གཅིག་	1,000
ཐིང་ཐིང་	adjective used to convey "completely" with certain colors
ཐོ་	a list; va. — རྒྱག་: to make a list, to record
ཐོག་ནས་	from on top
དང་མཉམ་དུ་	together with
དང་བསྟུན་	in accordance with
དང་མཐུན་པ་	compatible with

དང་འདྲ་བ་	similar to (with)
དང་ལྡན་པ་	possessing, having
དང་པོ་	first
དང་འབྲེལ་	related to, joined with
དང་སྦྲགས་	see སྦྲགས་
དང་མི་འདྲ་བ་	dissimilar to (with)
དང་ལྷན་རྒྱས་	together with (h.)
དུང་	conch shell
དུང་ཕྱུར་གཅིག་	100,000,000
དུང་ཕྱུར་བཅུ་	1,000,000,000
དེ་གར་	there
དེ་འདྲ་	like that
དོ་སྣང་བྱེད་	vi. to notice, to pay attention to
དོན་	seventies
དྲང་སྲོང་	an ascetic
དྲན་	vi. to remember
དྲུག་	six
དྲུག་ཁྲི་	60,000
དྲུག་བརྒྱ་	600
དྲུག་ཅུ་	60
དྲུག་ཆ་གཅིག་	one sixth
དྲུག་སྟོང་	6,000
དྲུག་པ་	sixth
དྲུག་འབུམ་	600,000
བདུན་	seven
བདུན་ཁྲི་	70,000
བདུན་བརྒྱ་	700
བདུན་ཅུ་	70
བདུན་སྟོང་	7,000
བདུན་སྟོང་ལྔ་བརྒྱ་ཉི་ཤུ	7,520
བདུན་པ་	seventh
བདུན་འབུམ་	700,000
སྡོད་	va. to stay, live, reside
ནག་ཐིང་ཐིང་	completely black
གནས་ཚུལ་	news, events, situation
རྣོ་པོ་	sharp
དཔོན་པོ་	lord
སྤོ་བོ་(ལགས་)	old man (h.)
ཕྱི་ཟླ་	Western month
ཕ་མ་	parents
ཕྱི་ཉིན་	the next day
ཕྱིས་	va. to wipe
བོད་ཟླ་	Tibetan (lunar) month
བྱིལ་	va. to stroke, caress
བྱིལ་བྱིལ་	stroking; va. — བྱེད་
བྱེ་བ་གཅིག་	10,000,000
བླ་མའི་དྲང་སྲོང་	an ascetic lama
བླངས་	va. p. of ལེན་: took
དབྱུགས་	va. to throw
སྦྲགས་	"together with" connective
མི་ཚེ་	life, a lifetime
མིག་ཆུ་	tears
མིག་ཆེན་པོ་གདང་(ས)་	va. to open one's eyes wide
མེད་པར་གྱུར་	vi. to come into a state of not existing
སྨ་ར་	beard
ཙ་	twenties
རྩོམ་	va. to write, compose, author
འཛུལ་	va. to enter
བརྫུས་	va. to pretend
ཞེ་	forties
ཞོགས་པ་	morning
ཞོར་	incidental particle
གཞན་	other, different
གཞི་ནས་	only then
བཞི་ཁྲི་	40,000
བཞི་བརྒྱ་	400
བཞི་ཅུ་	40

བཞི་ཆ་གཅིག་	one quarter
བཞི་ཆ་གསུམ་	three quarters
བཞི་སྟོང་	4,000
བཞི་པ་	fourth
བཞི་འབུམ་	400,000
ཟམ་པ་	bridge
གཟབ་གཟབ་	careful
ཡག་ཤོས་	best
ཡང་ཡང་	over and over
ཡར་	up, upwards
ཡར་ཀླུང་གཙང་པོ་	the (Yarlung) Tsangpo River
ཡིན་མིན་	whether is or is not
ཡུད་ཙམ་	a moment
གཡུག་གཡུག་བྱེད་	va. to shake
ཡོད་མེད་	whether exists or does not
རེ་	sixties
རེ་རེ་	each
ལན་བཏབ་	va. p. of ལན་འདེབས་
ལན་འདེབས་	va. to answer, respond, reply
ལམ་ཀ་	road
ཤུགས་ཆེན་པོ་	strong, tough; loud
ས་བདག་	landlord
ས་ཡ་གཅིག་ (or ཁྲི་བརྒྱ་ཐམ་པ་)	1,000,000
སུ་འདྲ་ཞིག་	like who; whoever; what kind of a
སུམ་ཅུ་	30
སེམས་ཁྲལ་	worries; va. — བྱེད་
སོ་	thirties
སྲིད་འཛིན་	president; rule; va. — བྱེད་: to act, serve as president; to rule
སློབ་དེབ་	textbook
གསུམ་ཁྲི་	30,000
གསུམ་བརྒྱ་	300
གསུམ་བརྒྱ་དང་བཞི་བཅུ་ཞེ་དགུ་	349
གསུམ་ཆ་གཉིས་	two thirds
གསུམ་སྟོང་	3,000
གསུམ་པ་	third
གསུམ་འབུམ་	300,000
གསེར་	gold
བསམ་	va. to think
ཧ་ཅང་	very
ལྷག་བསམ་	p.n. Lhaksam

PART TWO

Lesson Nine

9.1 Constructions with ཐབས་ ("way, means")

ཐབས་ (which was first introduced in 7.5.6) expresses the idea of "the means to do" or "the way to do" something. It is used with the present (or non-past) stem of verbs in the following format: Vb. (pres.) + ཐབས་ + existential verb (positive or negative). For example, འགྲོ་ཐབས་ཡོད་པ་མ་རེད་ conveys the idea that "there is no way or means to go."

a. སོན་གསར་པ་མེད་པར་བརྟེན། ཐོན་སྐྱེད་ཡར་རྒྱས་གཏོང་ཐབས་ཡོད་པ་མ་རེད།
Because there are no new seeds, there is no way to improve production.

b. ཁོ་རྒྱ་གར་ནས་འདིར་ཆུ་ཚོད་གཉིས་ནང་འབྱོར་ཐབས་མི་འདུག
There is no way for him to arrive here from India in two hours.

c. ཨེམ་ཆི་ལྷ་ས་ནས་འདིར་ཆུ་ཚོད་གཅིག་ནང་ཕེབས་ཐབས་མེད་སྐབས།
Because there was no way for the doctor to come here from Lhasa in an hour,
ནད་པ་དེ་སྨན་ཁང་ལ་བསྐྱལ་བ་རེད།
(They, he, she, etc.) took the patient to the hospital.

ཐབས་ is also commonly used in negative constructions with the verb བྲལ་ ("to separate") conveying the meaning of "no way to do the verbal action."

Vb. (non-past) + ཐབས་ +བྲལ་བ་རེད་

Vb. (non-past) + ཐབས་ +དང་ +བྲལ་བ་རེད་

d. ཁོ་བལ་ཡུལ་ནས་འདིར་ཆུ་ཚོད་གཉིས་ནང་འབྱོར་ཐབས་བྲལ་བ་རེད།
There was no way for him to arrive here from Nepal in two hours.

e. ནད་པ་དེ་སྨན་ཁང་ལ་སྐྱེལ་ཐབས་བྲལ་སྐབས། ཨེམ་ཆི་ཞིག་སྐད་བཏང་སོང་།
Because there is no way to take the patient to the hospital, (they, he, she, etc.) called a doctor (to come).

ཐབས་ is also sometimes used in conjunction with the verb བྱེད་ ("to do") where it conveys the idea of "trying to do." The pattern is: Vb. (non-past) + ཐབས་ + བྱེད་ + verbal complement.

f. ཁོ་ཚོས་གཞུང་གསར་པ་ཞིག་འཛུགས་ཐབས་བྱེད་ཀྱི་ཡོད་པ་རེད།
They are trying to establish a new government.

g. བོད་པ་མང་པོས་འབྲུག་ཡུལ་ནས་བལ་ཡུལ་བར་དུ་ཡོང་ཐབས་བྱས་པ་རེད།
Many Tibetans tried to come to Nepal from Bhutan.

h. ཁོས་བྲོས་ཐབས་བྱས་ཀྱང་། ཕྲུ་གུ་དང་སྐྱེ་དམན་ཡོད་སྐབས་བྲོས་མ་ཐུབ་པ་རེད།
Even though he tried to escape, because (he) had a wife and children, (he) was unable to escape.

ཐབས་ can also nominalize verb phrases and therefore can be used with indefinites such as ཅིག་:

i. འདིར་ཆུ་གཏོང་ཐབས་ཤིག་གནང་དང་།
Please irrigate here. (lit., Do or make a way/method so that one can irrigate here.)

9.2 The auxiliary verbs "to dare to": ཕོད་ and ནུས་

ཕོད་ and ནུས་ are used with verb stems to convey the meaning of "daring to do" the verbal action.

a. སློབ་གྲྭ་བ་ཚོས་དགེ་རྒན་ལ་དྲི་བ་འདྲི་ཕོད་ཀྱི་མ་རེད།
The students will not dare to ask the teacher questions.
b. སློབ་ཕྲུག་དེས་ཕྱི་རྒྱལ་གྱི་མི་དེ་ལ་དྲི་བ་མང་པོ་དྲིས་ཕོད་མ་སོང་།
That student did not dare to ask the foreigner many questions.
c. ངས་དེ་བྱེད་ནུས་ཀྱི་མི་འདུག།
I do not dare to do that.
d. དེང་སང་ཁོང་ཚོས་མི་དམངས་ལ་བརྙས་བཅོས་བྱེད་ཕོད་དམ།
Do they dare to abuse the people these days?
e. འབྲོག་པ་དེས་གནམ་གྲུའི་ནང་འགྲོ་ཕོད་ཀྱི་མེད་ཙང་། རྟ་བཞོན་སྐྱེ་ཕྱིན་སོང་།
Because the nomad did not dare to go into the airplane, (he) went riding a horse.
f. གྲོང་གསེབ་པ་འདིས་ནགས་ཚལ་ནང་འགྲོ་མ་ཕོད་སྐབས། ནང་ལ་བསྡད་པ་རེད།
Because this villager did not dare to go into the forest, (he) stayed at home.
g. དམག་མིས་གྲོང་གསེབ་དེ་ལ་རྙོག་ཁྲ་བཤད་ཕོད་དམ།
Did the soldier dare to cause trouble to that village?
h. གྲྭ་པས་གཡག་བསད་ཕོད་མ་སོང་།
The monk did not dare to kill the yak.

9.3 The "let alone/far from" clause connectives: ལྟ་བཞག་, ཕར་བཞག་, and ལྟ་ཅི་

ལྟ་བཞག་ and ཕར་བཞག་ both are generally preceded by རྒྱུ་ or ཡས་/ཡག་. They convey the meaning "let alone X , (they, he, etc.) did Y" or "far from X being done, Y was done.'

a. ང་ཚོར་རོགས་རམ་བྱེད་རྒྱུ་ཕར་བཞག་གནོད་སྐྱོན་བཏང་བ་རེད།
Let alone helping us, (they, he, etc.) did us harm. (Or, Far from helping us, they did us harm.)

b. ཕྲུ་གུ་ཁ་ཤས་བོད་ཡིག་སློབ་སྦྱོང་བྱ་རྒྱུ་ལྟ་བཞག་ལས་ཀ་ཡང་ཡག་པོ་བྱེད་ཀྱི་མེད།
Let alone studying written Tibetan, some children are not even doing (their) work

well. (Or, Far from studying written Tibetan. . . .)

c. ཁོས་དགེ་རྒན་ལ་ཡི་གེ་གཏོང་རྒྱུ་ཕར་བཞག་ཁ་པར་ཡང་གཏོང་གི་མི་འདུག།
Far from sending a letter to the teacher, (he) does not even call him (by phone).

d. གྲྭ་པ་དེས་དགོན་པར་སྡོད་རྒྱུ་ལྟ་བཞག་མཆོད་མཇལ་ལ་ཡང་འགྲོ་གི་ཡོད་པ་མ་རེད།
The monk does not even go for religious visits, let alone stay in the monastery.

e. ཕྱི་རྒྱལ་གྱི་ཡུལ་སྐོར་སྐྱོ་འཆམ་པ་དེས་བོད་པའི་ཁ་ལག་ཟ་རྒྱུ་ལྟ་ཅི་འབྲས་ཀྱང་ཟ་གི་མི་འདུག།
Let alone eating Tibetan food, that foreign tourist doesn't even eat rice.

Past tense constructions are typically formed by using past tense verb stems or past time words:

f. ཁོས་གྲོགས་པོར་ཡི་གེ་བཏང་རྒྱུ་ཕར་བཞག་ཁ་པར་ཡང་བཏང་མ་སོང་།
He did not even make a phone call, let alone sending a letter to his friend.

g. ན་ནིང་སོ་ནམ་པ་དེས་ཚགས་པར་བཀླགས་རྒྱུ་ལྟ་བཞག་ཡི་གེ་ཐུང་ཐུང་ཞིག་ཀྱང་བཀླགས་ཤེས་ཀྱི་ཡོད་པ་མ་རེད།
Last year, that farmer did not even know how to read a short letter, let alone reading a newspaper.

Note that even though example g. ends with a present tense verbal complement, it conveys past tense because of the initial time element ("last year" - ན་ནིང་)

h. ཁོང་ཚོས་ནད་པ་དེ་སྨན་ཁང་ལ་བསྐྱལ་རྒྱུ་ཕར་བཞག་སྨན་ཡང་མ་ཉོས།
Let alone taking the patient to the hospital, (they) did not even buy medicine (for him).

9.4 The "excluding" clause connective: ཕུད་

The particle ཕུད་ is used with nouns to convey "aside from," "not including," "with the exception of," "except for," and "excluding."

a. ཨ་ཞང་ཕུད་ནང་མི་དྲུག་ཡོད།
Excluding uncle, (I) have six family members.

b. སློབ་ཕྲུག་འགའ་ཤས་ཕུད་ཚང་མས་བོད་སྐད་སློབ་སྦྱོང་བྱས་པ་རེད།
Excluding several students, all studied Tibetan.

c. ཚེ་རིང་གིས་གཟའ་ཉི་མ་ཕུད་ཉིན་ལྟར་དཔེ་མཛོད་ཁང་ལ་དེབ་ཀློག་པར་འགྲོ་གི་འདུག།
Excluding Sunday, Tsering goes to the library to read books every day.

d. བཀྲིས་ཕུད་སློབ་ཕྲུག་ཚང་མ་ཚོགས་འདུར་སླེབས།
Excluding Tashi, all students arrived at (came to) the meeting.

e. གྲྭ་པ་གཅིག་ཕུད་གཞན་དག་ཚང་མས་ཤ་ཟས་སོང་།
With the exception of one monk, all the others ate meat.

When ཕུད་ is used with nominalized verbs it conveys the meaning of "not only" and "in addition to." It normally requires ཡང་ ("also/even") in the second clause.

f. ལྷ་སར་ཕྱིན་པ་ཕུད་ས་ཆ་གཞན་དག་ལ་ཡང་ཕྱིན།

Not only did (they, he, etc.) go to Lhasa, (they, he, etc.) also went to other places.

g. ལྷ་སར་འགྲོ་རྒྱུ་ཕུད་རྒྱལ་རྩེར་ཡང་འགྲོ་གི་རེད།

Not only will (they, he, etc.) go to Lhasa, (they, he, etc.) will also go to Gyantse.

h. མོས་ཚལ་ཉོས་པ་ཕུད་ཤིང་ཏོག་ཀྱང་མང་པོ་ཉོས་སོང་།

Not only did (she) buy vegetables, (she) even bought lots of fruit.

9.5 The "danger of" clause connective: ཉེན་

This particle comes from the word ཉེན་ཁ་—"danger." It is used primarily as a verbal auxiliary to convey that there is a danger that the verbal action is going to occur. For example:

a. ཡུལ་གཉིས་བར་དམག་ཡོང་ཉེན་ཡོད་པ་རེད།

There is a danger that war will break out (come) between those two countries.

b. ཁ་ལག་འདི་ཟས་ཚེ་ན་ཉེན་འདུག།

If (you, he, she, etc.) eat this food, there is a danger (you, he, etc.) will get sick.

c. དེང་སྐབས་མི་དམངས་རྣམས་སྐྱིད་པོ་ཡོད་ཙང་། ངོ་ལོག་རྒྱག་ཉེན་ཡོད་པ་མ་རེད།

Because people are happy these days, there is no danger of (them) revolting.

d. དམག་མི་དེ་ཚོས་གྲོང་གསེབ་ནང་བཙན་འཛུལ་བྱེད་ཉེན་བྱུང་སྐབས་མི་དམངས་རྣམས་ཚོགས་འདུ་འཚོགས་པ་རེད།

Because there was danger of soldiers invading the village, the people held a meeting.

9.6 The auxiliary verb མྱོང་: "to experience"

This verb is used with non-past verb stems to convey the idea of "having experience" with respect to the verb.

a. ཁོ་ཚོར་བོད་ཇ་འཐུང་མྱོང་ཡོད་པ་རེད།

They have experienced (the drinking of) Tibetan tea.
(They have drunk Tibetan tea.)

b. ང་བལ་ཡུལ་ལ་འགྲོ་མྱོང་ཡོད་ཀྱང་། དེར་ཡུན་རིང་སྡོད་མྱོང་མེད།

Even though I have gone to Nepal (experienced going to Nepal), I have not stayed there for a long time (have not had the experience of staying there for a long time).

c. གསར་འགྱུར་འདི་འདྲ་གོ་མ་མྱོང་།

(I) have not heard (any) news like this.

d. རི་བོང་ཆེན་པོ་འདི་འདྲ་སུས་ཀྱང་མཐོང་མྱོང་ཡོད་པ་མ་རེད།
    No one has ever seen a rabbit as big as this. (lit., even by whomever rabbit big like this seeing not experienced)

e. རྒྱ་མི་དེ་བོད་ལ་འགྲོ་མྱོང་ཡོད་ཀྱང་བོད་སྐད་ཤེས་ཀྱི་མི་འདུག།
    Even though the Chinese person has gone to Tibet (has had the experience of going to Tibet), he does not know Tibetan.

f. བསོད་ནམས་ཀྱིས་གྲྭ་པ་བྱེད་མྱོང་བ་རེད།
    Sonam has experienced being monk.

g. ཁོང་རྒྱ་གར་ལ་ཕེབས་མྱོང་ཡོད་སྐབས་གྲྭ་པ་མང་པོ་གཟིགས་པ་རེད།
    Because he (h.) has gone to India (had the experience of going to India), he saw (h.) many monks.

9.7 "Seem" constructions using བཟོ་

བཟོ་ is used with the non-past stem of verbs to convey the idea that "it seems" that the verbal action will occur.

a. ཆར་པ་གཏོང་བཟོ་འདུག།
    It seems as if it will rain.

In this usage, བཟོ་ actually forms a verbal noun: "What exists?—the likelihood that it will rain." The next example shows this nominalized verb ("increase"+ བཟོ་) modified by the adjective "big."

b. ཟ་ཆས་ཀྱི་གོང་ཚད་ནི་འཕར་བཟོ་ཆེན་པོ་འདུག།
    It seems very likely that the price of foodstuffs will increase. (There is a great likelihood that the price of foodstuffs will increase.)

c. ཁོ་ཚོ་མགྱོགས་པོ་ཡོང་བཟོ་འདུག།
    It seems as if they will come soon.

d. ཁོ་རྒྱ་གར་ལ་འགྲོ་བཟོ་འདུག།
    It seems he will go to India.

e. ལུང་པ་དེ་མགྱོགས་པོ་ཡར་རྒྱས་འགྲོ་བཟོ་མི་འདུག།
    It doesn't seem that country will develop quickly.

བཟོ་ sometimes joins with existential and linking verbs.

f. མོ་བོད་པ་མིན་བཟོ་འདུག།
    It doesn't seem as if she is a Tibetan.

g. ཁོ་པར་དངུལ་ཡོད་བཟོ་མི་འདུག།

It doesn't seem as if he has money.

བཟོ་ also occurs in more complex constructions:

h. གྲྭ་པས་ངོ་ལོག་རྒྱག་བཟོ་མཐོང་ཙང་། གཞུང་གིས་མི་མང་པོ་འཛིན་བཟུང་བྱས་པ་རེད།

Because (the government) saw that it seemed as if the monks would revolt, the government arrested many people.

Another way to express "seem/does not seem" is to add པ་/བ་ (མི་) འདུག་ to the present tense stem of verbs:

i. ཁོ་རྒྱ་གར་ལ་འགྲོ་པ་མི་འདུག།

It does not seem he will go to India.

བཟོ་ is also used in a construction consisting of the dative-locative + the verb "to look" + the conditional "if" (ལ་བལྟས་ན་) to convey the idea that "if one looks at how something seems," one can make an assessment about something else. It will often be translated as "based on. . . ."

j. ད་རང་གི་གནམ་གཤིས་དེའི་བཟོ་ལ་བལྟས་ན་དོ་དགོང་ཆར་པ་གཏོང་བ་འདུག།

Based on how this morning's weather seems, it will rain tonight.

k. མི་དེའི་བཟོ་ལ་བལྟས་ན་རྒྱ་གར་བ་རེད།

Based on how this person seems, (he) is an Indian.

9.8 The "completed/finished" auxiliary verbs: ཟིན་, ཚར་, and གྲུབ་

These verbs follow the past stems of active verbs and convey that the verbal action is completed or finished. The last of these, གྲུབ་, has an honorific connotation so generally is not used for oneself.

a. བོད་ནས་ཡོང་མཁན་རྣམས་ཀྱིས་ལས་ཀ་དེ་ཁ་ས་བྱས་ཟིན་པ་རེད།

The ones who came from Tibet completed that work yesterday.

b. དེབ་གསར་པ་བཀླགས་ཟིན་ནས་ངས་བརྙན་འཕྲིན་བལྟས་པ་ཡིན།

After finishing reading the new book, I watched television.

c. ཁོང་ཚོས་རྒྱ་མིའི་ཁ་ལག་ཟས་ཚར་སོང་ངས།

Have they finished eating the Chinese food?

d ཁོང་ཚོའི་ལས་ཀ་ཚང་མ་གནང་གྲུབ་ཙང་བོད་ལ་ཕེབས་ཐུབ་གྱི་རེད།

Because (they) have finished all their work, they are able to go to Tibet.

e. ཁོ་ལྷ་ས་ནས་ཐོན་ཟིན་སོང་ཞེས་ང་ཚོར་ལན་འབྱོར་བྱུང་།

We received the message, "He departed (finished departing) from Lhasa."

f. སློབ་གྲྭ་བ་ཚོས་ཇ་འཐུང་ཟིན་འཕྲལ་འཛིན་གྲྭར་ཕྱིན།

As soon as students finished drinking tea, (they) went to class.

g. ལས་ཀ་ཚང་མ་བྱས་མ་ཟིན་གོང་ལ་ནང་ལ་འགྲོ་ཐུབ་གི་མ་རེད།

(You) cannot go home before (you) finish all (your) work.

9.9 Emphatic negative adverbs: ནམ་ཡང་, གཏན་ནས་, གང་ཡང་, རྒྱུན་ནས་, ཙ་བ་ནས་, and ཁྱོན་ནས་

There are six common emphatic negatives: གཏན་ནས་, ནམ་ཡང་, གང་ཡང་, རྒྱུན་ནས་, ཙ་བ་ནས་, and ཁྱོན་ནས་.

When used with negative active and involuntary verbs, the term ནམ་ཡང་ means "never."

a. ཁོས་འཛིན་གྲྭར་ནམ་ཡང་ཕྱིན་པ་རེད།

He never went to class.

On the other hand, the term གང་ཡང་ expresses the idea of "not at all" or "not in any amount" when used with negative active and involuntary verbs.

b. ངས་མོ་ལ་དངུལ་གང་ཡང་གཏོང་གི་མ་རེད།

I will not give her any money at all.

The remaining particles can convey either meaning depending on context.

c ཁོ་ཚོ་བོད་ལ་ཁྱོན་ནས་ལོག་ཐུབ་ཀྱི་མ་རེད།

They will never be able to return to Tibet.

d. གྲྭ་པ་རྒན་པོ་དེས་རྫུན་ནམ་ཡང་ཤོད་པ་མ་རེད།

That old monk never tells lies.

e. ངས་མོ་ལ་དངུལ་ཁྱོན་ནས་གཏོང་གི་མིན།

I will never give money to her.

However, when these verbs are used with negative existential or linking verbs they convey the meaning of "not at all."

f. ལུང་པ་དེར་འབྲོག་པ་ཙ་བ་ནས་ཡོད་པ་མ་རེད།

There are no nomads at all in that place.

9.10 "Want" constructions using འདོད་, མོས་, སྤོ་, and སེམས་

འདོད་ ("want," "desire") generally follows the verb it modifies, with that verb being placed in the non-past stem. It is followed by an existential verb.

a. ཚོང་པ་ཚོར་ཚྭ་ཚོང་རྒྱག་འདོད་ཡོད་པ་རེད།

The traders want to trade (barter/sell) salt.

Note that the subject (ཚོང་པ་ཚོ་) may or may not be placed in the dative-locative.

b ཞིང་པ་ཚོ་ཀུང་ཧྲེ་ལ་ཞུགས་འདོད་ཡོད་པ་མ་རེད།

The farmers do not want to participate in the commune.

འདོད་ often occurs with the ཐུབ་ complement.

c. ཁོང་གཉིས་པེ་ཅིང་ལ་འགྲོ་འདོད་ཐུབ་མ་སོང་།

Those two did not want to go to Beijing.

འདོད་ is also used with the verb བྱེད་:

d. མོས་ཆང་ས་རྒྱག་འདོད་བྱེད་ཀྱི་མེད་ཙང་། ནང་ནས་བྲོས་ཕྱིན་པ་རེད།
Because she does not want to get married, (she) ran away from home.

This could also have been written:

e. མོས་ཆང་ས་རྒྱག་འདོད་མེད་ཙང་། ནང་ནས་བྲོས་ཕྱིན་པ་རེད།
Because she does not want to get married, (she) ran away from home.

f. གཞུང་གིས་སྐྱབས་བཅོལ་བར་རོགས་རམ་བྱེད་འདོད་མ་བྱས་པ་རེད།
The government did not want to help the refugees.

མོས་ ("to like"), བློ་ ("mind") and སེམས་ ("mind") are used interchangeably with འདོད་.

g. ཁོ་རྒྱ་གར་ལ་འགྲོ་མོས་ཡོད་པ་རེད།
He wants to go to India.

h. དགེ་རྒན་རྣམས་པེ་ཅིང་ལ་ཕེབས་སེམས་ཡོད་པ་རེད།
The teachers want to go to Beijing.

9.11 "Hope" constructions using རེ་, འདུན་, and བ་/པའི་རེ་བ་

འདུན་, རེ་, and བ་/པའི་རེ་བ་ are used in constructions that parallel those of འདོད་, མོས་, and སེམས་.

a. ཁོ་པེ་ཅིང་ལ་འགྲོ་རེ་ཡོད་པ་རེད།
He hopes to go to Beijing.

b. མོ་པེ་ཅིང་ལ་འགྲོ་བའི་རེ་བ་ཡོད།
She hopes to go to Beijing.

c. ངོ་ལོག་པས་གཞུང་གི་དམག་མི་དེ་ཚོ་རྩ་མེད་གཏོང་རེ་བྱས་པ་རེད།
The rebels hoped to annihilate those government soldiers.

d. ཁོས་ལས་ཀ་ཧུར་བརྩོན་བྱས་པར་བརྟེན། ཁོ་ལ་བྱ་དགའ་ཐོབ་འདུན་ཡོད་པ་རེད།
Because he worked diligently, he has hopes of winning a prize.

e. དང་མི་དེ་ལ་མའོ་ཀྲུའུ་ཞི་མཇལ་འདུན་ཆེན་པོ་བྱུང་བ་རེད།
That party member had great hopes of meeting Chairman Mao.

f. བཀྲིས་ཀྱིས་རྒྱ་གར་ལ་འགྲོ་འདུན་བྱེད་ཀྱི་འདུག
Tashi is hoping to go to India.

g. ཨ་མས་བུ་དེ་ཕྱི་རྒྱལ་ནས་མགྱོགས་པོ་ཡོང་རེ་བྱས་པ་རེད།
The mother hoped that her son will come quickly from abroad.

9.12 "Manner" constructions: སྟངས་, ལུགས་, and ཚུལ་

These three verbal particles are used immediately after the present (non-past) stem of the verbs they modify, conveying the idea of "the manner of doing" the verbal action. The resultant compounds function as derived nouns. For example, in sentence a. planting rice becomes "the way/manner of planting rice." It is then modified by the adjective "new," conveying the sense, "a new way of planting rice."

a. ཁོས་ཞིང་པ་ཚོར་འབྲས་འདེབས་སྟངས་གསར་པ་གཅིག་སློབ་སྟོན་བྱས་པ་རེད།
He taught the farmers a new way to plant rice.

b. ཁོ་ཚོས་གནམ་གྲུ་བཟོ་སྟངས་ཤེས་ཀྱི་ཡོད་པ་མ་རེད།
They don't know how (the way) to make airplanes.

c. གཡོག་པོས་ངོ་ལོག་བརྒྱབ་ཚུལ་གྱི་ལོ་རྒྱུས་བཤད་སོང་།
(They, he, she, etc.) told the history of how the servants rebelled.

d. ཁོས་མོའི་ལུང་པ་ཆེན་པོ་ཡོད་ལུགས་ཤོད་ཀྱི་འདུག
He is telling about the size of her country (the manner of its being big).

When one of these particles is used with an adjective stem (as in e.), the linking or existential verb is not required.

e. གུང་ཁྲན་རིང་ལུགས་ཡག་ཚུལ་དང་། མ་རྩའི་རིང་ལུགས་རྩ་མེད་བཟོ་དགོས་ལུགས་སོགས་ཁྱབ་བསྒྲགས་མང་པོ་བྱས་པ་རེད།
(They) made many announcements about (proclaiming) such things as how good communism is and how capitalism has to be annihilated.

These particles are often used in conjunction with ལ་ལྟས་ན་ ("if you look at").

f. ཁང་པ་འདི་ཚོའི་རྒྱབ་སྟངས་ལ་ལྟས་ན། ལྷ་ས་འདྲ་པོ་འདུག
If you look at how these houses are built, (they are) similar to (others in) Lhasa.

g. མི་དེའི་སི་སྨན་ཟ་སྟངས་ལ་ལྟས་ན། ཁོ་ཨ་མི་རི་ཀའི་མི་མ་རེད།
If you look at the manner in which that man eats hot chili, he is not American.

9.13 Perfect tense

The perfect tense is made by joining a verb directly to one of the existential verbs such as འདུག་ or ཡོད་པ་རེད་, i.e., vb. past stem + existential verb.

a. ཁོས་དེབ་དང་སྨྱུ་གུ་ཉོས་ཡོད་པ་རེད།
He has bought a book and a pen.

b. ཁོས་དེབ་དང་སྨྱུ་གུ་ཉོས་ཡོད་པ་རེད་པས།
Has he bought a book and a pen?

This, of course, could also have been:

c. ཁོས་དེབ་དང་སྨྱུ་གུ་ཉོས་ཡོད་པ་རེད་དམ།
Has he bought a book and a pen?

འདུག་ is also commonly used.

d. འབྲོག་པ་ཚོ་ལྷ་སར་སླེབས་མི་འདུག།
The nomads have not arrived in Lhasa.

e. འབྲོག་པ་ཚོ་ལྷ་སར་སླེབས་འདུག།
The nomads have arrived in Lhasa.

f. འབྲོག་པ་ཚོ་ལྷ་སར་སླེབས་འདུག་གམ།
Have the nomads arrived in Lhasa?

In spoken Tibetan the perfect tense particle ཤག་ is normally used in third person positive constructions. It is also sometimes utilized in written materials.

g. འབྲོག་པ་ཚོ་ལྷ་སར་སླེབས་ཤག།
The nomads have arrived in Lhasa.

Perfect tense is used in subordinate clauses as follows:

h. སྟག་དེས་ལུག་མང་པོ་བསད་ཡོད་ཙང་འབྲོག་པ་ཞིག་གིས་སྟག་དེར་མེ་མདའ་བརྒྱབ་པ་རེད།
Because that tiger has killed many sheep, a nomad shot the tiger.

i. གཞུང་གིས་མི་དམངས་ལ་རོགས་རམ་བྱས་ཡོད་ཙང་ཁོ་པ་ཚོས་གཞུང་ལ་རྒྱབ་སྐྱོར་བྱས་པ་རེད།
Because the government has helped the people, they supported the government.

First and second person "perfect" constructions use ཡོད and མེད་:

j. ངས་དེབ་དང་སྨྱུ་གུ་ཉོས་ཡོད།
I have bought a book and a pen.

k. ངས་དེབ་དང་སྨྱུ་གུ་ཉོས་མེད་།
I haven't bought a book and a pen.

l. ཁྱེད་རང་གིས་དེབ་དང་སྨྱུ་གུ་ཉོས་ཡོད་པས།
Have you bought a book and a pen?

9.14 "Would have" constructions

When པ་/བ་ཡོད་ is used with the past stem of verbs in conjunction with a subordinate verb in a perfect tense conditional ("if") construction (e.g., སྤྲད་ཡོད་ན་ - "if had given"), the idea of "would have" is conveyed.

a. ཕྱི་རྒྱལ་ནས་རོགས་རམ་སྤྲད་ཡོད་ན་ཁོ་ཚོར་དམག་ཐོབ་པ་ཡོད།
If help had been given from abroad, they would have won the war.

b. ཕྱི་རྒྱལ་ནས་རོགས་རམ་སྤྲད་ཡོད་ན་ཁོ་ཚོའི་དམག་ཤོར་བ་མེད།
If help had been given from abroad, they would not have lost the war.

c. རྡོ་རྗེ་ཁ་སང་སླེབས་ཡོད་ན་གནས་ཚུལ་ཚང་མ་ཤེས་པ་ཡོད།
If Dorje had arrived yesterday, (he) would have known all about the situation.

d. མོ་ནང་ལ་བསྡད་མེད་པ་ཤེས་ཡོད་ན་ང་ཚོ་མོའི་ནང་ལ་འགྲོ་བ་མེད།

If (we) had known that she was not staying at home, we would not have gone to her home.

e. ཡི་གེ་དེ་ཁ་ས་འབྱོར་ཡོད་ན་ངས་དེ་རིང་ཁ་པར་གཏོང་བ་མེད།

If the letter had been received yesterday, I would not have called today.

f. མི་དམངས་རྣམས་ནས་ཞིང་ལས་ཧུར་བརྩོན་བྱས་ཡོད་ན། གྲོང་གསེབ་དེ་ར་ཡར་རྒྱས་ཆེན་པོ་བྱུང་ཡོད་བཀྱི་རེད།

If people had worked hard, the village would have improved a lot.

When this form is used in constructions that are not conditional, the meaning of "will be" is conveyed. Such constructions are used when there is considerable certainty about the future action.

g. མོས་སང་ཉིན་ཁ་ལག་བཟོ་བ་ཡོད།

She will make food tomorrow.

9.15 The "be fit/worthy" particles: ཉན་, ལོ་, and རུང་

ཉན་ and ལོ་ are placed after verbs to convey being "fit" or "worthy" of the verbal action. For example:

a. ཤ་འདི་ཟ་ཉན་གྱི་རེད་པས།

Is this meat fit for eating?

b. ཐ་མག་འདི་འཐེན་ཉན་གྱི་མ་རེད།

This cigarette is not fit to smoke.

c. ཤ་འདི་རྙིང་པ་ཡིན་སྟབས་ཟ་ལོ་པ་མི་འདུག

Because this meat is old, it is not fit to eat.

d. གོས་ལོག་དེ་རྩ་བ་ཧྲལ་ཡིན་ཙང་གོན་ཉན་པ་མི་འདུག

Because the clothes are torn, they are not fit to wear.

ཉན་ is also used to convey the meaning of "allowed" when used in constructions conveying a general statement, for example, e. below.

e. ཐ་མག་འཐེན་ཉན་གྱི་མ་རེད།

One is not allowed to smoke cigarettes. (Or, Smoking cigarettes is not allowed.)

In this usage, ཉན་ functions identically with རུང་ ("allow").

f. ཐ་མག་འཐེན་རུང་གྱི་མ་རེད།

One is not allowed to smoke cigarettes.

Other examples of རུང་ are:

g. དགོན་པའི་ནང་དུ་ཆང་འཐུང་རུང་གི་མ་རེད།

One is not allowed to drink beer in the monastery.

h. དགོན་པ་འདིའི་ནང་ལ་གྲྭ་པས་ཤ་ཟ་རུང་གི་རེད།

In this monastery the monks are allowed to eat meat.

9.16 The "possible" auxiliary verb: སྲིད་

སྲིད་ is placed after verbs to convey its being "possible" to do the verbal action. It is more often used with a negative particle to convey that the verbal action is impossible.

a. ལས་ཀ་འདི་བྱེད་མི་སྲིད།
   It is not possible to do this work.

b. འདི་འདྲ་བྱས་ན་ཁེ་བཟང་ཆེན་པོ་ཡོང་སྲིད་ཀྱི་མ་རེད།
   If you do like this, it will not be possible to obtain a big profit.

c. ཁེ་བཟང་ཆེན་པོ་ཡོང་མི་སྲིད་ན་ཅ་ལག་རྙིང་མ་དེ་ཚོ་ཉོ་གི་མེད།
   If it is not possible to get a large profit, (I) will not buy those old things.

9.17 Reading exercises

Lengthy grammatical narrative analyses will no longer be utilized in Part Two . Instead, grammatical explanations will be provided via brief notes.

9.17.1 Reading number one: "The Wolf and the Hunter"

9.17.1.1 Tibetan text

སྤྱང་ཀི་དང་རྔོན་པ།

གཉན་རབས་ཆོའི་སོད་སྡོལ་ལ་1 གནའ་སྔ་མོ་ཞིག་ལ་སྤྱང་ཀི་ཞིག་ནགས་ཚལ་གྱི་ཁྲོད་དུ་ཟས་འཚོལ་བཞིན་ཡོད་པ་རེད2། བསམ་ཡུལ་ལས་འདས་པ་ཞིག་ལ་3 སྤྱང་ཀི་དེ་ཟས་འཚོལ་བའི་ལམ་བར་4 གློ་བུར་དུ་རྔོན་པས་བཀོས་པའི་དོང་རྔའི་ནང་དུ་ལྷུང་། སྤྱང་ཀིས་དོང་རྔའི་ནང་ནས་སྐད་ཤུགས་ཆེན་པོས་དགེ་བ་ཡོང་སྲོག་སྐྱོབ་རོགས་གནང་5 ཞེས་སྐད་ངན་རྒྱག་གི་ཡོད་པ་རེད། སྐབས་དེར་ར་ཞིག་གིས་ཐོས་ནས་དོང་རྔའི་ནང་ལྟ་སྐབས་དེའི་ནང་སྤྱང་ཀི་ཞིག་གིས་ངའི་ནང་ལ་ཕྲུ་གུ་གཅིག་ཕུར་ལུས་སོང་བས་ད་ནི་ལྟ་སྐྱོང་བྱེད་མཁན་མེད་སྐབས་6 ཚང་མ་ལྟོགས་ཤི་ཐེབས་ཀྱི་རེད་ཅེས་ཟེར་ནས་ངུ་བཞིན་ཡོད་པ་མཐོང་7། ར་དེས་དོགས་ཟོན་ཆེན་པོའི་ངང་8 སྤྱང་ཀིར་གལ་ཏེ་9 ད་ལྟ་ངས་ཁྱོད་བསྐྱབས་ན་ཁྱོད་ཀྱིས་ང་བཟའ་རྒྱུ་ཡིན་པས་སྐྱོབས་མི་ཉན་ཞེས་བཤད། སྤྱང་ཀིས་ལག་གཉིས་ཀྱི་ཐལ་མོ་སྦྱར་ནས་ཁྱེད་ཀྱིས་ང་བསྐྱབས་ན་བཀའ་དྲིན་མཚོ་ལས་ཟབ་པས་10 ངས་དཀོན་མཆོག་གསུམ་ལ་མནའ་སྐྱེལ་དམ་བཅའ་བཞག་ནས་11 དུས་ནམ་ཡང་ཁྱེད་ལ་གནོད་འཚེ་གང་ཡང་12 གཏོང་གི་མིན་ཞེས་ཞུ་བ་འཐེན་པ་རེད། སྤྱང་ཀིས་ཞུ་བ་ཡང་ཡང་འཐེན་སྐབས་ར་དེས་སེམས་ཀྱིས་མ་བཟོད་པར་མཐར་ཀོ་ཐག་ཅིག་བཙལ་ནས་ས་དོང་ནང་བཏང་སྟེ་སྤྱང་ཀི་ཐག་པར་ཟུངས་ཏེ་དོང་རྔའི་ཕྱི་རུ་བཏེགས་པ་རེད། སྤྱང་ཀིས་རང་ཉིད་དོང་རྔ་ལས་ཐར་མ་ཐག་13 ལམ་སེང་ར་བཟའ་སྐབས་མི་བདེ་བས14། ཁོས་ངག་འཇམ་ཚིག་མཁས་15 ཀྱི་སྒོ་ནས་ཁྱེད་ཀྱིས་ངའི་སྲོག་བསྐྱབས་པ་གནང་བའི་བཀའ་དྲིན་དེ་ངས་ནམ་ཡང་བརྗེད་མི་སྲིད16། འོན་ཀྱང་ད་ལྟ་ང་ལྟོགས་ཤི་ཐེབས་གྲབས་17 བྱེད་ཀྱི་འདུག་པས་ཁྱེད་ཀྱིས་སླར་ཡང་ངའི་སྲོག་སྐྱོབ་ཐབས་ཤིག

18 གནང་དང་ 19 ཞེས་བཤད་པ་རེད། ཞི་དུལ་སེམས་བཟང་གི་ར་དེས་སྤྱང་ཀིར་ཁྱོད་ཀྱིས་ང་ལ་གནོད་འཚེ་གང་ཡང་གཏོང་རྒྱུ་མེད་པའི་མནའ་བསྐྱལ་དམ་བཅའ་བཞག་སོང་ཞེས་བཤད་པས་སྤྱང་ཀིས་ང་ནི་ཤ་གཟན་སྲོག་ཆགས་ 20 ཡིན་པས་ཁྱོད་གློད་ན་ག་ནས་འགྲིགས་ 21 ཞེས་བཤད། ར་དེའི་སེམས་ལ་ད་ནི་སྤྱང་ཀིའི་ཁ་ནས་ཐར་ཐབས་བྲལ་སོང་སྙམ་ནས་སེམས་ནང་འགྱོད་པ་དྲག་པོ་སྐྱེད་དེ་སྡོད་པའི་ཚེ་གློ་བུར་དུ་རི་བོང་ཞིག་མཆོངས་རྒྱུ་དང་བཅས་ཏེ་ 22 མདུན་དུ་སླེབས་བྱུང་བས་རས་ལམ་སེང་རི་བོང་ལ་ཁྱེད་ཀྱིས་ད་ལྟ་འདིར་བྱུང་བའི་གནས་ཚུལ་ལ་ང་གཉིས་སུ་བདེན་གྱི་དཔང་པོ་ཞིག་གནང་རོགས་ཞེས་ 23 ཞུ་བ་འཐེན་པ་རེད། རི་བོང་གིས་ཐུག་ནོ་ཞིག་གི་སྐད་ལ་ལྟངས་ནས་རྣ་ཅོག་ཀྲོང་ཀྲོང་བྱས་ནས་ར་དང་སྤྱང་ཀིས་བཤད་པའི་གནས་ཚུལ་རྣམས་ཉན་རྗེས་ཁོས་ཁྱེད་གཉིས་ཀར་རྒྱུ་མཚན་འདུག་པས་ངས་ཁྱོད་གཉིས་སུའི་སྐད་ཆ་བདེན་པ་ཡིན་མིན་ 24 མ་ཤེས་པས་སྔོན་ལ་ཁྱོད་གཉིས་ཀྱིས་ཐོག་མའི་གནས་ཚུལ་བྱུང་ལུགས་རྣམས་ 25 ངས་མཐོང་སར་སྟོར་ཡང་ཐེངས་གཅིག་གྱིས་དང་ 26 ངས་གནས་ཚུལ་རྣམས་དངོས་སུ་མཐོང་རྗེས་གཞི་ནས་ 27 སུ་བདེན་ཤན་འབྱེད་བྱེད་ཐུབ་ཅེས་བཤད་པ་རེད། སྤྱང་ཀིས་སྔར་གྱི་དོང་རྐའི་ནང་མཆོངས་རྗེས་རང་ཉིད་དོང་གི་ཕྱི་ལ་ཐོན་ཐབས་མེད་པ་ཤེས་ 28 ཏེ་སྔར་ཡང་ར་འབོད་ 29 ནས་ང་སྐྱོབ་རོགས་ 30 ཞེས་ཞུ་བ་ཡང་ཡང་འཐེན་པ་རེད། སྐབས་དེར་རི་བོང་གིས་དོང་རྐའི་ཁ་ནས་མར་བལྟས་ཏེ་དྲིན་ལན་ལོག་འཇལ་བྱེད་མཁན་ 31 ཁྱོད་ཇོན་པས་སྐྱོབ་པར་ཡོང་བར་བསྒུགས་ 32 ནས་སྡོད་ཅིག་ 33 ཅེས་སྨྲས། དེ་ནས་རི་བོང་དང་ར་གཉིས་དགའ་སྤྲོའི་ངང་མཉམ་དུ་ནགས་ཚལ་གྱི་ཕྱོགས་སུ་བསྐྱོད་དོ་34 །།།

9.17.1.2 Translation

The Wolf and the Hunter

According to sayings (passed down) from previous generations, in ancient times there was a wolf who searched for food in a forest. Incredibly, that wolf suddenly fell into a pit-trap set by a hunter while on the road in search of food. The wolf shouted loudly in anguish, "Obtain merit. Please save me." At that time a goat heard (the shouts) and looked into the pit. When he did this, he saw a wolf crying. (The wolf said,) "(My) children are left at home alone and there is no one to look after them, so now they will all starve to death." That goat was very suspicious and said to the wolf, "If I help you now, you will eat me. You are not fit for saving." The wolf clasped his two hands together (in prayer-like fashion) and pleaded, "Because your kindness is as deep as the ocean, if you save me, I swear to konchosum that I will never harm you at all."

Because the wolf pleaded over and over again, the goat could not tolerate it and finally searched for a leather rope and threw it into the pit. The wolf grabbed the rope and (the goat) lifted him to the outside of the the pit. As soon as the wolf escaped from the pit, feeling uneasy about immediately eating the goat, he smoothly and cleverly said, "The gratitude (I have) for saving my life is impossible to forget. Nevertheless, because I am about to starve to death, now once again please take action to save me." That peaceful and kind goat said, "Didn't you, wolf, swear an oath that you would never harm me?" The wolf said, "Because I am a carnivore, how is it okay to let you go?" That goat thought, "I have no way to escape from the mouth of that wolf," and felt very regretful. While he was sitting there (like that), suddenly a rabbit, running and jumping, arrived before him. The goat at once pleaded to the rabbit (saying), "You now please act as a judge to say who is right regarding the events that have occurred here." The rabbit got up on top of a boulder (and with) his ears standing erect listened to the stories told by the goat and the wolf. After that he said, "Because both of you have reasons, I do not know which of your comments to believe. You two reenact how things first came to be, so that I can see it myself. Then and only then will I be able to say who is correct." The wolf then jumped into the former pit and after that knew that he couldn't get out (without help) and once again called, "Goat" and pleaded over and over, "Please save me." After that, the rabbit went to the edge of the pit and looked in. He said, "You, who are one who does not repay kindness, can wait until the hunter comes to save you!" Then the goat and rabbit happily went together in the direction of the forest.

9.17.1.3 Grammatical notes

1. བཤད་སྲོལ་ལ་ is a common phrase (pattern = vb. non-past.+ སྲོལ་ ("custom") + dat.-loc.) conveying "as is commonly said" or "according to what people traditionally say." Here it is modified by གནའ་རབས་ཚོའི་ to convey "as was traditionally said in past generations."

སྲོལ་ can also be used with non-past stems of verbs in the pattern: vb.+ སྲོལ་+ existential verb. Used this way it conveys the meaning "there is" or "there is not" a custom of. . . . For example, འབྲོག་པས་ཉ་ཤ་ཟ་སྲོལ་མི་འདུག། means "There is no custom of nomads eating fish." And རྒྱ་མིས་ཉ་ཤ་ཟ་སྲོལ་འདུག།་ means "There is a custom of Chinese eating fish."

2. In more sophisticated writings this would have been expressed as འཚོལ་བཞིན་པར་.

3. This is a common phrase used to mean "something that passes beyond the mind," i.e., that is unimaginable.

4. བར་ or བར་དུ་ means "in between" and is commonly used to mean "between" beginning and finishing the journey. In this sense it conveys the meaning "while on the road." A similar example is: གནམ་གྲུ་གནམ་བར་དུ་སྐྱོན་ཤོར་སོང་—"The plane got damaged on the way" (lit., in the sky between starting and finishing). བར་དུ་, however, also can mean "up to." For example, བོད་བར་དུ་མོ་མཉམ་དུ་འགྲོ་གི་ཡིན་—(I) will go together with her *up to* Tibet."

5. This construction disaggregates into two sentences: "Obtain merit" (དགེ་བ་ཡོང་) and "Please save me" (སྲོག་སྐྱོབ་རོགས་གནང་). For examples of རོགས་གནང་ constructions see 7.13.
6. The verb "left behind" (ལུས་) is modified by the adverb "alone" (གཅིག་པུར་), conveying that her children were left behind alone.

Following this there is a construction consisting of the active verb phrase "to look after" (ལྟ་སྐྱོང་བྱེད་), which has been transformed by the agentive particle (མཁན་) to convey "the one or person who looks after." Now functioning as a noun, this existential sentence means, "because there was no. . . ."
7. This is a long nominalized construction starting with "by a goat" (ར་ཞིག་གིས་). Thus a goat saw the wolf crying (while) saying. . . ."
8. The adverbializing particle ངང་ here converts the noun + adjective compound "great doubt" into an adverbial unit meaning "in the manner of having great doubt." It then modifies "say" (བཤད་) so that it explains how or in what manner he said it.
9. Recall that གལ་ཏེ་. . .ན་ is one of the "if" clause connectives.
10. མཚོ་ལས་ཟབ་ is a common phrase meaning "deeper than the ocean," with ཟབ་ coming from the adjective ཟབ་པོ་ ("deep," "profound"). The addition of the instrumental particle (མཚོ་ལས་ཟབ་པས་) adjusts the phrase so as to say, "*because* your kindness is deeper than the ocean. . . ."
11. མནའ་སྐྱེལ་དམ་མཅའ་བཞག་ is an example of a redundant construction in that both མནའ་སྐྱེལ་ and དམ་མཅའ་བཞག་ convey "taking an oath" or "swearing." Redundant constructions such as these are very common. This oath is taken "on" (ལ་) the དཀོན་མཆོག་གསུམ་ ("three precious things [the Buddha, the clergy and the doctrine]").
12. The "amount" or "quantity" emphatic negative གང་ཡང་ is discussed in 9.9. The construction means "never" will do it "in any amount."
13. མ་ཐག་ is one of the "as soon as" clause connectives (see 6.2).
14. The phrase སྟབས་བདེ་པོ་ means "convenient" or "easy to do" and is often used after active verb constructions to convey that it is "convenient" to do the verbal action. For example, དེང་སང་ཁ་པར་གཏོང་སྟབས་བདེ་པོ་འདུག་ means: "Nowadays it is convenient to telephone."

This construction is also often used as སྟབས་བདེ་བས་, where it means "because it is convenient." In this example this phrase is negativized to convey "inconvenient" or "hard to do" in the mental rather than physical sense. In other words, here it means "uncomfortable" rather than physically difficult—thus, "because it was hard (he was uncomfortable) to eat the goat at once."

15. ངག་འཇམ་ཚིག་མཁས་ consists of two noun + adjective constructions in which only the adjective stems (འཇམ་) and (མཁས་) are used. The conjunction "and" has been omitted. This type of construction is very common.
16. Here we see both an emphatic negative (ནམ་ཡང) and the "possible" auxiliary verb (སྲིད་), together emphatically conveying the idea, "it is not possible ever that I will forget."
17. སྐབས་ is explained in 7.11.
18. ཐབས་ཤིག་ is explained in 9.1.
19. གནང་དང་ is explained in 7.12.
20. ཤ་གཟན་སྲོག་ཆགས་ is a compound consisting of two nouns: "carnivore" (ཤ་གཟན་) and "sentient creature" (སྲོག་ཆགས་).
21. ག་ནས་འགྲིགས་ is a phrase asking, "How could that be okay?" It will be discussed in a later lesson.
22. དང་བཅས་ཏེ་ here conveys "along with" or "together with" (see 6.4 e.-h.).
23. The construction ང་གཉིས་སུ་བདེན་གྱི་དཔང་པོ་ཞིག་གནང་རོགས་ breaks down into the phrase ང་གཉིས་སུ་བདེན་ ("(between) we two, who (is) true/correct"), which is linked to དཔང་པོ་ཞིག་ ("a judge") by the genitive. The resultant phrase means "a judge who (will decide) which of us (we two) is correct."

གནང་རོགས་ is a polite imperative meaning "please do/act (as a judge)." Its use is explained in 7.12.

Semantic context indicates that སུ་ here is not the dat.-loc. particle but the interrogative "who." In other sentences it can convey the dat.-loc., e.g., ང་གཉིས་སུ་ཁོས་དངུལ་སྤྲད་བྱུང་། ("He gave money to we two").
24. ཡིན་མིན ("is is-not") conveys whether something "is" or "is not." For example, in the sentence འདི་ཆེན་པོ་ཡིན་མིན་ལྟ་, ཡིན་མིན is followed by the verb ལྟ ("to look") and means "look whether (this) is or is not (big)" (see 8.6).

In this story it is used with བདེན་པ་, meaning "is or is not true." The entire segment means "I do not know (མ་ཤེས་པ) (regarding) you two (ཁྱོད་གཉིས་) whose talk (སུའི་སྐད་ཆ་) is true (or not true) (བདེན་པ་ཡིན་མིན་)."
25. This construction uses ལུགས་ to transform the verbal phrase ཐོག་མའི་གནས་ཚུལ་བྱུང་ ("the first events came about") into "the manner in which the first events came about." The plural particle emphasizes that there are multiple events or actions.
26. This is a difficult clause. The main verb is གྱིས་, the imperative stem of the verb "do": བགྱིད་. Note that this is not the instrumental particle. This verb is followed by the polite imperative particle དང་ so that the two mean "please do!"

སླར་ཡང་ཐེངས་གཅིག་ functions adverbially, conveying that the verbal action was done "once again," or "one more time." མཐོང་སར་ means "to the place where something is seen," or "in my field of vision." The pattern whereby ས་ is used with verbs to convey "the place where the verbal action occurred" is discussed in 10.13.

27. གཞི་ནས་ is one of the connective particles that occur at the start of the second of two clauses. It conveys "then and only then." For example, དཔེ་ཀློག་ནས་གཞི་ནས་ཤེས་པ་རེད། — "Having read the book, then and only then did I know."

28. This use of the verb མེད་ plus the nominalizer པ་ plus ཤེས་ is common. It means "knew that there was no way" (see 6.6.2).

29. The verb འབོད་ means "to call" or "to cry out." Thus, what he called out was the word "goat." This would have been clearer if the direct quote particle had been used, for example, ར་ཅེས་འབོད་.

30. རོགས་ following a verb functions identically with གནང་རོགས་ (see note 23) meaning "please do the verbal action."

31. དྲིན་ལན་ལོག་འཇལ་བྱེད་མཁན་ is a construction that consists of the verb phrase དྲིན་ལན་འཇལ་ ("to show gratitude, to repay someone's kindness") plus ལོག་ ("opposite" or "backwards") which transforms it to དྲིན་ལན་ལོག་འཇལ་ ("not showing one's gratitude").

The addition of the verb བྱེད་ plus the agentive particle མཁན་ makes the whole thing a noun phrase modifying "you" (ཁྱོད་) and meaning, "You who are a person who does not repay kindness."

32. སྐྱབ་པར་ཡོང་བར་བསྒུགས་ is a verbal phrase consisting of two infinitives: "wait for (a hunter) *to* come *to* save (you)."

33. བསྒུགས་ནས་སྡོད་ཅིག་ consists of two verbs linked by the simultaneous gerundive ནས་ to mean "staying in the manner of waiting" (see 5.11.2). ཅིག་ is a particle used with verbs to convey the imperative. Here it means "stay!"

34. དོ་ is a sentence-ending construction made by adding an "o" vowel to the final letter of the sentence.

9.17.2 Reading number two: "The Brief History of Ramoche (Temple)'s Jo (Statue)"

9.17.2.1 Tibetan text

ར་མོ་ཆེའི་ཇོ་བོའི་ལོ་རྒྱུས་མདོར་བསྡུས་བཤད་པ།

ར་མོ་ཆེ་གཙུག་ལག་ཁང་ནི། གྲོང་ཁྱེར་ལྷ་སའི་བྱང་ཕྱོགས་སུ་གནས་ཡོད། རྒྱ་བཟའ་ཀོང་ཇོ་བོད་ལ་མནའ་མར་ཡོང་དུས་རྗེན་

སྐལ་དུ་ཇོ་བོ་ཤཱཀྱ་མུ་ནེ་དགུང་ལོ་བཅུ་གཉིས་ཀྱི་ཚད་གཞི་ལྟར་བྱས་པ་1 དེ་རྒྱ་ནག་ནས་བོད་ཀྱི་ལྷ་སར་གདན་དྲངས་པ་ཞིག་རེད། སྔར་གདན་དྲངས་དུས་ད་ལྟའི་ར་མོ་ཆེའི་ས་ཆ་དེར་ཤིང་རྟ་འཁོར་ལོ་བྱེ་ཐང་དུ་ལུས་ནས་མི་མང་པོས་དྲུད་ཀྱང་དྲུད་མ་ཐུབ་2 སྟབས་ས་ཆ་དེར་རྒྱ་བཟས་རྩིག་རྨང་གཏིང་ནས་ཨར་པོ་རྒྱབ་སྟེ་ད་ལྟའི་ར་མོ་ཆེ་3 གཙུག་ལག་ཁང་ཆགས། ཤོད་སྒྲོལ་ལ་དེའི་འོག་ལ་ཀླུའི་ཕོ་བྲང་ཡོད་ཟེར4། བོད་ཀྱི་རྒྱལ་པོ་སྲོང་བཙན་སྒམ་པོ་ལ་བཙུན་མོ་ལྔ་ཡོད་པ་དང་། བཙུན་མོ་རེ་རེར་གཙུག་ལག་ཁང་་རེ་5 ཡོད་6 རྒྱ་བཟའི་གཙུག་ལག་ཁང་ནི་ར་མོ་ཆེ་གཙུག་ལག་ཁང་ཡིན7། དེའི་ཁ་རྒྱ་ནག་ཏུ་ཤར་ལ་གཏད་ཡོད། སྲོང་བཙན་སྒམ་པོ་འདས་རྗེས་མང་སྲོང་མང་བཙན་གྱིས་སྲིད་འཛིན་པའི་དུས་སུ་རྒྱ་ནག་ནས་དམག་ཡོང་བའི་གཏམ་ཐོས་ཏེ་ཇོ་བོ་ཤཱཀྱ་མུ་ནེ་ར་མོ་ཆེ་ནས། བལ་བཟའི་གཙུག་ལག་ཁང་་ར་ས་འཕྲུལ་སྣང་གཙུག་ལག་ཁང་8 དུ་གདན་དྲངས་ནས་སྦས་པ་མ་ཟད། ད་དུང་སྒོ་ལ་ཞལ་བ་བྱས་ཏེ་དེའི་ཐོག་9 འཇམ་དཔལ་དབྱངས་ཀྱི་སྐུ་ཞིག་བྲིས་པ་རེད། རྒྱ་དམག་གིས་ཇོ་བོ་ནོར་ཏེ་འཕྲུལ་སྣང་གཙུག་ལག་ཁང་ནས་ཇོ་བོ་མི་བསྐྱོད་རྡོ་རྗེ་དེ་ལྷ་སའི་ཤར་ཕྱོགས་འོ་རྒྱལ་ཐང་བར་གདན་དྲངས་པའི་རྗེས་སུ། ས་ཆ་དེར་ཇོ་བོ་ཤཱཀྱ་མུ་ནེ་མིན་པ་ཤེས་ཏེ་བོར་བ་དང་། རྗེས་སུ་ཇོ་བོ་དེ་ར་མོ་ཆེར་གདན་དྲངས་ནས་བཞག་པ་རེད། སྦས་པའི་ཇོ་བོ་ཤཱཀྱ་མུ་ནེ་དེ་ར་ས་འཕྲུལ་སྣང་གཙུག་ལག་ཁང་དུ་བཞག་སྟབས། ལྷ་ཁང་གཉིས་ཀར་ཇོ་བོ་གཉིས་བརྗེ་འཕྲུལ་ཤོར་10 ཡོད།།།

9.17.2.2 Translation

The Brief History of Ramoche (Temple)'s Jo (Statue)

Ramoche temple is located in the north of Lhasa. When Kongjo, the Chinese bride (of King Songtsen Gambo), came as a bride to Tibet, she brought with her to Lhasa as part of her dowry a statue of the Shakyamuni Buddha at the age of 12. In the past, when they were transporting it, the horse cart (that was carrying it) got stuck in the sand at the place where the present day Ramoche is. Even though many people pulled (to free it), (they) were unable to free it, so at that place the Chinese bride laid the foundation stone and constructed what became the temple of Ramoche. According to oral legends, it is said that there was a nāga's palace beneath that spot. Tibet's king Songtsen Gambo had five queens. Each of the five queens had a temple. As for the Chinese bride's temple, it was Ramoche temple. Its door faced east to China. After Songtsen Gambo died, at the time Mangsong Mangtsen ruled, (he) heard news of war coming from China and moved the statue of Jo Shakyamuni from Ramoche to the Nepalese bride's temple, the Tsuglakang [i.e., today's Jokhang], and buried it. Not only that, but (he) also plastered over the door and on top of that drew (an image) of Manjusri. The Chinese soldiers, mistaking the statue of Jo Akshobhya for the Jo (Shakyamuni) statue, took it from the Tsuglakang and carried it to the he Ogyɛtaŋ plain in the east of Lhasa. At that place they realized that it was not the Shakyamuni statue and threw it away. Later, that Jo (Akshobhya) statue was taken to Ramoche and left there. The buried Jo Shakyamuni statue was left in the Tsuglakang temple. Consequently, the two Jo statues in the two temples came to be mistakenly exchanged.

9.17.2.3 Grammatical notes

1. ལྟར་བྱས་པ་ or ལྟར་བྱས་ནས་ has two basic functions. On the one hand it conveys the meaning intended here, namely, "just like." Thus ལྟར་བྱས་པ་ conveys that the statue was "just like" Shakyamuni when he was at the physical size (ཚད་གཞི་) of 12 years old. Another example of this usage is: མོས་རི་མོ་དེ་ལྟར་བྱས་ནས་བྲིས་པ་རེད། ("She drew it just like that picture").

In other contexts it also can mean "acting just like," conveying the idea that the subject is different from that which he or she is compared with. The "acting like" function of ལྟར་བྱས་ is seen in the following examples:

a. ཁོས་ར་ལྟར་བྱས་ནས་བྲག་ལ་འཛེགས།
He climbed the rock just like a goat. (indicates he is not a goat)

b. ཏང་མི་ལྟར་བྱས་ནས་མོས་མའོ་ལ་སྟོད་ར་བཤད།
She praised Mao just like a party member. (indicates she is not a party member)

2. The pattern དྲུད་ཀྱང་དྲུད་མ་ཐུབ་ conveys the idea that "even though they tried to do X, they were unable to do X." In this case, even though they tried to pull it out, they were unable to pull it out (free it). The first verb in such constructions is in the non-past stem (if it has one), and the second in the past tense stem. For example:

a. ཆུ་འདྲེན་ཀྱང་དྲང་མ་ཐུབ་
Even though (they, he, etc.) tried to irrigate, (they, he, etc.) were unable to irrigate (get the water to flow).

3. ར་ཆེ་ is an abbreviation for ར་མོ་ཆེ་, one of Lhasa's two most famous temples.

4. ཟེར་ here acts as a verb conveying "it is said."

5. Tibetan uses རེ་རེ་ ("each each") to convey that each X had a Y. The normal pattern is: X + རེ་རེར་ ("to each X") + Y + རེ་ ("each Y"). Thus, here, "to each queen, there existed a temple each."

6. The absence of any clause connective or even space after ཡོད་ is common.

7. རེད་ could be used here as well.

8. ར་སའི་འཕྲུལ་སྣང་གཙུག་ལག་ཁང་ is the full name of Lhasa's famous Cathedral or Tsuglakang.

9. ཐོག་ has many functions, one of which conveys "on top of." It is discussed in detail in Lesson 12.

10. The involuntary verb ཤོར་ means "to lose" something (either physical or a contest). However, it is also used with other verbs to convey the involuntary happening of something negative. In this case, the phrase བརྗེ་འཁྲུལ་ཤོར་ consists of "exchange" + "mistake" and ཤོར་. Together they mean "(involuntarily and) mistakenly came to be exchanged."

9.18 Vocabulary

ཀུང་ཧྲེ་ ch. commune
ཀོ་ཐག་ leather rope
ཀྲུའུ་ཞི་ ch. chairman
ཀྲོང་ཀྲོང་ standing erect
ཀླུའི་ཕོ་བྲང་ nāga's palace
དཀོན་མཆོག་གསུམ་ the three precious things (the buddha, the clergy, and the dharma)
བཀའ་དྲིན་ kindness
བཀྲིས་ abbr. of བཀྲ་ཤིས་
སྐད་ངན་ anguished cry; va. — རྒྱག་
སྐད་བཏང་ va. p. of སྐད་གཏོང་ called
སྐུ་ statue; body (h.)
སྐྱག་རྫུན་ a lie; va. — བཤད་
སྐྱབས་བཅོལ་བ་ refugee
སྐྱེད་ vi. to grow, increase, widen; see འགྱོད་པ་
བརྐོས་ va. p. of རྐོ་: dug
བསྐྱབས་ va. p. of སྐྱོབ་: saved
ཁ་ 1. mouth; 2. edge; 3. direction
ཁོ་པ་ཚོ་ they
ཁྱབ་བསྒྲགས་ announcement
ཁྱོན་ནས་ emphatic negative
ཁྲོད་ among
ག་ནས་འགྲིག་ how could that be okay?
གང་ཡང་ emphatic negative
གུང་ཁྲན་རིང་ལུགས་ communism
གོ་ vi. to hear
གོང་ཚད་ rate/level of price
གོན་ va. to wear
གྱིས་ va. imp. of བགྱིད་: did
གྲུབ་ 1. "completed/finished" auxiliary verb; 2. vi. to obtain, achieve
གྲོང་གསེབ་པ་ villager
དགུང་ལོ་ age (h.)
དགེ་བ་ཡོང་ vi. to get merit
འགྱོད་པ་ regret; vi. — སྐྱེད་
རྒན་རབས་ elder or previous generation
སྒང་ on, on top
རྒྱ་བཟའ་ཀོང་ཇོ་ p.n. (the Chinese wife named Kongjo)
རྒྱབ་སྐྱོར་ support; va. — བྱེད་
རྒྱུན་ནས་ emphatic negative
ངག་འཇམ་ཚིག་མཁས་ id. speaking gently and cleverly, smoothly
ངུ་ va. to cry
ངུས་ va. p. of ངུ་
ངོ་ཤེས་པ་ an acquaintance

དངོས་སུ་ really, truly, actually

གཅིག་པུར་ alone

ཆང་ beer

ཆང་ས་ marriage; va. — རྒྱག་

མཆོངས་རྒྱུག་ jumping and running

ཇོ་བོ་ Jo (name of the Buddha) (also used to refer to the famous statue in the Lhasa Cathedral)

ཇོ་བོ་མི་བསྐྱོད་རྡོ་རྗེ་ the Buddha (Jo) Akshobhya

ཇོ་བོ་ཤཱཀྱ་མུ་ནེ་ the Buddha (Jo)Shakyamuni (also used to refer to the famous statue in the Lhasa Cathedral)

འཇམ་དཔལ་དབྱངས་ Manjusri

རྗེས་ after

བརྗེ་འཕྱུལ་ mistakenly exchanged; vi. — ཤོར་

བརྗེད་ vi. to forget

ཉ་ཤ་ fish meat

ཉན་ 1."fit/worthy" particle; 2. vi. to listen

ཉེན་ "danger of" clause connective

ཉེན་ཁ་ danger

རྙོག་ཁྲ་ trouble, difficulty; va. — བཤད་ to cause trouble

སྙམ་ va. to think (h.)

སྨྱུ་གུ་ pen

བརྙན་འཕྲིན་ television

ཏང་མི་ party member

གཏད་ va. p. of གཏོད་: faced

གཏན་ནས་ emphatic negative

གཏམ་ news; conversation, talk; proverb

གཏོད་ 1. va. to aim at, face towards, direct towards; 2. vi. to hand over, give

བཏེགས་ va. p. of འདེག་: lifted

རྟེན་སྐལ་ dowry

ལྟ་སྐྱོང་ looking after, caring for; va. — བྱེད་

ལྟ་ཅི་ "let alone/far from" clause connective

ལྟ་བཞག་ "let alone/far from" clause connective

ལྟར་བྱས་ just like, as, like

ལྟོགས་ཤི་ starving to death; vi. — ཐེབས་

སྟངས་ "manner" particle

སྟབས་མ་བདེ་བ་ inconvenient; unfortunate

བལྟས་ va. p. of ལྟ་: looked

བསྟོད་ར་ praise; va.— གཏོང་

ཐག་པ་ rope

ཐབས་ way, means, methods

ཐབས་བྱེད་ (vb. + —) to try to do the verbal action

ཐབས་བྲལ་ (vb. + —) no way/means to do verbal action

ཐལ་མོ་སྦྱར་ va. to clasp one's hands together (as in show of devotion or respect)

ཐུང་ཐུང་ short

ཐོག་མ་ beginning, first, start

ཐོབ་ vi. to win; to get, obtain

མཐར་ finally, at last, in the end

མཐོང་ས་ the place where something is seen, the field of vision

འཐུང་ va. to drink

ད་རང་ this morning

དེའི་ of that

དེར་ there

དོ་ sentence-ending particle

དོང་	pit
དོང་རྙི་	pit trap
དྲངས་	va. p. of འདྲེན་
དྲི་བ་	a question; va. — འདྲི་: to ask
དྲིན་ལན་ལོག་འཇལ་	va. to act ungrateful, to not repay kindness
དྲིས་	va. p. of འདྲི་
དྲུག་	six
དྲུད་	va. p. of འདྲུད་: pulled, dragged
གདན་དྲངས་	va. p. of གདན་འདྲེན་: transported, carried
བདེན་	true, right
མདོར་བསྡུས་	brief, abbreviated
འདས་	vi. p. of འདའ་: died
འདི་འདྲ་	like that
འདུན་	"hope" particle
འདོད་	"want" particle
འདྲི་	va. to ask
འདྲེན་	1. va. to lead, pull, draw, bring, transport, convey; 2. to invite; 3. to quote
ལྡོག་	opposite
ནང་མི་	family (household) member
ནམ་ཡང་	emphatic negative
ནུས་	va. to dare to
གནང་	va. to do (h.)
གནའ་སྔ་མོ་	ancient time, in the past
གནོད་འཚེ་	harm, damage
མནའ་སྐྱེལ་དམ་བཅའ་	swearing an oath; va. — འཇོག་ (p. བཞག)
ན་ཅོག་	ear
པ་མི་འདུག་	"does not seem" pattern
དཔང་པོ་	witness; judge
ཕར་བཞག་	"let alone/far from" clause connective
ཕུད་	1. "excluding" clause connective; 2. va. to take off (clothes); 3. va. to expel; 4. va. p. of འཕུད་
ཕོད	va. "to dare to" auxiliary verb
ཕྱི་	outside
ཕྱོགས་	direction
འཕྲུལ་སྣང་གཙུག་ལག་ཁང་	p.n. of Lhasa Cathedral (sometimes called the Jokang in Western literature)
བར་	in between; up to
བར་དུ་	see བར་
བལ་ཡུལ་	Nepal
བལ་བཟའ་	name of the Nepalese bride of King Songtsen Gambo
བོད་སྐད་	Tibetan language
བོད་ཇ་	Tibetan tea
བོད་ཡིག་	written Tibetan, Tibetan writing
བོར་	va. p. of འབོར་: threw, flung
བྱང་	north
བྱེ་ཐང་	desert
བྲག་	rock, boulder
བྲག་རྡོ་	boulder
བྲལ་	separate; for its use with ཐབས་ see 9.1
བྲིས་	va. p. of འབྲི་: drew; wrote

བྲོས་	va. p. of འབྲོས་: fled
བློ་	mind; "want" particle
སྦས་	va. p. of སྦ་: buried
མ་རྩའི་རིང་ལུགས་	capitalism
མང་སྲོང་མང་བཙན་	p.n. of a Tibetan king
མོ་	she
མོའི་	her
མའོ་	p.n. Mao (Zedung)
མོས་	1. to like, agree; 2. by her (she+instrumental); 3. "want" particle
མྱོང་	auxiliary verb "to experience"
སྨྲས་	va. p. of སྨྲ་: said
གཙུག་ལག་ཁང་	temple; also used as abbr. for འཕྲུལ་སྣང་གཙུག་ལག་ཁང་
བཙལ་	va. p. of འཚོལ་: searched
བཙུན་མོ་	queen
ཙ་བ་ནས་	emphatic negative
ཙབ་ཧྲུལ་	torn, tattered
རྩིག་རྨང་	foundation of a building; va. — འདིངས་ (p. བཏིང་): to lay a foundation
ཚད་	a level, limit
ཚད་གཞི་	size, standard, criteria, rate
ཚར་	the "finished/completed" auxiliary verb
ཚུར་	hither, toward this side
ཚུལ་	"manner" particle
ཚྭ་	salt
མཚོ་ལས་ཟབ་པ་	deeper than the ocean
འཚོགས་	va. to assemble, convene, hold a meeting
འཚོལ་	va. to search, look for
འཛིན་གྲྭ་	a class (in school)
འཛིན་བཟུང་	arresting; va. — བྱེད་
འཛེགས་	va. to climb
ཞལ་པ་	plastered wall
ཞི་དུལ་སེམས་བཟང་	peaceful and kind
ཞུ་བ་འཐེན་	va. to make a request, beseech
གཞན་དག་	others, another
ཟ་	va. to eat
ཟས་	1. food; 2. va. p. of ཟ་
ཟིན་	the "completed/finished auxiliary verb
གཟའ་ཉི་མ་	Sunday
བཟོ་	1."seem" construction particle; 2. va. to make
བཟོད་པ་	tolerating; va. — སྒོམ་
འོ་རྒྱལ་ཐང་	p.n. of a plain near Lhasa
འོག་	beneath, under
ཡུན་རིང་	long time
ཡུལ་སྐོར་སྐྱོ་འཆམ་པ་	tourist
ཡོང་	va. to come
གཡོག་པོ་	servant (male)
ར་མོ་ཆེ་	Ramoche (name of a temple in Lhasa)
ར་ས་འཕྲུལ་སྣང་	p.n. for Lhasa Cathedral
རུང་	1. "be fit/worthy" particle; 2. even though
རེ་	"hope" particle
ལ་ཡང་	even to
ལམ་བར་	on the road
ལན་སློག་	va. to reply, answer in kind, act in response to, counter
ལུགས་	"manner" particle

ལུང་པ་ place; country

ལུས་ 1. vi. to be left behind, forgotten, left over; 2. vi. to get stuck, bogged down

ལོ་ "be fit/worthy" particle

ལོ་རྒྱུས་ history

ཤ་གཟན་ a meat eater, carnivore

ཤག་ third person perfect tense particle

ཤན་འབྱེད་ va. to separate, differentiate, distinguish between

ཤར་ 1. vi. to arise, rise; 2. east

ཤིང་ཏོག་ fruit

ཤིང་རྟ་འཁོར་ལོ་ horse cart

ཤེས་ va. to know

ཤོད་སྲོལ་ as is commonly said, according to a saying; according to an oral legend

ས་དོང་ pit; tunnel

སུས་ by whom

སི་སྤན་ hot chili, cayenne pepper

སེམས་ 1. mind; 2. "want" construction particle

སོ་ནམ་པ་ farmer

སྲིད་ vi. "possible" auxiliary verb

སྲོག་ཆགས་ living, animate, sentient creature/being

སྲོང་བཙན་སྒམ་པོ་ p.n. Songtsen Gambo (Tibetan king)

སྲོལ་ "way/custom of doing" particle

སློབ་སྟོན་ advice, teachings

བསམ་ཡུལ་ལས་འདས་པ་ incredibly, beyond one's imagination

ཨ་མ་ mother

ཨ་ཞང་ uncle (maternal)

ཨར་པོ་ construction; va. — རྒྱག་

Lesson Ten

10.1 The "while" clause connective ཤུལ་

ཤུལ་ is placed after non-past verb stems to signify "while" the verbal act was going on.

a. ང་ཚོ་ཁྲོམ་ལ་འགྲོ་ཤུལ་མོས་ཁ་ལག་བཟོས་པ་རེད།
While we were going to the market, she made the food.

b. ངས་ལྟད་མོ་ལྟ་ཤུལ་ཁོ་ནང་ལ་ལོག་པ་རེད།
While I was watching the show, he returned home.

c. ཁོ་ཚོས་ཁ་ལག་ཟ་ཤུལ་ངས་ཚགས་པར་བཀློགས་པ་ཡིན།
While they were eating food, I read the newspaper.

ཤུལ་ is also used with demonstratives:

d. ཁོ་ཚོས་ངོ་ལོག་བརྒྱབ་པ་རེད། དེའི་ཤུལ་དུ་. . . .
They rebelled. While that was going on. . . .

10.2 Past-present constructions

To express an action that was done (in the past) and is still being done (at present), the following pattern is employed: past stem of a verb + དང་ + the present (non-past) stem of the verb + བཞིན་ or མུས་ + a final complement or clause connective. For example:

a. དམག་མི་ཚོས་དམག་བརྒྱབ་དང་རྒྱག་བཞིན་པ་རེད།
The soldiers were and are fighting.

b. དམག་མི་ཚོས་དམག་བརྒྱབ་དང་རྒྱག་མུས་རེད།
The soldiers were and are fighting.

c. གྲྭ་པ་དེ་ཚོས་དཔེ་ཆ་བཀློགས་དང་ཀློག་བཞིན་པ་རེད།
Those monks were and are reading books.

d. གཞུང་གིས་ཁྲལ་བསྡུས་དང་སྡུ་མུས་རེད།
The government was and is collecting taxes.

e. གྲོང་འཁྱེར་དེ་རང་ཡར་རྒྱས་བཏང་དང་གཏོང་བཞིན་པ་ཡིན་ཙང་། ངས་ལྟ་པར་ཕྱིན་པ་ཡིན།
Because that city was and is improving, I went to see it.

10.3 Adjectives and adjectival constructions

10.3.1 Basic adjective form

Almost all true adjectives (i.e. non-derived ones) have a basic, a comparative, and a superlative stem. The basic stem is the one we have frequently encountered, for example, ཆེན་པོ་ ("big") and མང་པོ་ ("many"). The basic form, therefore, is normally disyllabic with the second syllable being པོ་. However, you will recall that we have encountered "irregular" adjectives that do not take པོ་, for example, གསར་པ་ ("new") and ཆུང་ཆུང་ ("small").

As indicated earlier, adjectives follow the noun they modify so that "red book" becomes "book red" in Tibetan (དེབ་དམར་པོ་). We have also seen that adjectives are used with existential and linking verbs, for example: དེབ་དེ་ཆེན་པོ་འདུག། ("That book is big") but དེབ་དེ་དམར་པོ་རེད། ("That book is red"). There is no simple rule regarding this but, with the exception of colors, adjectives normally take existential verbs.

When the adjective modifies a nominal, case endings normally are attached to it. For example, སློབ་ཕྲུག་གིས་བཙོས་སོང་། becomes སློབ་ཕྲུག་མང་པོས་བཙོས་སོང་།.

a. སློབ་ཕྲུག་མང་པོའི་ནང་ནས་ཁོ་ལ་བྱ་དགའ་ཐོབ་པ་རེད།
From among many students, he won a prize.

b. མི་མང་པོར་རྟ་འདུག།
Many people have horses. (To many people, there exist horses.)

10.3.2 The comparative form of adjectives

The comparative stem (adj. comp.) of most adjectives is the first syllable of the basic adjective form. For example, ཡག་ is the comparative stem of ཡག་པོ་ and མང་ of མང་པོ་. Some adjectives, however, have slightly different comparative stems, for example, ཆེ་ is the comparative stem of ཆེན་པོ་.

Comparative adjectival constructions of the type "X is bigger, whiter, etc. than Y" have the following pattern: X + ལས་ ("than") + adj. comp. plus an optional གི་རེད་.

a. ཕྲུ་གུ་འདི་ལས་དེ་ཡག་གི་རེད།
That child is better than this one. (Than this child, that one is better.)

b. ལུག་ལས་གཡག་ཆེ།
Yak are bigger than sheep.

The comparative idea can also be expressed by placing the པ་/བ་ nominalizing particles after the comparative stem, for example, ཆེ་བ་ ("the bigger one").

c. ཕྲུ་གུ་ཆེ་བ་དེ་སློབ་ཕྲུག་རེད།
The bigger (older) child is a student.

d. མོས་ཁྱི་མོ་ཡག་པ་དེ་ཉོས་སོང་།

She bought the better hat.

e. ང་ཚོའི་དགེ་རྒན་གྱིས་དགེ་རྒན་གཞན་དག་ལས་སྒྲུང་རིང་བ་ཞིག་འབྲི་གི་རེད།
Our teacher will write a longer story than the other teacher.

f. ཕྲུ་གུ་ཆེ་བ་དེ་ཚོས་ཞིང་ལས་བྱེད་མྱོང་བ་རེད།
The older children have done (experienced) agricultural work.

g. ཕྲུ་གུ་ཆེ་བ་དེའི་ཨ་མ་ཤི་བ་རེད།
The mother of the older children died.

Nominalized comparative adjectives also express the comparative degree when used with existential verbs.

h. ལྷ་ཁང་དེ་ལས་འདི་ཆུང་བ་ཡོད་པ་རེད།
This temple is smaller than that one.

Often ཀྱང་ ("also, even") is used after ལས་ for emphasis.

i. ལྷ་ཁང་དེ་ལས་ཀྱང་འདི་ཆུང་བ་ཡོད་པ་རེད།
This temple is even smaller than that one.

Nominalized comparative adjectives, however, do not always convey the comparative meaning. When they are part of relative clauses modifying a noun or nominal, they sometimes convey the adjectival meaning. Only context will differentiate these two meanings.

j. ངས་གནམ་གཤིས་གྲང་བའི་ལུང་པར་ཕྱིན་པ་ཡིན།
I went to a place which has a cold climate. [What kind of a place? — one which has a cold climate.]

But:

k. རྒྱ་ནག་ནང་གི་མགྲོན་ཁང་ཆེ་བའི་འགོ་ཁྲིད་རྣམས་རི་པིན་ལ་ལྟ་སྐོར་ལ་ཕྱིན་པ་རེད།
The heads (leaders) of the bigger hotels in China went on a (sightseeing) tour to Japan.

When the instrumental particle is used with nominalized adjectival stems, the meaning of "because . . . " is conveyed.

l. ཁོ་འཚོ་བ་སྐྱོ་བས་བརྙན་འཕྲིན་གསར་པ་ཞིག་ཉོ་མི་ཐུབ།
Because his livelihood is poor, (he) is unable to buy a new television set.

m. ཁོར་དངུལ་མང་བས་བརྙན་འཕྲིན་ཡག་པོ་ཞིག་ཉོ་ཐུབ་སོང་།
Because he has much money, (he) was able to buy a good television.

Dative-locative particles and verbs such as གཏོང་ ("to send"), བྱེད་ ("to do"), or འགྲོ་ ("to go") are often used together with comparative adjective stems (comp. adj. stem + dat.- loc. + vb.). These constructions convey the comparative meaning.

n. རྒྱ་ནག་གི་མི་འབོར་ཆེ་རུ་འགྲོ་གི་ཡོད་པ་རེད།
The population of China is increasing. (. . . is going bigger)

o. ང་ཚོས་བོད་རིག་པའི་ཞིབ་འཇུག་མང་དུ་གཏོང་དགོས།
We have (need) to do more Tibetological research.

However, when *nominalized adjectival stems* are used with the dative-locative instead of the simple comparative stem (ཆེ་བར་ versus ཆེ་རུ་), an adverbial meaning is conveyed.

p. ཁོས་གསལ་བར་མཐོང་བ་རེད།
He saw it clearly.

The dative-locative performs the same function with basic adjective stems:

q. ཁོས་གསལ་པོར་མཐོང་བ་རེད།
He saw it clearly.

10.3.3 Augmentation of nominalized adjective stems with the particles: ཆེས་, ཤིན་ཏུ་, ཞེ་དྲགས་, ཏོག་ཙམ་, ཕུན་ཕུ་, ཛེ་, and ཛེ་...ཛེ་.

ཆེས་ and ཤིན་ཏུ་ are placed in front of nominalized adjective stems to convey the meaning of "very" or "extremely" with regard to the adjectival meaning. For example, ཆེས་ཡག་པ་ means "extremely good."

a. ས་ཆ་ཆེས་མང་བར་བཟོ་གྲྭ་འདུག།
There are factories in very many places.

[In this example the basic noun-adjective unit is ས་ཆ་མང་པོ་ ("many places").]

b. ས་ཆ་ཤིན་ཏུ་ཆེ་བའི་ནང་ལ་བཟོ་གྲྭ་མང་པོ་འདུག།
There are many factories in this very big place.

ཞེ་དྲགས་ ("lots") is also used to modify and augment adjectives, but it conveys different meanings when joined to basic and comparative adjectival stems. With the basic adjective it conveys simply the idea of "very" or "extremely."

c. སྒྲུང་འདི་ཞེ་དྲགས་རིང་པོ་འདུག།
This story is very long.

However, when it is used with a nominalized adjective stem it conveys the idea of "very" but with respect to the comparative degree.

d. སྒྲུང་འདི་ཞེ་དྲགས་རིང་བ་འདུག།
This story is very much longer.

ཆེས་, ཞེ་དྲགས་, and ཤིན་ཏུ་ can be used with the གི་རེད་ comparative pattern to express "very, very much" or "much —er."

e. འདི་ལས་འདི་ཤིན་ཏུ་ཆེ་གི་རེད།
   This is much bigger than this.

f. དེབ་གཞན་དག་དེ་ལས་དེབ་འདི་ཞེ་དྲགས་རིང་གི་རེད།
   This book is much longer than that other book.

g. ཉ་ཤ་ལས་ལུག་ཤ་ཆེས་ཞིམ་གི་རེད།
   Mutton is much more delicious than fish.

Even greater emphasis can be conveyed when both ཆེས་ and ཤིན་ཏུ་ are used together.

h. འདི་ལས་འདི་ཆེས་ཤིན་ཏུ་ཆེ་གི་རེད།
   This is very much bigger than this.

i. གླང་ཤ་ལས་ལུག་ཤ་ཆེས་ཤིན་ཏུ་ཞིམ་གི་རེད།
   Mutton is very much more delicious than beef.

Less extreme augmentation is conveyed by the two words ཏོག་ཙམ་ and ཕྲན་བུ་, both of which mean "a little."

j. ཉ་ཤ་ལས་ལུག་ཤ་ཏོག་ཙམ་ཞིམ་གི་རེད།
   Mutton is a little more delicious than fish.

k. འདི་ལས་འདི་ཕྲན་བུ་ཆེ་གི་རེད།
   This is a little bigger than this.

Both ཆེས་ and ཇེ་ are used to augment the comparative constructions that consist of the comparative adjective stem + dat.-loc. + གཏོང་ and འགྲོ་, e.g., ཆེ་རུ་འགྲོ་ ("become bigger") and ཆེ་རུ་གཏོང་ ("make bigger").

l. རྒྱ་ནག་གི་མི་འབོར་ཇེ་ཆེ་རུ་འགྲོ་གི་ཡོད་པ་རེད།
   The population of China is increasing a lot. [. . . is becoming much bigger]

m. ང་ཚོས་བོད་རིག་པའི་ཞིབ་འཇུག་ཆེས་མང་དུ་གཏོང་དགོས།
   We have to do much more Tibetological research.

The idea of more and more (e.g., "greater and greater" or "bigger and bigger") is conveyed by the pattern: ཇེ་ + adjective comparative stem + ཇེ་ + adjective comparative stem + dative-locative:

n. རྒྱ་ནག་གི་མི་འབོར་ཇེ་ཆེ་ཇེ་ཆེ་རུ་འགྲོ་གི་ཡོད་པ་རེད།
   The population of China is increasing more and more. [. . . is becoming bigger and bigger]

o. ང་ཚོས་བོད་རིག་པའི་ཞིབ་འཇུག་ཇེ་མང་ཇེ་མང་དུ་གཏོང་དགོས།
   We have to do more and more Tibetological research.

p. གནམ་གྲུ་ཇེ་མཐོ་ཇེ་མཐོར་ཕྱིན་པ་རེད།
The plane went higher and higher.

For stylistic reasons, Tibetans sometimes use two different adjective stems with the same meaning in such constructions. For example, in sentence q. the adjectives ངན་ and སྡུག་, both of which mean "bad," are employed.

q. གནས་ཚུལ་ཇེ་ངན་ཇེ་སྡུག་ཏུ་ཕྱིན་སོང་།
The situation became worse and worse.

The same meaning can be conveyed by two other patterns:

1. comp. adj. stem + ནས་ + comp. adj. stem + dative-locative, or
2. comp. adj. stem + dative-locative + comp. adj. stem + dative-locative

For example:

r. ང་ཚོས་བོད་རིག་པའི་ཞིབ་འཇུག་མང་ནས་མང་དུ་གཏོང་དགོས།
We have to do more and more Tibetological research.

s. གནམ་གྲུ་མཐོ་རུ་མཐོ་རུ་ཕྱིན་པ་རེད།
The plane went higher and higher.

t. གནས་ཚུལ་ངན་དུ་སྡུག་ཏུ་ཕྱིན་སོང་།
The situation became worse and worse.

10.3.4 The superlative degree: ཤོས་

Superlative constructions are formed by adding ཤོས་ to the comparative adjective stem. For example, ཆེན་པོ་ becomes ཆེ་ཤོས་ ("biggest").

a. གཡག་ཆེ་ཤོས་བོད་ལ་ཡོད་པ་རེད།
The biggest yaks are in Tibet.

b. མེ་མདའ་འདི་ཆུང་ཤོས་རེད་དམ།
Is this the smallest gun?

10.3.5 Excessive constructions: དྲགས་ or སྒྲོན་

Constructions conveying "too much" of an adjectival meaning (e.g., "too big") are formed by :

1. placing the auxiliary verb དྲགས་ after the comparative stem of adjectives, either with or without a normal verbal complement

a. རྟ་འདི་ཆུང་དྲགས་གྱི་རེད།
This horse is too small.

b. རྟ་འདི་ཆུང་དྲགས།
This horse is too small.

c. རྟ་འདི་ཆུང་དྲགས་པ་རེད།
This horse was too small.

2. placing སྐྱོན་ after the comparatve adjective stem. It is followed by the various existential verbs or the verb བྱུང་.

d. རྟ་འདི་ཆེ་སྐྱོན་ཡོད་པ་རེད།
This horse is too big.

e. རྟ་འདི་ཆེ་སྐྱོན་བྱུང་བ་རེད།
This horse was too big.

10.3.6 Derived adjectives

Nouns and nominals are converted into adjectives in a variety of ways. One of the most common is by adding either ཆེན་པོ་ ("big") or ཚ་པོ་ ("hot") after a noun. For example, ཡོན་ཏན་ ("knowledge") is adjectivized by adding ཆེན་པོ་ so that ཡོན་ཏན་ཆེན་པོ་ means "knowledgeable."

a. མི་ཡོན་ཏན་ཆེན་པོ་འདི་གཉིས་ཀྱིས་དེབ་རྙིང་པ་ཞིག་ཉོས་པ་རེད།
The two knowledgeable persons bought an old book.

b. མི་འདི་ཡོན་ཏན་ཆེན་པོ་འདུག།
This person is knowledgeable.

In a similar fashion the noun སྐྱག་རྫུན་ ("lie") becomes adjectivized by adding ཚ་པོ་ so that སྐྱག་རྫུན་ཚ་པོ་ = "mendacious."

c. མི་སྐྱག་རྫུན་ཚ་པོ་འདི་སུའི་གྲོགས་པོ་རེད་དམ།
This mendacious person is whose friend?

Another way to adjectivize nominals is by placing ལྡན་པ་, དང་ལྡན་པ་, or ཅན་ after a noun. These constructions convey the meaning of "having" or "possessing" the nominal quality. For example, ནྲ་བརྩོན་ means "diligence" or "hard work," whereas ནྲ་བརྩོན་ཅན་ means "diligent" (having the quality of diligence).

d. མི་འདི་ནྲ་བརྩོན་ལྡན་པ་ཞིག་རེད།
This person (man) is diligent.

e. མི་ནྲ་བརྩོན་ཅན་འདི་ཕྱི་རྒྱལ་ལ་ཕྱིན་པ་རེད།
The diligent person went abroad.

f. མི་ནྲ་བརྩོན་དང་ལྡན་པ་འདིས་དེབ་གསུམ་ཉོས།

The diligent person bought three books.

g. སྙིང་བརྩོན་ཅན་གྱི་སློབ་ཕྲུག་ཚོར་བྱ་དགའ་སྤྲད་པ་རེད།
(They) gave the diligent students a prize.

Such adjectivized nominals can be modified by other adjectives.

h. ཁོས་རྒྱལ་ཁབ་ཡར་རྒྱས་ཅན་མང་པོར་ཕྱིན་པ་རེད།
He went to many developed countries.

The existential verb ཡོད་ can also be used to adjectivize nominals.

i. མི་སྙིང་བརྩོན་ཡོད་པ་འདི་འདིར་འདུག།
The diligent person is here.

There are also derived adjectives that use མེད་པ་ or དང་བྲལ་བ་ to convey the negation of the basic nominal meaning. For example, སྙིང་བརྩོན་མེད་པ་ and སྙིང་བརྩོན་དང་བྲལ་བ་ mean "not possessing the quality of diligence" or "lazy."

j. སློབ་ཕྲུག་བ་སྙིང་བརྩོན་མེད་པ་དེ་ཤི་བ་རེད།
That lazy student died.

k. ཤིང་ནགས་དང་བྲལ་བའི་རི་བོ་དེ་
That mountain which is without forests (i.e., that unforested mountain)

10.3.7 Conjunction of adjectives: དང་, ཞིང་, ལ་, and ཁར་

Adjectives are joined together in a number of different ways. One way is by means of the conjunction དང་ ("and").

a. སྒམ་འདི་དམར་པོ་དང་ཆུང་ཆུང་རེད།
This box is red and small.

Another more common construction places ཞིང་ (or one of its complementary forms ཅིང་ and ཤིང་) between the adjectives. The adjective occurring before ཞིང་ is usually the comparative stem, while that following ཞིང་ occurs in both the comparative and basic forms.

b. ལུང་པ་དེ་ཚ་ཞིང་རྒྱ་ཆེན་པོ་ཞིག་འདུག།
That place is (one that is) hot and large.

c. ཁོ་ནི་སེམས་ཤུགས་ཆེ་ཞིང་སྙིང་བརྩོན་ཅན་གྱི་འགོ་ཁྲིད་ཞིག་རེད།
He is a leader who is enthusiastic and diligent.

Another common conjunctive constructive uses ལ་ or ཁར་ in place of ཞིང་. It is usually translated by "as well as."

d. ཁོ་ནི་སེམས་ཤུགས་ཆེ་ལ་སྙིང་བརྩོན་ཅན་གྱི་འགོ་ཁྲིད་ཞིག་རེད།

He is a leader who is enthusiastic as well as diligent.

e. ལུང་པ་འདི་གནམ་གཤིས་གྲང་ཁར་ཐོན་སྐྱེད་ཆུང་བ་ཞིག་རེད།

This place is one that is cold as well as one that has poor production.

When one wants to modify a noun with two adjectives, sometimes the two are simply listed one after another. For example:

f. ཁོ་པས་ཚགས་པར་རྙིང་པ་མང་པོ་ཉོས་སོང་།

He bought many old newspapers.

g. མོས་དེབ་སྣན་རིང་པོ་ཅིག་བཀླགས།

She read a long and interesting book.

10.3.8 Adjectival constructions using ལོས་

When ལོས་ is used with the comparative stem of adjectives it conveys the interrogative meaning of "how much." For example,

a. རྟ་དེ་ཆེ་ལོས་འདུག

How big is that horse?

b. ཁོ་པས་མེ་མདའ་མང་ལོས་ཉོས་པ་རེད།

How many guns did he buy?

10.4 Verbal constructions with ལ་ and ཁར་

10.4.1 ལ་ as a verbal clause connective

One function of vb. + ལ་ parallels its use with adjectives by conveying the meaning of "as well as." Note that ཡང་ (ཀྱང་/ འང་-"also") is normally used in this type of construction.

a. ཚོགས་པ་དེའི་ནང་དུ་ཞིང་པ་ཡོད་ལ་འབྲོག་པ་ཡང་འདུག

There are nomads as well as farmers in that association.

b. ཁོ་ཚོས་ཞིང་ལས་བྱེད་ལ་ཚོང་ལས་ཡང་རྒྱག་བཞིན་ཡོད།

They do agricultural work as well as trading.

A second, less common function of ལ་ conveys the meaning of "with respect to" or "concerning" or "because" (see c.). Only context will differentiate these two meanings.

c. དཔེ་ཆ་དེ་ཚོ་དཔེ་མཛོད་ཁང་ནས་ཐོབ་མིན་ལ་བལ་ཡུལ་ནས་མགྱོགས་པོར་བསྐུར་ཐུབ་གྱི་རེད་དམ།

With respect to (my) not (being able to) obtain those books from the library, can (you, etc.) send them quickly from Nepal?

10.4.2 ཁར་ as a verbal clause connective

One function of ཁར་ parallels that of ལ་ in conveying the meaning of "as well as.'

a. ཁོ་པ་སློབ་གྲྭར་འགྲོ་ཁར་བཟོ་གྲྭ་ལའང་འགྲོ་བ་རེད།

He goes to school as well as to the factory.

In this usage ཁར་ is interchangeable with ལ་. Note also that འགྲོ་བ་རེད is the "usual" verb complement.

A second function of ཁར་ is to convey the meaning of "in addition to" or "on top of."

b. སྔར་ཡོད་བོད་པའི་དམག་མི་གསུམ་སྟོང་ཁར་ད་དུང་གཅིག་སྟོང་གསར་པ་བཙུགས་པ་རེད།

In addition to the 3,000 Tibetan soldiers that previously existed, (they) recruited 1,000 new ones.

c. དུད་ཚང་༢༨༠་ལ་གློག་འཛུགས་ཐུབ་པ་བྱུང་ཁར་ལམ་ཁ་གསར་པ་བཟོས་པ་རེད།

As well as being able to electrify (bring [put in] electricity) to 280 households, (they, he, etc.) built a new road.

A third function of ཁར་ is to convey the meaning of "just before." It is used with the non-past stem of verbs to accomplish this.

d. ཉལ་ཁར་སོ་འཁྲུད་དགོས།

Just before going to sleep, (you) have to brush (your) teeth.

e. ཕྲུ་གུ་དེ་སྐྱེ་ཁར་ཨ་མ་ཞི་དྲགས་ན་པ་རེད།

Just before that child was born, (its) mother was very sick.

Semantic context differentiates this meaning from the "as well as" meaning.

10.5 Verbal constructions using: མ་ + vb. (past stem) + ན་

This clause construction links two clauses to indicate that "if the verbal action does not occur," or "unless the verbal action is done," something will happen.

a. ཁྱེད་རང་ལས་ཀ་འདི་མ་བྱས་ན་དམག་མིས་རྡེས་ཀྱི་རེད།

If you do not do this work, the soldiers will beat you.

b. ཁོང་ལྷ་སར་ཟླ་བ་འདིའི་ནང་ལ་མ་ཕེབས་ན་བྱ་དགའ་རག་གི་མ་རེད།

If he (h.) does not go (h.) to Lhasa this month (i.e., unless he goes to Lhasa this month), (he) will not get the prize.

c. ཁྱེད་རང་ཤ་མ་ཟས་ན་གྲོད་ཁོག་ལྟོགས།

If you do not eat meat you will be hungry.

d. དགུན་ཁ་གོས་ལོག་མཐུག་པོ་མ་གོན་ན་ཁྱག་གི་རེད།

If you do not wear thick clothing in winter you will get cold.

e. ཁོ་བོད་ལ་མ་ཕྱིན་ན་ཇོ་བོ་རིན་པོ་ཆེ་མཇལ་མི་ཐུབ།

Unless he goes to Tibet, (he) will not be able to visit the Jo Buddha (the famous statue in the Jokang).

10.6 The "unless" clause connective: ན་/ནས་མ་གཏོགས་

One mode of expressing "unless" is by the pattern: vb. (past stem) + ན་མ་གཏོགས་ or ནས་མ་གཏོགས་.

a. ཁྱེད་རང་མགྱོགས་པོ་ཕྱིན་ན་མ་གཏོགས་གནམ་གྲུ་ཐོན་གྱི་རེད།
Unless you go quickly, the plane will leave.

The previous མ་ + vb. + ན་ construction could be substituted for this (see b.).

b. ཁྱེད་རང་མགྱོགས་པོ་མ་ཕྱིན་ན་གནམ་གྲུ་ཐོན་གྱི་རེད།
Unless you go quickly, the plane will leave.

c. ད་ལྟ་ཁ་ལག་ཟས་ནས་མ་གཏོགས་གྲང་མོ་ཆགས་གི་རེད།
Unless (you) eat the food now, it will become cold.

d. ཁོ་ཚོས་མེ་མདའ་གསར་པ་མང་པོ་བཟོས་ན་མ་གཏོགས་དམག་ཕམ་ཉེས་ཡོང་གི་རེད།
Unless they make many new guns, (they) will lose the war.

10.7 མ་གཏོགས་ as a clause connective expressing "except for"

When མ་གཏོགས་ is used together with the instrumental case and the པ་ཡོད་/བ་ཡོད་ and པ་མེད་/བ་མེད་ ("would have") subjunctive verbal complements, it conveys the meaning "except for X, Y would have (or would not have) occurred."

a. ཁོས་རོགས་རམ་བྱས་པས་མ་གཏོགས་ང་ཚོར་དཀའ་ལས་ཆེན་པོ་ཡོང་བ་ཡོད།
Except for the help he gave, we would have had great difficulties.

b. གནམ་གྲུའི་ནང་ལ་ཕྱིན་པས་མ་གཏོགས་དེ་རིང་སླེབས་པ་མེད།
Except for going by plane, (I) would not have arrived today.

10.8 "Each" constructions using རེ་རེ་... རེ་ or རེ་རེ་

Tibetan conveys the notion of "each" somewhat differently than English. Whereas English requires that only the object be accompanied by "each," e.g., "He gave *each* man a book," Tibetan requires that both the direct and indirect object be accompanied by "each." For example, "He gave *to each* man a book *each.*"

a. ཁོས་མི་རེ་རེར་དེབ་རེ་སྤྲད་པ་རེད།
He gave each man a book.

b. ཁང་པ་རེ་རེར་སྒོ་རྟགས་རེ་རེ་ཡོད་པ་རེད།
Each house has a house number.

The instrumental particle is also used:

c. མི་རེ་རེས་མེ་མདའ་རེ་བཟོས་པ་རེད།

Each person made a gun. (*By* each person, gun each made.)

Either རེ་ or རེ་རེ་ can be used in genitive case constructions (see d. below).

d. མི་རེ་རེའི་ཁང་པར་ཁ་གདན་རེ་ཡོད།

There is a rug in each person's house.

10.9 Constructions with the verb "to change, alter": འགྱུར་

The normal use of this verb is presented in examples a and b.

a. ང་ཕྱི་རྒྱལ་ལ་སྡོད་བཞིན་པར་དང་གི་སྲིད་ཇུས་ཐད་དེ་འགྱུར་སོང་།

While I was living abroad, the party's policy changed completely.

b. འདི་འདྲ་བྱས་ན་ཁོ་ཚོའི་བསམ་ཚུལ་འགྱུར་གྱི་མ་རེད།

If (you, etc.) act like that, their opinion will not change.

འགྱུར་ in its nominalized form (འགྱུར་བ་), however, is used with the verbs "to go" (འགྲོ་, etc.) and the verb to "send" (གཏོང་) to convey respectively, (1) to passively "get changed/altered," and (2) to actively "change or alter."

c. ཁོ་ཚོའི་བསམས་ཚུལ་ལ་འགྱུར་བ་ཕྱིན་པ་རེད།

Their opinion (got) changed.

d. ཁོས་ཁོ་ཚོའི་བསམས་ཚུལ་ལ་འགྱུར་བ་བཏང་བ་རེད།

He changed their opinion.

10.10 "Without" clause connective constructions using མ་ + vb. + བར་/པར་

This construction conveys the meaning of "without" doing a verbal action.

a. སློབ་གྲྭར་མ་ཕྱིན་པར་ཡི་གེ་ཤེས་ཐུབ་ཀྱི་མ་རེད།

Without going to school, (one, etc.) will not be able to know how to read (lit., not understand writing/letters).

b. யུན་རིང་མ་སོང་བར་ཁོ་ཚོ་འདིར་སླེབས་བྱུང་།

Without much time having passed, they arrived here.

c. ལས་ཀ་ཡག་པོ་མ་བྱས་པར་བྱ་དགའ་ཐོབ་ཀྱི་མ་རེད།

Without doing a good job, (one, etc.) will not get a prize.

d. གནམ་གྲུའི་ནང་མ་ཕྱིན་པར་ཉིན་གཉིས་ལ་རྒྱ་གར་ལ་སླེབས་ཐུབ་ཀྱི་མ་རེད།

Without going by airplane, (one, etc.) will not be able to arrive India in two days.

e. གྲྭ་པ་མ་བྱས་པར་དགོན་པའི་ནང་སྡོད་ཐུབ་གི་མ་རེད།

Without being monk, (one, etc.) will not be able to stay in the monastery.

This construction can also convey the related meaning of "so as not to."

f. མེ་ཤིང་མ་སྤྲོད་པར་དངུལ་སྤྲད་པ་རེད།
So as not to give (them) firewood, (he, she, etc.) gave money.

10.11 "Until" clause connective constructions using: མ་ + vb.+ བར་/པར་དུ་

It should be noted that with the exception of the dative-locative particle (དུ་), this construction is identical to that in 10.10.

a. ཁོ་འདིར་མ་ཡོང་བར་དུ་སྐྱིད་གསོ་སྤྲོད་ཀྱི་མ་རེད།
Until he comes here, (they) will not give him welfare.

b. གྲྭ་པས་ཞལ་འདོན་མ་གནང་བར་དུ་གསོལ་ཇ་འབུལ་གྱི་མ་རེད།
Until the monks pray (h.), (he,she, etc.) will not give (h.) (he, she, etc.) tea (h.) .

c. ངས་མེ་ཤིང་མ་འཐུ་བར་དུ་མེ་གཏོང་མི་ཐུབ།
Until I collect firewood, (I) am unable to make a fire.

10.12 Constructions with འཕྲོ་, འཕྲོར་, and འཕྲོས་ ("left over, uncompleted"): vb.+ འཕྲོ་ (འཕྲོར་, འཕྲོས་) + ལུས་ or བཞག་

a. དགེ་འདུན་ཆོས་འཕེལ་ལགས་ནས་བོད་ཀྱི་རྒྱལ་རབས་བྲི་འཕྲོར་ལུས་པ་རེད།
Gedun Chömphel did not complete writing a history of Tibet.

This could also have been written:

b. དགེ་འདུན་ཆོས་འཕེལ་ལགས་ཀྱིས་བོད་ཀྱི་རྒྱལ་རབས་བྲི་འཕྲོ་ལ་ལུས་པ་རེད།
Gedun Chömphel did not complete writing a history of Tibet.

c. རྡོ་རྗེ་ལགས་ཕྱག་ལས་གནང་འཕྲོས་བཞག་སྟེ་བོད་ལ་ཕེབས་པ་རེད།
Dorje left (his) work unfinished and went to Tibet.

This could also have been written:

d. རྡོ་རྗེ་ལགས་ཕྱག་ལས་གནང་འཕྲོ་ལུས་ཏེ་བོད་ལ་ཕེབས་པ་རེད།
Dorje left (his) work unfinished and went to Tibet.

e. དེབ་འདི་མགྱོགས་པོ་མ་ཀློག་ན་ཀློག་འཕྲོར་ལུས་ཀྱི་རེད།
If (he, she, they, you) don't read this book quickly, it will get left over (unread).

f. སློབ་གྲྭ་བ་དེས་ཇ་འཐུང་འཕྲོ་བཞག་སྟེ་འཛིན་གྲྭར་ཕྱིན་སོང་།
The student went to class leaving (his) tea unfinished.

g. མོས་ལས་ཀ་བྱེད་འཕྲོས་བཞག་མི་འདུག།
She didn't leave (her) work unfinished.

10.13 The "location" particles: ཡུལ་ and ས་

These particles are used with the non-past stem of verbs to express the idea of "the place where" or "a thing on/at/in/to which" or "a person to whom" the verbal action is done. Thus, ལས་ཀ་བྱེད་ས་ means "the place where the work is being done."

a. ཁོའི་ལས་ཀ་བྱེད་ས་ག་པར་ཡོད་པ་རེད།
   Where is the place he works at?
b. གྲོང་ཁྱེར་འདིར་ལྟད་མོ་ལྟ་ཡུལ་མང་པོ་འདུག།
   In this city, (there) are many places to see shows.
c. ཁོས་དམག་རྒྱག་སར་ཕྱིན་པ་རེད།
   He went to the place where the war (was being) fought.

This could also convey, depending on context, "He went to the place where the war is being fought."

d. ང་ཚོ་ཚོགས་འདུ་འཚོག་ས་དེར་མགྱོགས་པོར་འགྲོ་དགོས།
   We have to go quickly to the place where the meeting is convened.
e. མོས་སྐད་ཆ་ཤོད་ཡུལ་དེ་བཀྲིས་རེད་དམ།
   That person to whom she is talking, is it Tashi?
f. རི་མོ་འདིའི་འབྲི་ས་རས་རེད་པས།
   The thing on which this picture is painted, is it cloth?
g. མོའི་རོགས་བྱེད་ས་མང་ཆེ་བ་ཁྱིམ་ཚང་སྐྱོ་པོའི་བུ་ཕྲུག་ཚོ་རེད།
   Most of the persons whom she helps are children of poor families.

10.14 "Like what," "how," and "what kind of" constructions: ཇི་ལྟར་ or ཇི་ལྟ་བུ་

ཇི་ལྟར་ and ཇི་ལྟ་བུ་ can function as adverbial interrogatives literally asking "like what" or "how" with regard to the verbal action. In example a. ཇི་ལྟར་ modifies the verbal phrase "to trick" (མགོ་བསྐོར་བཏང་), asking "like what" or "how" did he trick.

a. ཨ་ཁུ་སྟོན་པས་ཁྱིམ་མཚེས་དེ་ལ་མགོ་བསྐོར་ཇི་ལྟར་བཏང་བ་རེད་དམ།
   How did Agu dönba trick that neighbor?
b. ཨ་ཁུ་སྟོན་པས་རྣམ་འགྱུར་ཇི་ལྟ་བུ་ཞིག་བསྟན་པ་རེད།
   What kind of an appearance (expression) did Agu dönba show?
c. སློབ་གྲྭ་བ་ཇི་ལྟ་བུ་ཞིག་ལ་བྱ་དགའ་ཐོབ་བམ།
   What kind of a student won the prize ?
d. ང་ཚོས་ཇི་ལྟར་བྱས་ནས་ཞིང་ལས་ཡར་རྒྱས་གཏོང་དགོས།
   What (like what) should we do to improve farm work?

These are also used with existential and linking verbs. For example:

e. ལུང་པ་འདི་ལ་ལུགས་སྲོལ་ཇི་ལྟ་བུ་ཞིག་ཡོད་དམ།
   What kind of customs do they have in this country?

ཇི་ལྟར་ and ཇི་ལྟ་བུ་ are also used in non-interrogative constructions, sometimes functioning as indefinite or relative clauses and sometimes meaning "just like. . . ."

f. བླ་མས་ཇི་ལྟར་གསུངས་པ་དེ་བཞིན་གྲྭ་པས་བྱེད་དགོས།
   Monks should do just like (whatever) the Lama said.

g. ཁྱོད་ར་སློབ་དེབ་ནང་ཇི་ལྟར་ཡོད་པ་དེ་ལྟར་བྱེད་ན་འགྲིག་གི་རེད།
   If you do just like what is in the textbook, it will be all right.

h. གྲོང་འཁྱེར་ནང་ཚོང་ཁང་ཇི་ལྟར་ཡོད་པ་ལྟར་གྲོང་གསེབ་ནང་ཡོད་པ་མ་རེད།
   There are no shops in villages like those in the city.

i. འཕྲུལ་འཁོར་དེ་བརྙན་འཕྲིན་ནང་ཇི་ལྟར་བསྟན་པ་ལྟར་ཡག་པོ་འདུག།
   This machine is as good as the one shown on TV.

j. ཁ་ས་ཁོང་ཚོ་སྐད་ཆ་ཇི་ལྟར་བྱུང་མེད་ངས་ཤེས་མ་བྱུང་།
   I did not know what kind of conversation they had (or didn't have) yesterday.

10.15 Reading exercises

10.15.1 Reading number one: "Agu dönba Cuts Down A Walnut Tree"

10.15.1.1 Tibetan text

༈ ཨ་ཁུ་སྟོན་པས་སྟར་སྡོང་བཅད་པ།

༄༅། སྔོན་ཨ་ཁུ་སྟོན་པའི་ཁྱིམ་མཚེས་ཕྱུག་པོ་ཞིག་ཡོད་པ་དེས་ཨ་ཁུ་སྟོན་པར་བརྙས་བཅོས་1 ཀྱིས་ཨ་ཁུའི་སྒེའུ་ཁུང་གི་འོག་ཏུ་སྟར་སྡོང་ཞིག་བཙུགས། ལོ་ལྟར་དབྱར་ཁ་ཤར་བ་དང་སྟར་སྡོང་གི་ལོ་འདབ་རྒྱས་ཏེ་ཨ་ཁུ་སྟོན་པའི་ཁྱིམ་གྱི་སྒེ་ཁུང་གི་དཀར་ཆ་བསྒྲིབས་ནས་ཉིན་མོའང་2 སྒྲོན་མེ་སྤར་དགོས་པའི་མཚམས་སུ་སླེབས། ཨ་ཁུ་སྟོན་པའི་བསམ་པར་ངན་པར་ངན་ལན་མ་བསློགས་ན3། བརྙས་བཅོས་བྱེད་མཁན་མང་དུ་འགྲོ་ངེས་རེད་སྙམ་ནས་ཉིན་ཞིག་ཤིང་རིང་པོ་ཕྲག་ཏུ་ཁུར་ནས་ཕྱུག་པོ་དེའི་སྒོའི་མདུན་ནས་4 སོང་། དེ་ཕྱུག་པོས་མཐོང་ནས། ཨ་ཁུ་སྟོན་པ། ཁྱོད་རང་ཤིང་ཕྲག་པར་ཁུར་ནས་གང་དུ་འགྲོ་རྩིས་ཡོད་དམ་ཞེས་དྲིས་པར5། ཨ་ཁུ་སྟོན་པས་ཏ་ལས་པའི་རྣམ་འགྱུར་ཞིག་བསྟན་ནས། ཁྱེད་ཀྱིས་ད་དུང་མ་མཁྱེན་ནམ6། དེ་རིང་ལྷ་ས་ནས་སྟར་ཤིང་ཉོ་མཁན་ཚོང་པ་འབྱོར་ནས་སྟར་ཤིང་འཛོམ་གང་7 རེར་སྒོར་མོ་བརྒྱ་རེ་སྤྲོད་ཀྱི་འདུག། ཁྱེད་ཀྱི་སྟར་སྡོང་དེ་བཙོང་ན་མ་མཐར་ཡང་དངུལ་སྒོར་ཕྲག8 མང་པོ་རག་གི་རེད། ཡིན་ནའང་མགྱོགས་པོ་མ་ཕེབས་ན་ཚོང་པ་འགྲོ་གྲབས་འདུག་ཅེས་ལབ། ཕྱུག་པོའི་བསམ་པར་ངའི་སྟར་སྡོང་དེ་ནི་སྦོམ་ལ་རིང་བས9 གོང་ཆེན་པོ་རག་རྒྱུ་ཐེ་ཚོམ་མེད10 བསམ་ནས་སྟར་སྡོང་དེ་ལམ་སེང་བཅད་དེ་ཚོང་ལ་སོང་། གྲོང་ཁྱེར་ལ་སླེབས་དུས་ཤིང་ཉོ་མཁན་གཅིག་ཀྱང་མེད11 སྐབས། ཕྱུག་པོ་ཁོང་བློ་ཚད་མེད་ལངས་ནས་ཤིང་དེ་བུད་ཤིང་དུ་བཙོང་ནས་བོང་བུར་བཞོན་ནས་ཁྱིམ་དུ་ལོག། དེའི་ཕྱི་ཉིན་ནོར་བདག་ལ་ཨ་ཁུ་སྟོན་པ་ཐུག་ནས་ཁོས་ཁོང་བློ་ཆེན་པོའི་སྒོ་ནས་ཁྱེད་ཀྱིས་ང་ལ་མགོ་སྐོར་བཏང་སྟེ། གྲོང་ན་ཤིང་ཉོ་མཁན་ཚོང་པ་གཅིག་ཀྱང་མི་འདུག་ཅེས་བཤད། ཨ་ཁུ་སྟོན་པས། ང་ཡིས་ཕྱུག་པོར་མགོ་སྐོར་གཏོང་ག་ལ་ཡོད12། མགྱོགས་ཙམ13 མ་ཕེབས་ན་ཤིང་ཉོ་མཁན་ཚོང་པ་འགྲོ་གྲབས་འདུག་ཅེས་ཞུས་མ་བྱུང་ངམ14། ཁྱེད་རང་ཕྱིས་དྲགས་པའི་རྐྱེན་གྱིས་རེད15 ཅེས་བཤད་

པས་ཕྲུག་པོ་ཁོ་ཅི་ཤོད་འདི་ཤོད་མེད་པར་ 16 བྱུར། ཨ་ཁུ་སྟོན་པའི་ཁང་པར་ཉི་མ་དྲོ་པོ་བྱུང་ཁར་ 17 དཀར་ཆ་ཡང་གསལ་པོ་བྱུང་ངོ་།

10.15.1.2 Translation

Agu dönba Cuts Down A Walnut Tree

Formerly, Agu dönba had a wealthy neighbor who took advantage of him by planting a walnut tree outside Agu's house's window. Every year, as soon as summer started, the leaves on the tree grew and blocked the light from (reaching) Agu's window, making it necessary to light a lamp even during the day. At this juncture, Agu thought, "If one does not respond in kind to bad deeds, those who abuse one will certainly increase." (So) one day, he put a long piece of wood on his shoulder (carried it) and went in front of the door of the wealthy man. The wealthy man saw him and asked, "Agu dönba, where are you planning to go carrying a pole like that on your shoulder?" Agu dönba showed the appearance of surprise and said, "You still do not know? Today, walnut tree buyers arrived from Lhasa who are paying 100 dollars for each arm's length of walnut wood. If you sell your walnut tree, at the very least, you will obtain many thousands of dollars. Nevertheless, if you do not go quickly, they are about to leave." The wealthy man thought, "Because my walnut tree is thick and tall, I will certainly get a high price for it." So he immediately cut down the tree and went to sell it. When he arrived in the city, because there was not one tree buyer, the wealthy man got angry and sold it as firewood and returned home riding on a donkey. The next day, the wealthy man met Agu dönba, and angrily said, "You deceived me! There was not even one buyer of wood in town." Agu dönba replied, "How could I deceive a wealthy man (like you)? Didn't I tell you, 'If you do not go quickly the traders who are buyers are ready to go?' It is because you were too late." The wealthy man was unable to retort. Agu dönba's house (from then on) was warm and light.

10.15.1.3 Grammatical notes

1. The term བརྙས་བཅོས་ is often translated as "abuse" but here it conveys not physical abuse but "taking advantage of one's position or power" or "bullying." It is adverbialized by the instrumental particle གྱིས་ and explains how the rich neighbor planted the tree. See 6.5.2 for an explanation of this kind of adverbialization.

2. འང་ is the form of ཀྱང་ and ཡང་ ("even, also") that is used after syllables ending in a vowel. It attaches directly to the stem. In this segment it conveys the meaning that "*even* in daytime, it had reached the point where there was a need to light a lamp."

3. The pattern of noun or adjective + ལན་བསློགས་ conveys "responding in kind" in the manner of the noun or adjective. Thus ངན་ལན་བསློགས་ conveys "respond with evil" and བཟང་ལན་བསློགས་ means "respond with kindness." Consequently, ངན་ལན་མ་བསློགས་ན་ conveys "unless (one) responds to evil."

4. The use of ནས་ here conveys "via" or "by," i.e., ཕྱུག་པོ་དེའི་སྒོའི་མདུན་ནས་སོང་ ("went by the front of the door of that rich person").

5. This use of the dative-locative with nominalized verbs (ཉིས་པར་) is explained in 6.6.3. རྩིས་, the "plan to" particle, is explained in 7.3.

6. མ་མཁྱེན་ནམ་ is a negative question meaning "don't you know?" Here it is joined to ད་དུང་ ("still") and means "You still don't know?"

7. གང་ is typically used in measurements to mean "one." For example, ངར་ཇ་དཀར་ཡོལ་གང་སྤྲོད་རོགས་གནང་ ("Please give me one cup of tea"). Similarly, with measurement units such as རྒྱ་མ་ (a *jin* or half kilogram) one would say རྒྱ་མ་གང་ for "one *jin.*"

8. ཕྲག་ has two meanings. Earlier we saw it meant "shoulder," but here it conveys round numbers in multiples of ten, i.e., "tens," hundreds," thousands," "ten thousands," and so on.

9. ལ་ in སྦོམ་ལ་རིང་བ་ ("thick as well as long") functions as an adjectival conjunctive meaning "as well as" (see 10.3.7). Note that the addition of the instrumental particle (རིང་བས་) here means "because."

10. The nominalized phrase གོང་ཆེན་པོ་རག་རྒྱུ་ conveys a future action: "the obtaining of a high price." It modifies the verbal phrase ཐེ་ཚོམ་མེད་ ("having no doubts"), explaining what it is he has no doubts about.

11. གཅིག་ཀྱང་མེད་ is a common phrase meaning "there was not even one" of something, in this instance, "buyers" (ཉོ་མཁན་).

12. ག་ལ་ཕོད is a pattern consisting of ག་ལ་ ("how could I") + ཕོད ("dare"), meaning "how could I dare." Other such ག་ལ་ phrases are presented in Lessons 11 and 12.

13. The use of ཙམ་ in མགྱོགས་ཙམ་མ་ཕེབས་ན་ conveys a meaning akin to "-ish" or "sort of" in English, in this instance, "if you do not go sort of quickly."

14. ཞུས་མ་བྱུང་ངམ་ is a negative rhetorical question construction: "Didn't I tell you?"

15. ཕྱིས་དགས་པའི་རྐྱེན་གྱིས་རེད་ is a common pattern consisting of adj. stem + དགས་པའི་རྐྱེན་གྱིས་རེད་. It conveys the meaning that "it is because of too much of the adjective,"here, "too late." For example, དེ་ནི་ཁྱེད་རང་སྒྱོ་དགས་པའི་རྐྱེན་གྱིས་རེད་—"As for that, it is because you are/were too

poor." Another example is: ང་རེས་ཡིག་ཚད་ཡག་པོ་བྱུང་པ་དེ་ནམ་རྒྱུན་སློབ་སྦྱོང་ཡག་པོ་བྱས་པའི་རྐྱེན་གྱིས་རེད། "The doing well on your examination this time is because you usually study hard (well)."

16. ཅི་ཤོད་འདི་ཤོད་མེད་པར་ is a pattern that consists of ཅི་ + vb. + འདི་ + vb. + མེད་པར་, meaning "to be unable to do anything regarding the verbal action." Here it conveys that he was unable to say anything (respond). Another example of this is: ཁོས་རྐུ་མ་རྐུ་དུས་ང་ནང་ལ་འབྱོར་དུ་ཁོ་ཅི་བྱེད་འདི་བྱེད་མེད་པར་སྒེའུ་ཁུང་ནས་མཆོངས་སོང་།—"I arrived home when he was (in the act of) stealing, and since there was nothing he could do, he jumped out of the window."

17. ཁར་ here functions as an adjectival conjunctive (see 10.3.7).

10.15.2 Reading number two: "The 'Prayer-Festival' Holiday"

10.15.2.1 Tibetan text

སྨོན་ལམ་དུས་ཆེན་

བོད་ཀྱི་སྐད་གྲགས་ལྡན་པའི་1 ལྷ་སའི་སྨོན་ལམ་ཆེན་མོ་ནི་སྤྱི་ལོ་ཆིག་སྟོང་བཞི་བརྒྱ་བཅུ་མེད་བཞིའི་ལོར་རྗེ་ཙོང་ཁ་པ་ཆེན་པོས་2 ལྷ་སའི་གཙུག་ལག་ཁང་དུ་གྲྭ་པ་སྟོང་ཕྲག་འགའ་ཞིག་ཞུགས་པའི་ཚོགས་ཆེན་ཞིག་གསར་འཛུགས་གནང་བ་དེ་3 རེད། ཏཱ་ལའི་བླ་མ་སྐུ་འཕྲེང་ལྔ་པ་མཆོག་ནས་སྨོན་ལམ་ཉིན་ཉི་ཤུ་རྩ་གཅིག་རིང་ལྷ་སའི་གླིང་བསྐོར་ནང་ཚུད་དུ་དབང་ཆ་ཆ་ཚང་འབྲས་སྤུངས་ཚོགས་ཆེན་ཞལ་ངོར་གནང་སྐབས་དེའི་རིང་4 ཁྲིམས་ཀྱི་དབང་ཆ་འབྲས་སྤུངས་ཚོགས་ཆེན་ཞལ་ངོ་ནས་བྱེད་པ་རེད།།

བོད་ཟླ་དང་པོའི་ཚེས་བཞི་ཉིན་5 སྨོན་ལམ་གྲལ་འཛིན་ཟེར་བ་བྱེད་ཀྱི་ཡོད་པ་རེད། གྲལ་འཛིན་ཟེར་6 བ་གྲྭ་པ་སོ་སོའི་7 སྡོད་ས་ག་པར་ཡོད་མེད་8 ངོ་སྤྲོད་བྱས་པ་རེད། ཚེས་ལྔ་ཉིན་ནས་བཟུང་9 སྨོན་ལམ་དངོས་གཞི་འགོ་ཚུགས་ཀྱི་རེད། དེའི་རིང་བོད་གཞུང་ནས་ཇ་ཐུག་འགྱེད་དངུལ་སོགས་10 དཀྲིགས་བཅར་11 གནང་པ་མ་ཟད། ད་དུང་ལྷ་སའི་ཕྱུག་པོ་ཁག་གིས་མང་ཇ་དང་འགྱེད་སོགས་འབུལ་ཡས་12 ཀྱི་ལུགས་སྲོལ་ཡོད། ཚེས་བཅོ་ལྔ་ནི་བཅོ་ལྔ་མཆོད་པ་ཟེར་བའི་གལ་ཆེའི་དུས་ཆེན་དེ་རེད། དེ་ཉིན་དགོང་དྲོ་ས་སྲིབ་མཚམས་སུ་ལྷ་སའི་བར་སྐོར་ནང་དུ་མཆོད་པ་མང་པོ་སྒྲིག་གཤོམ་བྱ་གི་རེད། མཆོད་པ་ཆེན་པོ་དེ་ཚོ་ནི་མར་ཚོན་ཁྲས་བཟོས་པའི་རིས་བཟོ་13 མཛེས་པོ་མང་པོ་ཤིང་སྒྲོམ་ཆེན་པོའི་སྟེང་དུ་བཀོད་པ་ཞིག་རེད། མཆོད་པ་འདི་ཚོའི་ཆེ་ཆུང་ཆ་སྙོམས་ལ་མིའི་ཏར་ ༡༥ ཙམ་ཡོད་པ་རེད། ཏཱ་ལའི་བླ་མ་མཆོག་གིས་མཆོད་པར་གཟིགས་པར་ཕེབས་པ་དང་། དེའི་རིང་བར་སྐོར་ནང་དུ་དམག་མི་བཀྲམ་ནས་མང་ཚོགས་རྣམས་བར་སྐོར་དུ་ཡོང་མི་ཆོག་14། ཏཱ་ལའི་བླ་མས་མཆོད་པར་གཟིགས་གྲུབ་རྗེས་མང་ཚོགས་རྣམས་མཆོད་པ་མཇལ་བར་ཡོང་གི་རེད།

སྤྱི་ཚོགས་རྙིང་པའི་སྐབས་ལ་སྨོན་ལམ་ལ་སེ་ར་ནས་གྲྭ་པ་སྟོང་བརྒྱད་ཀྱི་གཡས་གཡོན་15 དང་། འབྲས་སྤུངས་ནས་གྲྭ་པ་ཆིག་ཁྲི་ཙམ། དགའ་ལྡན་ནས་གྲྭ་པ་ལྔ་སྟོང་ཙམ་ཞུགས་གི་ཡོད་པ་མ་ཟད་ད་དུང་དགོན་ཁག་16 གཞན་དག་ནས་ཀྱང་17 དགེ་

འདུན་མང་པོ་ཕེབས་ཀྱི་འདུག་གོ།།

10.15.2.2 Translation

The "Prayer-Festival" Holiday

As for Lhasa's "Great Prayer-Festival," which is famous in Tibet, it is the prayer meeting in which thousands of monks participate in Lhasa's Cathedral (Tsuglakang) temple. It was established in the year 1404 by the great (lama) Tsongkaba. Because the Fifth Dalai Lama gave all power within Lhasa's outer circumambulation road to the Disciplinary Officers of Drepung, judicial decisions were made by the Drepung Disciplinary Officers for the 21 days of the festival (lit., during that time).

On the 4th day of the 1st Tibetan month, the event called "arranging the rows" is done. The (activity) called "arranging the rows" (involves) showing (lit., introduces) the monks where their seats are. From the 5th onwards, the "prayer festival" really begins. During the time (of the festival), the Tibetan government not only gives tea, stew, and money distributions (to the monks) but there was also the custom that rich people in Lhasa give tea and money gifts (to the monks) in accordance with traditional amounts. As for the 15th, it is the important festival known as the "Offering of the Fifteenth." On that day, at dusk, (they) erect many "offerings" in the Bargor (circular path) of Lhasa. As for these big "offerings," they consist of many beautiful artistic forms made from colored butter that have been put on a large scaffolding. These "offerings" on the average are 15 meters high. The Dalai Lama comes to view the "offerings" and at that time soldiers are stationed in the Bargor and the common people are not allowed to come into the Bargor. After the Dalai Lama has finished seeing the offerings, the people come to have an audience with the "offering."

During the old society, not only did about 8,000 monks from Sera, 10,000 from Drepung, and about 5,000 from Ganden participate in this, but many monks came even from other monasteries.

10.15.2.3 Grammatical notes

1. ལྡན་པ་ here adjectivizes སྙན་གྲགས་ ("fame"), making it སྙན་གྲགས་ལྡན་པ་ ("famous")—see 10.3.6. Note that the genitive links this phrase to the noun phrase it modifies.

2. Tsongkapa (ཙོང་ཁ་པ་) is the name of the founder of the Gelugpa sect. རྗེ་ ("lord") and ཆེན་པོ་ ("great") are commonly added to denote respect.

3. Note that the segment བོད་ཀྱི་སྐད་གྲགས་ལྡན་པའི་ལྷ་སའི་སྨོན་ལམ་ཆེན་མོ་ནི་སྤྱི་ལོ་ཆིག་སྟོང་བཞི་བརྒྱ་བཅུ་མེད་བཞིའི་ལོར་རྗེ་ཙོང་ཁ་པ་ཆེན་པོས་ལྷ་སའི་གཙུག་ལག་ཁང་དུ་གྲྭ་པ་སྟོང་ཕྲག་འགའ་ཞིག་ཞུགས་པའི་ཚོགས་ཆེན་ཞིག་གསར་འཛུགས་གནང་བ་དེ་རེད། is really nothing more than a linking verb construction: . . . ནི་ . . . དེ་རེད་ ("As for X, it is Y").

What makes this construction difficult, however, is its use of an object phrase that is a nominalized verbal construction (སྤྱི་ལོ་ཆིག་སྟོང་བཞི་བརྒྱ་བཅུ་མེད་བཞིའི་ལོར་རྗེ་ཙོང་ཁ་པ་ཆེན་པོས་ལྷ་སའི་གཙུག་ལག་ཁང་དུ་གྲྭ་པ་སྟོང་ཕྲག་འགའ་ཞིག་ཞུགས་པའི་ཚོགས་ཆེན་ཞིག་གསར་འཛུགས་གནང་བ་) that itself contains a nominalized verb construction functioning as a relative clause (སྤྱི་ལོ་ཆིག་སྟོང་བཞི་བརྒྱ་བཅུ་མེད་བཞིའི་ལོར་རྗེ་ཙོང་ཁ་པ་ཆེན་པོས་ལྷ་སའི་གཙུག་ལག་ཁང་དུ་གྲྭ་པ་སྟོང་ཕྲག་འགའ་ཞིག་ཞུགས་པའི་). The overall nominalized phrase is "the establishing newly of a meeting in 1404 by Tsongkapa which had several thousand monks participating in Lhasa's Tsuglakhang cathedral." It explains what "Tibet's famous Lhasa Great Prayer Festival" (བོད་ཀྱི་སྐད་གྲགས་ལྡན་པའི་ལྷ་སའི་སྨོན་ལམ་ཆེན་མོ་ནི་) is.

The nominalized sub-clause (i.e., the clause within the nominalized clause)—གྲྭ་པ་སྟོང་ཕྲག་འགའ་ཞིག་ཞུགས་པའི་ ("several thousand monks who participated ")—modifies ཚོགས་ཆེན་ ("meeting") describing what kind of a meeting it was, namely that it was a meeting "of several thousand monks." This could have been written: གྲྭ་པ་སྟོང་ཕྲག་འགའ་ཞིག་ཡོད་པའི་.

4. The syllable རིང་ here does not mean "long" but rather "duration," this function being related to its use as one of the "when" connectives discussed in 5.10. དེའི་རིང་ means, therefore, "for the duration of that" (the 21 days). Note that this phrase could have included a dative-locative particle: དེའི་རིང་ལ་.

5. This could be expressed in a less abbreviated manner as: བོད་ཟླ་དང་པོའི་ཚེས་པ་བཞི་གི་ཉིན.

6. ཟེར་བ་ here conveys the meaning "the one called" (see 5.17.4 13). Thus it translates as "They do that which is called སྨོན་ལམ་གྲལ་འཛིན་ on the 4th day of the Tibetan 1st month."

7. སོ་སོ་ here conveys the meaning of "each his own," "individually," "separately." Thus གྲྭ་པ་སོ་སོའི་སྡོད་ས་ means "each monk's individual residence (or the place where each lives)." སོ་སོ་ can also take the instrumental case particle, for example, གྲྭ་པ་སོ་སོས་སྨོན་ལམ་རྒྱོན་པ་རེད་—"Each monk prayed separately" and the dative-locative particles, for example, ངས་གྲྭ་པ་སོ་སོར་འགྱེད་རྒྱབ་པ་ཡིན་—"I gave alms to each monk (individually)." Note that སྡོད་ས་ consists of སྡོད་ + ས་, this pattern being explained in 10.12.

8. The pattern ག་པར་ཡོད་མེད་ is explained in 8.6.

9. The term ནས་བཟུང་ conveys "from X onwards." Thus, ཚེས་ལྔ་ཉིན་ནས་བཟུང་ means "from the fifth onwards."

10. This is a standard way to list an enumeration. ཇ་ཐུག་འགྱེད་དངུལ་སོགས་ consists of four items: ཇ་ (tea), ཐུག་ (porridge), འགྱེད་ (alms [can be goods in kind]), དངུལ་ (money). Use of སོགས་ indicates that the list is not complete so it is normally translated as "etc.".

11. དགྲིགས་བཅར་ is probably derived from Hindi. It refers to doing something in a usual or customary way.

12. ཡས་ is a verbal nominalizer that is explained in 6.7.

13. ཚོན་ཁྲུས་བཟོས་པའི་རིས་བཟོ་ is a common relative construction conveying "X which is made from Y." Here it means "shapes which are made from colored butter."

14. ཚོག་ is an auxiliary verb meaning "allowed" that is used after other verbs to indicate "allowed" or "not allowed" with respect to that verbal action. In this case, མི་ཚོག་ following ཡོང་ means "not allowed to come." This verb is presented in more detail in 11.9.

15. གཡས་གཡོན་ literally means "left and right" but with numbers conveys "more or less."

16. ཁག་ is a pluralizing particle that when used with nouns conveys a plurality of different kinds of unit, sections, sectors, or parts. Thus, མི་མདའ་ཁག་མང་པོ་འདུག་ means "many different kinds of guns." Here དགོན་ཁག་ means from different monasteries but not necessarily from all monasteries.

17. The combination of ནས་ཀྱང་ means "also from" or "even from."

10.16 Vocabulary

དཀའ་ངལ་	difficulties
དཀར་ཆ་	light
དཀར་ཡོལ་གང་	one cup
དགྲིགས་བཅར་	regularly, in a usual or customary way
བཀོད་	va. p. of འགོད་: put into, onto
བཀྲམ་	va. p. of འགྲེམས་: spread, distributed, stationed (soldiers)
སྐད་གྲགས་ལྡན་པ་	famous
སྐུ་འཕྲེང་ལྔ་པ་	fifth incarnation (in a line of incarnations)
སྐྱེ་	va. to give birth
སྐྱོན་	excessive particle
བསྐུར་	va. p. of སྐུར་: sent
ཁ་གདན་	small rug (usually 3' x 5')
ཁག་	pluralizing particle
ཁར་	conjunctive particle for adjectives, verbal clause connective
ཁྱེར་	va. p. of འཁྱེར་: carried
ཁྱོད་རང་	you
མཁྱེན་	va. to know (h.)
འཁྲུད་	va. to wash, brush (teeth)
འགྱུར་	vi. to be/get changed, altered
འགྱེད་	alms (gift usually of money) to monks; va. —རྒྱག་
གྲལ་འཛིན་	the rite of arranging the rows where monks sit

in the Great Prayer Ceremony

གྲོང་ town, city

གླིང་བསྐོར་ outer circumambulation road in Lhasa

གློག་འཛུགས་ va. to electrify, to put in electricity lines

དགེ་འདུན་ monk (h.)

དགེ་འདུན་ཆོས་འཕེལ་ p.n. (Gedun Chömphel)

དགོང་དོ་ evening

འགོ་ཚུགས་ va. to begin, start

འགྲིག་ vi. to be okay, all right

རྒྱ་ཆེན་པོ་ large

རྒྱལ་རབས་ history

རྒྱས་ vi. to become plentiful, abundant

སྒམ་ box

སྒེའུ་ཁུང་ window

སྒོ་ door

སྒོ་རྟགས་ house number

སྒོར་མོ་ dollar

སྒྲིག་གཤོམ་ erecting, arranging; va. — བྱེད་

སྒྲུང་ story

སྒྲོན་མེ་ lamp

བསྒྲིབས་ va. p. of སྒྲིབ་: blocked, covered, concealed

ངན་ bad

ངན་ལན་བསློགས་ va. to respond to evil with evil

དངོས་གཞི་ really

ཅན་ having, possessing

བཅུག་ va. p. of འཇུག་: put in, recruited

བཅོ་ལྔ་མཆོད་པ་ "offering on the fifteenth" (the butter sculpture ritual conducted on the 15th of 1st Tibetan month)

ཆ་སྙོམས་ average

ཆ་ཚང་ complete; all

ཆུང་བ་ younger; smaller

ཆེ་བ་ older; bigger

ཆེས་ augmentive particle

ཆོག་ 1. ready; 2. allow

མཆོག་ honorific word used after names and titles

མཆོད་པ་ an offering

ཇི་ལྟ་བུ་ "like what," "just like"

ཇི་ལྟར་ "like what," "just like"

ཇེ་ augmentive particle

རྗེ་ཙོང་ཁ་པ་ Je Tsongkaba (founder of the Gelukpa sect)

ཉིན་མ་ a day

ཉིན་མོ་ day time

བརྙན་འཕྲིན་ television

ཏཱ་ལའི་བླ་མ་ Dalai Lama

ཏོག་ཙམ་ a little bit

སྟར་སྡོང་ walnut tree

བསྟན་ va. to show

ཐུག་པ་ stew, porridge

ཐེ་ཚོམ་ doubt

མཐུག་པོ་ thick

དང་ and

དུས་ཆེན་ festival, holiday

དྲགས་ excessive particle ("too")

དྲོ་པོ་ warm

འདོམ་ a length measurement equal to a person's outstretched arms

ལྡན་པ་ having, possessing

སྡུག་	bad
ན་མ་གཏོགས་	the "unless" clause connective
ནང་ཚུད་	within
ནས་མ་གཏོགས་	the "unless" clause connective
ནས་བཟུང་	from X onwards
ནོར་བདག་	wealthy person
གནམ་གཤིས་	climate, weather
རྣམ་འགྱུར་	appearance
སྤར་	va. to light
སྤྱི་ཚོགས་	society, social
སྤྱི་ལོ་	a year in the Western calendar
ཕམ་ཉེས་ཡོང་	vi. to be defeated, lose
ཕྱིས་དྲགས་པ་	too late
ཕྲག་	even numbered units of ten, hundreds, thousands, etc.
ཕྲག་པ་	shoulder
ཕྲན་བུ་	a little
འཕྲོ་	left over, uncompleted
བར་བསྐོར་	the Barkor (circular path in Lhasa)
བུ་ཕྲུག་	child, children
བུད་ཤིང་	firewood
བོད་རིག་པ་	Tibetology, Tibetological
དབང་ཆ་	power
འབྲི་	va. to write
སྦོམ་	thick
མ་	1. "unless" clause connective; 2. "until" clause connective
མ་མཐར་ཡང་	at the very least
མ་གཏོགས་	clause connective expressing "except for"
མང་ཚོགས་	the people
མར་ཚོན་ཁྲ་	colored butter
མི་འབོར་	population
མིའི་ཊར་	eng. meter
སྨོན་ལམ་དུས་ཆེན་	Lhasa's Great Prayer Festival
ཚེས་	"th" as used with dates, i.e., the 10th of June
ཚོགས་ཆེན་ཞལ་ངོ་	head disciplinary officer in monastery
ཚོན་ཁྲ་	color
འཛིན་གྲྭ་	class (in a school)
ཞིང་	conjunctive particle for adjectives
ཞིབ་འཇུག་	research; va. — བྱེད་
ཞེ་དྲགས་	the augmentation particle
བཞོན་	va. to ride
ཡུལ་	the location particle
ཡོན་ཏན་	knowledge
གཡས་གཡོན་	left-right; both sides; approximately
རས་	cloth
རི་བོ་	hill, mountain
རི་མོ་	picture, drawing
རིང་པོ་	long
རིང་བ་	longer
རིས་བཟོ་	shape (of a drawing, sculpture)
རེ་རེ་	each
ལ་	1. conjunctive particle for adjectives; 2. verbal clause connector (see lesson)
ལན་བསློགས་	va. p. of ལན་སློག་: responded in kind

ལུགས་སྲོལ་	custom
ལོ་སྣར་	every year
ལོ་འདབ་	leaf
ལོས་	"how"—in adjectival constructions
ཤིང་སྒྲོམ་	scaffold
ཤིན་ཏུ་	the augmentation particle
ཤུལ་	the "while" connective
ཤོས་	the superlative degree particle
ས་	the location particle
ས་སྲིབ་མཚམས་	at dusk
སེ་ར་	Sera (monastery)
སོ་སོ་	each one's, individually, separately
སྲིད་ཇུས་	policy, strategy
གསར་འཛུགས་	newly establish
བསམ་ཚུལ་	thought, opinion
ཧ་ལས་	vi. to be surprised

Lesson Eleven

11.1 The "time to do" auxiliary verb: རན་

This verb follows the non-past stem of verbs to convey that "it is/was time" to do the verbal action.

a. ད་རྒྱལ་རྩེ་ལ་འགྲོ་རན་འདུག།
   Now it's time to go to Gyantse.

b. ད་ཁོང་ཚོ་ཞལ་ལག་མཆོད་རན་འདུག།
   Now it's time for them to eat dinner. (h.)

c. ཁྱེད་རང་ཐེབས་རན་སོང་ན་ང་ལ་གསུངས་རོགས་གནང་།
   Please tell me if it is time for you to leave. (h.)

d. ད་ལྷ་ཆང་འཐུང་རན་མི་འདུག།
   It's not time to drink beer now.

རན་ itself takes various verbal connectives:

e. ཐུགས་སྐྱོར་འགྲོ་མ་རན་གོང་ལ་འགྲོ་རྒྱུ་ཡོད་པ་མ་རེད།
   (One) should not go to the party until it's time to go.

11.2 Constructions using the phrases ག་ལ་ཡོད་, ག་ལ་རུང་, and ག་ལ་འགྲིགས་: "how can it be okay?"

ག་ལ་ཡོད་, ག་ལ་རུང་, and ག་ལ་འགྲིགས་ all convey the notion that some action is not acceptable or should not be done, implying an element of shock and/or disdain. These constructions generally convey conditional meaning: "Given X, how could it be all right/okay to do Y?"

a. སློབ་ཕྲུག་ཚོས་འཛིན་གྲྭ་མ་གྲོལ་གོང་ལ་ནང་ལ་ལོག་རྒྱུ་ག་ལ་ཡོད།
   How can it be okay for students to return home before class is over? (i.e., Students should not return home before class is over).

b. ཞིང་པས་དཔྱིད་ཀ་སོན་མ་བཏབ་པར་ལྷ་སའི་གྲོང་འཁྱེར་ནང་ལ་སྡོད་རྒྱུ་ག་ལ་ཡོད།
   How is it okay for farmers to stay in Lhasa and not sow their seeds in spring?

c. ལྷ་སར་སླེབས་ནས་ཇོ་བོ་མ་མཇལ་ན་ག་ལ་འགྲིགས།
   How could it be all right if you didn't visit the Jo Rimpoche statue after arriving in Lhasa?

d. དགོན་པར་སླེབས་ནས་མཆོད་མཇལ་མ་ཞུས་པར་ལོག་ན་ག་ལ་རུང་།
   How could it be okay to return without making a religious visit after arriving at the monastery?

e. བླ་མས་ཆོས་མ་ཤེས་ན་ག་ལ་འགྲིགས་

How could it be all right if a Lama does not know religion?

f. བླ་མས་རྫུན་གསུང་བ་ག་ལ་རུང་།

How could it be all right if a Lama tells lies?

11.3 Constructions using ག་ལ་+ vb. (non-past)

ག་ལ་ is also used directly with active verbs to ask "how can" such a thing as the verbal action occur. Again it conveys shock at the idea.

a. འབྲོག་པས་རྟ་ཤ་ག་ལ་ཟ།

How could nomads eat horse meat?

b. ལག་ཁྱེར་མེད་པར་བོད་ལ་ག་ལ་འགྲོ།

How can one go to Tibet without a permit?

c. དམག་མིས་ཕྲུ་གུར་མེ་མདའ་ག་ལ་རྒྱག།

How can the soldiers shoot children?

d. གྲྭ་པ་རྒན་འཁོགས་དེ་ལ་མེ་མདའ་རྒྱག་ག་ལ་ཕོད།

How can one dare to shoot that old monk?

e. ཕྲུ་གུ་ཆུང་ཆུང་དེས་མཚན་མོ་ཕྱི་ལ་འགྲོ་ག་ལ་ཕོད།

How can that small child dare to go out in the night?

Past tense is conveyed by context and past tense words. For example:

f. ན་ཉིན་དམག་རྒྱབ་དུས་སློབ་གྲྭ་བ་ཚོ་སློབ་གྲྭར་འགྲོ་ག་ལ་ཕོད།

How could the students dare to go to school during the war last year?

ག་ལ་ is also frequently used with སྲིད་ ("to be possible"), conveying the meaning of "how is it possible" to do the verbal action or for the verbal action to occur. It implies that there is no possibility or, sometimes, no custom for the action in question to occur. Note that the verbs are nominalized.

g. ཉི་མ་ནུབ་ནས་ཤར་བ་ག་ལ་སྲིད།

How is it possible for the sun to rise in the west?

h. གྲྭ་པས་དགོན་པའི་ནང་ཆང་ས་བརྒྱབ་པ་ག་ལ་སྲིད།

How is it possible for monks to marry in the monastery?

i. ལྷ་སར་སླེབས་ནས་བོད་པ་མ་མཐོང་བ་ག་ལ་སྲིད།

How is it possible to not see Tibetans after you arrive in Lhasa?

j. སློབ་གྲྭ་བས་རང་སྦྱོང་མ་བྱེད་པར་སློབ་གྲྭ་ཆེན་མོའི་ཡིག་ཚད་གཏོང་ཐུབ་པ་ག་ལ་སྲིད།

How is it possible for students to pass the college exam without doing homework?

11.4 Constructions using the phrase དོན་ཅི་ཡོད་

དོན་ཅི་ཡོད་ follows the non-past stem of verbs conveying "what is the point/reason/purpose" of doing the verbal action. In certain contexts it is also used to ask "why."

a. ཁྱེད་རང་འདིར་སླེབས་མ་ཐག་ཏུ་ཁོ་ལ་ཁ་པར་གཏོང་དགོས་དོན་ཅི་ཡོད།
   What is the point of needing to phone him as soon as you arrived here?

b. ཁོང་ཁྲོམ་ནས་མགྱོགས་པོ་དེ་འདྲ་ལོག་དགོས་དོན་ཅི་ཡོད་པ་རེད།
   Why does he have to return home from the market as fast as this?

c. ཁོ་དམག་མི་མིན་པར་དམག་སྒར་ནང་སྡོད་དགོས་དོན་ཅི་ཡོད།
   Because he is not a soldier, what is the point of (him) having to stay in the base?

d. ཁོང་གིས་དེ་འདྲ་གསུངས་དོན་ཅི་ཡོད། ངས་ཤེས་མ་སོང་།
   I didn't know what is the point of his saying that.

e. ལྟད་མོ་དེ་ང་ཚོས་ཐེངས་ཁ་ཤས་མཐོང་ཙང་། ཡང་བསྐྱར་ལྟ་དགོས་དོན་ཅི་ཡོད།
   Because we saw the show several times, what is the point of having to watch it again?

f. མི་དམངས་སྐྱིད་པོ་ཡོད་ན་ངོ་ལོག་རྒྱག་དོན་ཅི་ཡོད།
   If people are happy, what is the point of revolting?

11.5 Constructions using the pattern vb.+ རྒྱུ་གང་ཡོད་: "What is there to be . . ."

This pattern is used with the present (non-past) tense stem of verbs. It asks rhetorically what is the reason for doing the verbal action.

a. འདི་འདྲ་བྱས་ན་ཞེད་རྒྱུ་གང་ཡོད།
   What is there to be afraid of if you act (do) like this?

b. དགེ་རྒན་ལ་སྐད་ཆ་དྲིས་པར་ངོ་ཚ་རྒྱུ་གང་ཡོད།
   What is there to be embarrassed at if you ask the teacher questions?

c. ཉོ་ཆ་རྒྱག་དགོས་མེད་ན་ཚོང་ཁང་ནང་ལ་འགྲོ་རྒྱུ་གང་ཡོད།
   Why go to the store if you don't have to do shopping?

d. ཁྱེད་རང་གྲྭ་པ་མིན་པར་གྲྭ་ཆས་གོན་རྒྱུ་གང་ཡོད།
   Why wear monk's clothes if you are not a monk?

This pattern can also be used with the perfect tense complement in the first clause:

e. འདི་འདྲ་བྱས་ཡོད་ན་ཞེད་རྒྱུ་གང་ཡོད།
   If this is what you have done, what is there to be afraid of?

11.6 Constructions using ཐ་ན་: "even"

ཐ་ན་ is normally placed at the start of the second of two clauses and typically is accompanied by ཀྱང་ ("even/also").

a. སྒྲུང་དེ་མི་རྒན་པས་མ་ཟད། ཐ་ན་ཕྲུ་གུས་ཀྱང་ཧ་གོ་ཐུབ་ཀྱི་རེད།
   Let alone adults, even children are able to understand that story.

b. དཔེ་ཆ་དེ་བླ་མས་མ་ཟད། གྲྭ་བ་གསར་པ་ཞིག་གིས་ཀྱང་ཀློག་ཤེས་ཀྱི་རེད།
   Let alone Lamas, even a new monk knows how to read that book.
c. ཟ་འཐུང་ནི་དུད་འགྲོས་ཀྱང་ཤེས་ཀྱི་ཡོད་པ་རེད།
   Even animals know how to drink and eat. (lit., As for eating and drinking, even animals know.)
d. ཚོང་ཁང་དེའི་ནང་ཁ་ན་མུ་སི་ཡན་ཆད་ཚོང་རྒྱུ་ཡོད་པ་རེད།
   That shop sells even everything upwards from (larger than) matches.

ཡན་ཆད་ in example d. normally means "upwards of," or "above," or "more than," including the item mentioned; for example, བཅུ་ཡན་ཆད་ conveys the meaning "ten and above" and ཟླ་བ་བཅུ་པ་ཡན་ཆད་ means "from the tenth month onwards." In a parallel fashion, མུ་སི་ཡན་ཆད་ means "from matches upwards" or "everything from a match onwards," i.e., a match and everything larger.

11.7 Causative constructions

11.7.1 Constructions using འཇུག་ (p. བཅུག་)

There are several ways to form causatives. One places the verb འཇུག་ ("to put in" or "insert into") immediately after the non-past stem of a verb. This conveys the strongest, most coercive expression of causation (X made Y do something)—direct force or coercion. Such constructions sometimes include the dative-locative particle immediately after the non-past stem of the verb as in b. below.

a. གཞུང་གིས་གྲྭ་པ་རྣམས་ཞིང་ལས་བྱེད་བཅུག་པ་རེད།
   The government made the monks do agricultural work.
b. གཞུང་གིས་གྲྭ་པ་རྣམས་ཞིང་ལས་བྱེད་དུ་བཅུག་པ་རེད།
   The government made the monks do agricultural work.
c. སང་ལོ་གཞུང་གིས་གྲྭ་པ་རྣམས་ཞིང་ལས་བྱེད་དུ་འཇུག་གི་རེད།
   The government will make the monks do agricultural work next year.

11.7.2 Constructions using བཟོ་

A second causative construction uses དགོས་ and བཟོ་ after verb stems (non-past). It literally means "made it necessary for them to do the verbal action." This generally conveys the idea that the actor did something so that someone had to do the action in question.

a. གཞུང་གིས་གྲྭ་པ་རྣམས་ཞིང་ལས་བྱེད་དགོས་པ་བཟོས་པ་རེད།
   The government made the monks (have to) do agricultural work.

b. འགོ་ཁྲིད་ཚོས་ཁོ་ཚོ་ལམ་སེང་འགྲོ་དགོས་པ་བཟོ་གི་མ་རེད།

The leaders will not make them have to go immediately.

རྒྱུ་ is often used to indicate that the action that someone is being made to do is in the future.

c. གཞུང་གིས་གྲྭ་པ་རྣམས་ཞིང་ལས་བྱེད་དགོས་རྒྱུ་བཟོས་པ་རེད།

The government made monks have to do agricultural work (in the future).

In example c. the main verb ("made") is in the past tense (བཟོས་པ་རེད་), while the object of the verb, "the future doing of fieldwork," is in the present/future tense (ཞིང་ལས་བྱེད་དགོས་རྒྱུ).

རྒྱུ་ can also be used alone with བཟོས་:

d. གཞུང་གིས་གྲྭ་པ་རྣམས་ཞིང་ལས་བྱེད་རྒྱུ་བཟོས་པ་རེད།

The government made the monks do agricultural work (in the future).

Another way to express future tense is via the future tense stem of verbs:

e. གཞུང་གིས་གྲྭ་པ་རྣམས་ཞིང་ལས་བྱ་དགོས་བཟོས་པ་རེད།

The government made the monks have to do agricultural work (in the future).

When བཟོ་ is added to nominalized verb stems (non-past), a causative meaning is also conveyed.

f. གཞུང་གིས་གྲྭ་པ་རྣམས་ཞིང་ལས་བྱེད་པ་བཟོས་པ་རེད།

The government made the monks do agricultural work.

g. གཞུང་གིས་གྲྭ་པ་རྣམས་ཞིང་ལས་བྱེད་མཁན་བཟོས་པ་རེད།

The government made the monks agricultural workers.

h. གཞུང་གིས་གྲྭ་པ་རྣམས་ཞིང་ལས་བྱེད་མི་བཟོས་པ་རེད།

The government made the monks agricultural workers.

11.7.3 Constructions using བྱེད་

The verb བྱེད་ can be substituted for བཟོ་ to convey a causative meaning. Causative constructions using བྱེད་ follow nominalized verb stems and generally imply causation due to indirect means such as inducements or incentives rather than direct force or the threat of it. Thus in sentence a. below, the implication is that the doctor would have been ordered to come with the threat of force hanging over his head, while in sentence b., he would have been coaxed or induced to come.

a. ཁོས་ཨེམ་ཆི་འདི་འདིར་ལམ་སེང་ཡོང་དུ་བཅུག་པ་རེད།

He made this doctor come here at once.

b. ཁོས་ཨེམ་ཆི་དེ་འདིར་ལམ་སེང་ཡོང་བ་བྱས་པ་རེད།

He made (did something so that) that doctor come here at once.

A somewhat stronger causative voice than b. would be conveyed by:

c. ཁོས་ཨེམ་ཆི་འདི་འདིར་ལམ་སེང་ཡོང་དགོས་པ་བཟོས་པ་རེད།

He did something so that this doctor had to come here at once.

d. གཞུང་གིས་དགོན་པ་ཉམས་གསོ་བྱེད་ཐུབ་པ་བྱས་པ་རེད།

The government made (did something to make) it possible to repair the monastery.

e. ཞིང་པ་གསར་པ་ཚོས་ཐོན་སྐྱེད་བརྒྱ་ཆ་བཅུ་འཕར་བ་བྱེད་བཞིན་ཡོད་པ་རེད།

The new farmers are acting so that production can increase 10%.

f. ང་ཚོས་ཁོང་དབྱིན་སྐད་མགྱོགས་པོ་ཤེས་པ་བྱས་པ་ཡིན།

We made him learn English quickly. (We did things so that he learned [came to know] English quickly.)

11.8 "Let" or "allow" constructions using the verb འཇུག་

A source of confusion in reading Tibetan stems from the fact that འཇུག་ is also used to convey the meaning of "let do" or "allow" in grammatical constructions identical with the causative ones discussed above. Only context can differentiate the two.

a. ཁོ་ཚོས་མོ་ལྷ་སར་འགྲོ་རུ་བཅུག་པ་རེད།

They made her go to Lhasa. Or, They allowed her to go to Lhasa.

b. ཁོ་ཚོས་མོ་ལྷ་སར་འགྲོ་མ་བཅུག་པ་རེད།

They did not allow her go to Lhasa.

c. མོས་ཁྱི་འདི་ཤ་ཟ་དུ་བཅུག་པ་རེད།

She let the dog eat the meat.

While བཅུག་ in c. could be taken to convey "made," normally it would have been written with an extra modifier such as ཨུ་ཚུགས་རྒྱབ་ནས་ ("insist") if that was intended:

d. མོས་ཨུ་ཚུགས་རྒྱབ་ནས་ཁྱི་འདི་ཤ་ཟ་རུ་བཅུག་པ་རེད།

She made the dog eat the meat.

e. ངས་ཁོ་ལ་བརྡ་ཡིག་ཞིག་འབྲི་རུ་བཅུག་པ་ཡིན།

I let (or made) him write a letter.

Negative constructions, however, normally convey "not allowed":

f. གཞུང་གིས་དམག་མི་རྣམས་ལ་མེ་མདའ་རྒྱག་རུ་བཅུག་མ་སོང་།

The government did not allow the soldiers to shoot guns.

11.9 "Allow" constructions using the auxiliary verb ཆོག་

ཆོག་ is used with verbs to convey the idea of "allowing" or "permitting" the verbal action to occur. With some verbs, both the past and non-past stems can be used, but with others, only the past stem is permissible. For example, in example a. the non-past tense stem of the verb "talk" (ཤོད་) is not used but in b. and c. both stems of the verb are used.

a. དམག་མི་འདི་ཚོ་རང་ཚོས་སྐད་ཆ་བཤད་ཆོག་གི་མ་རེད།
We are not allowed to talk to these soldiers.

b. ལག་ཁྱེར་མེད་པར་རྒྱ་ནག་ལ་འགྲོ་ཆོག་གི་མ་རེད།
Without a permit (visa), (one) cannot go to China.

c. ལག་ཁྱེར་མེད་པར་རྒྱ་ནག་ལ་ཕྱིན་ཆོག་གི་མ་རེད།
Without a permit (visa), (one) cannot go to China.

d. ལྷ་ཁང་དེའི་ནང་ན་ཞྭ་མོ་གྱོན་ཆོག་གི་མ་རེད།
It is not permitted to wear a hat in that temple.

e. དེང་སང་བོད་ལ་ལྟ་སྐོར་བ་ཕྱིན་ཆོག་གི་ཡོད་པ་རེད་པས།
Are tourists allowed to go to Tibet these days?

f. ན་ནིང་བོད་ལ་ལྟ་སྐོར་བ་ཕྱིན་ཆོག་སོང་ངས།
Were tourists allowed to go to Tibet last year?

11.10 "I'll do" volunteering constructions using the auxiliary verb ཆོག་

When ཆོག་ is used at the end of a sentence following the past tense stem of verbs, it conveys the idea that "I volunteer to do" the verbal action.

a. ཁྱེད་རང་གི་ཕྲུ་གུ་སྐྱེ་སྐབས་ཁྱིམ་གྱི་ལས་ཀ་ཚང་མ་ངས་བྱས་ཆོག།
When your child is born, I'll do all the housework.

b. ཁྱེད་རང་ཁ་ལག་བཟོས་དགོས་ཡོད་སྐབས་ང་ཚོས་ཤ་ཉོ་བར་ཕྱིན་ཆོག།
Because you have to make the food, (if you want) we'll go to buy the meat.

Another way of expressing this is through the pattern: vb.+ པས་ཆོག་.

c. ངས་ད་ལྟ་ཆུ་ནང་ནས་སྟ་རེ་ལེན་པས་ཆོག་ཅེས་བཤད་པ་རེད།
(He) said, "I'll get the axe from the water now."

11.11 "Ready to do" constructions using: ཆོག་ and ཆོག་ཆོག་

ཆོག་ and ཆོག་ཆོག་ are also used with verb stems to convey the meaning of "ready to do the verbal action." Usually this means ready in the sense of having completed the packing and preparations for the trip or for some task.

a. ང་རྒྱལ་རྩེར་འགྲོ་ཆོག་ཡིན།
I am ready to go to Gyantse.

b. ཁྱོད་རྒྱལ་རྩེར་འགྲོ་ཆོག་ཡིན་པས།
Are you ready to go to Gyantse?

c. ཁ་སང་རྒྱལ་རྩེར་ཕྱིན་ཆོག་ཡིན་ཀྱང་། གནམ་གྲུ་སླེབས་མ་བྱུང་།

Even though I was ready to go to Gyantse yesterday, the plane did not come.

d. ཁ་ལག་བཟོས་ཚོག་ཡིན།

The food is ready to make.

11.12 "Approve" or "agree" constructions using the verb འཐུས་

When the verb འཐུས་ is used after another verb, it conveys the meaning of "approval" ("permission") being given for the action of the first verb. In example a. approval was given to establish monk soldiers.

a. གཞུང་གི་ཞབས་ཞུར་སེར་དམག་དང་བླངས་འཛུགས་འཐུས་བྱུང་བ་རེད།

It was approved to establish (enrolling) monk volunteer soldiers to serve the government.

b. ཁོང་ཚོས་དེ་ལྟར་གནང་ན་འཐུས་ཀྱི་རེད།

If they do (like) that, (it) will be approved. (h.)

c. བོད་ལ་ཕེབས་འཐུས་ཞེས་བཀའ་ཕེབས་ཤག།

An order has come that it was approved to go to Tibet.

d. ལས་ཀ་དེ་འདྲ་བྱས་ན་འཐུས་མིན་བཀའ་འདྲི་ཞུས་སོང་།

(They, he, etc.) asked whether (it) would be approved (or not) if (they, he, etc.) did work (like) that.

e. ང་ཚོས་དེ་ལྟར་གནང་འཐུས་ཁོང་ལ་ཞུས་པ་ཡིན།

We told him that we approved doing like that.

Sometimes context requires that འཐུས་ be translated as "all right."

f. ཁོའི་དྲི་བ་དེ་ལ་ཁྱོད་རས་ལན་དེ་འདྲ་ཞིག་རྒྱབ་ན་འཐུས་ཀྱི་རེད།

It will be all right if you answer his question like that.

An alternative form for this is འགྲིགས་.

g. ཁོའི་དྲི་བ་དེ་ལ་ལན་དེ་འདྲ་ཞིག་རྒྱབ་ན་འགྲིགས་ཀྱི་རེད།

It will be all right if (you) answer his question like that.

11.13 "No choice" and "no way" constructions using ཀ་མེད་, ཐབས་མེད་, ཐབས་བྲལ་, ཚད་མེད་, མཐུ་མེད་, ཚད་བྲལ་, and རང་

All but the last of the above terms is used in the following pattern: མ་ + vb. + —. They convey "no choice" but to do the verbal action.

a. ཁོ་འདིར་མ་ཡོང་ཀ་མེད་རེད།

He had no choice but to come here.

b. ང་བོད་ལ་ལོ་གཉིས་བསྡད་དགོས་བྱུང་སྐབས་བོད་སྐད་མ་བསླབས་ཐབས་མེད་བྱུང་།

Because I had to live in Tibet for two years, I had no choice but to learn Tibetan.

c. ངའི་གཞུང་གིས་གྲོས་མཐུན་དེ་ར་ཆ་འཛོག་མི་བྱེད་མཐུ་མེད་བྱུང་།

My government had no choice but to abide by that agreement.

Note that changing the stem of the verb in b. to non-past changes the overall tense (see c.).

d. ང་བོད་ལ་ལོ་གཉིས་སྡོད་རྒྱུ་ཡིན་སྟབས་བོད་སྐད་མ་སློབ་ཐབས་བྲལ་རེད།

Because I will live in Tibet for two years, I will have no choice but to learn Tibetan.

Another semantically identical "no choice" pattern consists of: མ་ + vb. + རང་ + vb.

e. ཁོང་འདིར་མ་ཕེབས་རང་ཕེབས་རེད།

He had no choice but to come here. (h.)

f. སྲིད་གཞུང་ཡག་པོ་མེད་ཙང་། ངོ་ལོག་མ་རྒྱབ་ཐབས་བྲལ་བྱུང་བ་རེད།

Because the government was not good, (they, he, etc.) had no choice but to rebel.

Note that ཡག་པོ་མེད་ཙང་ is translated as past tense because of the past tense of the second clause.

g. བག་ལེབ་མེད་པར་བརྟེན། ཁོ་ཚོ་འབྲས་མི་ཟ་ཐབས་མེད་རེད།

Because there is no bread, they have no choice but to eat rice.

h. ཁོར་ལས་ཀ་གཞན་དག་མེད་ཙང་། འདི་མ་བྱེད་རང་བྱེད་རེད།

Because he has no other work, he has no choice but to do this.

i. ཁོ་ཚོར་བཙན་གནོན་གཏོང་གི་ཡོད་པས། ཕྱི་རྒྱལ་ལ་སྐྱབས་བཅོལ་དུ་མི་འགྲོ་ཀ་མེད་ཡིན་པ་རེད།

Because (they, he, .etc.) are oppressing them, (they) have no choice but to seek refuge abroad.

When no negative precedes the verb, many of these can be used to convey that there is no way the verbal action can/could occur. For example:

j. ཤིང་སྡོང་སྦོམ་པོ་ཡིན་ཙང་གཅོད་ཐབས་བྲལ་བ་རེད།

Because the tree is thick, there is no way to cut it down.

11.14 Constructions expressing the idea of "about" and "concerning": སྐོར་ and ཐད་

སྐོར་ and ཐད་ are two important words that convey "about" and "concerning." They typically are linked to the words they modify by the genitive particle and often are followed by the dative-locative particles. In example a. below, སྐོར་ conveys what kind of a petition he submitted.

a. ཁོས་འབྲོག་པའི་འཚོ་བའི་སྐོར་སྙན་ཞུ་ཞིག་ཕུལ་བ་རེད།

He submitted a petition concerning the livelihood of the nomads.

In example b., however, སྐོར is part of an adjectivized nominal clause modifying "petition"

(སྙན་ཞུ་).

b. འབྲོག་པའི་འཚོ་བའི་སྐོར་གྱི་སྙན་ཞུ་འདི་ང་ཚོས་ཀློག་དགོས།

We must read this petition about the livelihood of the nomads.

c. དམག་མིས་མི་དམངས་དཀྱིལ་ལ་མེ་མདའ་བརྒྱབ་སྐོར་ཚགས་པར་ནང་བྲིས་ཡོད་པ་རེད།

The newspaper contained (an article) concerning the soldiers shooting amongst the people.

d. ཁོས་ན་ཉིན་བོད་ལ་ཡུལ་བསྐོར་སྤྱི་འཆམ་བྱས་སྐོར་གཏམ་བཤད་བྱས་སོང་།

He gave a speech concerning his visit to Tibet last year.

Note that if the writer had intended to convey that he gave the speech last year, the sentence would probably have been written: ཁོས་བོད་ལ་ཡུལ་བསྐོར་སྤྱི་འཆམ་བྱས་སྐོར་ན་ཉིན་གཏམ་བཤད་བྱས་སོང་།

e. ང་ཚོས་འབྲོག་ལས་ཡར་རྒྱས་གཏོང་རྒྱུའི་སྐོར་ལ་འཆར་གཞི་ཞིག་བཀོད་པ་ཡིན།

We made a plan concerning improving animal husbandry.

f. ཨ་མི་རི་ཀ་བ་དེས་ལྷ་སའི་གཙུག་ལག་ཁང་གི་སྐོར་ལ་དེབ་ཅིག་བྲིས་ཤག

The American has written a book concerning the Cathedral in Lhasa.

g. རྒྱལ་ཁབ་དེའི་སྐོར་ངས་གང་ཡང་ཤེས་ཀྱི་མེད།

I don't know anything (at all) about that nation.

ཐད་ performs the same function even though its use is not completely interchangeable with སྐོར.

h. གནས་ཚུལ་འདིའི་ཐད་ལ་ཁོས་བསམ་འཆར་བཤད་ཡོད་པ་མ་རེད།

He hasn't given (spoken) his opinion regarding this situation.

ཐད་ is also used to convey the meaning "by means of." In this role it generally occurs with ནས་, i.e., ཐད་ནས་.

i. བཟོ་ལས་ཀྱི་ཐད་ནས་ཁོ་ཚོ་གཞིས་ཆགས་བྱེད་ཀྱི་ཡོད་པ་རེད།

(They) are settling them by means of (giving them) industrial work.

11.15 Rhetorical negative constructions

Rhetorical negative constructions convey the idea "isn't it . . ." or "aren't there . . .?" or "are there not. . . ." For example:

a. བོད་མི་ནི་ཆོས་པ་མ་རེད་དམ།

As for Tibetans, aren't they (considered) "religious people?" (are they not religious people)

Note that if this were not in the negative, the simple interrogative idea would be conveyed:

b. བོད་མི་ནི་ཆོས་པ་རེད་དམ།

As for Tibetans, are they (considered) "religious people"?

c. བོད་ལ་དགོན་པ་ཆེན་པོ་མང་པོ་ཡོད་པ་མ་རེད་དམ།

Aren't there many big monasteries in Tibet?

d. ག་ས་ག་ལ་དམྱལ་བ་མ་རེད་པས།

Isn't there hell everywhere?

e. རོ་ཞིག་མཐོང་བས་པ་ཕའི་སྙིང་ནད་ལངས་པ་མིན་ནམ་བསམས།

(He) thought, "Because (father) saw a corpse, (perhaps) father's heart disease has started up?" [In colloquial = ñīŋnɛɛ̀ la̲ŋgi mɛ̱ɛ̀dro sām.]

f. བུས་ཨ་ཕའི་རྐང་པའི་རྨ་དེ་དྲག་མིད་དམ་བསམས།

The son thought, "(perhaps) the sore on father's leg is healing?"

If a conditional is used (e.g., g.), a probable future action is conveyed.

g. ཚ་ལུ་མ་ཁ་གཤགས་ན་ལྷ་མོ་གནམ་ལ་འཕུར་མི་ཡོང་ངམ་དགོངས་ནས་སྐྲག།

Thinking, "If (I) split open the orange, will not the goddess fly into the sky?" (he) was frightened. (If I split . . . .probably the goddess will fly . . . .)

h. རྒྱལ་སྲས་ཕྱིར་ལོག་ཕེབས་རྒྱུ་མི་འདུག་པས་འདྲེ་ཡིས་བཟས་པ་མ་ཡིན་ནམ།

Because the prince has not returned, might not a demon have eaten (him)? (perhaps a demon ate him)

i. གལ་ཏེ་ཨ་མ་དང་པ་ཕ་གཉིས་བསྡད་ཡོད་ན་གཏམ་བཟང་འདི་གོ་དུས་དགའ་པོ་ག་ཚད་ཡོང་གི་མ་རེད་དམ་བསམས།

(He) thought, "If mother and father were alive (lit., "living"), when (they) heard this good news how much gladness would they have not had? (i.e., they would have been so happy.)

Another function of this type of construction is to convey "didn't I. . . ?"

j. དམག་མི་ཡོང་གི་རེད་ཞེས་ངས་ཞུས་མ་བྱུང་ངམ།

Didn't I tell you that soldiers will come?

11.16 Double negatives

Tibetan makes frequent use of double negative constructions. There are several common past tense constructions:

1. མ་ + vb. (past) + པ་ + neg. linking verb—མ་བྱས་པ་མ་རེད་
2. vb. + མིན་པ་ +neg. linking verb—བྱེད་རྒྱུ་མིན་པ་མ་རེད་
3. མི་ + vb. (pres. or non-past) + པ་+ ཡོང་གི་མ་རེད་—མི་བྱེད་པ་ཡོང་གི་མ་རེད་
4. མ་ + vb. (past) + པ་ + neg. existential verb—མ་བྱས་པ་ཡོད་པ་མ་རེད་
5. མ་+ vb. (past) + པ་ + བྱུང་ + neg. existential verb—མ་བྱས་པ་བྱུང་མི་འདུག་ (or ཡོད་པ་མ་རེད་)

The first, second, and third of these express the idea that "it is not that the verbal action was not done."

a. ཁོ་ཚོས་ནུར་བརྩོན་མ་བྱས་པ་མ་རེད། དགེ་རྒན་ཡག་པོ་མི་འདུག།

It is not that they were not diligent, (they) did not have a good teacher (the teacher wasn't good). (i.e., it means they were diligent.)

b. ཁོས་ཁ་ལག་འདི་ལ་དགའ་པོ་མ་བྱས་པ་མ་རེད།་ ཁོ་ན་བ་རེད།

It is not that he did not like the food, he was sick.

c. ཁོ་ཚོས་ནུར་བརྩོན་མ་བྱས་པ་མིན་ཀྱང་། ཁོ་ཚོས་ནུར་བརྩོན་མ་བྱས་པ་རེད་ལབ་པ་རེད།

Even though it is not that they didn't work diligently, they said they did not work diligently.

d. ཁོས་ཁ་ལག་བཟོ་རྒྱུ་མིན་པ་མ་རེད།

It is not that he is not going to make food.

e. ཁོས་ངལ་རྩོལ་བྱེད་རྒྱུ་མིན་པ་མིན་ཀྱང་། ཞོར་ལ་སློབ་སྦྱོང་བྱེད་ཀྱི་རེད།

Even though it is not that he will not do (manual) labor (i.e., even though he will do manual labor,) (he)will study in his spare time.

f. ཁོས་བོད་ཀྱི་ལོ་རྒྱུས་མི་ཤོད་པ་ཡོང་གི་མ་རེད།

He will not not talk about Tibetan history. (i.e., he will talk about Tibetan history.)

The fourth and fifth constructions express the idea that "there is nothing with regard to the verbal action that was not done" or "there was nothing (or hasn't been anything) with regard to the verbal action that was not done."

g. ཁོ་ཚོས་ནུར་བརྩོན་མ་བྱས་པ་ཡོད་པ་མ་རེད།

There isn't anything (or there is nothing) they didn't work diligently at.

h. མོས་བོད་པའི་ཁ་ལག་མ་ཟས་པ་བྱུང་ཡོད་པ་མ་རེད།

There is not any Tibetan food that she has not eaten.

Double negative constructions are also used in subordinate clauses. Some typical examples are:

i. ཁོས་ནུར་བརྩོན་མ་བྱས་པ་མེད་ཀྱང་། གཞུང་གིས་ཁོར་བྱ་དགའ་མ་སྤྲད་པ་རེད།

Even though there isn't anything he hasn't done diligently, the government didn't give him a prize.

j. གཞུང་གིས་སྐྱབས་བཅོལ་བ་དེ་ཚོར་རོགས་རམ་མ་བྱས་པ་བྱུང་མེད་ཙང་། ཁོ་ཚོ་ཕྱུག་པོ་ཆགས་པ་རེད།

Because there hasn't been anything that the government hasn't done to help the refugees, they have become rich.

First person constructions take མེད་.

k. ངས་བོད་པའི་གཞས་མ་གོ་བ་མེད།

There isn't any Tibetan song I haven't heard.

Perfect tense double negatives are commonly formed as follows: vb. (past) + མེད་ + པ་ + neg. linking verb.

l. ཁོ་ཚོས་བྲོས་ཐབས་བྱས་མེད་པ་མ་རེད། པུ་ལི་སིས་འཛིན་བཟུང་བྱས་ཡོད་པ་རེད།

It isn't that they (have not tried or) did not try to flee, the police have arrested (them).

m. ཁོས་ལས་ཀ་བྱས་མེད་པ་མིན་པ་མ་ཟད། གྲུབ་འབྲས་ཀྱང་ཡག་པོ་ཐུང་འདུག།

Not only isn't it that they haven't worked, (they) have even achieved a lot [lit., they even got a good result].

By substituting མི་ for མ་, and by using the present (non-past) verb stem, present/usual tense double negative constructions are formed. Note should be made, however, that མ་+ vb. + མ་རེད་ constructions can also be used to express present time if context dictates.

n. ཁོ་ཚོས་ཧུར་བརྩོན་མི་བྱེད་པ་མ་རེད། དགེ་རྒན་ཡག་པོ་མི་འདུག།

It is not that they are not diligent, (they) don't have a good teacher.

o. ཁོས་ལས་ཀ་བྱེད་མི་དགོས་པ་མ་རེད། ཁོ་ན་གི་ཡོད་པ་རེད།

It isn't that he does not have/need to work, he is sick.

p. ཁོ་ཚོས་ཧུར་བརྩོན་མི་བྱེད་པ་མིན་ཡང་། གཞུང་གིས་བྱ་དགའ་སྤྲོད་ཀྱི་ཡོད་པ་མ་རེད།

Even though it isn't that they are not diligent, the government is not giving them a prize.

q. ཁོ་ཚོས་ཁ་ལག་མི་ཟ་བ་ཡོད་པ་མ་རེད།

There is not (does not exist any) food they do not eat.

Double negative constructions also occur with linking and existential verbs.

r. བོད་པའི་ནང་ལ་ནང་པ་མིན་པ་ཡོད་པ་མ་རེད།

Among Tibetans, there is not anyone who is not a Buddhist.

s. རྒྱ་ནག་ལ་གནམ་གྲུ་མེད་པ་མ་རེད།

It is not that China has no planes.

t. ཏང་ནང་ལ་ལོག་སྤྱོད་པ་མེད་པ་མིན་པར་བརྟེན། ལས་འགུལ་ཞིག་བྱེད་དགོས།

Because it is not that there are no reactionaries in the party, (we) must make a campaign (against them).

u. ལུང་པ་དེ་ལ་དམག་མེད་པ་བྱུང་མེད།

In that country, there has never been (a time) without war.

Present (usual) constructions are also formed by: vb. (pres. or non-past) + ཀྱི་མེད་ + པ་ + མ་རེད་.

v. ཁོ་ཚོས་འདེབས་ལས་ཡག་པོ་བྱེད་ཀྱི་མེད་པ་མ་རེད། ད་ལོ་ཆར་པ་ཞེ་དྲགས་བབས་མ་སོང་།

It isn't that they are not planting well, it did not rain a lot this year.

w. དེང་སང་ཁོ་ནང་ལ་སྡོད་ཀྱི་མེད་པ་མ་རེད། མཚན་ལས་བྱེད་པར་འགྲོ་གི་ཡོད་པ་རེད།

It is not that he is not living at home these days, (he) goes to work at night.

Constructions using མི་ + vb. (non-past) + པ་ + བྱེད་ + རྒྱུ་ + neg. existential verb convey the idea of "should not not do" or, put positively, that "the action should be done"

x. ཁྱེད་རང་གིས་མི་སྐྱོ་པོར་རོགས་རམ་མི་བྱེད་པ་བྱེད་རྒྱུ་མེད།

You shouldn't not help the poor people. (i.e., You should help. . . .)

y. ཁོ་ལ་སྐད་ཆ་མི་ཤོད་པ་བྱེད་རྒྱུ་ཡོད་པ་མ་རེད།

(You) shouldn't not talk to him. (i.e., You should talk . . .)

11.17 Double negative constructions with གཏན་ནས་, ཙ་བ་ནས་, ཁྱོན་ནས་, ཀྱོན་ནས་, and ནམ་ཡང་

These emphatic negative terms ("never," "not at all") when used in double negative constructions convey something less than the absolute negative sense. Thus, whereas གཏན་ནས་ཤེས་ཀྱི་མིན་ means "(I) don't know anything (about something)," གཏན་ནས་མ་ཤེས་པ་མིན་ means "it is not that (I) don't know anything (about something)" (i.e., I know a little).

a. གནས་བསྐོར་བ་དེ་ཚོས་ལམ་ཀ་གཏན་ནས་མ་ཤེས་པ་མིན་ཀྱང་། གསལ་པོ་ཤེས་ཀྱི་མི་འདུག།

Even though the pilgrims did not completely not know the road, (they) did not know it clearly.

b. ཁོང་བོད་ལ་ཐེངས་མང་པོ་ཕེབས་མེད་ཀྱང་། ཙ་བ་ནས་ཕེབས་མ་མྱོང་བ་མ་རེད།

Even though he hasn't gone to Tibet many times, it is not that (he) has never experienced going there.

c. བཀྲིས་ཀྱིས་ཆང་གཏན་ནས་མ་འཐུང་བ་མིན་ཀྱང་། ཞེ་དྲགས་འཐུང་གི་མི་འདུག།

Even though Tashi has not never drunk beer, he doesn't drink much.

d. འབྲོག་པས་ནམ་རྒྱུན་ཆང་འཐུང་གི་མེད་ཀྱང་། ཙ་བ་ནས་མ་འཐུང་བ་མ་རེད།

Even though nomads usually do not drink beer, it is not that (they) never drink it.

e. དེང་སང་ལྷ་སར་ལྟ་སྐོར་བ་མང་པོ་གཏོང་གི་ཡོད་པ་མ་རེད་དེ། ཙ་བ་ནས་མི་གཏོང་བ་མ་རེད།

Even though these days (they) are not sending (allowing) many tourists to go to Lhasa, it is not that (they) are completely not sending (them).

f. ཕྲུ་གུ་དེས་སློབ་གྲྭར་གཏན་ནས་མ་ཕྱིན་པ་བྱས་མེད་པ་མ་ཟད། དགོང་མོ་ནང་ལ་མ་ལོག་པ་ཡང་བྱེད་ཀྱི་ཡོད་པ་མ་རེད།

Not only does this child never not go to school, (he) even doesn't not return home in the evening. (He sometimes goes to school and returns home in the evening.)

11.18 Double negative constructions with ཐུབ་, དྲན་, མཐོང་, བསམ་, and ཤེས་

a. ཁོས་བོད་ཀྱི་ལོ་རྒྱུས་ཤོད་མི་ཐུབ་པ་ཡོང་གི་མ་རེད།

It won't come about that he won't be able to talk (about) Tibetan history.
(He will (definitely) be able to talk (about) Tibetan history.)

Note the difference when we switch to an existential verb:

b. ཁོས་བོད་ཀྱི་ལོ་རྒྱུས་ཤོད་མི་ཐུབ་པ་ཡོད་པ་མ་རེད།
There is nothing (about) Tibetan history he is unable to talk (about).

c. ཁོས་ངལ་རྩོལ་མ་ཐུབ་པ་མིན་ཙང་ང་ཚོས་མི་གླར་གླ་དགོས།
We have to hire (him) because he is not unable to do hard work.

d. ཁོ་ཡོང་མ་ཐུབ་པ་མ་རེད། མ་ཡོང་བ་རེད།
Its not that he was unable to come, (he) didn't come.

e. ཁོ་ཚོའི་ནང་ནས་བོད་ཡིག་འབྲི་ཀློག་མི་ཐུབ་པ་ཡོད་པ་མ་རེད།
There is no one among them who is unable to read and write Tibetan.

f. ཁོ་འདིར་ཡོང་རྒྱུ་མིན་པ་དྲན་མ་སོང་།
(He) didn't remember that he wasn't coming here.

g. ཁོས་ནང་ལ་མ་བསྡད་པ་མཐོང་མ་བྱུང་།
(I) didn't see him (when) he was not staying at home. (I never saw him not staying at home.)

h. ཁོས་བོད་ཀྱི་ལོ་རྒྱུས་མི་ཤེས་པ་མ་རེད། བཤད་འདོད་མེད་པ་རེད།
It is not that he doesn't know Tibetan history, (he) doesn't want to talk (about it).

11.19 Constructions with ག་: vb.+ ག་ + བྱེད་ or བྱས་

This pattern conveys a number of rather different meanings. The first is to "try to" do the verbal action.

a. ཁོས་དགག་པ་རྒྱབ་ག་བྱས་པ་རེད་དེ། མ་ཐོབ་པ་རེད།
Even though he tried to rebut (it), (he) did not win.

This conveys that the speaker did not really think he could win but tried anyway.

A second common meaning for this construction is to "pretend to" do the verbal action:

b. ཁོས་འགྲོ་ག་བྱས་ནས་ཉལ་བསྡད་པ་རེད།
Pretending to go (out), he slept.

c. ཁོས་བཙོང་ག་བྱས་ནས་སྦས་པ་རེད།
Pretending to sell it, he hid it.

A third usage conveys that the speaker does not like something or considers the action done to be inappropriate. For example:

d. ཁོས་ཁང་པ་རྒྱབ་ག་བྱས་ནས་རྣོགས་ཁྲ་བཟོས་པ་རེད།

Because he built a house it brought problems.
This sentence conveys that the writer feels the subject did not have to build the house.

11.20 Reading exercises

11.20.1 Reading number one: "The Urine of the Precious Gem"

11.20.1.1 Tibetan text

༄༅། །ནོར་གཅིན་བཏང་པ།1

སྔར་བོད་ཀྱི་ལྷོ་ཕྱོགས་སྨེ་གདོང་ཞེར་བའི་ཡུལ་ན་2 སྨེ་གདོང་རྒྱལ་པོ་ཞེར་བ་ཞིག་ཡོད་པ་དེར་3 བློན་པོ་ཉི་ཆོས་བཟང་པོ་ཞེར་བའི་བློ་རིག་ཏ་ཙང་བཀྲ་བ་ཞིག་4 ཡོད། ཉིན་ཞིག་ཉི་ཆོས་བཟང་པོས་རྒྱལ་པོར་ཞུས་པར5། རྒྱལ་པོ་རིན་པོ་ཆེ6། གཞན་གྱིས་རྒྱ་ཆེའི་ནོར་བུ་རྣམས་ཕྱིར་བཏོན་ནས་འོད་ཞེར་འཕྲོ་རུ་འཇུག7 གི་ཡོད་པ་དེ་ནི་8 བརྗིད་ཉམས་ལྡན་ཞིང་9 སྙན་གྲགས་ཆེན་པོ་འདུག། ང་ཚོའི་ནོར་བུ་རྣམས་བང་མཛོད་ནང་དུ་བཙུག་ནས་བཞག་པ་དེར་ཚོ་མེད་པ་ཞིག་རེད། ཅེས་ཞུས་པར། རྒྱལ་པོས་དེ་འདྲ་ཡིན་ན་ང་ཚོས་བང་མཛོད་ནང་ནས་ནོར་བུ་རྒྱ་བ་ཆེ་ཤོས་དེ་བཏོན་ཏེ་སང་ཉིན་ཉི་ཆོས་བཟང་པོ་ཁྱོད་ཀྱིས་འོད་ཞེར་འཕྲོ་རུ་འཇུག་དགོས་ཞེས་བཤད།

དེའི་སང་ཉིན་སྔ་དྲོ་ཉི་ཤར་གྱི་མཚམས་སུ་10 ཉི་ཆོས་བཟང་པོས་རྒྱལ་པོའི་ནོར་བུ་རྒྱ་འགངས་ཆེ་ཤོས་དེ་བང་མཛོད་ནང་ནས་བཏོན་ཏེ་རང་ཉིད་ཀྱི་ཁྱིམ་དུ་སྦས་རྗེས་ལམ་སེང་རྒྱ་འགྲམ་དུ་ཕྱིན་ནས་འཁྱག་པ་ཆེན་པོ་ཞིག་བཀོག་སྨེ་རྒྱལ་པོའི་ཕོ་བྲང་གི་ནུབ་ངོས་རི་ལྡིབས་ཤིག་གི་ཐོག་ཏུ་བསླངས་ནས་བཞག་པ་དེར་11 ཉི་འོད་ཕོག་པའི་སྐབས་སུ་དངོས་འབྲེལ་འོད་ཞེར་ཆེན་པོ་སྤྲོ་བཞིན་ཡོད། སྐབས་དེར་ཉི་ཆོས་བཟང་པོས་མགྱོགས་མྱུར་རྒྱལ་པོའི་དྲུང་དུ་རྒྱུགས་ཕྱིན་ནས།12 རྒྱལ་པོ་རིན་པོ་ཆེ། རྒྱང་ཤེལ་བསྣམས་ཏེ་ཕོ་བྲང་གི་ཡང་སྟེང་ནས་ནོར་བུའི་བརྗིད་ཉམས་ལྡན་པའི་འོད་ཞེར་ལ་གཟིགས་པར་ཕེབས་དང་།13 ཞེས་བཤད་པར། རྒྱལ་པོས་ཤེལ་འཚབ་དང་བློན་འཁོར་14 ཚང་མ་འཁྲིད་དེ་ཕོ་བྲང་གི་ཡང་སྟེང་ནས་ལྟ་སྐབས་རྒྱལ་པོའི་བསམ་པར་ནོར་བུའི་འོད་ཞེར་དངོས་འབྲེལ་འཕྲོ་བཞིན་འདུག་སྙམ་ཏེ་དགའ་ཐག་ཆོད་ནས་ཉིན་གུང་གི་ལྟོ་ཆས་ཀྱང་ཕོ་བྲང་གི་ཡང་སྟེང་དུ་བཟས་ཏེ་ཉིན་གང་བལྟས་པའི་མཐར་15 ཕྱི་དྲོ་ཉི་མ་བཞུད་ལ་ཉེ་བའི་སྐབས་སུ་16 ནོར་བུའི་འོད་ཞེར་ཆུང་དུ་ཆུང་དུ་འགྲོ་བཞིན་འདུག་པས་ཁྱོད་རང་ཕ་གིར་མགྱོགས་མྱུར་ལྟ་བར་རྒྱུགས་དང་ཞེས་བཤད་པ་ལྟར་17 ཉི་ཆོས་བཟང་པོས་ལྟ་བར་ཕྱིན་རྗེས་ཚུར་རྒྱུགས་ཡོང་18 ནས་ད་ནི་དཔེ་བསགས་འདུག། ནོར་བུས་ནོར་གཅིན་བཏང་ནས་བྲོས་ཕྱིན་འདུག། རྒྱལ་པོ་རིན་པོ་ཆེ། མགྱོགས་པོ་ཕ་གིར་ནོར་བུ་བཞག་སར་གཟིགས་པར་ཕེབས་དང་ཞེས་ཞུས་པར་རྒྱལ་པོས་སྐད་ཆ་དེ་ཐོས་འཕྲལ་ལྟ་བར་ཕྱིན།

ཕ་གིར་སླེབས་སྐབས་དངོས་འབྲེལ་འཁྱགས་པ་བཞུར་བའི་བཞའ་བརྟན་ཏོག་ཙམ་ལས་མེད་པ་མཐོང་སྐབས་རྒྱལ་པོས་ད་

ཉི་དཔེ་བསམགས་འདུག། ད་ཇི་ལྟར་བྱས་ན་ལེགས།19 དེའི་འདྲའི་ནོར་བུའི་ཕངས་པ་ལ་ཡང་20 ཞེས་བཤད་ནས་ག་བྱེད་འདི་
བྱེད་མེད་པར་གྱུར21 ༎

11.20.1.2 Translation

The Urine of the Precious Gem

Formerly, in the area in southern Tibet called Nedong, there was a king called King Nedong who had a very intelligent minister called Ñijösaŋbo. One day Ñijösaŋbo said to the king, "King Rimpoche, others take out their precious gems and make them sparkle in the light. As for that, it is a grand and fame-producing thing. Leaving our precious gems in our storeroom is senseless." The king said, "If that is so, then take out our most precious gem and you, Ñijösaŋbo, make it shine in the light tomorrow."

The next day, early, at the time the sun rose, Ñijösaŋbo took out the king's most precious gem from the treasury and took it to his house and buried it there. After this, he immediately went to the bank of a river, broke off a piece of ice, and (went) up the side of a hill to the west of the king's palace and left it standing up there. At the time when the sun's rays hit that, there really was a great glittering. At that time, Ñijösaŋbo quickly went running to the king and said, "King Rimpoche, bring a telescope. Come to see a glorious glittering gem from the roof of the palace."

The king hurried, taking along all his retinue and ministers. When they looked from the roof of the palace the king thought in his mind, "The gem's glitter is really shining," and was extremely happy. He even ate his noon meal on the roof, (staying) looking all day. Finally, in the late afternoon when the sun was close to setting, because the glitter from the gem was getting less and less, (the king) said, "You go quickly over there to look!" Accordingly, Ñijösaŋbo went to look and afterwards came running back and said, "Oh my goodness. The gem has urinated gem-urine and fled away. King Rimpoche, go at once to the place where the gem was left to see." The king went to look as soon as he heard this.

When he arrived over there, he really saw only (nothing other than) the wetness of the melted ice. He said at that time, "Now, oh my goodness. Now what is better to do? Oh, what a shame (to lose) a gem such as this." And there was nothing he could do.

11.20.1.3 Grammatical notes

1. The title is a cryptic phrase meaning "gem-urination." It is actually an abbreviation of the phrase ནོར་བུས་ནོར་གཅིན་བཏང་, which means "(by) the precious gem did a gem-urination." The normal term for "urinate" is གཅིན་པ་བཏང་ but here the story embellishes by indicating that a gem urinated, calling it a gem-urination, although at this point what that really means is not clear. Linguistically, the phrase is constructed by adding the first syllable of the word gem (ནོར་) to urine (ནོར་ + གཅིན་) and dropping the པ་ in གཅིན་པ་བཏང་.

2. ན་ as used here in ཡུལ་ན་ conveys neither the "if" verbal connective, nor the verb "be sick." Instead it is another of the dative-locative particles meaning "in," "at," "to."

3. དེར་ marks the subject in what is basically an existential sentence ("to the king, existed X"—སྣེ་གདོང་རྒྱལ་པོ་...དེར་...X...ཡོད). Between སྣེ་གདོང་རྒྱལ་པོ་ and དེར་ is the nominalized phrase ཟེར་བ་ཞིག་ཡོད་པ་, which means "was one who was called." Thus, the entire construction means "to that one who was called Nedong King. . . ."

4. The phrase བློ་རིག་དྲ་ཅང་བཀྲ་བ་ཞིག་ breaks down into བློ་རིག་ ("intellect"), དྲ་ཅང་ ("very"), བཀྲ་བ་ ("bright, sharp"), and ཞིག་ ("a/one"). Together they mean "one who was very intelligent." It is modified via the genitive to བློན་པོ་ཉི་ཆོས་བཟང་པོ་ཟེར་བའི་ ("who was called Minister Ñijösaŋbo"). These together convey "one who was very intelligent who was called Minister Ñijösaŋbo." They tell what the King had: "he had one who was very intelligent called. . . ."

5. The ར་ in ཞུས་པར་ is an example of the dative-locative used with nominalized verb stems to convey "concerning" the verbal action (see 6.6.3). Here it is used to introduce the minister's direct speech, i.e., what he said to the king. It would be translated literally as "concerning what the minister said to the king."

6. The use of རིན་པོ་ཆེ་ here does not convey that the king was an incarnate lama. It is used merely as a polite honorific.

7. See 11.7.1 for the explanation of འཇུག་. Here ཕྱིར་བཏོན་ནས་འོད་ཟེར་འཕྲོ་རུ་འཇུག་ conveys that after taking it out (of the treasury), he made it so that it shone.

8. The particle ནི་ marks the completion of the nominalized subject of this existential construction ("X is Y"). The X is "as for others making (their) precious gems shine" (གཞན་གྱིས་རྩ་ཆེའི་ནོར་བུ་རྣམས་ཕྱིར་བཏོན་ནས་འོད་ཟེར་འཕྲོ་རུ་འཇུག་གི་ཡོད་པ་དེ་ནི་).

9. The particle ཞིང་ functions here as an adjectival conjunctive (see 10.3.7), joining བརྗོད་

ཉམས་ལྡན་ and སྙན་གྲགས་ཆེན་པོ་.

10. The particle མཚམས་སུ་ is one of the "when" connectives (5.10).

11. The phrase བསྒྲངས་ནས་བཞག་ means "having set (it) up, left it." It is modified by a phrase indicating the location of the "setting up": ནུབ་ངོས་རི་ལྡེབས་ཤིག་གི་ཐོག་ཏུ་ ("on the face of a mountain in the west"). The last portion of the phrase (པ་དེར་) nominalizes it: བསྒྲངས་ནས་བཞག་པ་དེར་ ("to that which was set up and left ").

12. The combination རྒྱུག་ཕྱིན་ is a typical pattern conveying simultaneous action, in this case, "went running."

13. The particle དང་ functions here as a polite imperative conveying "please" come (7.12).

14. Tibetan authors frequently use abbreviations such as བློན་འཁོར་, which consists of the first syllables of both བློན་པོ་ ("minister") and འཁོར་བཅས་ ("retinue").

15. མཐར་ ("finally, in the end, at last") is a word that usually is placed at the start of the second of two syllables (མོས་བོད་ཡིག་ལོ་མང་པོ་སློབ་སྦྱོང་བྱས་པ་དང་། མཐར་བོད་ཡིག་ཤེས་པ་རེད་). It is used here, however, as a verbal clause connective being joined to the verb by the genitive particle. It conveys, "looked all day, and in the end. . . ."

16. (ལ་) ཉེ་བའི་སྐབས་སུ་ is a phrase conveying "at the time when it was close to. . . .."

17. ལྟར་ occurs with nominalized verbs to convey "like" or "in accordance with" or "in the manner of." Here it means "in accordance with what he said."

18. རྒྱུགས་ཡོང་—like རྒྱུག་ཕྱིན་—also conveys simultaneous action—"came running." Note that རྒྱུགས་ is sometimes spelled with a final "s."

19. ཇི་ལྟར་ + vb. + ན་ + ལེགས་ is a common construction that means, "how is it best to do the verbal action?"

20. ཕངས་པ་ལ་ཨང་ is a common spoken phrase meaning "Oh, what a shame."

21. ག་བྱེད་འདི་བྱེད་མེད་པར་གྱུར་ is a common phrase meaning"he came into a state in which there was nothing that could be done."

11.20.2 Reading number two: "The Origin of Shodön [The "Curd" or "Opera" Festival]"

11.20.2.1 Tibetan text

ཞོ་སྟོན་གྱི་ཡོང་ཁུངས་

ཞོ་སྟོན་ཞེས་པ་ནི་བོད་ཟླ་དྲུག་པའི་གནམ་གང་ནས་འགོ་བཙུགས་ཏེ་བདུན་ཕྲག་ཁ་ཤས་རིང་སྒྱུ་རྩལ་འཁྲབ་ནས་ལྷ་སར་སྤྲོ་སྐྱིད་གཏོང་བའི་དུས་སྟོན་ཞིག་རེད། སྔར་གཞུང་ས་དགའ་ལྡན་ཕོ་བྲང་གིས་1 ཞོ་སྟོན་བྱེད་སྒོ་ཁག་2 འབྲས་སྤུངས་དགོན་པར་བྱེད་སྲོལ་3 བྱུང་འདུག། དེའི་དུས་བོད་ལ་ལྷ་མོ་ཚོགས་པ་ཁག་བཅུ་གཉིས་ཡོད་པ་ཚང་མ་4 ལོ་ལྟར་དུས་ཚོད་དེར་འབྲས་སྤུངས་དགོན་པར་འཁྲབ་སྟོན་དུ་ཡོང་5 དགོས་ཀྱི་ཡོད་པ་རེད།

བོད་ཀྱི་ལྷ་མོ་ནི་སྔར་གྲུབ་ཐོབ་ཐང་སྟོང་རྒྱལ་པོ་ཟེར་མཁན་བོད་ལ་ལྕགས་ཐག་ཟམ་པ་ཁག་བརྒྱ་ལྷག་ཙམ་རྒྱབ་མྱོང་ཡོད་པ་དེས་6 ལྕགས་ཟམ་གྱི་འགྲོ་སོང་གཏོང་ཆེད་དུ། ལྷ་སའི་ནུབ་ངོས་ཀྱི་ཆུ་ཤུལ་ལྕགས་ཟམ་ལས་གྲྭ་7 ནས་ཕོ་མོ་མཛེས་པ་དང་སྐད་གདངས་ལེགས་པ་འདམ་གསེས་ཀྱིས་གླུ་གར་ཚོགས་པ་ཞིག་སྒྲིག་འཛུགས་བྱས། ཚོགས་པ་དེས་ལྷ་སའི་མང་ཚོགས་ལ་འཁྲབ་སྟོན་བྱས་སྐབས་མང་ཚོགས་རྣམས་ཧང་སངས་ཏེ་གླུ་གར་བ་རྣམས་ལྷ་ཡུལ་ནས་ཕེབས་པའི་ལྷ་མོ་ནང་བཞིན་འདུག་ཅེས་བསྔགས་བརྗོད་བྱས་པ་དེ་ནས་བཟུང་ལྷ་མོ་ཟེར་བའི་ཐ་སྙད་དེ་ཆགས་པ་རེད། ད་བར་ལྷ་མོའི་འཁྲབ་གཞུང་དུ། འགྲོ་བ་བཟང་མོ་དང་། སྣང་ས་འོད་འབུམ། གཟུགས་ཀྱི་ཉི་མ། པད་མ་འོད་འབར། ཆོས་རྒྱལ་ནོར་བཟང་། གཙུང་པོ་དོན་ཡོད་དོན་གྲུབ། དྲི་མེད་ཀུན་ལྡན། རྒྱ་བཟའ་བལ་བཟའ། རས་ཆུང་སོགས་ཡོད་པ་རེད།

དཔེར་ན་འགྲོ་བ་བཟང་མོའི་འཁྲབ་གཞུང་དུ་སྔར་མོན་དུ་རྒྱལ་པོ་ཀ་ལ་དབང་པོ་ཟེར་བ་ཞིག་ལ་བཙུན་མོ་ཧ་ཤང་བདུད་མོ་ཟེར་མཁན་ཞིག་ཡོད། ཉིན་ཞིག་རྒྱལ་པོ་རི་དྭགས་རྒྱག་པར་འགྲོ་དུས་རྒྱལ་པོའི་ཁྱི་བརླག་པ་འཚོལ་དུ་འགྲོ་སར་8 མི་ཚང་གཅིག་ལ་རྒན་རྒོན་གཉིས་དང་བུ་མོ་ཧ་ཅང་གི་མཛེས་མ་འགྲོ་བ་བཟང་མོ་ཟེར་བ་ཞིག་བཅས་9 ཡོད་པ་རེད། བུ་མོ་དེ་རྒྱལ་པོས་མཐོང་མ་ཐག་རྒྱལ་པོ་ཤིན་ཏུ་དགའ་ནས་ལམ་སེང་བཀའ་བཏང་སྟེ་བུ་མོ་དེ་རང་གི་མནའ་མར་བསྐོང་10 སྐྱེ་སྲས་སྲོས་ཡང་གཉིས་བྱུང་བ་རེད།

བཙུན་མོ་ཧ་ཤང་བདུད་མོས་དེ་ལ་མི་དགའ་བ་ཆེན་པོ་11 བྱས་ཏེ་རང་ལ་དགའ་བའི་12 བློན་པོ་དང་ངན་འབྲེལ་གྱིས་རྒྱལ་པོ་བཙོན་དུ་བཙུག་པ་དང་འགྲོ་བ་བཟང་མོ་གསོད་གྲབས་བྱས་13 ཀུང་མོ་རྫུ་འཕྲུལ་གྱིས་གནམ་ལ་འཕུར་སྐབས་བསད་མ་ཐུབ་པར་ཤོར།14 འོན་ཀྱང་ཕྲུ་གུ་གཉིས་བྲོས་མ་ཐུབ་སྐབས་ཧ་ཤང་བདུད་མོས་ལམ་སེང་ཐག་རིང་དུ་གསོད་པར་གཏོང་དུས་གསོད་མཁན་གྱིས་བུ་མོ་དེར་སྙིང་རྗེ་ནས་གསོད་མ་ནུས་པར་བཞག་པས་ལུས།15 བུ་དེ་ནི་རི་སྟེང་ནས་མར་དབྱུགས་ཀྱང་ཨ་མའི་སྤྲུལ་པ་རྒོད་དཀར་པོའི་གཤོག་པའི་སྟེང་དུ་བབས་པས་མ་ཤི་བ་རེད། བུ་ལྷ་སྲས་རྒྱལ་པོ་དེ་ཡུལ་པད་མ་ཅན་ཟེར་བར་སླེབས་སྐབས་ལུང་པ

དེའི་མི་སེར་རྣམས་ནས་ཁོང་རྒྱལ་པོར་བསྐོས། རྒྱལ་པོ་དེས་དམག་དྲང་ནས་ཏ་ཤང་བདུད་མོ་དང་དམག་འཐབ་མཐར་བདུད་མོ་ཕམ་ནས་ཤི་བ་དང་། རང་གི་ཕ་ཀ་ལ་དབང་པོ་བཙོན་ཁང་ནས་བཏོན་ཞིང་མ་འགྲོ་བ་བཟང་མོ་ནམ་མཁའ་ནས་ཕྱིར་ཕེབས་ཐུབ་པ་བྱུང་། རྒྱལ་བཙུན་གཉིས་ཀྱིས་ཀྱང་དུས་ཡུན་གང་ཙམ་ནས་བུ་མོ་ལྷ་གཅིག་ཀུན་བཟང་ཙད་ཆོད་ནས་རང་ཡུལ་དུ་འབྱོར། རྒྱལ་པོ་ཀ་ལ་དབང་པོས་ཐུར་བཞིན་རྒྱལ་སྲིད་བསྐྱངས་པས་མི་སེར་ཚང་མར་བདེ་སྐྱིད་ཆེན་པོ་བྱུང་བ་རེད།

རྗེས་སུ་རྒྱལ་བ་སྐུ་འཕྲེང་བདུན་པ་སྐལ་བཟང་རྒྱ་མཚོའི་སྐབས་ནས་ལྷ་མོ་མང་ཆེ་བ་འབྲས་སྤུངས་ནས་ནོར་བུ་གླིང་ཁར་སྤོས་ཏེ་ཞོ་སྟོན་ལྷ་མོ་འཁྲབ་ཡུལ་གཙོ་བོ་དེ་ནོར་བུ་གླིང་ཁར་གྱུར་པ་རེད།

ལྷ་མོ་བ་ཚང་མས་ཆོས་ཉི་ཤུ་དགུའི་ཉིན་ཙེ་ཕུག་ལས་ཁྲུངས་སུ་འགྱུར་ཕྱོ་བཀོད། དེ་ནས་འབྲས་སྤུངས་ཕོ་བྲང་དུ་གཟིགས་ཕུད་ཕུལ་ཏེ་འབྲས་སྤུངས་དགོན་པའི་ནང་འཁྲབ་གཞུང་མི་འདྲ་བ་ཁག་བགོས་ཀྱིས་འཁྲབ་སྲོལ་ཡོད། ལྷ་ས་དང་གྲོང་གསེབ་ཡས་མས་ནས་ལྟད་མོ་བ་མང་པོ་དེ་ཉིན་འབྲས་སྤུངས་དགོན་པར་འཛོམས་ཤིང་འབྲས་སྤུངས་པ་ཚོས་འགྲུལ་པ་ཚོར་སྐྱེ་ལེན་གང་ཟབ་16 བྱེད་ཀྱི་རེད། ཟེར་སྲོལ་ལ། འབྲས་སྤུངས་ཞོ་སྟོན་སྐད་གྲགས་ཆེན་པོ་དེས། གྲྭ་པ་གྲྭ་རྐྱང་17 སྤྲང་པོར་བཏང་།18 ཞེས་པའང་དེ་ནས་བྱུང་བ་རེད། ཞོ་སྟོན་དེ་ནི་འབྲས་སྤུངས་དགོན་པར་དགེ་འདུན་རྣམས་དབྱར་གནས་ཞེས་ཆར་དུས་ཀྱི་མཚམས་སུ་བཞུགས་པའི་སྐབས་དང་བསྟུན་གནའ་བོའི་དུས་སུ་ཞོ་ཡི་སྟོན་མོ་དྲངས་སྲོལ་ནས་ཞོ་སྟོན་ཞེས་གྲགས་པ་རེད།19

བོད་ཟླ་བདུན་པའི་ཚེས་གཅིག་ཉིན་ནོར་གླིང་20 ཕོ་བྲང་དུ་ཞལ་ཕུད་འབུལ་བ་དང་དེ་ནས་བདུན་གཅིག་རིང་ལྷ་མོའི་ལོ་རྒྱུས་རེ་21 ཉིན་གང་འཁྲབ་དེ་དགོང་མོ་དམག་སྒར་ཁག་ནས་རུ་སྒྲིག་ས་ལམ་ཡང་ཞུ་སྲོལ་ཡོད།

དེ་ནས་ལྷ་མོའི་ཚོགས་པ་ཁག་ཚོས་ལྷ་སའི་ནང་གི་སྐུ་དྲག་ཁག་དང་ལྟ་སྤྲང་ཁག་ལ་འཁྲབ་སྟོན་བྱེད་པ་དང་། འཁྲབ་སྟོན་སྐབས་ ལྷ་མོ་བ་ཚང་མར་ཁ་བཏགས་གཡོག་པ་དང་ཇ་འབྲུ་དངུལ་བཅས་ཀྱི་གསོལ་རས་ཆེན་པོ་གནང་ཡོང་།22 དེ་ནས་ལྷ་མོ་འཁྲབ་མཁན་ཁྲིས་ལྷ་རྒྱལ་འཐེན་པ་དང་། ད་དུང་སྦྱིན་བདག་ལ་བྱ་བ་ལམ་འགྲོ23 དང་། སྐུ་ཚེ་བར་ཆད་མི་ཡོང་བའི་སྨོན་འདུན་ཡང་ཞུ་གི་ཡོད་པ་རེད། ལྷ་མོ་བ་ཚོ་ལྷ་སར་ཡོང་དགོས་པའི་རྒྱུ་རྐྱེན་ནི་གཞུང་གི་ལྷ་མོའི་ཁྲལ་ཞིག་རེད།

སྤྱི་ཚོགས་རྙིང་པའི་ནང་དུ་སྐད་གྲགས་ཡོད་པའི་ལྷ་མོའི་ཚོགས་པ་སྐྱོར་མོ་ལུང་བ་ཕུད། དེ་མིན་24 ཚང་མ་གྲོང་གསེབ་ཁག་ནས་ཡོང་པ་ཤ་སྟག་25 རེད། དཔེར་ན་གྲོང་གསེབ་ནས་ཡོང་བའི་ལྷ་མོ་བ་ཚོས་ལྷ་སར་ལྷ་མོ་འཁྲབ་པའི་དུས་ཚོད་ཕུད། རྒྱུན་དུ་གྲོང་གསེབ་ནང་ཞིང་ལས་བྱེད་ཀྱི་ཡོད་པ་རེད། ལྷ་མོ་ཚོགས་པ་བཀྲིས་ཤོལ་པ་ནི་ལྷོ་ཁ་ཡར་ལུང་ནས་ཡིན་པ་དང་། དེ་བཞིན་གཙང་པ་ནི་སྟོད་ངམ་རིང་། རྒྱང་དཀར་བ་རིན་སྤུངས་ནས་རེད།

རིག་གནས་གསར་བརྗེ་ཆེན་པོའི་ནང་རྙིང་གཏོར་གསར་འཛུགས་ཟེར་བའི་ལས་འགུལ་ཚུགས་ནས་བོད་ཀྱི་ཆོས་ལུགས་དང་རིག་གནས་ཡུལ་སྲོལ་གཤིས་ལུགས་སོགས་ལ་གཏོར་བཤིག་ཚབས་ཆེན་བྱུང་སྐབས་བོད་དུ་ལྷ་མོ་ཡང་རྩ་བ་ནས་འཁྲབ་དུ་མ་

བཙུག་པ་རེད། ༡༩༨༠ ལོ་ནས་བཟུང་སྲིད་ཇུས་ལྷུག་ཏུ་སོང་ནས་ལྷ་མོ་རིམ་བཞིན་འཁྲབ་མགོ་ཚུགས་པ་དང་། ༡༩༨༥ ལོ་ནས་བཟུང་ཞོ་སྟོན་ཡང་བསྐྱར་གསོ་བྱུང་ཡོད་པ་རེད། ད་ལྟའི་སྐྱོ་མོ་ལུང་པ་ནི་བོད་ལྗོངས་ལྷ་མོ་ཚོགས་པ་ཡིན་པ་དང་། ལྷ་མོ་བ་ཚོའི་ཕོགས་ཀྱང་རྒྱལ་ཁབ་རང་ནས་སྤྲོད་ཀྱི་ཡོད་པ་རེད། དེ་མིན་ལྷ་མོ་ཚོགས་པ་གཞན་དག་ཚང་མ་ལས་ཞོར་ལྷ་མོ་ཚོགས་པ་རྐྱང་རྐྱང་རེད།།

11.20.2.2 Translation

The Origin of Shodön [The "Curd" or "Opera" Festival]

Shodön is the festival that begins on the 30th day of the 6th month of the Tibetan calendar. It goes on for several weeks after that (date), with artistic performances and picnics (being held) in Lhasa. In the past, the custom arose whereby the Tibetan government held this opera festival in Drepung monastery. All twelve opera (literally "goddess") associations had to gather annually at Drepung monastery to perform the operas at this time.

As for (the origin of the) Tibetan opera:

The yogin called Tangdong Gyebo, (the one) who had constructed more than one hundred iron-link bridges in Tibet, (began it) in the past in order to pay for the expenses of the iron bridges. He selected attractive girls and boys with good voices from a work site at Chushul (south of Lhasa) and organized (them into) a dance troupe. When they performed the opera in Lhasa, all the people were surprised and said that it was as if the performers had come from the realm of the gods. They received so much praise from the public that from that time onward the name "lhamo" ("goddess") came (into use for their performances) As of now, there (are a number of) opera stories such as: Drowasangmo, Nangsaömbum, Sugiñima, Pemeömbar, Chögyenorsang, Jungpo Dönyödöndrup, Drimegunden, Gyasabesa, and Rechung.

(To give an) example (of the plot of an opera, let us take) the play Drowasangmo: A long time ago in Mon there was a king called Galawangbo who had a queen called Hashangdümo. One day when the king was going hunting he lost his dog, and at the place where he was looking for it, he met a family consisting of an old couple and a very beautiful girl whose name was Drowasangmo. As soon as the king saw the girl he felt extremely happy and summoned the girl to the palace as his bride. After that they had two children.

Queen Hashangdümo did not like that at all and, conspiring with ministers who liked her, put the king in prison and tried to kill Drowasangmo. However, she flew into the sky and escaped, so they couldn't kill her. Nevertheless her two children were not able to run away. Hashangdümo immediately ordered them taken to a remote area and killed. At this time the men taking them felt compassion for the girl and did not dare to kill her. As for the boy, they threw him from a high mountain but a white vulture who was an emanation of his mother came at once and carried him on (its) wings, saving his life. When Lhasegyebo, the boy, reached the place called "Pemajen," the local people selected him as their king. He then sent his soldiers (to) battle with Hashangdümo. She was finally defeated and died. Then Lhasegyebo took his father, Galawangbo, out of prison and his mother, Drowasangmo, was able to return from the sky. Some years later, the king and queen were also able to find out about their daughter, Lhachikgünsang, and she arrived back home. King Galawangbo ruled his country like before, and because of this all the people were very happy.

Later, (during) the era of the 7th Dalai Lama, most of the operas moved from Drepung to Norbulingka, which became the main site of the Shodön opera performances.

On the 29th, all of the opera associations register their arrival with the Tseja Office. After that, they perform their "first day" show in the "Palace" at Drepung. Having done that, there is a custom that they divide into groups and perform different operas in Drepung monastery. On that day many guests from Lhasa and the nearby villages gather at Drepung, so the Drepungers (the monks) welcome the guests excellently (with generous hospitality). Thus there is a saying, "The famous Drepung opera festival makes a common monk a beggar." This opera festival is called Shodön because long ago at the time the monks stayed in the monastery during the rainy season at "summer retreat" there was a custom of inviting (them to a) party (at which) curds (were served), and therefore it became known as the "curd festival."

On the 1st day of the 7th month of the Tibetan calendar they have to perform the "offering show" at Norbulingka palace. After that, for one week, each opera is performed for a whole day. It is a tradition that in the evening (at the end of the performances), soldiers of the different regiments line up in rows to salute them (the performers).

After that, the troupes perform for aristocratic families and for high lamas at their residences in Lhasa. At the time of the performance, all the opera performers have scarves put around their necks and will be given a large present consisting of tea, barley, and money. The opera performers shout at this time, "May the gods be victorious," and also offer wishes for the patrons (donors) to have success in their business and no harm in their lives. The reason for these opera troupes having to come to Lhasa is that there was a government opera tax.

In the "old society," with the exception of the famous Gyomo lunga opera troupe, all the others came only from villages. The opera troupes who came from the villages were always (engaged in) doing agricultural work except when they come to Lhasa to perform. As for the opera association Tashishöpa, it is from Yarlung in Lhoka. Similarly, Jungba is from Ngamring in Dö, and Gyang karwa is from Rimpung.

During the Great Cultural Revolution a movement called "Destroy the old, begin the new" was started and such things as Tibetan religion, culture, and native customs were seriously destroyed. At this time in Tibet the opera performances also were absolutely not allowed. Since 1980, the government policy has become looser and opera performances were gradually started. Since 1985, the Opera Festival also started again. Gyomo lunga currently is the Tibet National Opera Association, their salary being paid by the state. Besides this, all the other groups are just spare-time opera associations.

11.20.2.3 Grammatical notes

1. དགའ་ལྡན་ཕོ་བྲང་ was the name of the Dalai Lama's residence in Drepung monastery at the time of the 5th Dalai Lama and became the name of the government he headed. གཞུང་ས་ means "place of the government" and is commonly used with དགའ་ལྡན་ཕོ་བྲང་ when the government is meant.

2. ཞོ་སྟོན་བྱེད་སྒོ་ཁག་ breaks down into ཞོ་སྟོན་ ("the name of the festival"), བྱེད་སྒོ་ ("activities, work, duties"), and ཁག་, the pluralizer described in 10.15.2.3.16. Together they mean the various activities of Shodön. A genitive particle could have been used here: ཞོ་སྟོན་གྱི་བྱེད་སྒོ་ཁག་.

3. སྲོལ་, as described in Lesson 9 (9.17.1.3.1), is used after verbs to convey "the custom" of doing the verbal action. Here it means that "the government made it the custom that the various activities of Shodön would be done at Drepung monastery."

4. The clause དེའི་དུས་བོད་ལ་ཟླ་མོ་ཚོགས་པ་ཁག་བཅུ་གཉིས་ཡོད་པ་ཚང་མ་ consists of the existential

sentence "there were twelve different opera troupes in Tibet at that time" (དེའི་དུས་བོད་ལ་ལྷ་མོ་ཚོགས་པ་ཁག་བཅུ་གཉིས་ཡོད་པ་རེད་), which was nominalized by ending it as (ཡོད་པ་). It then becomes the subject of the clause, being modified by "all" (ཚང་མ་). Thus, "all twelve of the Opera troupes that existed in Tibet at that time. . . ."

5. འཁྲབ་སྟོན་ is used here as a verb ("to perform a play"), so that the phrase འཁྲབ་སྟོན་དུ་ཡོང་ becomes "came to perform a play."

6. This phrase consists of the subject/actor ("the one called Siddhi [གྲུབ་ཐོབ་] Tangdong Gyebo" [ཐང་སྟོང་རྒྱལ་པོ་ཟེར་མཁན་]) plus a long nominalized phrase ("who had the experience of building") and then an instrumentalized demonstrative (དེས་) conveying: "by that Siddhi Tangdong Gyebo." Thus,"By that one, the Siddhi Tangdong Gyebo who had built. . . ."

Between གྲུབ་ཐོབ་ཐང་སྟོང་རྒྱལ་པོ་ཟེར་མཁན་ and དེས་ is a phrase (modifying the former) that says "who had built over 100 iron-link bridges in Tibet" (བོད་ལ་ལྕགས་ཐག་ཟམ་པ་ཁག་བརྒྱ་ལྷག་ཙམ་རྒྱབ་མྱོང་ཡོད་པ་).

7. This phrase could also be written with genitive particles: ཆུ་ཤུལ་གྱི་ལྕགས་ཟམ་གྱི་ལས་ཀ་.

8. The phrase རྒྱལ་པོའི་ཁྱི་བརླག་པ་འཚོལ་དུ་འགྲོ་སར་ breaks down into "to the place (where they were) going (འགྲོ་སར་) to search (འཚོལ་དུ་) for the king's lost dog (རྒྱལ་པོའི་ཁྱི་བརླག་པ་)." རྒྱལ་པོའི་ཁྱི་བརླག་པ་ is a nominalized phrase meaning "the king's dog which was lost."

9. The use of བཅས་ here conveys that the enumeration is complete, i.e., inclusive (see 6.4). Here it means that there were only the three of them in the household.

10. བུ་མོ་དེ་རང་གི་མནའ་མར་བསྐོང་ the dative-locative particle after མནའ་མ་ conveys "as"—"summoned that girl *as* his bride."

11. མི་དགའ་བ་ཆེན་པོ་ means "a great not liking," the syllable མི་ here functioning as a negative ("no") rather than the word "man." The use of བྱས་ verbalizes this.

12. The phrase རང་ལ་དགའ་བའི་ ("who liked self") refers to the queen and modifies and describes བློན་པོ་དང་ངན་འབྲེལ་ ("ministers and accomplices"): "the ministers and accomplices who liked (herself) the queen."

13. We encountered གྲབས་ in 7.11 where it conveyed "about" to do the verbal action. This clause reveals a second meaning for གྲབས་: "prepare" to do the verbal action. Thus, གསོད་གྲབས་བྱས་ཀྱང་ conveys "even though (they) prepared to kill (her)."

14. The dative-locative particle makes the phrase བསད་མ་ཐུབ་པར་ ("not able to kill") an

adverbial phrase modifying བྲོས་ ("escape"). Thus, "she escaped in the manner of not being able to be killed."

15. པས་ལུས་ is a pattern used with active verbs to convey that the subject was "left behind" or "left over." In this case it is redundant, emphasizing that the girl was left alive. Other examples of this are:

> དུས་ཚོད་དག་དག་མ་སླེབས་པས་ལུས་པ་རེད།
>
> (He, she, etc.) didn't arrive there at the exact time and was left behind.
>
> ཁང་པ་དེ་ཆུང་དྲགས་པས་ལུས།
>
> That house was too small so it was left (i.e., not sold or rented).

Sometimes the dative-locative is also used with ལུས་.

> ཁོའི་ལས་ཀ་ཚང་མ་བྱེད་མ་ཐུབ་པར་ལུས།
>
> He was unable to do all his work, and some was left (unfinished).

16. གང་ plus an adjective stem conveys "as X as possible." This གང་ཟབ་ means as good as possible and གང་མང་ means "as many as possible."

17. ཀྱང་ is used with nouns to mean "completely." The usual pattern is to take the first syllable of the noun and repeat it followed by ཀྱང་. Thus གྲྭ་པ་གྲྭ་ཀྱང་ means "completely a monk" or "a true monk." Similarly སྐུགས་པ་སྐུགས་ཀྱང་ means "a complete idiot."

18. This use of the noun + dative-locative + གཏོང་ parallels the adjective + dative-locative + གཏོང་ constructions seen in 10.3.2 q. Here གཏོང་/བཏང་ conveys "made into a beggar," whereas ཆེ་རུ་བཏང་ means "made bigger."

19. This segment is a bit confusing. དགོན་པར་དགེ་འདུན་རྣམས་དབྱར་གནས་ཞེས་ཆར་དུས་ཀྱི་མཚམས་སུ་བཞུགས་པའི་སྐབས་དང་བསྟུན་གནའ་བོའི་དུས་སུ་ཞོ་ཡི་སྟོན་མོ་དྲངས་སྲོལ་ནས་ཞོ་སྟོན་ཞེས་གྲགས་པ་རེད། breaks down first into དགོན་པར་དགེ་འདུན་རྣམས་དབྱར་གནས་ཞེས་ཆར་དུས་ཀྱི་མཚམས་སུ་བཞུགས་, which means "the monks stay in the monastery during the rainy season which is called 'yarne' (summer retreat)."

This is followed by སྐབས་དང་བསྟུན་, "in accordance with that time/condition," and then by གནའ་བོའི་དུས་སུ་ཞོ་ཡི་སྟོན་མོ་དྲངས་སྲོལ་, which conveys "in ancient times there was a custom of a yogurt banquet being brought." The last section says "from this it came to be known as 'shodön' (ཞོ་སྟོན་) Thus, the entire segment means: "in accordance with the monks in Drepung monastery staying during the rainy season in 'summer retreat,' in the past there was the custom of a yogurt banquet, and from this it came to be known as 'shodön.'"

20. ནོར་གླིང་ is a standard abbreviation for ནོར་བུ་གླིང་ཁ་.

21. The use of རེ་ ("each") in བདུན་གཅིག་རིང་ལྷ་མོའི་ལོ་རྒྱུས་རེ་ཉིན་གང་འཁྲབ་ conveys that "during one week each opera history (story) is performed for an entire day." Note that རིང་ here means "during."

22. This use of ཡོང་ immediately following a verb (གསོལ་རས་གནང་) is a common way to convey that the verbal action will occur or will come to be. Here it means "large gifts will be given" or "they will give large gifts." The recipients are all the performers (ལྷ་མོ་བ་ཚང་མར་).

23. བྱ་བ་ལམ་འགྲོ་ is a standard phrase meaning "may your deeds be successful."

24. This combination of ཕུད་ ("except for") and དེ་མིན་ ("besides that") is typical of the stylistic redundancy often used in literary Tibetan. It literally means "except for Gyomo lunga, beside that. . . ."

25. The use of ཤ་སྟག་ with nominalized verbs conveys that "only" the verbal action occurred or was done. Here it means "they come only from villages."

11.20.3 Reading number three: "Concerning the National Minorities in China"

11.20.3.1 Tibetan text

རྒྱ་ནག་ནང་གི་གྲངས་ཉུང་མི་རིགས་ཀྱི་སྐོར་

རྒྱ་ནག་ནང་གི་གྲངས་ཉུང་མི་རིགས་ཀྱི་མང་ཤོས་དང་ཉུང་ཤོས་སུ་ཡིན་ན་ཟེར་ན།1 རྒྱ་ནག་རྒྱལ་ཁབ་ལ་གྲངས་ཉུང་མི་རིགས་ལྔ་བཅུ་ང་ལྔ་ཡོད་པའི་ནང་ནས་མི་གྲངས་མང་ཤོས་ཀྱི་མི་རིགས་ནི་ཀྲོང་རིགས་ཡིན་ཞིང་། དེ་ལ་མི་གྲངས་ཁྲི་ ༡༣༠༠ ལྷག་ཙམ་ཡོད། མི་གྲངས་ཉུང་ཤོས་ཀྱི་མི་རིགས་ནི་ཧོ་ཀྲེ་རིགས་ཡིན་ཞིང་། དེ་ལ་མི་གྲངས་ ༡༩༠༠ ལྷག་ཙམ་ལས་མེད་། ཁྱབ་ཆེ་ཤོས་ཀྱི་མི་རིགས་ནི་ཧུའི་རིགས་ཡིན་པས་རྒྱལ་ཡོངས་ཀྱི་ས་ཆ་ཀུན་ལ་ཁྱབ་ཡོད་། རང་རྒྱལ་དུ་ས་ཁྱོན་2 ཆེ་ཤོས་ཀྱི་ཞིང་ཆེན་ནི་ཞིན་ཅང་ཡུ་གུར་རང་སྐྱོང་ལྗོངས་ཡིན་ཞིང་། དེའི་ས་ཁྱོན་ལ་སྤྱི་ལི་གྲུ་བཞི་ ༡༦༩༦༤༠༠ ཡོད། གྲངས་ཉུང་མི་རིགས་ཆེས་མང་བའི་ཞིང་ཆེན་ནི་ཡུན་ནན་ཞིང་ཆེན་ཡིན་ཞིང་། དེར་གྲངས་ཉུང་མི་རིགས་ཉི་ཤུ་རྩ་བཞི་གནས་ཡོད། གྲངས་ཉུང་མི་རིགས་ཆེས་མང་བའི་གྲོང་ཁྱེར་ནི་རྒྱལ་ས་པེ་ཅིན་ཡིན་ཞིང་། དབར་པེ་ཅིན་དུ་གྲངས་ཉུང་མི་རིགས་རིགས་ལྔ་བཅུ་ང་བཞི་ཡོད།།

11.20.3.2 Translation

Concerning the National Minorities in China

In China, if you ask which national minority (minority nationality) has the most population and which one has the least, from among China's 55 minorities the nationality with the biggest population is the Zhuang nationality. It has more than 13,000,000 people. The smallest population is the Hote nationality, which has only a little more than 1,400 people. As for the most widespread nationality, it is the Hui nationality. It has spread to all the areas of the nation. The Sinjiang Uighur Autonomous Region has the largest land area—1,646,800 square miles of land. The province with the most national minorities is Yunnan province. There are 24 national minorities living there. The city with the most national minorities is the capital, Beijing. Up to now, there are 54 national minorities in Beijing.

11.20.3.3 Grammatical notes

1. An interrogative such as སུ་ཡིན་ན་ + ཟེར་ན is a common way to ask a rhetorical question. It means: "If you ask which (or who) is. . . ." If we change the interrogative part to ག་རེ་རེད་ཟེར་ན་ the meaning conveyed is "if you ask what it is."

2. The particle ཁྱོན་ (all over; size in area) modifies ས་ (earth, land), indicating the area or size of the land. Thus ས་ཁྱོན་ཆེ་ཤོས་ཀྱི་ཞིང་ཆེན་ conveys "the province with the largest area."

11.21 Vocabulary

ཀ་མེད་	"no choice" (11.13)
ཀ་ལ་དབང་པོ་	p.n.
ཀུན་	all, entire, every
ཀྲོང་རིགས་	Zhuang nationality (found in southern China)
དཀར་པོ་	white
དཀྱིལ་	among
བཀའ་གཏོང་	va. to summon, order to come
བཀའ་ཞེབས་	vi. to receive an order/instructions, to have an order come or arrive
བཀོག་	va. p. of འགོག་: broke off
བཀོད་	va. p. of འགོད་: made; wrote
བཀྲ་བ་	bright, sharp
བཀྲིས་ཞོལ་པ་	p.n. of an opera troupe
རྐྱང་	noun or adjective + — conveys "completely" the nominal/adjectival meaning
རྐྱང་རྐྱང་	only

སྐད་གྲགས་ famous; fame

སྐད་གདངས་ལེགས་པ་ a good voice

སྐལ་བཟང་རྒྱ་མཚོ་ Kesang Gyatso (the p.n. of the 7th Dalai Lama)

སྐུ་དྲག་ noble, aristocrat (h.)

སྐུ་ཚེ་ life (h.)

སྐྱོང་ va. to rule, govern; to protect, take care of

སྐྱོར་མོ་ལུང་པ་ p.n. of an opera troupe

བསྐོང་ va. to summon, order to come

བསྐོས་ va. p. of བསྐོ་: appointed, selected as

བསྐྱངས་ va. p. of སྐྱོང་

བསྐྱར་གསོ་ recovery; restoration; va. —བྱེད་

སྐྲག་ va. to frighten

ཁ་བཏགས་ ceremonial scarf

ཁ་གཤགས་ va. to split open

ཁག་བགོས་ va. to divide into sections, parts

ཁྱབ་ vi. to spread, become widespread

ཁྱབ་ཆེ་ཤོས་ most widespread

ཁྱོན་ all, all over; size in area; all told

ཁྱོན་ནས་ negative emphatic term

འཁྱག་པ་ ice

ཁྲལ་ tax

འཁྲབ་སྟོན་ 1. performance, presentation, va. —བྱེད་; 2. va. to perform a show, play, opera

འཁྲབ་གཞུང་ script (story) for a play, opera, movie

ག་ "try to" and "pretend to" particle (va.+ག་+བྱེད་ or བྱས་)

ག་བྱེད་འདི་བྱེད་མེད་པར་གྱུར id. came into a state in which there was nothing that could be done

ག་ལ་ "how can" + vb. (non-past)

ག་ལ་འགྲིགས་ "how can it be okay"

ག་ལ་ཡོད་ " "

ག་ལ་རུང་ " "

ག་ལ་ཕོད་ "how could one dare"

ག་ས་ག་ལ་ everywhere

གང་ཙམ་ནས་ after some time (དུས་ཡུན་+ —)

གང་ཟབ་ as good as possible

གྲགས་ to be known as

གྲངས་ཉུང་མི་རིགས་ minority nationality

གྲྭ་ཆས་ monk's dress, clothes

གྲུབ་ཐོབ་ a great yogin, siddhi

གྲུབ་འབྲས་ achievement, result

གྲུ་བཞི་ square

གྲོལ་ vi. to be over, finished, to let out (e.g., a class or meeting)

གྲོས་མཐུན་ agreement

གླ་ va. to hire

གླས་ va. p. of གླ་

གླུ་གར་བ་ a performer

གླུ་གར་ཚོགས་པ་ musical association, dance troupe

དགག་པ་ rebuttal; va.— རྒྱག་

དགེ་འདུན་(པ་)	monk (h.)
དགོངས་	va. to think (h.)
འགོ་བཙུགས་	va. p. of འཛུགས་
འགྲུལ་པ་	traveler, passenger
འགྲོ་བ་བཟང་མོ་	p.n. of an opera
འགྲོ་སོང་	expenses; va.— གཏོང་ to pay expenses
རྒན་རྒན་	old person
རྒན་རྒན་གཉིས་	old couple
རྒོད་	vulture
རྒྱ་བཟའ་ བལ་བཟའ་	p.n. of an opera
རྒྱང་དཀར་བ་	p.n. of an opera troupe
རྒྱངས་ཤེལ་	telescope
རྒྱལ་སྲས་	prince
རྒྱལ་སྲིད་	reign, ruling a kingdom; va. — བསྐྱངས་ to rule, reign
རྒྱུ་གང་ཡོད་	"what is there to be"
རྒྱུ་རྐྱེན་	reason
རྒྱུག་	va. to run
རྒྱུན་དུ་	continuously, all the time, always
སྒྱུ་རྩལ་འཁྲབ་	va. to do an artistic performance
སྒྲིག་འཛུགས་	organization; va. — བྱེད་
ངན་འབྲེལ་	conspiring, plotting, collaborating (for evil); va. — བྱེད་
ངམ་རིང་	p.n. of a district in West Tibet
ངོ་ཚ་པ་	embarrassed, embarrassing
སྔ་དྲོ་	morning
སྔར་བཞིན་	as or like before
བསྔགས་བརྗོད་	praise; va. — བྱེད་
གཅིན་པ་	urine; va. — གཏོང་
གཅུང་པ་	p.n. of an opera troupe
གཅུང་པོ་དོན་ཡོད་ དོན་གྲུབ་	p.n. of an opera
ལྕགས་ཐག་ཟམ་པ་	iron link bridge
ལྕགས་ཟམ་	abbr. iron link bridge
ཆ་འཇོག་	abiding by; va. — བྱེད་
ཆུ་ཤུལ་	p.n. of a place south of Lhasa
ཆེ་ཤོས་	biggest; most
ཆོ་	sense, meaning
ཆོག་	1. "I will do it" particle; 2. allow; 3. ready to do
ཆོས་རྒྱལ་ ནོར་བཟང་	p.n. of an opera
ཆོས་པ་	religious person/ people
ཆོས་ལུགས་	a religion; religious doctrine
མཆོད་མཇལ་ཞུ་	va. to go on a religious visit to a monastery or temple to make offerings
མཆོད་མཇལ་ཞུས་	va. p. of མཆོད་མཇལ་ཞུ་
འཆར་གཞི་	a plan; va. — འགོད་
འཆར་གཞི་བཀོད་	va. p. of འཆར་གཞི་འགོད་
ཇི་ལྟར་	(like) what; how (to do)
འཛུག་	1. va. to put in, insert into; make do (p. བཙུགས་); 2. va. to let, allow
བརྗིད་ཉམས་ལྡན་པ་	grand, magnificent
ཉི་ཆོས་བཟང་པོ་	p.n.
ཉི་མ་བཞུད་	vi. to set (for the sun)

ཉི་འོད་	sunlight; va. — ཕོག་ to receive sunlight
ཉིན་གང་	all day
ཉིན་གུང་	noon
ཉུང་ཤོས་	least
ཉེ་བ་	close
རྙིང་གཏོར་གསར་འཛུགས་	slogan: "destroy the old, start the new"
རྙོག་དྲ་	problem, difficulty; va. — བཟོས་ to make problems, difficulties
སྙན་གྲགས་	fame
སྙིང་ནད་	heart disease
ཏག་ཏག་	exactly, precisely
ཏང་	party
གཏན་ནས་	emphatic negative term
གཏམ་བཟང་	good news
གཏམ་བཤད་	speech; va. — བྱེད་
གཏོར་བཤིག་	destroying; va. — གཏོང་
བཏང་ཡིག་	letter (correspondence)
བཏོན་	va. p. of འདོན་: took out
སྟོད་	the entire region of westernmost Tibet
སྟོན་མོ་	feast, banquet
ཐ་སྙད་	term, technical word
ཐ་ན་	"even"
ཐང་སྟོང་རྒྱལ་པོ་	p.n. of a famous lama
ཐད་	about, concerning
ཐབས་བྲལ་	"no choice" construction
ཐབས་མེད་	"no choice" construction
མཐུ་མེད་	"no choice" construction
འཐབ་	va. to fight, struggle
འཐུས་	vi. to be approved, to be agreed
དང་བླངས་	volunteer
དུས་སྟོན་	holiday, festival
དེ་ནས་བཟུང་	since that time
དེ་རང་	that itself
དོན་ཅི་ཡོད་	"what's the use," "why"
དྲག་	vi. to heal, get better, recover
དྲངས་	va. p. of འདྲེན་
དྲི་མེད་ཀུན་ལྡན་	p.n. of an opera and its main character
དྲུང་	presence, near
འདྲེ་	demon, ghost, evil spirit
བདུན་(ཕྲག་)	a week
བདེ་སྐྱིད་	happiness, joy, well-being
འདམ་གསེས་	1. choosing, selecting; va. — རྒྱག་; 2. va. to choose, select
འདེབས་ལས་	planting (work); va.— བྱེད་
འདྲེན་	va. to lead; to draw; to pull; to bring
ནང་པ་	a Buddhist
ནང་བཞིན་	like, similar to
ནམ་མཁའ་	sky
ནམ་ཡང་	emphatic negative term
ནུབ་	west
ནུབ་ངོས་	western side, direction
ནོར་བུ་	precious gem
ནོར་གླིང་	abbr. of ནོར་བུ་གླིང་ཁ་
ནོར་བུ་གླིང་ཁ་	Norbulingka ("the jewel park"—summer palace of Dalai Lama)
གནང་སྦྱིན་	gift, present
གནམ་གང་	thirtieth day of the month
གནའ་བོའི་	ancient time
སྣང་ས་འོད་འབུམ་	p.n. of an opera

སྣེ་གདོང་ p.n. of a place in southern Tibet
སྣེ་ལེན་ hospitality; va. — བྱེད་ receive guests, travelers
བསྣམས་ va. to take, bring, carry (h.)
པད་མ་ཅན་ p.n. of a place
པད་མ་འོད་འབར་ p.n. of an opera
པུ་ལི་སི་ police
དཔེ་བསགས་འདུག་ id. Oh my goodness!
དཔེར་ན་ for example
སྤོས་ va. p. of སྤོ་: moved, shifted residence
སྤྱི་ལི་ kilometer
སྤྱི་ལི་གྲུ་བཞི་ square kilometer
སྤྲུལ་པ་ an emanation
སྤྲོ་ vi. to sparkle, see འོད་ཟེར་
སྤྲོ་སྐྱིད་ party, recreation; va. — གཏོང་ to enjoy oneself
ཕངས་ vi. to feel regret, to be sorry
ཕངས་པ་ལ་ཨང་ id. a common spoken phrase meaning "Oh, what a shame."
ཕམ་ vi. to lose, be defeated
ཕོ་མོ་ male and female
ཕོ་བྲང་ 1. palace; 2. at Drepung, the term ཕོ་བྲང་ refers to the palace of the Dalai Lama, which is known as དགའ་ལྡན་ཕོ་བྲང་
ཕོག་ vi. to get, catch involuntarily (e.g., an illness)
ཕོགས་ salary
ཕྱི་ outside
ཕྱི་དྲོ་ (late) afternoon
འཕྲོ་ vi. to shine, radiate, emanate
བག་ལེབ་ bread
བང་མཛོད་ storeroom, treasury
བར་ཆད་ hindrance, obstruction
བྱ་བ་ལམ་འགྲོ་ good fortune in business/work
བྱེད་སྒོ་ activities, work, duties
བྲེལ་འཚབ་ hurry, rush
བླ་བྲང་ the "corporation" of a lama
བློ་རིག་ intellect
བློ་རིག་བཀྲ་བ་ intelligent
བློན་པོ་ minister
དབྱར་གནས་ the summer retreat of monks
དབྱིན་སྐད་ English language
འབྱོར་ཐོ་ arrival report, registration; va. — བཀོད་ to make an arrival report; to register
འབྲོག་ལས་ dairy work
སྦྱིན་བདག་ patron, donor
མང་ཆེ་བ་ the majority, mostly
མང་ཚོགས་ public, the masses
མང་ཤོས་ most
མི་གྲངས་ population, the number of people
མི་གླར་ hired person; worker; va. — གླ་ to hire a worker
མི་ཚང་ family

མི་འདྲ་བ་ different

མི་སེར་ serf; subject; citizen

མུ་སི་ matches (for fire making)

མོན་ p.n. of a place

དམག་སྒར་ military camp/ garrison

དམག་དྲངས་ va. p. of དམག་འདྲེན་

དམག་འདྲེན་ va. to wage war, to lead troops into battle

དམྱལ་བ་ hell

རྨ wound, sore

སྨོན་འདུན་ wish, desire; va. — བྱེད་

བཙན་གནོན་ oppressing; va.— གཏོང་

བཙོན་ prison

རྩ་འགངས་ valuable

རྩ་ཆེ་ precious; sacred

རྩ་བ་ནས་ with negative constructions = never, completely not

རྩད་ཆོད་ vi. to find out about something, to get information on something

རྩེ་ཕྱག་ལས་ཁུངས་ p.n. of a treasury office in traditional Tibetan government

ཚ་པོ་ 1. hot; 2. strong (answer)

ཚགས་པར་ newspaper

ཚད་བྲལ་ "no choice" term

ཚད་མེད་ "no choice" term

ཚབས་ཆེན་ serious, severe

ཚུགས་ vi. p. of འཚུགས་

མཚན་མོ་ night

མཚན་ལས་ night work; va. — བྱེད་ to work at night

འཚུགས་ vi. to get established, founded, started, begun

འཛམ་གླིང་ world

འཛུགས་ va. to establish, found, start, begin

འཛོམས་ va. to come together, to congregate, to assemble

རྫུ་འཕྲུལ་ miracle; magic

རྫུན་ lie

ཞབས་ཞུ་ service

ཞལ་ཕུད་ the first offering of something; va. — འབུལ་ to give/make the first offering [With respect to the opera festival it refers to giving a first performance, which is a sampler of the different plays.]

ཞིང་ཆེན་ province, state

ཞིན་ཅང་ཡུ་གུར་ Sinjiang Uighur (Autonomous Region)

ཞེད་ vi. to be afraid

ཞོ་ curd, yogurt

ཞོ་སྟོན་ opera festival

ཞོར་ spare time

གཞས་ song

གཞས་ཕུད་ first day performance of an opera [With respect to the opera festival it refers to giving a first performance, which is a sampler of the different plays.]

གཞུང་ས་དགའ་ལྡན་

ཕོ་བྲང་ p.n. of the traditional government of Tibet
གཞིས་ཆགས་ resettling, settling people; va. — བྱེད་
བཞའ་བརླན་ wetness, dampness, moisture
བཞུར་ vi. to melt
ཟེར་མཁན་ the one called
ཟེར་སྲོལ་ (ལ་) as the traditional/customary saying goes
གཟིགས་ཕུད་ first day performance of an opera; va. — འབུལ་ [With respect to the opera festival it refers to giving a first performance, which is a sampler of the different plays.]
གཟུགས་ཀྱི་ཉི་མ་ p.n. of an opera
བཟུང་ see glossary: ནས་བཟུང་
བཟོ་ 1. va. to make; 2. causative particle
བཟོ་ལས་ industrial work
འོད་ཟེར་ sparkling light; vi. — སྤྲོ་ to sparkle, glitter
ཡང་བསྐྱར་ again
ཡང་སྟེང་ on top; roof
ཡར་ལུང་ p.n. of a place in ལྷོ་ཁ་
ཡས་མས་ vicinity; up and down; about; approximately
ཡུན་ནན་ཞིང་ཆེན་ Yunnan province
ཡུལ་བསྐོར་སྤྲོ་འཆམ་ sightseeing visit, tour
ཡུལ་གོམས་གཤིས་ལུགས་ native customs, habits, way of life
ཡོང་ཁུངས་ origin; resources
གཡོགས་ va. to put something on someone, to dress someone
རང་ part of the "no choice" construction
རང་སྐྱོང་ལྗོངས་ an autonomous region
རང་སྦྱོང་ homework; self-study
རན་ "time to do" particle
རས་ཆུང་ p.n.
རིག་གནས་ culture
རིག་གནས་གསར་བརྗེ་ཆེན་པོ་ the "Great Cultural Revolution"
རིན་སྤུངས་ p.n. of a district in Tibet
རུ་སྒྲིག་ va. to march in formation, to line up in rows
རུ་སྒྲིག་ས་ལམ་ term used in traditional society for military salute, presenting of arms; va. — ཞུ་
རོ་ corpse
ལས་གྲྭ་ workshop; work site
ལས་འགུལ་ campaign
ལས་ཞོར་ spare time (after work)
ལོག་སྤྱོད་པ་ reactionaries
ཤ་སྟག་ only
ཤིང་ཅང་ཡུ་གུར་ Sinjiang Uighur (Autonomous Region)
ཤིང་བཟོ་བ་ carpenter
གཤོག་པ་ wings
ས་ཁྱོན་ area, size in area
ས་ལམ་ Hindi salutation: "salaam"
སང་ལོ་ next year

སེར་དམག་	monk soldiers
སྲས་སྲོས་	children (h.)
སྲིད་ཇུས་	policy
སྲོལ་	custom (vb.+ — = custom of doing the verbal action)
སློང་	va. to cause to stand up
བསློངས་	va. p. of སློང་
གསོལ་རས་	gift; tip (h.); va. — གནང་
བསམ་འཆར་	opinion
ཧ་གོ་	vi. to understand
ཧ་ཤང་བདུད་མོ་	p.n.
ཧང་སངས་	vi. to be surprised, be shocked
ཧུའི་རིགས་	Hui nationality
ཧོ་ཀྲི་རིགས་	Hote nationality
ལྷ་རྒྱལ་ལོ་	"May the gods be victorious"
ལྷ་གཅིག་ཀུན་བཟང་	p.n.
ལྷ་མོ་ཚོགས་པ་	opera association, troupe
ལྷ་ཡུལ་	realm, place of the gods
ལྷ་སྲས་རྒྱལ་པོ་	p.n.
ལྷག་ཙམ་	a little more
ལྷུག་(པོ་)	loose
ལྷོ་ཁ་	p.n. of region southeast of Lhasa
ལྷོ་ཕྱོགས་	southern direction, side
ཨ་ཕ་	father
ཨུ་ཚུགས་	insisting; va. — རྒྱག་

Lesson Twelve

12.1 Constructions with the particle ཐོག་

ཐོག་ is used to convey a variety of very different meanings and is one of the more confusing grammatical particles. The following sections explain its main uses.

12.1.1 The "on" function of ཐོག་

One of the main functions of ཐོག་ is to convey the idea of "on" or "on top of." When used in this manner it may immediately follow the noun it modifies (example a.) or may be preceded by a genitive particle (example b.). It may also be followed by a dative-locative particle as in a. and b.

a. ཆུ་ཐོག་ལ་སྡོད་པའི་མི་ཚོ་སྐྱོ་པོ་ཞེ་དྲགས་འདུག།

The people who live on the water are very poor.

b. ཡར་ཀླུང་གཙང་པོའི་ཐོག་ཏུ་ཆུ་གློག་ས་ཚིགས་ཤིག་བཙུགས་པ་རེད།

(They) established a hydro-electric station on the Yarlung Tsangpo River.

Sometimes ཐོག་ is best translated as "in," "at," or "among" in English.

c. ཞིང་པ་ཚོས་རྟ་བཞོན་ནས་བྱེ་ཐང་ཐོག་ཏུ་ཤིང་སོན་འདེབས་མུས་རེད།

The farmers are sowing tree seeds in the desert from horseback. (lit., Riding a horse, the farmers are sowing. . .)

d. བསམ་ཚུལ་འབྲི་དེབ་ཀྱི་ཐོག་ཏུ་ངས་བསམ་འཆར་ཞིག་བྲིས།

I wrote a suggestion in the "suggestion book."

e. མང་ཚོགས་ཐོག་སོ་པ་མང་པོ་འདུག།

There are many spies among the masses.

f. གསོལ་སྟོན་ཐོག་ཁོས་གཞས་བཏང་བ་རེད།

He sang a song at the banquet.

12.1.2 The "via" function of ཐོག་

ཐོག་ can also function to convey the meanings of "via," "by means of," and "through." Only semantic context differentiates these from the "on" function.

a. མོས་གནམ་ཐོག་ལ་བཏང་ཡིག་དེ་བཏང་།

She sent that letter by air.

When the "by means of" meaning is intended, ཐོག་ནས་ is usually used.

b. ཁོ་པས་གྲུའི་ཐོག་ནས་གྲོང་ཁྱེར་གསར་པར་སྤོས་པ་རེད།

He moved by boat to a new city.

However, in many cases such as the following example, the difference between "via" and "by means of" is indistinct.

c. ཁོས་མོར་ཁ་པར་ཐོག་ནས་སྐད་ཆ་བཤད་སོང་།

He spoke to her by telephone.

It should be noted that another way to convey the meaning of "via" is by means of a བརྒྱུད་ ནས་ construction.

d. ངས་རྒྱ་གར་བརྒྱུད་ནས་བོད་ལ་བཏང་ཡིག་ཁ་ཤས་བཏང་བ་ཡིན།

I sent several letters to Tibet via India.

12.1.3 The "in addition to" function of ཐོག་

Another use of ཐོག་ expresses the meaning of "in addition to." It can be used with nouns and verbs.

a. སྔོན་དུ་སྤྲད་པའི་དངུལ་ཐོག་སྒོར་ཁྲི་གཉིས་བསྐྱར་དུ་སྤྲད་པ་རེད།

In addition to the money which was given before, (they, he, etc.) again gave 20,000 dollars.

b. འཐུས་མིར་བདམས་ཐོག་ཁོས་ཏང་གི་ཏྲུའུ་ཅིའི་ལས་ཀ་བྱས་དགོས་བྱུང་སོང་།

In addition to being selected as a delegate, he had to do the work of party chairman.

Note that སྒང་ (cf. 5.10) also functions to convey "in addition to."

c. འཐུས་མིར་བདམས་པའི་སྒང་ལ་ཁོས་ཏང་གི་ཏྲུའུ་ཅིའི་ལས་ཀ་བྱས་དགོས་བྱུང་སོང་།

In addition to being selected as a delegate, he had to do the work of party chairman.

12.1.4 The "during," "at the time of," and "when" functions of ཐོག་

a. ཆུ་ཚོད་༡༠་ཐོག།

at ten o'clock

b. ཕྲུ་གུ་ཚོས་ལངས་ཐོག་རྒྱལ་གླུ་བཏང་བ་རེད།

The children sang the national anthem when they got up.

c. ཀུ་མ་དེ་མཚན་མོ་རྟོག་ཞིབ་ཐོག་འཛིན་བཟུང་བྱས་པ་རེད།

(They) arrested the thief during their evening inspection.

12.1.5 The "concerning" function of ཐོག་

Finally, ཐོག་ can also convey the meaning of "concerning," or "with regards to," or "about." When this is intended, ཐོག་ typically is preceded by the genitive and may or may not have a dative-locative particle following it.

a. འཆར་གཞི་དེའི་ཐོག་རྒྱ་གར་གཞུང་གིས་གྲོས་མོལ་གནང་བ་རེད།

The Indian Government held discussions about that plan.

b. ཁོ་ཚོའི་ཐོག་ལ་རྩད་གཅོད་བྱས་པའི་སྐབས་སུ་

At the time (they) did an investigation concerning them, ...

12.2 Verbal constructions using མདོག་ཁ་པོ་

This construction follows the non-past stem of verbs to mean "seems (or "doesn't seem") likely to occur" with respect to the verbal meaning.

a. སློབ་ཕྲུག་ཚོས་ད་ལོ་འབྲུག་ཡུལ་ལ་འགྲོ་མདོག་ཁ་པོ་རེད།

It seems that the students are going to go to Bhutan this year.

b. ན་ནིང་སླེབས་པའི་ལས་མི་ཚོས་མགྱོགས་པོ་ལོག་མདོག་ཁ་པོ་མི་འདུག།

It doesn't seem likely that the workers who came last year will return quickly.

c. སང་ཉིན་མོ་ཁྲོམ་ལ་འགྲོ་མདོག་ཁ་པོ་རེད།

It seems that she is going (to go) to the market tomorrow.

d. སློབ་ཕྲུག་དེས་སློབ་སྦྱོང་ཧུར་བརྩོན་བྱེད་མདོག་ཁ་པོ་འདུག།

It seems that the student studies diligently.

e. བུ་མོ་དེས་གཞས་གཏོང་མདོག་ཁ་པོ་མི་འདུག།

It doesn't seem likely that the girl will sing a song.

12.3 "Shouldn't" constructions: རྒྱུ་ + negative existentials

"Shouldn't" constructions are formed by combining the non-past stem of a verb + རྒྱུ་ + a negative existential verb.

a. གཞུང་གིས་ས་བདག་ལ་རོགས་རམ་བྱེད་རྒྱུ་ཡོད་པ་མ་རེད།

The government shouldn't help the landlords.

b. བཅིངས་འགྲོལ་བཏང་འཕྲལ་ཀྱང་རྫི་འཛུགས་རྒྱུ་མི་འདུག།

(You) shouldn't establish communes as soon as (an area has been) liberated.

"Shouldn't" constructions also occur in dependent clauses.

c. ཁྱེད་རང་ཀྱང་རྫི་འཛུགས་རྒྱུ་མེད་པ་མ་ཟད། མཉམ་འབྲེལ་ཚོང་ཁང་ཡང་འཛུགས་རྒྱུ་ཡོད་པ་མ་རེད།

Not only shouldn't you establish a commune, (you) also shouldn't establish a cooperative store.

12.4 "What kind of" constructions: གང་འདྲ་ཞིག་, ཅི་འདྲ་ཞིག་, and ཇི་འདྲ་ཞིག་

These are common interrogative phrases that follow nominals and demonstratives.

a. རླངས་འཁོར་འདི་གང་འདྲ་ཞིག་རེད།

What kind of car is this?

b. ཁོ་ལ་ལས་ཀ་ཅི་འདྲ་ཞིག་ཡོད་དམ།

What kind of work (job) does he have?

c. ཁོ་ཚོས་ལྟད་མོ་གང་འདྲ་ཞིག་ལ་ཕྱིན་པ་རེད།

What kind of a show did they go to?

d. རྒྱུ་མཚན་གང་འདྲ་ཞིག་གིས་ཟིང་འཁྲུག་བྱུང་བ་རེད།
What was the reason for the uprising?

These constructions, however, do not necessarily ask a question, for example:

e. འཕྲུལ་འཁོར་འདི་ཇི་འདྲ་ཞིག་ཡིན་ངས་ཤེས་ཀྱི་མེད།
I don't know what kind of a machine this is.

f. ཁོ་ལ་ཁང་པ་གང་འདྲ་ཞིག་ཡོད་ང་ལ་བཤད་མ་བྱུང་།
(He) didn't tell me what kind of a house he has.

When these are used with ཡང་ (or ཀྱང་), they convey the idea of "whatever" or "any kind."

g. ཁོས་ལས་ཀ་གང་འདྲ་ཞིག་ཡིན་ཡང་བྱས་པ་རེད།
He did whatever kind of work it was.

h. ཕྲུ་གུ་འདིས་དེབ་གང་འདྲ་ཞིག་ཀྱང་ཀློག་ཐུབ་ཀྱི་རེད།
This child will be able to read any kind of book.

12.5 "Lots of ways" constructions: གང་ཅི་ and གང་དང་ཅི་

These constructions precede verbs and convey the idea that the verbal action was done in a lot of different ways or with respect to many different things/aspects.

a. ཁོས་ཞིང་ལས་སློབ་སྦྱོང་གང་ཅི་བྱས་པ་རེད།
He studied lots of aspects of farming.

Note should be made that with regard to the difference between གང་ཅི་ and ཞི་དྲགས་ "lots," the latter conveys the idea that a great deal of studying was done, whereas གང་ཅི་ conveys the idea that a lot of different aspects or dimensions of the object were studied.

b. ཁོ་ཚོར་རོགས་རམ་གང་ཅི་ཐོབ་ཡོད་པ་རེད།
They got lots of kinds of aid.

c. ཁོས་ཞིང་པ་ཚོར་གང་དང་ཅིའི་སློབ་གསོ་བྱས་པ་རེད།
He educated the farmers in many things.

12.6 "By all means/ in all respects" constructions: གང་ཐད་ནས་, གང་ས་ནས་, གང་གི་ཐད་ནས་, གང་གི་ཐོག་ནས་, གང་ཅིའི་ཐད་ནས་, གང་ཅིའི་ཐོག་ནས་, and གང་གི་ཆ་ནས་

The constructions listed above can convey either the idea of "all sorts of means/ methods" or that of "all sorts of aspects." Context determines which is intended.

a. མོས་གང་ཅིའི་ཐད་ནས་ཕྲུ་གུ་དེ་སློབ་གྲྭར་གཏོང་ཐབས་བྱས་པ་རེད།
She tried all means to send the child to school.

b. ལུང་པ་འདིར་གང་ས་ནས་མཐུན་རྐྱེན་ཡག་པོ་འདུག།
In all respects, this country has good resources.

c. བོད་མི་ཚོ་གང་ཅིའི་ཐད་ནས་གཞིས་ཆགས་བྱས་ཡོད་པ་རེད།

(They) have resettled the Tibetans by all means.

12.7 "To whom" constructions (སུ་+ dative-locative): སུར་ and སུ་ལ་

a. ཁོ་ཚོས་སུ་ལ་རོགས་རམ་བྱེད་ཀྱི་ཡོད་པ་རེད།
Who are they helping? (They are helping whom?)

b. མི་འདིས་སུ་ལ་སྐད་ཆ་བཤད་སོང་ངམ།
To whom did this man talk?

c. མི་འདི་ཚོས་སུ་ལ་སྐྱོན་བརྗོད་བྱེད་ཀྱི་ཡོད་པ་རེད།
Who are these men criticizing?

d. འདི་སུ་ལ་སྤྲོད་དགོས་རེད།
To whom do (they, he, etc.) have to give this?

12.8 "Whose" (སུ་ + genitive: སུ་ཡི་ and སུའི་) and "by whom" (སུ་ + instrumental: སུས་ and སུ་ཡིས་) constructions

a. ཕྲུ་གུ་འདི་སུའི་རེད་དམ།
Whose child is this?

Note that དམ་ here is optional.

b. ཁོ་ཚོ་སུའི་དྲུང་དུ་ཕྱིན་པ་རེད།
Whom did they go to see? (To whose presence did they go?)

c. མི་འདི་ཚོས་སུའི་དོན་ལ་ངལ་རྩོལ་ཆེན་པོ་བྱེད་ཀྱི་ཡོད་པ་རེད།
For whose purpose/benefit are these men laboring so much?

d. འདི་སུའི་ཡིན་དྲིས་པ་རེད
(They, he, etc.) asked, "Whose is this?"

e. ལས་ཀ་འདི་སུའི་ཡིན་ངས་ཤེས་ཀྱི་མེད།
I don't know whose work this is.

f. ཁང་པ་འདི་སུས་ཉོས་པ་རེད།
Who bought this house?

g. ལས་ཀ་འདི་སུས་བྱེད་ཀྱི་རེད།
Who will do this work?

h. དེབ་འདི་སུས་སུ་ལ་སྤྲད་པ་རེད།
Who gave this book to whom?

i. དེབ་འདི་སུས་བྲིས་པ་རེད་དམ།
Who wrote this book?

The addition of the "even/also" particle conveys the meaning "even by whomever":

j. འདི་སུས་ཀྱང་བྱེད་ཐུབ་ཀྱི་རེད།
Anyone will be able to do this. (This can be done even by whomever.)

k. འདི་སུས་ཀྱང་ཟ་གི་མ་རེད།

No one will eat this. (This will not be eaten even by whomever.)

l. ཁོ་ལ་སུས་བཤད་ཀྱང་ཉན་གྱི་མ་རེད།

(He) won't listen whoever tells him.

m. བཙོན་པ་ཚོས་སུ་ཡི་ལས་དོན་ལ་ཡང་ཐེ་ཇུས་བྱེད་ཀྱི་མ་རེད།

The prisoners will not interfere even (in) whoever's work (i.e., in anyone's work).

n. སུས་གཞུང་ལ་སྐྱོན་བརྗོད་བྱས་ཀྱང་འཛིན་བཟུང་བྱེད་ཀྱི་ཡོད་པ་རེད།

Whoever criticizes the government is arrested.

སུ་འདྲ་ཞིག་ ("like whom") functions the same as སུ་ in indefinite constructions but conveys more emphasis.

o. མི་དེ་སུ་འདྲ་ཞིག་ཡིན་ཁོས་ཤེས་ཀྱི་ཡོད་པ་རེད།

He knows who that man is.

p. ཁོས་སུ་འདྲ་ཞིག་ལ་ཁ་པར་བཏང་བ་ཤོད་ཀྱི་མི་འདུག

He isn't saying whom he called.

q. མོས་སུ་འདྲ་ཞིག་ལ་ཡང་སྐད་ཆ་ཤོད་ཚོག་གི་མ་རེད།

She cannot talk to anyone.

r. སུ་འདྲ་ཞིག་ཡིན་ཡང་ལག་ཁྱེར་དགོས་ཀྱི་འདུག

Whoever (it) is, a permit is needed.

s. ཁོས་སུ་འདྲ་ཞིག་གི་ནང་ལ་བསྡད་པ་ཤེས་མ་བྱུང་།

(I) didn't know at whose house he stayed.

12.9 "Why" constructions: གང་ཡིན་ཅེ་ན་, གང་ཡིན་ཟེར་ན་, གང་གིས་ཤེ་ན་, ཅིས་ཤེ་ན་, ཅིའི་ཕྱིར་ཞེས་ན་, and ཅི་ལ་ཟེར་ན་

These all function to relate two clauses so that the latter explains the former. They can be translated literally as "if you ask why" (the preceding clause occurred).

a. ཁོ་རྒྱ་གར་ལ་སྐྱིད་པོ་བྱུང་མི་འདུག གང་གིས་ཤེ་ན། ཁོ་ཚ་བ་ལ་དགའ་པོ་མི་འདུག

He was not happy in India because he does not like the heat. (lit., If one asks why he does not like the heat, . . .)

b. བོད་ཟླ་དང་པོའི་ནང་གྲོང་ཁྱེར་ལྷ་སར་མི་མང་ཤོས་འཛོམས་ཀྱི་ཡོད་པ་རེད། གང་ཡིན་ཅེ་ན། ལྷ་ལྡན་སྨོན་ལམ་ཆེན་མོ་ཞེས་ཆོས་ལུགས་ཀྱི་དུས་ཆེན་ཆེ་ཤོས་དེ་ཚུགས་ཀྱི་ཡོད་པ་རེད།

Most people gather in Lhasa city in the first month of the Tibetan calendar. If you ask why, it is because it is the time when the biggest religious festival, the Monlam Chemo, starts.

c. དེང་སང་མི་མང་པོས་རི་པིན་གྱི་ཅ་ལག་ཉོ་གི་འདུག ཅིའི་ཕྱིར་ཞེས་ན། དེ་ཚོ་སྤུས་ཀ་དག་པོ་དང་གོང་ཁེ་པོ་ཡོད་པ་རེད།

These days many people are buying Japanese things. If you ask why, it is because they are of good quality and cheap.

d. བོད་མི་དམངས་ནས་གྲུབ་ཐོབ་ཐང་སྟོང་རྒྱལ་པོར་བསྔགས་བརྗོད་ཞུ་གི་ཡོད་པ་རེད། གང་ཡིན་ཟེར་ན། ཁོང་གིས་ལྕགས་ཐག་ཟམ་

པ་བརྒྱབ་སྟེ་མང་ཚོགས་ལ་ཕན་ཐོགས་ཆེན་པོ་བྱུང་ཡོད་པ་རེད།

The Tibetan people praise Siddhi Tangdong Gyebo because he constructed iron chain bridges that benefited the people greatly.

12.10 "Everywhere" construction: ག་ས་ག་ལ།

This is a colloquial expression that sometimes appears in writing to convey the idea of "everywhere."

a. ཁོས་ག་ས་ག་ལ་ཕྱིན་པ་རེད།

He went everywhere.

b. ག་ས་ག་ལ་རི་པིན་གྱི་རླངས་འཁོར་གསར་པ་མང་པོ་མཐོང་རྒྱུ་འདུག།

Many new Japanese cars can be seen everywhere.

12.11 "It's a pity" constructions: གང་དྭག་, ཅི་དྭག་, གང་ཞིག་དྭག་, and ཅི་ཞིག་དྭག་

These constructions are used as sentence final complements. They exclaim sorrow, sympathy, or regret. The nearest English equivalents are "oh," "too bad," and "what a pity.'

a. མི་མིག་མེད་པ་དེ་ཅི་དྭག།

That man without eyes, what a pity!

b. ཁོ་ཚོར་དཀའ་ངལ་བྱུང་ན་གང་དྭག།

It's a pity if they have difficulties.

c. སྐྱབས་བཅོལ་བ་དེ་ཚོར་རོགས་རམ་བྱེད་མི་ཐུབ་ཙང་གང་ཞིག་དྭག།

It's too bad that (I) am unable to help those refugees.

d. འབྲོག་པ་ཚོང་པ་སྐྱོ་པོ་དེ་ལ་ཁེ་བཟང་མ་རག་ན་ཅི་ཞིག་དྭག།

If that poor nomad trader doesn't get profit, what a pity!

12.12 "However much . . . that much" constructions: interrogative + ཙམ་ + vb.+ དེ་ཙམ་

These constructions express the idea that "however much one does the verbal action, that much of something else will happen." Common interrogatives used in these constructions are གང་, ཇི་, ཅི་, ག་ཚད་, གང་ཙམ་, and ག་ཚོད་.

a. ལས་ཀ་ཇི་ཙམ་བྱས་པ་དེ་ཙམ་གླ་ཆ་ཐོབ་ཀྱི་རེད།

However much (you) work, that much of a wage (you) will obtain.

b. དེབ་གང་ཙམ་ཀློག་པ་དེ་ཙམ་ཤེས་ཀྱི་རེད།

However many books (you) read, that much (you) will know.

c. གོམ་པ་གང་ཙམ་རྒྱབ་པ་དེ་ཙམ་གཟུགས་པོར་ཕན་ཐོགས་ཡོང་གི་རེད།

However much (you) walk, that much (your) body will benefit.

d. ལུང་པ་ཡར་རྒྱས་གང་ཙམ་བཏང་བ་དེ་ཙམ་མི་དམངས་རྣམས་སྐྱིད་པོ་ཡོང་གི་རེད།

However much a country is developed, that much happiness will come to the people.

12.13 "How could" constructions with ག་ནས་ and ག་པར་

These are used to convey the rhetorical question "how could . . .," even though the literal meaning of these particles is "where" and "from where."

a. ཁོ་ཚོས་ང་ཚོར་དམག་འཁྲུག་བྱེད་ག་ནས་ནུས་ཀྱི་རེད།
How could they dare to make war with us?

b. ངས་ཁྱེད་རང་ལ་རོགས་མ་བྱས་ན་ག་ནས་འགྲིགས།
How could it be all right if I did not help you?

c. ཕྲུ་གུ་འདི་གཅིག་པོར་ཁྲོམ་ལ་ག་པར་འགྲོ་ཐུབ་ཀྱི་རེད།
How could this child be able to go to the market alone?

12.14 Constructions with ཚད་(ལ་)

Depending on context, this construction conveys "whenever," "whoever," or "whatever."

a. ཁོས་མི་འཕྲད་ཚད་ལ་སྐད་ཆ་ཤོད་ཀྱི་འདུག།
He talks to whatever person (he) meets.

b. བླ་མ་དེས་དུས་ཚོད་བྱུང་ཚད་ལ་ཁ་འདོན་བྱེད་ཀྱི་འདུག།
Whenever the Lama gets time, (he) prays.

c. སློབ་གྲྭ་བ་དེས་དེབ་མཐོང་ཚད་ཀློག་གི་འདུག།
Whenever the student sees a book, (he) reads (it).

d. བསོད་ནམས་ཀྱིས་གསར་འགྱུར་གོ་ཚད་ཚང་མ་མོ་ལ་བཤད་སོང་།
Whatever news Sonam heard, (he) told her everything.

12.15 "According to" and "based on" constructions with ལ་གཞིགས་ཏེ་ and ལ་དཔག་སྟེ་ (ན་)

The meaning conveyed by these constructions is: "based on" or "according to" or "in accordance with" X, Y occurred or will occur.

a. ད་ལོའི་གནམ་གཤིས་ལ་གཞིགས་ན་ཐོན་སྐྱེད་ཡག་པོ་ཡོང་གི་རེད།
According to this year's climate, production will be good.

b. མི་མང་ཉུང་ལ་དཔག་སྟེ་ཁ་ལག་བཟོ་དགོས།
In accordance with the quantity (number) of people, (we) have to make food.

c. སློབ་ཕྲུག་དེའི་སློབ་སྦྱོང་བྱེད་སྟངས་ལ་གཞིགས་ཏེ་བྱ་དགའ་ཐོབ་ཀྱི་མ་རེད།
Based on the student's manner of studying, (he) will not win a prize.

d. ཚོང་པ་དེའི་ཁེ་བཟང་བྱུང་སྟངས་ལ་གཞིགས་ན་མགྱོགས་པོ་ཕྱུག་པོ་ཆགས་ཀྱི་རེད།
Based on that trader's manner of making profit, (he) will soon become rich.

12.16 "Go right ahead" constructions with རྐྱང་བྱེད་ or རྐྱང་གནང་

These རྐྱང་ constructions are used with verbs to tell someone to "go right ahead" and do the verbal action.

a. གལ་སྲིད་ང་ཆུ་ཚོད་བརྒྱད་པར་མ་སླེབས་ན་ཁྱེད་རང་ཕེབས་རྐྱང་གནང་རོགས་གནང་།
If I do not arrive at 8 o'clock, you please go right ahead and go.

b. ཁྱེད་རང་ཚོ་ཕྱག་རོགས་ཞུ་དགོས་འདུག་ན་གསུང་རྐྱང་གནང་རོགས་གནང་།
If you need to ask for help, please go right ahead and say it.

c. ལས་ཀ་དེ་བྱེད་རྐྱང་བྱས་ན་འགྲིག་གི་རེད།
If you go right ahead and do that work, it will be all right.

d སྐད་ཆ་དེ་འདྲ་བཤད་རྐྱང་བྱས་ན་འགྲིག་གི་མ་རེད།
If you go right ahead and speak like that, it will not be all right.

12.17 "Everything" constructions with གང་ན་ཅི་ཡོད་

This construction means "everything" or, more literally, "whatever exists."

a. ཁོའི་ཅ་ལག་གང་ན་ཅི་ཡོད་རྣམས་མོ་ལ་སྤྲད་པ་རེད།
He gave her whatever things he had.

b. ཚོང་ཁང་དེའི་ནང་གང་ན་ཅི་ཡོད་ཚང་མ་གོང་ཁེ་པོར་འཚོང་གི་འདུག།
Whatever is in that shop is being sold cheaply.

c. མོའི་འཇོན་ཆས་གང་ན་ཅི་ཡོད་སྔ་ལོ་ཁོ་ཚོས་ཉོས་སོང་།
They bought all her furniture last year (whatever furniture she had).

12.18 "Immediately" constructions with འཕྲལ་ + vb. + བྱེད་, གཏོང་, and རྒྱག་

འཕྲལ་ ("at once") was encountered earlier as a clause connective particle (6.2). Here it conveys the same meaning ("at once/immediately") but is used in constructions where it is placed before the main verb. In this role it adds "quickly/immediately" to the verbal meaning.

a. ངར་དངུལ་ཏོག་ཙམ་འཕྲལ་གཡར་བྱེད་རོགས་གནང་།
Please lend me a little money at once.

b. ཏར་འབྱོར་པ་དང་འཕྲལ་བསྐྱོད་བྱས་པ་ཡིན།
As soon as the telegram arrived, (I) immediately went.

12.19 "May it come" constructions: vb.+ པ་/བ་ or པར་/བར་ ཤོག་

These constructions are used to convey the exclamation "may something come (or not come) to pass."

a. སང་ཉིན་ཆར་པ་མ་གཏོང་བ་ཤོག།

May it not rain tomorrow.

b. འཛམ་གླིང་ཡོངས་ལ་ཞི་བདེ་ཡོང་བར་ཤོག།

May peace come to the entire world.

c. ང་ཚོའི་སློབ་གྲྭར་ལག་རྡེད་པོ་ལོའི་འགྲན་བསྡུར་གྱི་བྱ་དགའ་ཐོབ་པ་ཤོག།

May our school win the prize for the basketball competition.

12.20 Reading exercises

12.20.1 Reading number one: "The Love of the Male and Female Swan"

12.20.1.1 Tibetan text

ངང་པ་ཕོ་མོའི་མཛའ་གཅུགས།

མོན་ཏ་རེའི་གཤམ་དུ་གཞོན་ནུ་ཇོན་པ་དབུལ་པོ་1 ཞིག་ཡོད། ཁོང་གིས་ཡིད་འོང་མཛེས་སྡུག་ལྡན་པའི་2 གཞོན་ནུ་མ་ཞིག་ལ་སྙིང་ནས་བརྩེ་བ་དང་གཞོན་ནུ་མས་ཀྱང་ཁོ་པར་སྙིང་ནས་བརྩེ་པོ་ཡོད། གཞོན་ནུ་མའི་པ་ཕ་ནི་འདོད་ཧམས་ཏ་ཅང་ཆེན་པོ་ཡོད་པས། ཁོ་པས་གཞོན་ནུ་མར་རྒྱུ་དབང་གཉིས་འཛོམས་ཀྱི་ཕྱུག་པོ་ཞིག་གི་སར་བག་མར་འགྲོ་དགོས་ཟེར་ནས་གཞོན་ནུ་མ་དེ་ཁང་པའི་ནང་དུ་བཙུག་སྟེ་གཞོན་ནུ་ཇོན་པ་དེ་དང་ཐུག་འཕྲད་བྱེད་དུ་འཇུག་གི་མེད།3 མཚན་མོ་ཞིག་གཞོན་ནུ་མ་དེས་ཁྱིམ་ལས་བྲོས་ཏེ་ཇོན་པ་དང་མཉམ་དུ་ཐག་རིང་གི་ཕྱོགས་སུ་བདེ་སྐྱིད་ཀྱི་འཚོ་བ་འཚོལ་བར་སོང་།

གཞོན་ནུ་མའི་པ་ཕ་དང་ཕྱུག་པོ་གཉིས་པོས་རྟ་བཞོན་ནས་རྗེས་འདེད་གཏོང་བར་ཡོང་སྟེ། ཕྱུག་པོས་མདའ་འཕང་ཐེངས་གཅིག་ལ་4 གཞོན་ནུ་ཇོན་པ་བསད། གཞོན་ནུ་མས་རང་གི་སྙིང་གྲོགས་ལ་འཁྱུད་ནས་སེམས་སྡུག་ཆེན་པོས་མིག་ཆུ་བཏང་། གཞོན་ནུ་མའི་མཆི་མ་དེ་ཇོན་པའི་སྐ་ཁའི་ཐོག་ལྷུང་མ་ཐག་གཞོན་ནུ་ཇོན་པ་དེ་ངང་པ་དཀར་པོ་ཞིག་ཏུ་གྱུར་ནས་གཞོན་ནུ་མ་རྒྱབ་ཏུ་ཁུར་ཏེ་མཁའ་དབྱིངས་སུ་འཕུར་ནས་སོང་། ཁོང་གཉིས་ཐག་རིང་གི་ཕྱོགས་སུ་འཕུར་ཏེ་བྲག་ཕུག་ཅིག་གི་ནང་དབུལ་ཡང་སྐྱོ་བ་ལྡན་པའི་འཚོ་བ་སྐྱེལ་བཞིན་བསྡད།

སྟོན་དུས་ཤར་བས་ངང་པས་གཞོན་ནུ་མར་ང་ནི་ལྷོ་ལ་དགུན་དུས་སྐྱེལ་བར་འགྲོ་དགོས་པས་ཁྱེད་ཀྱིས་འདི་གར་སེམས་པ་སྐྱིད་པོའི་ངང་ང་སྒུག་སྡོད་བྱེད་རོགས། སྤང་རྒྱན་མེ་ཏོག་ཤར་མ་ཐག་ང་ཕྱིར་ལོག་ཡོང་ངེས་ཡིན། ཞེས་བཤད། དགུན་དུས་གྲང་ངར་ཏ་ཅང་ཆེ་ཞིང་། གཞོན་ནུ་མས་ཐག་རིང་གི་ཕྱོགས་སུ་ཕྱིན་པའི་ངང་པ་དྲན་ནས་སེམས་སྡུག་གིས་རྒྱན་པས་5 ནད་ཀྱིས་གདུངས།6

ཙེ་ཤིང་འདབ་ལོ་རྒྱས་ཤིང་མེ་ཏོག་བཞད་པའི་དཔྱིད་དུས་སུ་ངང་པ་ཕྱིར་ལོག་ཡོང་སྐབས་གཞོན་ནུ་མ་ནི་ནད་ཀྱིས་མནར་ཏེ་ཚེ་ལས་འདས་ཟིན་པ་མཐོང་། ངང་པ་སེམས་པ་སྐྱོ་ཐག་ཆོད་དེ་མིག་ཆུ་བཏང་། ཁོ་པའི་མིག་ཆུ་གཞོན་ནུ་མའི་མིག་གི་ཐོག་ལྷུང་མ་ཐག་གཞོན་ནུ་མ་དེའང་ངང་པ་དཀར་པོ་ཞིག་ཏུ་གྱུར་པས་མཉམ་དུ་ནམ་མཁའི་མཐོངས་སུ་འཕུར་ཏེ། དེ་ནས་བཟུང་ཁོང་གཉིས་དུས་ཆོད་སྐད

ཅིག་ཙམ་ཡང་ཁ་བྲལ་གྱི་མེད་པ་རེད།

12.20.1.2 Translation

The Love of the Male and Female Swan

There was a poor young hunter (living) at the foot of Montari. He loved a beautiful young girl with all his heart, and the girl loved him from her heart too. (But) because the young girl's father was a very greedy person, he told the young girl that she had to go as the bride of a man who was both powerful and wealthy. He kept (lit., put) the young girl in the house and did not allow her to meet the young hunter. One night, the young girl left her home and went with the hunter to a distant place to search for a happy life.

The girl's father and the rich man came riding horses in pursuit of them. The rich man shot one arrow and killed the young hunter. The young girl embraced her lover and cried with great sadness. As soon as the tears of the girl dropped on the opening of the young hunter's wound, the hunter turned into a white swan and flew away into the sky carrying the girl on his back. The two of them flew for a long distance and (then) lived happily in a cave even though they were poor.

Because autumn came, the swan said to the young girl, "I have to go south to spend the winter. Please wait here happily for me. I will definitely return as soon as the meadow flowers bloom." But because it was very cold during the winter and the young girl missed the white swan who had flown far away and was sad, she was afflicted with illness.

In springtime, (when) the leaves on the trees were growing and the flowers were blooming, the swan came back and saw that the young girl had died of illness. The swan felt extremely sad and cried. As soon as his tears dropped on the girl's eyes, she also became a white swan, and together (they) flew away into an opening in the sky. Ever since then, those two have never separated for even an instant of time.

12.20.1.3 Grammatical notes

1. གཞོན་ནུ་རྔོན་པ་ consists of the two nouns "young man" and "hunter." Together these describe a single person: "a young man who was a hunter." This is a common pattern with nouns describing types of persons (but not things), for example: དེར་གྲྭ་པ་འབྲོག་པ་གཅིག་འདུག་ "There is a monk who is a nomad here." Note that the first of the two nouns, in this case གཞོན་ནུ་ ("young man"), is considered more emphasized.

2. ཡིད་འོང་མཛེས་སྡུག་ལྡན་པའི་ consists of two nominals: ཡིད་འོང་ ("attractiveness") and མཛེས་སྡུག་ ("beauty"). These have been transformed to adjectivals by ལྡན་པ་ (see 10.3.6). The entire phrase then modifies བཞོན་ནུ་མ་ ("young girl").

3. ཐུག་འཕྲད་བྱེད་དུ་འཇུག་གི་མེད་ is the type of construction discussed in 11.8. འཇུག་ here conveys "allowed." Note that while grammatically this could also be translated as "did not make (her) meet the young hunter," it makes no semantic sense here. Note also that དང་ in this construction means "with."

4. ཐེངས་གཅིག་ལ་ is a standard construction conveying do/did the verbal action "one time." The verbal action here is "shot an arrow" (མདའ་འཕང་). For example, ཁོས་དེབ་ཀློག་ཐེངས་གཅིག་ལ་དོན་ལྷ་ཚང་མ་ཤེས་པ་རེད།—"Reading the book one time, he understood the meaning completely."

5. The རྐྱེན་ verbal connective constructions (conveying "because") are discussed in 5.9. Here རྐྱེན་ + the instrumental particle is used with a nominal སེམས་སྡུག ("sadness") to convey "because" or "by"—("because of sadness").

6. The cause of ནད་ཀྱིས་གདུངས་ ("suffer from illness") is conveyed in the two preceding clauses: དགུན་དུས་གྲང་ངར་ཧ་ཅང་ཆེ་ཞིང་ and གཞོན་ནུ་མས་ཐག་རིང་གི་ཕྱོགས་སུ་ཕྱིན་པའི་ངང་པ་དྲན་ནས་སེམས་སྡུག་གིས་རྐྱེན་པས་. Thus, she was sick because of the extreme cold and her sadness at missing the swan.

12.20.2 Reading number two: "The Wish-fulfilling Gem Necklace".

12.20.2.1 Tibetan text.

ཡིད་བཞིན་ནོར་བུའི་1 དོ་ཤལ།།

གནའ་རབས་སུ་རྒྱལ་པོ་ཞིག་ཡོད། ཁོང་དགུང་ལོ་བཞི་བཅུར་སོན་སྐབས་གཞི་ནས་སྲས་མོ་ཞིག་བྱུང་། སྲས་མོ་དེ་ནི་གཤིས་རྒྱུད་བཟང་ལ་བློ་གྲོས་ལྡན་པ་དང་། མཛེས་ཤིང་2 ཡིད་དུ་འོང་བ་ཞིག་ཡོད་པས་རྒྱལ་པོས་རང་གི་མིག་འབྲས་ལྟར་གཅེས་སྐྱོང་གནང་བ་མ་ཟད།3 བླ་མ་རྩ་ཆེན་ཞིག་གདན་དྲངས་ནས་སྲས་མོར་བཀྲ་ཤིས་ལྷ་མོ་ཞེས་མཚན་བཏགས། མི་རྣམས་ཀྱིས་ཁོང་ལ་སྲས་མོ་བཀྲས་ལྷ་4 ཞེས་འབོད་ཀྱི་ཡོད།

སྲས་མོ་བཀྲས་ལྷའི་སྐྱེ་སྐར་གྱི་རྟེན་འབྲེལ་དེ་ལོ་གསུམ་རེའི་ཐོག་ཐེངས་རེ་5 བྱས་ནས་རྒྱལ་པོ་དང་བཙུན་མོ་རྣམ་གཉིས་ཀྱིས་གསོལ་སྟོན་བྲ་རྒྱས་གཤོམ་གྱི་ཡོད། སྲས་མོ་བཀྲས་ལྷ་དགུང་ལོ་བཅུ་དགུར་སོན་པའི་ལོ་དེར་སྐྱེ་སྐར་གྱི་རྟེན་འབྲེལ་སྔར་ལས་བྲ་རྒྱས་བྱས། བརྗོད་ཉམས་ལྡན་པའི་རྒྱལ་པོའི་ཕོ་བྲང་ནང་རིན་ཆེན་ཕྲེང་དུ་བརྒྱུས་པ་ལྟར་6 དང་རྣམ་པར་བཀྲ་བའི་རྒྱན་མཆོར་གྱིས་བརྒྱན་པ་དང་། སྐུ་མགྲོན་ཚང་མ་དགའ་སྤྲོའི་ངང་ལ་རོལ་བཞིན་ཡོད་སྲས་མོ་བཀྲས་ལྷ་མུ་ཏིག་ལ་སོགས་པའི་རིན་ཆེན་སྣ་ཚོགས་ཀྱིས་བརྒྱན་ནས་ལྷ་ཡི་བུ་མོ་ལྟ་བུར་གྱུར་ཡོད། རྟེན་འབྲེལ་གྱི་སྟོན་འདུན་ཞུ་བའི་སྐྲའི་ཁྲིད་དུ་རྒྱལ་པོས་གཟི་མིག་དགུ་པ་བཅུ་

དགུ་དང་བྱུ་རུ་སུམ་ཅུ་སོ་གསུམ། གཡུ་དྲུག་ཅུ་རེ་དྲུག་བཅས་རིན་ཆེན་ལས་འགྲུབ་པའི་7 ཡིད་བཞིན་ནོར་བུའི་དོ་ཤལ་དེ་བྱམས་བརྩེའི་ངང་སྲས་མོ་བཀྲས་ལྷའི་མགུལ་ལ་བསྐོན།

མུ་ཏིག་སོགས་རིན་ཆེན་སྣ་ཚོགས་ཀྱིས་བརྒྱན་པའི་ཡོ་བྱང་གི་གཞས་མ་ཁྲུ་གཅིག་གིས་བསོད་ནམས་ལྡན་པའི་སྲས་མོར་བསྐོར་ཞིང་དགའ་སྤྲོའི་གླུ་གར་འཁྲབ། སྲས་མོ་བཀྲས་ལྷས་ཡབ་ཡུམ་གཉིས་ཀྱིས་དྲིན་གྱིས་སྐྱོང་བར་ཐུགས་རྗེ་ཆེ་ཞུ་ཆེད་སྐུ་ཚེ་ཡུན་ནས་ཡུན་དུ་གནས་པར་ཤོག་ཅེས་པའི་གླུ་བླངས་སོ།8

གློ་བུར་དུ་རླུང་དམར་ནག་པོ་འཚུབས་9 ནས་ནམ་མཁའ་འཐིབས་པ་དང་ས་གཞིར་མུན་པ་རུབ་པ་གློག་འཁྱུགས་པ་དང་། འབྲུག་སྒྲ་བསྒྲགས་པས་10 རྒྱལ་པོ་དང་བཙུན་མོ་གཉིས་སྐྲག་ཐག་ཆོད་ནས་རང་གི་གཟིམ་ཆུང་དུ་བྲོས། སྐབས་དེར་ཡ་མཚན་ཅན་གྱི་བྱ་གླག་གཅིག་གིས་སྲས་མོ་ཁྱེར་ཏེ་སྒེ་ཁུང་ནས་འཕུར་སོང་བ་རེད། རྒྱལ་པོ་དང་བཙུན་མོ་རྣམ་གཉིས་ནི་རང་གི་སྲས་མོ་བརླགས་པའི་སེམས་སྡུག་གིས་གདུངས་བའི་ཁྲོད་དུ་གནས། རི་མོ་མཁན་མཁས་པ་གདན་དྲངས་ཏེ་སྲས་མོ་བཀྲས་ལྷའི་སྐུ་བརྙན་ཚོན་ཁྲ་ཅན་ཞིག་བྲིས་ནས་གང་སར་སྦྱར་འགྲིམ་བྱས་པ་མ་ཟད། ད་དུང་གལ་ཏེ་སྲས་མོ་གང་ཡོད་ཤེས་ནས་11 སྙན་སེང་ཞུ་མཁན་ལ་གསོལ་རས་དངུལ་ཏྲ་སྨིག་པ་12 བཅུ་སྤྲོད་རྒྱུ་དང་། གལ་ཏེ་སྲས་མོ་སྐྱོབ་ཐུབ་མཁན་ཡོད་ན་དེར་མི་ཚེ་གཅིག་རིང་འདང་བའི་གསེར་ས་ཕག་བརྒྱ་ཐམ་པ་སྤྲོད་13 རྒྱུ། གལ་ཏེ་སྐྱོབ་མི་དེ་གཞོན་པ་ཡིན་ན་སྲས་མོའི་མག་པར་ཉར་རྒྱུ་བཅས་ཡིན་ཞེས་རྒྱ་ཆེར་བཀྲམ།

གྲོག་རོང་ཞིག་གི་ནང་དུ་དབུལ་ཞིང་ཕོངས་པའི་མ་བུ་དུད་ཚང་ཞིག་ཡོད་བྱམས་བརྩེ་ལྡན་པའི་ཨ་མའི་མིང་ལ་ཚེ་སྐྱིད་ཟེར་བ་དང་དཔའ་ཉམས་ལྡན་པའི་བུ་ཡི་མིང་ལ་བློ་ནོར་ཟེར་ཞིང་། ཐ་ཅང་མཐོང་བར་དཀོན་པའི་14 སེར་དྲག་ཆེན་པོ་དེས་ཤིང་ཁང་ཀྱག་ཀྱག་བཟོས་པ་དང་། ཞིང་ནང་གི་ལྗང་པ་རྣམས་སེར་བས་བརྡུངས་བར་བརྟེན་ཨ་མས་ཞིང་ནང་གི་ལྗང་པ་རྣམས་ཡར་སྐྱོར་བ་བུ་ཡིས་ཁང་པ་ཉམས་གསོ་བྱེད་བཞིན་ཡོད། ཨ་མ་ཚེ་སྐྱིད་ངལ་དུབ་ཀྱིས་ཁྱིམ་དུ་ཇ་འཐུང་ཤུགས་བཟས་15 བྱེད་པར་འགྲོ་དགོས་བསམས། ཕྱིར་ལོག་བྱེད་པའི་ལམ་བར་དྲེགས་ལྡན་སེང་གེའི་ང་རོ་སྐད་བརྒྱབ་པ་གློ་བུར་དུ་ཐོས་མ་ཐག་མགོ་ཡར་བཏེགས་ནས་ལྟ་སྐབས་གངས་ལས་དཀར་བའི་སེང་གེ་ཞིག་གིས་ཁ་ཆེས་ཆེར་གདངས་ནས་མདུན་དུ་མཆོང་ཡོང་གི་ཡོད་པ་མཐོང་བས་ཨ་མ་སྐྲག་ཐག་ཆོད་དེ་འགྱེལ་བ་དང་བུ་བློ་ནོར་བློ་ནོར་ཞེས་བོས། བུ་ཡིས་སེང་གེའི་ང་རོ་སྐད་དང་ཨ་མའི་འབོད་སྒྲ་ཐོས་མ་ཐག་སྟ་རེ་འཁུར་བཞིན་རྒྱུག་ཕྱིན། སེང་གེ་དཀར་མོས་ཨ་མའི་རྐང་པར་སོ་བརྒྱབ་ནས་འདྲུད་ཕྱིན་པས། བློ་ནོར་གྱིས་སྟ་རེ་གཞུ་སྐབས་སྟ་རེའི་མགོ་བུད་དེ་ཐག་རིང་སར་ཟགས་པ་16 དང་སྟ་རེའི་ཡུ་བ་སེང་གེའི་སྒལ་སྟེང་དུ་ཤུགས་ཆེ་ཐེབས་སྐབས་གཏུམ་དྲག་ཆེ་བའི་སེང་གེ་དཀར་མོ་དེས་དངངས་སྐྲག་གི་སྒོ་ནས་ཨ་མའི་ལྷམ་ཁྱེར་ནས་བྲོས་ཕྱིན། ཨ་མ་ཚེ་སྐྱིད་ལ་ལྷམ་ཆ་དེ་རང་ལས་མེད་པས་བུ་བློ་ནོར་གྱིས་རང་དགར་བསྐྱུར་ག་ལ་སྲིད། ཁོང་གིས་སྟ་རེ་ཡར་བསྒྲུགས་རྗེས་ཡུ་བ་བརྟན་པོར་བཟུང་ནས་གོམ་སྟབས་མགྱོགས་པོའི་ངང་རི་མཐོའི་ནགས་གསེབ་ཀྱི་ཁྲོད་དུ་རྗེས་འདེད་གཏོང་བར་ཕྱིན།

འདི་འཕྲོས་སློབ་ཚན་བཅུ་གསུམ་པར་གཟིགས་

12.20.2.2 Translation

The Wish-fulfilling Gem Necklace

In ancient times there was a king. When he reached the age of forty, only then did he get a daughter (was a daughter born to him). That daughter had good character, was wise, and was very beautiful. Because of this, the king took care of her like his own eyes. Not only that, he (also) invited a venerable lama who named her Tashi Lhamo ["auspicious goddess"]. (Afterwards) people called her Princess "Drelha."

Princess Drelha's birthday celebration was done every three years. (At this time) the king and queen prepared an elaborate banquet. On the year when Princess Drelha was 19 years of age, (they) made a birthday celebration more elaborate than in the past. The inside of the king's magnificent palace had been decorated with beautiful ornaments and with many precious jewels strung like beads on a rosary. All the guests were enjoying themselves. Princess Drelha was adorned with pearls and other different kinds of precious gems and had become like a daughter of the gods (goddess). In the midst of the exchange of good wishes, the king lovingly put on Princess Drelha's neck a precious gem necklace made from precious gems such as 19 nine-eyed *si* stones, 33 (pieces of) coral, and 66 (pieces of) turquoise.

(At this time) a group of the palace's female singers wearing pearls and many other precious gems surrounded the fortunate princess, singing and dancing. Princess Drelha sang a song in order to show gratitude to her parents (for their kindness), which said, "May (they) live forever!"

Suddenly it became stormy, the sky clouded over, the earth became dark and there was lightning and thunder. The king and the queen were very frightened and fled into their living quarters. At that time a strange eagle (appeared in the hall) and flew from the window carrying the princess. The king and queen were sad over the loss of their daughter. (They) summoned an expert artist who drew a color picture of Princess Drelha, which they put up everywhere. Beside that, they also disseminated an edict saying, "If anyone knows where the princess is and reports it, (he, she) will be rewarded with 10 horse-hoof-sized (ingots) of silver. If someone saves the princess, he will be rewarded with one hundred bricks of gold, a sum that will be sufficient for one's whole life. (And) if the one who saves her is a young man, he will be taken (into the family) as a bridegroom."

In a gorge there was a poor family (consisting) of a mother and son. The name of the kind mother was Tsekyi and the name of the brave son was Lodor. Due to a hailstorm of proportions rarely seen, their wooden house had become lopsided and the sprouts in the field had been beaten down. Because of this, the mother was working in the fields propping up the stalks and the son was repairing their house. The mother Tsekyi got very tired and thought, "I have to go home to drink tea and eat *pak* (roasted barley dough)." On the road (she was) returning (on), she suddenly heard the roar of a ferocious lion. As soon as (she) heard it, (she) lifted her head, looked, and saw a lion whiter than snow leaping towards her (to the front) with its mouth open very wide. She was extremely scared, collapsed, and called, "Son Lodor, Lodor." As soon as the son heard the shouts of his mother and the lion's roar, he took an axe and went running. Because the white lion had bitten his mother's leg and was dragging her (away), Lodor struck (a blow) at (the lion) with his axe. At that time the head of the axe became unstuck and flew off (lit., slipped off) far away. The handle (however) hit the lion hard on its back. The fierce white lion was frightened by this and fled carrying his mother's shoe. (Lodor thought,) "Since Mother Tsekyi had just that one pair of shoes, how could her son give it up?" After he picked up the axe (head), he fixed it on the handle firmly (and) then went quickly into the forest on the high mountain to chase after (the lion).

See Lesson 13 for the continuation.

12.20.2.3 Grammatical notes

1. The phrase ཡིད་བཞིན་ནོར་བུ་ means "wish-fulfilling gem" and by extrapolation is also used for the Dalai Lama. Here it refers to the gem.

2. This segment consists of 4 adjectivals: (1) གཤིས་རྒྱུད་བཟང་ལ་, (2) བློ་གྲོས་ལྡན་པ་དང་།, (3) མཛེས་ཤིང་, and (4) ཡིད་དུ་འོང་བ་ strung together by the conjunctives ལ་, དང་, and ཤིང་. See 10.3.7 for a discussion of adjective conjunction.

3. Although this placement of "not only" may seem semantically inappropriate here, there is nothing wrong with it in Tibetan semantics.

4. This is an abbreviation of the name བཀྲ་ཤིས་ལྷ་མོ་. Normally the first and third syllables are joined, but in this case Tibetan convention uses བཀྲས་ instead of བཀྲ་.

5. ཐོག་ in the phrase ལོ་གསུམ་རེའི་ཐོག་ཐེངས་རེ conveys "at" (see 12.1.4). The particle རེ་ ("each") was explained in 10.8.

6. The phrase བརྗོད་ཉམས་ལྡན་པའི་རྒྱལ་པོའི་པོ་བྲང་ནང་རིན་ཆེན་ཕྲེང་དུ་བརྒྱུས་པ་ལྟར་ illustrates three

common ways that Tibetans convey flowery descriptions. In the first segment, an adjectivized nominal (བརྗིད་ཉམས་ལྡན་པ) modifies "palace" through the genitive particle ("a palace that was magnificent—a magnificent palace"). In the second part, རིན་ཆེན་ཕྲེང་དུ་བརྒྱུས་པ་, ལྟར་ ("like") is used to create a simile—"precious gems strung like (beads) on a rosary." In the third part, རྣམ་པར་བཀྲ་བའི་, the adjective བཀྲ་བ ("beautiful") is modified by the adverbial རྣམ་པར་ ("completely"), which both are then linked to the noun "decorations" (རྒྱན་མཆོར་) through the genitive particle.

7. The phrase རིན་ཆེན་ལས་འགྲུབ་པ་ ("came from precious gems") modifies རྡོ་ཤལ་ ("necklace"). It should be noted that ལས་ here means "from" rather than its more usual "than."

8. Recall that སོ་ indicates the end of a sentence (see 6.10.3.14).

9. རླུང་དམར་འཚུབས་ means "to storm" and དྲག་པོ་ functions adverbially conveying "fiercely."

10. This is a common way to list a series of verbal actions (ནམ་མཁའ་འཕྱིབས་པ་དང་ས་གཞིར་ལྡན་པ་རྡབ་པ་གློག་འཁྱུགས་པ་དང་། འབྲུག་སྒྲ་བསྒྲགས་པས་). Four verb phrases are linked here by the པ་དང་ clause connective or just listed consecutively.

11. གལ་ཏེ་ . . . ནས་ ("if") is normally written གལ་ཏེ་ . . . ན་.

12. This literally means "silver made in the shape of a horse hoof."

13. This construction breaks down into མི་ཚེ་གཅིག་རིང་ ("for the duration of one lifetime") and འདང་བའི་གསེར་ས་ཕག་-བརྒྱ་ཐམ་པ་སྤྲོད་ ("give 100 bricks of gold which are/will be sufficient for").

14. ཧ་ཅང་མཐོང་བར་དཀོན་པའི་སེར་དྲག་ཆེན་པོ་ is an interesting construction. The core is the noun "hailstorm" (སེར་དྲག་), which is modified by both the adjective "big" (ཆེན་པོ་) and the preceding phrase via the genitive particle. That phrase starts with the adverb "very" (ཧ་ཅང་), which modifies "rare" (དཀོན་པ), which in turn modifies the nominalized verb "seeing" (མཐོང་བར་).

15. In this construction the verbal phrase "eat *ba* and drink tea" (ཇ་འཐུང་སྤགས་བཟས་) function as noun and thus are verbalized by བྱེད་. It could have also have been written ཇ་འཐུང་པ་དང་སྤགས་བཟས་པར་འགྲོ་.

16. In the phrase སྟ་རེའི་མགོ་ཐུད་དེ་ the verb ཐུད་ ("to come off, get unstrung") conveys that the head of the axe slipped off as he was in the action of striking the lion.

12.21 Vocabulary

ཀྱོག་ཀྱོག་	crooked, zig-zag
དཀོན་	rare, scarce
བཀྲ་བ་	multicolored, beautiful, lovely; bright
བཀྲ་ཤིས་ལྷ་མོ་	p.n.
བཀྲམ་	va. to spread out, disperse
བཀྲས་ལྷ་	abbr. བཀྲ་ཤིས་ལྷ་མོ་
ཀྱང་	"go right ahead" particle
རྐུ་མ་	thief; va.— རྐུ་ to steal
སྐད་ཅིག་	a moment, an instant
སྐུ་མགྲོན་	guest (h.)
སྐུ་བརྙན་	statue, image, portrait (h.)
སྐྱེལ་	1. va. to deliver; 2. va. to spend time
སྐྱེ་སྐར་	birthday
སྐྱོན་	1. "too" particle; 2. error, mistake; 3. damage, harm
སྐྱོར་	va. to support, prop up
བསྐོར་	va. to surround
བསྐྱར་	again
བསྐྱུར་	va. to give up, abandon, throw away
ཁ་བྲལ་	vi. to separate, to divorce
ཁུར་	va. p. of འཁུར་
ཁེ་པོ་	cheap
ཁྱུ་	herd, group
ཁྱེར་	va. p. of འཁྱེར་
མཁའ་དབྱིངས་	sky
འཁྱུད་	va. to embrace, hug
འཁྲབ་	va. to act, perform
ག་ནས་	"how could" construction
ག་པར་	"how could" construction
གང་གི་ཆ་ནས་	"by all means/in all respects" construction
གང་གི་ཐད་ནས་	"by all means/in all respects" construction
གང་གི་ཐོག་ནས་	"by all means/in all respects" construction
གང་གིས་ཤེ་ན་	"why" construction
གང་ཅི་	"lots of ways" construction
གང་ཅིའི་ཐད་ནས་	"by all means/in all respects" construction
གང་ཅིའི་ཐོག་ནས་	"by all means/in all respects" construction
གང་ཐད་ནས་	"by all means/in all respects" construction
གང་དང་ཅི་	"lots of ways" construction
གང་དྲག་	"it's a pity" construction
གང་འདྲ་ཞིག་	"what kind of" construction
གང་ན་ཅི་ཡོད་	"whatever exists" construction
གང་ས་ནས་	"by all means/in all respects" construction
གང་ཞིག་དྲག་	"it's a pity" construction
གང་ཡིན་ཅེ་ན་	"why" construction
གང་ཡིན་ཟེར་ན་	"why" construction
གང་སར་	everywhere, all over
གོམ་སྟབས་	step
གྲ་རྒྱས་	elaborate preparations; va. — བྱེད་; — གཤོམ་ to make elaborate preparations
གྲང་ངར་	cold, coldness
གྲུ་	boat
གྲུབ་ཐོབ་ཐང་སྟོང་	a great yogin, siddhi
གྲོག་རོང་	gully, gorge, deep ravine
གྲོས་མོལ་	discussion; va. — བྱེད་
གླུ་	song
གླུ་གར་	song and dance

གློག་འཁྱུགས་ lightning
དགུན་དུས་ winter time
མགུལ་ neck, throat
མགྲིན་དབྱངས་ voice
འགྱེལ་ vi. to fall, collapse
འགྲན་བསྡུར་ competition; va. — བྱེད་
འགྲིགས་ vi. to be all right, okay
འགྲུབ་ vi. to be achieved, fulfilled, completed; to be gathered, assembled
རྒྱ་དངུལ་ Chinese silver
རྒྱན་མཚར་ ornament, decoration
རྒྱལ་གླུ་ national anthem
རྒྱབ་དུ་ the back side
རྒྱས་ vi. to flourish, thrive, grow
རྒྱུ་ 1. "should not" particle; 2. va. to string beads, flowers, gems
རྒྱུ་དབང་ wealth and power
སྒར་ va. to fix, to put on a handle
སྒལ་ the back (of a person or animal)
སྒུག་སྡོད་ stay waiting; va. — བྱེད་
སྒོ་ door
སྒོར་ dollar or rupee or yuan
སྒྲོན་ va. to put on (h.)
བརྒྱན་ va. to adorn, decorate
བརྒྱུད་ via, through
བརྒྱུས་ va. p. of རྒྱུ་
བསྒར་ va. p. of སྒར་
བསྒྲོན་ va. p. of སྒྲོན་
ངང་པ་ swan
བསྔགས་བརྗོད་ praise; va. — བྱེད་
ཅི་དྲག་ "it's a pity" construction
ཅི་འདྲ་ཞིག་ "what kind of" construction
ཅི་ཞིག་དྲག་ "it's a pity" construction
ཅི་ལ་ཟེར་ན་ "why" construction
ཅིས་ཤེ་ན་ "why" construction
གཅེས་སྐྱོང་ taking care of, protecting, defending; va. — བྱེད་
བཅིངས་འགྲོལ་ liberation; va. — གཏོང་
ལྕགས་ཐག་ཟམ་པ་ iron-link bridge
ཆ་ pair, match
ཆུ་གློག་ hydroelectric
ཆུ་གློག་ས་ཚིགས་ hydroelectric station
ཆེས་ཆེར་ very much bigger
ཇི་འདྲ་ཞིག་ "what kind of" construction
རྗེས་འདེད་ chasing, pursuing; va. — གཏོང་
ལྗང་པ་ a sprout, a plant
ཉར་ va. to keep, hold
གཉིས་པོ་ the two together
མཉམ་འབྲེལ་ cooperation, cooperative
སྙན་སེང་ report; petition; va. — ཞུ་
སྙིང་གྲོགས་ bosom friend
ཏར་ telegram, cable; va. — གཏོང་
གཏུམ་དྲག་ fierce, savage, violent
བཏགས་ va. p. of འདོགས་
རྟ་མིག་ hoof of horse
རྟེན་འབྲེལ་ ceremony, celebration
རྟེན་འབྲེལ་གྱི་སྨོན་འདུན་ good wishes offered at a celebration (e.g., "best of luck, long life"), va. — ཞུ་
རྟོག་ཞིབ་ inspection; va. — བྱེད་
ལྟ་བུ་ similar, like
སྟོན་དུས་ autumn
ཐག་རིང་ distant, far
ཐུག་འཕྲད་ meet; va. — བྱེད་
ཐེ་ཇུས་ interference; va — བྱེད་
ཐེབས་ vi. to get hit, struck by

ཐོག་	1. on; 2. via; 3. in addition to; 4. during; at the time when; 5. concerning
མཐུན་རྐྱེན་	resource
མཐོངས་	opening, gap, hole
འཐིབས་	vi. to be overcast, cloudy
འཐུས་མི་	a delegate
དག་པོ་	good quality
དུས་ཆེན་	festival; occasion
དུས་ཚོད་	time
དེ་ནས་བཟུང་	from that time onwards
དེ་ཙམ་	"how ever much . . ., that much" construction
དོ་ཤལ་	necklace
དྲིན་གྱིས་སྐྱོང་	va. to look after with kindness, to be kind to
དྲེགས་	vi. to be arrogant, haughty; to be ferocious
གདན་དྲངས་	va. p. of གདན་འདྲེན་
གདན་འདྲེན་	1. va. to summon, call; 2. va to invite
གདུངས་	vi. to suffer from, be tormented by
བདམས་	va. p. of འདམ་
མདའ་	arrow; va. — རྒྱག་
མདོག་ཁ་པོ་	"seems likely to occur"
འདང་	vi. to suffice, to be enough
འདབ་ལོ་	leaf
འདི་གར་	here, over here
འདོད་རྔམས་	greed, avarice
འདོད་རྔམས་ཆེན་པོ་	greedy
འདྲུད་	va. to drag, pull
ལྡན་པ་	having, possessing
བརྡུངས་	va. p. of རྡུང་
ནགས་གསེབ་	forest, jungle
ནད་	illness, disease
ནམ་ཡང་	always
མནར་	vi. to suffer, to be oppressed
རྣམ་	honorific term used for second and third person
རྣམ་པར་	perfectly, completely
དཔའ་ཉམས་	heroic, courageous, spirited
དཔའ་ཉམས་ལྡན་པ་	heroic
སྤག་	name of the staple Tibetan food that is made from roasted barley flour and kneaded with tea or water
སྤང་རྒྱན་མེ་ཏོག་	meadow flower
སྤུས་ཀ་	quality
དཔྱིད་དུས་	springtime
སྤྲོ་བ་ལྡན་པ་	happy, joyful, cheerful
ཕོངས་	vi. to be destitute, devoid of
ཕྱག་རོགས་ཞུ་	va. to request help (h.)
ཕྲེང་	rosary; string of beads, jewels, flowers; va. — (དུ་) བརྒྱུས་ to string beads, jewels, flowers
འཕང་	va. to shoot, to fire a weapon
འཕྱར་	va. to hoist, raise, lift up
འཕྲད་	va. to meet
འཕྲལ་	at once, immediately
བག་མ་	bride
བུད་	vi. to come off, to become unstrung
བོད་མི་	Tibetan person
བྱ་རྒོད་	Tibetan eagle
བྱམས་བརྩེ་	love
བྱུ་རུ་	coral

བྲིས་	va. p. of འབྲི་
བློ་གྲོས་ལྡན་པ་	wise, understanding
བློ་རྡོར་	p.n.
འབྲུག་སྒྲ་བསྒྲགས་	vi. to thunder
སྦྱར་འགྲེམ་	a poster, va. — བྱེད་ to put up a poster
མ་བུ་	abbr. mother and son
མག་པ་	bridegroom who comes to live with wife's family
མང་ཉུང་	quantity, amount, number
མིག་འབྲས་	eyeball
མིང་	name
མུ་ཏིག་	pearl
མུན་པ་རུབ་	vi. to become dark, night, twlight
མོན་	p.n. of an area
ཙམ་	about, approximately
བཙོང་	va. p. of འཚོང་
བཙོན་པ་	prisoner
རྩ་ཆེན་	precious, sacred
རྩ་ཆིག་	public notice, edict, proclamation; va. — བཀྲམ་ to proclaim, announce an edict
རྩད་གཅོད་	investigation; va. — བྱེད་
རྩི་ཤིང་	a plant
བརྩེ་	va. to love
བརྩེ་བོ་	love
ཚ་བ་	heat
ཚད་	1. level, limit, scale; 2. also particle used in "every time/whenever/whoever/whatever" constructions
ཚུགས་	vi. p. of འཛུགས་
ཚེ་སྐྱིད་	p.n.
ཚོན་ཁྲ་	colored
མཚན་	a name (h.)
མཚན་འདོགས་	va. to name, give a name (h.)
མཚན་བཏགས་	va. p. of མཚན་འདོགས་
འཚོང་	va. to sell
མཛའ་གཅུགས་	love
མཛེས་ཤིང་ཡིད་དུ་འོང་བ་	beautiful, charming, attractive
མཛེས་སྡུག་	beauty
འཛམ་གླིང་	the world
འཛིན་བཟུང་	arrest; va. — བྱེད་
འཛོམ་	vi. to be collected together, to be congregated, to be gathered
འཛོམས་	vi. p. of འཛོམ་
ཞི་བདེ་	peace
གཞས་མ་	singer (female)
གཞུ་	va. to hit, strike
གཞིས་ཆགས་	resettling; va. — བྱེད་
གཞོན་ནུ་མ་	young girl
བཞད་	vi. to bloom (flower)
ཟགས་	vi. to fall (off something)
གཟི་	a type of precious stone that is black with dot-like designs that Tibetans refer to as "eyes"
གཟིམ་ཆུང་	living quarters, living room (h.)
བཟང་	kind, sincere, good
ཡ་མཚན་ཅན་	strange, unusual
ཡབ་ཡུམ་	parents; father and mother (h.)
ཡར་	upwards
ཡར་ཀླུང་གཙང་པོ་	name of the main east-west river in Tibet
ཡིད་དུ་འོང་བ་	beautiful, pleasing
ཡིད་བཞིན་ནོར་བུ་	precious gem

ཡིད་འོང་མཛེས་སྡུག་ལྡན་པ་	beautiful, pretty
ཡུ་བ་	handle
ཡུན་	duration
ཡུན་ནས་ཡུན་དུ་	forever, everlasting
གཡུ་	turquoise
རང་དགར་	1. leaving something as it is; va. — བསྐྱུར་ or བཞག་ to leave as it is; 2. on one's own, free
རི་ལྗོངས་	rivers and hills; country, side scenery
རི་མཐོ་	high mountain
རི་མོ་མཁན་	painter, artist
རིན་ཆེན་	precious, valuable
རོལ་	vi. to enjoy
རླངས་འཁོར་	car, automobile
རླུང་དམར་དྲག་པོ་	storm, hurricane, typhoon; vi. — འཚུབས་ to storm
ལ་དཔག་(སྟེ་)(ན་)	according to
ལ་གཞིགས་(ཏེ་)(ན་)	according to
ལག་ཏེད་སྤོ་ལོ་	basketball; va. — རྒྱག་
ལས་དོན་	work
ལས་མི་	worker
ལུང་པ་	place, country
ཤིང་ཁང་	wooden house
ཤིང་སོན་	tree seed
ཤུགས་	strength, power
གཤམ་ (དུ་)	beneath, below
གཤིས་རྒྱུད་	character, personality
གཤོམ་	va. to set out, to arrange, to prepare
ས་ཕག་	a brick
ས་ཚིགས་	station
ས་གཞི་	earth
སུ་འདྲ་ཞིག་	like who, like whom
སུ་ཡི་	"whose"
སུ་ཡིས་	"by whom"
སུ་ལ་	"to whom"
སུའི་	"whose"
སུར་	"to whom"
སུས་	"by whom"
སེར་བ་	hail
སེང་གེ་	lion
སེམས་སྡུག་	sadness, depression
སེར་དྲག་	hail storm; vi. — བབས་
སོན་	va. to reach, to receive
སྲས་མོ་	1, daughter (h.); 2. also a term of address for daughters of the aristocracy or royalty—In this case since it is the daughter of a king, it is translated as "princess."
གསོལ་སྟོན་	banquet, feast; va. — གཤོམ་ to give a banquet
བསམ་ཚུལ་འབྲི་དེབ་	suggestion book
བསོད་ནམས་	luck, merit, good fortune; person's name
ཀྲུའུ་ཞི་	ch. chairman
ལྷ་ལྡན་	Lhasa
ལྷམ་	boot, shoe
ལྷོ་	south

Lesson Thirteen

13.1 Word formation: introduction

As we have seen, virtually all Tibetan syllables have independent meanings. This "monosyllabic" nature of Tibetan affords tremendous flexibility not only in expressing new ideas and concepts, but also in expressing old ones in new ways. In fact, it is a mark of literary ability and accomplishment to manipulate and recombine syllables (morphemes) creatively. For the student, however, this means that you will often encounter new combinations even for very standard ideas. Thus, in order to read written Tibetan successfully, the basic structure underlying word formation must be understood and this will be the subject of the following sections.

13.1.1 Nominal compounds

Nominal compounds consist of two syllables,[1] each of which is a non-derived noun.

13.1.2 Synonymic compounds

These consist of two syllables which are synonyms. The meaning of the compound word is identical to the overall meaning of the component parts. For example, སྟོབས་ཤུགས་ ("power, strength") is comprised of two syllables: སྟོབས་ ("power, strength") and ཤུགས་ ("power, strength").

a. སྟོབས་ཀྱིས་ས་མང་པོ་བཟུང་བ་རེད།
(They) seized many areas by force.

b. སྟོབས་ཤུགས་ཀྱིས་ས་མང་པོ་བཟུང་བ་རེད།
same as a.

Other common synonymic compounds are:

གྲངས་འབོར་	quantity, number, amount	སྒྲ་སྐད་	sound, voices
དཀའ་ངལ་	difficulty	རེ་འདུན་	hope
དུས་སྐབས་	time, period	ངོ་གདོང་	face
བུ་ཕྲུག་	children	གྲལ་རིམ་	class (social)

13.1.3 Premodifying compounds

In these constructions the first syllable modifies the second. Thus, in the word སྨན་ཁང་ ("hospital"), the syllable སྨན་ ("medicine") describes what kind of a ཁང་ (པ་) (house,

[1] Four-syllable compounds will be discussed following the section on two syllable units.

establishment") it is. Some other common examples are:

གནམ་གྲུ་	sky + boat = airplane
ཞིང་ཆུ་	agricultural field + water = irrigation water
ས་བདག་	land + owner = land owner, landlord
སློབ་ཕྲུག་	school + children = student
དམག་མི་	war + person = soldier
གནམ་གཤིས་	sky + nature/character = weather, climate
གློག་འཕྲིན་	electricity + correspondence/communication = telegram

13.1.4 Conjunctive compounds

Like premodifying compounds, the component syllables in these compounds also have different meanings, but here the relationship between them is one of conjunction rather than modification. For example, "workers and farmers" consists of the first syllable of the word བཟོ་པ་ ("workers") and the first syllable of the word ཞིང་པ་ ("farmers"). The meaning is the combination of the two: "workers and farmers."

a. བཟོ་པ་དང་ཞིང་པ་མང་པོས་ཚོགས་འདུ་བྱས་པ་རེད།
Many workers and farmers held a meeting.

b. བཟོ་ཞིང་མང་པོས་ཚོགས་འདུ་བྱས་པ་རེད།
Many workers and farmers held a meeting.

Some other common conjunctive compounds are:

གནས་དུས་	place and time
ཞིང་འབྲོག་	farmers and nomads
དགེ་སློབ་	teachers and students
རྒྱ་བོད་	China/Chinese and Tibet/Tibetans
ལོ་ཟླ་	years and months
རྟ་དྲེལ་	horses and mules

13.1.5 Polar compounds

In these constructions each of the syllables has an opposite meaning, but the overall meaning of the compound is either conjunctive or an abstract notion deriving from both. For example, ཕ་མ་ literally consists of ཕ་ ("father") and མ་ ("mother") and as a compound can mean either "father and mother" or "parent(s)." Other common compounds are:

ཉིན་མཚན་	day + night; all the time
ཕོ་མོ་	male + female; sex
གཞུང་སྒེར་	government + private; everything

Adjectives are more commonly used as the components of polar compounds.

They are discussed in the next section.

13.1.6 Adjectival polar compounds

The polar type of adjectival compound functions the same as the nominal polar compound discussed above. It consists of two comparative adjective stems having opposite meanings. The overall meaning is either conjunctive or an abstract notion deriving from both. For example:

ཆེ་ཆུང་	big + small = size
རིང་ཐུང་	long + short = length, distance
ཚ་གྲང་	hot + cold = temperature
བཟང་ངན་	good + bad = quality
སྐམ་རློན་	dry + wet = dampness
མཐོ་དམན་	high + low = height

13.1.7 Adjectival postmodifying compounds

These consist of a noun in the first syllable slot and the first syllable of the basic adjective form in the second. The adjective in the second syllable describes the noun in the first, and the resultant compound is a new noun. The main difference between this construction and that of normal adjectival modification is that only the first syllable of the adjective is used. For example, ཚོགས་ཆེན་ ("big meeting, general assembly meeting, plenary meeting") consists of the noun ཚོགས་ ("meeting, assembly") and the first syllable of ཆེན་པོ་ ("big").

a. ང་ཚོགས་ཆེན་ལ་འགྲོ་གི་ཡིན།

I'm going to the general assembly meeting.

b. ཁོང་གིས་ཚོགས་ཆེན་ཐོག་གསུང་བཤད་གནང་བ་རེད།

He gave a speech at the big meeting.

Other common examples of this are:

རྒྱལ་ཡོངས་	nation/kingdom + all over/all = nationwide, national
བློ་མཐུན་	mind/thought/ + harmonious/similar/ friendly = state of having the same opinions/thoughts = comrade
ལས་གསར་	work/worker + new = new work/worker
མི་ངན་	man + bad/evil = evil person

13.1.8 Verbal compounds

Verbal compounds consist of N.-Vb., Adj.-Vb., and Vb.-Vb. combinations. In all of these, the resultant compound is a nominal, which then can be used with verbalizers such as

བྱེད་ or རྒྱག་ to make verbal constructions.

13.1.8.1 Premodifying compounds : Adj. -Vb.

As was the case with the earlier premodifiers, the first syllable (here the adjective stem) describes or modifies the second. For example, ལེགས་རྟོགས་ ("good/thorough understanding") consists of ལེགས་པོ་ ("good") and རྟོག་ ("to understand").

a. ཁོ་ཚོར་མི་དམངས་ཀྱི་བསམ་ཚུལ་ལེགས་རྟོགས་ཡོད་པ་མ་རེད།

They do not have (a) good understanding of public opinion.

This combination can also be used with a verbalizer.

b. ཁོ་ཚོས་མི་དམངས་ཀྱི་བསམ་ཚུལ་ལེགས་རྟོགས་མ་བྱས་པ་རེད།

They did not act (so as to) understand public opinion well.

Other common examples are:

གསར་བརྗེ་	new + change = revolution
དགའ་བསུ་	happy + receive = welcome
གསལ་སྟོན་	clear + show = demonstration
གསར་བཟོ་	new + make = new (i.e., not used) product
གསར་གཏོད་	new + create, found = invention, new creation
གསར་འཛུགས་	new + establish = (newly) establish, (new) construction

c. རྒྱ་ནག་གིས་མེ་ཤུགས་འཕུར་མདེལ་གྱི་རྟེན་གཞི་གཅིག་གསར་འཛུགས་བྱས་པ་རེད།

China has newly established a missile base.

13.1.8.2 Synonymic compounds: Vb.-Vb.

When the meaning of both syllables in the compound are the same, the original meaning does not change but a nominal is created.

For example, འགྲོ་བགྲོད་—go + go = going

a. ལྷ་སར་ཕྱི་རྒྱལ་མི་རིགས་འགྲོ་བགྲོད་བཀག་འདོམས་བྱས་པ་རེད།

(They) prohibited foreign nationalities (from) going to Lhasa.

b. ཁོ་ཚོས་ལྷ་སར་འགྲོ་བགྲོད་བྱས་པ་རེད།

They went to Lhasa.

Other examples are:

འཛིན་བཟུང་	hold/grasp+ hold/seize = arrest, seizure, capture
ཤེས་རྟོགས་	know + know = knowledge
མཇལ་འཕྲད་	meet + meet = meeting (h.)
གསུང་བཤད་	say + say = speech
འཕོ་འགྱུར་	change + change = change
འཕེལ་རྒྱས་	increase + increase = development

གཡོ་འགུལ་	shake/move + shake/move = shaking; moving

13.1.8.3 Verbal summation compounds: Vb.-Vb.

These compounds consist of syllables (verb stems) with different meanings. The overall meaning is the summation of the two independent ones. For example, བཅོས་བསྒྱུར་ ("reform") is comprised of བཅོས་ ("to correct") and བསྒྱུར་ ("to change"). Like the earlier example, these function as nouns and take the standard verbalizers. Some common compounds are:

འཛུགས་བསྐྲུན་	plant/erect + make = construction, building, development
འབོད་བསྐུལ་	call + urge/incite/demand action = appeal
སྲུང་བརྩི་	defend + respect = respect, honor
གསོག་འཇོག་	save + keep = deposit, savings
འཕུར་བསྐྱོད་	fly + go = flying

13.1.8.4 Verbal polar compounds: Vb.-Vb.

These compounds consist of verbs with opposite meanings. The overall meaning is usually the abstract idea derived from the two syllables, although it may also be simply the conjunctive meaning with each syllable retaining its independent meaning. For example, འགྲོ་སྡོད་ breaks down into "going" and "staying" and together means either "movement" or "going and staying" ཉོ་ཚོང་ ("buying + selling") has the general meaning of "trading."

a. ཁོའི་འགྲོ་སྡོད་སྐོར་སུས་ཀྱང་ཤེས་ཀྱི་མི་འདུག།
   Nobody knows (anything) about his movements.

b. ང་ཚོ་འགྲོ་སྡོད་ཐག་ཆོད་མ་སོང་།
   We didn't decide whether to go or stay.

Other examples of this type of compound are:

བཤད་ཉན་	telling + listening
འབྲི་ཀློག་	writing + reading
ཐོབ་ཤོར་	winning + losing
ཟ་བཏུང་	eating + drinking
སྐྱེལ་འདྲེན་	transport to + transport from = shipping

13.1.8.5 Verbal premodifying compounds: Vb. + N.

In these compounds the first syllable (verb) modifies the second syllable, e.g., སྡོད་ཁང་ = "live" + "house" with the overall meaning "a house to live in" or "residence." Some common examples are:

འགྲོ་ལམ་	go + road = a road (to go on)

རོགས་དངུལ་	help + money/finance = money to help, aid funds, relief money
རྨོ་ཕྱུགས་	plough + cattle = draft animals
འབྲི་དེབ་	write + book = book to write in, notebook

13.1.8.6 Verbal premodifying compounds: N. + Vb.

Like other premodifying constructions, the first syllable modifies the second. For example, "spring planting" breaks down into the first syllable དཔྱིད་ ("spring") (from དཔྱིད་ཀ་) and the verb འདེབས་ ("to plant/sow"). The first syllable tells us what kind of a planting it was: a "spring planting." This nominal compound can then be verbalized.

a. ཞིང་པ་ཚོས་དཔྱིད་འདེབས་ཀྱི་གྲ་སྒྲིག་བྱེད་ཀྱི་འདུག།
   The farmers are making preparations for spring planting.

b. ཞིང་པ་ཚོས་དཔྱིད་འདེབས་བྱེད་བཞིན་འདུག།
   The farmers are doing spring planting.

Other common examples of this are:

རང་སྐྱོང་	self + govern/rule = self-governing, autonomous
བཙན་འཛུལ་	force + enter = forceful entrance, invasion, aggression
སྨན་བཅོས་	medicine + treat = medicinal treatment
སྐྱོན་བརྗོད་	mistake + tell = criticism

13.1.8.7 Verbal sequential compounds: Vb.-Vb.

In these constructions the first verb takes the past stem (if it has more than one stem) and the second the non-past. The overall meaning derives from the action of the second verb on the first. For example, in བཅིངས་འགྲོལ་ the first syllable means "to bind" and the second "to release," with the overall meaning "to release or untie that which was bound." This compound is used to express the modern concept of political "liberation." Another example is ཉམས་གསོ་ ("repair, renovation"), which literally means "taking care of or rearing that which has become deteriorated."

Sequential compounds are usually idiomatic in the sense that the meaning is not easily derivable from the constituent elements. Like the other compounds cited earlier, they are verbalized by standard verbs such as བྱེད་.

13.1.9 Quadrisyllabic compounds

Quadrisyllabic compounds consist of two disyllabic compounds. The relationship between these two disyllabic units is that of premodification, i.e., the first disyllabic compound modifies the second. When a quadrisyllabic compound is encountered, each of the two disyllabic sub-units should be analyzed separately before the overall meaning is determined. The glossary will usually contain these. For example:

a. རྒྱ་བོད་ས་མཚམས།

Sino-Tibetan border (what kind of a border?—the Sino-Tibetan one)

We can substitute for either of the disyllabic compounds:

b. རྒྱ་བོད་དམག་མི་

Chinese and Tibetan soldiers

c. བལ་བོད་ས་མཚམས་

Tibeto-Nepalese border

Other examples are:

d. མི་དམངས་སྨན་ཁང་།

people's hospital

e. གནམ་གྲུ་འབབ་ཐང་།

airport

f. དམངས་གཙོ་བཅོས་བསྒྱུར།

democratic reform

13.2 "Time to do" particles: ལོང་ and ཁོམ་

These particles are used following the non-past stems of verbs. They convey that there was or was not "time to do" the verbal action.

a. ཁ་སང་ཨ་མས་ཁྲོམ་ནས་ཚལ་ཉོ་ལོང་བྱུང་མི་འདུག

Mother didn't have time to buy vegetables from the market yesterday.

b. བཀྲིས་ཞོགས་པ་སྔ་པོ་མ་ལངས་ཙང་། ཇ་འཐུང་ལོང་མེད་པར་སློབ་གྲྭར་འགྲོ་དགོས་བྱུང་བ་རེད།

Because Tashi didn't get up early in the morning, he had to go to school without having time to drink tea.

c. བསོད་ནམས་ལགས་གུང་གསེང་ལ་མ་གཏོགས་ཏན་ཧྲི་གཟིགས་ལོང་ཡོད་པ་མ་རེད།

Sonamla doesn't have time to watch television except during vacation.

d. མདང་དགོང་ང་ཚོས་གློག་བརྙན་ཆ་ཚང་བལྟ་ཁོམ་མ་བྱུང་། གང་གིས་ཞེས་ན་ཕྱིས་པོ་ཞེ་དྲགས་ཆགས་སོང་།

Last night we didn't have time to watch the movie completely. If you ask why, it is because it became too late.

e. སང་ཉིན་ཁྱེད་རང་ནང་ལ་བཞུགས་ཁོམ་ཡོད་པས།

Do you have time to stay at home tomorrow?

f. ན་ནིང་ང་བོད་ལ་འགྲོ་དུས་མཆོད་མཇལ་ཞུ་ཁོམ་བྱུང་།

Last year, when I went to Tibet, I had time to go on religious visits.

g. ཁ་སང་ངས་ཁོ་ལ་སྐད་ཆ་བཤད་ཁོམ་བྱུང་མ་སོང་།

I didn't have time to talk to him yesterday.

h. སང་དགོང་ཁོང་ཚོ་ནང་ལ་སྡོད་ལོང་ཡོད་པ་མ་རེད།

They will not have time to stay at home tomorrow night.

13.3 Vb. + ཁག་པོ་ constructions

ཁག་པོ་ is used after verbs to convey that it was difficult to do the verbal action.

a. སྐྱི་ཁུང་མེད་ན་དབུགས་གཏོང་ཁག་པོ་རེད།
If there is no window, it is difficult to breathe.

b. ལམ་ག་དེ་འགྲོ་ཁག་པོ་ཡོད་པ་རེད།
It is difficult to go on that road.

c. ཁོང་གི་ཕྱག་བྲིས་དེ་ཀློག་ཁག་པོ་ཡོད་པ་མ་རེད།
His letter (handwriting) is not difficult to read.

13.4 Vb. + བདེ་པོ་ constructions

These constructions parallel those with ཁག་པོ་ but convey that it was easy to do the verbal action.

a. སྐྱི་ཁུང་ཡོད་ན་དབུགས་གཏོང་བདེ་པོ་རེད།
If there is a window, it is easy to breathe.

b. ལམ་ག་དེ་འགྲོ་བདེ་པོ་ཡོད་པ་རེད།
It is easy to go on that road.

c. ཁོང་གི་ཕྱག་བྲིས་དེ་ཀློག་བདེ་པོ་ཡོད་པ་མ་རེད།
His letter (handwriting) is not easy to read.

13.5 Reading exercise: "The Wish-Fulfilling Gem Necklace," continued from Lesson 12

13.5.1 Tibetan text

སློབ་ཚན་བཅུ་གཉིས་པའི་འཕྲོས།

ན་གཞོན་བློ་རྡོར་གྱིས་དབུགས་དལ་བཞིན་པར་ནགས་གསེབ་ཀྱི་ཁྲོད་དུ་སེང་གེ་འཚོལ་བར་ཕྱིན་པ་དང་ནམ་མཁར་1 ཐུག་པ་ལྟ་བུའི་ཐང་ཤིང་ཆེན་པོ་ཞིག་གི་འོག་ཏུ་སླེབས་སྐབས་སེང་གེ་དཀར་མོ་དེ་གར་ཡིབས་ནས་བསྡད་2 ཡོད་པ་མཐོང་མ་ཐག་བློ་རྡོར་ཁོང་ཁྲོ་མི་ལྟར་འབར་ནས་3 སྣ་རེ་གཞུ་སྐབས་དང་ལང་ཞེས་པའི་སྒྲ་ཞིག་ཐོས་ནས་མི་སྣག་འཕྱུར་བ་དང་ལག་གཉིས་ཀྱང་སྒྲིད། ཡང་བསྐྱར་ཞིབ་པར་ལྟ་སྐབས་དེ་ནི་རྡོ་ཡི་སེང་གེ་ཞིག་ཡིན་པ་རེད།4 འཛིག་རྟེན་ཐོག་ལ་མཚན་ཅན་གྱི་བྱ་བ་འདི་འདྲ་ཡོད་པ་སྙེ་5 ཨ་མའི་ལྷམ་ནི་རྡོ་ཡི་སེང་གེའི་ཁའི་ནང་དུ་ཡོད། ན་གཞོན་བློ་རྡོར་གྱིས་ཞིབ་ཚགས་ངང་ལྷམ་ཚུར་བླངས་ནས་ཨམ་ཕྲག་ནང་དུ་བཅུག་པ་དང་སྤྲགས་དགའ་བའི་འཛུམ་མདངས་ཕྱུར།

ན་གཞོན་བློ་རྡོར་གྱིས་མགོ་བོ་གྱེན་དུ་བདེགས་ཏེ་ལྟ་སྐབས་མིག་ལམ་དུ་དོ་ཤལ་ཞིག་ཐང་ཤིང་གི་ཡལ་གའི་སྟེང་དུ་དཔྱངས་

ནས་6 ཡོད་པ་མཐོང་7། ཁོ་པས་ཡང་བསྐྱར་ཞིབ་པར་ལྟ་སྐབས་ཡ་མཚན་ཆེ་བའི་བསམ་པ་སྐྱེས་8། ཀློ་རྡོར་གྱིས་ཡར་ལངས་ནས་དོ་ཤལ་ལེན་དགོས་སྙམ་ཡང་9 ལག་གིས་སྟོབ་ཀྱི་མེད། ཤིང་སྡོང་གི་རྩེ་ལ་འཛེག་བསམ་ཀྱང་ཤིང་སྡོང་སྡོམ་པས་འཁྱུད་ཐབས་བྲལ། དེས་ན་ཁོ་པས་ཤིང་སྡོང་ཐོག་སྤྲ་རེས་ཁ་ཞོ་ཁ་ཤས་བཏོན་ཏེ་ཡར་འཛེགས་ན་འཛེག་བདེ་པོ་10 ཡོང་སྙམ་བཞིན་པར་སྤྲ་རེ་ཞིག་གཞུས་མ་ཐག་འཛིགས་རྫམ་དགོད་སྒྲས་11 གྲོག་རོང་གཡོ་བ་དང་ནམ་མཁར་བྲག་ཅ་འཁོར། དུས་མཚུངས་སྤྲ་རེ་ཡང་ཚུར་འཕར་ཡོང་བ་རེད། ཀློ་རྡོར་ཟུ་ཐུག་ཐབས་ཟད་དེ་ཅི་བྱ་གཏོལ་མེད་དུ་གྱུར་ནས་ཁོང་ཁྲོའི་ངང་སྤྲ་རེ་གཡུགས་ཏེ་རྡོ་ཡི་སེང་གེའི་ཐོག་ཏུ་བརྡུང་ནས་རྟན་ཐོར་བཞིན་པར་དེའི་མགོ་ལ་ཐྲིལ་ཐྲིལ་བཏང་།

ཨེ་མ་ཡ་མཚན་ཆེ་བ་ཞིག་ལ་12 ཕོ་གཞོན་དེས་རྡོ་ཡི་སེང་གེའི་མིག་གཉིས་ནས་འོད་ཟེར་འཕྲོ་བ་དང་ཁ་ཆེན་གདངས་པ་དང་སྤྲུགས་འོད་ཆེམ་ཆེམ་འཕྲོ་བའི་སྤྲ་རེ་གཅིག་སྐྱུག་ཡོང་བ་མཐོང་། དགའ་བ་རབ་ཏུ་འཕེལ་བའི་ཕོ་གཞོན་དེས་གསེར་གྱི་སྤྲ་རེ་ཡར་བསྒྲུགས་ཏེ་ཤིང་སྡོང་ལ་བརྒྱབ་པས་ཚ་ཤག་ཅེས་པའི་སྒྲ་དང་བཅས་13 ཐང་ཤིང་དེ་ཕྱེད་གཤགས་སུ་ཕྱིན་14 ནས་གཞོགས་གཅིག་ཏུ་འགྱེལ། ཀློ་རྡོར་གྱིས་མགྱོགས་མྱུར་དོ་ཤལ་ཚུར་བླངས་ཏེ་ཡིད་ཆགས་ནས་འཇོག་འདོད་མེད་པ་ལྟ་བུར་15 གྱུར། གློ་བུར་དུ་ལྷུང་དམར་དྲག་པོ་འཚུབས་ནས་ཤིང་ལོ་16 ཚང་མ་བཤྲིལ་བས་ཀློ་རྡོར་དངངས་སྐྲག་ཤིན་ཏུ་ཆེན་པོ་སྐྱེས། དེ་མ་ཐག་ཆེ་ཆུང་སྣར་ཁ་ཙམ་གྱི་17 སེར་དྲག་ཆེས་ཆེར་བཏང་།18 ཁོ་སྐྲག་ཐག་ཆོད་ནས་རྡོ་ཡི་སེང་གེའི་སྒོ་འོག་ཏུ་འཛུལ་ནས་བསྡད། གློག་འཁྱུག་པ་དང་འབྲུག་སྒྲ་རབ་ཏུ་བསྒྲགས་ཏེ་ཡ་མཚན་ཅན་གྱི་བྱ་གླག་དེ་ནམ་མཁའ་ནས་མར་འབབ་ཡོང་19 ཞིང་། བྱ་གླག་དེས་གཤོག་པ་བརྡབ་ཙམ་20 བྱས་པ་དང་སྤྲུགས་སྐད་ཤུགས་ཆེན་པོས་ང་ཡི་བླ་ཤིང་གཙོད་མཁན་སུ་རེད་དམ། ང་ཡི་ཡིད་བཞིན་ནོར་བུའི་དོ་ཤལ་འཕྲོག་མཁན་སུ་རེད་དམ་ཞེས་སྐད་ཅོར་བརྒྱབ། སྐད་སྒྲ་དེ་ནི་ཐོག་བརྒྱབ་པ་ལྟར་ཐང་ཤིང་གི་ཡལ་ག་རྣམས་གཡོ་ཞིང་ས་ལ་ལྷུང་། ཕོ་གཞོན་དེས་ཡ་མཚན་ཅན་གྱི་བྱ་གླག་དེར་ལྟ་བཞིན་པར་ནན་རབས་ཆོས་རྒྱུན་དུ་སེར་དྲག་ནི་ལོ་ཏོག་རྡུང་བ་དང་ར་ལུག་གསོད་པའི་གདུག་རྩུབ་ཅན་གྱི་གདོང་འདྲེ་ཞིག་རེད་ཅེས་གོད་སྐྱོལ་ཡོད་པ་དེ་བློ་ལ་ཤར་ནས་ཁོང་ཁྲོ་ཚད་མེད་ལངས། ཀློ་རྡོར་གྱིས་རྡོ་ཡི་སེང་གེའི་འོག་ནས་མར་ཐོན་ཏེ་སྐད་ཤུགས་ཆེན་པོས་མ་ཡིས་གཟིག་གསོད་རྒྱུའི་ཆེད་དུ་ང་སྐྱེས། ཕ་ཡིས་འདྲེ་མེད་པ་བཟོ་རྒྱུའི་ཆེད་དུ་ང་གསོས་ཞེས་བཤད་ནས་སྤྲ་རེ་གཡུགས་པས་དེ་མ་ཉིད་དུ་ནག་འཁྲིགས་པ་དང་སྤྲུག་སྐད་བརྒྱབ་ནས་བྱ་གླག་དེ་ནགས་གསེབ་སྟུག་པོའི་ཁྲོད་དུ་གར་སོང་མེད་གྱུར།

ཀློ་རྡོར་གྱིས་གསེར་གྱི་སྤྲ་རེ་འཕྱུར་བཞིན་པར་མགྱོགས་མྱུར་རྗེས་འདེད་གཏོང་བར་འགྲོ་སྐབས་ཤུགས་དང་ལྡན་པའི་ལག་གཅིག་གིས་ཁོང་བཟུང་བས་ཁོ་པས་ཁ་ཕྱིར་གཏུས་ཏེ་ལྟ་སྐབས་མགོ་བོ་དང་སྨ་ར་དུང་ལས་དཀར་བའི་སྤྱི་བོ་ཞིག་ཡོད་པ་མཐོང་། ཁོང་གིས་སྤྱི་བོ་ལགས་ལ་གུས་འདུད་ཅིག་ཕུས་ཤིང་། སྤྱི་བོ་ལགས་ཀྱིས་ཕོ་གཞོན་དེའི་དཔུང་པར་བཙག་ཙམ་21 བྱས་རྗེས་འཛུམ་མུལ་དང་ངོ་གསར་ཁྱེད་ཀྱང་སེང་གེ་ངར་མ་ཞིག་རེད་འདུག་22 ཅེས་བཤད། ཀློ་རྡོར་གྱིས་ཕར་ལྟ་སྐབས་རྡོ་ཡི་སེང་གེ་དེ་གར་སོང་མེད་སྐབས་23 བགྲེས་སོང་གི་ལག་ནས་འཛུས་ཏེ་ཁྱེད་ཉིད་རྡོ་ཡི་ཨ་ཁུ་སེང་གེ་དེ་ཡིན་ནམ་ཞེས་དྲིས། ཨ་ཁུ་སེང་གེས་འཛུམ་མདངས་འཕྱེན་བཞིན་པར་འགྱེལ་བའི་ཐང་ཤིང་གི་རྩ་བའི་ཐོག་བསྡད་ནས་ཀྱང་ཤ་དོད་པོས་སྣ་ཐག་འཐེན་ཞིང་། ཕོ་གཞོན་ཀློ་རྡོར་

གྱིས་ཡིད་བཞིན་ནོར་བུའི་དོ་ཤལ་དང་གསེར་གྱི་སྐ་རེ་སེང་གེ་ནད་པོར་ཕུལ། སེང་གེ་ནད་པོས་མགོ་བོ་གཡུག་བཞིན་པར་གསེར་གྱི་སྐ་རེ་དེ་ངས་ཁྱེད་ལ་ཕྱག་རྟགས་སུ་ཕུལ་བ་ཡིན་དོ་ཤལ་དེ་ཁྱེད་ཀྱིས་དོ་བདག་ལ་ཕྱིར་སྤྲོད་བྱེད་དགོས་པ་ཞིག་རེད་ཅེས་བཤད། བློ་ནོར་གྱིས་འཕྲུལ་མར་དོ་བདག་གང་དུ་ཡོད་དམ་ཞེས་དྲིས། ནད་པོས་དལ་པོའི་ངང་ཐག་རིང་ཤར་ཕྱོགས་སུ་ཡོད་ལ་སྡོང་པོའི་འོག་ཏུའང་24 ཡོད་པས་སྔོན་ལ་ཐག་རིང་གྱི་དོ་བདག་དེ་འཚོལ་བར་འགྲོ་དགོས་པ་དང་། དེ་རྗེས་སྡོང་པོའི་འོག་གི་མི་དེ་སྐྱོབ་ཐབས་བྱེད་དགོས་ཞེས་ལན་བཏབ།

ཕོ་གཞོན་གྱིས་བསམ་པ་རྣམ་དག་གི་སྙིང་ནས་ངས་ཐག་རིང་གི་དོ་བདག་ཇི་ལྟར་བྱས་ནས་25 འཕྲད་པ་བྱེད་26 ཐུབ་བམ་ཞེས་དྲིས། ནད་པོས་གད་མོ་དགོད་བཞིན་པར་ཁྱེད་ཀྱིས་རྒྱ་འབྲས་བརྩིས་ཏེ་27 འཚོལ་བར་འགྲོ་དགོས་ཞེས་བཤད། ཕོ་གཞོན་གྱིས་མགོ་བོ་ལྡུག་ལྡུག་ཡང་ཡང་བྱེད་བཞིན་པར་ནད་པོར་ཞལ་གྱིས་ཞུས། ཁོང་ཁྱིམ་དུ་ཕྱིར་ལོག་བྱས་རྗེས་ཨ་མར་འབྱུང་རྒྱུ་28 ཟེམ་དགུ་བླངས་པ་དང་རྩམ་པ་སྒྲེ་མོ་དགུ་བདགས་རྗེས་རྩ་ཆེའི་ཡིད་བཞིན་ནོར་བུའི་དོ་ཤལ་དེ་ཁྱེར་ནས་སྐྱིད་པར་འོད་ཆེམ་ཆེམ་འཕྲོ་བའི་གསེར་གྱི་སྐ་རེ་གཟེར་ནས་ཐག་རིང་དུ་དོ་ཤལ་གྱི་བདག་པོ་འཚོལ་དུ་ཕྱིན།

བློ་ནོར་གྱིས་ཉིན་ཞག་མང་པོ་འགྲུལ་བཞུད་བྱས་ཏེ་གྲོང་ཚོ་མང་པོར་སྐད་ཆ་དྲིས་ཤིང་། མཐར་རྒྱལ་པོ་ཡོད་སའི་གྲོང་ཁྱེར་དུ་འབྱོར། ཁྲོམ་གཞུང་དུ་མི་ཡིས་ཁེངས་པ་དང་ཁྲོམ་ར་ནི་ཧ་ཅང་འཁྲུག་པོ་ཡོད། མི་རྣམས་ཀྱིས་རྩ་ཆེག་ཐོག་གི་ཚོན་ཁྲ་ཅན་གྱི་སྲས་མོ་བཀྲས་ལྷའི་འདྲ་པར་ལ་ལྟ་བཞིན་ཡོད། ལྷག་པར་དུ་སྲས་མོའི་མགུལ་གྱི་ཡིད་བཞིན་ནོར་བུའི་དོ་ཤལ་ལ་ཕོ་གཞོན་དོ་སྣང་ཆེན་པོ་བྱུང་བས་ཁོང་གིས་ཨམ་ཕྲག་ནང་ནས་དོ་ཤལ་དེ་མར་བཏོན་ཏེ་གཉིས་སྦྱར་སྐབས་ཁྱད་པར་སྒྲ་ཙམ་ཡང་མེད་སྐབས་ཁོང་རང་དབང་མེད་པར་སྒྲོ་བ་འཕེལ་ཞིང་འཛུམ་མདངས་ཤུང་། ཕོ་གཞོན་གྱིས་ལག་གཉིས་པོས་ཚོན་ཁྲ་ཅན་གྱི་སྲས་མོ་བཀྲས་ལྷའི་འདྲ་པར་དེ་མར་བླངས་མ་ཐག་སྲུང་དམག་གཉིས་ཡོང་ནས་བློ་ནོར་ཕོ་བྲང་ནང་དུ་ཁྲིད་ནས། རྒྱལ་པོ་དང་བཙུན་མོར་མི་གཅིག་ལ་29 སྲས་མོ་བཀྲས་ལྷའི་དོ་ཤལ་རྙེད་འདུག་ཅེས་སྙན་སེང་ཞུས་རྗེས་རྒྱལ་པོ་དང་བཙུན་མོ་གཉིས་བྲེལ་འཚུབ་ངང་ཕྱིར་ཐོན་ཡོང་། ཕོ་གཞོན་གྱིས་གུས་ཞབས་ཆེན་པོས་ཕུས་མོ་ས་ལ་བཙུགས་ནས་དོ་ཤལ་དེ་ཇི་ལྟར་རྙེད་ལུགས་རྣམས་རྒྱལ་པོར་ཞིབ་པར་སྙན་སེང་ཞུས། རྒྱལ་པོ་དང་བཙུན་མོ་གཉིས་དགའ་ཐག་ཆོད་ནས་ཕོ་གཞོན་བློ་ནོར་གྱིས་ཕྱག་མཛོད་ཆེ་མོ་དང་སྐུ་སྲུང་སུམ་བརྒྱ་དྲུག་ཅུ་རེ་དགུའི་ལམ་སྣེ་འཁྲིད་ནས་འཕྲལ་དུ་ནོག་ཐོན་གྱིས་སྲས་མོ་སྐྱོབ་པར་འགྲོ་དགོས་པའི་བཀའ་ཕབ།

འདིའི་འཕྲོས་སློབ་ཚན་བཅུ་བཞི་པར་གཟིགས་རོགས་གནང་།

13.5.2 Translation

Continued from Lesson Twelve

The young man Lodor was sighing as he went into a forest to search for the lion. When he reached (a spot) under a huge pine tree that seemed to be stuck into the sky, he saw the white lion hiding there. As soon as he saw that, Lodor got angry like a flame igniting and struck with the axe. At that time, he heard the sound "tanglang," and sparks flew. His hands become numb. When he looked again carefully (at the lion), it was a stone lion. 'There are really astonishing things like this in the world' (he thought), 'mother's shoe is in a stone lion's mouth.' Then young man Lodor carefully took the shoe out (of the stone lion's mouth) and put it in his pocket and a smile of joy appeared (on his mouth).

When young man Lodor raised up his head and looked, he saw in his field of vision a necklace hanging on the branch of the pine tree. He looked again carefully and very weird thoughts occurred (concerning what was going on). Lodor got up and even though he thought he should take the necklace, his hand could not reach it. He thought he would climb to the top of the tree, but the tree was too thick to cling to [lit., he had no way to cling to it because it was thick]. Consequently, he thought that if he could make some notches (in the tree trunk) with his axe it would be easy to climb. As soon as he started to hit the tree with his axe, a frightening laughing sound (occurred) that made the ravine shake and filled the sky with its echo. At the same time the axe also bounced back to him [i.e., did not stick in the tree trunk]. Lodor was desperate. He had no way to do anything, so became stymied and angrily threw away his axe and sat stunned on the lion and absent-mindedly stroked its head.

Oh my, it was amazing. That young man saw light shining from the two eyes of the stone lion and saw it open its big mouth and vomit out a glittering axe. That extremely joyous youth picked up the golden axe and struck the tree making the sound "tsashag." The pine tree split into two pieces and fell down to one side. Lodor quickly took the necklace, and liking it [becoming attached to it], didn't want to leave it. Suddenly a storm arose and all the leaves got rolled up, so Lodor became extremely frightened. At this moment [lit., immediately], a hail storm with (hail) as big as walnuts came and fell stronger and stronger [lit., bigger and bigger]. He was terrified and so he moved underneath the stone lion's belly and sat there. While it was lightning and thundering a lot, a strange big bird came down from the sky. That bird flapped its wings and roared in a loud voice, "Who is the one who cut down my 'soul tree'? Who is the one who took away my precious gem necklace?" That voice [lit., noise], shook the leaves of the pine tree like lightning (making them) fall onto the ground. While the young man was looking at the weird bird, (he) remembered [lit., it came to his mind] that previous generations customarily said, "Heavy hail is a ferocious ghost which damages crops and kills sheep and goats," and got extraordinarily angry. Lodor came out from underneath the lion and in a loud voice said, "My mother gave birth to me to kill leopards, and my father brought me up to annihilate ghosts." Then he threw the axe and immediately the bird became black, made a cry of anguish, and vanished into the thick forest.

When Lodor raised the golden axe and went quickly to pursue the big bird, a strong hand seized him. As he turned back and looked, he saw an old man with a head and beard whiter than a conch shell. He gave a respectful greeting to the old man, and the old man patted the young man's shoulder and said smilingly, "You also are a powerful lion." When Lodor looked back the stone lion had disappeared. He took hold of the old man's hand and asked him, "Are you the stone 'uncle' lion?" Uncle lion, giving a smile, sat down at the bottom of the fallen down pine tree and took some snuff in a lively fashion. The young man Lodor gave the precious gem necklace and the golden axe to the old lion. The old lion, shaking its head, said, "I gave the axe to you as a gift. That necklace is one which you have to give back to its owner." Lodor immediately asked, "Where is the owner?" The old man slowly answered, "It is far away in the east—under a tree. At first you should go to search for the distant owner; after that you should try to save the person who is under the tree."

The young man asked sincerely, "What should I do so as to be able to meet that far away owner?" The old man laughed and said, "You have to search in accordance with karmic law." The young man nodded again and again left the old man. After returning home he brought nine wooden barrels of drinking water and ground nine sacks of tsamba (barley flour) for his mother. Then, carrying the precious gem necklace with him, he stuck the glittering golden axe in his belt and left to search far away for the owner of the necklace.

Lodor traveled for many days and asked questions in many villages. Finally, he arrived in the city of a king. The market area was full of people and the marketplace was flourishing and lively. The people were looking at the colored picture of Princess Drelha on an edict. The young man in particular paid great attention to the precious gem necklace on the princess's neck. He took the necklace out of his pocket and compared the two. When he did that, because there was no difference, not even so much as a single strand of hair, he spontaneously became happy and smiled. The young man took the picture of Princess Drelha with his two hands, and as soon as he did that, two policemen came and took Lodor to the palace. (They) reported to the king and queen, "A person has found the princess's necklace." The king and queen hurriedly came out. The young man (bowed), putting his knee on the floor to show respect, and reported in detail to the king how he found the necklace. The king and queen were extremely happy and ordered the youth Lodor to lead the chief steward with 369 bodyguard troops and depart immediately to save the princess.

See Lesson 14 for the continuation.

13.5.3 Grammatical notes

1. Note that ནམ་མཁར་ is ནམ་མཁའ་ + the dative-locative particle.

2. ནས་ here joins ཡིབས ("hide") and བསྡད ("stayed"), conveying that both are occurring simultaneously—"staying (there) hiding." See 5.11.2.

3. X + མེ་ལྟར་འབར་ is a commonly used simile meaning "X caught fire like a flame." Here, X is his anger (ཁོང་ཁྲོ་).

4. The use of ཡིན་པ་རེད་ here conveys some uncertainty, i.e., "It seems it is. . . ."

5. The use of ནི་ in ཡོད་པ་ནི་ conveys the "defining function" discussed in 5.11.3. In other words, what follows ཡོད་པ་ནི་ explains what the amazing deed was—namely, that the stone lion had his mother's shoe in its mouth.

6. ནས་ acts here as a simultaneous clause connector—"hanging it existed." See 2., above, and 5.11.2.

7. This core of this segment is ན་གཞོན་བློ་ནོར་གྱིས་ . . . མཐོང་ ("the youth Lodor saw . . ."). What he saw in his field of vision when he raised his head and looked was the existence of the necklace hanging on the branch of a pine tree.

8. བསམ་པ་སྐྱེས་ means " a thought was born." ཡ་མཚན་ཆེ་བའི་ conveys what kind of a thought—"(a thought) of great amazement." Together these mean he "was amazed."

9. ཡང་ here acts not as "also" but as the "even though" clause connective. Thus སྙམ་ཡང་ means "even though he thought."

10. Here the use of ཡོང་ in ཡར་འཛེགས་ན་འཛེག་བདེ་པོ་ཡོང་ conveys future action—"if I climb up, it will be easy to climb."

11. The use of སྒྲ་ following the verb དགོད་ ("to laugh") is a common pattern of vb.+ noun. In it the verb modifies the noun, explaining something about it. Thus, here it conveys "the sound of laughing" (what kind of sound?—a sound of laughing). This joins with འཛིགས་རྔམ་ to become a quadrisyllabic compound—"a frightful laughing sound."

12. ཨེ་མ་ཡ་མཚན་ཆེ་བ་ཞིག་ལ་ is an idiomatic phrase meaning "How strange."

13. དང་བཅས་ conveys "along with"; see 6.4 e.-h.

14. We have seen how the verb "to go" joins with the comparative stem of adjectives and the dative-locative particle to convey "becoming bigger" (ཆེ་རུ་འགྲོ་). It also can be linked with verb stems to convey "become. . . ." Thus ཕྱེད་ག་ཤགས་སུ་ཕྱིན་ here means "became split in half."

15. ལྟ་བུར་ in the clause ཡིད་ཆགས་ནས་འཇོག་འདོད་མེད་པ་ལྟ་བུར་བྱུར་ conveys the added meaning of "it seems." The author is conveying that "it seems he didn't want to leave it."

16. Written Tibetan abounds in abbreviations. ཤིང་ལོ་ is a typical one in that it combines the first syllables of two words, here—ཤིང་སྡོང་ and ལོ་མ་.

17. The phrase ཆེ་ཆུང་སྟར་ཁ་ཙམ་ means "size approximately that of a walnut."

18. སེར་དྲག་ཆེས་ཆེར་བཏང་ is a pattern in which ཆེས་ augments a comparative construction (see 10.3.3 l.-m.). Here it means, "hail was increasing a lot."

19. ཡོང་ conveys two simultaneous actions: "descending coming" (see 8.10.3.19).

20. The use of ཙམ་ in the phrase གཤོག་པ་བརྡབ་ཙམ་བྱས་ illustrates a common pattern: vb. + ཙམ་ + བྱེད་. It is used to refer to "a little" of the first verbal action; in this case it conveys that the eagle flapped its wings once or twice.

21. ཙམ་ here functions the same as it did in note 20 above.

22. The combination of རེད་ + འདུག་ conveys somewhat more certainty than རེད་ by itself.

23. གར་སོང་མེད་ is a standard idiomatic construction meaning literally "where he went, no exist." It conveys that someone vanished and the narrator does not knows where.

24. The particle ལ་ in the clause ཐག་རིང་ཤར་ཕྱོགས་སུ་ཡོད་ལ་སྡོང་པོའི་འོག་དུའང་ acts as a clause connective meaning "as well as" (see 10.4.1). Thus, "as well as being far away in the east, it was also under a tree."

25. ཇི་ལྟར་བྱས་ནས་ is used to convey "how or what should be done." Here it means, "What should I do so as to be able to meet the owner?" (See also 10.14.)

26. This "causative" use of nominalized verb + བྱེད་ conveys the meaning of "doing something to achieve the action of the first verb" (i.e., doing something so as to meet the owner) (See 11.7.3).

27. The phrase རྒྱུ་འབྲས་བརྩིས་ literally means "to abide by or adhere to the law of karma" (cause and effect), but really means to do the honest and proper thing, in this case, searching for the real owner of the necklace.

28. As we saw in note 11, here again he have a vb.+ noun compound: འཐུང་ཆུ་ It conveys the meaning of "water for drinking."

29. ལ་ is required in མི་གཅིག་ལ་ ("to a person" or "to someone") because the verb "to find" requires the person who found something to be marked by the dative-locative.

13.6 Vocabulary

བཀག་འདོམས་	prohibition; va. — བྱེད་	སྐད་ཅོར་	shouting, clamor; va. —
བཀའ་ཕབ་	va. p. of བཀའ་འབེབས་		རྒྱག་ to shout
བཀའ་འབེབས་	va. to order, to command	སྐུ་སྲུང་	bodyguard

སྐམ་རློན་	dry + wet = dampness
སྐེད་པ་	waist
སྐྱུག་	vi. to vomit
སྐྱེལ་འདྲེན་	transporting, transportation, shipping
སྐྱེས་	vi. p. of སྐྱེ་
ཁ་ཕྱིར་གཙུས་	va. to turn one's body backward (e.g., to look at something)
ཁ་ཤོ་	harelip; gap, rift
ཁེངས་	vi. p. of འཁེངས་
འཁེངས་	vi. to be full (with)
ཁོམ་	"time to do" particle
ཁྱད་པར་	difference
ཁྲོམ་གཞུང་	main street, business section
ཁྲོམ་ར་	market, market place
འཁྲུག་པོ་	lively, active
གར་སོང་མེད་	id. disappearance, vanishing
གུང་གསེང་	holiday
གུས་འདུད་	respect, reverence; va. — ཞུ་ (h.)
གུས་ཞབས་	respect, reverence
གྱེན་	uphill, upwards
གྲལ་རིམ་	class (social)
གྲངས་འབོར་	quantity, number, amount
གྲུང་ཤ་དོད་པོ་	alert, lively, active
གྲོང་ཚོ་	town, village
དགའ་བ་	happiness
དགེ་སློབ་	teachers and students
བགྲེས་སོང་	an older person (h.)
འགྲུལ་བཞུད་	traveling, traffic
འགྲོ་བསྐྱོད་	go + go = going
འགྲོ་སྡོད་	go + stay = movement
འགྲོ་ལམ་	go + road = road (to go on)
རྒྱ་བོད་	China/Chinese and Tibet/Tibetans
རྒྱལ་ཡོངས་	nationwide, national
རྒྱུ་འབྲས་	cause and effect, karma; vi. — བརྩིས་ to do the proper, honorable, moral, upright thing
རྒྱུན་དུ་	always, at all times
སྒྱེ་མོ་	bag, sack
སྒྲ་	sound
སྒྲ་སྐད་	sound, voice
བསྒྲིལ་	va. to roll up, to wind up
ངར་མ་	strong, powerful
ངོ་གདོང་	face
ཅི་བྱ་གཏོལ་མེད་	helpless, without a viable alternative, stymied; vi. — འགྱུར་
གཅུས་	va. to turn
བཅག་	va. p. of གཅོག་
བཅིངས་འགྲོལ་	liberation, va. — གཏོང་
བཅོས་བསྒྱུར་	reform; va. — གཏོང་ to reform
ལྷོག་ལྷོག་	nod, nodding; va. — བྱེད་
ཆེ་ཆུང་	big + small = size
ཆེད་བསྐུལ་	special appeal
ཆེམ་ཆེམ་	glittering
མཇལ་འཕྲད་	meet + meet = meeting (h.)
འཇིག་རྟེན་	the world (of samsara)
འཇིགས་རྫམས་དགོད་སྒྲ་	frightening laugh
འཇུས་	va. p. of འཇུ་

འཇོག་	va. to leave; to put
ཉིན་མཚན་	day and night, 24-hour period
ཉིན་ཞག་	day (including night—24-hour day)
རྙེད་	vi. to find, to discover
སྙོབ་	vi. to be able to reach something, to be able to touch
ཏང་ལང་	tanglang (a sound)
ཏན་ཧྲི་	ch. television
བཏགས་	va. p. of འདོགས་
རྟ་དྲེལ་	horses and mules
རྟེན་གཞི་	base
སྟར་ཁ་	walnut
སྟོབས་	power, strength
ཐག་ཆོད་	vi. to be decided
ཐང་ཤིང་	pine, fir tree
ཐོག་	lightning
ཐོབ་ཤོར་	winning and losing
མཐོ་དམན་	high + low; height
འཐུང་ཆུ་	drinking water
དལ་པོ་	slow, leisurely
དུས་སྐབས་	time, period
དུས་མཚུངས་	at the same time; contemporaneously
དེ་མ་ཉིད་དུ་	immediately, at once
དེ་མ་ཐག་	suddenly
དོ་བདག་	owner
དྲི་ལན་	answer a question, reply
གདངས་	va. to open (one's mouth)
གདུག་རྩུབ་བ་ཅན་	cruel, ferocious, savage
གདོང་འདྲེ་	ghost
བདེ་པོ་	easy
མདང་དགོང་	last night
འདྲ་པར་	picture, portrait; photograph
རྡོ་	stone, rock
རྡོག་ཐོན་	leaving a place for good; va. —བྱེད་
སྡུག་སྐད་	complaining, grumbling
སྡོང་པོ་	tree
བརྡབ་	va. to beat against; to bang
བསྡུར་	va. to compare
ནག་འཁྲིགས་	vi. to become dark
གནམ་གྲུ་འབབ་ཐང་	airport
གནས་དུས་	place and time
སྣ་ཐག་	snuff; va. —འཐེན་
པུས་མོ་	knee
དཔུང་པ་	shoulder
དཔུང་ཚོགས་	troops, military force
དཔྱངས་	vi. to be hanging, dangling
དཔྱིད་འདེབས་	spring planting
སྤུ་ཙམ་	a little bit, lit., about one hair (in size)
སྤྲོ་བ་འཕེལ་	vi. to have happiness be increased
ཕ་	father
ཕར་	over there, thither
ཕོ་འགྱུར་	change
ཕོ་མོ་	male + female; sex
ཕོ་གཞོན་	young man
ཕོ་གསར་	young man
ཕྱག་རྟགས་	present, gift (h.)
ཕྱག་བྲིས་	letter (h.)
ཕྱག་མཛོད་	steward, treasurer, manager

ཕྱི་པོ་	late
ཕྱིར་	back
ཕྱུང་	va. p. of འབྱིན་
ཕྱུར་	va. p. of འཕྱུར་
ཕྱེད་ག་ཤགས་	split in half; vi. — (སུ) འགྲོ to become split in half; va. — (སུ) གཏོང་ to split in half
འཕར་	vi. to bounce up; to fly up
འཕུར་བསྐྱོད་	flying
འཕེལ་	vi. to increase, to multiply; to develop
འཕེལ་རྒྱས་	development, improvement
འཕོ་འགྱུར་	changing, altering
འཕྱུར་	vi. to raise up, to hoist
འཕྱུར་	vi. to rise, swell upwards (like waves or smoke or sparks)
འཕྲད་	va. to meet
འཕྲལ་མར་	at once, immediately
བལ་བོད་	Tibeto-Nepalese
བུ་ཕྲུག་	children
བྲག་ཅ་	echo; vi. — འཁོར་ to echo
བླ་ཤིང་	soul tree (tree in which one's བླ་ resides)
བློ་མཐུན་	comrade
བློ་ལ་ཤར་	vi. to come to mind
དབང་མེད་པར་	involuntarily, spontaneously
དབུགས་ཧལ་	vi. to sigh
འབབ་སྟང་	station
འབར་	vi. to ignite, catch fire
འབོད་བསྐུལ་	appeal; va. — བྱེད་
འབྱིན་	va. to make; to produce; to cast, throw
འབྲི་ཀློག་	writing and reading
འབྲི་དེབ་	book to write in, notebook
སྦོ་	side of the body; belly
སྦྲིད་	vi. 1. to become numb; 2. vi. to sneeze
མ་	mother
མི་ངན་	evil person
མི་རིགས་	race; nationality
མིག་ལམ་	field of vision
མེ་	fire; vi. — འབར་ to burn
མེ་སྟག་	spark
མེ་ཤུགས་འཕུར་མདེལ་	missile
དམངས་གཙོ་	democratic
རྨོ་ཕྱུགས་	draft animals
སྨན་བཅོས་	medicinal treatment
རྩ་བ་	root, base
རྩེ་	top, tip, peak
བརྩིས་	va. p. of བརྩི་: adhered to, acted in accordance with
ཚ་གྲང་	hot and cold; temperature
ཚ་ཤག་	tshashak (a sound)
ཚོགས་ཆེན་	general assembly
འཛུགས་སྐྲུན་	construction, building, development
འཛུམ་མདངས་	smiling demeanor; va. — འཕྱུར་; — འབྱིན་
འཛུམ་མུལ་	a smile, a laugh
ཞལ་བྲིས་	vi. to separate, part, split (h.)
ཞལ་ལག་	food (h.)
ཞིང་ཆུ་	irrigation
ཞིང་འབྲོག་	farmers and nomads

གཞུང་སྒེར་	government and private; everything
གཞོགས་	the side (of)
ཟ་བཏུང་	eating + drinking; food
ཟུག་	1. vi. to be stuck (in) 2. pain; vi. — ཟུག་; 3. vi. to be pricked
ཟོམ་	wooden barrel
གཟིག་	leopard
གཟེར་	va. to wear, put on
བཟང་ངན་	good and bad; quality
བཟུང་	va. to seize, hold
ཨུ་ཐུག་ཐབས་ཟད་	desperate, helpless
ཡ་མཚན་	surprise, wonder, amazement
ཡལ་ག་	branch
ཡིད་ཆགས་	vi. to get, become attached to
ཡིབས་	va. to hide
གཡུགས་	va. to throw
གཡོ་	va. to move, shake
གཡོ་འགུལ་	moving, shaking
རང་སྐྱོང་	self governing, autonomous
རན་	time to do
རབ་ཏུ་	thoroughly; completely
རིང་ཐུང་	long and short; length, distance
རེ་འདུན་	hope; va. — བྱེད་ to hope for
རོགས་དངུལ་	aid/relief money
ལག་	hand
ལམ་སྟེ་	guiding, leading; va. — འཁྲིད་
ལས་གསར་	new work
ལེགས་རྟོགས་	good understanding
ལོ་ཟླ་	year and month
ལོང་	"time to do" particle
ཤིང་སྡོང་	tree
ཤིང་ལོ་	tree and leaf
ཤེས་རྟོགས་	knowledge
བཤད་ཉན་	telling + listening
སང་དགོང་	tomorrow night
སྲུང་དམག་	bodyguard troops
སྲུང་བརྩི་	respect, honor, abide by
གསར་གཏོད་	invention, new creation
གསར་བཟོ་	make newly; new product
གསལ་སྟོན་	demonstration
གསུང་བཤད་	speech (h.)
གསོག་འཇོག་	deposit, saving
གསོས་	va. to rear, feed, nourish
བསམ་པ་རྣམ་དག་	sincere, earnest, genuine
བསམ་ཚུལ་	thought; opinion
ཧོན་ཐོར་	vi. to be shocked, surprised
ཨ་ཁུ་	uncle (paternal)
ཨམ་ཕྲག་	pocket formed by fold of dress
ཨེ་མ་	oh my

Lesson Fourteen

14.1 Constructions using the verb ཕྱིན་ as an auxiliary

These constructions consist of vb. + ཕྱིན་. They convey two different meanings, the first of which can be either "whatever," "whichever," "whoever," or "all kinds of" with regard to the verb modified.

a. བླ་མའི་བཀའ་སློབ་ཡིན་ཕྱིན་ལག་ལེན་བསྟར་དགོས།
Whatever the lama's advice is, (one) should put it into practice.

b. གནད་ཆེ་བའི་དོན་ཡིན་ཕྱིན་ངས་ཨ་ཕ་ཁྱེད་ལ་འདྲི་བར་ཡོང་གི་ཡིན།
Father, for all kinds of important issues, I'll come to ask you.

c. ལྷ་སར་སླེབས་ཕྱིན་པོ་ཏཱ་ལ་མ་མཐོང་བ་མ་སྲིད་པ་རེད།
Whoever arrives in Lhasa, it is impossible not to see the Potala.

d. སོ་ནམ་པ་ཡིན་ཕྱིན་ཞིང་ལས་བྱེད་དགོས་པ་རེད།
Whoever is a farmer has to do field work.

e. ཁྲིམས་འགལ་བྱས་ཕྱིན་བཙོན་ཁང་ལ་འགྲོ་རྒྱུ་མ་གཏོགས་ཡོད་པ་མ་རེད།
Whoever breaks the law, there is no other way but to go to jail.

f. ལྟད་མོ་དེ་མཐོང་ཕྱིན་སུ་ཡིན་ཀྱང་དེ་ལ་མི་དགའ་བ་ཡོང་གི་མ་རེད།
Whoever sees that show, there is nobody who doesn't like it.

Sometimes the meaning is better translated as "if X, then Y."

g. ཕ་ལམ་འཁྲུལ་མེད་ཡིན་ཕྱིན་གོང་ཆེན་པོ་བྱེད་ཀྱི་རེད།
If the diamond is real, (it) will be expensive.

h. གནས་ཚུལ་འདི་ཚགས་པར་ནང་བཀོད་ཕྱིན་མི་ཚང་མས་ཤེས་ཀྱི་རེད།
If this situation is written (about) in the newspaper, everybody will know (about it).

i. བོད་པ་ཡིན་ཕྱིན་རྩམ་པ་ཟ་མྱོང་ཡོད་པ་རེད།
If (he) is a Tibetan , (he) has experienced eating tsamba (parched barley flour).

14.2 The "do it again" particle: སྐྱོར་

This particle is used following the present or non-past stem of verbs: vb. + སྐྱོར་ + རྒྱག or བྱེད་. It conveys that the verbal action was repeated.

a. ཁོས་བཏང་ཡིག་དེ་ཀློག་སྐྱོར་ཐེངས་གསུམ་བརྒྱབ་པ་རེད།
He repeated reading that letter three times.

b. ཁོས་ལས་ཀ་དེ་བྱེད་སྐྱོར་བྱེད་དགོས་བྱུང་བ་རེད།
He had to do that work again.

c. མོས་སློབ་གྲྭར་གཏོང་རྒྱུའི་ཡི་གེ་དེ་བྲི་སྐྱོར་བྱེད་དགོས་བྱུང་སོང་།
She had to again write the letter which (she) is going to send to the school.

d. བཀའ་མོལ་དེ་གསུང་སྐྱོར་ཞིག་གནང་དང་།

Please say it again.

e. ཁ་སར་རྒྱ་གར་ནས་འབྱོར་བའི་ཚགས་པར་དེའི་ནང་གསར་འགྱུར་སྙན་པོ་ཞིག་འདུག། ཅུས་ཙང་ངས་ཀློག་སྐྱོར་བརྒྱབ་པ་ཡིན།

There was some interesting news in the newspaper that I received from India yesterday, so I read it again.

14.3 The auxiliary verb ཐལ་

One main use of ཐལ་ is to convey involuntary action in the sense that something was not intended to happen but did.

a. སྐད་ཆ་དེ་ཤོད་ཡག་མིན་ཀྱང་ཁ་ནས་ཐལ་བ་རེད།

That speech was not for telling but it just (got) blurted out.

In the next example, the subject didn't intend to go, but did so because he met his friend.

b. ཁ་སང་ལྟད་མོར་འགྲོ་ཡག་མིན་ཀྱང་གྲོགས་པོ་ཐུག་ནས་མཉམ་དུ་འགྲོ་བར་ཐལ་སོང་།

Even though I wasn't intending to go to the show yesterday, I met (my) friend and went together (with him).

A second major use of ཐལ་ is to convey "an excess of" something.

c. ཆང་ཐལ་ཆེ་བ་འཐུང་ན་ན་གི་རེད།

If (you) drink too much (an excessively large amount of) beer (you) will get sick.

d. མོ་ཊོར་མགྱོགས་ཐལ་ཆེ་བ་བཏང་ན་པུ་ལི་སིས་འཛིན་བཟུང་བྱེད་ཀྱི་རེད།

If (one) drives too fast, the police will arrest (you).

e. ལས་ཀ་ཇི་འདྲ་ཞིག་ཡིན་ཀྱང་ཐལ་མ་དྲགས་པ་བྱེད་གལ་ཆེན་པོ་རེད།

It is important that whatever work you do, you should not do it to excess.

14.4 Hypothetical constructions: དཔང་དུ་བཏང་ན་, ཆ་བཞག་ན་, and ཆ་ནས་མཚོན་ན་

These constructions convey the meaning "if we hypothetically say X, then Y."

a. གྲོང་གསེབ་དེར་དུད་ཚང་ ༢༠༠༠ ཡོད་པའི་དཔང་དུ་བཏང་ན་དེའི་ནང་བརྒྱ་ཆ་ ༡༥ ཙམ་ཚོང་པ་རེད།

If we say hypothetically that there are 2,000 families in that village, then about 15% of them are traders.

b. སྐུ་མགྲོན་ཚང་མ་ཕེབས་པར་ཆ་བཞག་ན་མི་གྲངས་ ༡༥༠ ཙམ་བྱེད་ཀྱི་རེད།

Hypothetically, if all the guests come, then there will be about 150 people.

c. ལུང་པ་དེའི་ཐོན་སྐྱེད་འཕེལ་རྒྱས་ཀྱི་ཆ་ནས་མཚོན་ན་མི་དམངས་ཚང་མ་ཕྱུག་པོ་ཆགས་དགོས་ཀྱི་རེད།

If (we) say hypothetically that production in that country will increase, then all the people have to (should) become rich.

d. ལུང་པ་དེའི་ཐོན་སྐྱེད་འཕེལ་རྒྱས་བྱུང་བའི་ཆ་ནས་མཚོན་ན་མི་དམངས་ཚང་མ་ཕྱུག་པོ་ཆགས་དགོས་ཀྱི་རེད།

If (we) say hypothetically that production in that country has increased, then all the people have to (should) get rich.

e. ཁོ་རྒྱ་གར་ལ་ཕྱིན་པའི་དཔང་དུ་བཏང་ན་ཡང་རྒྱུན་རིང་པོ་སྡོད་ཐུབ་ཀྱི་མ་རེད།

Even if we hypothetically say that he will go to India, (he) won't be able to stay long.

14.5 "For example" constructions: དཔེར་ན་ and དཔེར་ན་ཆ་བཞག་ན་

དཔེར་ན་ and དཔེར་ན་ཆ་བཞག་ན་ convey "for example."

a. བོད་ལ་ལྷ་མོའི་ཚོགས་པ་མང་པོ་ཡོད་པ་རེད། དཔེར་ན། སྐྱོར་མོ་ལུང་པ། གཅུང་པ། རྒྱངས་དཀར་བ་སོགས་ཡོད་པ་རེད།
In Tibet there are many opera associations. For example, Gyomo lunga, Chungba, Gyangkarwa, etc.

b. སྔོན་མ་བོད་ལ་གྲྭ་པ་ཏ་ཅང་མང་པོ་ཡོད་པ་རེད། དཔེར་ན་ཆ་བཞག་ན། འབྲས་སྤུངས་གཅིག་པུར་གྲྭ་པ་ཆིག་ཁྲི་ཙམ་ཡོད།
Formerly, there were very many monks in Tibet. For example, in Drepung alone there were about 10,000 monks.

14.6 Constructions using ཇུས་

ཇུས་ is used after the present (non-past) stems of verbs to convey "planning" or "making plans" to do the verbal action.

a. མོས་མགྱོགས་པོ་ཆང་བཟའ་རྒྱག་ཇུས་བྱེད་ཀྱི་འདུག།
She is making plans to get married quickly.

b. ན་ཉིན་ཁོས་སློབ་གྲྭར་འགྲོ་ཇུས་བྱས་པ་རེད།
Last year he made plans to go to school.

c. ཁོང་ཚོ་ཁང་པ་སྤོ་ཇུས་བྱེད་ཀྱི་འདུག
They are planning to move their residence.

14.7 Constructions with ཆེད་

ཆེད་ is used before verbs to convey that the verbal action was specially done.

a. ཁོ་ཚོང་རྒྱག་པར་རྒྱ་གར་ལ་ཆེད་ཐོན་བྱས་སོང་།
He left for India specially to do trading.

b. དེའི་སྐོར་ལ་ཁོ་ལ་ཁ་པར་ཆེད་གཏོང་བྱེད་ཀྱི་ཡིན།
(I) will specially telephone him regarding that.

c. ཞྭ་མོ་བཟོ་རྒྱུར་རས་ཆེད་ཉོས་བྱས་པ་རེད།
(They, he, etc.) specially bought material to make a hat.

14.8 Reading exercise: "The Wish-Fulfilling Gem Necklace," continued from Lesson 13

14.8.1 Tibetan text

སློབ་ཚན་བཅོ་གསུམ་པའི་འཕྲོས་

དེ་ལྟར་ངང་ཉིན་མཚན་བསྒྱུད་དེ་སྐྱོད་པས་མཐར་ཉིན་བཅོ་ལྔ་ལས་མ་འགོར་བར་ 1 རྟ་དམག་དཔུང་ཚོགས་རྣམས་གདོན་འདྲི་སྟོད་སའི་ནགས་ཚལ་གྱི་ཁྲོད་དུ་འབྱོར་བ་དང་འགྲིལ་ཟིན་པའི་ཐང་ཤིང་སྡོང་པོའི་འགྲམ་དུ་སླེབས་སྐབས་དམག་མི་རྣམས་རྟ་

ཐོག་ནས་བབས་ཏེ་ཐང་ཆད་ནས་ནུས་ཤུགས་མེད་པར་2 ས་ཐོག་ཏུ་ཉལ་གྱི་ཡོད་ཅིང་། ཕྱུག་མཛོད་ཆེ་མོས་སྣང་ཆུང་གི་སྒོ་ནས་3 ཐང་ཤིང་སྡོང་པོ་དེའི་འོག་ཏུ་ཡོད་པ་རེད་དམ་ཞེས་སྐད་ཆ་དྲིས། ལྷོ་རྡོར་ཁྱིས་ཧ་སྣ་བཤུས་པ་དང་ཧ་སློད་རྗེས་གཞི་ནས་ཁ་པར་བསྒོགས་ཏེ་དེ་གར་རེད། སྐུ་ངོ་། ཐང་ཤིང་སྡོང་པོ་དེའི་འོག་ཏུ་རེད་ཅེས་ལན་བཏབ། ཕྱུག་མཛོད་ཆེ་མོས་ངལ་དུབ་ཀྱིས་མནར་བའི་དམག་མི་རྣམས་ལ་ཧ་ལྷུག་གཞུ་བ་དང་སྦྲགས་ད་དུང་སྐད་ཤུགས་ཆེན་པོས་ ངད་འགྲོ་ཆོ། མགྱོགས་པོ་ཡར་ལངས་ཏེ་ཤིང་སྡོང་དེ་ཕར་དབོར་ཞིག་4 ཅེས་ཁ་རྡུང་བཏང་། ཤིང་སྡོང་ཏ་ཅང་སྦོམ་པོ་དེ་སྒུལ་ཙམ་ཡང་5 བྱེད་ཐབས་བྲལ་བར་བརྟེན་ཕོ་གཞོན་རིས་གསེར་གྱི་སྟ་རེས་ཤིང་སྡོང་དེ་དུམ་བུར་བཅད་པ་དང་དམག་མི་རྣམས་ཀྱིས་ཤིང་དུམ་དེ་ཚོ་དབོར།

དེ་ནས་བྲག་ཁུང་ཆེན་པོ་ཞིག་མངོན་པས་དམག་མི་རྣམས་ཧོན་ཐོར་བ་དང་ཕྱུག་མཛོད་ཆེ་མོས་མར་ལྟ་སྐབས་མུན་པ་ནག་ཅིང་འཇིགས་སུ་རུང་བ་ཞིག་ཡོད་པས་ཁོ་པ་སྐྲག་ཐག་ཆོད་ནས་འདར་གསིགས་ཤོར་6། ཡིན་ནའང་ཕྱུག་མཛོད་ཆེ་མོས་མིག་ཏྲིག་ཏྲིག་བྱས་ནས་ཁྲིལ་གད་དགོད་བཞིན་པར་ཕོ་གཞོན་ལ་མགྱོགས་པོ་མར་འབབས་ཤིག་7། སྲས་མོ་སྐྱོབ་ཐུབ་པ་ཡིན་ན་8 སྲས་མོའི་མག་པ་ཁྱེད་ཀྱིས་བྱེད་ཆོག་9། འོན་ཀྱང་ཁྱོད་ཀྱིས་གུས་ཞབས་ཞུས་པ་བྱས་10 དེ་སྲས་མོ་སྡོད་ལ་ཡར་གཏོང་དགོས་ཞེས་བཤད། དེ་རྗེས་དམག་མི་ཆོར་མི་གཅིག་ཤོང་བའི་ཀོ་བའི་ཁྲིན་སྐྱོགས་ཤིག་བཟོ་རུ་བཅུག། དེ་ནས་ལྷོ་རྡོར་བྲག་ཁུང་ནང་དུ་མར་བཏང་། མུན་པ་ནག་པའི་འདྲེ་ཡི་བྲག་ཁུང་དེ་ནི་བཞའ་ཚན་ཆེ་ལ་འཇིགས་སུ་རུང་བ་ཞིག་ཡོད། ཡ་མཚན་ཅན་གྱི་བྲག་ཁུང་དེའི་ནང་ཟོག་གི་མགོ་དང་མི་རུས་ཀྱིས་ཁེངས་ནས་ཡོད། མི་ཕུང་ནང་ཤིང་དུམ་བུ་འགའ་ཞིག་ལ་མེ་ཆུང་ཆུང་འབར་བཞིན་ཡོད་མི་མདངས་དེ་ས་ཐོག་ཏུ་འགྱེལ་བའི་སྲས་མོ་བཀྲས་ལྷའི་ལུས་པོར་འཕྲོ་བཞིན་ཡོད། ཁོ་མོས་སྐད་ཤུགས་ཆུང་ངུས་སྐྱོ་གླུ་ལེན་བཞིན་ཡོད་པ་རེད།

གཞོགས་བྱང་ངོས་སུ་བྲག་ཁུང་ཆུང་ཆུང་ཞིག་ཡོད་ཅིང་གདོན་འདྲེ་དེ་དེའི་ནང་ཡིབས་ནས་རྨ་ཁ་གསོ་བཞིན་11 བསྡད་ཡོད། ཁོ་པས་སྲས་མོ་བཀྲས་ལྷའི་སྐྱོ་གླུ་ཐོས་རྗེས་སྙིང་སྣང་ཆེན་པོ་བྱེད་བཞིན་པར་རོ་ཟ་རྒྱུ་12 ཀུན་པོ་ཆུང་ཆུང་ཁྱོད། ད་དུང་གཞན་ཐོངས་དང་13 ངའི་རྨ་ཁ་གསོས་རྗེས་ཁྱོད་ཤ་ཐོར་རུས་ཐོར་བཟོ་རྒྱུ་ཡིན་ཅེས་སྐད་ཤུགས་ཆེན་པོས་གཤེ་གཤེ་བཏང་། སྲས་མོ་སྐྲག་ཐག་ཆོད་ནས་འདར་བ་དང་ཁྲུར་ཁྱུར་ངང་ཡར་ལངས་ནས་ཕྱོགས་བཞིར་གསོན་ལམ་འཚོལ་སྐབས་གློ་བུར་དུ་དངོས་པོ་ནག་ཏྲིལ་ཏྲིལ་ཞིག་མར་འབབ་ཡོང་བ་མཐོང་སྲས་མོའི་སེམས་པར་སྔར་ཡང་གདོན་འདྲེ་གསར་པ་ཞིག་ཡོང་གི་འདུག་སྙམ་ནས་དེ་བས་སྐྲག་ཐག་ཆོད་དེ་ཁྲིལ་འཚབ་ངང་ཡིབས་ནས་བསྡད།

གདོན་འདྲེས་མི་ཡི་རྡོག་སྒྲ་ཐོས་མ་ཐག་ཁོང་ཁྲོ་ལངས་ནས་མར་ཐོན་པས་དེ་ནི་ཁོ་པར་རྨས་སྐྱོན་གཏོང་མཁན་གྱི་ཕོ་གཞོན་དེ་ཡིན་པ་མཐོང་། ཁོ་པས་གདུག་རྩུབ་ཆེ་བའི་སྒོ་ནས་གད་མོ་དགོད་བཞིན་པར་ཡག་པོ་བྱུང་ ཡག་པོ་བྱུང་ སྒོ་རྩ་ར་སྐྱེ ཁྱིར་ནས་ཞུགས་པ་ཏོ་བར་སྐྱིབས་བྱུང་ངས་14 ཁྱེད་ལ་གོད་རྒྱུར་15 བུད་མེད་སུམ་བཅུ་སུམ་ཙ་སོ་གསུམ་བཟས་པ་ཡིན་ སྐྱེས་པ་དགུ་བཅུ་དགུ་བཅུ་གོ་དགུ་བཟས་པ་ཡིན།། དེ་རིང་ཁྱོད་བཟས་ན་གྲངས་ཚད་ལོན་སོང་ཞེས་བཤད། གདོན་འདྲེས་སྐད་ཆ་བཤད་ཚར་རྗེས་ཧུར་སྒྲ་དང་བཅས་པའི་སྒོ་ནས་འཕུར་ཏེ་གཤོག་པ་རྡེབ་བཞིན་པར་ཆེ་ཆུང་སྐར་ཁ་ཙམ་གྱི་སེར་དྲག་ཕབ་སྟེ་ཕོ་གཞོན་

དང་སྲུས་མོའི་མགོ་སེར་པས་བརྡུངས། སློ་རྡོར་གྱིས་ལག་གཡོན་མས་སྲུས་མོར་སྲུང་སྐྱོབ་དང་། ལག་གཡས་པས་གསེར་གྱི་སྒ་རེ་མཐོན་པོར་འཕྱར་ནས་སེར་པ་བཀག་པས་གདོན་འདྲེ་ཁོང་ཁྲོ་ཆེན་པོ་ལངས་ནས་གཤོག་པ་བརྡབས་ཏེ་སེར་བ་སྤྲར་ལས་ཆེ་བ་ཕབ་སྟེ་བྲག་ཕུག་ནང་སེར་བ་གང་སར་འཕར་བཞིན་ཡོད།

ཕོ་གཞོན་དེའི་བསམ་པར་སེར་དྲག་གི་འོག་འཆི་བ་ལས་གདོན་འདྲེ་དང་ཤི་གསོན་གྱི་འཐབ་རྩོད་བྱས་ན་དགའ་སྙམ་སྟེ་སྐད་ཆེན་པོ་ཞིག་བརྒྱབ་པ་དང་སྤྲགས་ནུས་ཤུགས་ཡོད་ཚད་བཏོན་ནས་སྒ་རེ་གཡུགས་པས་གདོན་འདྲེ་དེ་ཕྱེད་གཤགས་སུ་བཏང་བ་དང་གདོན་འདྲེའི་ཁྲག་དེ་སློ་རྡོར་གྱི་གདོང་དང་ལུས་པོ་ཡོངས་ལ་འཐོར། བསམ་ཡུལ་ལས་འདས་པ་ཞིག་ལ་གདོན་འདྲེའི་ཁྲག་ལ་དུག་ཡོད་པར་བརྟེན་ཕོ་གཞོན་དེའི་གདོང་པ་འཚིགས་ནས་སོལ་བ་ལྟ་བུར་གྱུར། ཕོ་གཞོན་དེས་ལུས་ཀྱི་ན་ཟུག་དྲག་པོ་བཟོད་བཞིན་པར་ནུས་ཤུགས་གང་ཡོད་ཀྱིས་ཨམ་ཕྲུག་ནང་ནས་འོད་ཆེམ་ཆེམ་འཕྲོ་བའི་ཡིད་བཞིན་ནོར་བུའི་དོ་ཤལ་དེ་མར་བཏོན་ནས་སྲུས་མོའི་མགུལ་ལ་སྒྲོན་ཏེ་གུས་པར་འབེས་པའི་སྲུས་མོ་ལགས། ཁྱེད་ཉིད་འཕྲལ་དུ་གདོན་འདྲེའི་བྲག་ཁུང་ལས་ཞལ་གྱིས་དགོས་ཅེས་བཤད་པས་སྲུས་མོའི་ཐུགས་ལ་གཡོ་འགུལ་ཚད་མེད་ཐེབས་ཏེ་རང་དབང་མེད་པར་སྤྱན་ཆབ་ལྷུང་། སྲུས་མོ་རང་ཉིད་གཅིག་པུར་ཡར་འགྲོ་འདོད་མེད་ཀྱང་སེམས་པ་བཟང་བའི་ཕོ་གཞོན་དེས་ཨུ་ཚུགས་བརྒྱབ་མཐར་སྲུས་མོ་བཀྲས་ལྷ་ཀོ་བའི་ཁྲོན་སྐྱོགས་ནང་ཡར་འཛུལ། སྲུས་མོས་རང་ཉིད་ཀྱི་རིན་ཆེན་ཕ་ལམ་གྱི་སོར་གདུབ་དེ་མར་ཕུད་ནས་ཕོ་གཞོན་དེའི་མཛུབ་མོར་གཡོགས་ཤིང་། བརྩེ་སེམས་ཅན་མོའི་ངང་འདི་ནི་བཞེས་རོགས་གནང་། ང་ཁྱེད་དང་མཉམ་དུ་ཕོ་བྲང་ནང་དུ་ཕྱིར་ལོག་བྱེད་ཀྱི་ཡིན་ཞེས་བཤད།

སློ་རྡོར་སེམས་འཁྱུལ་ཐེབས་བཞིན་པར་སོར་གདུབ་ཕར་ཕུལ་ཏེ་ང་ལ་ལག་རྟགས་མི་དགོས། དང་པོ་ནས་ང་ལ་བསམ་དོན་གཅིག་ཁོ་ན་16ལས་མེད། དེ་ནི་གདོན་འདྲེ་མེད་པ་བཟོ་རྒྱུ་དེ་ཡིན་ཅེས་ལན་བཏབ། དེས་ན་སྲུས་མོ་བཀྲས་ལྷས་ཕོ་གཞོན་དེའི་ལག་ནས་བཟུང་སྟེ་ཨུ་ཚུགས་ཀྱིས་སོར་གདུབ་དེ་སློ་རྡོར་གྱི་མཛུབ་མོར་གཡོགས་སོང་། སྐབས་དེར་ཁྲོན་སྐྱོགས་ལ་འཁྱུལ་སྐྱོད་ཐེབས་པས་དྲིལ་བུའི་སྒྲ་གྲགས་ཤིང་། བྲག་ཁུང་གི་ཁར་སྐྱུང་ནས་སྡོད་པའི་དམག་མི་ཚོས་དྲིལ་སྒྲ་ཐོས་མ་ཐག་སྲུས་མོ་བཀྲས་ལྷ་ཡར་འཐེན། ཕོ་གཞོན་དེའི་བསམ་པར་དམག་མི་ཚོས་སྲུས་མོ་ཡར་འཐེན་རྗེས་ལམ་སེང་ཁྲོན་སྐྱོགས་དེ་མར་གཏོང་ངེས་ཡིན་སྙམ། འོན་ཀྱང་བསམ་ཡུལ་ལས་འདས་པ་ཞིག་ལ་བྲག་ཁུང་གི་ཁ་དེ་འུང་ཞེས་པའི་སྒྲ་དང་བཅས་རྡོ་ཆེན་ཞིག་གིས་བཀག་པ་དང་སྤྲགས་ཕུག་མཛོད་ཆེན་མོས་བཀའ་ཕབ་པའི་སྒྲ་དང་ཏ་ཡི་རྨིག་པའི་སྒྲ་ཐག་རིང་དུ་སོང་བ་བཅས་ཐོས། སློ་རྡོར་ཁོང་ཁྲོ་ཤིན་ཏུ་ཆེན་པོ་ལངས་ནས་གསེར་གྱི་སྒ་རེས་ཕ་བོང་ཚང་མ་གཏོར་ཀྱང་ཕྱིར་ཐོན་མི་ཐུབ་སྐབས་ཕོ་གཞོན་དེ་བུ་ཐབས་ཟད་པའི་གནས་སུ་ལྷུང་སྐབས་གློ་བུར་དུ་གདོན་འདྲེའི་བྲག་ཕུག་ཚུང་ཚུང་ནང་ནས་འོད་དཀར་པོ་ཞིག་འཕྲོས་ཡོང་བ་མཐོང་། སློ་རྡོར་གྱི་བསམ་པར་གདོན་འདྲེ་དེ་སླར་ཡང་གསོས་པ་རེད་སྙམ་ནས་མགྱོགས་པོར་གསེར་གྱི་སྒ་རེ་གཞུ་བར་འགྲོ་སྐབས་བྲག་ཕུག་ཚུང་ཚུང་དེའི་ནང་ནས་བྱམས་བརྩེ་ལྡན་པའི་སེང་གེ་རྒད་པོ་མར་ཐོན་ཡོང་ནས་ཁྱེད་ལ་བཀྲིས་བདེ་ལེགས་ཞུ་རྒྱུ་ཡིན། ཁྱེད་ཀྱིས་མི་དམངས་ཀྱི་དོན་དུ་གནོད་འཚེ་ཞིག་མེད་པ་བཟོས་པ་མ་ཟད། ཕ་ལམ་གྱི་སོར་གདུབ་གཅིག་ཀྱང་ཐོབ་འདུག་ཅེས་བཤད་དེ་གད་མོ

བགད། ཀློ་རྡོར་གྱིས་གུས་བཏུད་གཅིག་ཞུས་ནས་སེམས་སྐྱོ་པོའི་ངང་གལ་ཏེ་ཁྱེད་ཀྱིས་ང་གདོན་འདྲེའི་བྲག་ཁུང་འདི་ནས་ཕྱིར་ཐོན་ཐུབ་པ་གནང་ 17 ན་ངས་རིན་ཆེན་སོར་གདུབ་འདི་ཁྱེད་ལ་འབུལ་རྒྱུ་ཡིན་ཞེས་བཤད། སེང་གེ་ནད་པོས་གད་མོ་དགོད་བཞིན་པར་ཡིད་ཐང་ཆད་རྒྱུ་ག་ལ་ཡོད་ 18 ཅེས་ལན་བཏབ། དེ་ནས་ནད་པོ་དེས་འགྲེ་ལོག་ཅིག་བརྒྱབ་མ་ཐག་གངས་ལྟར་དཀར་བའི་སེང་གེ་ཞིག་ལ་གྱུར་ཏེ་ས་ཐོག་ལ་ཙོག་པུར་བསྡད། ཀློ་རྡོར་གྱིས་སེང་གེར་བཞོན་སྐབས་སེང་གེས་སྐད་སྒྲ་སྒྲོག་སྟེ་བར་སྣང་མཐོངས་སུ་འཕུར་ནས་བྲག་ཁུང་འགྲམ་དུ་འབྱོར་བ་དང་ཕོ་གཞོན་གྱིས་གསེར་གྱི་སྦ་རེས་རྡོ་ཆེན་གཏོར་ནས་སེང་གེས་ཁོ་བྲག་ཁུང་གི་ཕྱི་ལ་བསྐྱལ། བྲག་ཁུང་གི་ཕྱི་ལ་ཐོན་མ་ཐག་སེང་གེ་དེ་ནད་པོ་ཞིག་ཏུ་གྱུར་ནས་ཕོ་གཞོན་དེར་ཕེབས་ཤིག རྒྱལ་པོའི་གྲོང་དུ་ཕེབས་ཤིག ཁྱེད་ལ་བདེ་སྐྱིད་སྤྲོད་མཁན་ཞིག་ཡོང་གི་རེད་ཅེས་བཤད། ཀློ་རྡོར་སེམས་འགྱུལ་ཐེབས་བཞིན་པར་གོམ་ཞིང་ཆེན་པོས་གྲོང་ཁྱེར་གྱི་ཕྱོགས་སུ་སོང་།

ཕྱུག་མཛོད་ཆེ་མོས་སྐྱུང་ཀྲུང་འཛོམས་ཤིང་མཛེས་སྡུག་ལྡན་པའི་སྲས་མོ་བཀྲས་ལྷའི་སྲོག་བསྐྱབས་པ་རེད་ཅེས་གྲོང་མི་ཚོས་གོ་ཐོས་བྱུང་བ་དང་། རྒྱལ་པོ་དང་བཙུན་མོ་གཉིས་པོས་ཕོ་བྲང་གི་མདུན་དུ་མི་མང་པོའི་ཁྲོད་ན་ཕྱུག་མཛོད་ཆེ་མོ་སྲས་མོའི་མག་པར་བསྡུ་བཞིན་ཡོད། མི་རྣམས་ཀྱིས་དགའ་སྤྲོ་ཚད་མེད་ཀྱི་སྒོ་ནས་རེ་འགས་ལག་ཏུ་ཁ་བཏགས་འཁྱེར་བ་དང་། རེ་འགས་ཆང་གི་དམ་བི་བཏེགས་པ། རེ་འགས་སྐད་གསང་མཐོན་པོའི་སྒོ་ནས་གཞས་གཏོང་བ་དང་ཞབས་བྲོ་རྒྱག་བཞིན་པར་འཚང་ཀ་ཤིག་ཤིག་ངང་ཕོ་བྲང་གི་སྒོའི་མདུན་དུ་ཡོང་བཞིན་ཡོད། རྒྱལ་པོའི་ཕོ་བྲང་གི་སྒོ་མོའི་མདུན་དུ་དུས་ཆེན་གྱི་རྣམ་པ་ལྡན་ཞིང་། སྐུ་སྲུང་བ་ཚོས་བརྗིད་ཉམས་ལྡན་པའི་སྒོ་ནས་རུ་བསྣར་གཉིས་བསྒྲིགས། རྒྱལ་པོ་དང་བཙུན་མོ་གཉིས་སྤྲོ་སྣང་གི་འཛུམ་མདངས་སྟོན་བཞིན་པར་ཁྲི་ཐོག་ཏུ་བཞུགས།

ཕྱུག་མཛོད་ཆེ་མོ་བྲང་ཁོག་ཕྱིར་བཞིན་པར་རང་ཆེ་རང་བཀུར་གྱི་སྒོ་ནས་གོམ་པ་རེ་རེ་བྱས་ཏེ་སེའུ་རྣམས་འཛེགས། རྒྱལ་པོ་སྐུ་ངོ་མས་ཕྱུག་མཛོད་ཆེ་མོར་གསེར་དངུལ་ལ་སོགས་པའི་ནོར་བུའི་རིགས་དང་། དཔོན་གོས། རལ་གྲི་བཅས་གསོལ་རས་གནང་། སྐབས་དེར་བཙུན་མོས་ཕོ་བྲང་ནང་གི་གཡོག་མོ་རྣམས་ལ་སྲས་མོ་བཀྲས་ལྷ་གདན་འདྲེན་ཞུ་བར་བཏང་བ་དང་ཚང་མའི་མདུན་དུ་ཕྱུག་མཛོད་ཆེ་མོ་དང་ 19 གཉེན་སྒྲིག་བྱེད་རྒྱུའི་བཀའ་ཕབ། སྐབས་དེར་དགའ་འབོད་ཀྱི་སྒྲས་ཁེངས་པ་དང་སྲས་མོ་བཀྲས་ལྷ་ཕོ་བྲང་ནང་ནས་མར་ཡོང་སྐབས་ཕྱུག་མཛོད་ཆེ་མོས་གྱོན་ཆས་གྱོན་ཡོད་པ་མཐོང་བ་ལས་གདོན་འདྲེའི་དུག་ཁྲག་གིས་ཐམས་སྐྱོན་བྱུང་བའི་ཕོ་གཞོན་དེ་མཐོང་རྒྱུ་མེད་པ་རེད། ཁོ་མོས་ཕྱུག་མཛོད་ཆེན་མོའི་མགོ་སྐོར་འོག་ཚུད་པ་གཞི་ནས་གསལ་པོ་ཤེས་པ་དང་ཁོང་ཁྲོ་ཚད་མེད་ལངས་ནས་གློ་བུར་དུ་ཁོ་མོ་དྲན་པ་བོར་ནས་འགྱེལ།

རྒྱལ་པོས་གཡོག་མོ་རྣམས་ལ་སྲས་མོ་མགྱོགས་མྱུར་ཡར་སྐྱོར་དགོས་པའི་བཀའ་གནང་བ་དང་དེའི་རྒྱུ་མཚན་གང་ཡིན་ཞིབ་དཔྱོད་བྱེད་པའི་སྐབས་འདིར་མདོག་ད་ཅང་ངན་པའི་ 20 མི་ཞིག་གིས་ལག་གཉིས་པོས་སྲས་མོ་བཀྲས་ལྷའི་རིན་ཆེན་ཕ་ལམ་གྱི་སོར་གདུབ་མཐོན་པོར་བཏེགས་ནས་རྒྱལ་པོའི་མདུན་དུ་ཡོང་སྟེ་གུས་ཕྱག་དང་བཅས་སྲས་མོ་ཕལ་ཆེར་རིན་ཆེན་ཕ་ལམ་གྱི་སོར་གདུབ་འདི་བོར་བརླག་ཏུ་སོང་བའི་རྐྱེན་གྱིས་མིན་ནམ 21། ངས་མགྱོགས་པོ་འབུལ་བར་ཡོང་བ་ཡིན་པས་སྲས་མོས་འདི་ཉེས་

བཞེས་རོགས་གནང་ཞེས་ཞུས། སྐད་ཆ་དེ་བཤད་ཚར་རྗེས་པོ་གཞོན་དེས་སོར་གདུབ་ཕར་ཕུལ་ནས་བློ་ཐག་ཆོད་པོའི་ངང་ཕྱིར་ལོག་སོང་ཞིང་། བློན་པོ་རྣམས་ཧོན་ཐོར་ནས་གཡས་གཡོན་དུ་མིག་ཅེ་རེར་བལྟས་དེ་བསྡད། སྲས་མོས་གཟབ་གཟབ་བྱས་དེ་ལྟ་སྐབས་པོ་གཞོན་དེ་ངོ་ཤེས་ཤིང་ཁོང་ནི་ ཁོང་ནི་ ཁོང་ནི་ང་ཡི་སྲོག་སྐྱོབ་མཁན་དྲིན་ཆེན་ངོ་མ་དེ་རེད་ཅེས་བསྐྱུད་མར་བཤད།

རྒྱལ་པོ་དང་ བཙུན་མོ་ བྲན་འཁོར། བློན་པོ་བཅས་ཚང་མ་ཧང་སངས་པ་དང་། དེར་ཡོད་ལྟད་མོ་ལྟ་མཁན་གྱིས་ཀྱང་སྐད་ཤུགས་ཆུང་ངུས་གཏམ་གླེང་སྣ་ཚོགས་བྱེད་བཞིན་ཡོད། རྒྱལ་པོས་པོ་གཞོན་དེ་འཕྲལ་དུ་ཡར་ཕྱིན་ཤོག་ཅེས་བཀའ་བསྩལ་བ་དང་བློན་པོར་བློ་ཇོར་ལ་གསོལ་རས་རྒྱ་དངུལ་ཏ་མིག་པ་བརྒྱ་ཐམ་པ་སྤྲོད་ཅེས་བཀའ་གནང་། དེས་ན་པོ་གཞོན་བློ་ཇོར་གྱིས་མི་མང་པོའི་ཁྲོད་དུ་སྐད་ཤུགས་ཆེན་པོས་རྒྱལ་པོས་ང་ལ་གསོལ་རས་གནང་བར་22 ཐུགས་རྗེ་ཆེ་ཞུ་རྒྱུ་ཡིན། འོན་ཀྱང་ངས་སྲས་མོ་སྐྱོབ་པ་ནི་དངུལ་གྱི་དོན་དུ་མ་ཡིན་པར་རྒྱལ་པོའི་བཀའ་དྲིན་བསམ་ཤེས་དང་མི་དམངས་ཀྱི་དོན་དུ་གནོད་འཚེ་མེད་པ་བཟོ་རྒྱུའི་ཆེད་དུ་ཡིན་ཞེས་ཞུས་ནས་སླར་ཡང་ཕྱིར་ལོག་སོང་།

མཛེས་ལྡན་སྲས་མོས་བློ་བུར་དུ་པོ་གཞོན་དེར་འཁྱུད་དེ་གུས་མོ་སྐྱོབ་མཁན་པོ་གཞོན་སུ་ཡིན་ལ་མ་ལྟོས་པར་23 དེ་མག་པར་བཞེས་རྒྱུའི་ཡབ་ཀྱི་བཀའ་ཡོད། ཁྱེད་ཕྱིར་ལོག་སོང་ན་ག་ནས་འགྲིག་ཅེས་ངུ་བཞིན་པར་བཤད། དེས་ན་བློན་པོ་འཁོར་དང་བཅས་པ་དགའ་སྤྲོ་རབ་ཏུ་འཕེལ་ཞིང་། ཕྱག་མཛོད་ཆེ་མོ་ནི་ངོ་ཚ་ཁ་སྐྱེངས་ཀྱི་གནས་སུ་གྱུར། སྲས་མོས་དེ་བས་སེམས་འགུལ་ཐེབས་པའི་ངང་གཞོན་པར་ཡིད་སྨོན་དང་བརྩེ་གདུང་གི་སེམས་པ་འཆང་བཞིན་པར་གུས་མོས་ཁྱེད་ཀྱི་དཔའ་ངར་དང་། ལྷག་བསམ་ཟོལ་མེད་དེར་དགའ་ཞེན་ཞུ་བཞིན་ཡོད། ཁྱེད་ཀྱིས་གུས་མོའི་གཡོ་ལྷད་མེད་པའི་བསམ་པར་ཡིད་ཆེས་གནང་རྒྱུའི་རེ་བ་ཡོད། ཁྱེད་ཀྱི་རྣམ་པ་ཇི་ལྟར་ངན་པ་དང་ཁྱིམ་གཞི་ཇི་ལྟར་ཉམ་ཐག་ཡིན་རུང་གུས་མོ་བདག་ནི་ཁྱེད་དང་མཉམ་དུ་འགྲོ་བར་འདོད་ཅེས་པའི་སྙིང་གཏམ་ཤོད་བཞིན་པར་ལག་གཉིས་པོས་པོ་གཞོན་གྱི་གདོང་ལ་བྱིལ་བྱིལ་ཡང་ཡང་བྱས། སྲས་མོའི་ཕྱག་གིས་བྱིལ་བྱིལ་བྱེད་སྐབས་ཕྱག་གང་དུ་རེག་སར་རྨ་ཁ་རྣམས་གསོས་ཏེ་པོ་གཞོན་གྱི་གདོང་པ་སྔར་ལྟར་འདྲ་ཆགས་པོར་གྱུར།

རྒྱལ་པོ་སྤྲོ་བ་རབ་ཏུ་འཕེལ་ནས་ཁོང་སྐུ་ངོ་མས་གཞོན་པ་དེ་ཁྲི་ཐོག་ཏུ་གདན་དྲངས་ནས་རང་ཉིད་དང་བཙུན་མོའི་དབུས་སུ་བཞག། རྒྱལ་པོས་ཡར་བཞེངས་ནས་ཁོང་ཁྲོ་ཆེན་པོས་ཕྱག་གི་འཁར་བ་ཡར་བཏེགས་ནས་དྲག་དམག་ལ་གཡོ་སྐྱོ་ཆེ་བའི་ཕྱག་མཛོད་ཆེ་མོ་མར་ཁྲིད་དེ་མག་པའི་གྲོན་ཆས་རྣམས་འབུད་དགོས་པ་དང་གསོལ་རས་སྤྲད་པ་རྣམས་ཚུར་བླངས་ནས་ཚང་མ་པོ་གཞོན་དེར་སྤྲོད་དགོས་པའི་བཀའ་ཕབ། རྒྱལ་པོ་དང་བཙུན་མོ་རྣམ་གཉིས་སྐུ་ངོ་མས་པོ་གཞོན་དང་སྲས་མོ་གཉིས་ཀྱི་གཉེན་སྒྲིག་བག་སྟོན་གྱི་གཙོ་གཉེར་གནང་བ་དང་། གཉེན་སྒྲིག་བག་སྟོན་མཇུག་བསྒྲིལ་རྗེས་པོ་གཞོན་དེས་སྐུ་སྐྱུང་ཁྲིད་ནས་བྱམས་བརྩེ་ལྡན་པའི་ཨ་མ་ཆེ་སྐྱིད་བསུ་བར་ཡོང་། དེ་ནས་བཟུང་སྲས་མོ་དང་ལྷན་དུ་བདེ་སྐྱིད་ཕུན་སུམ་ཚོགས་པའི་འཚོ་བ་བསྐྱལ་ནས་སྡོད་རྒྱུ་བྱུང་བ་རེད། །

14.8.2 Translation

Continued from Lesson 13

Finally, by going continuously day and night, the cavalry force arrived after only 15 days had elapsed at the side of the fallen pine tree in the forest where the demon lived. At this time, the soldiers dismounted and, being exhausted and bereft of energy, lay down on the ground. The chief steward asked in a demeaning tone, "Is it below this pine tree?" Lodor took off his saddle and let his horse loose and only then turned back and answered, "It is here. Your lordship, it is under this pine tree." The chief steward hit his fatigued soldiers with his whip and in a loud voice verbally abused them saying, "Animals, get up quickly. Move this tree away." (However), they could not move that very thick tree even a little bit, so the youth cut the tree into pieces with his golden axe. The soldiers carried the pieces away.

Then a large cave became visible. The soldiers were astonished. When the chief steward looked down into it, it was scary and dark and he got frightened and started shaking. Nevertheless, the chief steward, wide-eyed, gave a sarcastic laugh and told the young man, "Go down! If you are able to save the princess, it is okay for you to become the princess's husband. Nevertheless, you should show [lit., know] respect and send the princess up first." After that he made the soldiers make a well-bucket of leather that would hold one person. Then they lowered Lodor into the cave. As for that black cave of the demon, it was humid and scary. The inside of that weird cave was filled full with cattle heads and human bones. There was a small fire with several pieces of wood burning, and the fire's glow was glittering on the body of Princess Drelha, who had collapsed on the floor. She was softly singing a sad song.

On the north side there was a small cave in which the demon was hiding while his wounds healed. When he heard Princess Drelha's sad song he was very annoyed and scolded (her) loudly, "You corpse-eating small thief, (go ahead and continue to) sing! After my wound is healed, I'll annihilate you [lit., destroy your bones and flesh]." The princess was very frightened and shivered. She got up unsteadily and looked in all four directions seeking a way to stay alive. When (she did this) suddenly she saw a round black thing descending toward her. She thought, "another demon is coming," and got very scared. She hurriedly hid.

As soon as the demon heard the sound of a person's feet he got angry and came out (lit., down). As he saw that the noise was the young man who had wounded him, he laughed viciously and said, "It's good. It's good. Having brought your neck to the door, have you come to buy a lasso? I have something to tell you. I have eaten 333 women and 999 men. Today if I eat you, I'll reach my goal (i.e., 1000)." After the demon finished speaking, he flew off making the sound "hurdra." He flapped his wings and made hail the size of walnuts fall. The heads of the youth and princess were pelted by hail. Lodor protected the princess with his left hand and with his right hand raised the golden axe high and blocked the hail. The demon was very angry at this and flapped his wings so that hail even bigger than before fell. In the cave, hail bounced about everywhere.

The youth thought that rather than dying under the hail it would be better to have a life or death battle with the demon. He yelled loudly and threw the axe with all his strength. The demon was split in half, its blood splattering all over Lodor's face and body. Incredibly, the demon's blood had poison in it so the youth's face burned and became like coal. The youth, tolerating (his) body's extreme pain with whatever strength he had left, took out the glittering "wish-fulfilling gem" necklace from his pocket and put it on the princess's neck and said, "You, princess, who are worthy of respect, you have to leave this cave immediately." The princess was moved immeasurably by this and cried uncontrollably. The princess herself did not want to go up alone, but the kind youth insisted and finally Princess Drelha entered into the leather bucket. The princess took off her precious diamond ring and put it on the youth's finger. With deep love, she said, "As for this, please take it. I shall return to the palace together with you."

Lodor was deeply moved and gave the ring back answering, "I do not want any gift. From the start, I have had only one wish. As for that, it is to completely destroy the demon." Consequently, Princess Drelha seized the youth's hand and, insisting, put that ring onto Lodor's finger. At that time the bucket moved a bit and its bell rang. The soldiers who were guarding the edge of the cave pulled up the princess as soon as they heard the ringing. The youth thought that the soldiers would definitely send the bucket down immediately after they brought up the princess. However, incredibly, (he) heard the sound "ung" at the edge of the cave and a big boulder blocked the opening. And (he heard) the sound of the chief steward's orders and the sound of the horses' hooves growing distant. Lodor became furious and broke up all the boulders with his golden axe. But he was unable to get out. He was left without the means for doing anything. At this time he suddenly saw a white light coming out from the small cave of the demon . Lodor thought that the demon had again recovered. He was going quickly to hit him with the golden axe when the loving old man-lion came out from the small cave and said, "Greetings to you. You not only have destroyed that demon, benefiting the people, you have also obtained a diamond ring." And then he laughed. Lodor showed his respect and said sadly, "If you are able to get me out of this demon's cave, I will give you this precious gem ring." The old man-lion answered laughing, "What is there to be discouraged about?" Then the old man rolled over and as soon as he did this he became the lion as white as snow. He sat crouched on the ground. When Lodor mounted the lion, the lion yelled and flew into the sky arriving at the edge of the cave. The youth (then) destroyed the big rock with his golden axe and the lion delivered him outside of the cave. As soon as he arrived outside the cave the lion became the old man and said to the youth, "Go! Go to the king's city! You will meet a person who will give you happiness." Lodor was touched and went toward the city quickly (lit., with big steps).

"The chief steward saved the clever and beautiful princess," the villagers heard, and the king and queen both were in the front of the palace in the midst of many people to welcome the chief steward as the princess's groom. The people were extremely happy, crowding into the front of the door of the palace, some carrying ceremonial scarves in their hands, others carrying flasks of beer, and others dancing and singing songs with loud and clear voices. The front of the main door of the palace had the appearance of a festival with the bodyguard troops lined up grandly in two rows. The king and queen, smiling happily, sat on top of (their) thrones.

The chief steward threw out his chest and proudly climbed the stairs step by step. The king himself gave the chief steward precious things such as gold and silver, the outfit of a lord's clothes, and a sword. At that time, the queen ordered the palace servants to ask Princess Drelha to come and (decreed) that (she will) marry the chief steward in front of all. At that time, when happy sounds filled the air, Princess Drelha came down from the palace. When she saw that it was not the youth who had been wounded by the demon's blood but only the chief steward all dressed up, only then did she understand that she had been tricked by the chief steward. She got extremely angry and suddenly fainted and fell.

The king ordered the maidservants to prop up the princess quickly, and when they inquired as to the reasons for this, a very ugly person held up the princess's diamond ring high in the air with his two hands and came to the king. He did the show of respect and said, "Probably the princess lost this diamond ring (so) I came quickly to give it (to her). Princess, please take it." After he said that the youth gave (her) the ring and decisively returned (started to leave). The chief steward was stunned and stayed staring wide-eyed to the left and right. The princess carefully looked and recognized the youth and said repeatedly, "As for him. As for him. As for him. The person who saved me (lit., my saving person), the real one to whom I owe gratitude, it is that one."

The king, queen, serfs, servants, and ministers all were shocked and the people who were there to watch the show were also quietly discussing (this). The king immediately ordered, "Bring the youth here at once." (He then) ordered the ministers to give Lodor 100 ingots of silver as a gift. Because of that, Lodor, who was in the midst of many people, said loudly, "King, I thank you for giving me a gift. Nevertheless, as for my saving the princess, it was not for silver. It was to eliminate harm to the people and through thoughts of gratitude for the king." (Having said this, he) again (began to) leave.

The beautiful princess suddenly hugged the youth and crying, said, "Respected savior, young man, regardless of who you are, taking you (lit., that one) as my bridegroom is the order of my father. How is it okay for you to return?" Consequently, the ministers and the retinue became very happy. As for the chief steward, he became embarrassed. The princess, holding thoughts of love and desire for the youth even more than before, expressed her innermost thoughts saying, "I give to you ,who are completely sincere and courageous, my love and loyalty. I hope that you will believe my completely deceitless thoughts. However ugly your appearance, and however humble your social background, I want to go with you." (Saying this she) caressed the youth's face with her two hands again and again. When the princess's hand caressed (his face), wherever the hand touched, the wounds healed and the youth's face became handsome like before.

The king became extremely happy and personally invited the youth to the throne and put (him) between himself and the queen. Then the king stood up and angrily lifted his walking stick, ordering the soldiers to bring the deceitful chief steward, take off his bridegroom's clothes, and give his gifts all to the youth. The king and queen themselves personally took charge of the marriage celebration of the princess and the youth. After the marriage celebration, the youth took (some) bodyguard troops and came to welcome (bring) his loving mother Tsekyi. From then on (they) lived happily together with the princess.

14.8.3 Grammatical notes

1. འགོར་ is an involuntary verb that conveys "time elapsed/passed." Thus ཉིན་བཅོ་ལྔ་འགོར་ means "15 days passed." In this story a common construction is used to convey "only 15 days elapsed" (ཉིན་བཅོ་ལྔ་ལས་མ་འགོར་བར་). Literally this translates as, "than 15 days, did not elapse."

ཉིན་མཚན་བརྒྱུད་དེ་སྐྱོད་ is a simultaneous construction meaning "going continuously night and day."

2. The pattern of noun + མེད་པར་ negativizes and adverbializes the nominal. Thus ནུས་ཤུགས་མེད་པར་ means "in the manner of being without strength." Similarly ཁོང་ཁྲོ་མེད་པར་བཤད་ would mean "said (it) without anger."

3. This is another adverbial construction conveying doing something in the manner of "looking down" on someone or something.

4. This use of ཞིག་ after a verb (དཔོར་) conveys the imperative (2.5.2).

5. The pattern of vb.+ ཙམ་བྱེད is explained in 13.5.3.20. It conveys that just a little of the verbal action was done. The addition of ཡང་ and a negative (or ཐུབ་) conveys that "even" a little bit was not done. Here the phrase means, "There was no way they were able to move that very thick tree even a little."

6. ཤོར་ is an involuntary verb that is used with nouns to convey that an action involuntarily or uncontrollably occurred. Thus, here he "involuntarily shivered." Similarly མིག་ཆུ་ཤོར་ conveys that "(he, she, etc.) involuntarily cried." When used with respect to games and contests, however, ཤོར་ means "to lose."

7. Note that in the construction ཕེབས་ཤོག་, the verb is an imperative stem.

8. སྐྱོབ་ཐུབ་པ་ཡིན་ན་ conveys the same meaning as སྐྱོབ་ཐུབ་ན་.

9. ཆོག་ here means "allowed" (see 11.9).

10. The phrase ཤེས་པ་བྱས་ here conveys the meaning "know." The larger clause means, "You know how to act respectful and. . . ." Another example of this pattern is:

ལུགས་སྲོལ་ཤེས་པ་བྱས་ནས་སྙན་ཞུ་བོད་ཡིག་ཐོག་འབྲི་དགོས།

Knowing the customs, you should write the report in Tibetan.

This pattern also, however, can convey the more active notion that you should *make* yourself know or do something to *find out* about something. For example:

འཛིན་གྲྭར་མ་འགྲོ་གོང་ལ་སློབ་གྲྭའི་སྒྲིག་ལམ་ཤེས་པ་བྱེད་དགོས།

Before you go to class you should know (do something to find out) the school's rules.

ལུང་པ་དེའི་གནམ་གཤིས་ཤེས་པ་བྱས་ནས་གོས་ལོག་ཁྱེར་དགོས།

You should know about the weather in that area and take clothes (accordingly).

11. In the phrase རྨ་ཁ་གསོ་བཞིན་བསྡད་ཡོད་ the particle བཞིན་ conveys that he was staying there "while" his wound was healing.

12. རོ་ཟ་ཐྲུ་ is a derogatory slang phrase meaning "corpse eater."

13. This is another colloquialism that is comprised of the imperative stem of the verb གཏོང་ (ཐོངས་) and the polite imperative particle དང་. It is used here in the sense of a dare: "Go ahead and do that, and I'll. . . .".

14. This is another colloquial expression that conveys sarcasm. The first part—ཡག་པོ་བྱུང་ ཡག་པོ་བྱུང་—means "very good, very good." It is followed by a traditional saying used when someone brings about his own destruction: "Carrying one's neck, arriving at the doorstep

to buy a lasso."

15. The use of ཞོད་རྒྱུར་ here is idiomatic, conveying, "I have something to tell you." For example, a common construction using this is ངས་ཁྱེད་ལ་ཞོད་རྒྱུར་ . . . ("I have something to say, . . ."), followed by what the person has to say.

16. The main pattern here is ང་ལ་གཅིག་ལས་མེད་—Than one, I do not have" or "I have only one." The addition of ཁོ་ན་ ("only") emphasizes having *only* one.

17. The vb.+ ཐུབ་པ་ + གནང་ means "do something so as to be able to do or achieve the verbal action." In this instance the phrase means: "if you are able to do something to get me out of this demon's cave."

18. See 11.2.

19. དང་ here mean "with."

20. Although ངན་པ་ normally means "evil" or "mean," with མདོག་ in this context it means ugly.

21. The use of the negative linking verb and the interrogative particle (མིན་ནམ་) here conveys a negative rhetorical question which means, "probably it is . . . ." (see 11.15).

22. The use of the dative ར་ after གནང་བ་ indicates the object or reason for the youth's thanks. In other words, "Thanks *for* . . . ."

23. མ་ལྟོས་པར་ conveys "regardless of" through a variety of constructions that generally include "whether something is X or Y" or "whether something happens or does not happen." For example,

སང་ཉིན་ཆར་པ་གཏོང་མིན་ལ་མ་ལྟོས་པར་ཁོང་ཚོ་གླིང་ཁར་ཐེབས་རྩིས་འདུག།

Regardless of whether it rains tomorrow, they plan to go to the park.

སློབ་ཕྲུག་ཧུར་བརྩོན་ཆེ་ཆུང་ལ་མ་ལྟོས་པར་ཚང་མར་གསོལ་རས་རག་པ་རེད།

Without regard to the students' diligence, all received prizes.

14.9 Vocabulary

ཀོ་བ་	leather
བཀག་	va. p. of འགོག་
བཀའ་ཕབ་	ordered, commanded
བཀའ་བསྒྱུལ་	va. to give an order
བཀའ་སློབ་	advice; va. — གནང་ (h.)
བཀྲིས་བདེ་ལེགས་	congratulations, greetings; va. — ཞུ་
རྐུན་པོ་	thief
སྐད་གསང་	clear voice
སྐུ་ངོ་	title of address for government officials (in Tibet)
སྐུ་ངོ་མ་	in person (h.)
སྐེ་	neck, throat
སྐྱེས་པ་	man, male
སྐྱོ་གླུ་	song of sadness; tragic drama
སྐྱོད་	va. to go
སྐྱོར་	"do it again" particle
སྐྲག་	vi. to be scared, afraid
རྐྱོང་	va. p. to stretch, to

	extend, to raise (hand)
བརྐྱངས་	va. p. of རྐྱོང་
ཁ་སྐྱེངས་	vi. to be embarrassed, ashamed
ཁ་ཕར་ཟློག་	va. to face/turn backwards, to reverse direction
ཁ་ཕར་བཟློགས་	va. p. of ཁ་ཕར་ཟློག་
ཁས་བླངས་	va. p. of ཁས་ལེན་
ཁེངས་	full
ཁྱད་པར་	difference
ཁྱར་ཁྱོར་	abbr. ཁྱར་རེ་ཁྱོར་རེ་
ཁྱར་རེ་ཁྱོར་རེ་	unsteady, precarious, unstable
ཁྱིམ་གཞི་	property, wealth
ཁྱེད་ཉིད་	you (h.)
ཁྲག་	blood
ཁྲི་	throne
ཁྲིམས་འགལ་	vi. to break/violate the law
ཁྲེལ་གད་	jeering, ridiculing, laughing at
ཁྲོན་སྐྱོགས་	ladle for use in a well
བཀའ་ཕབ་	va. to order, command
འཁོར་	vi. to get (an idea, thought)
འཁྲིད་	va. to take, lead, guide
འཁྲུལ་མེད་	real, genuine
གང་ཙམ་	"however much" constructions
གལ་	important
གུས་	1. respect; reverence; 2. humble term for "I"
གུས་བཏུད་	respect; reverence; va. — ཞུ་
གུས་ཞུག་	respect, reverence
གུས་མོ་	humble term for "I" (for females)
གོ་ཐོས་	vi. to hear
གོམ་ཞེང་	the width/size of a step or stride
གྱོན་	va. to dress, put on clothes
གྱོན་ཆས་	clothes
གྲངས་ཚད་	quantity, number, rate
གྲོང་མི་	resident of a- གྲོང་ཚོ་
གྲོང་ཚོ་	village, town
དགའ་ཞེན་	love and loyalty; va. — ཞུ་
མགོ་སྐོར་འོག་འཚུད་	vi. to be or get tricked, duped
འགལ་	vi. to be in violation, contradict
འགུལ་	va. to move, shake
འགུལ་སྐྱོད་	moving, shaking; vi. — ཐེབས་
འགོར་	vi. to elapse, pass (of time)
འགྲེ་ལོག་	tumbling, rolling over (on ground or floor, etc.); va. — རྒྱག་
རྒྱུ་ནོར་	wealth, riches, property
སྒུལ་	va. to move, shake
བསྒྲིགས་	va. p. of སྒྲིག་
ངང་པ་	yellowish, cream-colored
ངན་སེམས་	evil-mindedness, cruelty, meanness
ངོ་མ་	in person
ངོས་	side, direction
མངོན་	vi. to become visible, evident, to appear
རྔམ་བརྗིད་	majestic, splendid, grand

ཅན་ having, possessing
བཅངས་ va. p. of འཆང་
བཅོས་ 1. va. to make, create; 2. to treat
ལྕགས་རིགས་ metal(s)
ཆ་བཞག་ན་ "hypothetical" construction
ཆ་ནས་མཚོན་ན་ "hypothetical" construction
ཆུ་ཞག་ tears
ཆེད་ "specially" particle
འཆང་ va. to hold, keep (in mind)
འཆི་ vi. to die
ཇུས་ "planning" particle
འཇིགས་སུ་རུང་བ་ scary, frightening
ཉམ་ཐག་ misery, misfortune
ཉིན་ཞག་ twenty-four-hour day; day and night
གཉེན་སྒྲིག་བག་སྟོན་ marriage celebration
རྙེད་ vi. to find, discover
སྙན་པོ་ interesting
སྙེག་ va. to pursue, run after
བསྙེགས་ va. p. of སྙེག་
གཏམ་གླེང་ conversation, discussion; va. — བྱེད་
གཏེར་ཁ་ a mine
རྟ་སྒ་ saddle
རྟ་ལྕག་ horsewhip
རྟ་དམག་ mounted troops, cavalry
སྟོན་ va. to show
བསྟར་ va. to put into practice
བསྟུད་ va. to do successively, in succession, repeatedly
བསྟུད་མ་ successively, one after another, repeatedly
ཐང་ཆད to be tired, fatigued
ཐལ་ the involuntary action verb ("too much" or "too fast")
ཐལ་འཚུབ་ dust storm
ཐུགས་ mind (h.)
ཐུགས་སྒྲོ་ party (h.)
ཐེབས་ vi. to undergo; to get hit; to reach
ཐོངས་ va. imp. of གཏོང་
མཐོན་པོ་ high
འཐབ་རྩོད་ struggling, fighting; va. — བྱེད་
འཐེན་ va. to pull, drag
འཐོར་ vi. to be scattered, dispersed
དམ་པེ་ flask (usu. for beer, wine)
དར་ཞིང་རྒྱས་པ་ flourishing, prosperous
དུག་ poison
དུམ་བུ་ part, portion, piece, section
དེ་ལྟར་ in that manner, like that
དེ་ལྟར་དང་ in that manner, like that
དེ་ཙམ་ that much
དོན་ issue, question, matter
དྲན་པ་ཐོར་ vi. to lose consciousness
དྲིལ་བུ་ bell
གདོང་(པ་) face
གདོན་འདྲེ་ demon
མདངས་ complexion, radiance; shade of color
འདབ་ times
འདར་ vi. to tremble, shake, shiver
འདར་གསིག་ shivering
འདྲ་ཆགས་པོ་ good-looking, handsome

འདྲ་པར་ photograph

རྡེབ་ va. to beat against, bang against, to clap, flap (wings)

རྡོ་སོལ་ coal

རྡོག་(པ་) 1. a step, stride; 2. sole of shoes

རྡོག་སྒྲ་ sound of a step

སྡུག་བསྔལ་ suffering, misery

བསྡུ་ va. to gather

ན་ཟུག་ pain, illness

ནག་ཧྲིལ་ཧྲིལ་ black and round (thing)

ནུས་ཤུགས་ strength, power

གནད་ཆེ་ important

མནར་གཅོད་ oppression, torture

རྣམ་ཤེས་ soul, mind, consciousness

སྣ་ལྔ་ five kinds

སྣང་(བ་) impression, feeling, sensation

སྣང་ཆུང་ low esteem, low regard; va. — བྱེད་ to show contempt, disdain

སྣར་ va. to stretch

བསྣར་ va. p. of སྣར་

པོ་ཊཱ་ལ་ Potala (Dalai Lama's palace in Lhasa)

དཔའ་ངར་ heroic, brave, courageous

དཔུང་ཚོགས་ military force, troops

དཔེར་ན་ for example

དཔེར་ན་ཆ་
བཞག་ན་ same as དཔེར་ན་

དཔོན་གོས་ clothes for a lord, chief, aristocrat

ལྤགས་ skin (of people as well as of foods)

སྤུང་སྤུང་

འཛོམས་པོ་ intelligent, clever

སྤྱན་ཆབ་ tears (h.); vi. — ཤོར་ to shed tears, cry

སྤྲོ་བ་ joy, happiness; vi. — འཕེལ་ to increase/develop joy and happiness

ཕབ་ va. p. of འབེབས་: caused to descend/come down

ཕར་ thither, away, over there

ཕུན་སུམ་ཚོགས་ id. all the good things

ཕུད་ va. p. of འབུད་

ཕེབས་སྒུག་ wait; va. — ཞུ་ (h.)

ཕྱིན་ "all kinds of" verbal auxiliary

ཕྱིར་ back, back to (usu. with ལོག་ = return back)

འཕེལ་རྒྱས་ increasing, an increase, development

བབས་ vi. p. of འབབ་: descended, fell down (as with snow), landed, dismounted

བུད་མེད་ woman, female

བོབས་ vi. imp. of འབབ་

བོར་བརླག་ loss, losing, theft; vi. — ཏུ་སོང་ or — ཤོར་

བྱ་བ་ work, deeds, actions

བྱ་ཐབས་ཟད་ vi. to be without the means of doing, to be unable to do

བྲག་ཁུང་ cave

བྲན་འཁོར་ abbr. serfs and servants/attendants

བྲང་ཁོག་ chest; vi. — སྒྱེར་ to stick out one's chest (with pride)

བློ་ཐག་ཆོད་པོ་	decisive
དབང་ཆེན་	p.n.
དབང་དུ་བཏང་ན་	"hypothetical" construction
དཔོར་	va. to transport, move from one location to another
འབུད་	va. to take off
དབྱིབས་	shape, form, figure
མི་རུས་	human bone
མིག་ཧྲིག་ཧྲིག་	wide-eyed, fixed stare
མུན་པ་	darkness, ignorance
མེ་ལྕེ་	a flame
མེ་ཕུང་	heaped up fire
མེད་པར་བཟོ་	va. to destroy, annihilate
མོ་ཊར་	car
རྨས་སྐྱོན་	injury; va. — གཏོང་
སྨིན་མ་	eyebrow
ཙམ་	a little
ཙོག་པུར་	crouching, squatting
གཙོ་གཉེར་	chief guest
བཙོན་ཁང་	prison, jail
རྗེས་བཞེས་	va. to take over (h.)
བརྩེ་གདུང་	love
ཚིག་འཇམ་	gentle, kind, pleasant talk
ཚུད་	vi. p. of འཚུད་
ཚོད་མེད་	immense, boundless, limitless
མཚམས་སྤྲིན་	colored clouds
མཚོན་བྱེད་	representative, indicator, symbolic
འཚང་ཀ་ཤིག་ཤིག་	crowded, squashed in
འཚིགས་	vi. to get burned
འཚུད་	vi. to get put into/under
མཛེས་སྡུག་ལྡན་པ་	beautiful
ཞགས་པ་	lasso; va. — རྒྱག་
ཞིབ་དཔྱོད་	investigating, examining, checking; va. — བྱེད་
བཞའ་ཆན་	wetness, moisture, humidity
བཞེང་	1. va. to get up, arise; 2. to build, erect (h.)
བཞེངས་	va. p. of བཞེང་
བཞེས་	va. to take (h.)
ཟབ་མོ་	deep, profound, thorough
ཟོག་	livestock, cattle
བཟོ་	"it seems to" particle
ཐུང་	a sound
འོད་	light
འོས་པ་	worthwhile, worthy, appropriate
ཡིད་	mind, thought
ཡིད་ཕང་ཆད་	vi. to be discouraged, disappointed, sad
ཡོད་ཆད་	all, everything
ཡོབ་རྡུང་	spurring
གཡས་	right
གཡས་པ་	the right one (e.g., for hands)
གཡོ་སྒྱུ་	cunning, deceit
གཡོ་ལྷད་	dishonesty, deception
གཡོག་མོ་	servant (female)
གཡོན་	left
གཡོན་མ་	the left one (e.g., for hands)
རང་ཆེ་རང་བཀུར་	conceit(ed)
རང་དབང་	freedom, liberty, independence
རང་དབང་ མེད་པར་	uncontrollably (lit., in the manner of without

freedom)

རན་ vi. to be time to do

རལ་གྲི་ sword

རས་ woven cotton or synthetic material, fabric

རིགས་ kind, category, thing

རུ་བསྟར་ a line, row

རུ་སྣེ་ leader or head of a column, line, row

རེ་འགས་ some, several

རེག་ va. to touch

ལག་ལེན་ practice

ལམ་སྟོན་ leadership, guidance; va. — འཁྲིད་

ལུས་པོ་ body

ལོན་ vi. to reach, to get

ཤ་ཐོར་རུས་ཐོར་ destroying flesh and bone, ripping to sheds, annihilating

ཤི་གསོན་ dead or alive

ཤོང་ vi. to fit, hold, have room

བཤུ་ va. to peel, skin, take off

སིའུ་ step (on stairs)

སུན་སྣང་ irritated, bothered, fed up; va. — བྱེད་

སེམས་སྐྱོ་པོ་ sad

སེམས་འགུལ་ moved emotionally; vi. — ཐེབས་

སེམས་པ་ thoughts

སེམས་འཚབ་ worried, anxious, nervous

སོར་གདུབ་ ring (for finger)

སོལ་བ་ coal

སྲབ་ bridle

སྲུང་ va. to guard, defend, protect

སྲུང་སྐྱོབ་ defending, safe-guarding, protecting; va. — བྱེད་

སྲུང་དམག་ guards, bodyguards, defending troops

གསོ་ vi. to heal

གསོན་པོ་ live, alive

གསོན་ལམ་འཚོལ་ va. to seek a way to stay alive

བསམ་དོན་ desire, wish, goal

བསུ་ va. to receive, to welcome

བསློགས་ va. p. of སློག་

ཧུར་སྒྲ་ hurdra (a sound)

ལྷག་བསམ་རྣམ་དག་ sincere, genuine, cordial

ལྷག་བསམ་ཟོལ་མེད་ complete sincerity, openness

ཨུ་ཚུགས་ insistence, persistence

Lesson Fifteen

15.1 ཤས་ཆེ་ constructions

ཤས་ཆེ་ is placed at the end of a sentence to mean "maybe" or "perhaps."

a. ཁ་སང་ང་ཚོར་དགོན་པའི་ནང་ཐུག་པའི་གྲྭ་པ་གཞོན་གཞོན་དེ་ཨེམ་ཆི་ཡིན་ཤས་ཆེ།
Perhaps the young monk we met in the monastery yesterday is a doctor.

b. རྒྱ་གར་ནས་སླེབས་པའི་ཚོང་པ་དེ་ལ་ཅ་ལག་རྙིང་མ་འཚོང་རྒྱུ་ཡོད་ཤས་ཆེ།
Maybe the merchant who came from India has old things (antiques) to sell.

c. སང་ཉིན་འདིར་ཚོགས་འདུར་ཕེབས་རྒྱུའི་མཁས་པ་དེས་དེང་དུས་འཛམ་གླིང་གི་དཔལ་འབྱོར་སྐོར་གྱི་གསུང་བཤད་ཅིག་གནང་ཤས་ཆེ།
Maybe the expert who will be coming to the meeting here tomorrow will give a speech regarding the world's current economy.

d. ཁང་པ་དེའི་ནང་སྡོད་མཁན་མེད་ཤས་ཆེ།
Perhaps there is no one living in this house.

15.2 Constructions using vb. + པས་རེད་

When པས་རེད་ is used at the end of sentences it conveys the notion of "because."

a. ཟ་ཁང་དེར་རྟག་པར་མི་མང་པོ་ཡོང་བ་དེ་ཁ་ལག་ཞིམ་པོ་ཡོད་པས་རེད།
Many people are always coming to that restaurant because the food is delicious.

b. མོས་ཁྱེད་རང་ལ་ཡང་ཡང་ཁ་པར་གཏོང་ཡས་དེ་མོ་ཁྱེད་རང་ལ་དགའ་པོ་ཡོད་པས་རེད།
Her calling you often is because she loves (likes) you.

c. དེང་སང་ཡུལ་དེར་ལྟ་སྐོར་བ་མང་པོ་མི་འགྲོ་བ་ནི་ལྷིངས་འཇགས་མེད་པས་རེད།
As for many tourists not going to that country these days, it is because there is no peace there.

15.3 "Manner of" constructions using ཕྱོགས་

ཕྱོགས་ is used after the present or non-past stem of verbs to convey the "manner" of doing the verbal action. It functions the same as སྟངས་ (9.12).

a. མི་དེའི་སྐད་ཆ་ཤོད་ཕྱོགས་ལ་ཉན་ན་ཁོ་གཙང་པ་ཡིན་པ་འདྲ།
If you listen to the manner in which that person talks, he probably is from Tsang.

Note that འདྲ་ (which normally = "similar") conveys that something or some action is "probable" or "seems to be" when used after verbs. For example, ཨ་མི་རི་ཀའི་ནང་ལ་དམག་མི་མང་པོ་ཡོད་པ་འདྲ།—"There probably are many soldiers in America." Similarly, ཁོ་ཁ་སང་བོད་དུ་ཕེབས་པ་འདྲ།—"It seems he probably went to Tibet yesterday."

b. དེང་སྐབས་ཀྱི་སྲིད་ཇུས་འགྲོ་ཕྱོགས་དང་བསྟུན་ནས་ལས་ཀ་བྱེད་དགོས་པ་རེད།
One should work in accordance with the manner in which policy is going these days.
c. ལས་བྱེད་པ་དེས་ལས་ཀ་ར་ཏྲར་བརྩོན་བྱེད་ཕྱོགས་ལ་གཞིགས་ན་ཁོ་ལ་བྱ་དགའ་ཐོབ་རྒྱུ་ཐག་གཅིག་རེད།
Based on the way that cadre did his work diligently, he will definitely get an award.

15.4 གསལ་ constructions

གསལ་ is used after verbs (and before linking and existential verbs) to convey that the verbal action occurred "clearly. "

a. དམག་མིས་མེ་མདའ་བརྒྱབ་པ་ང་ཚོ་ཚང་མས་མཐོང་གསལ་ཡིན།
We all clearly saw the soldiers shooting guns.
b. དེང་སང་རྒྱ་ནག་ལ་ཟིང་ཆ་ཡོད་པ་ཤེས་གསལ་རེད།
It is clearly known that there are disturbances in China these days.
c. ཁོང་གི་ཕྱག་ཡིག་ནང་འཁོད་གསལ་ཁོང་གང་མགྱོགས་ཕེབས་ཀྱི་ཡིན་གསུང་ཤག།
According to what was clearly written in his letter, he has said he will come as soon as possible.
d. ཞིང་པས་སྙན་ཞུ་ཕུལ་གསལ་ལ་གཞིག་ན་ཐོན་སྐྱེད་ཡག་པོ་བྱུང་ཤག།
Based on what was clear in the farmers' report, they have got a good crop yield.
e. གནས་ཚུལ་དེ་འབྱོར་གསལ་ལྟར།
According to the news (we) clearly received, ...

15.5 Alternative ན་ constructions

ན་ normally follows the past stem of verbs to convey "if." However, it also has another very different meaning that can be discerned only by context. Sometimes, as the following examples illustrate, ན་ conveys the meaning of "because" or "as" something happened.

a. ཁོང་དེ་རིང་ཕེབས་ཀྱི་མིན་གསུངས་བྱུང་ན་ ང་ཚོས་ཕེབས་སྒུག་ཞུ་དགོས་མི་འདུག།
As he said that he wouldn't come today, we do not have to wait for him.
b. འདི་གར་མཐུན་རྐྱེན་འཛོམས་པོ་འདུག་ན་ང་རང་ད་དུང་ལོ་རེ་ཟུང་སྡོད་འདོད་འདུག།
Because there are plentiful resources here, I still want to stay a couple of years more.
c. ཁ་སྔ་བསོད་ནམས་ཀྱིས་ཁ་པར་བཏང་བྱུང་ན་ཁོང་སང་ཉིན་བོད་ལ་ཐོན་རྒྱུ་གཏན་འཁེལ་འདུག།
Because Sonam called me yesterday, (it means) he has decided to leave for Tibet.
d. འདི་ཕྱོགས་ཕུན་རང་གཟུགས་པོ་བདེ་ཐང་ཡོད་ན་ཐུགས་ཁྲལ་གཏན་ནས་གནང་མི་དགོས།
As I am feeling very well here (lit., this side), (you) don't have to worry at all.

15.6 སྐད་ constructions

སྐད is used after verbs to convey "it is said" that the verbal action exists or occurred.

a. ཁོ་ལ་དངུལ་མང་པོ་ཡོད་སྐད་འདུག།

It is said that he has a lot of money.

b. ན་ཉིན་བལ་ཡུལ་དང་རྒྱ་གར་གཉིས་བར་རྙོགས་ཁྲ་བྱུང་སྐད་འདུག།
   It is said that there was a disturbance between Nepal and India last year.

15.7 བསྐྱར་ constructions

བསྐྱར་ constructions consist of བསྐྱར་ + vb. + བྱེད་ and convey a sense of "repeating" or "redoing" the verbal action.

a. གནས་ཚུལ་དེ་ཚོ་ཚོགས་འདུར་བསྐྱར་བཤད་བྱས་པ་རེད།
   Those events were re-discussed at the meeting.
b. མོས་སློབ་ཚན་ཚང་མ་བསྐྱར་སྦྱོང་བྱེད་ཀྱི་རེད།
   She will restudy all the lessons.
c. ཁོས་ཡི་གེ་དེ་བསྐྱར་བྲིས་བྱེད་དགོས་བྱུང་སོང་།
   He had to rewrite the letter.
d. ཁོའི་ཞྭ་མོ་ཚོང་ཁང་ནང་ལུས་ཙང་། ཁོ་བསྐྱར་ལོག་བྱེད་དགོས་བྱུང་བ་རེད།
   Because he left his hat at the store, he had to return again.

15.8 Reading exercise: "Chapter One: Meeting the Jowo"

This reading selection is taken from Chapter One of གཙུག་གཡུ་ ("The Turquoise Headpiece"), a wonderful novel published in Tibet in 1985. Its author, Penjor Langdun, originally wrote the chapters as magazine stories and only later wove them into a full-length novel.

"The Turquoise Headpiece" tells the story of an old man and his son who leave their home in Amdo (Qinghai Province) to make a pilgrimage to the statue of the Buddha (called the Jo Rimpoche) in Lhasa's Cathedral. Their goal is to present the turquoise headpiece stone of the old man's late wife to the Jo as a religious offering.

The section presented in this lesson deals with the last leg of their journey to Lhasa. It starts with the father in the temple of the goddess Gungthang, which is located about 5 miles east of Lhasa. This selection has been slightly abbreviated and altered.

15.8.1 Tibetan text

ལེའུ་དང་པོ།　　ཇོ་བོ་མཇལ་བ།

༄༅། །　ཕ་ནན་ཕུན་ཚོགས་ཀྱིས་སྟོང་ནན་ས་ལ་འགྲིལ་བ་ལྟར་གྱི་བརྐྱང་ཕྱག་གསུམ་འཚལ་རྗེས་སུ་པུས་མོའི་ལྷ་ང་ས་ལ་བཙུགས་དེ་ཐལ་མོ་སྤྱི་བོར་བཀོད་ནས་གསོལ་བ་འདི་ལྟར་བཏབ་བོ།　"1 ཀུང་ཐང་ལྷ་མོས་མཁྱེན་ནོ།　བདག་ཅག་ནི་དལ་རྟེན་མི་ལུས་ཐོབ་ཀྱང་སྐྱེ་བ་སྔོན་མ་བསོད་ནམས་མ་བསགས་པའི་རྐྱེན་གྱིས་ད་བར་སྡུག་དཀའ་ལས་2 ཁོ་ནའི་ངང་མི་ཚེ་འདས། ད་ནི་ཚེ་ཕྱི་མའི་དོན་ཕྲན་བུ་བསྒྲུབ་ཕྱིར་གནས་སྐོར་ལ་ཡོང་ནས་ལྷ་སའི་ཇོ་བོའི་ཞལ་མཇལ་ཙམ་བྱ་རྒྱུའི་འདུན་པ་ཁོ་ན་འཆང་བཞིན་

ཕ་ཡུལ་ནས་ཐོན་ཏེ་དུས་ཡུན་ཟླ་བ་དྲུག་ཙམ་གྱི་རིང་ལ་དགོན་སྡེ་དང་གནས་ཆེན་བཞི་བཅུ་ཙམ་བསྐོར་ཟིན་པ་དང་། ད་ནི་ལྷ་མོ་ཁྱེད་ཀྱི་སྐུ་གམ་དུ་ལྷགས། སང་ཉིན་ས་ག་ཟླ་བའི་ཆོས་ཆེན་བཅོ་ལྔ་ལ་ཇོ་བོའི་ཞལ་རས་མཇལ་རྒྱུའི་དུས་སུ་སླེབས་པས། ལྷ་མོ་ཁྱེད་ཀྱིས་ང་གཉིས་ཕ་བུ་གཉིས་ལ་དེའི་བར་དུ་བར་ཆད་མི་ཡོང་བའི་སྐྱབས་འཇུག་ཅི་ནས་ཀྱང་ཡོད་པ་ཞུ།" ཞེས་སྨོན་ལམ་བཏབ་ཇེས།

ལྷ་ཁང་གི་ཕྱི་རོལ་དུ་ཐོན། དེ་མ་ཐག་ཏུ་འབྲུག་སྐད་ལྡིར་ལྡིར་དུ་སྒྲོག་ཅིང་ནམ་མཁའ་ནས་གློག་འཁྱུགས། ནད་པོ་ཕུན་ཚོགས་ཀྱིས་གནམ་ལ་བལྟས་པས་སྤྲིན་ནག་ལང་ལོང་དུ་གཡོ་བཞིན་པ་མཐོང་ནས་འཕྱུལ་དུ་དྲག་ཆར་ཞིག་འབབ་རྒྱུར་ངེས་3 སོ་བསམས་ཏེ་ཉེ་འགྲམ་དུ་མི་ཚང་ཞིག་ཡོད་པ་དེའི་སྒོའི་འོག་ཏུ་འཛུལ་ནས་བསྡད། ཕ་ནད་ཕུན་ཚོགས་ཀྱིས་ལག་པ་གཡས་པས་ཕྱིང་བ་གཏོང་བཞིན་དུ་ཁ་ནས་མ་ཎི་འདོན། མ་ཎི་ཕྱིང་སྐོར་གཅིག་མ་འཁོར་གོང་ནས་4 དྲག་ཆར་ཆེན་པོ་ཞིག་བབས་པས་མགྱོགས་མྱུར་བུ་ཚུང་དེ་པང་དུ་ཁུར་ནས་ཕྱི་སྒོའི་ཐོག་5 འོག་ཏུ་མ་ཎི་འདོན་བཞིན་དུ་ཆར་དྲག་འདི་གང་མགྱོགས་ཆད་ན་ཅི་མ་རུང་6 སྙམ་པའི་སྐབས་སུ་མི་ཚང་དེའི་ཁྱིམ་འཛིན་མ་སྐྱེ།7 ན་ཚོད་དར་ལ་བབས་པའི་8 བུད་མེད་ཅིག་གིས་རང་གི་ཕྱི་སྒོའི་ཐོག་འོག་ཏུ་ཕྱི་མི་ཡོད་པ་ཤེས་ནས་ལྟ་བར་ཡོང་དུས་བཀྲིས་སྐམ་དང་ངལ་དུབ་ཀྱིས་མནར་བས་མདོག་སྐྱོ9 ལ་ཤ་རིད་པའི་ནད་པོ་ཞིག་གིས་པང་དུ་བུ་ཆུང་ངུ་ཞིག་ཁུར་ནས་ཕ་བུ་གཉིས་གཅིག་གིས་གཅིག་ལ་འཐམས་ནས་བསྡད་ཡོད་པ་མཐོང་།

དེ་ནས་ཁྱིམ་འཛིན་མ་དེས་ཕོ་གཉིས་གང་ནས་ཡོང་བ་དང་། གང་དུ་འགྲོ་བ། དོན་ཅི་བསྒྲུབ་ཕྱིར་ཡོང་བ་སོགས་ཞིབ་ཕྲ་དྲིས་པ་ལ་ཕ་ནད་ཕུན་ཚོགས་ཀྱིས་ལན་ཇི་མ་ཇི་བཞིན་10 དྭང་པོར་སྨྲས་པས་གནས་ལུགས་རྣམས་རྟོགས་ཤིང་། ཕོ་གཉིས་ལ་མགོ་ནས་མཇུག་བར་ཞིབ་པར་ལྟ་དུས་ཕ་ནད་ཀྱི་ཕྱུ་པ་ནི་ལྷན་པས་ཁེངས་ཤིང་རྐང་པའི་ལྷམ་མོ་གཉིས་དོར་མའི་ཕྱི་ལ་ཕྱུང་། ལྷམ་མཐིལ་ཟད་ནས་རྐང་མཐིལ་ས་ལ་རེག། བུ་དེ་ནི་རྐང་ལྷམ་གྱོན་རྒྱུ་ལྟ་ཅི། ཐ་ན་དོར་མའང་མེད་པར་རས་གོས་ཐུང་ཐུང་ཟད་རྡུལ་ཞིག་གོན། སྐྲ་ལོ་ནི་འཕྱིངས་ནས་རལ་པར་གྱུར། གདོང་ལ་སོལ་བ་བསྐུས་པ་ལྟར་གྱི་དྲིག་པ་ཆགས་བཞིན་འདུག བདག་དངོས་ཀྱི་ཆ་ནས་མཚོན་ན་11 ཕ་ནད་ཀྱི་ཨམ་ཕྲག་ཏུ་ཕོར་པ་ཁ་ཆག་གཅིག་དང་། ཕྲུ་པའི་གོང་བར་ལྷུགས་ཁབ་གཉིས་དང་། ལག་པར་འཁར་བ་དང་ཁྲི་སྣུང་གཅིག་ལྕོགས་12 ཀྱི་དབྱུག་པ་ཞིག་ལས་ཅི་ཡང་མེད་པ་མཐོང་། ཚུལ་དེ་མཐོང་བས་ཁྱིམ་འཛིན་མའི་སེམས་ལ་སྙིང་རྗེ་དབང་མེད་དུ་སྐྱེས་པ་དང་། ཁོང་གི་བསམ་པར་འདི་ནས་ལྷ་སར་ཕྱིན་ཏེ་ཇོ་བོའི་ཞལ་མཇལ་ཞུ་བར་ཞོགས་ལས་གཅིག་གི་དུས་ཚོད་ལས་མི་འགོར་ཡང་། ང་ནི་ད་བར་མཆོད་མཇལ་ཐེངས་གཉིས་ལས་ཞུ་མ་མྱོང་། ཕ་བུ་འདི་གཉིས་ནི་ཇོ་བོའི་ཞལ་མཇལ་ཐེངས་གཅིག་འཐོབ་ཕྱིར་ཟླ་བ་དྲུག་ཙམ་གྱི་རིང་དཀའ་བ་སྤྱད་ནས་ཡོང་བའི་སྙིང་རུས་དེ་ལྟ་བུ་བསྐྱེད་པའི་རྒྱུ་ནི་དམ་པའི་ཆོས་ཁོ་ན་ཡིན་པས། གནས་སྐོར་བ་ཕ་བུ་འདི་གཉིས་ལ་སྦྱིན་པ་བཏང་ན་རང་ཉིད་ཕྱིན་པ་དང་ཁྱད་པར་མ་མཆིས་བསམས་ནས་ཕ་བུ་གཉིས་རང་ཁྱིམ་དུ་ཡར་ཤོག13 ཅེས་བརྗོད་ནས་ཇ་དང་། ཙམ་པ། ཐུག་པ་སོགས་ཚིམས་པར་14 བྱིན།

དེའི་ཚེ་ཉི་མ་བཞུད་ཟིན་པས་ན་ཕོ་གཉིས་ལ་དོ་ནུབ་འདིར་ཉལ་ཅིག15 ཅེས་སྨྲས་ཏེ་གཟན་ཁང་དུ་ཁྲིད་ཐོག་ཉལ་གཟན་རྙིང་པ་ཞིག་ཀྱང་གཡར་པོ་བཏང་། དེའི་དགོང་མོ་ཕ་བུ་གཉིས་ཁ་ངོམས། གྲོད་པ་རྒྱགས། གཟན་པ་གདན་དུ་བཏིང་ནས

ཉལ་གཟན་ཞིག་ཀྱང་གོན་རྒྱུ་ཡོད་པས་བུ་ཆུང་དེ་ནི་ཉལ་བ་ཙམ་ནས་16 གཉིད་ལ་ཤོར། འོན་ཀྱང་ཕ་རྒན་ཕུན་ཚོགས་ནི་རང་གི་ཚེ་གཅིག་གི་འདུན་པ་སྟེ་17 ཇོ་བོ་ཤཱཀྱ་མུ་ནེའི་ཞལ་མཇལ་རྒྱུའི་ཉིན་མོ་དེ་ནི་ཁ་འགྲམ་དུ་བཅར་བའི་དགའ་ཚོར་གྱིས་གཉིད་ནི་ག་ལ་ཁུག། རིམ་བཞིན་རང་གི་བཟའ་ཟླའི་གདོང་ཡང་མིག་གི་མདུན་དུ་ཁྲ་ལྷིམ་ལྷིམ་དུ་འཁོར་ནས་འདི་སྐམ་དུ་བསམས་18 སོ།

ངའི་ཟླ་བོ་འཇོམས་པ་ནི་ལོ་བཅུ་དྲུག་ནས་ང་དང་འགྲོགས་ཤིང་། ལོ་བཞི་བཅུ་ཙམ་གྱི་རིང་ལ་ཐོག་མཐའ་བར་གསུམ་དུ་བདག་ལ་གཡོ་མེད་དུ་བརྩེ་བ་དང་། ངའི་སྙིང་གི་གཙོང་ནད་དེ་ཡང་ཡང་ལངས་བའི་སྐབས་སུ་འཇོམས་པ་ནི་མིག་གཉིས་མཆི་མས་ཁེངས་བཞིན་དུ་ངའི་ཁ་ལ་ལྷོ་ཆས་སྦུར་མ་རེ་རེ་བཞིན་དུ་བླུགས་པ་དང་ནད་གཡོག་གང་དགོས་བྱེད་ཅིང་། ཐ་ན་འཇོམས་པ་རང་ཉིད་ན་ནིང་ནད་ཀྱིས་མནར་ནས་འདི་ཕྱི་གཉིས་ཀྱི་མཚམས་སུ་སླེབས་ནའང་ད་དུང་ངའི་ལག་པ་ནས་བཟུང་སྙིང་ནི་གསོན་རེ་བྲལ་19 སོང་ཨ་ཕོ་ཕུན་ཚོགས། ཁྱོད་ཀྱི་སྙིང་ལ་གཙོང་ནད་ཡོད་པས་གཟབ་གཟབ་གྱིས་ཨང་20 ཞེས་རང་གི་ན་ཟུག་ལས་ཀྱང་ང་ལ་དོ་འཁུར་ཆེ་བ་བྱེད་པ་དང་། འཇོམས་པའི་མི་ཚེ་ཧྲིལ་པོར་རང་སྙིར་གྱི་འདོད་རེ་གང་ཡང་འདོན་མ་སྨྲོང་རུང་འཆི་ཁར་བུའི་འགྲམ་པར་བྱིལ་བྱིལ་བྱས་ནས་ཁ་ཆེམས་སུ་ང་གཉིས་ཀྱི་བུ་གཅིག་པུ་དཔལ་ལྡན་འདི་ཁྲིད་ནས་ལྷ་སའི་ཇོ་བོ་ཐེངས་གཅིག་མཇལ་བ་བྱེད་21 རོགས་ཞེར་བཞིན་དུ་རང་གི་སྒྲི་གཙུག་ནས་གཙུག་གཡུ་གཅིག་རང་ཡོད་པ་དེ་བཀྲོལ་ནས་ངའི་ལག་ཏུ་བླུགས་ཤིང་། མིག་ནས་མཆི་མ་ཏོག་ཁ་ཤས་ཤིག་བཏང་སྟེ་ཨ་ཕོ་ཕུན་ཚོགས་ཁྱོད་ཀྱིས་འདི་ཇོ་བོའི་སྐུ་མདུན་དུ་ཕུལ་ནས་ང་གཉིས་ཀྱི་བུ་དཔལ་ལྡན་སྐྱིད་པོ་ཡོང་བའི་སྨོན་ལམ་རྒྱག་རོགས་ཞེས་ཟེར་ནས་གྲོངས། ད་ནི་སང་ཉིན་ཇོ་བོ་མཇལ་ཐུབ་ལ་རང་གི་བཟའ་ཟླ་འདས་པོ་འཇོམས་པའི་བསམ་འདུན་ཡང་འགྲུབ་ཐུབ་ངེས་རེད་བསམས་ཏེ་དགའ་ཚོར་ཆེན་པོ་སྐྱེས།

ཡུད་ཙམ་ཞིག་ནས་གློ་བུར་དུ་ཕུན་ཚོགས་ཀྱི་སྙིང་ཁ་འཕར་ཤུགས་ཇེ་ཆེར་22 སོང་ཞིང་། དཔྲལ་བ་ནས་རྔུལ་ཆུའི་ཐིགས་པ་ཟགས། དབུགས་ཀྱང་གཏོང་འཐེན་དཀའ་བའི་གནས་སུ་གྱུར་བས་ཨུ་ཏུ་ལགས། བསོད་ནམས་མེད་པའི་མི་ངའི་སྙིང་གི་གཙོང་ནད་དེ་ཡང་ལངས་ཡོང་གི་འདུག། ད་ཅི་དྲག་བསམས་ནས་དངངས་འཚབ་ཆེན་པོ་སྐྱེ་བའི་སྐབས་དེར། གནས་མོས་མདང་ནུབ་ཀྱི་ཐུག་ལྷག་དེ་ཐབ་ལ་བཀབ། ཛ་སྦྱབ་མ་ཕོག་ཕྱིར་གང་བཟོས་ནས་གཟན་ཁང་དུ་གནས་སྐོར་བ་གཉིས་འབོད་པར་ཡོང་དུས་ཕུན་ཚོགས་ནི་ནད་མནར་གྱིས་དབུགས་ལྷིམ་ལྷིམ་དུ་བསྡད་ཡོད་པ་མཐོང་། གནས་མོས་འཕྲལ་དུ་མི་ཕོག་གཅིག་ཁྲིར་ནས་ཕུན་ཚོགས་ཀྱི་མདུན་དུ་རྩམ་གསུར་བདུག་པ་དང་། མགྱོགས་མྱུར་ཐུག་ལྷག་ཆ་པོ་གང་23 སྟེར་བས་རིམ་བཞིན་ཕུན་ཚོགས་དྲན་པ་གསོས་པ་མ་ཟད། སྙིང་གི་འཕར་ཚད་ཀྱང་འཇགས། དེ་ནས་གནས་མོས་བུ་དཔལ་ལྡན་གཉིད་ལས་སད་དེ་ཁོ་གཉིས་ལ་ཇ་དང་སྤག་རྒྱགས་ཚད་སྟེར་བས་ཨ་ཕ་ཕུན་ཚོགས་ནི་ནུས་པ་དང་ལྡན་པའི་སྨན་བཟས་པ་བཞིན་དུ་དྲག་སྐྱིད་བྱུང་བ་མཐོང་ནས་གནས་མོས་"གལ་ཏེ་ཨ་ཕོ་རང་གཟུགས་པོ་ཨའུ་ཙམ་འདུག་ན། དེ་རིང་ས་ག་ཟླ་བའི་ཚེས་པ་བཅོ་ལྔ་ལ་ཇོ་བོ་མཇལ་ཚེ་དཔག་ཏུ་མེད་པའི་བསོད་ནམས་གསོག་ཐུབ། ད་ལྟ་བུ་སྐད་གཉིས་པ་རྒྱག་རྒྱུ་རེད། ཁྱོད་གཉིས་སྔོན་ན་ཉི་མ་ཤར་མཚམས་སུ་ཇོ་བོ་མཇལ་ཐུབ་" ཅེས་ལབ་པས་ཨ་ཕ་ཕུན་ཚོགས་ཀྱིས་"གནས་མོ་ཐུགས་རྗེ་ཆེ། ཁྱེད་ལ་བུ་བ་ལམ་འགྲོ་ཡོང་བར་ཤོག། ངས་ཇོ་བོའི་སྐུ་མདུན་དུ་སྨོན་ལམ་བརྒྱབ་ཆོག། ཁྱེད་སྐུ་ཚེ་རིང་"ཞེས་བརྗོད་ནས་བུ་དཔལ་ལྡན་ཁྲིད་དེ་ལམ་ལ་ཞུགས་སོ།

ཤན་ཁའི་གྲུ་ཁར་སླེབས་ནས་ཀོ་བའི་ནང་དུ་འཛུལ་སྐབས་ལྷ་སར་གང་མགྱོགས་འགྱོར་ན་སྙམ་པའི་དངངས་སྐྲག་གིས་ཀང་པ་འདེགས་ཤུགས་ཆེ་དྲགས་སྐབས་ལམ་བར་ཀང་པ་གཡས་པའི་ཀྲུ་རིལ་ལ་འཐྲིག་པའི་ཁྱིས་རྨུགས་པའི་རྨ་དེའི་རྨ་ཁ་བྱེ་སྐྱེ། གུ་ཐུང་ཉོལ་པའི་ཁུང་བུ་ནས་ཁྲག་རྣག་འཛགས་པ་བུ་དཔལ་ལྡན་གྱིས་ཟླ་བའི་འོད་ཀྱི་མདངས་ལ་མཐོང་བས་ཨ་ཕ། ཀང་པ་ནས་ཁྲག་དོན་གྱི་འདུག "ཟེར་བས་ཕས་དཔལ་ལྡན་ལ་"ཁྱོད་སེམས་ཁྲལ་མ་བྱེད། ཇོ་བོ་མཇལ་ན་དྲག་འོང་ཟེར་བཞིན་བུ་པང་དུ་བཏེགས་ཏེ་ཀོ་བར་འཛུལ།

ཕ་བུ་གཉིས་རིམ་གྱིས་ལྷ་སའི་གླིང་སྐོར་ལམ་དུ་སླེབས་པ་ན་24 ནམ་ལངས་ཐང་གསལ་བས། གླིང་སྐོར་ལམ་གྱི་གཡས་ཟུར་ལ་མི་མང་པོ་ཞིག་གྲལ་བསྒྲིགས་ཏེ་ས་ལ་བསྡད་ཡོད་པ་མཐོང་། འགྲམ་དུ་ཕྱིན་ནས་ལྟ་དུས་ལ་ལས་ཁ་དོན་འདོན་བཞིན་མདུན་དུ་རས་ལྷེ་པ་གཅིག་བཏིང་ནས་སྦྱིན་པའི་རེ་སྐུལ་བྱེད། དེའི་གཤམ་དུ་ཀང་ལུགས་བརྒྱབ་པ་དང་། སྐེ་ལ་ཤིང་སྒོ་གཡོགས་པ་སོགས་ཀྱི་བཙོན་པ་སྣར་པ་གཅིག གང་ལྟར་མིག་གིས་མ་ཟིན་པའི་སའི་བར་སྣང་མཁན་གྱིས་ཁེངས། གླིང་སྐོར་ལ་འགྲོ་མཁན་ནི་གཅིག་རྗེས་གཉིས་མཐུད་ཀྱིས་བར་མི་ཆད། སྐྱེ་བོ་མང་པོ་ཞིག་གིས་ནི་ཆེད་མངགས་སྤྲང་པོར་སྦྱིན་པ་གཏོང་བར་ཡོང་ནས་གཅིག་རྗེས་གཉིས་མཐུད་ཀྱིས་རྒྱལ་པ་སོགས་སྣོད་འདྲ་མིན་གྱི་ནང་ནས་སྤྲང་པོ་མི་རེ་ངོ་རེར་དངུལ་རྩམ་པ་སོགས་སྟེར་བཞིན་དུ་གླིང་སྐོར་སྐོར་བར་བྱེད། ལ་ལ་ནི་གཟབ་མཆོར་དང་རིན་པོ་ཆེ་སྣ་ཚོགས་ཀྱིས་བརྒྱན། ལ་ལ་ནི་ལུས་ཀྱི་ངོ་ཚ་སྒྲིབ་ཐུབ་ཙམ་གྱི་ཆས་གོས་གྱོན་པ། དེ་བཞིན་མི་རིགས། ཆ་ལུགས། རྣམ་པ་བཅས་འདྲ་མིན་སྣ་ཚོགས་ཀྱི་མིའི་ཁྱུ་ཚོགས་ནི་ཆུ་རྒྱུན་བཞིན་དུ་ཕྱོགས་གཅིག་ཏུ་རྒྱུ་བའི་ཚུལ་ལ། ཨ་ཕ་ཕུན་ཚོགས་དང་བུ་དཔལ་ལྡན་གཉིས་ཀ་ལས་དོན་ཐོར་གྱིས་ཡུད་ཙམ་ལྷོད་མེར་མགོ་འཁོར། གློ་བུར་དུ་ཨ་ཕ་ཕུན་ཚོགས་དྲན་པ་གསོས་པ་བཞིན་དུ་དཔལ་ལྡན་གྱི་ལག་པ་ནས་འཐེན་ཏེ་མི་གཞན་ལ་ལམ་འདྲི་བཞིན་དུ་གོམ་ཞིང་ཆེན་པོས་བསྐྱོད་པས་མི་རིང་བར་ལྷ་ལྡན་གཙུག་ལག་ཁང་གི་སྒོ་འགྲམ་དུ་སླེབས། མཆོད་མཇལ་ཞུ་མིའི་གྲལ་སྟར་ནི་ཇོ་བོ་དབུ་སྐུའི་འོག་བར་འདུག། གྲལ་སྟར་གྱི་མཇུག་མཐར་ཕ་བུ་གཉིས་ལངས་ནས་ངང་གིས་མདུན་དུ་བསྐྱོད་དོ།

15.8.2 Translation

Chapter One: Meeting the Jowo

The old father Phuntsog, like an old tree that fell to the ground, did three prostrations (fully stretched out on the ground). Then he bowed, placing one knee on the ground, and put his hands together in the gesture of prayer and prayed, "Gungtang Lhamo knows! As for us, even though we have obtained human life, because we did not accumulate merit in our former lives, up to now we have lived only with suffering and difficulties. Now, for the purpose of obtaining a little bit [of merit] for our future life, we have come on (this) pilgrimage. Holding only the hope that we will be able to see the Jo of Lhasa in person, we have left our homeland and for 6 months have traveled visiting along the way about 40 monasteries and holy sites. Now we have arrived in your presence, Goddess. Tomorrow, on the great 15th day of Sagadawa [the specially holy 4th Tibetan month], the time has arrived to see the face of the Jo. Consequently, please would you Goddess see to it that no harm befalls my son and me until we get there."

After that they went outside the temple. Immediately it began to thunder and lightning. The old father Phuntsog looked at the sky and saw black clouds slowly moving about and thought, "A powerful rainstorm will definitely fall immediately," and entered and sat down beneath the outer door of a nearby household. Old father Phuntsog's right hand was counting on a rosary and he was intoning "mani" (prayers). Before he could complete one round of mani prayers on his rosary, the rainstorm came. He quickly took his small son into his lap and sat under the roof of the door counting his rosary and thinking, "How nice it would be if the rain quickly stopped." At that time, the lady who was the head of that household (came). She was a young woman who knew that some strangers were under the roof of her door and had come to look. She saw an old man who was thin, of poor complexion, and oppressed by hunger, thirst and hardship. He was holding a small boy in his lap, each one hugging the other.

The lady of the house asked a lot of detailed questions such as where are you from, where are you going and for what reason have you come. The old father Phuntsog explained everything truly, and she then understood all the circumstances. She looked at the two of them carefully from head to toe and saw that the old man's dress was filled with patches, both his knees hung out from his (torn) pants, and the soles of his boots were so worn that the soles of his feet touched the ground. As for the son, let alone having boots to wear, he did not even have pants and wore a short (small) and very tattered dress. His braids were matted and had become long and wild. His face was full of dirt as if charcoal had been applied. If we use their possessions as an example, the old father had only a chipped (wooden tea) bowl in his pocket, two iron needles on his lapel, and a wooden stick in his hand that served both as a cane and as a stick to protect against dogs. Seeing that situation, the lady of the house spontaneously felt compassion and thought, "(Going) from here to Lhasa to visit the Jo takes only one morning. (But) up to now I have only visited it twice. These two, father and son, have traveled for 6 months, undergoing great difficulties just to be able to visit the Jo once. The cause of them having such determination can only be pure religion. So, if I give give alms to these two pilgrims, father and son, it will be the same as if I myself went (to visit the Jo)." Then she said, "You two, father and son, come into my house!" (She then) satiated (their hunger) by giving them tea, tsamba, and stew.

At that time, because the sun had set, the lady of the house said,"Tonight sleep here." And she took them to the hay storage room and lent them old bedding. That evening because the old man and the boy had their thirst quenched, their stomachs full, and a bed of straw and also blankets, the boy fell asleep as soon as he lay down. However, the old father Phuntsog was so happy thinking about his lifetime dream—being so near to the day of meeting the Jo Shakyamuni. How could he sleep? Gradually, his wife's face came glittering before his eyes, and he thought about this.

My wife Dzomba was my friend since (she was) sixteen years of age. For about 40 years, she loved me at all times without deceit. Time after time when my heart disease arose, with tears filling her eyes, Dzomba would feed me spoonfuls of food and do whatever nursing work was needed. Finally, last year Dzomba herself got sick and was on the point of death, but still she took my hand and said, "I am at the end of my life, Phuntsog. Because you have heart disease, be careful." Rather than (think) about her own pain, she had great concern for me. Throughout her whole life she never wished things for herself, but at the point of death she stroked her son's cheek and as her last will said, "Please take our only son Panden to Lhasa to see the Jo once." And then she took off her the large turquoise headstone from the crown of her head and put it into my hand. She shed a few tear drops and said, "Phuntsog, give this to the Jo and pray (to him) that our son Panden will have a happy life." Then she died. Now, tomorrow, I will see the Jo as well as definitely fulfill the wish of my deceased wife. Thinking in this manner, he became very happy.

A moment later, Phuntsog's heart suddenly started to palpitate stronger and stronger and sweat drops fell from his forehead. It was difficult to breathe. Phuntsog thought, becoming very frightened, "Oh my! Unfortunate person that I am, my heart disease is starting to rise again. Now what is best?" The lady of the house had heated some left-over stew and made a teapot of butter tea, and had come at that time to the hay room to call the two pilgrims (to eat). She saw Phuntsog panting due to his heart attack and immediately brought a hibachi-like container in front of Phuntsog and (pouring some tsamba on the coals) caused the air to be filled with the smell of burning tsamba. She quickly gave him a hot bowl of the leftover stew and gradually, Phuntsog not only regained consciousness, but his heart palpitation also decreased. Then the lady of the house woke up Panden and gave the two a large helping of tea and *ba* (tsamba mixed with tea into a dough-like consistency) to make them full, and Phuntsog recovered as if he had eaten a powerful medicine. When the lady of the house saw this, she said, "If your health is not too bad, today is the 15th of Sagadawa and if you see the Jo (on this day) you will be able to collect measureless merit. Now the second cock's crow is yet to come. If you two depart, you will be able to see the Jo by about sunrise." Phuntsog replied, "Thank you, lady of the house. May everything you do be successful! I will pray in this way before the Jo. Long life to you!" Then he took his son Panden and set off (lit., entered) the road.

When they arrived at the Shanka boat landing they got on a coracle (ferry) boat, and at that time, because they were anxious to get to Lhasa quickly, Phuntsog lifted his foot too energetically and opened a wound on his right calf that had been made when he was bitten by a nomad's dog on the trip. From a hole in his pants, pus and blood seeped through. Panden saw it in the moonlight and said, "Father, blood is coming out of your foot." The father told Panden, "Do not worry. When I see the Jo, it will be cured." And then he took his son in his lap and lifted him on to the boat.

When the father and son finally (lit., in stages) reached Lhasa's Outer Circumambulation Road, it was dawn and a clear day. On the right corner of the Outer Road they saw there were many people sitting in a line. When they went up to them and looked, some were praying with a cloth spread out in front of them waiting hopefully for alms. Below them was a line of crippled individuals and prisoners with their feet shackled and their necks bound with wood cangues. Wherever one looked, as far as the eye could see, it was full of beggars. As for the people walking on the Outer Road, they were going one after another without break. Many people had specially come to give alms to the beggars. They had sacks and other containers, and from these gave each and every beggar such things as money or tsamba as they did their circumambulation. Some were all dressed up with jewels and fine clothes. Some had just enough clothes to cover their private parts. Similarly, there were different nationalities and customs (clothes, etc.) among the mass of people who were moving like flowing water in one direction. Father Phuntsog and his son Panden were utterly amazed and stood watching for a moment absorbed. Suddenly, as if regaining consciousness, Phuntsog took Panden's hand, and asking someone directions, went walking quickly. Not long after that they arrived at the door of Lhasa's Cathedral. The line of people waiting to do the religious visit was up to the tree called "Jo's hair" and the father and son went to the end of that line and gradually moved forward/toward the entrance of the Cathedral.

15.8.3 Grammatical notes

1. Some contemporary publications in Tibet use quotation marks in addition to the traditional markers of direct speech.
2. སྡུག་དཀའ་ལས་ is an abbreviation of སྡུག་པོ་ and དཀའ་ལས་ ("suffering and hardship").
3. ངེས་ here is used as an involuntary verb meaning "to be certain."
4. འཁོར་ is an involuntary verb that means "to return" or "come back" to some place or position. Thus, with regard to doing prayers on a rosary it refers to the completion of one

turn (སྐོར་གཅིག་). In this example it is modified by the "before" clause connective (མ་+ vb. + གོང་ནས་, see 7.4).

5. ཐོག་ here does not function as the preposition "on" but rather as a noun meaning "roof." This is obvious from context and from its being followed by the preposition "under" (འོག་ ཏུ་).

6. ཅི་མ་རུང་ is commonly used at the end of clauses to ask "wouldn't it be nice" if something were to come to pass. It conveys this in a hopeful vein. In this case, "Wouldn't it be nice if it stopped raining quickly?"

7. This use of ནི་ has the defining function (see 5.11.3).

8. ན་ཚོད་དར་ལ་བབས་པའི་ is a common literary phrase meaning "young." When it is placed before the nominal it modifies, it is linked to it by the genitive particle.

9. མདོག་སྐྱ་ is an abbreviation, the longer form being མདོག་སྐྱ་པོ་: "poor color" (of the skin). ལ་, of course, here conveys the conjunctive meaning "as well as."

10. ཇི་མ་ཇི་བཞིན་ is used to mean "exactly what something is or is not" (or "was or was not"). In this sentence it conveys that he answered truly, saying exactly what happened and did not happen. Another example is:

ཞིང་པ་ཚོས་སྔོན་མའི་དགོན་པ་དེ་ཇི་མ་ཇི་བཞིན་ཞིག་བརྒྱབ་པ་རེད།

The farmers made the monastery exactly like it was previously.

11. ཆ་ནས་མཚོན་ན་ normally is used to convey hypothetical statements such as "if we hypothetically say X, then Y." Here, however, it means simply "taking something as an example." Thus, this clause says, "for example, with regard to his things, he had. . . ."

12. གཅིག་ཕྱོགས་ is used to convey the idea that one thing or person has two jobs or functions. Here the stick was used for two things: as a cane *and* to ward off dogs. It is used with respect to offices or positions as follows: སྐད་བསྒྱུར་དང་དྲུང་ཡིག་གཅིག་ཕྱོགས་ "combined interpreter and secretary."

13. The author here uses the traditional non-honorific speech form (ཡར་ཤོག་ rather than ཡར་ཕེབས་) to convey realism since it was these forms that were used when speaking to beggars and people of the lower social strata.

14. ཚིམ(ས)་ is used both as a verb and as an adverb. In this construction (ཚིམས་པ་བྱིན) it functions adverbially to convey that the verbal action, "giving," was done in the manner of trying to satisfy or satiate.

15. Here the imperative form (ཉོལ་) of the verb (ཉལ་) is used with the imperative particle ཅིག་ to convey the traditional style of speech to inferiors. It is not a real imperative statement.

16. The ཙམ་ནས་ in ཉལ་བ་ཙམ་ནས་ conveys that they laid down "for just a moment."

17. See note 7.

18. སྙམ་དུ་བསམས་ is a redundant phrase meaning "thought thinking." This juxtaposition of two equivalent involuntary verbs is stylistic and adds no new meaning.

19. རེ་བྲལ་ means རེ་བ་བྲལ་, "separated from the hope" of doing something. The "something" here is གསོན་, which is really an adjective meaning "living" or "being alive." Thus together they mean, "As for me, I have no hope of staying alive."

20. ཨང་ is a spoken term that is used with verbs to convey a polite imperative. Here it is used with the imperative གྱིས་ ("do!") and གཟབ་གཟབ་ ("be careful") to mean: "Take care of yourself!"

21. This type of construction conveys causation—"doing something so that he can meet . . . " (see 11.7.3).

22. See 10.3.3.

23. གང་ here means "one" rather than its more normal meaning of "what." This is discussed in 7.14.1.4.2.

24. པ་ན་ when used after verb stems means "when" the verbal action occurred.

15.9 Vocabulary

ཀོ་བ་	boat made from hide
དཀའ་བ་སྤྱད་	vi. to undergo, hardship
བཀབ་	va. p. of འགེབས་
བཀོད་	va. p. of འགོད་
བཀྲེས་སྐོམ་	hunger and thirst
བཀྲོལ་	va. p. of འགྲོལ་: untied, set loose, undid knots
རྐང་ལྕགས་	leg-irons, shackles, fetters
རྐང་མཐིལ་	sole (of foot)
རྐྱལ་པ་	skin/leather bag
སྐད་	"it is said" particle
སྐུ་གམ་	in/at the presence of (h.)
སྐོར་	1. about, concerning; 2. va. to surround, encircle; to go around; circumambulate
སྐྱབས་འཇུག་	a request, favor; va. — ཞུ་
སྐྱེ་བ་	a lifetime
སྐྱེ་བ་སྔོན་མ་	a former life
སྐྱེ་བོ་	person; people, mankind
སྐྲ་ལོ་	plait (of hair)
བརྐྱངས་ཕྱག་	type of prostration where hands are completely stretched out in front; va. — འཚལ་
བསྐུས་	va. p. of སྐུད་: put on ointment, oil, etc.
བསྐོར་	va. p. of སྐོར་
བསྐྱར་	"repeating" particle
ཁ་འགྲམ་	nearby, close to
ཁ་ངོམས་	vi. to quench (thirst)
ཁ་ཆག་	chipped edge; broken
ཁ་ཆེམས་	will, last testament
ཁ་དོན་	praying; va. — འདོན་
ཁག་པོ་	hard, difficult
ཁུང་བུ་	small hole
ཁོག་ཕྱིར་	teapot
ཁྱིམ་འཛིན་མ་	housewife; female household head
ཁྲ་ལྷིམ་ལྷིམ་	glittering, sparkling

ཁྲག་དོན་ vi. to bleed
ཁྲག་རྣག་ blood and pus
འཁར་བ་ walking stick
འཁོད་ vi. to be written
གང་དགོས་ whatever is needed
གོ་ཐུང་ pants
གུང་ཐང་ལྷ་མོ་ p.n. of a goddess (housed at Gungtang near Lhasa)
གོང་བ་ collar
གོམ་ཞེང་ width of step
རྒྱག་ཚད་ a lot, enough to satisfy
གྲལ་བསྒྲིགས་ va. to line up
གྲལ་སྟར་ row, line
གྲོངས་ vi. to die
གྲོད་པ་རྒྱགས་ vi to be full/ satisfied (with food)
དགའ་ཚོར་ happy
དགོན་སྡེ་ monastery
མགོ་འཁོར་ vi. to be fooled, to be deceived
འགེབས་ 1. va. to put on; 2. to cover, conceal
འགོར་ vi. to take (time), to elapse (of time)
འགྲམ་པ་ cheek, jaw
འགྲོགས་ va. to associate with, to have a close relationship with
རྒྱུག་ vi. to flow, run (of water)
སྒེར་ private, personal
སྒྲིབ་ va. to cover, conceal
སྒྲུབ་ va. to achieve, accomplish, obtain, fulfill
བསྒྲུབ་ va. f. of སྒྲུབ་
བསྒྲུབས་ va. p. of སྒྲུབ་
ངང་གིས་ gradually, slowly
དངངས་འཚབ་ fright, dread, panic
རྔུལ་ཆུ་ sweat, perspiration
ཅི་ནས་ཀྱང་ by all means, in all ways
ཅི་མ་རུང་ how nice
གཅིག་སྡོགས་ combined
གཅིག་རྗེས་གཉིས་མཐུད་ one after another
གཅོང་ནད་ chronic disease
བཅར་ va. to meet someone of a high status (h.)
ལྕགས་ཁབ་ iron needle
ཆ་ལུགས་ style of dress/costume, fashion
ཆད་ vi. to be cut off, to stop (e.g., rain)
ཆས་གོས་ costumes, clothes, garments
ཆུ་རྒྱུན་ the flow of rivers, current
ཆུང་ངུ་ small
ཆེད་མངགས་ specially, exclusively
མཆིས་ existential verb (= ཡོད་)
ཇ་སྲུབ་མ་ butter tea
ཇི་མ་ཇི་བཞིན་ exactly what it was
ཇོ་བོ་དབུ་སྐྲ་ p.n. place at the main door of the Jokang temple
མཇུག་ the end, the last
འཇགས་ vi. to calm down, to settle down
ཉ་རིལ་ calf (of leg)
ཉག་གཅིག་ certainly, surely
ཉལ་གཟན་ blanket
ཉེ་འགྲམ་ close to, nearby
ཉོལ་ va. imp. of ཉལ་
གཉིད་ལ་ཤོར་ vi. to fall asleep
སྙིང་རུས་ diligence, fortitude; va. — བསྐྱེད་
བཏིངས་ va. p. of འདིང་
རྟག་པར་ always

རྟོགས་	understanding, comprehension
སྟར་པ་	line, row
ཐབ་	stove, fireplace
ཐིགས་པ་	a drop
ཐུག་ལྷག་	left over porridge, stew
ཐུགས་ཁྲལ་	worry (h.)
ཐུར་མ་	spoon
ཐོག་	roof
ཐོག་མཐའ་བར་གསུམ་	at all times, from beginning to end
འཐམས་	va. p. of འཐམ་
དམ་པའི་ཆོས་	the dharma
དལ་རྟེན་མི་ལུས་	human life
དུས་ཡུན་	duration, time
དོ་འཁུར་	notice; va. — བྱེད་
དོར་མ་	pants
དྲག་སྐྱིད་	healing, getting better; vi.— བྱུང་ or ཡོང་
དྲག་ཆར་	rainstorm
དྲག་འོང་	vi. to get well, to recover (from illness)
དྲང་པོ་	true
དྲན་པ་གསོས་	vi. to remember; to recall
དྲེག་པ་	dirt
གདན་	mattress
བདག་ཅག་	we
བདུག་	va. to fill with scent
བདེ་ཐང་	well, in good health (usu. used after གཟུགས་པོ་)
བདེ་པོ་	well, in good health
བདོག་དངོས་	things, possessions
མདང་ནུབ་	last night
འདས་	vi. p. of འདའ་
འདས་པོ་	deceased
འདི་གར་	here
འདི་ཕྱི་གཉིས་	both this life and the next life
འདི་ཕྱོགས་	this side, this direction, here
འདེགས་	va. to lift, to raise up
འདུན་པ་	hope
འདོན་	va. to say; to read; to intone
འདྲ་	1. like, similar; 2. vb. + པ་ + — probably
རྡོལ་པ་	torn, tattered
ལྡིར་ལྡིར་	roaring (thundering) noise
སྡུག་དཀའ་ལས་	suffering and difficulties
སྡོང་རྒན་	old tree
ན་	"because," "as" particle
ན་ཚོད་དར་ལ་བབས་	young age
ནད་གཡོག་	a nurse; va. — བྱེད་
ནམ་ལངས་ཐང་གསལ་	dawn and a clear day
ནུས་པ་	power, strength; effectiveness
གནས་བསྐོར་བ་	pilgrim
གནས་ཆེན་	holy site
གནས་མོ་	inkeeper (female), hostess
གནས་ལུགས་	situation, condition
སྣོད་	vessel, container, receptacle
པང་	lap
པས་རེད་	"because" construction
དཔག་ཏུ་མེད་པ་	immeasurable
དཔལ་ལྡན་	p.n.
དཔྲལ་བ་	forehead
སྤྱི་པོ་	top, apex
སྤྱི་གཙུག་	top, apex, crown
སྤྲིན་ནག་	black cloud
ཕ་རྒན་	old father
ཕ་བུ་	abbr. father and son
ཕ་ཡུལ་	homeland
ཕོར་པ་	wooden bowl (for eating and

drinking)	
ཕྱི་སྒོ་	main door
ཕྱི་མ་	next (life)
ཕྱི་རོལ་	outside
ཕྱུ་པ་	Tibetan style dress
ཕྱོགས་	"manner of" particle
འཕྱིངས་	vi. to become matted together (fur, hair, wool)
ཕྲན་ (རང་)	I; myself
བར་མི་ཆོད་	without a break
བུ་ཆུང་	small son
བྱ་སྐད་	cock's crow
བྱིན་	va. p. of སྦྱིན་
བྱི་	vi. p. of འབྱི
ལྡུགས་	va. to pour
དབང་མེད་(དུ་)	without control/choice/ freedom
དབུགས་ལྷེམ་ལྷེམ་	panting
དབྱུག་པ་	stick, club
འབྲུག་སྐད་	thunder; vi. — རྒྱག་
སྦྱིན་པ་	charity, alms; va. — གཏོང་
མ་ཎི་	mani prayer
མི་རེ་ངོ་རེ་	each and everyone
མི་ཚེ་འདའ་	vi. to pass one's life
མེ་ཁོག་	hibachi like firepot
ཟུགས་	va. to bark
སྨོན་ལམ་	a prayer; va. — རྒྱག་ or འདེབས་
སྨྲས་	va. p. of སྨྲ་
གཙུག་གཡུ་	turquoise headstone
རྩམ་གསུར་	smell of tsamba burning
ཚིམས་	vi. to be satisfied
ཚེ་ཕྱི་མ་	the next life
ཚེས་	date
ཚེས་ཆེན་བཅོ་ལྔ་	name of the 15th of the 4th month (the holiest day of the holiest month)
ཚོགས་དང་བསོད་ནམས་	virtue, merit
འཚལ་	va. to prostrate
འཛགས་	vi. to drip, to leak
འཛོམས་པ་	p.n.
འཛོམས་པོ་	abundant, plentiful
ཞལ་	face (h.)
ཞལ་མཇལ་	face to face meeting, meeting in person; va. — གནང་ (h.)
ཞལ་རས་	face; va. — མཇལ་ to meet in person, face to face (h.)
ཞིབ་ཕྲ་	in detail
ཞོགས་ལས་	morning work
ཞྭ་མོ་	hat
གཞིགས་	in accordance
གཞོན་གཞོན་	young; youth
བཞུད་	vi. to set (for sun and moon)
ཟད་རྫུལ་	worn out
ཟིང་ཆ་	disturbance, unrest, riot
ཟླ་བོ་	spouse
གཟན་ཁང་	hay storage room
གཟན་པ་	hay
གཟབ་མཆོར་	dressing up
བཟའ་ཟླ་	spouse; husband and wife
རལ་པ་	locks of hair; matted hair
རས་གོས་	cotton clothing
རིན་པོ་ཆེ་	precious, valuable
རིམ་བཞིན་	successively, gradually
རེ་ཟུང་	a couple (of things)
ལ་ལ་	some, a few, several
ལང་ལོང་	sluggish, languid
ལེའུ་	a chapter
ཤ་རིད་པ་	thin, emaciated
ཤན་ཁ་གྲུ་ཁ་	p.n. the Shanka boat landing
ཤས་ཆེ་	"maybe" particle
གཤམ་དུ་	below, beneath

ས་ག་ཟླ་བ་ the name of the 4th Tibetan month

སློང་མཁན་ beggar

སློབ་ཚན་ lesson

གསལ་ to become clear; as was (seen or known)

གསོན་རེ་བྲལ་སོང་ "no hope of surviving"

གསོལ་བ་ prayer; va. — འདེབས་

གསོལ་བ་བཏབ་ va. p. of གསོལ་བ་འདེབས་

བསགས་ va. p. of གསོག་

ཧྲིལ་པོ་ whole

ལྷ་ང་ kneecap

ལྷག་ left-over

ལྷགས་ vi. to come, arrive

ལྷན་པ་ a patch

ལྷམ་མཐིལ་ sole of boot, shoe

ལྷིང་འཇགས་ peaceful

ལྷི་པ་ slice, sliver

ཨ་ཕོ་ a title (use mostly by Eastern Tibetan people)

ཨང་ polite imp. particle

ཨམ་ཕྲག་ the pocket made by the belt and fold of traditional Tibetan dress

ཨའུ་ཙམ་ not too bad, so-so

ཨུ་ཏུ་ལགས་ Oh my!

Lesson Sixteen

16.1 Introduction

This lesson contains extracts from two recent historical essays written in Tibet by Tsewang Dorje Lhalu, one of the highest officials in the traditional Tibetan government. They appeared in 1983 and 1985 as part of a program in which former government officials were encouraged to write accounts of historically significant events of which they had firsthand knowledge.

Extract number one is about Reting, the young incarnate lama who served as the first regent after the death of the 13th Dalai Lama in 1933. The essay deals with his disagreement with Langdün, the Prime Minister, and explains the events leading to the latter's resignation.

The second extract talks about the life of Lhalu's father, the famous Dzibön Lungshar. He was a major figure in Tibet in the 1920's and early 1930's and ultimately had his eyes plucked out in 1934 as a result of political machinations.

16.1.1 Reading number one: "The Sequence of Events Regarding the Problems Between Reting and Takdra, and the Summoning of the Ex-Regent Reting from Reting Monastery" (by) Lhalu, Tsewang Dorje

16.1.1.1 Tibetan text

རྭ་སྟག་གཉིས་ཀྱི་འགལ་རྐྱེན་དང་། རྒྱལ་ཚབ་རྭ་སྒྲེང་ལྷ་སར་སྐོང་
འགུག་བྱེད་པར་བསྐྱོད་པའི་བརྒྱུད་རིམ།
ལྷ་ཀླུ་ཚེ་དབང་རྡོ་རྗེ།

ཏཱ་ལའི་བླ་མ་བཅུ་གསུམ་པ་སྐུ་གཤེགས་རྗེས་རྒྱལ་ཚབ་རྭ་སྒྲེང་ལ་བསྐོས་པ་དང་། དེ་རྗེས་རྭ་སྒྲེང་དགོངས་ཞུ་གནང་སྟེ་སྟག་བྲག་ལ་
སྲིད་སྐྱོང་བསྐོས་པ།

༄༅།། སྤྱི་ལོ་ ༡༩༣༣ བོད་ཆུ་བྱ་ཟླ་བ་ ༡༠ པར་ཏཱ་ལའི་བླ་མ་བཅུ་གསུམ་པ་སྐུ་གཤེགས་རྗེས་བོད་ལྗོངས་ཚོགས་འདུ་
རྒྱས་འཛོམས་གྲོས་བསྡུར་གྱིས་རྗེ་འཕགས་པ་ལོ་ཀི་ཤྭ་རའི་སྤྱན་སྔར་བོད་རྗེ་རྒྱལ་ཚབ་གསར་བསྐོའི་འོས་ 1 ཁོངས་སུ་རྭ་སྒྲེང་ཧོ་
ཐོག་ཐུ་ཐུབ་བསྟན་འཇམ་དཔལ་ཡེ་ཤེས་དང་། དགའ་ལྡན་ཁྲི་པ་མི་ཉག་ཡེ་ཤེས་དབང་ལྡན། ཕུར་ལྕོག་ཡོངས་འཛིན་སྤྲུལ་སྐུ་
བྱམས་པ་ཐུབ་བསྟན་ཚུལ་ཁྲིམས་བཅས་གཟན་བརྟག་ཞུས་པར། རྭ་སྒྲེང་བཟང་ཕེབས་བྱུང་བར་བརྟེན་བོད་ལྗོངས་ཚོགས་འདུས་
རྭ་སྒྲེང་ཧོ་ཐོག་ཐུས་རྒྱལ་ཚབ་ཀྱི་ཐུགས་འགན་སྐྱེད་དགོས་དང་། སྲིད་བློན་གླང་མདུན་ཀུན་དགའ་དབང་ཕྱུག་སྔར་ནས་ཡོད་མུས་ 2

དང་།   ཐུགས་འགན་མཉམ་བཞེས་ཡོང་བ་ཞུས་དོན་བཞིན3 རྭ་སྒྲེང་ཧོ་ཐོག་ཐུས་རྒྱལ་ཚབ་ཀྱི་ཐུགས་འགན་བཞེས་དེ་སྲིད་བློན་གླང་མདུན་དང་། སྲིད་འགན་མཉམ་བཞེས་གནང་།

སྲིད་བློན་ཀུན་དགའ་དབང་ཕྱུག་དང་ལྷན་སྦྲེལ་ལོ་ལྔ་ཙམ་གནང་རྗེས་རྭ་སྒྲེང་དང་།   གླང་མདུན་གཉིས་གཞུང་སྒེར་ཕྱུག་ལས་ཐད་ཕན་ཚུན་གོ་བསྡུར་གནང་སྐབས་འགལ་བ་བྱུང་བར་བརྟེན་རྭ་སྒྲེང་རྒྱལ་ཚབ་ཀྱིས་བཀའ་ཤག་ལ་རྒྱལ་ཚབ་ཀྱི་འགན་འཁུར་དགོངས་པ་དགོས་ཚུལ་གསུང་སྐབས་བཀའ་ཤག་གིས་སྤྱི་ཁྱབ་མཁན་པོ་དང་།   དྲུང་རྩིས། གདན་ས་གསུམ་གྱི་མཁན་པོར་གྲོས་བསྡུར་ཐོག་རྭ་སྒྲེང་ལ་ལྷ་རབ་ཏཱ་ལའི་བླ་མ་བཅུ་བཞི་པས་ཆོས་སྲིད་ལུགས་གཉིས་ཀྱི་ཐུགས་འགན་མ་བཞེས་བར་དང་།   མཐར་སྲིད་ཁྲི་མངའ་གསོལ་མ་གྲུབ་བར་མཛད་འཁུར་རང་འཛགས་ཡོང་བ་དང་།   ང་ཚོས་ཅི་གསུང་བཀའ་སྒྲུབ་ཞུ་རྒྱུའི་4 ཁས་ལེན་ཞུས་དེ་སྲིད་བློན་གླང་མདུན་དང་།   བཀའ་བློན།   སྤྱི་མཁན།   དྲུང་རྩིས།   གདན་ས་གསུམ་གྱི་མཁན་པོ་ལས་ཟུར། གཞུང་ཞབས་སེར་སྐྱ་ཚང་མས་རྭ་སྒྲེང་རྒྱལ་ཚབ་ལ་ཅི་གསུང་བཀའ་སྒྲུབ་ཞུ་རྒྱུའི་གན་རྒྱ་འབུལ་འཛོག་ཞུས།

སྤྱི་ལོ་ ༡༩༣༩ ལོའི་དཔྱིད་དུས་ཙམ་ལ་རྒྱལ་ཚབ་རྭ་སྒྲེང་གིས་བཀའ་ཤག་བརྒྱུད་བོད་ལྗོངས་ཚོགས་འདུར་དགོངས་འཆར་གསུང་དོན།5 དེ་སྔོན་རྒྱལ་ཚབ་རིམ་པར་ལས་སྒྲིབ་མེད་རུང་།   ང་རང་ལ་ལས་སྒྲིབ་ཡོད་པ་འདི་ནི་བསྟན་པ་གཅིག་ལ་སྐྱོན་པ་གཉིས་ལྷ་བུས་ཏཱ་ལའི་བླ་མའི་ཡང་སྲིད་རིན་པོ་ཆེ་གདན་ཞུ་བྱ་རྒྱུ་སོགས་ལ་འགོག་རྐྱེན་མཛད་དཀའ་ཡོང་ལུགས་གསུངས་པས། བཀའ་ཤག་གིས་གོང་གསལ་གསུང་བབས6 དེ་ཚོགས་འདུར་བཤད་དེ་གྲོས་བྱེད་བཙུག་པར་ཚོགས་འདུ་ནས་རྭ་སྒྲེང་དང་གླང་མདུན་གཉིས་ཐུགས་སྣང་མཐུན་མིན་གྱིས་ཏཱ་ལའི་བླ་མའི་ཡང་སྲིད་རིན་པོ་ཆེ་གདན་ཞུ་བྱ་རྒྱུ་སོགས་ལ་འགོག་རྐྱེན་མཛད་དཀའ་བྱུང་ཡོད་ཚེ་མཛད་འཁུར་མཉམ་བཞེས་གནང་རྒྱུ་འགྲིག་མིན་སོགས་བཤད་དེ་གླང་མདུན་ཀུན་དགའ་དབང་ཕྱུག་སྲིད་དབང་ཕྱིར་འཐེན་གྱིས་སྲིད་ཟུར་གྱི་གདན་ཐོབ་དང་།   ཡོགས་ཐོབ་རང་འཛགས་སྩད་དེ་བཞག།

16.1.1.2 Translation

Extract from: "The Sequence of Events Regarding the Problems Between Reting and Takdra, and the Summoning of the Ex-Regent Reting from Reting Monastery"
(by) Lhalu, Tsewang Dorje

After the 13th Dalai Lama died, Reting was appointed Regent, and after that, Reting resigned and Takdra ruled.

In 1933, in the 10th month of the Water Bird year, the 13th Dalai Lama died. After that, the Full National Assembly discussed (the matter) and held a divine lottery in the presence of the Avaloketisvara (statue) in the Potala to appoint a new regent. The candidates were Reting Hotoktu, Tubden Jamyan Yeshe, the Ganden Triba Minya Yeshe Wangden, and Purbujo Tutor Trulku Jamba Tubden Tsultrim. Reting was the name that came out from the lottery (lit., came well). Consequently, the National Assembly said that Reting Hotoktu had to take the responsibility of being regent , and that Prime Minister Langdün Kunga Wangchuk would continue as before. Both together would jointly share the responsibility. In accordance with that, Reting Hotoktu took the responsibility of being regent and ruled jointly with Langdün.

After they worked jointly for about 5 years, Reting and Langdün had differences when they were conferring back and forth about government and individual matters. Consequently, Reting Regent told the Kashak that he had to resign from the Regent's responsibilities. At that time the Kashak discussed this with the Cigyab khembo, the drungtsi, and the abbots of the 3 Great Gelugba monasteries (Drebung, Ganden and Sera). They decided to request Reting to continue until the great 14th Dalai Lama takes religious and secular responsibility, i.e., until his coronation is finished. We [the officials] also took an oath to obey whatever Reting said. Prime Minister Langdün, the Kalöns, the Cigyab, the Drungtsi, the 3 Great Gelugba monasteries' abbots and ex-abbots, and the government officials (lay and monk) all left a guarantee that they would obey whatever Reting Regent said.

In about springtime in 1939, Reting Regent made a suggestion to the National Assembly via the Kashak (that said), "Even though there was no joint regency in the past, I had a joint regency. As for that, it is like one teaching (Buddhism), but two Buddhas. It is making it difficult to carry out such things as the finding of the Dalai Lama." The Kashak told the National Assembly what he said and made them discuss (the matter). The Assembly said a number of things, such as that because Reting and Langdün do not have harmonious relations, if this makes difficulties and problems for finding the Dalai Lama it is not acceptable to have joint responsibility. (Consequently), Langdün Kunga Wangchuk withdrew from power. (He) received the position of ex-Prime Minister and was given salary as before.

16.1.1.3 Grammatical notes

1. The term འོས་ literally means "worthy" but is also used to mean "a candidate" for a position. འོས་ is linked by the genitive to the phrase བོད་རྗེ་རྒྱལ་ཚབ་གསར་བསྐོ་, which explains what kind of a candidate it was, i.e., it was a candidate for "appointing as the new regent of Tibet."

2. The use of སྡུས་ here emphasizes that the action was continuing; that he was "existing (in his position) as before."

3. དོན་བཞིན means "in accordance with the meaning (of something preceding it)." What precedes it here is ཐུགས་འགན་མཉམ་བཞེས་ཡོང་བ་ཞུས་. In this phrase the verb ཞུས་ means

"requesting" or "saying" something to someone higher, and ཞུགས་འགན་མཉམ་བཞེས་ཡོང་བ་ conveys what was requested, i.e., that they "jointly take the responsibility." Together these mean, "in accordance with requesting (they) take responsibility together. . . ."

4. The future nominalizing particle རྒྱུའི་ here links the past tense verb phrase "agreed" (ཁས་ལེན་བྱས་) by the genitive to the phrase ཅི་གསུང་བཀའ་སྒྲུབ་ཞུ་ ("doing whatever [you] say"). Thus, together they mean, "(they) agreed (in the future) to do whatever (he) said."

5. རྡོན in this instance functions to introduce direct discourse or some explanation of what was said or written. Thus here it conveys that the content of the suggestion made to the Assembly is explained immediately afterwards.

6. This use of བབས་ conveys "in accordance with the verbal action."

16.1.2 Reading number two: "Recollections of My Father Dorje Tsegye Lungshar

(by) Lhalu, Tsewang Dorje"

16.1.2.1 Tibetan text

ངའི་ཕ་ལུང་ཤར་རྡོ་རྗེ་ཚེ་རྒྱལ་དྲན་གསོ་བྱས་པ།

ལྷ་ཀླུ་ཚེ་དབང་རྡོ་རྗེ།

༄༅ ॥ ལུང་ཤར་ནི་དྭ་ལའི་བླ་མ་སྐུ་ཕྲེང་ལྔ་པའི་དུས་ས་གནས་སྲིད་གཞུང་གི་དཔོན་རིགས་ནང་ཞུགས། མི་རྒྱུད་རིམ་པ་ནས་སྲིད་གཞུང་གི་ཞབས་སྡོད་ཞུས། ལུང་ཤར་ནི་གཞིས་རྩེ་ཀུན་རྒྱས་བཞད་མཐོང་སྨོན་རྫོང་ཁོངས་ཧ་ནག་ཁུལ་གྱི་སྣེར་པའི་གྲས་ཤིག་རེད། ངའི་མེས་པོ་སྲིད་གཞུང་གི་དྲུང་འཁོར་ལུང་ཤར་ལྷུན་གྲུབ་རྡོ་རྗེ་དང་། སྐྱོའི་བདེ་ཆེན་པད་མོ་གཉིས་ཀྱི་བུར་བོད་ལྕགས་སྦྲུལ་ (༡༨༨༡) ལོར་ཕ་དམ་པ་དེ་འཁྲུངས་ཤིང་། མཚན་ལ་རྡོ་རྗེ་ཚེ་རྒྱལ་ཞེས་བཏགས།

ཁོང་དགུང་ལོ་བརྒྱད་ཙམ་ལ་སླེབས་དུས་ཡབ་གཤེགས་འདུག་ཀྱང་། ཡུམ་ནས་གཅེས་པར་བསྐྱངས་ཏེ་འཚར་ལོངས་བྱུང་ཞིང་། ཤེས་ཡོན་རིག་གནས་སློབ་སྦྱོང་ཐད་ལའང་ཡུམ་གྱིས་ཐུགས་འཁུར་གནང་སྟེ་དགེ་རྒན་མང་པོ་བསྟེན་སྐབས་སྦྱང་འབྲས་ཧ་ཅང་ཡག་པོ་བྱུང་འདུག། དེར་བརྟེན་ཁོང་གིས་ཡུམ་ལ་ཐོག་མཐའ་བར་གསུམ་དུ་གུས་བརྩེ་ཧ་ཅང་ཆེན་པོ་གནང་གི་འདུག།

ངའི་ཕ་ནི་བོད་ལུགས་གསོ་བ་རིག་པ་སྦྱོང་རྒྱུར་དགའ་པོ་ཡོད་སྐབས་དགེ་རྒན་བསྟེན་གདུགས་ཀྱིས་1 སྨན་དཔྱད་བྱེད་སྒོ་སློབ་སྦྱོང་ཧུར་བརྩོན་གནང་རྗེས་ལག་རྩལ་ཡག་ཙམ་2 ཤེས་ཐུབ་པ་བྱུང་གཤིས་རྗེས་སུ་ང་ཚོ་ལོ་ན་སོན་དུས་ཀྱང་པཱ་ལགས་ནས་ལས་ཞོར་ནད་པར་རྩ་རྒྱ་བརྟག་དཔྱད་དང་། བོད་ལུགས་ཀྱི་སྨན་སྦྱོར་བ་སོགས་གནང་གི་འདུག། དེ་བཞིན་ཁོང་དགུང་ལོ་ཆུང་དུས་ནས་གཞས་དང་ཞབས་བྲོ་ལའང་ཧ་ཅང་དགའ་པོ་ཡོད་སྐབས་རྒྱུན་དུ་རྟོའི་ཅན་དང་ཡང་ཅིན་གཏོང་གནང་བ་མ་

ཟད། སྐབས་འགར་ལྷ་སར་ཡོད་པའི་རོལ་ཆ་གཏོང་མི་རྣམས་བསྡུ་རུབ་གནང་སྟེ་མཉམ་གཏོང་སྐྱོ་སྐྱིད་ཡང་ཡང་གནང་གི་འདུག

དགུང་གྲངས་ཉི་ཤུ་སྐོར་ལ་ཕེབས་དུས་རྟ་ནག་སྨིར་ལྷད་ཁྲིད་པའི་བུ་མོ་མདུན་ཐབས་སུ་བཞེས་པ་དེ་ལ་ཕྲུ་གུ་ཆ་པ་རྟ་ཐུར་དབང་ཆེན་གཡུ་ལྷ་དང་། སྒྲོལ་མ་ཕུག་པད་མ་གཉིས་བཅས། དེ་ནས་སྲིད་སྐྱོང་གི་དྲུང་འཁོར་ཞུ་བར་ལྷ་སར་ཕེབས་དེ་དཔོན་རིགས་ཁོངས་ཞུགས། ཁོང་ཡིག་རྩིས་ཡག་ཙམ་ཡོད་སྟབས་མི་རིང་བར་རྩིས་ཁང་ལས་ཁུངས་ཀྱི་རྩིས་པ་བསྐོ་བཞག་བྱས་འདུག རྩིས་པའི་ལས་འགན་ལོ་བཅུ་ཙམ་གནང་རིང་ལས་ཀར་དྲུར་བརྩོན་ཆེ་ཞིང་། འཛིན་གྲང་ཆེན་པོ་ཡོད་མཁན་ཞིག་ཡིན་འདུག་གསུངས། རྩིས་པ་ལུང་ཤར་ཞེས་མིང་གྲགས་ཐོག་མར་ཐོན།

པུ་ལགས་ཀྱི་སྐུ་ཟླ་དེ་ཉིད་ལུང་ཤར་གཞིས་སུ་སྡོན་བསྡུའི་ཕྱག་ལས་གནང་བར་ཕེབས་སྐབས་ཤིག་ལ་3 སྟབས་མ་ལེགས་པར་གཞིས་སུ་སྐུ་གཤེགས། དེ་ནས་ལོ་གསུམ་ཙམ་སོང་བའི་རྗེས་སུ་ངའི་ཨ་མ་བསྟན་འཛིན་སྒྲོལ་དཀར་ལགས་དང་གཉེན་སྒྲིག་གནང་། ཕྲུ་གུ་ང་ཚོ་བུ་ལྔ་དང་། བུ་མོ་གཅིག་བྱུང་།

༡༩༡༡ ལོར་ཏཱ་ལའི་བླ་མ་སྐུ་ཕྲེང་ ༡༣ པ་ཉིད་དྷར་ཕེབས་བཞུགས་རིང་ཕྱི་རྒྱལ་གྱི་གནས་ཚུལ་མང་ཙམ་ཞིག་མཁྱེན་རྟོགས་བྱུང་རྐྱེན་བོད་ལྗོངས་ཡར་རྒྱས་འགྲོ་བར་རིག་གསར་འཕེལ་རྒྱས་གཏོང་དགོས་པ་དེ་དགོངས་པར་འཁོར་ནས་སྤྱི་ལོ་ ༡༩༡༣ ལོར་སྐུ་དྲག་གི་བུ་ཕྲུག་ཁོངས་ནས་ན་གཞོན་ཁ་ཤས་འདེམས་སྒྲུག་གནང་སྟེ་ཕོ་ཚོ་དབྱིན་ཡུལ་དུ་སློབ་སྦྱར་སྐྱེལ་བར་འགྲོ་མཁན་གྱི་འགོ་གཙོ་ངའི་པུ་ལགས་ལ་རེམ་བཞིའི་གོ་གནས་དང་ཐུགས་ལས་འགན་གནང་། བུ་ཕྲུག་ཁོངས་སྨོན་གྲོང་མཁྱེན་རབ་ཀུན་བཟང་། བྱང་ངོས་པ་རིག་འཛིན་རྡོ་རྗེ། སྐྱིད་སྡུག་པ་དབང་འདུས་ནོར་བུ། སྒོག་མཁར་བ་བསོད་ནམས་མགོན་པོ་བཅས་གཏོང་གནང་མཛད་པ་ཁོང་ཚོ་དང་མཉམ་དུ་དབྱིན་ཇིའི་རྒྱལ་ས་ལོན་ཀྲོན་དུ་ཕེབས། དབྱིན་གཞུང་ནས་སྟེ་ཤན་རྒྱལ་ཊ་ས་ཧེབ་དང་། སྐད་སྒྱུར་ལེགས་ལྡན་ས་ཧེབ (བོད་རིགས) གཉིས་བཙུགས་དེ་སྣེ་ལེན་བྱས་འདུག བོད་ས་གནས་སྲིད་གཞུང་གིས་བསྐུར་བའི་ཡི་གེ་དང་ལག་རྟགས་སོགས་སྤྲོད་ཅིང་། ཕྲུ་གུ་བཞི་ཨིང་ལན་དུ་རག་བྱིའི་ཞེས་པའི་སློབ་གྲྭར་བཙུག

རྗེས་སུ་ཕྲུ་གུ་རྣམས་ལ་ཆེད་ལས་ཡོན་ཏན་རེ་རེ་བསླབས་པ་ནི། སྨོན་གྲོང་མཁྱེན་རབ་ཀུན་བཟང་ལ་ས་གཏེར་འཚོལ་འདོན་སྐོར་དང་། བྱང་ངོས་པ་རིག་འཛིན་རྡོ་རྗེར་གློག་གི་ལས་ཀ། སྐྱིད་སྡུག་པ་དབང་འདུས་ནོར་བུར་དར་གཏོང་དང་ས་ཐིག་ལེན་རྒྱུའི་ལས་ཀ། སྒོག་མཁར་བ་བསོད་ནམས་མགོན་པོར་དམག་དོན་ལས་ཀ་བཅས་སློབ་སྦྱོང་བྱས་དེ་ཚང་མ་སློབ་ཐོན་གྱིས་བོད་ལ་ཕྱིར་ལོག་ཡོང་བ་རེད།

སྐབས་དེར་ངའི་པུ་ལགས་དང་ཨ་མ་ལགས་གཉིས་ནས་ཀྱང་དབྱིན་ཇིའི་སྐད་ཡིག་ཕྲན་བུ་བསླབས་ཤིང་། ཕ་རན་སི་དང་། ཨི་ཀྲར་ལི་སོགས་ལ་བལྟ་སྐོར་དུ་འང་ཕེབས་འདུག་པ་བཅས་བརྒྱུད་ངའི་པུ་ལགས་ལ་ཕྱི་རྒྱལ་གྱི་བྱེད་སྟངས་ཐད་ནས་ཤུགས་རྐྱེན་ཆེ་ཙམ་ཐེབས་དེ་བོད་ཀྱི་ལམ་ལུགས་རྙིང་པ་དེར་ཕན་བུའི་བཅོས་སྒྱུར་མ་བྱས་ཚེ་ཉེན་ཁ་ཡོད་པའི་བསམ་བློ་འཁོར་ཡོད་འདུག གང་ཡིན་ཞེ་ན། རྗེས་སུ་པུ་ལགས་ནས་དུས་ཚོད་བྱུང་རིམ་བཞིན་དབྱིན་ཡིག་གི་ལོ་རྒྱུས་དེབ་ལ་རྟག་པར་བལྟ་ཀློག་གནང་བ་དང་། ང་ཚོ་ནང་མི་འཛོམས་དེ་སྐོར་སྐབས་པུ་ལགས་ཀྱིས་དེ་སྔོན་ཕ་རན་སིར་དུས་འགྱུར་གྱིས་ཕ་རན་སིའི་རྒྱལ་པོ་གཏོར་བ་དང་། ཨི་ཀྲར་ལིའི་རྒྱལ་པོ་གཏོར་བའི་ལོ་རྒྱུས་སྐོར་སྐྲུང་གཏམ་ལྟ་བུར་གསུང་གི་འདུག

པཱ་ལགས་བོད་དུ་ཕྱིར་ལོག་གནང་རྗེས་ཏཱ་ལའི་བླ་མས་དམིགས་བསལ་གཟིགས་སྐྱོང་གནང་སྟེ་རྩིས་དཔོན་གྱི་གོ་གནས་གནང་། དེ་དུས་བོད་དམག་སྒྲིག་གཞི་རྒྱ་སྐྱིད་བྱེད་སྐབས་ཡིན་ཙང་། དམག་ཡོགས་ལྷིང་གི་མེད་སྐབས་འབྲུ་རིགས་འཕར་མ་བསྡུ་རྒྱུའི་འཆར་གཞི་བཟོས་ཏེ་འབབ་ཞིབ་ལས་ཁུངས་ཞེས་པ་གསར་བཙུགས་ཐོག་དེ་དམ་དྲུང་ཡིག་ཆེན་མོ་བློ་བཟང་བསྟན་སྐྱོང་དང་། ངའི་ཕ་རྩིས་དཔོན་ལུང་ཤར་རྡོ་རྗེ་ཚེ་རྒྱལ་གཉིས་ལ་བསྐོ་བཞག་གནང་རྒྱུར་ཏཱ་ལའི་བླ་མས་ཆོག་མཆན་གནང་། དེར་བརྟེན་འབབ་ཞིབ་འགེལ་ཡུལ་སྡེ་དཔོན་མི་དྲག་དང་། ཡབ་གཞིས་ཁག་ སྐྱེར་པ། ཆོས་གཞིས་བཅས་ལ་ས་ཞིང་ཐྲུག་བཟོས་འཕར་མ་ཡོད་རིགས་དང་། བཀའ་གཞིས། མདའ་གཞིས། སྐྱེར་པ་ཞབས་སྡོད་མ་ཐུབ་པའི་ཕ་གཞིས་སོགས་ལ་ཞིབ་འཕར་འབྲུ་རིགས་འཕར་འགེལ་བྱས་ཏེ་མི་ཚང་ཆེ་རིགས་ལ་འབྲུ་ཁལ་སྟོང་ཕྲག་བཞི་ལྔ་དང་། དེ་འོག་ལ་ཁལ་བརྒྱ་ཕྲག་ཁ་ཤས་འགེལ་དགྲི་བྱས་སྐབས་ས་གནས་སྲིད་སྐྱོང་ལ་འབྲུ་རིགས་ཏ་ཙང་ཡོན་འབོར་ཆེན་པོ་བྱུང་སྟེ་རྗེས་སུ་ཏཱ་ལའི་བླ་མའི་སྐུ་ཚེའི་སྨད་ཆར་སླེབས་དུས་འབྲུ་ཁང་རྙིང་པ་ཕལ་ཆེར་ཁེངས་ཏེ་ས་གནས་ཁ་ཤས་ལ་བཀར་ཁང་ནང་འབྲུ་འཛུག་ཡུལ་མེད་པ་ལྟ་བུ་བྱུང་བ་རེད།

སྐབས་དེར་འབྲུ་རིགས་འབབ་བཟོ་བྱེད་ཡུལ་སྡེ་དཔོན་མི་དྲག་ཆེ་གྲས་ཁག་ལ་འབབ་འཕྲི་ཆེན་པོ་བྱུང་སྐབས་མཐོ་རིམ་ཁག་གཅིག་ནས་ངའི་ཕ་རྩིས་དཔོན་ལུང་ཤར་ལ་མ་དགའ་བའི་གླིང་ཕྱོགས་ཆེན་པོ་བྱུང་འདུག་ཀྱང་དེའི་དུས་ཏཱ་ལའི་བླ་མའི་གཟིགས་བསྐྱངས་ཆེན་པོ་ཡོད་སྐབས་རྒྱབ་རྩ་བཟང་བས་སུས་ཀྱང་གནོད་འཚེ་གཏོང་ཐུབ་མི་འདུག འོན་ཀྱང་དེའི་རྐྱེན་པས་རྗེས་སུ་ལུང་ཤར་ལ་གཤམ་གསལ་ལྟར་ཆག་སྒོ་ཆེན་པོ་འཕྲད་པ་རེད།

16.1.2.2 Translation

Recollections of My Father Dorje Tsegye Lungshar
(by) Lhalu, Tsewang Dorje

As for (the) Lungshar (family), (it) joined the ranks of government officials at the time of the 5th Dalai Lama and continued to serve as government servants one generation after another. It is an aristocratic family from Tanag area in Shey Tongmön district in Shigatse Prefecture. In the year of the Iron-Snake (1881), my late father was born to my grandfather, the lay official Lungshar Lhundrub Dorje, and (to my) grandmother Dechen Bemo. (They) gave him the name Dorje Tsegye.

When he was about eight years old, his father died. However, his mother cared for him and he grew up. (His) mother took concern even about his intellectual studies, and (he) studied with many teachers. Consequently, he achieved an excellent result (i.e., became knowledgeable). Because of that, he showed great respect and love for his mother all the time.

Because my father liked studying Tibetan medicine, (he) worked with teachers and studied medical activities very diligently and became skilled. Thereafter, even when we were young, father in his spare time did such things as examine the urine and stool of patients and give out Tibetan medicine. Similarly, from small he liked singing and dancing, and not only always played the hojin and yangjin, but occasionally gathered together with musicians in Lhasa and played with them again and again for pleasure.

When he reached the age of about 20, he took as (his) bride a girl (from the) aristocratic family of Lheguba in Tanag, and she [lit., that one] bore two children: Chaba Rusu Wangchen Yulha, and Bema Dromapug. After that, he went to Lhasa to petition to become a lay official in the old government and joined the ranks of officials. Because he was good in writing and arithmetic, he was soon appointed as Dziba ("accountant") in the Revenue Office. During the 10 years that he held the position of "accountant," he worked diligently. Because he was very capable, he first came to be famous as "Dziba" Lungshar [i.e., people first came to refer to him by the name Dziba Lungshar].

Once when father's wife went to Lungshar's estate for doing the autumn harvest [i.e., overseeing it], she unfortunately died there. After about 3 years passed, (he) married my mother Dendzin Droma. (She) got (bore) us children, 5 boys and one girl.

In 1911, while the 13th Dalai Lama was living in India, he became cognizant of much foreign news and consequently came to think that to improve Tibet we have to spread new (kinds of) knowledge. In 1913, he selected several youths from among the aristocracy, and gave my father the task of being in charge of them—of going and delivering them to school in England. Together with this, (he gave him) the rank of Rimshi. (The Dalai Lama) sent (among these children) Khenrab Günsang Möndrong, Rinzin Dorje Changöba, Wangdü Norbu Kyibugba, and Sonam Gombo Gonggarwa. (Lungshar) went together with them to the English capital London. The English government appointed Gould Sahib as liaison officer and Lengden Sahib (a Tibetan) as interpreter and received (the Tibetans). The Tibetan Government gave them (the boys and Lungshar) identification papers and letters, etc. The four children were placed in the school called Rugby in England.

As for the special training that each child was taught (in England): Khenrab Günsang Möndrong was (taught) mining, Rinzin Dorje Changöba was taught electricity, Wangdü Norbu Kyibugba was taught telegraphy and mapping, and Sonam Gombo Gonggarwa was taught military affairs. After they all finished their studies (graduated), (they) returned to Tibet.

At that time, my father and mother studied spoken and written English a little and also went on tour to places such as France and Italy. My father was very influenced by foreign ways of doing things and came to think that unless Tibet reforms its old system a little, there was a danger. If you ask why (this was needed)? Later, father, whenever he had time read histories in English and when we household members were assembled and seated, he would tell us about history in story fashion—of how in the past in France the king of France was destroyed because of changed circumstances and about the destruction of the king of Italy.

After father returned to Tibet, the Dalai Lama treated him specially and gave him the position of Revenue Head (Dzibön). At that time, they were in the midst of expanding the Tibetan military organization, but there was insufficient income for the military salaries and consequently a plan was made to collect extra grain. The Babshi Office was established (to collect it). Concerning it, the Dalai Lama approved the appointment of Drunyichemmo Losang Tenkyong and my father Dzibön Dorje Tsegye Lungshar to be its heads. They imposed extra grain levies on such sources as council ministers' estates, generals' estates, aristocratic estates that were not the one for which the official served the government. (Similarly, they were levied) on all those among the religious sector and the Debön midra, the Yabshi and other aristocrats who had extra estates that had been obtained without proper title. (In this manner) the large families had to pay extra levies of 4-5,000 ke of grain, and the families beneath (them) levies of several hundred ke. Because of this, the old government got a very large amount of grain. Afterwards, toward the end of the Dalai Lama's life, the old grain storage places (of the government) were basically full. In some regions there was even no place to store all the grain.

Because the target of the extra grain levies was the larger Debön midra (families), negative public opinion concerning my father Dzibön Lungshar was disseminated from one group of the highest officials. Nevertheless, because the Dalai Lama looked after (him) at that time, he had good support and nobody was able to harm (him). However, because of that, afterwards, as explained below, he met a great misfortune.

16.1.2.3 Grammatical notes

1. ཙམ་ literally means "a little" but here is used as a convention to convey modesty on the part of the writer about his father's knowledge.
2. མཉམ་གཏོང་ and སྣོ་སྐྱིད་ both go with the verb གཏང་, conveying that they "played together" and "made merry." ཡང་ཡང་ functions as an adverb.
3. སྐབས་ཤིག་ལ་ is simply a version of the "when" connective. It conveys "at one time" with respect to the verbal action; thus ཕེབས་སྐབས་ཤིག་ལ་ means "at one time when (she) went."

16.2 Vocabulary

ཀུན་དགའ་
  དབང་ཕྱུག་ — p.n.
ཀྲོན་ཆུས་ — ch. prefecture (a political unit in contemporary Tibet equivalent to a province)
བཀའ་སྒྲུབ་ — following or obeying orders; va. — ཞུ་ or — བྱེད་
བཀའ་བློན་ — minister in traditional Tibetan government
བཀའ་གཞིས་ — estate held by council ministers while in office
བཀའ་ཤག་ — the Council of Ministers
བཀར་ཁང་ — storehouse, warehouse, treasury
སྐད་སྒྱུར་ — interpreter, translator
སྐབས་འགར་ — sometimes, occasionally
སྐུ་ཟླ་ — spouse (h.)
སྐུ་གཤེགས་ — vi. to die (h.)
སྐོང་འགུག་ — summon; va. — བྱེད་
སྐྱིད་སྡུག་པ་ — p.n. (of an aristocratic family)
བསྐོ་བཞག་ — appointment, assignment; va. — བྱེད་ or — གནང་
ཁལ་ — a standard measure of volume equal to about 25-30 pounds
ཁུལ་ — region, area
མཁན་པོ་ — abbot
མཁྱེན་རྟོགས་ — understanding, knowing; vi. — ཐུང་ (h.)
འཁྲུངས་ — vi. to be born (h.)
གན་རྒྱ་ — written agreement, contract; va. — འཛོག་ to sign a contract
གུས་བརྩི་ — respect and love; va. — གནང་ (h.)
གོ་བསྡུར་ — consultation, discussion; va. — བྱེད་
གོ་གནས་ — rank, position
གོང་གསལ་ — as is clear above
གྲས་ — kind, type, sort
གྲོས་བསྡུར་ — discussion, talk; va. — བྱེད་
གླང་མདུན་ — p.n. (of aristocratic family)
གླེང་ཕྱོགས་ — public opinion
གློག་ — electricity
དགའ་ལྡན་ཁྲི་པ་ — head of Gaden monastery
དགུང་གྲངས་ — age (h.)
དགེ་མཚན་ — advantages, good points, benefits
དགོངས་འཆར་ — suggestion, opinion; va. — གསུང་ or — གནང་ (h.)
དགོངས་ཞུ་ — taking leave, resigning; va. — གནང་ (h.)
འགལ་རྐྱེན་ — unfavorable condition, obstruction, hindrance; va. — བཟོ་ or — གཏོང་
འགལ་བ་ — contradiction
འགེལ་དཀྲི་ — loading, imposing, putting on; va. — བྱེད་
འགེལ་ཡུལ་ — place to put on, place to impose on
འགོ་གཙོ་ — headman, foreman
འགོག་རྐྱེན་ — obstacle, barrier,

	hindrance; va. — བཟོ་ or — གཏོང་
འགྲིག་མིན་	whether it's all right or not
ཀུལ་ཊ་ས་ཧེབ་	p.n. Gould Sahib
རྒྱ་སྐྱེད་	expansion; va. — བྱེད་
རྒྱབ་རྩ་	one who stands behind giving support
རྒྱལ་ཚབ་	regent
རྒྱལ་ཟུར་	ex-regent
རྒྱལ་ས་	capital
རྒྱས་འཛོམས་	plenary session, full or large session/meeting
སྒེར་པ་	nobility, aristocracy
སྒྲིག་གཞི་	construction, structure
སྒྲུང་གཏམ་	folklore, tale
སྒྲོལ་མ་ཕུག་	p.n.
སྒོག་མཁར་བ་	p.n. of an aristocratic family
བརྒྱུད་	through, via
བརྒྱུད་རིམ་	sequence of events
མངའ་གསོལ་	enthronement
ཅི་གསུང་བཀའ་སྒྲུབ་	willingly accepting instruction/orders, obedient (h.)
གཅེས་པར་སྐྱོང་	va. to take care of, look after, rear
གཅེས་པར་བསྐྱངས་	va. p. of གཅེས་པར་སྐྱོང་
ལྕགས་སྦྲུལ་	iron-snake (year)
ཆ་པ་རྟུ་ཟུར་	p.n.
ཆག་སྒོ་	calamity, catastrophe, misfortune; vi. — འཕུད་
ཆེད་ལས་ཡོན་ཏན་	special knowledge, professional study
ཆོག་མཆན་	approval, authorization, sanction
ཆོས་སྲིད་ལུགས་གཉིས་	the system in which the religious and secular are combined (i.e. the Tibetan government)
མཆོད་གཞིས་	monastic estate
མཉམ་བཞེས་	taking something together, cooperating together; va. — གནང་ (h.)
གཉེན་སྒྲིག་	marrige; va. — བྱེད་
གཏུགས་	va. to go to meet
གཏོར་	va. to destory, demolish
རྟ་ནག་	p.n. of a place in Tsang area
སྟག་བྲག་	Takdrak (a monastery near Lhasa)
སྟོན་བསྡུ་	autumn harvest
སྟོན་པ་	a religious teacher, Buddha
བརྟག་དཔྱད་	study, research, examination; va. — བྱེད་
བསྟན་པ་	the doctrine or teachings of the Buddha
བསྟན་འཛིན་སྒྲོལ་དཀར་	p.n.
བསྟེན་	va. to study with a teacher; to check with a doctor
ཐུགས་འཁུར་	concern, care; va. — བཞེས་ or གནང་
ཐུགས་འགན་	responsibility; va. — ཁྱེར་ or — བཞེས་ (h.)
ཐུགས་སྣང་	impression, feeling,

sensation (h.)

ཐུབ་བསྟན་འཇམ་དཔལ་ཡེ་ཤེས་ p.n. of Reting Rinpoche

ཐོད་ above, over

མཐུན་མིན་ not in harmony, incompatible, disagreement

མཐོ་རིམ་ high level

དམ་པ་ late, deceased

དུས་འགྱུར་ change

དེ་སྔོན་ previously, before that

དེ་ཉིད་ that itself

དེར་བརྟེན་ therefore, because of that

དོ་དམ་ commissioner, official in charge, supervisor, custodian

དྲན་གསོ་ a commemoration, rememberance; va. — བྱེད་

དྲུང་འཁོར་ lay official (in traditional Tibetan government)

དྲུང་རྩིས་ monastic and secular officials of the traditional Tibetan government

དྲུང་ཡིག་ཆེན་མོ་ high official in the monk official segment of the traditional Tibetan government

གདན་ཐོབ་ seat (in parliament/ congress)

གདན་ཞུ་ 1. inviting, act of inviting to take a post; 2. in the case of the Dalai Lama it means to search for or discover the new incarnation; va. — ཞུ་ (h.)

གདན་ས་གསུམ་ the three great monasteric seats of the Gelukpa Sect (Sera, Drepung, and Ganden)

བདེ་ཆེན་པད་མོ་ p.n.

མདའ་གཞིས་ estate held by generals while in office

མདུན་ཐབས་ bride

འདེམས་སྒྲུག་ selection, choosing

རྡོ་རྗེ་ཚེ་རྒྱལ་ p.n.

ལྡང་ vi. to suffice; to be sufficient/ enough

སྡེ་དཔོན་མི་དྲུག་ the highest level of aristocrats

བསྡུ་རུབ་ collecting, assembling, gathering; va. — བྱེད་ or — གནང་

སྣེ་ཤན་ guide, liaison officer

པཱ་ལགས་ father (h.)

པད་མ་ p.n.

དཔོན་ chief, lord, ruler

དཔོན་རིགས་ officials, lords, authorities

སྤྱན་སྔར་ in the presence of, in person, in an audience (h.)

སྤྱི་ཁྱབ་མཁན་པོ་ a high-ranking monk official in the traditional Tibetan government

སྤྱི་མཁན་ abbr. སྤྱི་ཁྱབ་མཁན་པོ་

སྤྲུལ་སྐུ་ an incarnate lama

ཕ་རན་སི་ France

ཕན་ཚུན་ each other, one another, back and forth, here

and there
ཕུར་ལྕོག་ name of a monastery near Lhasa and its incarnation
ཚོན་འབོར་ quantity, amount, number
ཕྱིར་འཐེན་ withdrawing, pulling back; va. — བྱེད་
འཕགས་པ་ལོ་ཀི་
ཤྭ་ར་ title of Takdra
འཕར་འགེལ་ levying something extra (such as a tax)
འཕར་མ་ extra
བོད་རྗེ་ king of Tibet
བོད་ལྗོངས་ Tibet
བོད་ལུགས་ Tibetan customs, ways, manner
བྱང་ངོས་པ་རིག་
འཛིན་རྡོ་རྗེ་ p.n.
བྱམས་པ་ཐུབ་བསྟན་
ཚུལ་ཁྲིམས་ p.n.
བྱེད་སྒོ་ activities, duties, work
བྱེད་སྟངས་ the manner or method of doing things
བློ་བཟང་བསྟན་སྐྱོང་ p.n.
དབང་ཆེན་གཡུ་ལྷ་ p.n.
དབང་འདུས་ནོར་
བུ་ p.n.
དབྱིན་གཞུང་ government of England
དབྱིན་ཡུལ་ England
འབབ་ཞིབ་འཕར་
མ་ extra tax levy
འབབ་ཞིབ་ལས་
ཁུངས་ Babshi office
འབབ་བཟོ་བྱེད་ va. to impose a tax
འབུལ་འཛོག་ agreement, guarantee; va. — བྱེད་

འབྲུ་ཁང་ granary
འབྲུ་རིགས་ grains
ཐུག་བཟོས་ something that was taken over but was not officially given, something held without proper title
སྦྱང་ va. to study
སྦྱང་འབྲས་ the fruit of one's studies, the result
མང་ཙམ་ a little more
མི་རྒྱུད་ lineage, descendents
མི་ཉག་ཡེ་ཤེས་
དབང་ལྡན་ p.n.
མི་དྲག་ aristocracy
མི་རིང་བར་ soon, before long
མིང་གྲགས་ famous, well known
མེས་པོ་ 1. ancestor; 2. grandfather
དམག་དོན་ military, military affairs
དམག་ཕོགས་ military salary/pay
དམིགས་བསལ་ special(ly)
རྨོ་འོ་ grandmother
སྨད་ཆ་ the second of two parts in a book; later part of a lifetime
སྨན་དཔྱད་ medical examination, medical check-up; va. — བྱེད་
སྨོན་གྲོང་མཁྱེན་རབ་
ཀུན་བཟང་ p.n.
བཙས་ va. p. of བཙའ་
ཅོ་ཆུ་ urine and feces
རྩིས་ཁང་ revenue bureau in traditional Tibetan government
རྩིས་པ་ accountant, book-keeper

	in Tibetan Revenue Office
རྩིས་དཔོན་	one of the four heads of the Revenue Office
ཚེ་དབང་རྡོ་རྗེ་	p.n.
མཚན་	name (h.)
འཚར་ལོངས་	vi. growing up; vi. — བྱུང་
འཚོལ་འདོན་	searching and extracting, exploration and mining; va. — བྱེད་
མཛད་དཀའ་	difficulty, problem (h.)
མཛད་འཁུར་	responsibility (h.)
ཞབས་སྡོད་	government servant or official; va. — ཞུ་ to serve as a government official
ཞབས་བྲོ་	dance; va. — རྒྱག་
ཞིབ་འཕར་	abbr. འབབ་ཞིབ་འཕར་མ་
ཞེས་གྲགས་	vi. to be called
གཞུང་འབྲུ་	government grain/barley
གཞུང་ཞབས་	government official
གཞིས་རྩེ་	abbr. Shigatse
བཞད་མཐོང་སྨོན་	p.n. of a district
བཞུགས་ཡུལ་	place of residence (h.)
ཟུར་ཚུང་ཤེས་རབ་གྲགས་པ་	lineage of a Lama
གཟན་བརྟག་	divine lottery (rolling dough balls within which have been placed answers on a plate before a deity (statue). When one ball falls off the plate it is considered to have been chosen by the deity as the correct choice); va. — འདྲིལ་ or བསྒྲིལ་ to choose something by means of a divine lottery
གཟིགས་སྐྱོང་	taking care of, looking after (h.)
བཟང་ཕེབས་	vi. to be selected as the correct /best one by divine lottery
འོས་ཁོངས་	among the candidates
ཡག་ཙམ་	a little better
ཡང་ཅིན་	ch. a musical instrument called "yangjin"
ཡང་སྲིད་	reincarnation
ཡབ་གཞིས་	title of families who have provided Dalai Lamas
ཡིག་རྩིས་	knowledge (lit., letters and math)
ཡོངས་འཛིན་	teacher, tutor (of an incarnation) (h.)
རག་བི་	Rugby (a school in England)
རང་འཇགས་	as before, unchanged
རིག་གསར་	new science
རིམ་བཞི་	fourth rank official in traditional Tibetan government
རིམ་པར་	gradually, in series, in stages, one after another
རོལ་ཆ་	music; va. — གཏོང་
རྭ་སྒྲེང་	Reting (a monastery north of Lhasa)
རྭ་སྟག་	abbr. Reting and Takdra

ལག་རྟགས་ present, gift
ལག་རྩལ་ craft, dexterity, skill
ལམ་ལུགས་ way, system
ལས་ཁངས་ office
ལས་འགན་ task, responsbility, duty; va. — འཁུར་ or — བཞེས་
ལས་སྦྲེལ་ assistant, helper
ལས་ཟུར་ present and former holder of an office
ལུང་ཤར་ p.n.
ལེགས་ལྡན་ས་དེབ་ p.n.
ལོ་ན་ age; vi. — སོན་ to grow older
ལོན་ཀྲོན་ London
ཤུགས་རྐྱེན་ influence, effect; vi. — ཐེབས་
ཤེས་ཡོན་ knowledge, education
གཤམ་གསལ་ listed, presented, cited below
གཤེགས་ vi. to die (h.)
ས་གཏེར་ minerals
ས་ཐིག་ a demarcation line, boundary line
ས་གནས་སྲིད་གཞུང་ 1. local government; 2. the term that is used in the Tibet Autonomous Region for the traditional government of the Dalai Lamas
སེར་སྐྱ་ monks and laymen
སྲིད་སྐྱོང་ regent
སྲིད་འགན་ political responsibility; va. — བཞེས་
སྲིད་རྙིང་ abbr. of སྲིད་གཞུང་རྙིང་པ་: old government (i.e., the government before 1959)
སྲིད་བློན་ prime minister
སྲིད་དབང་ political power, secular power
སྲིད་གཞུང་ government
སྲིད་ཟུར་ ex-prime minister
གསུང་བབས་ in accordance with what was said
གསེར་ཁྲི་ golden throne
གསོ་བ་རིག་པ་ science of medicine
བསོད་ནམས་མགོན་པོ་ p.n.
བསླབས་ va. p. of སློབ་
ཧིན་དྷུ་ India, Hindu
ཧོ་ཐོག་ཐུ་ Hotoktu (highest rank of incarnations)
ཧོའོ་ཅིན་ ch. a musical instrument called "hojin"
ལྷ་ཀླུ་ p. n.
ལྷ་རབ་ best
ལྷད་ཁུད་པ་ p.n.
ལྷན་སྦྲེལ་ together (h.)
ལྷུན་གྲུབ་རྡོ་རྗེ་ p.n.
ཨི་ཀྲར་ལི་ Italy

PART THREE

Tibetan-English Glossary

The Glossary consists of all the words and grammatical particles used in the lessons. To enable this book to be used as a reference grammar, the lesson and section where each grammatically relevant particle is explained are included in the glossary entry. For example, ཙང་ is listed as *causal connective (5.9)*, the number in parenthesis indicating that the explanation of ཙང་'s usage can be found in Lesson 5, section 9.

Grammatically relevant constructions such as བའི་རྗེས་སུ་ are also included even though they really consist of two or more grammatically definable components: བ + འི་ + རྗེས་ + སུ་. Citing such constructions as units, i.e., under བའི་རྗེས་སུ་ as well as under the main particle རྗེས་, will ease the user's task of finding such compounds in the glossary.

Nouns that convey verbal meanings when used with verbalizing verbs (e.g. noun = a telephone; noun + གཏོང་ = verb = to telephone) will be listed in a single entry under the main noun. The following example illustrates this:

ཁ་པར་ telephone; va. — གཏོང་

ཁ་པར་ in this example is the noun "telephone." The verbal meaning "to telephone" (ཁ་པར་ གཏོང་) is indicated by listing the verbalizing verb (གཏོང་) after the meaning of the noun. The fomat of "va. — གཏོང་" breaks down as follows: "va." = active verb," the em dash (—) indicates the main entry. Verbal meanings such as "to telephone" will only be translated in cases where the meaning of the compound is not clear. In the above case, the meaning is self evident.

ཀ་	infinitive particle (5.15)
ཀ་མེད་	"no choice" (11.13)
ཀ་ལ་དབང་པོ་	p.n.
ཀུང་ཧྲེ་	ch. commune
ཀུན་	all, entire, every
ཀོ་ཐག་	leather rope
ཀོ་བ་	1. leather; 2. boat made from hide
ཀོང་ཏུང་	ch. Guangdong
ཀོང་པོ་	Kongpo (a region southeast of Lhasa)
ཀྱང་	1. also, even (4.6.4.7); 2. "even though" clause connective (7.2); 3. with གཅིག་ and negatives (7.14.1.4.2)
ཀྱང་...མ་ཐུབ་	see 9.17.2.3.2
ཀྱི་	1. genitive particle (5.14); 2. relative clauses (6.6.1.j.-ff)
ཀྱི་འདུག་	present tense complement (3.5)
ཀྱི་ཡིན་	see གི་ཡིན་
ཀྱི་ཡོད་(པ་) རེད་	present tense complement (3.5)
ཀྱི་རེད་	see གི་རེད་
ཀྱིན་འདུག་	present tense complement (3.5)

ཀྱིན་ཡོད་(པ་) རེད་ present tense complement (3.5)
ཀྱིས་ 1. instrumental particle (3.1); 2. adverbializer (6.5.2)
ཀྱོག་ཀྱོག་ crooked, zig-zag
ཀྲུང་གོ་ ch. China
ཀྲུང་དབྱང་ཨུ་ཡོན་ལྷན་ཁང་ ch. Central Committee
ཀྲུང་ཡོ་ ch. abbr. of ཀྲུང་གོ་དང་ཡོ་ནན་: China and Vietnam, Sino-Vietnamese
ཀྲུང་ཨུ་ ch. abbr. of ཀྲུང་ཨུ་ཚང་འཛོམས་གྲོས་ཚོགས་
ཀྲུང་ཨུ་ཚང་འཛོམས་གྲོས་ཚོགས་ ch. plenary session of the Central Committee
ཀྲུའུ་ཞི་ ch. chairman
ཀྲོང་ཀྲོང་ standing erect
ཀྲོང་རིགས་ p.n. of a nationality
ཀྲོན་ཆུས་ ch. prefecture (a current political unit equivalent to a province in traditional Tibet)
ཀྲའོ་ཙི་དབྱང་ p.n. Zhao Ziyang
ཀླ་ཀློ་ barbarian, savage
ཀླུའི་ཕོ་བྲང་ palace of ཀླུ་ (nāga)
ཀློག་ va. to read
དཀའ་ངལ་ sm. དཀའ་ལས་
དཀའ་བ་སྤྱད་ vi. p. of དཀའ་བ་སྤྱོད་
དཀའ་བ་སྤྱོད་ vi. to undergo hardship, difficulties
དཀའ་ཚེགས་ difficulties, hardships; vi. — སེལ་ to overcome difficulties
དཀའ་ལས་ difficulties, hardship, problems; vi. — ཁ་ to undergo difficulties, hardship, problems; to get tired
དཀར་ཆ་ light
དཀར་པོ་ white
དཀར་ཡོལ་གང་ one cup
དཀོན་(པོ་) rare, scarce
དཀོན་མཆོག་གསུམ་ the three precious things: the Buddha, the dharma, and the clergy
དཀྱིལ་ among, middle
ཀྲིག་ཙར་ doing something in a usual, regular or customary way
དཀྲིགས་བཙར་ sm. ཀྲིག་ཙར་
བཀག་ va. p. of འགོག་
བཀག་འགོག་ sm. བཀག་འདོམས་
བཀག་འདོམས་ prohibiting, stopping, blocking, obstructing; va. — བྱེད་
བཀབ་ va. p. of འགེབས་
བཀའ་སྒྲུབ་ following, obeying orders; va. — ཞུ་ or — བྱེད་
བཀའ་བརྒྱུད་པ་ the Kagyupa sect
བཀའ་གཏོང་ va. to summon, order to come
བཀའ་དྲིན་ kindness; va. — བྱེད་
བཀའ་འདྲི་ asking, questioning; va. — ཞུ་ (h.)
བཀའ་ཕབ་ va. p. of བཀའ་འབེབས་ (h.)
བཀའ་ཕེབ་ an order, instructions
བཀའ་ཕེབས་ vi. to have an order or instructions come or arrive
བཀའ་བློན་ member of the Council of Ministers in traditional Tibetan government
བཀའ་འབེབས་ va. to order, command (h.)

བཀའ་མོལ་	talk, conversation, discussion; va. — གནང་ (h.)
བཀའ་སྩོལ་	va. to give an order (h.)
བཀའ་བསྩལ་	va. p. of བཀའ་སྩོལ་
བཀའ་གཞིས་	estate given to a བཀའ་བློན་ while he is in office
བཀའ་ཤག་	the Council of Ministers in the traditional Tibetan government
བཀའ་སློབ་	advice (h.); va. — གནང་
བཀར་ཁང་	storehouse, warehouse, treasury
བཀལ་	va. p. of འགེལ་
བཀོག་	va. p. of འགོག་
བཀོད་	va. p. of འགོད་
བཀྲ་བ་	multicolored; beautiful, lovely, bright
བཀྲ་ཤིས་	p.n.
བཀྲམ་	va. to spread out, disseminate, disperse
བཀྲམས་	va. p. of བཀྲམ་
བཀྲིས་	abbr. of བཀྲ་ཤིས་
བཀྲིས་བདེ་ལེགས་	1. phrase used to convey congratulations; 2. phrase used as a greeting; va. — ཞུ་ to convey one's greetings or congratulations
བཀྲིས་ཞོལ་པ་	p.n. of an opera troupe
བཀྲིས་ལྷ་མོ་	p.n.
བཀྲེས་སྐོམ་	hunger and thirst
བཀྱོལ་	va. p. of འཁྱོལ་
བཀླགས་	va. p. of ཀློག་
རྐང་ལྕགས་	leg-irons, shackles, fetters
རྐང་མཐིལ་	sole (of foot)
རྐང་པ་	foot; leg
རྐང་བཙུགས་ནས་	purposely (8.10.3.21)

རྐུ་	va. to steal
རྐུ་མ་	thief; va. — རྐུ་ to steal
རྐུན་པོ་	thief
རྐོ་	va. to dig
རྐོ་མ་	pick axe
རྐྱང་	1. wild ass; 2. go right ahead construction: va. + རྐྱང་ (12.16); 3. noun or adj.+ — conveys "completely the nominal meaning" (11.20.2.3.17)
རྐྱང་རྐྱང་	only
རྐྱང་ཐང་སྒང་	p.n. of place near Lhasa
རྐྱལ་པ་	skin/leather bag
རྐྱེན་	"causal" clause connective (5.9)
རྐྱོང་	va. to stretch, extend (e.g., hand); to raise (hand)
ལྐུགས་པ་	idiot
སྐད་	1. noise, a shout, a yell; va. — རྒྱག་; 2. "it is said" particle (15.6)
སྐད་གྲགས་ (ལྡན་པ་)	famous
སྐད་སྒྱུར་	interpreter, translator
སྐད་ངན་	cry of anguish; va. — རྒྱག་
སྐད་ཅིག་	a moment, an instant
སྐད་ཅོར་	shouting, yelling; va. — རྒྱག་
སྐད་ཆ་	conversation, talk; va. — བཤད་
སྐད་གཏོང་	va. to invite
སྐད་བཏང་	va. p. of སྐད་གཏོང་
སྐད་གདངས་ལེགས་པ	a good voice
སྐད་ཡིག་	spoken and written language

སྐད་ཤུགས་ཆེན་པོ་	loud voice, loud noise
སྐད་གསང་(པོ་)	clear voice
སྐམ་རློན་	dry + wet; dampness
སྐབས་	1. "when" connective (5.10); 2. a time—e.g., with numbers, the xth time (སྐབས་བརྒྱད་པ་ = the eighth time something took place)
སྐབས་འགར་	sometimes, occasionally
སྐབས་ཅིག་	one time
སྐབས་ཤིག་ལ་	"at one time" verbal connective (16.2.3.3)
སྐལ་བཟང་རྒྱ་མཚོ་	p.n. of the 7th Dalai Lama
སྐུ་	body; statue (h.)
སྐུ་གམ་	in or at the presence of (h.)
སྐུ་གོང་མ་	the previous one (for positions, incarnations) (h.)
སྐུ་མགྲོན་	guest (h.)
སྐུ་ངོ་	old title of address for government officials (in Tibet)
སྐུ་ངོ་མ་	in person (h.)
སྐུ་ཆས་	things, belongings (h.)
སྐུ་བརྙན་	image, statue (h.)
སྐུ་དྲག་	nobility, aristocracy; noble, aristocrat (h.)
སྐུ་འཕྲེང་ལྔ་པ་	the fifth in a line of incarnations
སྐུ་ཚེ་	life (h.)
སྐུ་ཟླ་	spouse (h.)
སྐུ་གཟུགས་	body (h.)
སྐུ་གཟུགས་བདེ་པོ་ ཡིན་པས་	idiom. How are you? (h.)
སྐུ་རབ་པ་	p.n. (of an aristocratic family in Tibet)
སྐུ་གཤེགས་	vi. to die (h.)
སྐུ་སྲུང་	bodyguard
སྐུད་	va. to apply, put on (ointment, oil, etc.)
སྐེ་	neck, throat
སྐེ་ལ་ཤིང་སྒོ་ གཡོགས་པ་	neck cangues
སྐེད་པ་	waist
སྐོ་	va. to appoint, select
སྐོང་འགུག་	summon; va. — བྱེད་
སྐོམ་	vi. to be thirsty (usu. ཁ་སྐོམ་)
སྐོམ་པ་	thirst; thirsty person
སྐོར་	1. about, concerning (11.14); 2. va. to surround, encircle; to go around, circumambulate
སྐྱ་སེར་	laymen and monks
སྐྱག་རྫུན་	lie; va. — བཤད་
སྐྱབས་བཅོལ་བ་	refugee
སྐྱབས་འཇུག་	requesting help, asking for a favor; va. — ཞུ་ or — གནང་ (h.)
སྐྱིད་པོ་	happy, glad, enjoyable
སྐྱིད་སྡུག་པ་	p.n. (of an aristocratic family)
སྐྱིད་ཤོད་པ་	p.n. (of an aristocratic family)
སྐྱུག་	vi. to vomit
སྐྱེ་	1. vi. to grow; 2. vi. to be born
སྐྱེ་སྐར་	birthday
སྐྱེ་དམན་	woman, female
སྐྱེ་བ་	a lifetime
སྐྱེ་བ་སྔོན་མ་	a former life
སྐྱེ་བོ་	person, people, mankind
སྐྱེ་སྲིད་	reincarnation

སྐྱེད་ vi. to grow, increase, widen; also see འཕྱོད་པ་

སྐྱེད་མེད་ interest-free

སྐྱེས་པ་ man, male

སྐྱེལ་ 1. va. to deliver; 2. vi. to spend time

སྐྱེལ་འདྲེན་ transportation, shipping; va. — བྱེད་

སྐྱེས་ vi. p. of སྐྱེ་

སྐྱེས་སྐར་ birthday

སྐྱོ་གླུ་ song of sadness

སྐྱོ་པོ་ poor

སྐྱོང་ 1. va. to rule, govern; 2. va. to protect, take care of

སྐྱོད་ va. to go

སྐྱོན་ 1. mistake, defect, harm; vi. — ཤོར་ to get harmed/ damaged; 2. excessive particle (10.3.5)

སྐྱོན་བརྗོད་ criticism; va. — བྱེད་

སྐྱོབ་ va. to save, defend, protect; to rescue

སྐྱོབ་གསོ་ welfare; va. — སྤྲོད་ to give/provide welfare

སྐྱོར་ 1. va. to support, prop up; 2. "do it again" particle (14. 2)

སྐྱོར་མོ་ལུང་པ་ p.n. of Tibetan opera troupe

སྐྲ་ hair on head

སྐྲ་ལོ་ pleat (of hair)

སྐྲག་ vi. to be scared, afraid

བརྐོས་ va. p. of རྐོ་

བརྐྱངས་ va. p. of རྐྱོང་

བརྐྱངས་ཕྱག་ type of prostration where hands are completely stretched out in front of body; va. — འཚལ་

བསྐུར་ va. to send

བསྐུས་ va. p. of སྐུད་

བསྐོ་བཞག་ appointment (to a position, job); va. — བྱེད་ or གནང་

བསྐོང་ va. to summon, to order to come

བསྐོར་ va. p. of སྐོར་

བསྐོས་ va. p. of སྐོ་

བསྐྱངས་ va. p. of སྐྱོང་

བསྐྱབས་ va. p. of སྐྱོབ་

བསྐྱར་ 1. again; 2. vb. + — བྱེད་ to repeat, do again (15.7)

བསྐྱར་གསོ་ restoring, putting back in original form; va. — བྱེད་

བསྐྱལ་ va. p. of སྐྱེལ་

བསྐྱུར་ va. to give up, abandon, throw away

བསྐྱོད་ va. p. of སྐྱོད་

བསྐྲུན་ va. to publish

ཁ་ 1. mouth; 2. edge; 3. direction; 4. vi. to befall, to involuntarily happen

ཁ་སྐྱེངས་ embarrassed, ashamed

ཁ་ཁར་ quietly

ཁ་འགྲམ་ close (to)

ཁ་ངོམས་ vi. to get quenched (thirst)

ཁ་ཆག་ chipped, broken edge

ཁ་ཆེམས་ will, last testament

ཁ་འཆམ་ 1. agreement, consent; 2. also used as a verb: va. to agree upon

ཁ་ཏོན་ praying; va. — འདོན་

ཁ་བཏགས་ ceremonial scarf

ཁ་དན་ 1. oath, promise; 2. see ཞི་བདེའི་ཁ་དན་

ཁ་གདང་ va. to open one's mouth

ཁ་གདན་ rug

ཁ་འདོན་ praying; va. — བྱེད་

ཁ་བརྡུང་ verbal abuse; va. — གཏོང་

ཁ་པར་ telephone; va. — གཏོང་; — རྒྱག་

ཁ་ཕྱིར་གཙུ་ va. to turn one's body backward (e.g., to look at something), to reverse direction

ཁ་ཕྱིར་གཙུས་ va. p. of ཁ་ཕྱིར་གཙུ་

ཁ་ཕྱིར་སློག་ sm. ཁ་ཕྱིར་གཙུ་

ཁ་བ་ snow; vi. — བབས་

ཁ་བྲལ་ 1. separated, split up; 2. also used as a verb: vi. to become separated, split up, divorced

ཁ་ར་ཆི་ Karachi

ཁ་ལ་ཁར་ "about to" clause connective (7.11)

ཁ་ལག་ food

ཁ་ལེན་ approval, acceptance, acknowledgement; va. — བྱེད་

ཁ་ཤས་ several, a few

ཁ་ཤོ་ harelip; gap, rift

ཁ་གཤོག་ va. to split open, cleave

ཁ་གཤགས་ va. p. of ཁ་གཤོག་

ཁ་ས་ yesterday

ཁ་སང་ yesterday

ཁག་ pluralizing particle (10.15.2.3.16)

ཁག་བགོ་ va. to divide into sections, parts

ཁག་བགོས་ 1. va. p. of ཁག་བགོ་; 2..division, classification; va. — བྱེད་

ཁག་པོ་ 1. difficult; 2. with verbs, see 13.3

ཁང་པ་ house; va. — རྒྱག་ to build a house

ཁད་ see ལ་ཁད་ལ་

ཁམས་ p.n. of Eastern Tibet

ཁར་ 1. "about to" clause connective (7.11); 2. adjective conjunctive particle (10.3.7); 3. verbal clause connective (10.4.2)

ཁལ་ a standard Tibetan volume measure equal to about 25-30 lbs.

ཁལ་རྒྱབ་ a load

ཁལ་གཡག་ a carrying/transport yak

ཁས་བླངས་ va. p. of ཁས་ལེན་

ཁས་ལེན་ 1. a guarantee, promise; va. — བྱེད་; 2. also used as a verb: va. to guarantee, promise

ཁུང་བུ་ small hole

ཁུངས་འཛིན་ verification, authentication

ཁུངས་བཙན་ reliable, authentic

ཁུར་ va. p. of འཁུར་

ཁུལ་ 1. "pretend" particle (6.8); 2. region, area

ཁུལ་བྱས་ sm. ཁུལ་, 1

ཁེ་པོ་ cheap

ཁེ་བཟང་ profit

ཁེ་ལས་ commercial enterprise, business, company

ཁེངས་ vi. p. of འཁེངས་

ཁོ་ he

ཁོ་ན་ only

ཁོ་པ་ he

ཁོ་ཚོ་ they

ཁོག་ལྷིར་ teapot

ཁོང་ he (h.)

ཁོངས་ part of, belonging to

ཁོངས་འཕེར་ verification, authentication

ཁོང་ཁྲོ anger; vi. — ཟ་ to get angry

ཁོམ་ "time to do" particle (13.2)

ཁོའི་ his (he + gen.)

ཁོར་ to him (he + dat. loc.) (4.5)

ཁོས་ by him (he + instrumental) (3.1)

ཁྱག་ vi. to be/get cold

ཁྱད་དུ་གསོད་ va. to ignore, disdain, scorn, show contempt for

ཁྱད་དུ་བསད་ p. of ཁྱད་དུ་གསོད་

ཁྱད་པར་ difference

ཁྱད་པར་ཅན་ extraordinary

ཁྱབ་ vi. to spread, become widespread

ཁྱབ་ཁོངས་ area, region, field

ཁྱབ་ཆེ་ཤོས་ most widespread

ཁྱབ་བསྒྲགས་ announcement, notice; va. — བྱེད་

ཁྱབ་སྤེལ་ widespread, disseminated; vi. — (དུ་) འགྲོ་ to be widespread, widely disseminated; va. — གཏོང་

ཁྱར་ཁྱུར་ abbr. of ཁྱར་རེ་ཁྱུར་རེ་

ཁྱར་རེ་ཁྱུར་རེ་ unsteady, precarious, unstable

ཁྱི་ dog

ཁྱིམ་ home, household

ཁྱིམ་དུད་ family, household

ཁྱིམ་མཚེས་ neighbor

ཁྱིམ་འཛིན་མ་ housewife, female head of household

ཁྱིམ་གཞི་ property, wealth

ཁྱུ་ a herd/group of animals

ཁྱེད་ you (h.)

ཁྱེད་རང་ you (h.)

ཁྱེད་ཉིད་ you (h.)

ཁྱེར་ 1. va. p. of འཁྱེར་; 2. also sometimes used as non-past stem, va. to carry

ཁྱོད་ you

ཁྱོད་ར་ you

ཁྱོན་ all over, all (usu. of an area), all told (11.20.3.3.3)

ཁྱོན་ནས་ 1. emphatic negative adverb (9.9); 2. in double negative constructions (11.17)

ཁྲ་ལྷེམ་ལྷེམ་ glittering, sparkling

ཁྲག་ blood; vi. — འདོན་. to lose blood, to bleed

ཁྲག་རྣག་ blood and pus

ཁྲལ་ a tax, duty

ཁྲི་དགུ་དང་སྟོང་ཕྲག་དྲུག་ 96,000

ཁྲི་ 1. throne; 2. ten thousand

ཁྲི་གཅིག་ (one) 10,000

ཁྲི་སྟོང་ 10,000,000

ཁྲི་པ་ 1. chairman, head of a committee; 2. abbot of Ganden monastery

ཁྲི་ལོ་ year in the reign of a dynasty

ཁྲིམས་ law

ཁྲིམས་འགལ་ 1. illegal, in violation, a breach of the law; va. — བྱེད་ to violate, break the

	law; 2. vi. to be in violation of the law
ཁྲིད་	va. p. of འཁྲིད་
ཁྲིང་ཏུའུ་	ch. Chengtu (capital of Sichuan)
ཁྲེལ་གད་	jeering, sarcasm, ridicule; va. — བྱེད་ to jeer, laugh at, ridicule; 2. also used by itself as an active verb
ཁྲེལ་ཀོད་	sm. ཁྲེལ་གད་
ཁྲོད་	among, in the midst of
ཁྲོན་སྐྱོགས་	ladle used at a well
ཁྲོན་པ་	a well
ཁྲོན་བོད་	Sichuan-Tibet
ཁྲོམ་	market
ཁྲོམ་གཞུང་	main street; business section
ཁྲོམ་ར་	market, marketplace
མཁན་	"agentive" particle (5.16); 2. future particle (5.16 g)
མཁན་པོ་	abbot
མཁའ་དབྱིངས་	sky
མཁའ་རླུང་	air; atmosphere
མཁའ་རླུང་སླབ་པོ་	thin/rarefied air
མཁར་རྔ་	gong
མཁར་འབོ་	volume measure equal to about 25-30 lbs.
མཁས་པ་	an expert
མཁས་པོ་	expert
མཁས་དབང་	authorities
མཁོ་སྒྲོད་	supplies; va. — བྱེད་
མཁྱེན་	va. to know (h.)
མཁྱེན་རྟོག་	understanding, knowing (h.)
མཁྲིགས་བཟུང་	persistence; va. — བྱེད་
འཁར་བ་	walking stick, cane
འཁུར་	va. to carry, to shoulder
འཁེངས་	vi. to be full (with)
འཁེལ་	vi. to occur, to involuntarily get, to fall on (a date)
འཁོད་	vi. to be written
འཁོར་	1. vi. to spontaneously get (an idea, thought); 2. retinue, attendant; 2. vi. to return, come back (15.8.3.4)
འཁོལ་	vi. to be/get boiled
འཁྱག་ཀླུང་	ice field, glacier
འཁྱག་པ་	ice
འཁྱུད་	va. to embrace, hug
འཁྱེར་	va. to carry, take (inanimate objects)
འཁྱེར་སོ་	demeanor, bearing, manner, way
འཁྲབ་	va. to act, perform
འཁྲབ་སྟོན་	performance of a play or entertainment, presentation
འཁྲབ་གཞུང་	script (story) of a play
འཁྲིད་	1. va. to lead, to guide; 2. va. to take
འཁྲུག་རྐྱེན་	provocation, challenge, incitement; va. — སློང་
འཁྲུག་པོ་	lively, active
འཁྲུངས་	va. to give birth (h.)
འཁྲུད་	va. to wash; to brush (teeth)
འཁྲུལ་མེད་	genuine, true, real
ག་	1. "try to" particle (11.19); 2. infinitive particle (5.15)
ག་གི་	which
ག་དུས་	when (2.9)
ག་འདྲ་	how (2.9)
ག་འདྲ་ཞིག་	what kind (2.9; 5.17.4.5)
ག་ན་	where (2.9)
ག་ནས་	1. from where (2.9); 2. "how could" (12.13)

ག་ནས་་འགྲིག་ (འགྲིགས་)	"how could that be okay?" (9.17.1.3.21)
ག་པར་	1. where (2.9); 2. "how could" (12.13)
ག་བྱེད་	vb. + — try to do (11.19).
ག་བྱེད་འདི་བྱེད་མེད་པར་གྱུར	id., "came into a state in which there was nothing that could be done" (11.20.1.3.21)
ག་ཚད་	how much (2.9)
ག་ཚོད་	how much (2.9)
ག་རུ་	where (2.9)
ག་རེ	what (2.9)
ག་རེ་རེད་ཟེར་ན་	if you ask what it is (11.20.3.3.1)
ག་ལ་	1.where (2.9); 2. "how could" (11.3)
ག་ལ་འགྲིག་(ས་)	"how can it be okay?" (11.2)
ག་ལ་ཡོད་	"how can it be okay?" (11.2)
ག་ལ་རུང་	"how can it be okay?" (11.2)
ག་ལ་ཕོད་	"how could one dare?" (11.3 d,e,f)
ག་ས་ག་ལ་	everywhere
གང་	1. what (2.9); 2. one (7.14.1.4.2; 10.15.1.3.7) 3. — + adj. stem: "as x as possible" (11.20.2.3.16)
གང་གི་ཆ་ནས་	by all means, in all respects (12.6)
གང་གི་ཐད་ནས་	by all means, in all respects (12.6)
གང་གི་ཕྱོགས་ནས་	by all means, in all respects (12.6)
གང་གིས་སྙེ་ན་	why (12.9)
གང་ཅི་	lots of ways (12.5)
གང་དགོས་	whatever is needed
གང་ཅིའི་ཐད་ནས་	by all means, in all respects (12.6)
གང་ཅིའི་ཕྱོགས་ནས་	by all means, in all respects (12.6)
གང་ཐད་ནས་	by all means, in all respects (12.6)
གང་ཐུབ་བྱེད་	va. (vb. + —) to do as much as one can regarding the verbal action (Appendix C, #1.)
གང་དང་ཅི་	"lots of ways" construction (12.5)
གང་དུ་	where (2.9)
གང་དྲག་	"it's a pity" construction (12.11)
གང་འདྲ་ཞིག་	"what kind of" construction (12.4)
གང་ན་	where (2.9)
གང་ན་ཅི་ཡོད་	""whatever exists" construction (12.17)
གང་ནས་	from where (2.9)
གང་ཙམ་	1. how much (2.9); 2. however much (14.9)
གང་ཙམ་ནས་	after some time (དུས་ཡུན་ + —)
གང་ཞིག་དྲག་	sm. གང་དྲག་
གང་ཟབ་	sm. གང་གཟབ་
གང་གཟབ་	as good as possible
གང་ཡང་	emphatic negative adverb (9.9)
གང་ཡིན་ཅི་ན་	"why" construction (12.9)
གང་ཡིན་ཟེར་ན་	"why" construction (12.9)
གང་ཡོད་	1. where something is/exists; 2. རྒྱུ་ + — "what is the reason for?" (11.5)
གང་ལ་	where (2.9)

གང་ས་ནས་	"lots of ways," "by all means" construction (12.6)
གང་སར་	everywhere, all over
གངས་	snow; vi. — འབབ་
གད་མོ་	a laugh, laughing; va. — དགོད་
གན་རྒྱ་	written agreement, contract; va. — འཛོག་ to sign an agreement or contract
གབ་	va. to hide
གམ་	1. question particle (2.9c); 2. "or" particle (8.6); 3. presence
གར་	where (2.9)
གར་སོང་མེད་པ་	disappearing, vanishing (13.5.3.23)
གལ་	important
གལ་ཏེ་—ན་	"if" clause connective (6.1)
གལ་ཏེ་—ཚེ་	"if" clause connective (6.1)
གལ་སྲིད་—ན་	"if" clause connective (6.1)
གལ་སྲིད་—ཚེ་	"if" clause connective (6.1)
གས་	question particle (2.6)
གི་	genitive particle, see ཀྱི་ (5.14)
གི་འདུག་	present tense complement (see ཀྱི་འདུག་)
གི་ཡིན་	future tense complement (3.7)
གི་ཡོད་པ་རེད་	present tense complement (see བགྱི་ཡོད་པ་རེད་)
གི་རེད་	future tense complement (see ཀྱི་རེད་)(3.7)
གིས་	1. instrumental particle (3.1); 2. adverbializer (6.5.2; 6.6.3 d)
གུ་ཐུང་	pants
གུང་ཐང་ལྷ་མོ་	the Gungtang goddess (located at Gungtang near Lhasa)
གུང་ཁྲན་ཏང་	ch. the communist party
གུང་ཁྲན་རིང་ལུགས་	communism
གུང་གསེང་	holiday
གུས་	1. respect, reverence; 2. humble term for "I"
གུས་བཏུད་	respect; reverence; va. — ཞུ་ (h.)
གུས་འདུད་	respect, reverence va. — ཞུ་ (h.)
གུས་ཕྱག་	respect, reverence
གུས་བརྩི་	respect and love; va. — བྱེད་; — གནང་
གུས་ཞབས་	respect, reverence
གོ་	1. vi. to hear; 2. vi. to understand; 3. nineties particle (8.1)
གོ་སྐབས་	opportunity
གོ་ཐོས་	1. hearing; 2. vi. to hear
གོ་བསྡུར་	consultation, discussion; va. — བྱེད
གོ་གནས་	rank, position
གོ་མིན་ཏང་	ch. Kuomintang
གོག་པོ་	old, beat-up
གོང་	1. price; 2. "before" clause connective (7.4)
གོང་བ་	collar
གོང་མ་	emperor
གོང་ཚད་	price or rate level
གོང་གསལ་	as is clear above
གོན་	va. to wear
གོམ་	step

གོམ་པ་	a step, a stride; va. — རྒྱག་ or — བྱེད་ to walk
གོམ་ཞེང་	width, size of a step or stride
གོམས་གཤིས་	habits, customs
གོས་ལོག་	clothing
གྱ་	eighties particle (8.1)
གྱར་	vi. to get, fall into (a situation or state)
གྱི་	see ཀྱི་ (5.14)
གྱིས་	1. see གིས་ (3.1; 6.5.2; 6.6.3 d); 2. va. p. of བགྱིད་ (9.17.1.3.26)
གྱུར་	vi. p. of འགྱུར་
གྱེན་	uphill, upwards
གྱོན་	va. to dress, put on clothes
གྱོན་ཆས་	clothes
གྱོན་ནས་	1. emphatic negative adverb ("never") (9.9); 2. in double negative constructions (11.17)
གྲྭ་པ་	monk
གྲྭ་ཆས་	monk's clothing/robes
གྲ་རྒྱས་	elaborate preparations; va. — བྱེད་
གྲ་སྒྲིག་	preparations; va. — བྱེད
གྲང་	cold
གྲང་ངར་	cold
གྲང་མོ་	cold
གྲངས་ཉུང་མི་རིགས་	minority nationality
གྲངས་འབོར་	quantity, number, amount
གྲངས་ཚད་	quantity, number, rate
གྲབས་	1. "about to" clause connective (7.11); 2. "prepare to do" (11.20.2.3.13)
གྲབས་བྱེད་	"about to" clause connective (7.11)
གྲམ་པ་	river shore, bank
གྲལ་སྒྲིག་	1. arranging into rows; 2. va. to line up, to arrange in rows
གྲལ་བསྒྲིགས་	va. p. of གྲལ་སྒྲིག་
གྲལ་སྣར་	row, line
གྲལ་འཛིན་	va. to arrange the seating at monk's prayer ceremony
གྲལ་རིམ་	class (socio-political)
གྲས་	kind, class, type, sort
གྲུ་	boat
གྲུ་ཁ་	harbor, port, ferry landing, wharf, shipyard
གྲུ་གཟིངས་	ship, boat
གྲུང་ཤ་དོད་པོ་	alert, lively, active
གྲུབ་	1. the "completed" auxiliary verb (9.8); 2. vi. to obtain, achieve
གྲུབ་ཐོབ་	a great yogin, siddhi
གྲུབ་འབྲས་	achievement, result, accomplishment
གྲུ་བཞི་	square
གྲོ་	wheat
གྲོ་ཞིབ་	flour (from wheat)
གྲོག་རོག་	ravine
གྲོག་རོང་	gully, gorge
གྲོགས་པོ་	friend
གྲོང་ཁྱེར་	city, town
གྲོང་བརྡལ་	a town
གྲོང་ཚོ་	village, town
གྲོང་གསེབ་	village
གྲོང་གསེབ་པ་	villager
གྲོངས་	vi. to die

གྲོད་ཁོག་ stomach; vi. — ལྟོགས་ to be hungry

གྲོད་པ་ stomach; vi. — རྒྱགས་ to be full/satisfied (for food)

གྲོལ་ vi. to be over/let out (class/meeting)

གྲོས་འཆམ་ (འཆམས)་ agreement, resolution (usu. one that is adopted at a meeting); va. — བྱེད་

གྲོས་མཐུན་ agreement

གྲོས་བསྡུར་ discussion; talk; va. — བྱེད་

གྲོས་མོལ་ discussion; va. — བྱེད་

གླ་ va. to hire, rent

གླ་ཆ་ wage

གླ་ཤ་ beef

གླང་མདུན་ p.n.

གླས་ va. p. of གླ་

གླས་པ་ hired person or thing

གླིང་བསྐོར་ outer circumambulation road in Lhasa

གླུ་ song; va. — གཏོང་

གླུ་གར་ song and dance

གླུ་གར་བ་ song and dance performer

གླུ་གར་ཚོགས་པ་ musical association, dance troupe

གླིང་ཕྱོགས་ public opinion

གློ་བུར་དུ་ sudden(ly) (6.5.5)

གློག་ electricity; va. — འདོན་- to generate electricity

གློག་སྐུད་ electric wire, electric cable

གློག་འཁྱུགས་ lightning

གློག་རྒྱུན་ electric current

གློག་སྒུལ་ electrically operated

གློག་བརྙན་ movie

གློག་འདོན་འཕྲུལ་འཁོར་ electric generator; va. — གཏོང་

གློག་སྤྱོད་ electricity use

གློག་འཕྲིན་ cable, telegram

གློག་ཤུ་ electric light, electricty; flashlight

གློད་ 1. va. to release, let go; 2. va. — གཏོང་

དགག་པ་ rebuttal; va. — རྒྱག་

དགའ་ vi. to like

དགའ་མཆོངས་ jumping for joy; va. — རྒྱག་

དགའ་ཐག་ཆོད་ being extraordinarily happy

དགའ་ལྡན་ཁྲི་པ་ head abbot of Ganden monastery

དགའ་ལྡན་ཕོ་བྲང་ name of the traditional Tibctan government

དགའ་སྣང་ happiness

དགའ་པོ་ like

དགའ་སྤྲོ་ happiness

དགའ་ཚོར་ happy

དགའ་ཞེན་ love and loyalty; va. — ཞུ་

དགའ་བསུ་ welcoming, va. — ཞུ་

དགུ་ nine

དགུ་ཁྲི་ 90,000

དགུ་བརྒྱ་ 900

དགུ་བརྒྱ་དང་བརྒྱད་ཅུ་གྱ་བདུན་ 987

དགུ་བཅུ་ 90

དགུ་སྟོང་ 9,000

དགུ་པ་ ninth

དགུ་འབུམ་ 900,000

དགུང་གྲངས་ age (h.)

དགུང་ལོ་ age (h.)

དགུན་ཁ་ winter

དགེ་རྒན་ teacher

དགེ་འདུན་ monk (h.)

དགེ་འདུན་ཆོས་

འཕེལ་ p.n.
དགེ་བ་ཡོང་ vi. to get, obtain merit
དགེ་མཚན་ advantages, good points, benefits
དགེ་ལུགས་པ་ Gelugpa (sect)
དགེ་སློབ་ abbr. teacher and student
དགོང་མོ་ night
དགོངས་ va. to think (h.)
དགོངས་ཁྲོལ་ permission (h.)
དགོངས་འཆར་ suggestion, opinion; va. — གསུང་ or གནང་ (h.)
དགོངས་པ་ thought (h.)
དགོངས་པ་ཞུ་ va. to resign, to take a leave of absence
དགོངས་ཞུ་ taking leave, resigning; va. — གནང་
དགོད་ va. to laugh
དགོད་སྒྲ་ sound of laughing
དགོན་སྡེ་ monastery
དགོན་པ་ monastery
དགོན་རུལ་ ruins of a monastery
དགོས་ 1. va. to have to, want to, need to (7.5); 2. used in conjunction with active verbs (7.5.2; 7.5.6)
དགོས་མཁོ་ need, necessity; va. — སྐོང་ to fill a need
དགྲ་བོ་ enemy
དགྲ་ཤ་ revenge; va. — ལེན་
བགྱི་འདུག་ present tense complement (3.5)
བགྱི་ཡོད་པ་རེད་ present tense complement (3.5)
བགྱིད་ va. to do
བགྲེས་སོང་ older person (h.)
མགུལ་ neck, throat
མགོ་ head
མགོ་སྐོར་ tricking, deceiving; va. — གཏོང་
མགོ་འཁོར་ vi. to be fooled, be deceived
མགོ་སྒུར་ bowing down, surrendering
མགོ་མཇུག་ head and tail
མགོ་མཇུག་ལྡོག་ va. to overthrow, to topple, to turn upside down
མགོ་བོ་ head
མགོ་རྩུགས་ sm. འགོ་རྩུགས་
མགྱོགས་མྱུར་ quickness, quickly
མགྱོགས་པོ་ quick, quickly
མགྲིན་གཅིག་ with one voice, unanimously
མགྲིན་དབྱངས་ voice
མགྲོན་ཁང་ hotel, guest house
འགག་མེད་ without obstacle/hindrance/impediment
འགན་ཁུར་ 1. responsibilty; 2. va. p. of འགན་འཁུར་
འགན་འཁུར་ va. to take responsibility
འགན་ལེན་ guarantee, pledge; va. — བྱེད་
འགམས་ va. to eat tsamba
འགའ་ཞིག་ several
འགའ་ཤས་ several
འགལ་རྐྱེན་ unfavorable condition, obstruction, hindrance; va. — བཟོ་ to obstruct, hinder
འགལ་ 1. vi. to be contrary, to contradict, violate; 2. vi. to exceed, to be beyond/over a limit
འགལ་བ་ contradiction
འགུལ་ va. to move, shake
འགུལ་སྐྱོད་ moving, shaking; vi. — ཐེབས་ to be moved,

shaken

འགེབས་ va. to put on, to cover

འགེལ་དཀྲི་ loading, imposing, putting on; va. — བྱེད་

འགེལ་ཡུལ་ place to put on, impose

འགོ་འཁྲིད་ leader

འགོ་གཙོ་ headman, foreman

འགོ་བཙུགས་ va. p. of འགོ་འཛུགས་

འགོ་ཚུགས་ vi. to begin, to get started

འགོ་འཛུགས་ va. to begin, start; to found

འགོག་ va. to block, obstruct, ban; to break

འགོག་རྐྱེན་ obstacle, barrier, hindrance; va. — བཟོ་ or — གཏོང་

འགོག་རྒོལ་ resistance; va. — བྱེད་

འགོད་ 1. va. to record, write down, sign; 2. va. to draw up, formulate a plan; 3. va. to put in, insert

འགོར་ vi. to elapse, pass (of time) (14.8.3.1)

འགྱིང་ཉམས་ dignity

འགྱུར་ vi. to become, change into (6.5.3; 10.9)

འགྱུར་ལྡོག་ a change

འགྱེད་ money given as gift/alms to monks; va. — རྒྱག་; va.— གཏོང་

འགྱེད་སྐལ་ monk's share of money given as alms to monks

འགྱེལ་ 1. vi. to faint; 2. vi. to fall; 3. to collapse

འགྱོད་པ་ regret; vi. — སྐྱེད་ to feel regret

འགྱོད་བཤགས་ repentance, repenting; va.— བྱེད་

འགྲན་ va. to compete

འགྲན་བསྡུར་ competition, match; va. — བྱེད་

འགྲམ་དུ་ near (usu. noun + genitive + —)

འགྲམ་པ་ cheek, jaw

འགྲིག་མིན་ whether it's all right or not

འགྲིགས་ vi. to be all right, okay

འགྲུབ་ vi. to achieve, fulfill, complete

འགྲིམ་ va. to travel

འགྲིམ་འགྲུལ་ communications, traffic

འགྲུལ་པ་ traveler, passenger

འགྲུལ་བཞུད་ traveling, traffic

འགྲེ་ལོག་ tumbling, rolling over; va. — རྒྱག་

འགྲོ་ 1. va. to go (5.7.1); 2. with adjectives (10.3.2); 3. with other verbs. (13.5.3.14); 4. in simultaneous constructions (8.10.3.19)

འགྲོ་བསྐྱོད་ going

འགྲོ་སྐྱོད་ movement

འགྲོ་བ་བཟང་མོ་ p.n. of an opera and character in the opera

འགྲོ་ལམ་ road (to go on); way

འགྲོ་སོང་ expenses; va. — གཏོང་ to pay or meet expenses

འགྲོགས་ va. to associate with, to have a close relationship with

འགྲོལ་ 1. vi. to untie, set loose, undo knots; 2. vi. to set free, release, liberate

རྒད་པོ་ old man

རྒན་ཁོག་ (—འཁོགས་, —གོག་) old person

རྒན་རྒོན་ old person

རྒན་རྒོན་གཉིས་	old couple
རྒན་པ་	an elder; a headman
རྒན་རབས་	previous generations (elders)
རྒལ་	va. to cross/pass over (rivers, etc.)
རྒུལ་ཊ་ས་ཧེབ་	Gould (Basil) Sahib
རྒོད་	vulture
རྒོལ་ལན་	counter attack, retaliation attack
རྒྱ་སྐྱེད་	expansion; va. — སྐྱེད་
རྒྱ་ཁྱོན་	area, size
རྒྱ་གར་	India
རྒྱ་དངུལ་	Chinese silver
རྒྱ་ཆེ་	larger, more extensive
རྒྱ་ཆེན་པོ་	large, spacious, expansive
རྒྱ་ནག་	China
རྒྱ་བོད་	China-Tibet, Chinese-Tibetan
རྒྱ་མ་	1/2 a kilogram (in Chinese this measure is called *jin)* (10.15.1.3.7)
རྒྱ་མི་	Chinese person, a Han
རྒྱ་མོ་དངུལ་ཆུ་	Salween River
རྒྱ་མཚོ་	ocean
རྒྱ་མཚོའི་ངོས་ལས་ མཐོ་ཚད་སྨི་	meters above sea level
རྒྱ་བཟའ་ཀོང་ཇོ་	the Chinese bride of king Srongtsen gambo
རྒྱ་བཟའ་ བལ་བཟའ་	p.n. of an opera
རྒྱ་རིགས་	Chinese person, Han
རྒྱག་	va. auxiliary verb (build; shoot; do) (5.6)
རྒྱག་ཚད་	a lot, enough; satiating (of food)
རྒྱང་དཀར་བ་	p.n. of an opera troupe
རྒྱངས་	va. to stuff, fill up, cram in

རྒྱངས་ཤེལ་	telescope, binoculars
རྒྱན་	va. to adorn, decorate
རྒྱན་མཆོར་	ornament, decoration
རྒྱབ་	1. va. p. of རྒྱག་ (5.6); 2. behind (5.17.4.10)
རྒྱབ་སྐྱོར་	support; va. — བྱེད་
རྒྱབ་ཏུ་	the back side, on the back
རྒྱབ་ཙ་	one who stands behind giving support
རྒྱབ་རི་	the hill behind something
རྒྱལ་ཁ་	victory, success
རྒྱལ་ཁབ་	nation
རྒྱལ་གླུ་	national anthem
རྒྱལ་པོ་	king
རྒྱལ་པོའི་སྲས་མོ་	princess
རྒྱལ་རྩེ་	p.n. of a town in Tibet (Gyantse)
རྒྱལ་ཚབ་	regent
རྒྱལ་མཚམས་	international border
རྒྱལ་ཟུར་	ex-regent
རྒྱལ་ཡོངས་	nationwide, national
རྒྱལ་རབས་	history
རྒྱལ་ས་	capital
རྒྱལ་སྲས་	prince
རྒྱལ་སྲིད་	state affairs, government
རྒྱས་	vi. to flourish, thrive, increase
རྒྱས་འཛོམས་	plenary session, full or large session/meeting
རྒྱུ་	1. nominalizing particle (6.7); 2. future tense particle (6.7.1); 3. "should not" construction particle (12.3); 4. va. to string, put into a hole
རྒྱུ་མཚན་	reason
རྒྱུ་གང་ཡོད་	"what is there to be" construction (11.5)

རྒྱུ་ནོར་	wealth, riches, property
རྒྱུ་དབང་	wealth and power
རྒྱུ་འབྲས་	cause and effect
རྒྱུ་མཚན་	reason
རྒྱུག་	va. to run
རྒྱུག་ཁྱི་	id. running dog
རྒྱུག་འགྲོའི་བྱེ་མ་	shifting sand desert
རྒྱུགས་	sm. རྒྱུག་
རྒྱུད་	edge, side, bank, shore
རྒྱུན་དུ་	always, at all times, continuously
རྒྱུན་ནས་	1. emphatic negative adverb (9.9); 2. in double negative constructions (11.17)
རྒྱུན་རིང་	long time
རྒྱུའི་ཆེད་དུ་	"purposive" connective (5.13)
སྒང་	1. on, on top of, in addition to (8.9); 2. at the point/time of, when (5.10)
སྒམ་	box
སྒར་	va. to attach (e.g., a handle)
སྒལ་	the back of a person, animal
སྒུག་	va. to wait
སྒུག་སྡོད་	staying waiting; va. — བྱེད་
སྒུལ་	va. to move, shake
སྒེའུ་ཁུང་	window
སྒེར་	private, personal
སྒེར་གྱིས་བདག་གཉེར་	private management
སྒེར་པ་	noble family, aristocrat
སྒོ་	door
སྒོ་རྟགས་	house number
སྒོ་ནས་	adverbializer (in the manner of, by means of) (6.5.1)
སྒོག་མཁར་བ་བསོད་ནམས་མགོན་པོ་	p.n.
སྒོར་	dollar, rupee
སྒྱིད་ལུག་	lazy; va. — བྱེད་ to act/be lazy
སྒྱུ་རྩལ་འཁྲབ་	va. to do an artistic performance
སྒྱུར་	va. to change, transform, alter
སྒྱེ་	sack
སྒྱེ་མོ་	bag, sack
སྒྲ་	sound
སྒྲ་སྐད་	sound, voice
སྒྲ་ལེན་འཕྲུལ་འཁོར་	radio
སྒྲིག་	va. to arrange, set up, put in order
སྒྲིག་འཛུགས་	organization
སྒྲིག་གཞི་	structure, way something is organized, composition
སྒྲིག་ལམ་	discipline, law and order
སྒྲིག་གཤོམ་	erecting for exhibition, displaying, showing; va. — བྱེད་
སྒྲིབ་	va. to cover, to conceal
སྒྲིལ་	va. to roll up; to wind up
སྒྲུག་	va. to pick up, to collect/gather
སྒྲུང་	story
སྒྲུང་གཏམ་	folklore, tale
སྒྲུབ་	va. to achieve, accomplish, obtain, fulfill
སྒྲོག་	va. to shout, call out
སྒྲོན་	1. va. to put on; 2. to set/lay out; 3. to build (h.)
སྒྲོན་མེ་	lamp
སྒྲོལ་མ་ཕུག་	p.n.
བརྒྱ་ཆ་	percent

བརྒྱ་ཆ་གཅིག་	one percent
བརྒྱ་ཆ་གཉིས་	two percent
བརྒྱ་ཆ་བཅུ་	ten percent
བརྒྱ་ཆ་ལྔ་བཅུ་	fifty percent
བརྒྱ་(ཐམ་པ་)	100
བརྒྱ་དང་བརྒྱད་	108
བརྒྱངས་	va. p. of རྒྱངས་
བརྒྱད་ཁྲི་	80,000
བརྒྱད་ཁྲི་ལྔ་སྟོང་ དྲུག་བརྒྱ་དགུ་བཅུ་ གོ་ལྔ་	85,695
བརྒྱད་བརྒྱ་	800
བརྒྱད་ཅུ་	eight
བརྒྱད་ཆ་ལྔ་	five eighths
བརྒྱད་སྟོང་	8,000
བརྒྱད་པ་	eighth
བརྒྱད་པར་	(at) eight o'clock
བརྒྱད་འབུམ་	800,000
བརྒྱན་	va. p. of རྒྱན་
བརྒྱབ་	va. p. of རྒྱག་, same as རྒྱབ་
བརྒྱུད་	via, through
བརྒྱུད་རིམ་	sequence of events
བརྒྱུས་	va. p. of རྒྱུ་
བསྒར་	va. p. of སྒར་
བསྒུགས་	va. p. of སྒུག་
བསྒྱུར་	va. p. of སྒྱུར་
བསྒྱུར་བཅོས་	change, reform, transformation; va. — བྱེད་ to change, to reform, to transform; vi.— འགྱུར་ to be reformed, to be transformed
བསྒྲིགས་	va. p. of སྒྲིག་
བསྒྲིབས་	va. p. of སྒྲིབ་
བསྒྲིལ་	va. p. of སྒྲིལ་
བསྒྲུག་	va. f. of སྒྲུག་
བསྒྲུགས་	va. p. of བསྒྲུག་
བསྒྲུབ་	va. f. of སྒྲུབ་
བསྒྲུབས་	va. p. of སྒྲུབ་
བསྒྲོན་	va. p. of སྒྲོན་ (h.)
བསྒྲོགས་	va. p. of སྒྲོག་
ང་	1. I; 2. fifties particle (8.1)
ང་ཚོ་	we
ང་རང་	I (myself)
ང་རོ་	a roar; va. — སྒྲོག
ངག་འཇམ་ཚིག་མཁས་	id. speaking smoothly and cleverly (9.17.1.3.15)
ངང་གིས་	gradually, slowly
ངང་(ནས་)	adverbializer (in the manner of) (6.5.1)
ངང་པ་	1. swan; 2. yellowish color, cream color
ངན་	bad, evil
ངན་པ་	bad, evil
ངན་འབྲེལ་	conspiring, plotting, collaborating (for evil)
ངན་རོགས་	cohort, accomplice (pejorative)
ངན་ལན་སློག་	id. to respond to evil
ངན་ལན་བསློགས་	va. p. of ངན་ལན་སློག་
ངན་སེམས་	evil-mindedness, cruelty, meanness
ངམ་རིང་	p.n. of a district in west Tibet
ངའི་	my (i + gen.)
ངར་	1. to me (i + dat. loc.); 2. violent, volatile, fierce
ངར་སྐད་	a shout, roar, yell
ངར་མ་	strong, powerful, vigorous
ངལ་དུབ་	tired
ངལ་བ་	difficulty, hardship; va. — བཟོད་ to tolerate or to

	endure difficulties/ hardships
ངལ་རྩོལ་	manual labor, hard work; va. — བྱེད་
ངལ་རྩོལ་མི་དམངས་	laboring/working people
ངས་	by me (i + inst.)
ངུ་	va. to cry
ངུས་	va. p. of ངུ་
ངེས་	1. certainty particle (7.8; 15.8.3.3) , 2. vi. to be certain (15.8.1., note 3)
ངེས་པར་དུ་	certainly, surely, definitely
ངེས་པ་མེད་	uncertain, unpredictable
ངོ་རྒོལ་	opposing, struggling against; va. — བྱེད་
ངོ་གདོང་	face
ངོ་སྤྲོད་	introduction to people or topics; va. — བྱེད་
ངོ་མ་	in person
ངོ་ཚ་བ་	embarrassed
ངོ་མཚར་ཅན་	wonderous, miraculous
ངོ་ལོག་	rebellion, uprising; va. — རྒྱག་
ངོ་ལོག་རྒྱབ་གཏོད་	treason; va. — བྱེད་
ངོ་ཤེས་པ་	acquaintance
ངོམས་	va. to show off
ངོས་	side, direction
ངོས་འཛིན་	recognition, acceptance, identification
དངངས་སྐྲག་	fright, dread
དངངས་འཚབ་	fright, dread, panic
དངུལ་	silver; money
དངུལ་ཁང་	bank
དངོས་གནས་	really
དངོས་འབྲེལ་	really
དངོས་གཞི་	really
དངོས་སུ་	really, truly, actually
མངའ་ཁོངས་	territory belonging to or subject to a polity
མངའ་རིས་	area in W. Tibet
མངའ་གསོལ་	enthronement
མངར་མོ་	sweet
མངོན་	vi. to become visible, evident; to appear
རྔ་	drums
རྔན་པ་	gift, present, tip
རྔམ་བརྗིད་	majestic, splendid, grand
རྔུལ་ཆུ་	sweat, perspiration
རྔོན་པ་	hunter
ལྔ་	five
ལྔ་ཁྲི་	50,000
ལྔ་བརྒྱ་	500
ལྔ་བཅུ་	50
ལྔ་ཆ་གཉིས་	two fifths
ལྔ་ཆ་བཞི་	four fifths
ལྔ་སྟོང་	5,000
ལྔ་པ་	fifth
ལྔ་འབུམ་	500,000
སྔ་རྗེས་ (སྔ་)	1. at different times; 2. one after the other (lit., before and after)
སྔ་དྲོ་	morning
སྔ་པོ་	early
སྔ་སྨིན་	early ripening; — འབྲས་ early ripening paddy
སྔ་གཡར་	an advance, a short-term loan
སྔ་ལོ་	last year
སྔར་	formerly, in the past
སྔར་ལས་	than before, than in the past
སྔར་རྒྱུན་ (སྔར་)	like before
སྔར་བཞིན་	like before
སྔོ་ཚལ་	vegetable

སྔོན་ཆད་ formerly, in the past
སྔོན་དུ་ formerly, in the past
སྔོན་པོ་ blue
སྔོན་མ་ formerly, in the past
བསྔགས་བརྗོད་ praise; va. — བྱེད་
ཅ་ལག་ things
ཅང་ཤིང་ ch. name of commune
ཅན་ having, possessing, adjective particle (10.3.6)
ཅི་ what (2.9)
ཅི་...འདི་... མེད་པར་ nothing left to do or say (10.15.1.3.16).
ཅི་དྲག་ "it's a pity" construction (12.11)
ཅི་འདྲ་ཞིག་ "what kind of" construction (12.4)
ཅི་ནས་ཀྱང་ by all means, in all ways
ཅི་ཕྱིར་ why (8.10.3.7)
ཅི་བྱ་གཏོལ་མེད་ helpless, without a viable alternative, stymied; vi. — འགྱུར་
ཅི་མ་རུང་ how nice (15.8.3.6)
ཅི་ཙམ་ how much (2.9)
ཅི་ཞིག་དྲག་ "it's a pity" construction (12.11)
ཅི་ལ་ཟེར་ན་ "why" construction (12.9)
ཅི་གསུང་བཀའ་སྒྲུབ་ willingly accepting instruction/orders, obedient
ཅིག་ 1. a, one (2.6.1); 2. imperative particle (3.2.1; 9.17.1.3.33)
ཅིང་ 1. verbal conjunctive connective (5.12); 2. with adjectives (10.3.7); 3. ch. name of a minority group in S. China
ཅིའི་ཕྱིར་ཞེས་ན་ "why" construction (12.9)
ཅིས་ཤེ་ན་ "why" construction (12.9)
ཅུང་ཟད་ a little, a few, slightly
ཅེ་རེ་ see མིག་ཅེ་རེ་
ཅེས་ quotation marker (4.4)
གཅིག་ one; a (2.6.1)
གཅིག་ཁྲི་ 10,000
གཅིག་གྱུར་ unification, unity
གཅིག་ཕྱོགས་ combined (15.8.3.12)
གཅིག་མཇུག་གཉིས་མཐུད་ one after another
གཅིག་རྗེས་གཉིས་མཐུད་ one after another
གཅིག་སྟོང་ 1,000
གཅིག་པུར་ alone
གཅིག་པོ་ alone
གཅིན་པ་ urine; va. — གཏོང་
གཅུང་པ་ p.n. of an opera troupe
གཅུང་པོ་དོན་ཡོད་དོན་གྲུབ་ p.n. of an opera
གཅུས་ va. to turn
གཅེས་སྐྱོང་ taking care of, protecting; defending; va. — བྱེད་
གཅེས་པར་སྐྱོང་ va. to look after, take care of
གཅེས་པར་བསྐྱངས་ va. p. of གཅེས་པར་སྐྱོང་
གཅོང་ནད་ chronic disease
གཅོག་ 1. va. to break; 2. va. to pat (e.g., a shoulder or head)
གཅོད་ va. to cut
བཅག་ va. p. of གཅོག་
བཅངས་ va. p. of འཆང་
བཅད་ va. p of གཅོད་

བཅར་ va. to go to meet someone of high status (h.)
བཅས་ 1. enumerative particle (6.4); 2. along with (6.4 f)
བཅས་པའི་ including (6.4.d)
བཅིངས་འགྲོལ་ liberation; va. — གཏོང་
བཅུ་ ten
བཅུ་དགུ་ nineteen
བཅུ་གཅིག་ eleven
བཅུ་གཅིག་པ་ eleventh
བཅུ་གཉིས་ twelve
བཅུ་གཉིས་པ་ twelfth
བཅུ་དྲུག་ sixteen
བཅུ་བདུན་ seventeen
བཅུ་པ་ tenth
བཅུ་མིད་ ten's place in a number (8.1)
བཅུ་བཞི་ fourteen
བཅུ་གསུམ་ thirteen
བཅུག་ va. p. of འཇུག་
བཅོ་ལྔ་ fifteen
བཅོ་ལྔ་མཆོད་པ་ butter sculpture offering ritual—done on the fifteenth of the first Tibetan month in Lhasa
བཅོ་བརྒྱད་ eighteen
བཅོམ་ va. to loot, plunder
བཅོས་ va. to make, create
བཅོས་བསྒྱུར་ reforming, transforming; va. — གཏོང་
ལྕགས་ iron
ལྕགས་ཁབ་ iron needle
ལྕགས་ཁྱི་ iron-dog year
ལྕགས་ཐག་ཟམ་པ་ iron-link chain bridge
ལྕགས་པོ་རི་ p.n. of hill (near Potala palace in Lhasa)
ལྕགས་སྦྲུལ་ iron-snake (year)
ལྕགས་རིགས་ metal
ལྕགས་ལམ་ railroad
ལྕགས་ལུག་ iron-sheep (year)
ལྕོག་ལྕོག་ nod
ཆ་ 1. pair; match; 2. fraction particle (8.3)
ཆ་རྐྱེན་ conditions, circumstances, facilities
ཆ་འཛོག་ abiding by; va. — བྱེད་
ཆ་སྙོམས་ average, on the average
ཆ་ནས་མཚོན་ན་ "hypothetical" construction (14.4; 15.8.3.11)
ཆ་པ་རུ་ཟུར་ p.n. of a family
ཆ་ཚང་ complete; all
ཆ་བཞག་ན་ "hypothetical" construction (14.4)
ཆ་ལུགས་ style of dress, costume, fashion
ཆག་སྒོ་ calamity, catastrophe, misfortune; va. — འཕྲད་ to meet misfortune, calamity, catastrophe
ཆག་ཡང་ concession, reduction; va. — གཏོང་; — གནང་
ཆགས་ vi. to become, change into
ཆང་ beer
ཆང་ཁང་ bar, tavern
ཆང་ས་ marriage; va. — རྒྱག་
ཆད་ 1.vi. to be short of, to be missing an amount; 2. vi. to stop raining/ snowing
ཆན་ཝ་ ch. kilowatts
ཆབ་སྲིད་ politics, political
ཆབས་ཅིག་ "together with" clause connective (7.9)
ཆབས་སྦྲགས་ "together with" clause connective (7.9)

ཆར་པ་	rain; vi. — གཏོང་
ཆས་གོས་	costumes, clothes, garments
ཆིག་སྟོང་	1,000
ཆིག་འབུམ་	100,000
ཆིང་གོང་མ་	Ch'ing Emperor
ཆིངས་འགྲིགས་	arbitration, mediation, intervention
ཆིངས་དངུལ་	indemnity
ཆུ་	water
ཆུ་བཀག་གཏོང་	va. to cut off (a/the) water supply
ཆུ་འཁོལ་	vi. to be boiled (water)
ཆུ་གློག་	hydroelectric
ཆུ་གློག་ས་ཚིགས་	hydroelectric station
ཆུ་རྒྱུན་	the flow of rivers, current
ཆུ་འདྲེན་	va. to irrigate
ཆུ་འདྲེན་ས་ཁུལ་	irrigated area
ཆུ་སྤྲེ་	water-monkey (year)
ཆུ་བྱ་	water-bird (year)
ཆུ་བྱི་	water-mouse (year)
ཆུ་འབྲས་	irrigated paddy (rice)
ཆུ་དམར་	Chumar River
ཆུ་ཚོད་	watch, clock
ཆུ་མཛོད་	reservoir, dam
ཆུ་ཞག་	watering of the eyes; vi. — འཁོར་ to have one's eyes water or tear
ཆུ་ཤུལ་	p.n. of a place south of Lhasa
ཆུང་ངུ་	small
ཆུང་ཆུང་	small
ཆུང་བ་	younger; smaller
ཆེ་ཆུང་	size
ཆེ་གྲས་	large-scale, big, high ranking
ཆེ་བ་	older; bigger
ཆེ་ཙམ་	a little bigger
ཆེ་རིགས་	larger type/kind
ཆེ་རུ་	+ vb. = increase (make or become bigger)
ཆེ་ཤོས་	biggest; most
ཆེད་ (དུ་)	1. purposive connective (5.13); 2. before verbs (14.7)
ཆེད་མངགས་	specially, exclusively
ཆེད་བསྐུལ་	special appeal
ཆེད་དོན་	special
ཆེད་ལས་ཡོན་ཏན་	special knowledge; professional study
ཆེན་པོ་	1. big; 2. for use as adjectivizer, see 10.3.6
ཆེམ་ཆེམ་	glittering
ཆེས་	very (for use with adjectives, see 10.3.3)
ཆེས་ཆེར་	very much; much bigger
ཆོ་	sense
ཆོག་	1. ready to do (11.11); 2. to allow (11.9); 3."I will do" (11.10)
ཆོག་ཆོག་	ready to do (11.11)
ཆོག་མཆན་	approval, authorization, sanction; va. — བཀོད་ to approve, authorize, endorse, sanction
ཆོད་གཏམ་	thesis
ཆོས་དད་	religious faith, religion
ཆོད་དོན་	decision, resolution
ཆོས་	religion
ཆོས་འཁོར་རྒྱལ་	p.n. of a place northeast of Lhasa
ཆོས་རྒྱལ་ནོར་བཟང་	p.n. of an opera
ཆོས་ལྡན་	p.n.
ཆོས་པ་	religious person
ཆོས་ར་	debating area in a monastery

ཆོས་ལུགས་	a religion; religious doctrine
ཆོས་བཤད་	va. to give religious teachings
ཆོས་གསུང་	va. to give religious teachings (h.)
ཆོས་སྲིད་ལུགས་གཉིས་	the traditional political system that combined religious and secular interests
མཆི་མ་	tears; vi. — གཏོང་
མཆིས་	existential verb, same as ཡོད་པ་རེད་
མཆེ་གཙིགས་སྡེར་བགྲད་	id. baring fangs and claws
མཆོངས་	va. to jump
མཆོངས་རྒྱུག་	jumping and running
མཆོད་	va. to eat (h.)
མཆོད་མཇལ་	religious visit; va. — ཞུ་ to make a visit to a temple or monastery (to make offerings)
མཆོད་གཞིས་	monastic estate
འཆང་	va. to hold, to keep in mind
འཆར་གཞི་	plan; va. — འགོད་ to make a plan
འཆི་	vi. to die
ཇ་	tea
ཇ་རོ་	used tea leaves
ཇ་སྲུབ་མ་	Tibetan style tea (with butter and salt churned in)
ཇི་ལྟ་བུ་	sm. ཇི་ལྟར་
ཇི་ལྟར་	1. like what (10.14); 2. how to do (11.20.1.3.19)
ཇི་འདྲ་ཞིག་	"what kind of" construction (12.4)
ཇི་མ་ཇི་བཞིན་	exactly what it was (15.8.3.10)
ཇི་ཙམ་	how much (2.9)
ཇུས་	planning particle (14.6)
ཇེ་	more (for use with adjectives, see 10.3.3)
ཇེ་...ཇེ་	more (for use with adjectives, see 10.3.3)
ཇོ་བོ་	1. Jo (the Buddha); 2. the famous statue of the Buddha in the Lhasa Cathedral (Jokang)
ཇོ་བོ་དབུ་སྐྲ་	a place (at the main door of the Cathedral)
ཇོ་བོ་མི་བསྐྱོད་རྡོ་རྗེ་	Jo Akshobhya
ཇོ་བོ་ཤཀྱ་མུ་ནེ་	Jo Shakyamuni
མཇལ་	va. to meet (h.)
མཇལ་འཕྲད་	meeting; va. — གནང་ (h.)
མཇུག་	the end, the last
འཇགས་	vi. to calm down, settle down
འཇམ་དཔལ་དབྱངས་	Manjusri
འཇིག་རྟེན་	the external, physical world
འཇིག་རྟེན་མི་རྣམས་	human beings
འཇིགས་བསྐུལ་	intimidating, threatening; va. — བྱེད་
འཇིགས་རྫམས་དགོད་སྒྲ་	the sound of a frightening laugh
འཇིགས་སུ་རུང་བ་	scary, frightening
འཛུ་	va. to hold, to catch
འཛུག་	1. va. to put in, insert into, to recruit (11.7.1); 2. to "let" or "allow" (11.8)
འཛུས་	p. of འཛུ་
འཛོག་	va. to leave something, to put something down

འཛོན་ཐང་	capability
རྗེ་ཙོང་ཁ་པ་	p.n. of the founder of the Gelugpa sect
རྗེས་	1. temporal connective (4.3); 2. after
རྗེས་འདེད་	chasing, pursuing; va. — གཏོང་
རྗེས་སྒྲིལ་	depending on; based on
ལྗང་པ་	a sprout; a plant
བརྗིད་ཉམས་ལྡན་པ་	grand, splendid, magnificent
བརྗེ་འཕྱུལ་	mistakenly exchanged; vi. — ཤོར་, ཐེབས་
བརྗེད་	vi. to forget
བརྗོད་ན་	see 7.14.2.4.2
ཉ་	fish
ཉ་ཤ་	fish meat
ཉག་གཅིག་	certainly, surely (with verbs see 15.3 c)
ཉན་	1. fit/worthy particle (9.15); 2. va. to listen
ཉམ་ཐག་	misery, misfortune
ཉམས་	elegance, charm, dignity; va. — བྱེད་
ཉམས་བཟང་ལྡན་	elegant, dignified, stylish
ཉམས་གསོ་	repairing; va. — བྱེད་
ཉར་	va. to keep
ཉལ་	va. to lie down to sleep
ཉལ་གཟན་	blanket
ཉི་མ་	the sun; a day
ཉི་མ་བཞུད་	vi. to set (the sun)
ཉི་འོད་	sunlight; vi. — ཕོག་ to shine on something (sunlight)
ཉི་ཤུ་	twenty
ཉིད་དུ་	"as soon as" clause connective (6.2)
ཉིན་	day
ཉིན་གང་	all day

ཉིན་གུང་	noon
ཉིན་སྟར་(ལྟར)	every day
ཉིན་མོ་	daytime
ཉིན་མཚན་	day + night = all the time
ཉིན་ཞག་	twenty-four-hour day; day and night
ཉིན་ཤས་	several days
ཉིས་ཁྲི་	20,000
ཉིས་བརྒྱ་	200
ཉིས་བརྒྱ་དང་ལྔ་བཅུ་ང་དྲུག་	256
ཉིས་སྟོང་	2,000
ཉིས་འབུམ་	200,000
ཉུང་ཉུང་	few, small amount
ཉུང་ཤས་	a few
ཉུང་ཤོས་	least
ཉེ་	"about to/close to" clause connective (7.11)
ཉེ་འགྲམ་	close
ཉེ་བ་	close
ཉེ་བའི་སྐབས་སུ་	close to the time of (11.20.1.3.16)
ཉེན་	"danger of" clause connective (9.5)
ཉེན་ཁ་	danger
ཉེར་	"about to" clause connective (7.11)
ཉེས་	va. to beat, hit
ཉེས་ཆད་	punishment; va.— གཅོད་ to punish
ཉེས་བརྡུང་	beating; va. — གཏོང་
ཉེས་པ་	punishment, va. — གཏོང་
ཉོ་	va. to buy
ཉོ་ཆ་	shopping; va. — རྒྱག་
ཉོལ་	va. imp. of ཉལ་
ཉོས་	va. p. of ཉོ་

ཉ་རིལ་	calf (of leg)
གཉལ་	p.n. of a place
གཉིད་ཁུག་	vi. to fall asleep
གཉིད་ལ་ཤོར་	vi. to fall asleep
གཉིས་	two
གཉིས་ཀ་	two together
གཉིས་པ་	second
གཉིས་པོ་	the two together
གཉེན་སྒྲིག་	marriage; va. — བྱེད་
གཉེན་སྒྲིག་བག་སྟོན་	marriage celebration
གཉེན་ཚན་	relative
མཉམ་དུ་	together (see 7.9)
མཉམ་འབྲེལ་	cooperative
མཉམ་བཞེས་	cooperation (h.); va. — གནང་
མཉམ་ལས་	cooperation, cooperative labor; va. — བྱེད་
མཉེས་པོ་	like (h.)
རྙི་	a trap, snare; va. — རྒྱག་
རྙིང་གཏོར་གསར་འཛུགས་	slogan: "Destroy the old, start the new"
རྙིང་པ་	old
རྙིང་མ་	old (in the sense of an antique)
རྙེད་	vi. to find, to discover
རྙོག་འཛིང་ཆེ་བ་	complicated, intricate, difficult
རྙོགས་དྲ་	trouble, problem, disturbance; va. — བཟོ་ or བཤད་ to cause problems, troubles
སྙན་གྲགས་	fame
སྙན་ཞུ་	report, petition; va. — ཞུ་; — འབུལ་
སྙན་པོ་	interesting
སྙན་སེང་	report, petition; va. — ཞུ་
སྙམ་	va. to think
སྙིང་	heart
སྙིང་གྲོགས་	bosom friend
སྙིང་རྗེ་	compassion
སྙིང་གདམ་	secrets, innermost feelings, thoughts
སྙིང་སྟོབས་	courage
སྙིང་ནད་	heart disease
སྙིང་རུས་	diligence, fortitude; va. — བསྐྱེད་
སྨྱུ་གུ་	pen
སྙུང་	vi. to get sick (h.)
སྙོབ་	va. to reach by stretching out hand or foot
བརྙན་འཕྲིན་	television
བརྙས་བཅོས་	bullying; va. — གཏོང་ or བྱེད་
བསྙེགས་	va. to pursue, run after
དཱ་ལའི་བླ་མ་	Dalai Lama
དག་དག་	exactly, precisely
དང་	ch. party (political)
དང་མི་	party member
དང་ལང་	tanglang (a sound)
དུང་ཞིང་	ch. p.n. of ethnic group
དན་ཧྲི་	ch. television
དར་	telegram, cable; va. — གཏོང་
དུ་	see ཏུ་
དེ་	gerundive connective (5.11)
དོག་ཙམ་	1. a little; 2. for use with adjectives, see 10.3.3
གདད་	va. p. of གདོད་
གདན་འཁེལ་	va. to decide
གདན་ནས་	1. emphatic negative adverb (9.9); 2. in double negative constructions (11.17)
གདན་འབེབས་	settled, decided

གཏན་ཚིགས་
མཁར་རྫ་ a volume measure weighing about 25 to 30 pounds for barley
གཏམ་ news; talk, conversation; proverb
གཏམ་གླེང་ conversation, discussion; va. — བྱེད་
གཏམ་བཟང་ good news
གཏམ་བཤད་ speech, talk; va. — བྱེད་
གཏིང་ depth
གཏིང་ཟབ་ deep and profound
གཏིང་ཟབ་པོ་ deep
གཏུག་ va. to meet, reach, touch, join
གཏུགས་ va. p. of གཏུག་
གཏུམ་དྲག་ fierce, savage, violent
གཏེར་ཁ་ a mine
གཏོང་ va. to send (5.6)
གཏོད་ 1. va. to aim at, face towards, direct towards; 2. va. to hand over, give
གཏོར་ va. to destroy, demolish
གཏོར་བཤིག་ destroying, destruction; va. — གཏོང་
གཏོར་བཤིག་པ་ saboteur
བཏགས་ va. p. of འདོགས་; 2. va. to grind
བཏང་ va. p. of གཏོང་
བཏང་ཡིག་ letter (correspondence)
བཏབ་ va. p. of འདེབས་ (see ལན་ —)
བཏིངས་ va. p. of འདིངས་
བཏེགས་ va. p. of འདེགས་
བཏོན་ va. p. of འདོན་
རྟ་ horse
རྟ་སྒ་ saddle
རྟ་ལྕག་ horsewhip
རྟ་དྲེལ་ horses and mules
རྟ་ནག་ p.n. of a place in Tsang area
རྟ་དམག་ mounted troops, cavalry
རྟ་རྨིག་ hoof of horse
རྟག་ཏུ་ always
རྟག་པར་ always
རྟགས་མཚན་
མཚོན་ vi. to express/show a sign or symbol, to symbolize
རྟགས་མཚན་ sm. རྟགས་མཚན་མཚོན་
རྟེན་སྐལ་ dowry
རྟེན་འབྲེལ་ ceremony, celebration; omen
རྟེན་འབྲེལ་གྱི་
སྨོན་འདུན་ good wishes offered at a celebration (e.g.,"best of luck, long life"); va. — ཞུ་
རྟེན་གཞི་ base
རྟོག་ vi. to understand, comprehend; to perceive
རྟོག་ཞིབ་ inspection; va. — བྱེད་
རྟོགས་ 1. understanding, comprehension; 2. vi. p. of རྟོག་
ལྟ་ va. to look
ལྟ་སྐོར་ sightseeing, touring; a tour; visit; va. — བྱེད་
ལྟ་སྐྱོང་ looking after, caring for; va. — བྱེད་
ལྟ་ཅི་ "let alone/far from" clause connective (9.3)
ལྟ་བ་ conceited
ལྟ་བུ་ similar, like, as (7.14.1.4.4)
ལྟ་ཚུལ་ viewpoint
ལྟ་བཞག་ "let alone/far from" clause connective (9.3)

ལྟད་མོ་ a show
ལྟར་ similar, like, as , in accordance with (7.14.1.4.4; 7.14.1.4.8; 11.20.1.3.17)
ལྟར་བྱས་ just like, as, like (9.17.2.3.1)
ལྟར་བྱས་ནས་ sm. ལྟར་བྱས་
ལྟོ་སྐལ་ share of food
ལྟོ་ཆས་ food
ལྟོགས་ vi. to be hungry; see གྲོད་ཁོག་
ལྟོགས་ཤི་ starving to death; vi. — ཐེབས་ to starve to death
ལྟོས་པར་ see མ་ལྟོས་པར་
སྟ་རེ་ axe
སྟག་ tiger
སྟག་བྲག་ 1. p.n. of a monastery near Lhasa; 2. p.n. of the incarnation who was regent in Tibet from 1941-1950
སྟག་འཚེར་ p.n. of a place in Amdo
སྟག་ལུང་ p.n. of a place northeast of Lhasa
སྟངས་ manner particle (9.12)
སྟབས་ causal connective (5.9)
སྟབས་བདེ་པོ་ simple, convenient (9.17.1.3.14)
སྟབས་མི་བདེ་བ་ inconvenient, unfortunate (9.17.1.3.14)
སྟབས་བསྟུན་ see དང་ (7.10)
སྟབས་ལེགས་པ་ཞིག་ལ་ fortunately
སྟར་ཁ་ walnut
སྟར་སྡོང་ walnut tree
སྟར་པ་ line, row
སྟུག་པོ་ thick
སྟེ་ gerundive connective (5.11; 5.17.4.7)
སྟེང་ on, on top of; the upper part
སྟེང་གི་བཀོད་པ་ superstructure
སྟེར་ va. to give
སྟོང་པ་ empty
སྟོང་ཕྲག་གཅིག་ one thousand
སྟོད་ 1. p.n. of Far Western Tibet; 2. the upper, higher part
སྟོད་མངའ་རིས་ p.n. of Far Western Tibet
སྟོད་ལུང་ p.n. of a place near Lhasa
སྟོན་ va. to show
སྟོན་ཐོག་ crop
སྟོན་དུས་ autumn
སྟོན་བསྡུ་ autumn harvest; va. — བྱེད་
སྟོན་པ་ a religious teacher; the Buddha
སྟོན་མོ་ banquet, feast
སྟོབས་ power, strength
སྟོབས་ཤུགས་ power, strength
བརྟག་དཔྱད་ study, research, examination; va. — བྱེད་
བརྟག་ཞིབ་ inspection; va. — བྱེད་
བརྟན་པོ་ firmly
བརྟན་སྲུང་ defence; va. — བྱེད་
བརྟེན་ 1. because (5.9); 2. with the dat.-loc. + — + ནས་ = basing/based on, depending on
བལྟ་ va. fut. of ལྟ་
བལྟས་ va. p. of བལྟ་
བསྟན་ va. p. of སྟོན་
བསྟན་པ་ the doctrine or teaching of the Buddha
བསྟན་འཛིན་སྒྲོལ་དཀར་ p.n.

བསྟན་སྲིད་ religion and politics, dual government

བསྟར་ va. to put into practice

བསྟུད་ va. to do successively, in succession, repeatedly

བསྟུད་མ་ successively, one after another, repeatedly

བསྟུན་ 1. "together with" clause connective (7.9); 2. "according to" clause connective (7.10); 3. in accordance with (8.7; 11.20.2.3.19)

བསྟུན་ནས་ see བསྟུན་

བསྟུམ་ va. to cover; to wrap

བསྟུམས་ va. p. of བསྟུམ་

བསྟེན་ va. to study with a teacher; to check with a doctor

བསྟོད་ར་ praise; va. — གཏོང་

ཐ་སྙད་ terminology; technical term

ཐ་ན་ "even" particle (11.6)

ཐ་མག་ cigarette; va. — འཐེན་ to smoke

ཐ་ལི་མུ་གཞོང་ས་ Tarim Basin

ཐག་ཆོད་ 1. used with adjectives: "very," "extremely" (7.6); 2. vi. to be decided

ཐག་ཉེ་ near, close

ཐག་རིང་ distant, far

ཐང་ཆད་ vi. to be tired, fatigued

ཐང་ཤིང་ pine tree; fir tree

ཐད་ 1. about, concerning (11.14); 2. by means of (12.6)

ཐན་ abbr. of ཐན་པ་

ཐན་པ་ drought

ཐན་སྐྱོན་ drought damage

ཐན་འགོག་ drought prevention

ཐབ་ stove; fireplace

ཐབས་ means, way, methods particle (9.1)

ཐབས་བྲལ་ "no choice," "no way" (11.13)

ཐབས་མེད་ "no choice," "no way" (11.13)

ཐམ་པ་ hundreds particle (8.1)

ཐམས་ཅད་ all

ཐབས་ཤེས་ means, method

ཐར་ vi. to escape, to get free

ཐལ་ vi. too much or too fast (14.3)

ཐལ་མོ་ palm of the hand; va. — སྦྱར་ or འགོད་ to clasp one's hands together in a show of respect or devotion

ཐལ་འཚུབ་ dust storm

ཐིགས་པ་ a drop (of a liquid);. vi. — རྒྱག་ to drip

ཐིང་ཐིང་ completely (with respect to a color) (8.10.3.14)

ཐུག་ va. to meet; to reach

ཐུག་པ་ stew, porridge

ཐུག་ལྷག་ left over porridge, stew

ཐུག་འཕྲད་ meeting; va. — བྱེད་

ཐུགས་ mind (h.)

ཐུགས་ཁྲལ་ worry; va. — གནང་ (h.)

ཐུགས་འཁུར་ concern, care; va. — བཞེས་ or གནང་

ཐུགས་འགན་ responsibility; va. — སྐྱོང་ or བཞེས་ (h.)

ཐུགས་རྗེ་ཆེ་ thank you

ཐུགས་སྣང་ impression, feeling, sensation (h.)

ཐུགས་སྐྱོ་ party (for entertainment) (h.)

ཐུང་ཐུང་ short

ཐུབ་ — 1. vi. to be able to do (6.9); 2. with ཀྱང་ + neg. see ཀྱང་མ་ཐུབ་

ཐུབ་བསྟན་འཇམ་དཔལ་ཡེ་ཤེས་ — p.n. of Reting Rinpoche

ཐུར་མ་ — spoon

ཐེ་ཇུས་ — interference; va. — བྱེད་

ཐེ་ཚོམ་ — doubt

ཐེངས་ — time (as in "one time"); with numbers, the xth time (ཐེངས་བརྒྱད་པ་ = the eighth time something took place)

ཐེབས་ — vi. to get hit, struck by; to undergo; to reach

ཐེར་འདོན་ — exposing, laying bare; va. — བྱེད་

ཐོ་ — list; va.— རྒྱག་ to make a list, to record

ཐོག་ — 1. the "on" function (12.1.1); 2. the "via" function (12.1.2); 3. the "in addition to" function (12.1.3); 4. the "when" function (12.1.4); 5. the "concerning" function (12.1.5); 6. lightning; 7. roof (15.8.3.8)

ཐོག་མཐའ་བར་གསུམ་ — at all times, from beginning to end

ཐོག་ནས་ — from on top (of)

ཐོག་མ་ — first, beginning, start

ཐོག་མར་ — initially, at the beginning

ཐོངས་ — va. imp. of གཏོང་

ཐོད་ — above, over

ཐོན་ — 1. vi. to be produced, get (as in a yield); 2. va. to depart, leave; 3. to graduate (a school)

ཐོན་སྐྱེད་ — production; va. — བྱེད་

ཐོན་ཚད་ — production level

ཐོབ་ — 1. vi. to win; 2. vi. to get, obtain

ཐོབ་ཤོར་ — winning and losing

ཐོབས་ — va. imp. of འདེབས་

ཐོས་ — vi. to hear

མཐའ་འཁོབ་ — wilderness, boondocks

མཐའ་དག་ — all, every

མཐར་ — finally, at last, in the end (11.20.1.3.15)

མཐུ་མེད་ — "no choice" (11.13)

མཐུ་རྩལ་ — competition of strength; va. — འགྲན་

མཐུག་པོ་ — thick

མཐུན་ — see དང་མཐུན་པ་

མཐུན་རྐྱེན་ — resources

མཐུན་སྒྲིལ་ — unity

མཐུན་མིན་ — not in harmony, incompatible, disagreement

མཐོ་གནོན་ — high tension, high pressure

མཐོ་གནོན་གློག་སྐུད་ — high tension electric wire/cable

མཐོ་པོ་ — high

མཐོ་དམན་ — high + low; height

མཐོ་ཚད་ — height

མཐོ་རིམ་ — high level

མཐོང་ — vi. to see

མཐོང་ས་ — field of vision, place where something is seen (9.17.1.3.26)

མཐོངས་ — opening, gap, hole

མཐོན་པོ་	high
འཐབ་	va. to fight
འཐམ་	va. to hug, embrace
འཐམས་	va. p. of འཐམ་
འཐབ་རྩོད་	a physical struggle; fighting; va. — བྱེད་
འཐིབས་	vi. to be cloudy, overcast
འཐུ་	va. to gather, collect, pick
འཐུང་	va. to drink
འཐུང་ཆུ་	drinking water
འཐུས་	1. vi. to be approved, to be agreed; 2. p. of འཐུ་; 3. approve/agree constructions (11.12)
འཐུས་མི་	delegate
འཐེན་	1. see ཐ་མག་; 2. va. to pull; to drag
འཐོར་	vi. to become scattered, dispersed
ད་	now
ད་ཆ་	now
ད་ལྟ་	now
ད་དུང་	still (4.6.4.9)
ད་ནི་	now
ད་བར་	until now
ད་རང་	this morning
ད་རེས་	this time
ད་ལོ་	this year
དག་	plural particle (3.2.2)
དག་པོ་	good quality, unblemished
དང་	1. and; 2. see པ་དང་; 3. polite verbal imperative (7.12); 4. conjunction of adjectives (10.3.7); 5. with (8.7)
དང་བཅས་ (དེ་)(པ་)	along with, together with (6.4. e-h)
དང་ཆབས་ཅིག་	"together with" clause connective (7.9)
དང་མཉམ་དུ་	"together with" clause connective (7.9)
དང་སྦྲགས་བསྟུན་	1. according to , in accordance with (7.10); 2. "coincidental" construction (8.8)
དང་བསྟུན	according to, in accordance with (7.10; 8.7; (11.20.2.3.19)
དང་མཐུན་པ་	compatible with (8.7)
དང་འདྲ་བ་	similar to (with) (8.7)
དང་ལྡན་པ་	possessing, having (8.7)
དང་པོ་	first
དང་བླངས་	sm. དང་ལེན་
དང་འབྲེལ་	1. related to, joined with (8.7); 2. "together with" connnective (7.9)s
དང་སྦྲགས་	see སྦྲགས་
དང་མི་འདྲ་བ་	dissimilar to (with) (8.7)
དང་ལེན་	voluntarily, volunteering; va. — བྱེད་ or ཞུ་
དང་ལྷན་རྒྱས་	together with (h.)
དྭང་བླངས་	see དང་ལེན་
དད་གུས་	faith and respect; reverence
དད་པ་	faith
དམ་	1. question particle (1.11); 2. "or" particle (8.6)
དམ་བཅའ་	oath; va. — འཇོག་ to take an oath
དམ་པ་	the late, the deceased
དམ་པོ་	tight, close
དམ་པའི་ཆོས་	the dharma
དར་ཆ་	flag

དར་ཆ་དམར་པོ་གསུམ་	the "Three Red Flags": the Great Leap Forward, the people's commune, and the Socialist Main Line
དར་ཞིང་རྒྱས་པ་	flourishing, prosperous
དལ་རྟེན་མི་ལུས་	human life
དལ་ཞོལ་ལི་	p.n.
དལ་པོ་	slow
དུ་	see ཏུ་
དུ་མ་	many
དུག་	poison
དུང་	conch shell
དུང་ཕྱུར་གཅིག་	100,000,000
དུང་ཕྱུར་བཅུ་	1,000,000,000
དུད་འགྲོ་	animal
དུད་ཚང་	family
དུམ་བུ་	part, portion, piece, section
དུས་	1. "when" connective (5.10); 2. time
དུས་སྐབས་	time, period, era
དུས་འགྱུར་	a change
དུས་ཆེན་	festival, holiday, occasion
དུས་གཏན་དུ་	permanently
དུས་སྟོན་	holiday, festival
དུས་ཐོག་ཏུ་	regularly, on schedule
དུས་ཚོད་	time
དུས་མཚུངས་	at the same time; contemporary
དུས་ཟིང་	disturbance, unrest, turmoil
དུས་ཡུན་	duration; time
དུས་རིམ་	period, stage
དེ་	1. gerundive connective (5.11); 2. even though clause connective (7.2)
དེ་གར་	there
དེ་སྔ་	previously, before
དེ་སྔོན་	previous(ly)
དེ་ཉིད་	that itself
དེ་ལྟར་	like that
དེ་འདྲ་	like that (with adjectives see 8.10.3.19)
དེ་ནས་	then; after that (4.6.4.9)
དེ་ནས་བཟུང་	since that time, from then onwards
དེ་མ་ཉིད་དུ་	immediately, at once
དེ་མ་ཐག་	suddenly
དེ་མིན་	besides that (4.6.4.9)
དེ་ཙམ་	"how ever much . . . . that much" construction (12.12)
དེ་ཚོ་	those
དེ་བཞིན་	similarly (4.6.4.9)
དེ་རང་	that one itself
དེ་རིང་	today
དེ་ལས་ལྡོག་(སྣེ་)	the opposite
དེང་སྐབས་	these days, nowadays
དེང་དུས་	currently, these days
དེང་སང་	these days, nowdays
དེད་	va. to drive (a herd), to herd
དེབ་	book
དེའི་	1. of that; 2. even though clause connective (7.2)
དེའི་ཤུལ་དུ་	in the meanwhile, while that (was going on)
དེར་	there
དེར་བརྟེན་	therefore, because of that
དེས་	by that
དེས་ན་	therefore (4.6.4.9)
དེས་མ་ཚད་	not only that (4.6.4.9)
དོ་	sentence-ending particle (9.17.1.3.34)

དོ་འཁུར་	concern; va. — བྱེད་
དོ་དགོང་	tonight
དོ་དམ་	official in charge, supervisor, custodian; va. — བྱེད་ to take care of, to supervise
དོ་བདག་	owner
དོ་ནུབ་	tonight
དོ་སྣང་	vi. to notice; also: vi. — བྱེད་
དོ་པོ་	a load
དོ་ཕོག་	effect; vi. — བྱུང་
དོ་ཤལ་	necklace
དོང་	pit (in ground)
དོང་རྐྱེ་	pit, trap
དོན་	1. seventies particle (8.1); 2. purpose, meaning; 3. purposive connective (5.13); 4. in newspapers (7.14.2.4.2); 5. issue, question, matter
དོན་ཅི་ཡོད་	what's the use, why (11.4)
དོན་གཅོད་ཁང་	bureau office
དོན་ལྟར་ན་	see 7.14.2.4.2
དོན་ལྟ་	meaning, point (of something)
དོན་དུ་	1. purposive connective (5.13); 2. in newspapers (7.14.2.4.2)
དོན་ཚན་	article, point, clause (in an agreement)
དོར་མ་	pants
དྭགས་པོ་	p.n. of a region southeast of Lhasa
དྭོགས་འཆར་	doubt, suspicion, fear
དྭོགས་ཟོན་	suspicion; va. — བྱེད་
དྲག་	vi. to heal, get better/well
དྲག་སྐྱིད་	healing, getting better; vi. — བྱུང་ or ཡོང་
དྲག་ཆར་	rainstorm
དྲག་ཆས་སྒྲིམས་	id. armed with
དྲག་དུ་	fiercely, strongly
དྲག་པོ་	fierce, harsh, strong
དྲག་འོང་	sm. དྲག་
དྲགས་	excessive particle (10.3.5)
དྲགས་པའི་རྐྱེན་ གྱིས་རེད་	"too much of" construction (10.15.1.3.15)s
དྲང་པོ་	true, honest
དྲང་སྲོང་	an ascetic, siddhi
དྲངས་	va. p. of འདྲེན་
དྲན་	1. vi. to remember, recall; 2. to miss
དྲན་པ་བོར་	vi. to become unconscious, to faint
དྲན་པ་གསོས་	vi. p. of དྲན་པ་གསོ་
དྲན་པ་གསོ་	1. vi. to regain consciousness, to get revived; 2. vi. to remember
དྲན་གསོ་	a commemoration, remembrance; va. — བྱེད་
དྲི་བ་	a question; va. — དྲི་ to ask questions, to question
དྲི་མེད་ཀུན་ལྡན་	p.n. of an opera
དྲི་ལན་	answer (to a question), reply
དྲིན་	kindness, favor, grace
དྲིན་གྱིས་སྐྱོང་	va. to look after with kindness, to be kind to
དྲིན་ལན་	repaying or returning kindness
དྲིན་ལན་ ལོག་འཇལ་	id. va. to not repay kindness
དྲིལ་བུ་	bell

དྲིས་	va. p. of འདྲི་
དྲུག་	six
དྲུག་ཁྲི་	60,000
དྲུག་བརྒྱ་	600
དྲུག་ཅུ་	60
དྲུག་ཆ་གཅིག་	one sixth
དྲུག་སྟོང་	6,000
དྲུག་འབུམ་	600,000
དྲུང་ (དྲུ་)	presence of, near to
དྲུང་འཁོར་	lay official (in traditional Tibetan government)
དྲུང་རྩིས་	secular and monastic officials in the traditional Tibetan government
དྲུང་ཡིག་ཆེན་མོ་	four heads of the Yigtsang Office in traditional Tibetan government
དྲུད་	va. p. of འདྲུད་
དྲེག་པ་	dirt
དྲེགས་	vi. to be arrogant, haughty
གདང་	see ཁ་ — and མིག་ —
གདངས་	va. p. of གདང་
གདན་	mattress
གདན་ཐོབ་	seat (in a parliament/ congress)
གདན་དྲངས་	va. p. of གདན་འདྲེན་
གདན་འདྲེན་	1. va. to summon, call; 2. va. to invite; 3. va. to transport, carry (h.)
གདན་ཞུ་	inviting, act of inviting to take a post; va. — ཞུ་ (h.)
གདན་ས་གསུམ་	the three great monasteries of the Gelukpa Sect (Sera, Drepung, and Ganden)
གདབ་	va. f. of འདེབས་
གདུག་རྩུབ་ཅན་	cruel, ferocious, savage
གདུངས་	vi. to suffer from, to be tormented by
གདོང་	face
གདོང་རིས་	face, true nature
གདོན་འདྲེ་	ghost
བདག་	I
བདག་ཅག་	we
བདག་གཉེར་	management, supervision; va. — བྱེད་
བདག་པོ་	owner
བདག་དབང་	sovereignty, right of ownership
བདམས་	va. p. འདེམས་
བདུག་	vi. to be filled with scent, odor
བདུན་	seven
བདུན་ཁྲི་	70,000
བདུན་བརྒྱ་	700
བདུན་ཅུ་	70
བདུན་སྟོང་	7,000
བདུན་སྟོང་ལྔ་བརྒྱ་ཉི་ཤུ་	7,520
བདུན་པ་	seventh
བདུན་ཕྲག་	week
བདུན་འབུམ་	700,000
བདེ་སྐྱིད་	happiness, joy, well-being
བདེ་ཐང་	well, in good health (usu. used after གཟུགས་པོ་)
བདེ་པོ་	1. well, in good health; 2. with verbs, see 13.4
བདེན་	truth; true, right, correct
བདོག་དངོས་	things, possessions
མདང་དགོང་	last night
མདང་ནུབ་	last night
མདངས་	complexion, radiance, color

མདའ་ arrow; va. — རྒྱག་ to shoot an arrow

མདའ་གཞིས་ an estate given to a general while he is in office

མདུན་(དུ་) (in) front (5.17.4.5)

མདུན་ཐབས་ bride

མདོག་ 1. appearance, looks; 2. "seems" construction (12.2); 3. "pretend," "act as if" construction (6.8)

མདོག་སྐྱོ་ poor color, poor complexion

མདོག་ཁ་པོ་ "seems likely to occur" (12.2)

མདོག་ངན་པ་ ugly

མདོག་མདོག་ "pretend" particle (6.8)

མདོར་བསྡུས་ brief, abbreviated

འདང་ vi. to be enough, sufficient, to suffice

འདབ་ times; double

འདབ་ལོ་ leaf

འདམ་སེང་ lion

འདམ་གསེས་ choose, select; va. — རྒྱག་

འདར་ vi. to tremble, shake, shiver

འདར་གསིག་ shivering; va. — རྒྱག་

འདའ་ 1. vi. to pass (time); 2. vi. to die; 3. vi. to disobey, violate, break a promise

འདས་ vi. p. of འདའ་

འདས་པོ་ deceased

འདི་ this

འདི་གར་ here, over here

འདི་འདྲ་ like that

འདི་ཕྱི་གཉིས་ both this life and the next life

འདི་ཕྱོགས་ this side

འདི་ཚོ་ these

འདི་ཡང་ this also, this even

འདི་ལོ་ this year

འདིང་(ས)' 1. va. to lay, spread out; 2. to formulate (a plan)

འདིར་ here

འདིས་ by these

འདུ་ཤེས་ ideology; va. — འཛིན་ to have/adhere to an ideology

འདུག་ existential verb (2.6)

འདུན་ "hope" particle (9.11)

འདུན་པ་ hope

འདུལ་ va. to overcome, vanquish, subdue

འདེག་ sm. འདེགས་

འདེགས་ va. to lift, raise up; to prop up

འདེབས་ va. to plant, sow

འདེབས་ལས་ planting, sowing; va. — བྱེད་

འདེམ་སྒྲུག་ selection, choosing; va. — བྱེད་

འདེམས་ va. to choose, select, elect

འདོགས་ 1. va. to tie, fasten; 2. to put on, wear; 3. to name (usu. མིང་ or མཚན་ + —)

འདོད་ want particle (9.10)

འདོད་ཛམ་ཅན་ greedy

འདོན་ va. to say, read, intone

འདོམ་ a length measure equal to the length of outstretched hands

འདྲ་ 1. like, similar; 2. vb. + པ་ + — probably (15.3 a)

འདྲ་ཆགས་པོ་ good-looking, handsome

འདྲ་པར་ photograph, portrait

འདྲ་བ་ like, similar to (5.17.4.6)

འདྲི་ va. to ask

འདྲུད་ va. to drag, pull

འདྲེ་ demon, ghost, evil spirit

འདྲེན་	1. va. to lead, pull, draw, bring, transport, convey; 2. to invite; 3. to quote
རྡུང་	va. to beat, strike
རྡེབ་	va. to beat against, bang against; to clap, flap (wings)
རྡོ་	stone, rock
རྡོ་རྗེ་	p.n.
རྡོ་སོལ་	coal
རྡོག་ (པ་)	1. a step, stride; 2. sole of shoes
རྡོག་ སྒྲ་	sound of a step
རྡོག་ཐོན་	leaving a place for good; va. — བྱེད་
རྡོལ་པ་	torn, tattered
ལྡང་	sm. ལྡེང་
ལྡན་པ་	having; possessing (10.3.6)
ལྡིར་ལྡིར་	roaring noise, thundering noise
ལྡེང་	vi. to suffice, be sufficient/ enough
ལྡེབས་	side or face of a mountain/ hill
ལྡོག་	opposite (also: དེ་ལས་ལྡོག་སྟེ་)
སྡུག་	bad
སྡུག་དཀའ་ལས་	suffering and difficulties (15.8.3.2)
སྡུག་སྐད་	complaints, grumbling; va. — རྒྱག་
སྡུག་བསྔལ་	suffering, misery
སྡུད་	va. to collect, assemble, gather
སྡེ་པ་	person in charge of an estate/ province
སྡེ་དཔོན་མི་དྲག་	the higher stratum of the aristocracy
སྡེ་སྲིད་	regent
སྡོང་རྙིང་	old tree
སྡོང་པོ་	tree
སྡོད་	va. to stay, live; to sit
སྡོད་ཁང་	residence, home
བསྡད་	va. p. of སྡོད་
བརྡབ་ (བརྡབས)	va. f./p. of རྡེབ་
བརྡུངས་	va. p. of རྡུང་
བསྡུ་	va. f. of སྡུད་
བསྡུ་རུབ་	collect, assemble, gather; va. — བྱེད་ or གནང་
བསྡུར་	va. to compare
བསྡུས་	va. p. of སྡུད་
སྡོམ་ཁྲིམས་	covenant
བསྡོམས་	1. va. to total, add up; 2. the total
ན་	1. vi. get sick; 2. conditional ("if") clause connective (6.1); 3. "as" or "because" construction (15.5); 4. in, at, to (dative-locative particle) (11.20.1.3.2); 5. see པ་/བ་ན་
ན་ནིང་	last year
ན་མ་གཏོགས་	the "unless" clause connector (10.6)
ན་ཚ་	illness; vi. — གཏོང་ to be ill, get sick
ན་ཚོད་དར་ལ་བབས་	young age (15.8.3.7)
ན་གཞོན་	a youth
ན་ཟུག་	pain; illness
ན་ཡང་	"even though" clause connective (7.2)
ནག་འཁྲིགས་པ་	becoming dark
ནག་ཉེས་	crime

ནག་ཐིང་ཐིང་	completely black
ནག་པོ་	black
ནག་རིལ་རིལ་	a black and round thing
ནགས་ཚལ་	forest
ནགས་གསེབ་	forest; jungle
ནང་	1. inside, in; 2. home
ནང་ཁུལ་	internal, domestic
ནང་པ་	a Buddhist
ནང་མ་	1. a type of Tibetan song; 2. inside
ནང་མི་	family member
ནང་ཚུད་	within
ནང་བཞིན་	like, similar to
ནང་ཟུལ་པ་	traitor, one who commits treason
ནད་	illness, disease
ནད་པ་	sick person, patient
ནད་གཡོག་	a nurse; va. — བྱེད་
ནན་ཏན་	emphatically
ནན་པོ་	serious, firm, strict
ནམ་	1. interrogative particle after the letter ན་ (14.8.3.21); 2. when, whenever (usu. ནམ་ — རུང་)
ནམ་མཁའ་	sky
ནམ་རྒྱུན་	usually
ནམ་ཡང་	1. emphatic negative adverb (never) (9.9); 2. in double negative constructions (11.17)
ནམ་ཡིན་རུང་	whenever
ནམ་ལངས་	vi. to be dawn
ནམ་ལངས་ཐང་གསལ་	dawn and a clear day
ནམ་ཕྱེད་	midnight
ནའང་	sm. ན་ཡང་
ནས་	1. from; 2. gerundive clause connective (5.11); 3. by (instrumental particle) (3.1)
ནས་མ་གཏོགས་	sm. ན་མ་གཏོགས་ (10.6)
ནས་བཟུང་	from then onwards (10.15.2.3.9)
ནི་	as for (1.10)
ནུབ་ངོས་	west side, west direction
ནུས་	the auxiliary verb "to dare to" (9.2)
ནུས་པ་	power, strength, effectiveness
ནུས་པ་ཐོན་	vi. to be effective
ནུས་ཤུགས་	strength, power
ནོར་འཁྲུལ་	mistake; va. — བྱེད་
ནོར་གླིང་	abbr. of ནོར་བུ་གླིང་ཁ་
ནོར་བུ་	precious gem, jewel
ནོར་བུ་གླིང་ཁ་	Norbulingka (jewel park)
ནོར་བདག་	wealthy person
གནང་	va. to do (h.)
གནང་སྦྱིན་	gift, present (h.)
གནད་འགག་ཆེ་བ་	important
གནད་ཆེ་	important
གནམ་	sky
གནམ་གང་	thirtieth day of the lunar month
གནམ་གྲུ་	airplane; va. — གཏོང་
གནམ་གྲུ་འབབ་ཐང་	airport
གནམ་གཤིས་	climate
གནའ་སྔ་མོ་	ancient time, in the past
གནའ་རབས་	in ancient times, long ago
གནས་	va. to live, stay
གནས་སྐོར་	pilgrimage
གནས་བསྐོར་བ་	pilgrim
གནས་ཆེན་	holy site
གནས་དུས་	place and time

གནས་མེད་ཡུལ་ཁྱར་	homeless and wandering around
གནས་མེད་ཡུལ་ཁྱུར་	sm. གནས་མེད་ཡུལ་ཁྱར་
གནས་མོ་	innkeeper (female), hostess
གནས་ཚུལ་	news, event, situation
གནས་ལུགས་	situation, condition
གནོད་སྐྱོན་	harm, damage; va. — གཏོང་
གནོད་འཚེ་	harm, damage; va. — བྱེད་
མནའ་སྐྱེལ་དམ་བཅའ་	swearing an oath; va. — འཛུགས་
མནའ་མ་	bride; va. — ལེན་ to take a bride; va. — གཏོང་ to send as a bride
མནར་	vi. to suffer, be oppressed
མནར་གཅོད་	oppression, torture; va. — གཏོང་
མནལ་ཁུག་	vi. to fall asleep (h.)
རྣ་ཅོག་	ear
རྣམ་	honorific term used for second and third person
རྣམ་འགྱུར་	appearance
རྣམ་རྒྱལ་	p.n.
རྣམ་པ་	1. type, kind, form; 2. face, looks, appearance
རྣམ་པ་སྣ་ཚོགས་	all kinds of, all sorts of
རྣམ་པར་	perfectly, completely
རྣམ་པར་རྒྱལ་	vi. to be completely victorious
རྣམ་ཤེས་	soul, mind, consciousness
རྣམས་	plural particle (3.2.2)
རྣོ་པོ་	sharp
སྣ་ཁུ་	nose
སྣ་ལྔ་	five kinds
སྣ་ཐག་	snuff
སྣ་ཚོགས་	various
སྣང་	impression, feeling, sensation
སྣང་ཆུང་	low esteem, low regard; va. —བྱེད་ to show low regard or esteem, to act contemptuous; to look down on
སྣང་ཚུལ་	appearance, look; vi. — འཆར་ to show/manifest an appearance/look
སྣང་ས་འོད་འབུམ་	p.n. of an opera
སྣེ་གདོང་	p.n. of a place in southern Tibet
སྣེ་ལེན་	hospitality
སྣེ་ཤན་	guide, host, liaison person; va. — བྱེད་ to serve as guide, liaison person
སྣོད་	vessel, container, receptacle
སྣོན་	va. to add to, augment
བསྣན་	va. p. of སྣོན་
བསྣམས་	va. to take, bring (h.)
བསྣར་	va. to stretch
པ་	1. agentive particle (5.16); 2. part of past complement (3.4); 3. in nominalized constructions (6.6)
པ་ཀི་སི་ཐན་	Pakistan
པ་དག་	"as soon as" clause connective (6.2)
པ་དང་	1. "and" clause connective (4.2); 2. "as soon as" connective (6.2)
པ་དང་ཆབས་ཅིག་	"together with" clause connective (7.9)
པ་དང་སྟབས་བསྟུན་	1."together with" clause connective (7.9); 2.

	"according to" clause connective (7.10)
པ་དང་བསྟུན་	1. "together with" clause connective (7.9); 2. "according to" clause connective (7.10)
པ་དང་སྦྲགས་	"together with" clause connective (7.9)
པ་དེ་མ་ཐག་	"as soon as" clause connective (6.2)
པ་ན་	1. when connective (5.10; 15.8.3.24); 2. conditional connective (6.1)
པ་ཕ་	father
པ་ཙམ་ན་	"as soon as" clause connective (6.2)
པ་ཙམ་ནས་	"as soon as" clause connective (6.2)
པ་བཟོ་མི་འདུག་	"does not seem" construction (9.7 e)
པ་ཡིན་	past complement (3.4)
པ་ཡོད་	see བ་ཡོད་
པ་རེད་	past complement (3.4)
པཱ་ལགས་	father (h.)
པང་	lap
པད་མ་	p.n.
པད་མ་ཅན་	p.n. of a place
པད་མ་འོད་འབར་	p.n. of an opera
པན་	ch. a board with writing that is hung on the door or window
པན་ཆེན་ཨེར་ཏི་ནི་	Panchen Erdini (name of the Panchen Lama)
པའམ་	"or" particle (8.6)
པའི་སྐབས་སུ་	"when" connective (5.10)
པའི་སྐད་ལ་	see སྐད་
པའི་ཆེད་དུ་	see བའི་ཆེད་དུ་
པའི་རྗེས་སུ་	"temporal" connective (4.3)
པའི་དུས་སུ་	"when" connective (5.10)
པའི་དབང་གིས་	"causal" connective (5.9)
པའི་རིང་ལ་	"when" connective (5.10)
པའི་རེ་བ་	hope construction (6.11)
པར་	see བར་
པར་བརྟེན་	"causal" connective (5.9)
པར་ལུས་	see ལུས་
པས་	1. question particle (1.11; 3.8); 2. "causal" connective (5.9); 3. adverbializer (6.5.2)
པས་ན་	because connective (7.14.1.4.15)
པས་ནའོ་	because construction (7.14. 1.4.15)
པས་ན་རེད་	because construction (7.14.1.4.15)
པས་རེད་	because construction (7.14.1.4.15; 15.2)
པས་ལུས་	see ལུས་
པུ་ལི་སི་	police
པུས་མོ་	knee
པེ་ཅིང་	ch. Beijing
པེ་ལུན་ཆུ་བོ་	Pelun River
པོ་ཏ་ལ་	Potala (palace in Lhasa)
དཔག་	see ལ་དཔག་སྟེ་/ན་
དཔག་ཏུ་མེད་པ་	immeasurable
དཔང་རྟགས་	evidence, proof
དཔང་པོ་	witness
དཔའ་ངར་	heroic, brave, courageous
དཔའ་བོ་	hero
དཔའ་མཛངས་རྩལ་ཡོད་	courage
དཔལ་	splendor, magnificence, glory
དཔལ་ལྡན་	p.n.

དཔལ་འབྱོར་ economy
དཔུང་པ་ shoulder
དཔུང་ཚོགས་ troops, military force
དཔེ་ཆ་ book (Tibetan style)
དཔེ་མཛོད་ཁང་ library
དཔེ་རིས་ plan (drawing), blueprint, designs
དཔེ་བསགས་འདུག་ id. "oh my goodness"
དཔེར་ན་ for example (14.5)
དཔེར་ན་ཆ་བཞག་ན་ for example (14.5)
དཔོན་ chief, lord, ruler
དཔོན་གོས་ clothes of a lord, chief, aristocrat
དཔོན་ངན་ bureaucrat (lit., bad master)
དཔོན་ངན་མ་རྩའི་ཁེ་ལས་ bureaucratic-capitalist enterprises
དཔོན་པོ་ lord
དཔོན་དམག་ officers and men
དཔོན་རིགས་ officials, lords, authorities
དཔྱངས་ vi. to be hanging, dangling
དཔྱིད་དུས་ spring
དཔྱིད་འདེབས་ spring planting
དཔྲལ་བ་ forehead
ལྤགས་ skin (of people as well as of food, fruits)
སྤག་ staple Tibetan food
སྤང་རྒྱན་མེ་ཏོག་ 1. meadow flower; 2. p.n. of a Lhasa newspaper
སྤར་ va. to light, set on fire
སྤུ་ཙམ་ small, slight, little
སྤུ་ཧྲེང་ p.n. town in W. Tibet
སྤུན་མཆེད་ relative
སྤུས་ཀ་ quality
སྤེལ་ 1. va. to increase, to enlarge, to expand; 2. va. to spread, disseminate
སྤོ་ va. to move, shift residence
སྤོ་བོ་ལགས་ old man (grandfather)
སྤོས་ va. p. of སྤོ་
སྤྱང་ཀི་ wolf
སྤྱང་གྲུང་འཛོམས་པོ་ intelligent, clever
སྤྱད་ va. p. of སྤྱོད་
སྤྱན་སྔར་ in the presence of, in person; an audience (h.)
སྤྱན་ཆབ་ tears (h.); va. — ཤོར་ to cry
སྤྱི་ཁྱབ་མཁན་པོ་ a high-ranking monk official in the traditional Tibetan government
སྤྱི་མཁན་ abbr. of སྤྱི་ཁྱབ་མཁན་པོ་
སྤྱི་ཕན་ public welfare
སྤྱི་བོ་ top, apex
སྤྱི་གཙུག་ top, apex, crown
སྤྱི་ཚོགས་ society
སྤྱི་ཚོགས་རིང་ལུགས་ socialism
སྤྱི་ཟླ་ Western month
སྤྱི་ལི་ ch. kilometer
སྤྱི་ལི་གྲུ་བཞི་ square kilometer
སྤྱི་ལོ་ Western year
སྤྱོད་ va. to use, to employ, to make use of
སྤྲང་པོ་ beggar
སྤྲད་ va. p. of སྤྲོད་
སྤྲིན་པ་ cloud
སྤྲུལ་སྐུ་ incarnate lama
སྤྲུལ་པ་ an incarnation, emanation
སྤྲོ་ va. to sparkle, see: འོད་ཟེར་

སྤྲོ་སྐྱིད་ partying; enjoying oneself, recreation; va. — གཏོང་

སྤྲོ་བ་ joy, happiness; vi. — འཕེལ་ to have joy/ happiness

སྤྲོ་བ་ལྡན་པ་ happy, joyful, cheerful

སྤྲོད་ va. to give

ཕ་ father

ཕ་གི་ over there

ཕ་རྒན་ old father

ཕ་བུ་ father & son

ཕ་མ་ parents, lit., father and mother

ཕ་ཡུལ་ homeland

ཕ་རན་སི་ France

ཕ་ལམ་ diamond

ཕངས་ vi. to feel regret, be sorry

ཕངས་པ་ལ་ཨང་ a common spoken phrase meaning "oh, what a shame" (11.20.1.3.20)

ཕན་ཐོགས་ benefit

ཕན་པོ་ beneficial

ཕན་ཚུན་ each other, one another, back and forth, here and there

ཕབ་ va. p. of འབེབས་

ཕམ་ vi. to lose, be defeated

ཕམ་ཉེས་ཡོང་ vi. to be defeated, to lose

ཕར་ over there, thither

ཕར་རྒོལ་ attacking, assaulting; va. — བྱེད་

ཕར་བཞག་ "let alone/far from" clause connective (9.3)

ཕུང་དཀྲུག་ disturbance; va. — བྱེད་

ཕུད་ 1. "excluding" clause connective (9.4); 2. va. to take off (clothes); 3. va. to expel; 4. va. p. of འབུད་

ཕུན་ཚོགས་ p.n.

ཕུན་སུམ་ཚོགས་ id. all the good things

ཕལ་ཆེར་ probably, almost

ཕུའུ་དུང་ the sound "phuthung" (of a splash)

ཕུར་ལྕོག་ p.n. of a monastery near Lhasa

ཕུལ་ va. p. of འབུལ་

ཕེབས་ va. to come, to go (h.)

ཕེབས་སྒུག་ waiting (h.); va. — ཞུ་

ཕོ་མོ་ male and female; sex

ཕོ་བྲང་ palace

ཕོ་གཞོན་ young man

ཕོ་གསར་ young man

ཕོགས་ salary

ཕོངས་ vi. to be destitute, devoid of

ཕོད་ the auxiliary verb "to dare to" (9.2)

ཕོན་འབོར་ quantity, amount, number

ཕོར་པ་ small wooden eating/ drinking bowl

ཕྱག་ hand (h.)

ཕྱག་རྟགས་ present, gift (h.)

ཕྱག་དེབ་ book (h.)

ཕྱག་བྲིས་ letter (h.)

ཕྱག་མཛོད་ steward

ཕྱག་རོགས་ help; va. — གནང་ to help (h.); — ཞུ་ to request help (h.)

ཕྱག་ལས་ work; va. — གནང་ (h.)

ཕྱི་ outside

ཕྱི་སྒོ་ main door

ཕྱི་རྒྱལ་ foreign

ཕྱི་ཉིན་ the next day

ཕྱི་དྲོ་ (late) afternoon

ཕྱི་ནང་ Buddhist and non-Buddhist; outside and inside
ཕྱི་པོ་ late
ཕྱི་མ་ next life
ཕྱི་རོལ་ outside
ཕྱི་ལོ་ next year
ཕྱིན་ 1. va. p. of འགྲོ་; 2. in adjective constructions (6.5.3; 13.5.3.14); 3. in verbal constructions, all kinds of, whatever, whoever (14.1); 4. in simultaneous constructions (8.10.3.19)
ཕྱིར་ 1. the "purposive" clause connective (5.13); 2. back, back to (usu. with ལོག་)
ཕྱིར་འཐེན་ withdraw, pulling back; va. — བྱེད་
ཕྱིར་འབུད་ expulsion; va. — བྱེད་
ཕྱིར་ལོག་(བྱེད་) va. to return
ཕྱིས་ va. to wipe
ཕྱིས་དྲགས་ to be too late
ཕྱུ་པ་ a dress (Tibetan style)
ཕྱུག་པོ་ rich
ཕྱུགས་ར་ livestock/ dairy farm
ཕྱུང་ va. p. of འབྱིན་
ཕྱུར་ va. p. of འཕྱུར་
ཕྱེད་གཤགས་ split in half
ཕྱོགས་ 1. direction; 2. "manner of" construction (15.3)
ཕྱོགས་ཁག་ faction, party, clique
ཕྲ་མ་ window
ཕྲག་ 1. sm. ཕྲག་པ་; 2. round number particle (10.15.1.3.8)
ཕྲག་པ་ shoulder
ཕྲད་ va. p. of འཕྲད་
ཕྲན་ (རང་) I (myself)
ཕྲན་བུ་ a little; for use with adjectives (10.3.3)
ཕྲུ་གུ་ child
ཕྲེང་ a rosary, string of beads
ཕྲོགས་ va. p. of འཕྲོག་
འཕགས་པ་ exalted, sublime; a bodhisattva
འཕང་ va. to shoot, to fire a weapon
འཕན་པོ་ p.n. of a place north of Lhasa
འཕར་ 1. vi. to increase; 2. vi. to bounce up, to fly up
འཕར་འགེལ་ making an extra tax levy
འཕར་མ་ extra
འཕུར་ va. to fly
འཕུར་འགྲོད་ flying
འཕེལ་ vi. to increase, multiply; to develop
འཕེལ་རྒྱས increase, development, progress; vi. — འགྲོ་; va. — གཏོང་
འཕོ་འགྱུར་ changing, altering, alterations; va. — གཏོང་
འཕྱུར་ va. to hoist, raise up
འཕྱིངས་ vi. to become matted together (fur, hair, wool)
འཕྱུར་ vi. to rise, swell upwards, come forth (like waves or smoke or a smile)
འཕྲད་ va. to meet
འཕྲལ་(དུ་) 1."as soon as" clause connective (6.2); 2. for use before verbs, see 12.18
འཕྲལ་མར་ at once, immediately

འཕྲུལ་འཁོར་ machine

འཕྲོ་ 1. vi. to be left over, uncompleted (10.12); 2. vi. to shine, radiate; emanate

འཕྲོག་ va. to steal, plunder, take away by force

འཕྲོག་བཅོམ་ robbery, plundering; va. — བྱེད་

འཕྲོར་ see 10.12

འཕྲོས་ see 10.12

བ་ see པ་

བ་དང་ see པ་དང་

བ་དག་ see པ་དག་

བ་དི་མ་ཐག་(ཏུ་) see པ་དི་མ་ཐག་(ཏུ་)

བ་ན་ see པ་ན་

བ་ཙམ་ན་ "as soon as" clause connective (6.2)

བ་ཙམ་ནས་ "as soon as" clause connective (6.2)

བ་ཡིན་ see པ་ཡིན་

བ་ཡོད་ following verbs, see 9.14

བ་རེད་ see པ་རེད་

བག་མ་ bride

བག་ལེབ་ bread

བང་མཛོད་ storeroom, treasury

བབས་ 1. vi. p. of འབབ་; 2. vi. to fall, land, come down, descend; 3. following verbs = in accordance with some verbal action (16.1.1.3.6)

བའི་སྐབས་ལ་ see སྐབས་

བའི་ཆེད་དུ་ the purposive connective (5.13)

བའི་རྗེས་སུ་ the temporal connective (4.3)

བའི་དབང་གིས་ see པའི་དབང་གིས་

བའི་རེ་བ་ hope construction (6.11)

བར་ 1. བ་ + dative-locative (5.15); 2. up to (7.14.2.4.1; 7.14.2.4.3); 3. in between (9.17.1.3.4); 4. infinitive usage (5.15)

བར་བསྐོར་ the Barkor (the circular path in Lhasa) that goes around the Cathedral

བར་ཆད་ hindrance, obstruction, harm

བར་བརྟེན་ see པར་བརྟེན་

བར་དུ་ see བར་

བར་སྣང་ space, atmosphere

བར་མི་ཆོད་ without break

བར་ཤོག་ "may it come" verbal construction (12.19)

བལ་བོད་ Tibeto-Nepalese, Nepal and Tibet

བལ་ཡུལ་ Nepal

བལ་བཟའ་ the Nepalese bride of King Srongtsen gambo

བས་ see པས་

བས་རེད་ see པས་རེད་

བུ་ son; young boy

བུ་བཙོལ་ཁང་ nursery

བུ་ཆུང་ small son

བུ་ཕྲུག་ children

བུ་མོ་ daughter; young girl

བུ་ཡུག་ snow storm, blizzard

བུད་ vi. to come off, get unstrung

བུད་མེད་ women; female

བུད་ཤིང་ firewood

བེད་སྤྱོད་ using, putting to use; va. — བྱེད་ or — གཏོང་

བོང་བུ་ donkey

བོད་ Tibet
བོད་སྐད་ Tibetan language
བོད་བསྐྱོད་ Tibet bound
བོད་ཇ་ Tibetan tea
བོད་ལྗོངས་ Tibet
བོད་རྗེ་ king of Tibet
བོད་པ་ Tibetan
བོད་ཟླ་ Tibetan (lunar) month
བོད་ཡིག་ written Tibetan
བོད་རིག་པ་ Tibetological
བོད་ལུགས་ Tibetan customs, way, manner
བོབས vi. imp. of འབབ་
བོར་ 1. vi. to lose; 2. va. p. of འབོར་
བོར་བརླག་ loss, losing; vi. — ཤོར་
བོས་ va. p. of འབོད་
བྱ་ va. f. of བྱེད་
བྱ་སྐད་ cock's crow
བྱ་གླག་ a big bird of prey, Tibetan eagle
བྱ་དགའ་ prize
བྱ་ཐབས་ཟད་ vi. to be without the means of doing, be unable to do
བྱ་བ་ work, deeds, action
བྱ་བ་ལམ་འགྲོ་ good fortune in business (11.20.2.3.23)
བྱང་ north
བྱང་ངོས་པ་རིག་འཛིན་རྡོ་རྗེ་ p.n.
བྱང་ཐང་ p.n. of Tibetan northern plateau
བྱམས་བརྩེ་ love
བྱས་ va. p. of བྱེད་
བྱས་རྗེས་ result, achievement
བྱས་ན་ well then
བྱས་ཙང་ because, consequently (4.6.4.9)
བྱིན་ va. p. of སྦྱིན་
བྱིལ་ va. to stroke, caress
བྱིལ་བྱིལ་ stroking, rubbing; va. — གཏོང་; བྱེད་
བྱུ་རུ་ coral (the gem)
བྱུགས་ va. to smear, apply a cream
བྱུང་ 1. vi. got (5.3); 2. auxiliary verb for first person involuntary constructions (5.1)
བྱེ་ vi. p. of འབྱེ་
བྱེ་ཐང་ desert
བྱེ་བ་གཅིག་ 10,000,000
བྱེད་ va. to do (5.6)
བྱེད་སྒོ་ activities, duties, work
བྱེད་སྟངས་ the manner of doing things
བྲག་ rock
བྲག་ཁུང་ cave
བྲག་ཅ་ echo; vi. — འཁོར་
བྲག་རྡོ་ boulder
བྲག་ཕུག་ cave
བྲག་རི་ rocky mountain
བྲང་ཁོག་ chest; vi. — ཕྱིར་ to stick out one's chest (with pride)
བྲལ་ 1. vi. to separate ; 2. with ཐབས་ and ཚད་ (9.1; 11.13)
བྲིན་ཚོང་ selling well
བྲིས་ va. p. of འབྲི་
བྲེལ་འཚབ་ hurried, rushed
བྲོས་ va. p. of འབྲོས་
བྲོས་བྱོལ་ refugee
བླ་མ་ lama
བླ་མའི་དྲང་སྲོང་ ascetic lama, a siddhi

བླ་བྲང་ the "corporation" of a lama
བླ་ཤིང་ soul tree
བླ་སྲོག་ soul, life essence
བླངས་ va. p. of ལེན་
བླུགས་ va. to pour
བློ་ 1. mind; 2. "want" particle (9.10)
བློ་གྲོས་ལྡན་པ་ understanding, wise; intellectual
བློ་ཐག་ཆོད་པོ་ decisive
བློ་མཐུན་ 1. having the same opinions, thoughts; 2. comrade
བློ་རྡོར་ p.n.
བློ་རིག་བཀྲ་བ་ intelligent
བློ་ལ་ཤར་ vi. to come to mind
བློན་པོ་ minister
དབང་གིས་ the causal connective (5.9)
དབང་བསྒྱུར་ power, domination, rule
དབང་ཆ་ power, ownership
དབང་ཆེན་ p.n.
དབང་ཆེན་གཡུ་ལྷ་ p.n.
དབང་དུ་བཏང་ན་ "hypothetical" construction (14.4)
དབང་དུ་བསྡུ་ va. to bring under power/ control, to dominate, conquer
དབང་མེད་(དུ་) without control, choice; involuntarily, spontaneously
དབང་འཛིན་པ་ person in authority, authorities
དབང་ཤུགས་ tyranny, excessive use of power, authority; va. — བྱེད་
དབུ་ཅན་ the type of Tibetan script used in books and newspapers
དབུགས་ breathing, respiration; va. — གཏོང་
དབུགས་རིང་ sighing; va. — གཏོང་
དབུགས་ཧལ་ va. to sigh
དབུགས་ལྷིམ་ལྷིམ་ panting
དབུལ་པོ་ poor
དབུས་ center, middle
དབུས་མ་ middle; see ཕར་གླིང་
དབོར་ va. to transport, move from one location to another
དབྱངས་སྐྱིད་ p.n.
དབྱར་དུས་ summertime
དབྱར་གནས་ the summer retreat of monks
དབྱིན་སྐད་ English language
དབྱིན་ཇི་ English; Englishman
དབྱིན་གཞུང་ government of England
དབྱིན་ཡུལ་ England
དབྱིབས་ shape, form, figure
དབྱུག་པ་ stick, club
དབྱུགས་ va. to throw
འབད་བརྩོན་ effort, diligence, striving; va. — བྱེད་
འབབ་ vi. to land, come down, descend
འབབ་ཐང་ airport, station
འབབ་ཞིབ་ལས་ཁུངས་ investigation office in traditional Tibetan government
འབབ་བཙོ་བྱེད་ va. to impose tax
འབར་ vi. to burn, catch fire
འབུད་ 1. va. to take off; 2. va. to expell
འབུལ་ va. to give (h.)
འབུལ་འཛོག་ agreement, guarantee; va. — བྱེད་

འབེབས་ va. to make or cause to descend, to bring down

འབོད་ va. to call out, shout

འབོད་བསྐུལ་ an appeal; va. — བྱེད་

འབོར་ 1. va. to throw, fling; 2. an amount

འབོར་ཆེན་ large quantity, amount, number

འབྱིན་ va. to throw out; to take out, produce

འབྱེ་ vi. to open, to come apart

འབྱོར་ vi. to arrive, to be received (5.7.2)

འབྱོར་ཐོ་ arrival report, registration; va. — བཀོད་

འབྱོར་ལྡན་གྲལ་རིམ་ bourgeoisie, bourgeois

འབྱོར་མེད་གྲལ་རིམ་ the proletariat, proletarian class

འབྲས་ rice

འབྲས་སྤུངས་ Drepung (monastery)

འབྲས་བུ་ fruit; result

འབྲི་ va. to write; draw

འབྲི་ཀློག་ writing + reading

འབྲི་ཆུ་ Yangtse river

འབྲི་དེབ་ notebook

འབྲིང་པ་ middle one; mediocre

འབྲུ་ barley; grain

འབྲུ་ཁང་ granary

འབྲུག་སྐད་ thunder; vi. — རྒྱག་

འབྲུག་སྒྲ་བསྒྲགས་ vi. to thunder

འབྲུམ་ནད་ smallpox

འབྲུ་རིགས་ grains

འབྲུག་ཡུལ་ Bhutan

འབྲེལ་ 1. "together with" clause connective (7.9); 2. the "according to" clause connective (7.10)

འབྲོག་པ་ nomad

འབྲོག་ལས་ dairy or pastoral work

འབྲོས་ va. to flee, run away

རྦ་རླབས་ waves (of water)

རྦད་དེ་ completely

སྦ་ va. to bury

སྦར་མོ་གང་ a handful

སྦས་ va. p. of སྦ་

སྦུག་བཙོས་ something that was obtained but not officially/ legally given

སྦོ་ 1. side of the body; belly; 2. vi. to swell up, get distended

སྦོམ་ thick

སྦྱངས་ va. p. of སྦྱོང་

སྦྱང་འབྲས་ the fruit or result of one's studies

སྦྱར་ p.n. of place

སྦྱར་འགྲེམ་ poster; va. — བྱེད་

སྦྱིན་ va. to give

སྦྱིན་བདག་ patron, donor

སྦྱིན་པ་ charity, alms; va. — གཏོང་

སྦྱོང་བརྡར་ training

སྦྲགས་ "together with" connective (7.9)

སྦྲིད་ 1. vi. to become numb; 2. vi. to sneeze

སྦྲེལ་ va. to connect

སྦྲེལ་ཐག་ connection, relation (lit., a connecting rope); va.— གཏོང་ to create relations, to extend a relationship

མ་	1. negative particle (2.8); 2. mother
མ་རྐང་	share (stock)
མ་...གོང་ལ་	"before" clause connective (7.4)
མ་གཏོགས་	1. "unless" clause connective (10.6); 2. "except for" clause connective (10.7)
མ་ལྟོས་པར་	disregarding; regardless of (14.8.3.23)
མ་ཐག་	"as soon as" clause connective (6.2)
མ་མཐར་ཡང་	even at the very last
མ་མཐུན་པ་	incompatible; unfriendly
མ་...ན་	"if don't do" clause connective (10.5)
མ་ཎི་	(mani) prayer
མ་...བར་དུ་	1. "without" clause connective (10.10); 2. "until" clause connective (10.11)0
མ་བུ་	abbr. mother and son
མ་རྩ་	capital
མ་རྩའི་རིང་ལུགས་	capitalism
མ་ཚད་	see མ་ཟད་
མ་ཟད་	"not only" clause connective (7.1)
མ་རེད་	is/am not; no (2.8)
མག་པ་	bridegroom
མང་པོ་	many
མང་ཆེ་བ་	the majority, the most part
མང་ཉུང་	quantity, amount, number
མང་ཙམ་	a little more
མང་ཚོགས་	public, the masses
མང་ཤོས་	most
མང་སྲོང་ མང་བཙན་	p.n. of a Tibetan king
མན་ཆད་	downwards of something or some number, under, lower than
མའོ་(ཙེ་ཏུང་)	Mao (Zedong)
མར་	1. down, downwards, downhill; 2. butter
མར་ཚོན་ཁྲ་	colored butter
མལ་གྲོ་	p.n. of a place east of Lhasa
མི་	1. person; 2. negative particle (2.8; 6.3); 3. agentive particle (5.16)
མི་གྲངས་	population, the number of people
མི་གླ་	hired laborer, worker
མི་རྒྱུད་	lineage, descendents
མི་ངན་	bad, evil person
མི་མཐུན་པ་	contradictory, incompatible, in conflict
མི་དྲག་	gentry, aristocracy; prominent citizens
མི་འདྲ་བ་	different
མི་སྣ་	personnel, people
མི་འབོར་	population
མི་དམངས་	people, masses
མི་དམངས་ཀུང་ཧྲེ་	people's commune
མི་དམངས་བཅིངས་འགྲོལ་དམག་	people's liberation army
མི་ཚང་	family
མི་ཚད་	sm. མ་ཟད་
མི་ཚེ་	life, a lifetime; vi. — འདས་ to pass, live a lifetime
མི་རིགས་	nationality, ethnic group
མི་རིགས་སྲིད་ཇུས་	nationality/minority policy
མི་རིང་བར་	soon, before long
མི་རེ་ངོ་རེ་	each and everyone
མི་རུས་	human bone

མི་སེམས་ people's minds; va. — འདུལ་ to capture people's minds

མི་སེར་ serf; citizen; subject

མིག་ eye; va. — ལྟ་ to look at

མིག་ཅེ་རེ་ wide-eyed; va. — ལྟ་ to look, stare at wide-eyed

མིག་ཆུ་ tears; vi. — ཤོར་ to shed tears

མིག་ལྟ་ va. to look at

མིག་བལྟས་ p. of མིག་ལྟ་

མིག་གདང་ va. to open one's eyes

མིག་འབྲས་ eyeball

མིག་ལམ་ field of vision

མིག་ཧྲིག་ཧྲིག་ wide-eyed; staring at someone or something

མིང་ name

མིང་གྲགས་ famous, well-known

མིད་པ་ throat

མིན་ 1. negative particle (2.8; 6.3); 2. with verbs to convey "whether or not" (8.6); 3. see དེ་མིན་

མིན་པས་སོ་ because something "is not" (7.14.1.4.15)

མུ་ཏིག་ pearl

མུ་མཐུད་(ནས་) continuously, without a break or interruption (6.5.5; 8.10.3.17)

མུ་སི་ matches

མུན་པ་ darkness; ignorance

མུན་པ་རུབ་ vi. to become night, dark, twilight

མུའུ་ ch. "mu" — a Chinese area measurement equal to 0.1647 acres

མུས་ present tense particle (3.5)

མུས་ཡིན་ present tense complement (3.5)

མུས་ཡིན་འདུག་ present tense complement (3.5)

མུས་ཡོད་ present tense complement (3.5)

མུས་ཡོད་(པ་)རེད་ present tense complement (3.5)

མུས་རེད་ present tense complement (3.5)

མེ་ fire

མེ་ཁོག་ hibachi-type stove

མེ་གོ་ ch. America

མེ་ལྕེ་ a flame

མེ་ཏོག་ flower

མེ་ལྟར་འབར་ caught fire like a flame (13.5.3)

མེ་སྟག་ spark; va. — འཕྲོ་ to spark

མེ་མདའ་ gun; va. — རྒྱག་ to shoot a gun

མེ་ཕུང་ bonfire

མེ་སྦྲུལ་ fire-snake (year)

མེ་ཤིང་ firewood

མེ་ཤུགས་འཕུར་མདེལ་ missile

མེད་ 1. negative existential verb (2.8; 6.3); 2. with verbs to convey "whether or not" (8.6)

མེད་པ་རེད་ no exist (2.8)

མེད་པར་ noun + —: "without" (14.8.3.2)

མེད་པར་འགྱུར་ vi. to come to be without, to come into the state of not existing (8.10.3.16)

མེད་པར་བཟོ་ va. to destroy, annihilate

མེད་པས་སོ་ because something does "not exist" (7.13.1.4.15)

མེས་པོ་ 1. grandfather; 2. forefather, ancestor

མེས་རྒྱལ་ fatherland

མོ་ she

མོ་ཊོར་ car

མོད་ "even though" clause connective (7.2)

མོན་ད་རི་ p.n. of a place

མོའི་ her (she + genitive)

མོར་ to her (she + dative-locative)

མོས་ 1. to like, agree; 2. by her (she + instrumental); 3. "want" particle (9.10)

མྱོང་ auxiliary verb "to experience" (9.6)

དམག་ war; va. — རྒྱག་

དམག་བསྐུལ་ military recruitment

དམག་བསྐྱོད་ march, marching (for the military); va. — བྱེད་

དམག་འཁྲུག་ war; vi. — ཤོར་ to have a war break out; va. — བྱེད་; va. — རྒྱག་ to wage war; va. — སློང་ to provoke a war

དམག་འཁྲུག་གི་ཉེས་ཅན་ war criminal

དམག་སྒར་ military camp

དམག་དོན་ military, military affairs

དམག་དྲངས་ va. p. of དམག་འདྲེན་

དམག་འདྲེན་ va. to lead troops into battle

དམག་དཔུང་ military forces, troops

དམག་ཕོགས་ military salary, pay

དམག་མི་ soldier

དམག་རོགས་ relief troops, reinforcement

དམག་ཤུགས་ military force, strength

དམངས་གཙོ་ democratic

དམངས་གཙོ་སྤྱི་མཐུན་རྒྱལ་ཁབ་ democratic republic

དམའ་ low

དམར་མོ་ red

དམིགས་ཡུལ་ goal, aim, hope

དམིགས་བསལ་ special, specially

དམྱལ་བ་ hell

རྨ་ wound, sore

རྨ་ཁ་ the surface of a wound, sore

རྨང་གཞི་ foundation, basis

རྨང་གཞིའི་དཔལ་འབྱོར་ economic foundation, basis

རྨས་སྐྱོན་ injury; va. — གཏོང་

རྨུགས་ va. to bark

རྨོ་ཕྱུགས་ draft animals

རྨོ་ཞིང་ arable land, land under cultivation

རྨོན་པ་རྒྱག་ va. to plow

རྨོའོ་ grandmother

སྨ་ར་ beard

སྨང་ཅེ་ p. n. of a city in Vietnam

སྨད་ཆ་ the second of two parts (e.g., in a book or a lifetime)

སྨན་ medicine

སྨན་ཁང་ hospital

སྨན་བཅོས་ medical treatment

སྨན་དཔྱད་ medical examination, medical check-up

སྨི་ meter

སྨིན་མ་ eyebrow

སྨོན་འདུན་ wish, desire; va. — བྱེད་

སྨོན་ལམ་ prayer for something; va. — རྒྱག་ or འདེབས་

སྨོན་ལམ་ཆེན་མོ་ the "great prayer festival" in Lhasa

སྨོན་ལམ་དུས་ཆེན་ sm. སྨོན་ལམ་ཆེན་མོ་

སྨྲ་ va. to say, to tell

སྨྲས་ va. p. of སྨྲ་

ཙ་ན་ causal connective (5.9)

ཙང་ causal connective (5.9)

ཙམ་ 1. about, approximately (7.14.1.4.9; 7.14.2.4.8); 2. "how ever much . . . that much" constructions (12.12); 3. a little; 4. + བྱེད་ in verbal constructions see (13.5.3.20); 5. as modestly particle (16.1.2.3.1)

ཙམ་ནས་ with verbs (15.8.3.16)

ཙམ་ཡང་ with negatives (14.8.3.5)

ཙི་ཙི་ mouse

ཙོང་ཁ་པ་ Tsongkapa

ཙོག་པུར་ crouching, squatting

གཙང་ region in Tibet

གཙང་པ་ person from གཙང་

གཙང་སེལ་ clean-up, purge; va. — བྱེད་

གཙུག་གཡུ་ turquoise headstone worn by Amdo women

གཙུག་ལག་ཁང་ temple; the Cathedral temple (Jokang) in Lhasa

གཙོ་གཉེར་ chief guest

གཙོ་བོ་ main

བཙལ་ va. p. of འཚོལ་

བཙན་རྒྱལ་རིང་ལུགས་ imperialism

བཙན་གནོན་ oppressing; va. — གཏོང་

བཙན་པོ་ secure, safe

བཙན་འཛུལ་ invasion; va. — བྱེད་

བཙའ་ vi. to give birth, to bear

བཙས་ va. p. of བཙའ་

བཙུགས་ va. p. of འཛུགས་

བཙུན་མོ་ queen

བཙོང་ va. f. of འཚོང་

བཙོངས་ va. p. of འཚོང་

བཙོན་ prison, jail

བཙོན་ཁང་ prison, jail

བཙོན་པ་ prisoner

རྩ་ twenties particle (8.1)

རྩ་ཆུ་ urine and feces

རྩ་ཆེ་ precious, sacred; invaluable, rare

རྩ་བ་ root

རྩ་བ་ནས་ 1. emphatic negative adverb "never" (9.9); 2. in double negative constructions (11.17)

རྩ་ཁྲིམས་ constitution

རྩ་འགངས་ valuable

རྩ་གཏོར་ annihilation, complete destruction; va. — (བཏང་) གཏོང་

རྩ་མེད་ annihilation; va. — གཏོང་

རྩ་ཆིག་ public notice; va. — བཀྲམ་ to distribute, announce a public notice

རྩྭ grass

རྩ་ལ་ to/in the presence (of) (5.17.4.7)

རྩད་གཅོད་ 1. investigation; va. — བྱེད་; 2. va. to investigate

རྩད་བཅད་ p. of རྩད་གཅོད་

རྩབ་ཧྲལ་ torn, tattered

རྩམ་སྒྲེ་ small bag for carrying tsamba

རྩམ་པ་ roasted barley flour

རྩམ་གསུར་ smell of tsamba burning

རྩི་ཤིང་ a plant

རྩིག་རྨང་ foundation (of building)

རྩིས་ 1. "plan/intend to" clause connective (7.3); va. — རྒྱག་ to calculate, add up

རྩིས་ཁང་ revenue bureau in traditional Tibetan government

རྩིས་ཐོ་ accounting records, account books

རྩིས་པ་ accountant, book-keeper, cashier

རྩིས་དཔོན་ finance minister, finance secretary

རྩིས་བཞེས་ p. of རྩིས་ལེན་

རྩིས་ལེན་ taking over, assuming control; va. — བྱེད་

རྩེ་ 1. va. to play; 2. top; tip; peak

རྩེ་ཕྱག་ལས་ཁངས་ a treasury office in traditional Tibetan government

རྩེད་མོ་ playing, a game; va. — རྩེ་ to play

རྩེས་ va. p. of རྩེ་

རྩོམ་ va. to author, compose

སྩོལ་ va. to give, bestow

བརྩད་ཆོད་ investigating; va. — བྱེད་

བརྩི་སྲུང་ respecting, abiding by; va. — བྱེད་

བརྩིས་ in accordance with

བརྩེ་ va. to love

བརྩེ་གདུང་ love

བརྩེ་བ་ love

བརྩེ་སེམས་ love

བརྩོན་འགྲུས་ diligence; va. — བྱེད་

བསྩལ་ va. p. of སྩོལ་

ཚ་གྲང་ hot + cold; temperature

ཚ་པོ་ 1.hot; 2. strong (e.g., an answer, wind)

ཚ་བ་ heat

ཚ་ལུ་མ་ orange (fruit)

ཚ་ཤག་ "tshashak" (a sound)

ཚགས་པར་ཁང་ newspaper office

ཚགས་ཡིག་ records, documents

ཚང་མ་ all

ཚང་འཛོམས་ plenary

ཚང་འཛོམས་གྲོས་ཚོགས་ plenary session

ཚད་(ལ་) 1. every time, whenever, whoever, whatever construction: va. + ཚད་ (12.14); 2. level, limit

ཚད་ see མ་ཚད་

ཚད་ཐུལ་ "no choice" (11.13)

ཚད་མེད་ 1. limitless, boundless; 2. "no choice" (11.13)

ཚད་གཞི་ size, standard, criteria, rate

ཚབས་ཆེན་ serious, severe

ཚར་ the completed/finished auxiliary verb (9.8)

ཚལ་ vegetable

ཚིག་འཇམ་ gentle, kind, pleasant talk

ཚིག་ཐག་གཅོད་ va. to assert, say emphatically, state definitely

ཚིག་ཐག་བཅད་ va. p. of ཚིག་ཐག་གཅོད་

ཚིམས་ vi. to be satisfied (15.8.3.14)

ཚུགས་ vi. p. of འཚུགས་

ཚུད་ vi. p. of འཚུད་

ཚུར་ hither (5.17.4.11)

ཚུལ་ 1. "manner" particle (9.12); 2. pretend particle (6.8)

ཚུལ་བྱས་ "pretend" construction (6.8)

ཚེ་ 1. life; 2. "when" connective (5.10); 3. conditional connective (6.1)

ཚེ་ཕྱི་མ་ the next life

ཚེས་	date
ཚོ་	pluralizing particle (3.2.2)
ཚོ་ཆུང་	subcommittee, small group
ཚོགས་	va. p. of འཚོགས་
ཚོགས་ཆེན་ཞལ་ངོ་	head disciplinary officer in monastery
ཚོགས་དང་བསོད་ནམས་	virtue, merit
ཚོགས་འདུ་	meeting
ཚོང་ཁང་	shop
ཚོང་པ་	trader
ཚོང་ལས་	business transaction; va. — བྱེད་ to transact business, to engage in commerce
ཚོད་མེད་	immense, boundless, limitless
ཚོན་	paint; va. — གཏོང་
ཚོན་ཁྲ་	colored
ཚོན་ལྡན་	colorful, colored
ཚྭ་	salt
མཚན་	name (h.)
མཚན་བཏགས་	va. p. of མཚན་འདོགས་
མཚན་འདོགས་	va. to name, give a name (h.)
མཚན་མོ་	night
མཚན་ལས་	night work
མཚམས་ (སུ་)	"when" connective (5.10)
མཚམས་འདྲི་	a visit; va. — བྱེད་ or ཞུ་ to visit
མཚམས་མཚམས་	sometimes
མཚམས་སྤྲིན་	colored clouds
མཚོ་སྔོན་	Lake Kokonor
མཚོ་སྔོན་ཞིང་ཆེན་	Qinghai Province
མཚོ་བོད་	Qinghai-Tibet
མཚོ་ལས་ཟབ་པ་	deeper than the ocean (9.17.1.3.10)
མཚོན་བྱེད་	an object used to illustrate or symbolize something
འཚང་ཀ་ཤིག་ཤིག་	crowded, squashed in
འཚར་ལོངས་	growth; vi. — ཡོང་ (བྱུང་) to grow (up)
འཚལ་	1. va. to prostrate; 2. to exist; 3. "I beg", "please", "I request"
འཚིག་	vi. to get burned
འཚུགས་	vi. to get established, found, started, begun
འཚུད་	vi. to get put into, under; to get admitted, included in; to fit into
འཚོ་	va. to look after, to take care of
འཚོ་བ་	livelihood, subsistence; va. — སྐྱེལ་ to earn one's livelihood
འཚོགས་	va. to assemble, convene, hold a meeting
འཚོང་	va. to sell; to barter, trade
འཚོལ་	va. to search, look for
འཚོལ་འདོན་	searching and extracting, exploration and mining; va. — བྱེད་
མཛད་	va. to do (h.)
མཛད་དཀའ་	difficulty, problem (h.)
མཛད་འཁུར་	responsibility (h.)
མཛའ་གཅུགས་	love
མཛའ་བཤེས་	friendship
མཛུབ་ཁྲིད་	direction; guidance; va. — བྱེད་
མཛུབ་མོ་	finger
མཛེས་	pretty, beautiful
མཛེས་སྡུག་	beauty
མཛེས་སྡུག་ལྡན་པ་	beautiful
མཛེས་པོ་	pretty, beautiful

མཛེས་ཤིང་ཡིད་དུ་འོང་བ་	beautiful, charming, attractive, fascinating
མཛོད་ཁང་	a warehouse
འཛགས་	vi. to drip, leak
འཛམ་གླིང་	world
འཛམ་གླིང་གི་ཡང་སྟེང་	"roof of the world"
འཛིན་	va. to seize, hold
འཛིན་ཁོངས་	ownership
འཛིན་གྲྭ་	a class (in school)
འཛིན་ཆས་	furniture
འཛིན་བཟུང་	arrest; va. — བྱེད་
འཛུགས་	1. va. to start, found, establish; 2. va. to set up, hoist, put up; 3. va. to stick in, poke, plant
འཛུགས་བསྐྲུན་	construction, building, development; va. — བྱེད་
འཛུམ་མདངས་	smiling demeanor; va. — འཕྱུར་
འཛུམ་མུལ་	a smile, a laugh; va. — བྱེད་
འཛུལ་	va. to enter
འཛེགས་	va. to climb
འཛེམས་	shyness, restraint
འཛོམ་	vi. to be collected together, be congregated, be gathered
འཛོམས་	vi. p. of འཛོམ་
འཛོམས་པོ་	abundant, plentiful
རྫུ་	va. to pretend, impersonate
རྫུ་འཕྲུལ་	miracle
རྫུན་	lies
རྫོགས་	vi. to be exhausted, finished, out of
རྫོང་	district
རྫོང་ཆེན་	big district; big castle
རྫོང་ཕྲན་	small district; small castle
བརྫུས་	va. p. of རྫུ་
ཞག་སྡོད་	overnight stop, halting place on trip
ཞགས་པ་	lasso; va. — རྒྱག་
ཞན་	ch. county
ཞབས་འདེགས་	service, serving; va. — ཞུ་
ཞབས་སྡོད་	government servant or official; va. — ཞུ་ to serve as a government official
ཞབས་བྲོ་	dance, dancing; va. — རྒྱག་
ཞབས་ཞུ་	service
ཞལ་	face (h.)
ཞལ་གྲེས་	va. to separate, depart, leave (h.)
ཞལ་ལྕེ་	decision, judgment (h.)
ཞལ་མཇལ་	face to face meeting, meeting in person; va. — གནང་ (h.)
ཞལ་འདོན་	prayer; va. — གནང་ (h.)
ཞལ་ཕུད་	the first offering of something; va. — འབུལ་ to give/make the first offering [With respect to the opera festival it refers to giving a first performance, which is a sampler of the different plays.]
ཞལ་པ་	plastered surface; wall
ཞལ་རས་	face (h.); va. — མཇལ་ to meet in person, face to face
ཞལ་ལག་	food (h.)
ཞི་དུལ་སེམས་བཟང་	peaceful and kind
ཞི་བདེ་	peace

ཞི་བདེའི་ཁ་དན་ peace offer
ཞི་བ་ peaceful, peace
ཞི་བའི་བཅིངས་འགྲོལ་ peaceful liberation
ཞིག་ 1. one, a (2.6.1); 2. imperative particle (7.14.1.4.16)
ཞིང་ 1. verbal conjunctive clause connective (5.12); 2. with adjectives (10.3.7)
ཞིང་ཁ་ farm, field
ཞིང་ཆུ་ irrigation; va. — གཏོང་
ཞིང་ཆུ་འདྲེན་གཏོང་ irrigation; va. — བྱེད་
ཞིང་ཆེན་ province, state
ཞིང་པ་ farmer
ཞིང་བྲན་བདག་པོ་ serf owners
ཞིང་འབྲོག་ farmers and nomads
ཞིང་ར་ farm
ཞིང་ལས་ farm/agricultural work
ཞིང་ལས་ཐོན་སྐྱེད་ agricultural production
ཞིན་ཅང་ཡུ་གུར་ Xinjiang Uighur (Autonomous Region)
ཞིན་བོད་ Xinjiang-Tibet
ཞིབ་པ་ details, in detail (7.14.1.4.4)
ཞིབ་འཇུག་ research; va. — བྱེད་
ཞིབ་དཔྱོད་ investigating, checking, examining; va. — བྱེད་
ཞིབ་ཕྲ་ details, in detail
ཞིབ་ཚགས་ 1. precise, detailed, thorough; 2. careful
ཞིབ་བཤེར་ investigation; va. — བྱེད་
ཞིབ་བཤེར་སྙན་ཞུ་ investigatory report
ཞིམ་པོ་ delicious (for food)
ཞུ་ va. to say, tell, ask, request (7.7) (h.)
ཞུ་བ་འདྲེན་ va. to make a request, beseech
ཞུས་ va. p. of ཞུ་ (h.)
ཞུགས་ va. to participate, join, enter
ཞུམ་བུ་ cat
ཞེ་ forties particle (8.1)
ཞེ་དྲགས་ 1. very, a lot; 2. the adjectival "augmentation" particle (10.3.3)
ཞེད་ vi. to be afraid
ཞེས་ quotation marker (4.4)
ཞེས་གྲགས་ vi. to be called
ཞེས་བྱ་བ་ that called (4.4. d.)
ཞོ་སྟོན་ name of the opera festival in Lhasa
ཞྭ་མོ་ hat
ཞོགས་པ་ morning
ཞོགས་ལས་ morning work
ཞོར་ 1.spare time; 2. "coincidental" particle (8.8)
གཞན་ other, another; different
གཞན་དག་ others, another
གཞས་ song; va. — གཏོང་
གཞས་བཏང་ va. p. of གཞས་གཏོང་
གཞས་ཤུད་ first day performance of an opera
གཞས་མ་ singer (female)
གཞི་ནས་ only then (7.14.1.4.10; 8.10.3.17)
གཞི་བཟུང་ "according to" connective (7.10)
གཞིགས་ see ལ་གཞིགས་ཏེ་/ན་
གཞིར་བཟུང་ sm. གཞི་བཟུང་
གཞིས་ཀ་ estate
གཞིས་ཀ་རྩེ་ Shigatse

གཞིས་ཆགས་ resettlement camp
གཞིས་རྩེ་ abbr. གཞིས་ཀ་རྩེ་
གཞུ་ va. to hit, strike
གཞུག་ va. to take part in, to participate in
གཞུང་ government
གཞུང་སྒེར་ government and private; everything
གཞུང་འབྲུ་ government grain/barley
གཞུང་ཞབས་ government official
གཞུང་བཞེས་ confiscation; va. — གཏོང་
གཞུང་ལམ་ highway, main road
གཞུང་ས་དགའ་ལྡན་ཕོ་བྲང་ p.n. of traditional government of Tibet (11.20.2.3.1)
གཞིས་ནིང་ the year before last
གཞོགས་ the side (of)
གཞོན་གཞོན་ young; youth
གཞོན་ནུ་ youth
གཞོན་ནུ་མ་ young girl
གཞོན་པ་ youth
བཞག་ va. p. of འཇོག་
བཞད་ vi. to bloom (flower)
བཞད་མཐོང་སྨོན་རྫོང་ p.n. of a district
བཞའ་ཚན་ wetness, moisture, humidity
བཞའ་བརླན་ wetness, moisture, humidity
བཞི་ four
བཞི་ཁྲི་ 40,000
བཞི་བརྒྱ་ 400
བཞི་བཅུ་ 40
བཞི་ཆ་གཅིག་ one quarter
བཞི་ཆ་གསུམ་ three quarter
བཞི་སྟོང་ 4,000
བཞི་པ་ fourth
བཞི་འབུམ་ 400,000
བཞིན་ like, as (7.14.1.4.10)
བཞིན་དུ་ (ཡོད་པ་རེད་) 1. present tense complement (3.5); 2. "while" (6.5.4)
བཞིན་འདུག་ present tense complement (3.5)
བཞིན་པ་ཡིན་པ་རེད་ present tense complement (3.5)
བཞིན་པར་ 1. present tense complement (3.5; 4.6.4.8; 4.6.4.11); 2. the "while" adverbializer (4.6.4.8; 6.5.4)
བཞིན་པ་རེད་ present tense complement (3.5)
བཞིན་ཡོད་(པ་)རེད་ present tense complement (3.5; 5.17.4.2; 5.17.4.5)
བཞུགས་ va. to stay, live, sit (h.)
བཞུགས་ཡུལ་ place of residence (h.)
བཞུད་ vi. to set (for sun and moon)
བཞུར་ va. to melt
བཞེང་ 1. va. to get up, arise; 2. to build, erect (h.)
བཞེངས་ va. p. of བཞེང་
བཞེས་ va. to take (h.)
བཞོན་ va. to ride (an animal)
ཟ་ va. to eat
ཟ་ཁང་ restaurant
ཟ་ཆས་ foodstuffs
ཟ་བཏུང་ food; eating and drinking
ཟགས་ vi. to fall (off something)
ཟད་ see མ་ཟད་
ཟད་རྡུལ་ worn out
ཟབ་མོ་ deep, profound
ཟམ་པ་ bridge
ཟམ་ཆེན་ large bridge
ཟས་ 1. food; 2. va. p. of ཟ་

ཟི་ལིང་	ch. Silling (city)
ཟིང་འཁྲུག་	disturbance, unrest, riot, uprising; vi. — ལངས་
ཟིང་ཆ་	disturbance, unrest, riot, uprising; vi. — ལངས་
ཟིན་	the "completed/finished" auxiliary verb (9.8)
ཟུག་	1. to be stuck (in); 2. pain; vi. — རྒྱག་ to be in pain; 3. vi. to be pricked
ཟུར་འཇོག་	va. to set, put aside
ཟུར་ཟ་	satire, sarcasm
ཟེར་	sm. ཟེར་, 2 and 3
ཟེར་	1.va. to say (4.6.4.9); 2. vi. to be called (4.4 c); 3. direct speech particle
ཟེར་མཁན་	the one called
ཟེར་བ་	that one called (4.4 c; 5.17.4.13; 8.10.3.1)
ཟེར་སྲོལ་	a traditional, customary saying
ཟོག་	livestock, cattle
ཟོག་གོང་	price of merchandise
ཟོམ་	wooden barrel
ཟོར་ར་	sickle
ཟོལ་	"pretend" particle (6.8)
ཟླ་ཉིན་	last year
ཟླ་བ་	the moon; month
ཟླ་བོ་	spouse
གཟན་ཁང་	hay storage room
གཟན་བརྡུག་	lottery; va. — འཕུལ་ or བསྒྲིལ་
གཟན་པ་	hay
གཟན་རྩྭ་	hay and straw
གཟབ་མཚར་	dressing up, dressed up
གཟབ་གཟབ་	careful(ly); va. — བྱེད་ to be careful or do carefully
གཟའ་ཉི་མ་	Sunday
གཟའ་སྤེན་པ་	Saturday
གཟར་ཅན་	sm. གཟར་པོ་
གཟར་པོ་	steep
གཟི་	a type of precious stone
གཟིག་	leopard
གཟིགས་	1. va. to look; 2. va. to buy (h.)
གཟིགས་སྐོར་	tour (h.)
གཟིགས་སྐྱོང་	taking care of, looking after (h.)
གཟིགས་ཤུད་	first day performance of an opera (preview of operas)
གཟིམ་	va. to sleep (h.)
གཟིམ་ཆུང་	living room (h.)
གཟུགས་ཀྱི་ཉི་མ་	p.n. of an opera
གཟུགས་པོ་	body
གཟེར་	1. nail; 2. va. to wear, put on (e.g., a knife); 3. vi. to pain, hurt
བཟང་	kind, sincere, good
བཟང་ངན་	good + bad = quality
བཟང་ཕེབས་	vi. to be selected as the correct /best one by divine lottery
བཟང་ལན་སློག་	va. to respond with kindness
བཟང་ལན་བསློགས་	va. p. of བཟང་ལན་སློག་
བཟའ་ཟླ་	spouse; husband and wife
བཟུང་	va. p. of འཛིན་
བཟོ་	1. "seem" constructions (9.7); 2. va. to make; 3. causative particle (11.7.2)
བཟོ་ཀུན་	a strike-breaker, scab
བཟོ་གྲྭ་	factory
བཟོ་བཅོས་	repair
བཟོ་བཅོས་རིང་ལུགས་	revisionism

བཟོ་པ་	worker
བཟོ་མི་འདུག་	"does not seem" construction (9.7 e)
བཟོ་ཚོང་ཞིང་ཕྱུགས་	abbr. industry, commerce, agriculture, and animal husbandry
བཟོ་ལ་བལྟས་ན་	see 9.7 j-k
བཟོ་ལས་	industrial work
བཟོད་པ་	tolerating; va. — སྒོམ་
བཟོས་	va. p. of བཟོ་
འ་མན་རི་	p.n.
འང་	see ཀྱང་ (10.15.1.3.2)
འམ་	"or" (8.6)
འི་	see ཀྱི་
ཧ་ལྷག་ཐབས་ཟད་	desperate, helpless
ཧུང་	a sound
ཧུད་ཤོབ་	bragging; va. — ཤོད་ to brag
འོ་	sentence final marker (3.9)
འོ་རྒྱལ་ཐང་	p.n. of a plain near Lhasa
འོག་	beneath, under
འོད་	light
འོད་ཀྱེམ་ཀྱེམ་	glittering
འོད་སྔོང་	brilliant, splendid; vi. — འབར་ to burn brilliantly
འོད་མདངས་	light, brightness, shine
འོད་ཟེར་	sparkling light, light rays
འོན་ཀྱང་	nevertheless (4.6.4.9)
འོས་ཁོངས་	among the candidates
འོས་པ་	worthwhile, worthy, appropriate; a candidate in an election
ཡ་མཚན་ཅན་	strange, unusual
ཡག་	nominalizing particle (6.7); 2. adjective stem of ཡག་པོ་
ཡག་ཉེས་	quality
ཡག་པོ་	good
ཡག་ཙམ་	a little better
ཡག་ཤོས་	best
ཡང་	see ཀྱང་
ཡང་བསྐྱར་	again
ཡང་ཅིན་	ch. a Chinese musical instrument
ཡང་སྟེང་	on top; roof
ཡང་དག་པ་	correct, perfect, accurate
ཡང་ན་	or, either or
ཡང་པོ་	light (in weight)
ཡང་ཡང་	1. over and over again (8.10.3.15); 2. often, frequestly
ཤ ཤཡང་སེ་	often, frequently
ཡང་སྲིད་	reincarnation
ཡན་	above, over
ཡབ་གཞིས་	title of families who have produced a Dalai Lama
ཡབ་យུམ་	parents; father and mother (h.)
ཡའོ་	ch. Yao (a minority group in South China)
ཡར་	upwards, up
ཡར་རྒྱས་	development, progress; va. — གཏོང་ to develop
ཡར་ལུང་	p.n. of a place in southern Tibet
ཡར་ལུང་གཙང་པོ་	p.n. of main east-west river in Tibet
ཡལ་	vi. to vanish, disappear
ཡལ་ག་	branch
ཡས་	nominalizing particle (6.7)
ཡས་མས་	vicinity, up and down, about, approximately
ཡི་	see ཀྱི་

ཡི་གེ་	letter
ཡིག་སྐྱེལ་	postal service
ཡིག་རྩིས་	knowledge (lit., letters and mathematics)
ཡིག་ཚད་	exam
ཡིད་	mind, thought
ཡིད་ཆགས་	vi. to get, become attached to
ཡིད་ཕང་ཆད་	vi. to be discouraged, disappointed, sad
ཡིད་དུ་འོང་བ་	beautiful, pleasing
ཡིད་བཞིན་ནོར་བུ་	precious wish-fulfilling gem (12.20.2.3.1)
ཡིད་འོང་མཛེས་སྡུག་ལྡན་པ་	beautiful, pretty
ཡིན་	the linking verb "is" (1.10)
ཡིན་ན་ཡང་	nevertheless (5.17.4.4)
ཡིན་ནའང་	see ཡིན་ན་ཡང་
ཡིན་པ་རེད་	linking verb construction (1.10; 13.5.3.4)
ཡིན་པས་སོ་	because is (7.14.1.4.15)
ཡིན་མིན་	""whether or not" interrogative (8.6; 9.17.1.3.24)
ཡིབས་	va. to hide
ཡིས་	instrumental particle (3.1)
ཡུ་བ་	a handle
ཡུག་གཅིག་ཏུ་	in one piece
ཡུད་ཙམ་	a moment
ཡུད་ཙམ་སོང་	after a moment passed
ཡུན་	duration; for a time
ཡུན་ནན་ཞིང་ཆེན་	Yunnan province
ཡུན་ནས་ཡུན་དུ་	forever
ཡུན་རིང་	long time
ཡུལ་	1. place, area, region, country; 2. location particle (10.13)
ཡུལ་སྐོར་སྤྲོ་འཆམ་	visiting, sight seeing
ཡུལ་སྐོར་སྤྲོ་འཆམ་པ་	tourist
ཡུལ་གོམས་གཤིས་ལུགས་	native customs, habits, way of life
ཡུལ་གྱུར་	vi. to move from place to place, wandering about, exile
ཡུལ་བྲོལ་	taking refuge, going into exile, fleeing
ཡུལ་སྲོལ་	customs of an area/ region
ཡོ་ནན་	ch. Vietnam
ཡོང་	1. va. to come; 2. as an auxiliary verb (11.20.2.3.22); 3. in simultaneous verb constructions (8.10.3.19)
ཡོང་ཁུངས་	origin
ཡོང་འབབ་	income
ཡོངས་	all, overall
ཡོངས་གྲགས་	well-known, famous
ཡོངས་འཛིན་	teacher, tutor (usu. of Dalai Lama) (h.)
ཡོངས་རྫོགས་	all, entire, whole
ཡོད་	existential verb (2.6)
ཡོད་པ་རེད་	existential verb (2.6)
ཡོད་པ་ཡིན་པས་ན་རེད་	see ཡོད་པས་རེད་
ཡོད་པ་ཡིན་པས་ནའི་	see ཡོད་པས་རེད་
ཡོད་པ་ཡིན་ཙང་རེད་	see ཡོད་པས་རེད་

ཡོད་པས་དབང་གིས་རེད་	see ཡོད་པས་རེད་
ཡོད་པས་རེད་	because (something) exists (7.14.1.4.15)
ཡོད་པས་སོ་	see ཡོད་པས་རེད་
ཡོད་མེད་	"whether or not" interrogative (8.6)
ཡོད་ཚད་	all, everything
ཡོན་ཏན་	knowledge
ཡོན་ཚང་	standard of knowledge or education; qualification (education)
ཡོན་ཚད་	ability, qualifications, standards
ཡོབ་རྡུང་	spurring on; va.— གཏོང་
གཡག་	yak
གཡང་གཟར་ཅན་	precipitous
གཡར་	va. to loan, lend
གཡས་	right (direction)
གཡས་པ་	the right one (usu. for hands)
གཡས་གཡོན་	left and right; with respect to numbers, this conveys "more or less"
གཡུ་	turquoise
གཡུག་གཡུག་	shaking (one's head no); va. — བྱེད་ (usu. མགོ་བོ་--)
གཡུགས་	va. to throw
གཡོ་	va. to move, shake
གཡོ་འགུལ་	shaking, moving; vi. — ཐེབས་ to be shaken, moved (including emotionally moved)
གཡོ་སྒྱུ་	cunning, deceit
གཡོ་ཟླད་	dishonesty, deception
གཡོག་པོ་	servant (male)
གཡོག་མོ་	servant (female)
གཡོགས་	va. 1. put on clothing, etc.; 2. to blame
གཡོན་	left (direction)
གཡོན་མ་	the left one (usu. for hands)
ར་	1. dative-locative particle (2.6.1); 2. goat; 3. adverbializing particle (6.5.3; 6.5.4); 4. with nominalized verb stems (6.6.3; 6.6.4)
ར་ཚེ་	abbr. of ར་མོ་ཚེ་
ར་སྤྲུགས་	confronting/exposing a person's misdoings in the presence of the person and others; proving something; va. — གཏོང་
ར་སྤྲོད་	proof, evidence; va. — བྱེད་
ར་མོ་ཚེ་	p.n. of a temple in Lhasa
ར་ས་འཕྲུལ་སྣང་	name of the Cathedral temple
རག་	vi. to obtain
རག་སྦི་	Rugby (a school in England)
རང་	1. self, oneself; 2. "no choice" construction (11.13)
རང་སྐྱོང་	self-governing; autonomous
རང་སྐྱོང་ལྗོངས་	autonomous region
རང་སྐྱོང་ཤན་	autonomous county
རང་གྲུབ་བཙན་ས་	natural barrier
རང་དགར་	leaving something as it is; free
རང་རྒྱལ་	our country
རང་ཚེ་རང་བཀུར་	conceit(ed)
རང་འཇགས་	as before, unchanged
རང་ཉིད་	itself, oneself (5.17.4.4)
རང་ཉེས་	own crime/fault
རང་སྟོབས་ རང་ཁྲིལ་	self-reliance and hard work; va. — བྱེད་
རང་འབབ་གི་ཆུ་	tap water, water supply

རང་བྱུང་ཁམས་	nature
རང་དབང་	freedom, liberty, independence
རང་དབང་མེད་པར་	uncontrollably
རང་སྦྱོང་	homework
རང་བཙན་	independence
རང་ཡུལ་	one's own country/area
རན་	"time to do" particle (11.1)
རབ་ཏུ་	thoroughly, completely
རབ་བྱུང་	the sixty-year cycle in the Tibetan calendar
རལ་གྲི་	sword
རལ་པ་	long hair; matted hair
རས་	woven cotton or synthetic material, fabric
རས་གོས་	cotton clothing
རས་ཆུང་	p.n. of an opera
རི་	hill, mountain
རི་ཀླུང་	rivers and hills; countryside scenery
རི་མཐོ་	high mountain
རི་དྭགས་	herbivorous wild animal; va. — རྒྱག་ to hunt
རི་པིན་	Japan
རི་བོང་	rabbit
རི་མོ་མཁན་	painter, artist
རིག་གནས་	culture
རིག་གནས་སློབ་གསོའི་ལས་ཁུངས་	cultural and educational institution
རིག་གནས་གསར་བརྗེ་	the Cultural Revolution
རིག་གནས་(ཀྱི་)གསར་བརྗེ་ཆེན་པོ་	the Great Cultural Revolution
རིག་རྩལ་	art and literature
རིག་གཞུང་	culture; academic
རིག་གསར་	new sciences
རིགས་	1. kind, category, thing; 2. race, ethnic group, nationality
རིང་	"when" connective (5.10); 2. during (11.20.2.3.21)
རིང་ཐུང་	long and short; length, distance
རིང་པོ་	long
རིང་བ་	longer
རིན་ཆེན་	precious, valuable
རིན་པོ་ཆེ་	1. precious, valuable; 2. title of an incarnation
རིན་སྤུངས་	p.n. of a place in west Tibet
རིམ་པར་	gradually, in series, in stages, one after another
རིམ་བཞི་	fourth rank official in traditional Tibetan government
རིམ་བཞིན་	successively, gradually
རིམ་པར་	gradual in series, in stages, one after another
རིའུ་མིག་	chart, diagram
རིལ་	vi. to fall down
རིལ་པོ་	1. whole; 2. round
རུ་	1. dative-locative particle (2.6.1); 2. adverbializing particle (6.5.3; 6.6 5); 3. with nominalized verb stems (6.6.3; 6.6.4)
རུ་སྒྲིག་	va. to march in formation, to line up in rows
རུ་སྒྲིག་ས་ལམ་	term used in traditional society for military salute, presenting of arms; va. — ཞུ་

རུ་བསྟར་	a line, row
རུ་སྣེ་	leader or head of a column, line, row
རུང་	1. "even though" clause connective (7.2); 2. "fit/ worthy" particle (9.15)
རེ་	1. "hope" particle (9.11); 2. sixties particle (8.1); 3. "each" particle (10.8)
རེ་འགས་	some, several
རེ་འདུན་	hope
རེ་བ་	hope
རེ་བཞིན་	every, each
རེ་ཟུང་	a couple of, a few
རེ་རེ་	"each" particle (10.8)
རེ་རེའི་	"of each" (10.8)
རེ་རེར་	"to each" (10.8; 9.17.2.3.5)
རེ་རེས་	"by each" (10.8)
རེག་	va. to touch
རེད་	linking verb (1.10)
རེད་འདུག་	see 13.5.3.22
རོ་	corpse
རོ་ཟ་	pejorative phrase: corpse-eater
རོ་ལངས་	1. lit., zombie; 2. slang: make a comeback; vi.— རྒྱག་
རོགས་སྐྱོར་	help; va. — བྱེད་
རོགས་དངུལ་	money to help, aid/ relief money
རོགས་གནང་	va. to help (7.13) (h.)
རོགས་བྱེད་	va. to help (7.13) (h.)
རོགས་རམ་	help; va. — གནང་ or བྱེད་
རོགས་རམ་ ཚོགས་པ་	relief, aid agency
རོལ་	va. to enjoy
རོལ་ཆ་	music; va. — གཏོང་
རྭ་སྒྲེང་	p.n. of a monastery north of Lhasa
རྭ་སྟག་	abbr. Reting and Taktra (2 regents after the death of the 13th Dalai Lama)
རླངས་འཁོར་	car, automobile
རླབས་ཆེན་	great
རླུང་	wind
རླུང་དམར་དྲག་པོ་	hurricane, typhoon, cyclone, vi. — འཚུབས་ (12.20.2.3.9)
རླུང་མགྱོགས་	fast, quick
རློག་	va. to destroy, smash, to lose
བརླགས་	vi. p. རློག་
ལ་	1. to (the dative-locative particle) (2.6.1) (also see ར་); 2. conjunctive of adjectives ("as well as") (10.3.7); 3. as a clause connector (10.4.1); 4. a mountain pass; va. — རྒྱག་ to cross a mountain pass
ལ་ཁད་ལ་	"about to" clause connective (7.11)
ལ་ཁར་	"about to" clause connective (7.11)
ལ་དཔག་ (སྟེ་) (ན་)	"according to" construction (12.15)
ལ་གཞིགས་ (ཏེ་) (ན་)	"according to" construction (12.15)
ལའང་	even
ལ་ཡང་	even
ལ་ལ་	some, a few, several
ལག་	hand
ལག་འཁྱེར་	permit
ལག་ཆ་	tool

ལག་རྟགས་ present
ལག་པ་ hand
ལག་རྩལ་ craft, dexterity, skill
ལག་རྩེད་སྤོ་ལོ་ basketball
ལག་ལེན་ practicing, putting into practice
ལག་ཤེས་བཟོ་གྲྭ་ handicraft center/factory
ལགས་ honorific word used after personal names or titles
ལང་ལོང་ sluggish, languid
ལངས་ va. to start; to get up, arise
ལངས་ཕྱོགས་ position
ལན་ 1. answer, reply, message; va. — སྐྱེལ་ or སློག་ or འདེབས་; 2. times
ལན་སློག་ va. to reply, answer in kind, act in response to, counter; 2. noun or adjective + — see (10.15.1.3.3)
ལན་བསློགས་ va. p. of ལན་སློག་
ལབ་ va. to say
ལམ་ག་ road
ལམ་རྒྱུད་ area on both sides of a road
ལམ་སྟོན་ leading, guiding; va. — འཁྲིད་
ལམ་བར་ on the road
ལམ་གཟུར་ side of a road; va. — འཛུག་ to divert, to make an object or person move aside
ལམ་བཟོ་ road construction
ལམ་ལུགས་ way, system
ལམ་སང་ sm. ལམ་སེང་
ལམ་སེང་ at once, immediately
ལས་ 1. than (7.14.1.4.14; 8.10.3.7); 2. from
ལས་ཀ་ work; va. — བྱེད་
ལས་ཁུངས་ office, department
ལས་གྲྭ་ workshop, work site
ལས་འགན་ task, responsibility, duty; va. — འཁུར་ or གནང་/བཞེས་
ལས་འགུལ་ campaign, movement
ལས་དོན་ work , business
ལས་བྱེད་པ་ official, cadre, worker, clerk
ལས་སྐྱེལ་ assistant, helper
ལས་མི་ worker
ལས་ཞོར་ spare time
ལས་ཟུར་ present and former (office holder)
ལས་བཟོ་ abbr. of ལས་བྱེད་པ་ and བཟོ་པ་ (officials and workers)
ལས་རིགས་ trades, occupations of all kinds
ལས་གསར་ new work
ལིའུ་ཧྲའོ་ཆི་ Liu Shaoqi
ལུག་ sheep
ལུགས་ "manner" construction particle (9.12; 9.17.1.3.25)
ལུག་ཁྱུ་ herd of sheep
ལུགས་སྲོལ་ custom
ལུག་རྫི་ shepherd
ལུང་པ་ place, country
ལུང་ཤར་ p.n. of a noble family in Tibet
ལུས་ 1. vi. to be left behind, left over; 2. vi. to get stuck, bogged down; 3. with verbs (see 11.20.2.3.15)
ལུས་རྩལ་ physical exercise
ལུས་རྩལ་བྱེད་ས་ athletic field
ལུས་པོ་ body
ལུས་སྲོག་ life
ལི་དབར་ ch. kilometer

ལེགས་འགྲུབ་	vi. to achieve well
ལེགས་བཅོས་	reform; va. — བྱེད་ to reform
ལེགས་རྟོགས་	good understanding
ལེགས་ལྡན་ས་ཧེབ་	p.n.
ལེགས་སྦྱར་	speech
ལེན་	va. to take, to get
ལེའུ་	chapter
ལོ་	1. year; 2. "be fit /worthy" particle (9.15)
ལོ་རྒྱུས་	history
ལོ་ཏོག་	crop
ལོ་སྟར་	every year
ལོ་ཟླ་	year and month
ལོ་འདབ་	leaf
ལོ་ན་	age; vi. — སོན་ to grow old
ལོ་མ་	leaf
ལོ་གསར་	new year
ལོག་	va. to return
ལོག་སྤྱོད་ཅན་	reactionary
ལོག་སྤྱོད་པ་	a reactionary
ལོག་སྤྱོད་སྲིད་གཞུང་	reactionary government
ལོང་	"time to do" particle (13.2)
ལོན་	vi. to reach, to get
ལོན་ཀྲོན་	London
ལོས་	1. "certainty" particle (7.8); 2. in adjectival constructions (10.3.8)
ཤ་	meat
ཤ་གཟན་	meat-eater
ཤ་སྟག་	1. only; 2. with verbs, see 11.20.2.3.25
ཤ་ཐོར་རུས་ཐོར་	destroy flesh and bones, rip to sheds, annihilate
ཤ་རིད་པ་	thin, emaciated
ཤག་	1. "certainty" particle (7.8); 2. perfect tense particle (9.13)
ཤད་	the vertical line marking the end of clauses
ཤན་ཁ་གྲུ་ཁ་	the "Shenka" boat landing
ཤན་འབྱེད་	va. to separate, differentiate, distinguish between
ཤར་	1. vi. to arise, rise; 2. east ; 3. direct, straight; va. — གཏོང་ to send directly
ཤར་གླིང་དབུས་མ་	Middle East
ཤས་	several (abbr. of ཁ་ཤས་)
ཤས་ཆེ་	"maybe" particle (15.1)
ཤི་	vi. to die
ཤི་གསོན་	dead or alive
ཤིག་	1. imperative particle (7.14.1.4.16); 2. a, one (2.6.1)
ཤིང་	1.verbal conjunctive clause connective (5.12); 2. with adjectives (10.3.7); 3. wood
ཤིང་ཁང་	wooden house
ཤིང་གླང་	wood-ox year
ཤིང་སྒྲོམ་	scaffold
ཤིང་ཅང་ཡུ་གུར་	Xinjiang Uighur (autonomous region)
ཤིང་ཏོག་	fruit
ཤིང་རྟ་འཁོར་ལོ་	horse cart
ཤིང་སྡོང་	tree
ཤིང་ནགས་	forest
ཤིང་སྦྲུལ་	wood-snake (year)
ཤིང་བཟོ་བ་	carpenter
ཤིང་ལོ་	tree leaf
ཤིང་སོན་	tree seeds

ཤིན་ཏུ་	1. very; 2. with adjectives (10.3.3)
ཤུགས་	strength, power
ཤུགས་རྐྱེན་	influence, effect; vi. — ཐེབས་ to have an effect, to be influenced
ཤུགས་བསྐྱེད་སྤོབས་སྐྱེལ་	energetically, vigorously; va. — བྱེད་
ཤུགས་ཆེན་པོ་	big, strong, loud
ཤུགས་སྣོན་	reinforcement; va. — རྒྱག་
ཤུལ་	"while" clause connective (10.1)
ཤུལ་མེད་	without a trace, without remains
ཤེད་ཤུགས་	strength
ཤེས་	1. va. to know; 2. question marker (4.4)
ཤེས་རྟོགས་	knowledge, understanding
ཤེས་པ་བྱེད་	see 14.8.3.10
ཤེས་ཡོན་	knowledge, education
ཤོག་	1. come!; 2. in "may it come" constructions (vb. + པ་ + —) (12.19)
ཤོང་	vi. to fit, hold, have room for
ཤོད་	va. imp. of བཤད་
ཤོད་སྲོལ་ལ་	id. as is commonly said, according to oral legend (9.17.1.3.1)
ཤོར་	1. vi. to lose; 2. vi. to escape, get loose (11.20.2.3.14); 3. vi. verb conveying involuntary action (9.17.2.3.10; 14.8.3.6)
ཤོས་	the superlative particle (10.3.4)
གཤམ་དུ་	below, beneath
གཤམ་གསལ་	listed, presented, cited below
གཤིས་	causal connective (5.9)
གཤིས་རྒྱུད་	character, personality
གཤེ་གཤེ་	scolding; va. — གཏོང་
གཤེགས་	vi. to die (h.)
གཤོག་པ་	wings
གཤོམ་	va. to set out, arrange, prepare for
བཤད་	va. to tell, say
བཤད་ཉན་	telling and listening
བཤུ་	va. to peel, skin, take off
བཤུ་གཞོག་གྲལ་རིམ་	the exploitive class
ས་	1. ground, earth; 2. location particle (10.13)
ས་ཁུལ་	region, zone
ས་ཁོངས་	territory
ས་ཁྱོན་	size of an area
ས་ག་ཟླ་བ་	name of the 4th Tibetan month
ས་ཆ་	place
ས་གཏེར་	minerals
ས་ཐིག་	a line of demarcation, boundary line
ས་བདག་	landlord
ས་གནས་	regional, local
ས་གནས་སྲིད་གཞུང་	1. local government; 2. the term that is used in the Tibet Autonomous Region for the traditional government of the Dalai Lamas
ས་ཕག་	brick
ས་ཚིགས་	station
ས་མཚམས་	border
ས་གཞི་	earth

ས་ཡ་གཅིག་ one million
ས་ལམ་ salutation
ས་གཤིས་ཀྱི་གནས་ཚུལ་ geological structure/features
ས་སྲིབ་མཚམས་ at dusk
སང་དགོང་ tomorrow night
སང་ཉིན་ tomorrow
སང་ཕོད་ next year
སི་ཁྲོན་ Sichuan
སི་སྤན་ hot chili
སིཁུ་ step (on stairs)
སུ་ 1. who; 2. dative-locative particle (2.6.1)
སུ་འདྲ་ཞིག་ whoever
སུ་ཡི་ whose (12.8)
སུ་ཡིས་ by whom (12.8)
སུ་ལ་ to whom (12.7)
སུན་སྣང་ annoyed, bothered, fed up; va. — བྱེད་
སུམ་ཅུ་ thirty
སུའི་ whose (12.8)
སུར་ to whom (12.7)
སུས་ by whom (12.8)
སེ་འབྲས་ Sera and Drepung monasteries
སེ་འབྲས་དགེ་གསུམ་ Sera, Drepung, and Ganden monasteries
སེ་ར་ Sera monastery
སེང་གེ་ lion
སེམས་ 1. mind; 2. "want" particle (9.10)
སེམས་སྐྱོ་པོ་ sad
སེམས་ཁྲལ་ worry; va. — བྱེད་
སེམས་འགུལ་ emotionally moved, touched; vi. — ཐེབས་ to be moved, touched
སེམས་ཅན་ sentient being, animal
སེམས་སྡུག་ sadness, depression
སེམས་པ་ thoughts
སེམས་འཚབ་ vi. to be worried, anxious, nervous
སེམས་ཤུགས་ enthusiasm; va. — བྱེད་
སེར་སྐྱ་ monks and laymen
སེར་དྲག་ hailstorm
སེར་དྲག་བབས་ vi. to hail
སེར་སྣ་ avaricious, greedy
སེར་པོ་ yellow
སེར་དམག་ monk soldiers
སོ་ 1. tooth; va. — རྒྱག་ to bite; 2. sentence final particle; 3. thirties particle (8.1)
སོ་ 1.thirties particle (8.1); 2. sentence final particle (6.10.4.15)
སོ་སོ་ each his own, individually, separately (10.15.2.3.7)
སོ་ནམ་པ་ farmer
སོ་པ་ spy
སོག་པོ་ Mongolian
སོགས་ enumerative particle (6.4)
སོང་ 1. past tense particle (3.4); 2. va. p. of འགྲོ་
སོད་ va. imp. of གསོད་
སོན་ 1. seed; 2. va. to arrive, come, receive
སོར་གདུབ་ ring
སོལ་བ་ coal
སོས་པ་ fresh
སྲ་བརྟན་ firm, stable, strong

སྲབ་ 1. bridle; 2. adj. comp. of སྲབ་པོ་
སྲབ་པོ་ thin
སྲས་མོ་ daughter (h.)
སྲས་སྲོས་ children (h.)
སྲིད་ "possible" auxiliary verb (9.16)
སྲིད་སྐྱོང་ regent
སྲིད་འགན་ political responsibility; va. — བཞེས་ to take political responsibility
སྲིད་ཇུས་ policy
སྲིད་རྙིང་ old (former) government
སྲིད་བློན་ prime minister
སྲིད་དབང་ political power, secular power
སྲིད་འཛིན་ president; va. — བྱེད་ to serve/ act as/be president; 2. va. — བྱེད་ to rule
སྲིད་གཞུང་ government
སྲིད་ཟུར་ ex-prime minister
སྲུང་ va. to guard, defend, protect
སྲུང་སྐྱོང་ protection; va. — བྱེད་
སྲུང་སྐྱོབ་ defending, safe-guarding, protecting; va. — བྱེད་
སྲུང་དམག་ bodyguards, bodyguard troops; defending troops
སྲུང་བརྩི་ respect, honor, abiding by
སྲོག་ life
སྲོག་སྐྱོབ་ va. to save someone's life
སྲོག་ཆགས་ living, animate, sentient creature/being
སྲོང་བཙན་སྒམ་པོ་ p.n. of a Tibetan king
སྲོལ་ "way/ custom of doing" particle (9.17.1.3.1; 11.20.2.3.3)

སླང་ roasting pan
སླད་ purposive connective (5.13)
སླར་ཡང་ once again (7.14.1.4.3; 7.14.1.4.17)
སླེབས་ vi. to arrive (5.7.2)
སློག་ 1. va. to turn upside down; 2. va. to send back
སློང་ 1. va. to cause to stand up; 2. va. to beg; 3. va. to incite, cause to start, provoke
སློང་མཁན་ beggar
སློབ་ va. to study; to learn
སློབ་གྲྭ་ school
སློབ་གྲྭ་བ་ student
སློབ་སྟོན་ advice, teachings
སློབ་ཕྲུག་ student
སློབ་སྦྱོང་ study; va. — བྱེད་
སློབ་ཚན་ lesson
སློབ་གསོ་ education; va. — བྱེད་
བསླངས་ va. p. of སློང་
གསད་ va. f. of གསོད་
གསར་འགྱུར་ news
གསར་བརྗེ་ revolution; va. — བྱེད་
གསར་བརྗེར་ངོ་ལོག་ counter-revolution(ary)
གསར་གཏོད་ invention, new creation
གསར་པ་ new
གསར་འཛུགས་ newly established; va. — བྱེད་
གསར་བཟོ་ new, newly made; va. — བྱེད་
གསལ་ 1. clear (7.14.2.4.2); 2. in verbal constructions (15.4); 3. for its use in newspaper stories, see 7.14.2.4.2
གསལ་ལྷར་ see 7.14.2.4.2
གསལ་སྟོན་ demonstration

གསལ་པོ་	clear, clearly
གསུང་	va. to say (h.)
གསུང་རྩོམ་	writings, works (literary) (h.)
གསུང་བཤད་	speech
གསུངས་	va. p. of གསུང་ (h.)
གསུམ་	three
གསུམ་ཁྲི་	30,000
གསུམ་བརྒྱ་	300
གསུམ་བརྒྱ་དང་བཞི་བཅུ་ཞེ་དགུ་	349
གསུམ་ཆ་གཉིས་	two thirds
གསུམ་སྟོང་	3,000
གསུམ་པ་	third
གསུམ་འབུམ་	300,000
གསེར་	gold
གསེར་ཁྲི་	golden throne
གསོ་	1. vi. to heal; 2. va. to rear, raise, feed
གསོ་བ་རིག་པ་	the science of medicine
གསོག་	va. to save up, accumulate
གསོག་འཇོག་	saving, accumulating; va. — བྱེད་
གསོད་	va. to kill
གསོན་ལམ་འཚོལ་	va. to seek a way to stay alive
གསོན་པོ་	alive
གསོལ་	va. to make an offering to a god
གསོལ་སྟོན་	banquet, feast; va. — གཤོམ་
གསོལ་བ་	prayer; va. — འདེབས་
གསོལ་བ་བཏབ་	va. p. of གསོལ་བ་འདེབས་
གསོལ་རས་	gift, tip (h.); va. — གནང་
གསོས་	va. p. of གསོ་
བསགས་	va. p. of གསོག་
བསད་	va. p. of གསོད་
བསམ་	va. to think
བསམ་འཆར་	opinion; va. — གནང་
བསམ་དོན་	desire, wish, goal
བསམ་པ་རྣམ་དག་	sincere, earnest, genuine
བསམ་བློ་	thinking; va. — གཏོང་
བསམ་ཚུལ་	thoughts, opinion
བསམ་ཚུལ་བྲི་དེབ་	suggestion book
བསམ་ཡུལ་ལས་འདས་པ་	incredible, beyond one's imagination (9.17.1.3.3)
བསམ་ཤེས་	understanding, consciousness
བསམས་	va. p. of བསམ་
བསུ་	va. to receive, welcome
བསོད་ནམས་	1. p.n.; 2. merit (in Buddhist sense), good fortune, luck
བསླད་སྐྱོན་	corruption; va. — གཏོང་ to corrupt
བསླབས་	va. p. of སློབ་
བསློགས་	va. p. of སློག་
བསླངས་	va. p. of སློང་
བསྲུས་མ་	Tibetan style tea
ཧ་ཧ་	""he he," "ha ha"
ཧ་གོ་	vi. to understand
ཧ་ཅང་	very
ཧ་ལས་	vi. to be surprised
ཧ་ཤང་བདུད་མོ་	p.n.
ཧང་སངས་	vi. to be surprised, shocked
ཧིན་དུ་	India; Hindu
ཧུའི་རིགས་	Hui nationality
ཧུར་བརྡ་	hurda (a sound)
ཧུར་ཐག་	energetically
ཧུར་བརྩོན་	diligence, diligently, energetically
ཧོ་ཀྲེ་རིགས་	Hote nationality
ཧོ་ཐོག་ཐུ་	Hotoktu (highest rank for incarnate lamas)
ཧོའོ་ཅིན་	ch. a Chinese musical instrument

ཧོན་ཐོར་ vi. p. of ཧོན་འཐོར་

ཧོན་འཐོར་ vi. to be shocked, stunned, surprised

ཧྲི་ཡོན་ ch. commune member

ཧྲིལ་ཧྲིལ་ round (for objects)

ཧྲིལ་པོ་ whole

ཧྲུ་ཅི་ ch. chairman

ཧྲུའུ་ཅི་ ch. chairman

ལྷ་ a god, deity

ལྷ་ཀླུ་ p.n. of a noble family in Tibet

ལྷ་སྐུ་ statue of a diety

ལྷ་ཁང་ temple

ལྷ་རྒྱལ་ལོ་ "May the gods be victorious"

ལྷ་ང་ kneecap

ལྷ་གཅིག་ཀུན་བཟང་ p.n.

ལྷ་ལྡན་ Lhasa

ལྷ་མོ་ goddess

ལྷ་མོ་ཚོགས་པ་ opera association

ལྷ་ཡུལ་ heaven

ལྷ་རབ་ best

ལྷ་ས་ Lhasa

ལྷག་ left-over

ལྷག་པར་(དུ་) moreover, in particular (4.6.4.9); particularly (6.5.5)

ལྷག་ཙམ་(དུ་) a little more, a little over

ལྷག་བསམ་ p.n.

ལྷག་བསམ་རྣམ་དག་ sincere, genuine, cordial

ལྷག་བསམ་ཟོལ་མེད་ complete sincerity, openness

ལྷགས་ vi. to come, arrive

ལྷད་ཁྲུད་པ་ p.n. (of aristocratic family)

ལྷན་ together with (h.)

ལྷན་རྒྱས་ together with (h.)

ལྷན་པ་ a patch

ལྷན་སྒྲིལ་ together (h.)

ལྷབ་ལྷུབ་དུ་གཡོ་ vi. to be waving, to be fluttering, to be flapping

ལྷམ་ shoe

ལྷམ་མཐིལ་ sole of boots, shoes

ལྷིངས་འཇགས་ quiet, peaceful

ལྷུག་ loose, easy

ལྷུང་ vi. to fall

ལྷེ་པ་ slice, sliver

ལྷོ་ཁ་ p.n. of region in southern Tibet

ལྷོ་ཕྱོགས་ southern direction, side

ཨ་ཁ་ "oh my," "too bad"

ཨ་ཁུ་ uncle

ཨ་ཁུ་སྟོན་པ་ p.n.

ཨ་མཆོག་ ear

ཨ་ཕ་ father

ཨ་ཕོ་ a title (use mostly by eastern Tibetan people)

ཨ་མ་ mother

ཨ་མེ་རི་ཀ་ America

ཨང་ imp. particle (15.8.3.20)

ཨབ་གྷ་ནི་སི་ཐན་ Afghanistan

ཨམ་ཕྲག་ pocket (formed by fold of traditional dress)

ཨར་པོ་ construction; va. —རྒྱག་

ཨར་ལས་ construction, building work

ཨི་ཀྲར་ལི་ Italy

ཨུ་ ch. abbr. of ཨུ་ཡོན་ལྷན་ཁང་

ཨུ་ཡོན་ལྷན་ཁང་ ch. committee, council

ཨུ་ཚུགས་ insistence, persistence; va. —རྒྱག་

ཨ་ཅི་ཨ་ཅི་ "oh my!

ཨ་ཞང་ uncle (maternal)

ཨའུ་ཙམ་ not too bad, so-so

ཨུ་ཚུགས་ insisting; va. —རྒྱག་

ཨུ་ཧུ་ལགས་	"oh my
ཨེ་མ་	"oh my
ཨེམ་ཆི་	doctor
ཨེར་ལང་རི་བོ་	p.n. of a mountain range in Eastern Tibet

Appendix A

VERB DECLENSION TABLE

Present	Past	Future	Imperative
ཀླུབ་	བཀླུབས་	བཀླུབ་	ཀླུབས་
ཀློག་	བཀླགས་	བཀླག་	ཀློག་
དཀྲོལ་	དཀྲོལ་	དཀྲོལ་	དཀྲོལ་
བཀའ་འབེབས་	བཀའ་ཕབ་	བཀའ་དབབ་	བཀའ་ཕོབ་
ཀྲུ་	བཀྲུས་	བཀྲུ་	ཀྲུས་
ཀྲོ་	བཀྲོས་	བཀྲོ་	ཀྲོས་
སྐྱོང་	བསྐྱངས་	བསྐྱང་	སྐྱོངས་
སྐྱེལ་	བསྐྱལ་	བསྐྱལ	སྐྱོལ་
སྐྱེ་	སྐྱེས་	སྐྱེ་	
སྐྱོབ་	བསྐྱབས་	བསྐྱབ་	སྐྱོབས་
སྐྱོར་	བསྐྱོར་	བསྐྱོར	སྐྱོར་
སྐུར་	བསྐུར་	བསྐུར་	སྐུར་
སྐུད་	བསྐུས་	བསྐུ་	སྐུས་
སྐོང་	བསྐངས་	བསྐང་	སྐོངས་
སྐོར་	བསྐོར་	བསྐོར་	སྐོར
སྐོ་	བསྐོས་	བསྐོ་	སྐོས་
སྐྱོང	བསྐྱངས	བསྐྱང་	སྐྱོངས་
སྐྱུར་"	བསྐྱུར་	བསྐྱུར་	སྐྱུར
སྐྱེངས་	སྐྱེངས	སྐྱེངས	
སྐྱོད་	བསྐྱོད་	བསྐྱོད	སྐྱོད་
འཁུར་	ཁུར་	འཁུར་	ཁུར་
འཁོར་	འཁོར་	འཁོར་	
འཁོལ་	བཀོལ་/ཁོལ་	བཀོལ་/འཁོལ་	ཁོལ་
ཁྱབ་	ཁྱབ་	ཁྱབ་	
མཁྱེན་	མཁྱེན་	མཁྱེན	མཁྱེན
འཁྱུད་	འཁྱུད	འཁྱུད	འཁྱུད
འཁྱེར་	ཁྱེར་	འཁྱེར་	ཁྱེར་
འཁྲབ་	འཁྲབས་	འཁྲབ	འཁྲོབས་
འཁྲིད་	ཁྲིད་	འཁྲིད	ཁྲིད་
འཁྲུང་	འཁྲུངས་	འཁྲུང་	

Present	Past	Future	Imperative
འཁྲུད་	བཀྲུས་	བཀྲུ་	ཁྲུས་
གྱུར་	གྱུར་	གྱུར་	
གྱོན་	གྱོན	གྱོན	གྱོན
འགྱུར་	གྱུར་	འགྱུར	
གྲོལ་	གྲོལ	གྲོལ	
གླ་	གླས་	གླ་	གློས་
གློད་	གློད	གློད	གློད
དགོད་	བགད་	བགད་	དགོད་
འགམ་	འགམས་	འགམ	འགོམས་
འགུལ་	འགུལ་	འགུལ་	
འགེལ་	བཀལ་	དགལ་	ཁེབས་
འགོག	བཀོག་	དགོག་	ཁོགས་
འགོད་	བཀོད་	དགོད་	ཁོད་/འཁོད་
འགེབས་	བཀབ་	དགབ་	ཁེབས་
འགོར་	འགོར་	འགོར་	
འགྲེལ་	འགྲེལ	འགྲེལ	
འགྲན་	འགྲན	འགྲན	འགྲན
འགྲིག་	འགྲིགས་	འགྲིག་	
འགྲོ་	ཕྱིན་	འགྲོ་	སོང་
འགྲུབ་	གྲུབ་	འགྲུབ་	
འགྲོལ་	བཀྲོལ་	དགྲོལ་	ཁྲོལ
འགྲོག་	འགྲོགས་	འགྲོག་	
རྒྱག་	བརྒྱབ་	བརྒྱག་/རྒྱག་	རྒྱོབ་
རྒྱུག་	བརྒྱུགས་/རྒྱུགས་	བརྒྱུག་/རྒྱུག་	རྒྱུགས་
སྒྲུག་	བསྒྲུགས་	བསྒྲུག་	སྒྲུགས་
སྒྲུལ་	བསྒྲུལ་	བསྒྲུལ	སྒྲུལ་
རྒྱན་	བརྒྱན་	བརྒྱན་	རྒྱན
རྒྱུད་	བརྒྱུས་	བརྒྱུ་	རྒྱུས་
རྒྱོང་	བརྒྱངས་	བརྒྱང་	རྒྱོངས་
སྒྲར་	བསྒྲར་	བསྒྲར	སྒྲོར་
སྒྲུར་	བསྒྲུར་	བསྒྲུར་	སྒྲུར་
སྒྲོག་	བསྒྲགས་/བསྒྲོགས་	བསྒྲག་/བསྒྲོག་	སྒྲོགས་
སྒྲག་	བསྒྲགས་	བསྒྲག་	སྒྲགས་
སྒྲིབ་	བསྒྲིབས་	བསྒྲིབ་	སྒྲིབས་

Present	Past	Future	Imperative
སྒྲུབ་	བསྒྲུབས་	བསྒྲུབ་	སྒྲུབས་
སྒྲིལ་	བསྒྲིལ་	བསྒྲིལ་	སྒྲིལ་
སྒྲོན་	བསྒྲོན་	བསྒྲོན་	སྒྲོན་
ངུ་	ངུས་	ངུ་	ངུས
ངོམས་	ངོམས	ངོམས	ངོམས
མངོན་	མངོན	མངོན	
གཅར་	བཅར་	གཅར་	གཅོར་
གཅུ་	གཅུས་	གཅུ་	གཅུས་
གཅོད་	བཅད་	གཅད་	ཆོད་
འཆག་	ཆགས་/འཆགས་	འཆག་	
མཆོང་	མཆོངས་	མཆོང	མཆོངས་
མཆོད་	མཆོད	མཆོད	མཆོད
འཆང་	བཅངས་	བཅང་	ཆོངས་
འཆད་	བཤད་	བཤད་/འཆད་	ཤོད་
འཆི་	ཤི་	འཆི་	
འཆོར་	ཤོར་	འཆོར་	
འཆོས་	བཅོས་	བཅོས	ཆོས་
མཇལ་	མཇལ་	མཇལ་	མཇོལ་
འཇུག་	བཅུག་/ཞུགས་	གཞུག་/འཇུག་	ཆུག་/ཞུགས་
འཇུ་	འཇུས་/ཞུ་	འཇུ་	འཇུས
འཇོག་	བཞག་/བཞོགས་	གཞག་/གཞོག་	ཞོག་/ཞོགས་
རྗེད་	བརྗེད་	བརྗེད་	རྗེད
ཉར་	ཉར	ཉར	ཉོར་
ཉལ་	ཉལ་	ཉལ་	ཉོལ་
ཉེས་	ཉེས	ཉེས	
ཉོ་	ཉོས་	ཉོ་	ཉོས
གཉིད་ཁུག་	གཉིད་ཁུགས་	གཉིད་ཁུག་	
མཉེས་	མཉེས	མཉེས	
སྙེ་རྒྱག་	སྙེ་བརྒྱབ་	སྙེ་བརྒྱག་/རྒྱག་	སྙེ་རྒྱོབ་
སྙེད་	སྙེད	སྙེད	
སྙམ་	སྙམ་	སྙམ་	
སྙུང་	བསྙུངས་	བསྙུང་	སྙུངས་
སྙོབ་	བསྙབས་	བསྙབ་	སྙོབས་
སྙེག་	བསྙེགས་	བསྙེག་	སྙེགས་

Present	Past	Future	Imperative
གཏོད་	བཏོད་/གཏད་	གཏོད་/གཏད་	གཏོད་
གཏན་འཁེལ་	གཏན་ཁེལ་	གཏན་འཁེལ་	
གཏོང་	བཏང་	གཏང་	ཐོང་
གཏོར་	གཏོར་	གཏོར་	གཏོར་
ལྟ་	བལྟས་	བལྟ་	ལྟོས་
སྟེན་	བསྟེན་	བསྟེན་	སྟེན་
སྟེར་	སྟེར	སྟེར	སྟེར
སྟོན་	བསྟན་	བསྟན་	སྟོན
སྟོར་	བསྟར་	བསྟར་	སྟོར་
སྟུད་	བསྟུད་	བསྟུད་	སྟུད་
ཐར་	ཐར་	ཐར་	
ཐལ་མོ་སྦྱོར་	ཐལ་མོ་སྦྱར་	ཐལ་སྦྱར་	ཐལ་མོ་སྦྱོར་
ཐུག་	ཐུག་	ཐུག་	
ཐུབ་	ཐུབ་	ཐུབ་	
ཐེབས་	ཐེབས་	ཐེབས་	
ཐོ་རྒྱག་	ཐོ་བརྒྱབ་	ཐོ་བརྒྱག་/རྒྱག་	ཐོ་རྒྱོབ་
ཐོས་	ཐོས་	ཐོས་	
མཐོང་	མཐོང་	མཐོང་	
འཐག་	བཏགས་	བཏག་	
འཐབ་	འཐབ་	འཐབ་	
འཐམ་	འཐམས་	འཐམ་	
འཐོབ་	ཐོབ་	འཐོབ་	
འཐེབས་	འཐེབས་	འཐེབས་	
འཐུ་	བཏུས་/འཐུས་	བཏུ་/འཐུ་	ཐུས་/འཐུས་
འཐུང་	བཏུངས་	བཏུང་	འཐུངས་
འཐུལ་	འཐུལ་	འཐུལ་	
འཐེན་	འཐེན་	འཐེན་	འཐེན་
འཐོར་	འཐོར་	འཐོར་	
འདེད་	བདས་	བདའ་	དེད་
འདེབས་	བཏབ་	གདབ་	ཐོབས་
དྲག་	དྲག་	དྲག་	
དྲན་	དྲན་	དྲན་	དྲོན་
དྲན་པ་གསོ་	དྲན་པ་གསོས་	དྲན་པ་གསོ་	
དྲན་མེད་དུ་རྒྱལ་	དྲན་མེད་དུ་རྒྱལ་	དྲན་མེད་དུ་རྒྱལ་	
དྲིན་གྱིས་སྐྱོང་	དྲིན་གྱིས་བསྐྱངས་	དྲིན་གྱིས་སྐྱོང་	

Present	Past	Future	Imperative
འདྲི་	དྲིས་	དྲི་	དྲིས
འདྲུད་	དྲུད་	འདྲུད	དྲུད་
འདྲི་	འདྲིས་	འདྲི་	
འདྲེན་	དྲངས་	དྲང་	དྲོངས་
གདང་	གདངས་	གདང	གདོངས་
གདུང་	གདུངས་	གདུང	
འདམ་	བདམས་/བཏམ་	བདམ་/གཏམ་	འདོམས་/ཐོམ་
འདིང་	བཏིངས་	གདིང་	ཐིང་
འདེགས་	བཏེགས་	གདེག་	ཐེགས་
འདེབ	བཏབ་	གདབ་	ཐོབ་
འདོན་	བཏོན་	གདོན་	ཐོན་
རྡེབ་	བརྡབས་	བརྡབ་	རྡོབས་
ལྡིར་	ལྡིར	ལྡིར	
ལྡུག་	ཀླུགས་	ཀླུག་	ཀླུགས་
ལྡོག་	ལོག	ལྡོག་	ལོག་
སྡོད་	བསྡད་	བསྡད་	སྡོད་
རྡུང་	བརྡུངས་	བརྡུང་	རྡུངས་
སྡུད་	བསྡུས་	བསྡུ་	སྡུས་
སྡུར་	བསྡུར་	བསྡུར་	སྡུར་
སྡོམ་	བསྡོམས་	བསྡོམ་	སྡོམས་
གནང་	གནང	གནང	གནོངས
མནར་	མནར་	མནར་	
མནལ་ཁུག་	མནལ་ཁུགས་	མནལ་ཁུག	
སྣོམ་	བསྣམས་	བསྣམ་	སྣོམས་
སྣར་	བསྣར་	བསྣར་	སྣོར་
སྣོན་	བསྣན་	བསྣན་	སྣོན་
དཔྱོང་	དཔྱངས་	དཔྱང་	དཔྱོངས་
སྤེལ་	སྤེལ་	སྤེལ་	
སྤོར་	སྤར་	སྤར་	སྤོར་
སྤོ་	སྤོས་	སྤོ་	སྤོས་
སྤྲོ་	སྤྲོས་	སྤྲོ་	སྤྲོས་
སྤྲོད་	སྤྲད	སྤྲད	སྤྲོད་
ཕངས་	ཕངས་	ཕངས་	
ཕུད་	ཕུད	ཕུད	ཕུད
ཕོང་	ཕོངས་	ཕོང་	

Present	Past	Future	Imperative
ཕེབས་	ཕེབས་	ཕེབས་	ཕེབས་
འཕམ་	ཕམ་	འཕམ་	
འཕར་	འཕར་	འཕར་	
འཕུར་	ཕུར་	འཕུར་	ཕུར་
འཕྲད་	ཕྲད་	འཕྲད་	
འཕེན་	འཕངས	འཕང་	འཕོངས་
འཕེལ་	འཕེལ་	འཕེལ་	
འཕྱུར་	ཕྱུར་	འཕྱུར་	ཕྱོར་
འཕྱུར་	འཕྱུར་	འཕྱུར་	
འཕྲད་	ཕྲད་	འཕྲད་	
འཕྲོ་	འཕྲོས་	འཕྲོ་	
འཕྲོག་	ཕྲོགས་	དཕྲོག་	ཕྲོགས་
བྱེད་	བྱས་	བྱ་	བྱོས་
དབོར་	དབོར་	དབོར་	
དབུག་	དབུགས་	དབུག་	དབུགས་
བོར་	བོར་	བོར་	
འབུད་	བུད་/བུས་	འབུད་	བུད་/བུས
འབབ་	བབ་	འབབ་	བོབ་
འབར་	འབར་	འབར་	
འབོར་	བོར་	བོར་	
འབུལ་	ཕུལ་	དབུལ་	ཕུལ་
འབོད་	བོས་	འབོད་	བོས་
འབེབས་	ཕབ་	དབབ་	ཕོབ་
འབྱེད་	ཕྱེས་/བྱེད་	དབྱེ་/འབྱེད་	ཕྱེས
འབྱུག་	བྱུགས་	བྱུག་	བྱུགས་
འབྱུང་	བྱུང་	འབྱུང་	
འབྱོར་	འབྱོར་	འབྱོར་	
འབྱིན་	ཕྱུང་	དབྱུང་	ཕྱུང་
འབྱིལ་	བྱིལ་	འབྱིལ་	བྱིལ་
འབྲི་	བྲིསཔ་/བྲི་བ་	བྲི་/འབྲི་	བྲིས་
འབྲོས་	བྲོས་	འབྲོས	བྲོས
སྦེད་	སྦས་	སྦ་	སྦོས་
སྦྱིན་	བྱིན་	སྦྱིན་	བྱིན་
སྦྱོང་	སྦྱངས	སྦྱང་	སྦྱོངས་
སྦིད་	སྦིད་	སྦིད་	

Present	Past	Future	Imperative
དམག་འདྲེན་	དམག་དྲངས་	དམག་འདྲེན	
སྨུག་	སྨུགས་	སྨུག་	
སྨྲ་	སྨྲས་	སྨྲ་	སྨྲོས་
བཙའ་	བཙས་	བཙའ་	
རྩེ་	བརྩེས་	བརྩེ་	རྩེས་
རྩོམ་	བརྩམས་	བརྩམ་	རྩོམས
བརྩེ་	བརྩེ་	བརྩེ་	
ཚིམ་	ཚིམས་	ཚིམ་	
ཚུད་	ཚུད་	ཚུད་	
འཚལ་	བཙལ་	འཚལ་	
འཚིག་	ཚིག་	འཚིག་	
འཚོ་	འཚོ་	འཚོ་	
འཚོགས་	ཚོགས་	འཚོགས་	ཚོགས་
འཚོང་	བཙོངས་	བཙོང་	ཚོངས
འཚོལ་	བཙལ་	བཙལ་	ཚོལ་
མཛད་	མཛད་	མཛད་	མཛོད་
འཛག་	ཟགས་	འཛག་	
འཛུགས་	བཙུགས་	གཟུགས་	ཚུགས་
འཛུལ་	འཛུལ་	འཛུལ་	འཛུལ་
འཛེག་	འཛེགས་	འཛེག་	འཛེགས་
འཛིན་	བཟུང་	གཟུང་	ཟུང་
འཛོམ	འཛོམས་	འཛོམ་	འཛོམས་
ཛོགས་	ཛོགས་	ཛོགས་	
ཛུ་	བཛུས་	བཛུ་	ཛུས་
ཞུ་	ཞུས་	ཞུ་	ཞུས་
ཞུགས་	ཞུགས་	ཞུགས་	
ཞེད་	ཞེད་	ཞེད་	
གཞུ་	གཞུས་	གཞུ་	གཞུས་
གཞུར་	བཞུར	བཞུར་	གཞུར་
བཞད་	བཞད་	བཞད་	
བཞུགས་	བཞུགས་	བཞུགས་	
བཞུད	བཞུད	བཞུད	
བཞེས་	བཞེས་	བཞེས་	
ཟ་	བཟས་	བཟའ་	ཟོ་
ཟག་	ཟགས་	ཟག་	

Present	Past	Future	Imperative
ཟུག་	ཟུག་	ཟུག་	
ཟེར་	ཟེར་	ཟེར་	
གཟིགས་	གཟིགས་	གཟིགས་	གཟིགས་
གཟིམས་/གཟིམ་	གཟིམས་	གཟིམས་/གཟིམ་	གཟིམས་
གཟེར་	གཟེར་	གཟེར་	
བཟོ་	བཟོས་	བཟོ་	བཟོས་
ཡིབ་	ཡིབས་	ཡིབ་	ཡིབས་
གཡུག་	གཡུགས་	གཡུག་	གཡུགས་
གཡོ་	གཡོས་	གཡོ་	
གཡོག་	གཡོགས་	གཡོག་	གཡོགས་
རག་	རག་	རག་	
རིལ་	རིལ་	རིལ་	
རླག་	བརླགས་	བརླག་	རློགས་
ལང་	ལངས་	ལང་	ལོངས་
ལེན་	བླངས་	བླང་	ལོངས་
ལོན་	ལོན་	ལོན་	
ཤན་འབྱེད་	ཤན་ཕྱེ་	ཤན་དབྱེ་	ཤན་ཕྱེ་
ཤེས་	ཤེས་	ཤེས་	
ཤོག་	ཤོག་	ཤོག་	
ཤོང་	ཤོང་	ཤོང་	
གཤེགས་	གཤེགས་	གཤེགས་	
ཤོམ་	བཤམས་	བཤམ་	ཤོམས་
བཤུ་	བཤུས་	བཤུ་	ཤུས་
སྐྱིབ	བསྐྱིབས་	བསྐྱིབ་	སྐྱིབས་
སྐྱོག་	བསྐྱོགས་	བསྐྱོག་	སྐྱོགས་
སྐྱོང་	བསྐྱངས་	བསྐྱང་	སྐྱོངས
སྐྱོབ	བསྐྱབས	བསྐྱབ་	སྐྱོབས་
གསོད་	བསད་	གསད	སོད་
གསུང་	གསུངས་	གསུང་	གསུངས་
གསོ་	གསོས་	གསོ་	
གསོལ་	གསོལ་	གསོལ་	
བསུ་	བསུས་	བསུ་	སུས་
ལྷགས་	ལྷགས་	ལྷགས་	ལྷགས་

Appendix B

Pronunciation Drills

The following sets of words demonstrate examples of minimal pairs of vowels, consonants, and tone combinations in Tibetan. They should be used in conjunction with the tape recording.

The letter "g"

1. ga (saddle–སྒ་)
2. gā (order–བཀའ་)
3. gāā (pillar–ཀ་བ་)
4. gāà (block–བཀག་)
5. gān (mainly–ཀྱང་)
6. gan (on top–སྒང་)
7. gɔ̄ɔ̄ (leather–ཀོ་བ་)
8. gɔɔ (elapse–འགོར་)
9. gɔ̄ɔ̀ (rip out–བཀོག་)
10. gɔɔ̀ (want–དགོས་)
11. gɔ̄p (time–སྐབས་)
12. göögo (needs–དགོས་མགོ་)
13. göö̀ (catch disease–འགོས་)
14. gȫȫ (boil–བཀོལ་)
15. gön (monastery–དགོན་)
16. gu (nine–དགུ་)
17. gūū (send–བསྐུར་)

Although example 15 has an "n" written immediately after the vowel, the nasal sound occurs simultaneously with the vowel. Such nasal or nasalized vowels normally lengthen the vowel they accompany. Consequently, example 15 would linguistically normally be written: gö̃ö̃. Similarly, nasalized falling tones such as those cited in examples 5 and 6, linguistically would be written gã̄à̃ and gãà̃ .

18. gū (body–སྐུ་)
19. gūù (bend–བཀུག་)
20. guù (wait–བསྒུགས་)
21. gēba (waist–སྐེད་པ་)
22. gewa (merit–དགེ་བ་)
23. gɛ̄ɛ̄ (hang up བཀལ་)
24. gɛ̄ɛ̄baa (phonograph–སྐད་ཕྱར་)
25. gɛ̄ɛ̀ (language–སྐད་)
26. gōŋji (governor of kongpo–ཀོང་སྤྱི་)
27. goŋa (egg–སྒོ་ང་)

The letter "k"

1. kā (mouth–ཁ་)
2. kāà (kinds–ཁག་)
3. kāŋla (rent–ཁང་གླ་)
4. kaŋdaa (anyway–གང་ལྟར་)
5. kan (snow–གངས་)
6. kē (profit–ཁེ་)
7. keeñiì (garbage–གད་སྙིགས་)
8. kēēri (kidney–མཁལ་རིལ་)
9. kɛ̄ɛ̄ (a volume measure–ཁལ་)
10. kɛ̄ɛ̀ (at the point of–ཁད་)
11. kɛɛ (important–གལ་)
12. kō (he–ཁོ་)
13. ko (to hear–གོ་)
14. kōō (gravy–ཁུ་བ་)
15. kɔ̄ɔ̄ (to conceive–འཁོར་)
16. kȫȫ (to boil–འཁོལ་)

The letter "ng"

1. ŋa (I–ང་)
2. ŋā (5–ལྔ་)
3. ŋaa (to me–ངར་)
4. ŋāāmo (sweet–མངར་མོ་)
5. ŋaà (speech–ངག་)
6. ŋāà (mantra–སྔགས་)
7. ŋüü (silver–དངུལ་)
8. ŋüù (to cry–ངུས་)
9. ŋɛɛ (my–ངའི་)
10. ŋɛɛ̀ (by me–ངས་)
11. ŋɛ̄ɛ̀ (to cut–བརྔས་)
12. ŋɛɛso (to rest–ངལ་བསོ་)
13. ŋɛ̄ɛ̄maà (previously–སྔས་མ་)

The letter "j"

1. ja (rainbow–འཇའ་)
2. jaa (to stick–འབྱར་)
3. jāā (to go to–བཅར་)
4. jaà (tongue–ལྗགས་)
5. jan (to practice–སྦྱང་)
6. jāŋgu (wolf–སྤྱང་ཀི་)
7. jaŋgu (green–ལྗང་ཁུ་)
8. jaabu (blow–ལྗགས་བུ་)
9. jāāri (fence–ལྕགས་རི་)
10. jīmbə (urine–གཅིན་པ་)
11. jimbə (alms–སྦྱིན་པ་)
12. jū (ten–བཅུ་)
13. jūù (to put into–བཅུག་)
14. jūù (to twist–གཅུས་)
15. jüù (to catch–འཇུས་)
16. jɛɛ (to meet–མཇལ་)
17. jɛ̄ɛ̀ (to cut–བཅད་)
18. jē (tongue–ལྕེ་)
19. jetsün (nun–རྗེ་བཙུན་)
20. jeema (afterwards–རྗེས་མ་)
21. jöö (to entrust–བཅོལ་)
22. jööŋɛn (misbehaving–སྤྱོད་ངན་)
23. jöömo (type of bird–མཇོལ་མོ་)
24. jibu (heavy–ལྗིད་པུ་)
25. jīgbu (alone–གཅིག་པུ་)

The letter "ch"

1. cha (tea–ཇ་)
2. chāgya (mudra–ཕྱག་རྒྱ་)
3. chasha (chicken meat–བྱ་ཤ་)
4. chāà (hand–ཕྱག་)
5 chūū (to fit into–འཆུར་)
6. chū (water–ཆུ་)
7. chuù (to spread–བྱུག་)
8. churu (coral–བྱུ་རུ་)
9. chūūjuu (rhubarb–ཕྱུར་ཕྱུར་)
10. chuujuu (to stroke–བྱུར་བྱུར་)
11. chūbə (dress–ཕྱུ་པ་)
12. chūù (to get twisted–འཆུས་)
13. chüù (strategy–ཇུས་)
14. chɛɛ̀ (to do–བྱས་)
15. che (to get opened–བྱེ་)
16. chē (to open–ཕྱེ་)

17. chēr (big–ཆེར་)
18. che̲mə (sand–བྱེ་མ་)
19. chō (meaning–ཆོ་)
20. cho̲ (older brother–ཇོ་)

The letter "ñ"

1. ña̲ (fish–ཉ་)
2. ña̲a̲ (to keep–ཉར་)
3. ñɛ̄ɛ (to put to sleep–སྙོལ་)
4. ñɛ̲ɛ̲ (to lie down to sleep–ཉལ་)
5. ñēbə (steward–གཉེར་པ་)
6. ñe̲bə (punishment–ཉེས་པ་)
7. ñēēbo (happy–མཉེས་པོ་)
8. ñe̲e̲bo (ugly–ཉེས་པོ་)
9. ñēè (to tan–མཉེད་)
10. ñe̲è (to beat–ཉེས་)
11. ñɛ̲ɛ̲daà (opium–ཉལ་ཐག་)

The letter "d"

1. dā (horse–རྟ་)
2. da̲ (arrow–མདའ་)
3. dāà (tiger–སྟག་)
4. dāwa (doctrine–ལྟ་བ་)
5. da̲wa (month–ཟླ་བ་)
6. dār (telegram–ཏར་)
7. da̲r (to shiver–འདར་)
8. dəp (to plant–བཏབ་)
9. də̲p (to bang against–རྡབ་)
10. di̲ (this–འདི་)
11. di̲i̲ (of this–འདིའི་)
12. dɛ̄ɛ̄ (navel–ལྟེ་བ་)
13. dēē (to give–སྟེར་)
14. dɛ̲ɛ̀ (to sit–བསྡད་)
15. de̲è (to herd–འདེད་)
16. dɛ̄ɛ̀ (to look at–བལྟས་)
17. dō (food–ལྟོ་)
18. do̲ (stone–རྡོ་)
19. do̲psoò (mason–རྡོ་བཟོ་བ་)
20. dōpshuù (power–སྟོབས་ཤུགས་)
21. dȫȫ (to burst–བརྡོལ་)
22. dö̲ö̲ (to get burst–རྡོལ་)
23. dȫö̀ (West Tibet–སྟོད་)
24. dö̲ö̀ (to sit–སྡོད་)

The letters "t" and "n"

1. tā (edge–མཐའ་)
2. ta̲ (now–ད་)
3. tāà (distance–ཐག་)
4. tāā (to escape–ཐར་)
5. tūū (downhill–ཐུར་)
6. tūù (to meet–ཐུག་)
7. tu̲ù (poison–དུག་)
8. tōbo (high–མཐོ་པོ་)
9. to̲bo (a load–དོ་པོ་)
10. tɔ̄ɔ̀ (roof–ཐོག་)
11. tɔ̄ɔ̄ (hammer–ཐོ་བ་)
12. na̲ (to be sick–ན་)
13. nā (oath–མནའ་)
14. nāà (pus–རྣག་)
15. nāmaà (airforce–གནམ་དམག་)
16. nāma (bride–མནའ་མ་)

The letters "b" and "p"

1. bā (baboon–སྤྲ་)
2. bāā (to light–སྦར་)
3. b<u>aa</u> (goitre–ལྦ་བ་)
4. b<u>a</u>à (mahjong–སྦག་)
5. b<u>a</u>n (to soak–སྦངས་)
6. bān (to renouce–སྤངས་)
7. bū (hair–སྤུ་)
8. b<u>u</u> (worm–འབུ་)
9. bōmbo (lord–དཔོན་པོ་)
10. b<u>o</u>mbo (thick–སྦོམ་པོ་)
11. bōō (old man–སྤོའོ་)
12. b<u>oo</u> (foam-ལྦུ་བ་)
13. pū (upper valley–ཕུ་)
14. p<u>u</u> (son–བུ་)
15. pāā (away–ཕར་)
16. pāà (pig–ཕག་)
17. p<u>a</u>à (to cut–བྲིག་)

The letter "m"

1. mā (sore–རྨ་)
2. m<u>a</u> (mother–མ་)
3. m<u>aa</u> (butter–མར་)
4. māà (war–དམག་)
5. māābo (red–དམར་པོ་)
6. mābo (low–དམའ་པོ་)
7. mīgbə (hoof–རྨིག་པ་)
8. m<u>i</u>gbə (throat–མིད་པ་)

The letters "dz" and "ts"

1. dzā (grass–རྩྭ་)
2. dzāga (pastureland–རྩྭ་ཁ་)
3. dz<u>a</u> (clay pot–རྫ་)
4. dzāā chēmbo (sacred–རྩ་ཆེན་པོ་)
5. dzāà (to strain–བཙགས་)
6. dz<u>a</u>à (to climb–འཛེགས་)
7. dz<u>u</u>gu (finger–མཛུབ་མོ་)
8. dzūbu (rough–རྩུབ་པོ་)
9. dzɛ̄ɛ̄ma (harvest–བཙས་མ་)
10. dz<u>ɛɛ</u>go (ceremony–མཛད་སྒོ་)
11. dzē (top–རྩེ་)
12. dz<u>e</u> (leprosy–མཛེ་)
13. dzēēmo (playing–རྩེད་མོ་)
14. dz<u>ee</u>bo (pretty–མཛེས་པོ་)
15. dzōn (onion–བཙོང་)
16. dz<u>o</u>n (district–རྫོང་)
17. dzȫȍ (to cook–བཙོས་)
18. dzȫȫbo (to hurry up–རྩོལ་པོ་)
19. tsā (salt–ཚྭ་)
20. tsāā (finish–ཚར་)
21. tsāà (strainer–ཚག་)
22. tsɛ̄ɛ̄ (vegetables–ཚལ་)
23. tsɛ̄ɛ̀ (measure–ཚད་)
24 tsē (life–ཚེ་)
25. tsēè (day–ཚེས་)

The letters "tr" and "dr"

1. trā (hawk–ཁྲ་)
2. trāà (blood–ཁྲག་)
3. dra̲ (enemy དགྲ་)
4. tra̲à (boulder–བྲག་)
5. trō (cauldron–ཁྲོ་)
6. tro̲ (wheat–གྲོ་)
7. tri̲ (knife–གྲི་)
8. tri̲i̲ (bell–དྲིལ་)
9. tri̲ì (asked–དྲིས་)
10. trīì (took–འཁྲིད་)
11. drī (1st cream–སྤྲི་)
12. dri̲ (female yak–འབྲི་)
13. dri̲ì (get mixed–འགྲིས་)
14. dri̲i̲ (merge–འགྲིལ་)

The letters "gy" and "ky"

1. gya̲ (hundred–བརྒྱ་)
2. gyāā (oar–སྐྱ་བ་)
3. gyāà (to lift–བཀྱག་)
4. gyāgba (excrement–སྐྱག་པ་)
5. gya̲gba (fat–རྒྱག་པ་)
6. gyūūmu (sour–སྐྱུར་མོ་)
7. gyǖǖmə (regular–དཀྱུས་མ་)
8. gyǖǜ (to string beads–སྐྱུད་)
9. gyü̲ǜ (descent line–རྒྱུད་)
10. gyɛ̲ɛ̲ (faint–བརྒྱལ་)
11. gyɛ̲ɛ̀ (eight–བརྒྱད་)
12. gyɛ̲n (bet–རྒྱན་)
13. gyēè (to be born–སྐྱེས་)
14. gyɛ̲ɛ̲mo (queen–རྒྱལ་མོ་)
15. gyēēsa (birthplace–སྐྱེས་ས་)
16. gyɛ̄ɛ̄ (to deliver–བསྐྱལ་)-
17. kyū (herd–ཁྱུ་)
18. kyūù (cursive script–ཁྱུག་)
19. kyǖǜ (to cling–འཁྱུད་)

The letters "w" and "y"

1. wə̲njuù (blouse–འོག་འཇུག་)
2. wānyöö̀ (bully–དབང་ཡོད་)
3. wö̲ö̀ (shine–འོད་)
4. wɔ̲ɔ̀ (under–འོག་)
5. wɔ̲ɔ̲mo (fox–ཝ་མོ་)
6. yāŋ (vowel–དབྱངས་)
7. ya̲ŋla (wax–ཡང་ལྭ་)
8. yāā (to lend–གཡར་)
9. ya̲a̲ (up–ཡར་)
10. yāà (yak–གཡག་)
11. yāāga (summer–དབྱར་ཁ་)
12. ya̲a̲gyaà (pestle–ཡ་བཀྱག་)
13. yə̄ŋdri (jade-like stone–གཡང་ཏི་)
14. yə̲ŋji (weight–ཡང་ཀྱི་)
15. yū (turquoise–གཡུ་)
16. yūù (to throw–གཡུག་)
17. yü̲ü̲gɛɛ̀ (dialect–ཡུལ་སྐད་)
18. yǖǖlɛɛ̀ (threshing–གཡུལ་ལས་)
19. yɛ̲ɛ̲ (to disappear–ཡལ་)
20. yɛ̄ɛ̀ (right–གཡས་)

Appendix C

Supplementary Readings in the Genre of Communist Political Essays

1. Reading number one

ཀྲུང་གོའི་གུང་ཁྲན་ཏང་གི་ཀྲུང་དབྱང་ཨུ་ཡོན་ལྷན་ཁང་གི་འགྱུར་མེད་
གྲལ་རིམ་གྱི་རིག་གནས་ཀྱི་གསར་བརྗེ་ཆེན་པོའི་
སྐོར་གྱི་ཆོད་དོན།

(1966ལོའི་ཟླ་ 8 ཚེས་ 8 ཉིན་གྲོས་འཆམས་བྱུང་བ་)

དང་པོ། སྤྱི་ཚོགས་རིང་ལུགས་ཀྱི་གསར་བརྗེའི་དུས་རིམ་གསར་པ།

དེང་སྐབས་ཁྱབ་ཁྱོན་དུ་འགྲོ་བཞིན་པའི་འགྱུར་མེད་གྲལ་རིམ་གྱི་རིག་གནས་ཀྱི་གསར་བརྗེ་ཆེན་པོ་འདི་ནི་མི་རྣམས་ཀྱི་བློ་སྲོག་ལ་ཐུག་པའི་གསར་བརྗེ་ཆེན་པོ་ཞིག་དང་། རང་རྒྱལ་གྱི་སྤྱི་ཚོགས་རིང་ལུགས་ཀྱི་གསར་བརྗེ་འཕེལ་རྒྱས་འགྲོ་བའི་དུས་རིམ་གསར་པ་སྔར་ལས་ཀྱང་གཏིང་ཟབ་པ་ཞིག་དང་སྔར་ལས་ཀྱང་རྒྱ་ཆེ་བ་ཞིག་རེད།

བློ་མཐུན་མའོ་ཙེ་ཏུང་གིས་ཏང་གི་སྐབས་བརྒྱད་པའི་ཀྲུང་ཨུ་ཚང་འཛོམས་གྲོས་ཚོགས་ཐེངས་བཅུ་པའི་ཐོག་གསུང་དོན་དུ། སྲིད་དབང་ཞིག་མགོ་མཇུག་སློག་བསམས་ན་རྣམ་ཡིན་ཟུར་ཐོག་མར་གླེང་ཕྱོགས་ཤིག་བཟོ་ཐབས་དང་། རྣམ་ཡིན་ཟུར་ཐོག་མར་འདུ་ཤེས་འཛིན་སྟངས་ཐད་ཀྱི་ལས་ཀ་བྱེད་དགོས་པ་རེད། གསར་བརྗེ་བྱེད་མཁན་གྱི་གྲལ་རིམ་གྱིས་དེ་འདྲ་བྱེད་ཀྱི་ཡོད་པ་རེད་ལ། གསར་བརྗེར་ངོ་རྒོལ་བྱེད་མཁན་གྱིས་ཀྱང་དེ་འདྲ་བྱེད་ཀྱི་ཡོད་པ་རེད་ཅེས་གསུངས་ཡོད་པ་རེད། ལག་ལེན་གྱི་ཐོག་ནས་བློ་མཐུན་མའོ་ཙེ་ཏུང་གི་ཆོད་གཏམ་དེ་ཐད་དེ་ཡང་དག་པ་ཞིག་ཡིན་པའི་ར་སྤྲོད་བྱུང་བ་རེད།

འགྱུར་ལྡན་གྲལ་རིམ་མགོ་མཇུག་བསློག་ཚར་ནའང་ཁོ་ཚོས་བཤུ་གཞོག་གྲལ་རིམ་གྱི་བསམ་བློ་རྙིང་པ་དང་། རིག་གནས་རྙིང་པ། ཡུལ་སྲོལ་རྙིང་པ། གོམས་གཤིས་རྙིང་པ་བཅས་ལ་བརྟེན་ནས་མང་ཚོགས་ལ་བསླད་སྐྱོན་གཏོང་ཐབས་དང་མི་སེམས་འདུལ་ཐབས་བྱས་ཏེ་ཁོ་ཚོའི་རོ་ལངས་རྒྱག་རྒྱུའི་དམིགས་ཡུལ་དེ་འགྲུབ་གང་ཐུབ་བྱེད་ཀྱི་ཡོད་པ་རེད། འགྱུར་མེད་གྲལ་རིམ་གྱིས་དེ་ལས་དག་དག་ལྡོག་སྟེ་ངེས་པར་དུ་འགྱུར་ལྡན་གྲལ་རིམ་གྱིས་འདུ་ཤེས་འཛིན་སྟངས་ཀྱི་ཁྱབ་ཁོངས་ནང་བསླངས་པའི་འཁྲུག་རྐྱེན་མཐའ་དག་ལ་རྒོལ་ལན་ཚ་ཐག་ཆོད་ཅིག་སྤྲད་ཐོག འགྱུར་མེད་གྲལ་རིམ་རང་ཉིད་ཀྱི་བསམ་བློ་གསར་པ་དང་། རིག་གནས་གསར་པ། ཡུལ་སྲོལ་གསར་པ། གོམས་གཤིས་གསར་པ་བཅས་ལ་བརྟེན་ནས་སྤྱི་ཚོགས་ཡོངས་པོའི་བསམ་པའི་འཁྱེར་སོ་དེ་བསྒྱུར་བཅོས་བྱེད་དགོས་པ་རེད། དེང་སྐབས་ང་རང་ཚོའི་དམིགས་ཡུལ་ནི་མ་རྩའི་རིང་ལུགས་ཀྱི་ལམ་དུ་འགྲོ་མཁན་གྱི་དབང་འཛིན་པ་རྣམས་གཏོར་རྒྱུ་དང་། འགྱུར་ལྡན་གྲལ་རིམ་གྱི་རིག་གཞུང་ཐད་ཀྱི་"མཁས་དབང་"ལོག་སྤྱོད་ཅན་རྣམས་ལ་དགག་པ་རྒྱག་

རྒྱུ། འབྱོར་ལྡན་གྲལ་རིམ་དང་བཤུ་གཞོག་གྲལ་རིམ་གཞན་དག་རྣམས་ཀྱི་འདུ་ཤེས་འཛིན་སྟངས་ལ་དགག་པ་རྒྱག་རྒྱུ། སློབ་གསོ་བཅོས་བསྒྱུར་བྱེད་རྒྱུ། རིག་རྩལ་བཅོས་བསྒྱུར་བྱེད་རྒྱུ། སྤྱི་ཚོགས་རིང་ལུགས་ཀྱི་རྨང་གཞིའི་དཔལ་འབྱོར་དང་མི་མཐུན་པའི་སྟེང་གི་བཀོད་པ་ཚང་མ་བཅོས་བསྒྱུར་བྱེད་རྒྱུ་བཅས་ལ་བརྟེན་ནས་སྤྱི་ཚོགས་རིང་ལུགས་ཀྱི་ལམ་ལུགས་དེ་སྲ་བརྟན་དང་འཕེལ་རྒྱས་འགྲོ་རྒྱུར་ཕན་པ་ཞིག་བྱེད་རྒྱུ་དེ་རེད།

Translation

Resolution of the Central Committee of the
Communist Party of China Concerning the
Great Proletarian Cultural Revolution
(Adopted August 8th, 1966)

A NEW STAGE IN THE SOCIALIST REVOLUTION

The great proletarian cultural revolution that is now becoming widespread is a great revolution that reaches to the souls of people. It is a new stage in the development of the socialist revolution in our country — a deeper and more extensive stage.

At the Tenth Plenary Session of the Eighth Central Committee of the Party, Comrade Mao Zedong said, "To overthrow a political power, first of all one has to create (mould) public opinion and to do work with ideology." This (approach) is done by the revolutionary class as well as by the counter-revolutionary class." This thesis of comrade Mao Zedong has been proved completely correct in practice.

Even though the bourgeoisie has been overthrown, because they hold and adhere to the old ideas, culture, customs, and habits of the exploiting class, they are doing whatever they can to achieve their aim of trying to corrupt the masses, subdue their minds, and stage a comeback. The proletariat, doing precisely the opposite of this, must effectively counterattack all challenges of the bourgeoisie in the ideological field. Employing the new ideas, culture, customs and habits of the proletariat itself, it must reform the mental outlook of the whole society. At present, our goal is to do something beneficial to facilitate the consolidation and development of the socialist system based on destroying those persons in authority who are taking the capitalist road, criticizing (repudiating) the reactionary bourgeois academic "authorities," criticizing (repudiating) the ideology of the bourgeoisie and the other exploiting classes, transforming education and the arts, and transforming all parts of the superstructure that are incompatible with the economic foundation of socialism.

2. Reading number two

ལིའུ་ཧྲའོ་ཆིའི་སྐོར་

ཚང་འཛོམ་གྲོས་ཚོགས་གིས་[1]ཀྲུང་དབྱང་ཆེད་དོན་ཞིབ་བཤེར་ཚོ་ཆུང་གི་ངོ་ལོག་པ་དང་། ནང་རྡུལ་པ། བཟོ་རྐུན་བཅས་ཡིན་པའི་ལིའུ་ཧྲའོ་ཆིའི་ནག་ཉེས་སྐོར་གྱི་ཞིབ་བཤེར་སྙན་ཞུ་ལ་ཆོག་མཆན་བཀོད་པ་ཡིན། སྙན་ཞུ་འདིས་དཔང་རྟགས་ཁུངས་བཙན་ཡོད་པའི་ཐོག་ནས་ཞིབ་བཤེར་བྱས་གསལ། ཏང་ནང་མ་རྩའི་རིང་ལུགས་གྱི་ལམ་ལ་འགྲོ་མཁན་དབང་འཛིན་པ་ཆེ་ཤོས་ལིའུ་ཧྲའོ་ཆི་ནི་ཏང་ནང་གབ་ནས་བསྡད་པའི་ངོ་ལོག་པ་དང་། ནང་རྡུལ་པ། བཟོ་རྐུན་བཅས་དང་། བཙན་རྒྱལ་རིང་ལུགས་དང་། དེང་རབས་གྱི་བཟོ་བཅོས་རིང་ལུགས། གོ་མིན་ཏང་ལོག་སྤྱོད་ཕྱོགས་ཁག་བཅས་གྱི་རྒྱུགས་ཁྲི་ནག་ཉེས་ཚབས་ཆེན་ཡོད་མཁན་ཅིག་རེད།

ཚང་འཛོམ་གྲོས་ཚོགས་གིས་ངོས་འཛིན་བྱས་དོན། འགྱུར་མེད་གྲུབ་རིམ་གྱི་རིག་གནས་གསར་བརྗེ་ཆེན་པོའི་ནང་དང་དང་གསར་བརྗེའི་མང་ཚོགས་གིས་ལིའུ་ཧྲའོ་ཆིའི་གསར་བརྗེ་རང་ངོ་རྟོལ་གྱི་གདོང་རིས་ཐེར་འདོན་བྱས་པ་དེ་ནི་མའོ་ཙེ་ཏུང་དགོངས་པའི་རྒྱལ་ཁ་ལྷབས་ཆེན་ཅིག་དང་། འགྱུར་མེད་གྲུབ་རིམ་གྱི་རིག་གནས་གསར་བརྗེ་ཆེན་པོའི་རྒྱལ་ཁ་ལྷབས་ཆེན་ཅིག་རེད།

ཚང་འཛོམ་གྲོས་ཚོགས་གིས་ལིའུ་ཧྲའོ་ཆིའི་གསར་བརྗེ་རང་ངོ་རྟོལ་གྱི་ནག་ཉེས་ལ་གསར་བརྗེའི་ཁོང་ཁྲོ་ཧ་ཅང་ཆེན་པོ་བཟས་ནས་མགྲིན་གཅིག་གིས་ཆོད་དོན་གྲོས་འཆམ་བྱས་དོན། ལིའུ་ཧྲའོ་ཆི་ཏང་གི་ནང་ནས་དུས་གཏན་དུ་ཕྱིར་འབུད་བྱས་པ་དང་། ཏང་ཕྱི་ནང་གི་ཁོ་པའི་གོ་གནས་ཡོད་ཚད་མེད་པ་བཟོས་པའི་ཐོག མུ་མཐུད་ནས་ལིའུ་ཧྲའོ་ཆི་དང་ཁོ་པའི་ངན་རོགས་ཚོས་ཏང་ལ་ངོ་ལོག་རྒྱབ་གཏོད་དང་རྒྱལ་ཁབ་ལ་ངོ་ལོག་རྒྱབ་གཏོད་བྱས་པའི་ནག་ཉེས་རྣམས་ར་སྤྲགས་གཏོང་དགོས།

ཚང་འཛོམ་གྲོས་ཚོགས་གིས་ཏང་ཡོངས་གྱི་བློ་མཐུན་རྣམས་དང་རྒྱལ་ཡོངས་མི་དམངས་རྣམས་གིས་མུ་མཐུད་དེ་གཏིང་ཟབ་པོའི་སྒོ་ནས་གསར་བརྗེའི་དགག་པ་ཆེན་པོ་ཁྱབ་སྤེལ་བཏང་དེ་ལིའུ་ཧྲའོ་ཆི་སོགས་ཏང་ནང་མ་རྩའི་རིང་ལུགས་གྱི་ལམ་ལ་འགྲོ་མཁན་དབང་འཛིན་པ་ཆེ་ཤོས་ཉུང་ཤས་དེའི་གསར་བརྗེ་རང་ངོ་རྟོལ་གྱི་བཟོ་བཅོས་རིང་ལུགས་གྱི་བསམ་བློ་གཙང་སེལ་བྱེད་དགོས་པའི་འབོད་སྐུལ་བྱས་པ་ཡིན།

Translation

Concerning Liu Shaoqi

The Plenary Session approved the investigatory report of the special central investigatory subcommittee concerning the crimes of the renegade, traitor and scab Liu Shaoqi. In this report which is based on reliable evidence, it is stated that Liu Shaoqi, the

---

[1] Note that this essay utilizes a style wherein the genitive and instrumental particles are written གིས་ and གི་ regardless of the preceeding final.

highest personage in the party taking the capitalist path, is a serious criminal who is a running dog of the imperialists, the modern revisionists and the Kuomintang clique, and a renegade, traitor, and scab who has stayed hidden within the party.

The Plenary Session recognized that the exposure of the counter-revolutionary face of Liu Shaoqi by the party and the revolutionary masses in the Great Proletarian Cultural Revolution is great victory for the thought of Mao Zedong and is a great victory for the Great Proletarian Cultural Revolution.

The Plenary Session, feeling great revolutionary anger at the counter-revolutionary crimes of Liu Shaoqi, unanimously adopted a resolution to expel Liu Shaoqi permanently from the party, to strip him of his posts within and outside of the party, and to continue to expose the crimes of treason of Liu Shaoqi and his accomplices to the country and to the party.

The Plenary Session appealed to all the party comrades and to the people of the whole nation to continue to spread revolutionary refutation diligently, and to deeply cleanse the counter-revolutionary revisionist thoughts of the few great "authorities" in the party such as Liu Shaoqi who are pursuing the path of capitalism.

3. Reading number three

ཀྲུང་ཡོའི་མཛའ་བཤེས་ལས་བྱུང་བའི་ཏུང་ཞིང་ཆུ་མཛོད་དང་། ཆུ་གློག་ས་ཚིགས།

ཀོང་ཏུང་ཞིང་ཆེན་ཁོངས་ཏུང་ཞིང་མི་རིགས་ཁག་གི་རང་སྐྱོང་ཞན་གྱི་ཙང་ཡིང་མི་དམངས་ཀུང་ཧྲེར་འཛུགས་སྐྲུན་བྱེད་པའི་སོ་ཞིང་མུའུ་སུམ་ཁྲི་ལྔ་སྟོང་ལྷག་ཙམ་དུ་ཆུ་འདྲེན་ཐུབ་པ་དང་གློག་ཆན་ཝ་བརྒྱད་བརྒྱ་ཉི་ཤུ་རྩ་ལྔ་འདོན་ཐུབ་པའི་ཏུང་ཞིང་ཆུ་མཛོད་དང་ཆུ་གློག་ས་ཚིགས་དེ་ ༡༩༦༣ ལོར་ལེགས་གྲུབ་བྱུང་ཞིང་། དེ་ནི་ཏུང་ཞིང་གི་ཡའོ་དང་། ཀྲོང་། ཅིང་ལ་སོགས་པའི་མི་རིགས་ཁག་གི་མི་དམངས་རྣམས་ཀྱིས་དར་ཆ་དམར་པོ་གསུམ་གྱི་མཛུབ་ཁྲིད་འོག་རང་སྟོབས་རང་སྐྱེལ་དང་ཤུགས་བསྐྱེད་སྟོབས་སྐྱེལ་བྱས་པ་ལས་བྱུང་བའི་རྒྱལ་ཁའི་འབྲས་བུ་ཞིག་རེད།

ཆུ་མཛོད་དང་ཆུ་གློག་ས་ཚིགས་ཀྱི་འཛུགས་སྐྲུན་ལེགས་གྲུབ་བྱུང་བ་དེས་རང་སྐྱོང་ཞན་གྱི་ཞིང་ལས་ཐོན་སྐྱེད་ཀྱི་རྣམ་པ་ཆེར་ཆེར་འགྱུར་བ་རེད། ༡༩༦༣ ལོ་ཆུ་མཛོད་ཀྱི་ཨར་ལས་འགྲུབ་ཏུ་ཉེ་བའི་སྐབས་སུ་ཤུགས་ཆེན་པོས་ཐུ་སྨིན་འབྲས་ཀྱི་ཐན་འགོག་འཐབ་རྩོད་ལ་རོགས་སྐྱོར་བྱས་པར་བརྟེན་ཙང་ཡིང་ཀུང་ཧྲེའི་ས་ཁོངས་ཀྱི་སོ་ཞིང་མུའུ་ཉིས་ཁྲི་ལྷག་ཙམ་ཞིག་ལ་ཐན་སྐྱོན་གྱི་གནོད་ཚེ་མ་འཁེལ་བར་མ་ཟད། སྔར་ཡང་སོ་ཞིང་གི་རྒྱ་ཁྱོན་ཆེ་རུ་བཏང་སྟེ་ཆུ་འདྲེན་ས་ཁུལ་གྱི་ཆུ་འབྲས་ཐོན་ཚད་བརྒྱ་ཆ་སུམ་ཅུ་སོ་བཞི་འཕར་བ་རེད།

སྔོན་ཆད་ཏུང་ཞིང་གྲོང་བརྡལ་དུ་གློག་ཤུགས་མི་ལྡང་བའི་དབང་གིས་གློག་ཞུ་གསལ་པོ་མེད་པ་མ་ཟད། སྒྲ་ལེན་འཕྲུལ་འཁོར་ཡང་བེད་སྤྱོད་གཏོང་ཁག་པོ་རེད། དེང་སང་ཏུང་ཞིང་ཆུ་གློག་ས་ཚིགས་ཀྱིས་བཏོན་པའི་གློག་ཤུགས་དེས་ཞན་དེ་ཉིད་ཀྱི་གློག་སྤྱོད་དགོས་མཁོ་སྐོང་ཐུབ་པས་མི་ཚད། ད་དུང་ཡོ་ནན་དམངས་གཙོའི་སྤྱི་མཐུན་རྒྱལ་ཁབ་ཀྱི་སྨང་ཅེ་གྲོང་ཁྱེར་དང་སྨང་ཅེ་ཞན་དུ་གློག་ཤུགས་ཁག་གཅིག་གཏོང་གི་ཡོད་པ་རེད། ཏུང་ཞིང་ཆུ་གློག་ས་ཚིགས་ཀྱིས་དངོས་སུ་སྨང་ཅེར་གློག་ཤུགས་གཏོང་འགོ་ཚུགས་པའི་ཉིན་དེར་རྒྱལ་མཚམས་སུ་གནས་པའི་ཏུང་ཞིང་དང་སྨང་ཅེ་གྲོང་ཁྱེར་གཉིས་བར་ནས་འབབ་པའི་པེ་ལུན་ཆུ་བོའི་སྟེང་དུ་བརྒྱབ་པའི་ཀྲུང་ཡོའི་མཛའ་བཤེས་ཟམ་ཆེན་ཐོག་ཚོན་ལྡན་དར་ཆ་ལྷབ་ལྷབ་ཏུ་གཡོ་བ་དང་། རྔ་དང་མཁར་རྔའི་སྒྲས་བར་སྣང་ཁེངས་དེའི་ཐོག་ནས་དུས་ཆེན་གྱི་སྣང་ཚུལ་ཞིག་འཆར་གྱི་འདུག། ཆུ་གློག་ས་ཚིགས་ཀྱི་བཟོ་པ་རྣམས་ཀྱིས་གློག་འདོན་འཕྲུལ་འཁོར་བཏང་མ་ཐག་གློག་རྒྱུན་དེ་མཐོ་གནོན་གློག་སྐུད་བརྒྱུད་ནས་སྨང་ཅེ་ཞན་ཁོངས་ཀྱི་ས་ཞིང་མུའུ་ཆིག་ཁྲི་བརྒྱད་སྟོང་ཡན་ལ་ཆུ་འདྲེན་ཐུབ་པའི་གློག་སྐྱེལ་ཞིང་ཆུ་འདྲེན་གཏོང་ས་ཚིགས་སྨང་ཅེ་གྲོང་ཁྱེར་ནང་དུ་སླེབས་པ་རེད། མཚན་མོར་པེ་ལུན་ཆུ་བོའི་འགྲམ་གཉིས་སུ་སྡོད་པའི་ཁྱིམ་དུད་ཁྲི་སྟོང་གི་གློག་ཞུའི་འོད་མདངས་རབ་ཏུ་བཀྲ་བ་དེའི་ཐོག་ནས་ཀྲུང་ཡོ་རྒྱལ་ཁབ་གཉིས་ཀྱི་སྤུན་ཟླ་ལྟ་བུའི་མཛའ་མཐུན་དེ་ཉིན་རེ་བཞིན་ཇེ་བརྟན་ཇེ་རྒྱས་སུ་འགྲོ་བའི་རྟགས་མཚན་གྱི་ཡོད་པ་རེད།

Translation

The Dongxing Reservoir and Hydro-Electric Station —

A Result of Sino-Vietnamese Friendship

The Dongxing reservoir and hydro-electric station were completed in 1963. They are able to generate 824 watts of electricity and to supply irrigation water for over 35,000 *mu* of land that have been made arable in the Jangping People's Commune of the Dongxing minority groups' (Dongxing) Autonomous County of Guangdong Province. The construction of the reservoir and hydro-electric station is a victorious accomplishment made possible because people of different nationalities such as the Yu, Dong, and Qing have worked vigorously and self-reliantly.under the guidance of the "Three Red Flags."

Agricultural production in that autonomous county has increased a lot as a result of the successful completion of the construction of the reservoir and hydro-electric station. In 1963, when construction of the reservoir was nearly completed, it helped in the struggle to prevent drought damage to the early-ripening rice crops, and because of this, over 20, 000 *mu* were not harmed by drought. Moreover, it enabled new fields to be opened, increasing rice production by 34%.

Similarly, before the construction of the hydro-electric station, insufficient electric power in Dongxing town caused lights to be dim and the use of radios difficult. Now, not only is there sufficient electricity for Dongxing, but there is also enough to supply Mong Cai city and district in the Democratic Republic of Vietnam.

On the day when they actually began to transmit electricity from Dongxing station, a festive mood prevailed along the Sino-Vietnamese Friendship Bridge spanning the Pelum River which flows between Dongxing and Mong Cai city. Multicolored flags fluttered in the wind and the sound of drums and gongs filled the air. As soon as the workers of the hydro-electric station started the generator, electric current arrived via high tension cables at the electric irrigation station in the district of Mong Cai. This station is able to irrigate over 18,000 *mu* of land and Mong Cai town.

In the evening, the lights from the tens of thousands of homes situated on the banks of the Pelum River shine brightly and are a symbol of the ever-increasing brotherly friendship between China and Vietnam.

4. Reading number four

མཐུན་སྒྲིལ་དང་བདེ་སྐྱིད་ཀྱི་གསེར་ཟམ།

བོད་ཞི་བའི་བཅིངས་འགྲོལ་ཐོབ་ནས་ལོ་བཅུ་ལྷག་ཙམ་གྱི་རིང་ལ་ཀྲུང་གོའི་མི་དམངས་བཅིངས་འགྲོལ་དམག་བོད་བསྐྱོད་དམག་དཔུང་དང་བོད་བསྐྱོད་ལས་བཟོ་རྣམས་ཀྱིས་ཧྲང་དང་མའོ་ཀྲུའུ་ཞིའི་རླབས་ཆེན་གྱི་འབོད་བསྐུལ་དང་ལེན་ཞུས་ཏེ་བོད་དུ་དམག་བསྐྱོད་བྱས་ནས་བོད་ལྗོངས་འཛུགས་སྐྲུན་བྱེད་ཀྱི་ཡོད་ཅིང་། ཕོ་ཆོས་བོད་རིགས་མི་དམངས་དང་མིས་རྒྱལ་མི་རིགས་ཁག་གི་མི་དམངས་རྣམས་ཀྱི་ཤུགས་ཆེན་གྱི་རྒྱབ་སྐྱོར་འོག་དཀའ་ངལ་ཚད་མེད་ཀྱིས་འབད་བརྩོན་བྱས་ནས་སྔ་རྗེས་སུ་འཛམ་གླིང་གི་ཡང་སྙིང་དུ་ཁྲོན་བོད་དང་། མཚོ་བོད། ཞིན་བོད་བཅས་ཀྱི་གཞུང་ལམ་གསར་བཟོ་བྱས་པ་རེད། ད་ལྟ་བོད་ཀྱི་རྒྱ་ཆ་ ༩༠ ཡན་གྱི་ཞན་ཁག་ལ་རླངས་འཁོར་ཤར་གཏོང་ཐུབ་ནས་འགྲིམ་འགྲུལ་སྐྱེལ་འདྲེན་གྱི་ལས་དོན་དང་དེ་མིན་གྱི་ལས་དོན་གཞན་དག་ལ་གྲུབ་འབྲས་རླབས་ཆེན་ཞིག་ཐོབ་ཡོད་པ་རེད། གྲུབ་འབྲས་དེ་དག་ནི་མའོ་ཙེ་ཧྲང་གི་དགོངས་པའི་རྒྱལ་ཁ་འོད་སྣང་འབར་བ་ཞིག་དང་། ཧྲང་གི་མི་རིགས་སྲིད་ཇུས་ཀྱི་རྒྱལ་ཁ་འོད་སྣང་འབར་བ་ཞིག་རེད།

དེ་སྔ་ལམ་བཟོའི་དམག་དཔུང་དང་། རྒྱ་ཁྲབ་ལས་བཟོ་དང་བོད་རིགས་མི་དམངས་བཅས་ཀྱིས་དཀའ་བ་ཆེན་པོ་སྤྱད་པ་དང་ངལ་བ་ཆེན་པོ་བཟོད་པའི་གསར་བརྗེའི་སྙིང་སྟོབས་སྤེལ་བ་དང་། རི་མཐོན་པོ་མགོ་སྒྲར་དུ་འཛུག་པ་དང་ཆུ་ཆེན་པོ་ལམ་གཟུར་དུ་འཛུག་པའི་དཔའ་བོའི་འཕྲིང་ཉམས་བསྟན་ནས་གཅིག་འཛུག་གཉིས་མཐུད་དུ་བྱུང་བའི་དཀའ་ངལ་རྣམས་ཁྱད་དུ་བསད་པ་དང་། དཀའ་ཚེགས་ཆེ་བའི་འཐབ་རྩོད་བྱས་ཏེ་གཞུང་ལམ་དེ་དག་བཟོ་གི་ཡོད་པ་རེད། ཁྲོན་བོད་གཞུང་ལམ་ལ་ཆ་བཞག་ན་སི་ཁྲོན་ཞིང་ཆེན་ཁོངས་ཁྲིང་ཏུའུ་གྲོང་ཁྱེར་ནས་བོད་ཀྱི་ལྷ་ས་གྲོང་ཁྱེར་གྱི་ལམ་རྒྱུད་དུ་རྒྱ་མཚོའི་ངོས་ལས་མཐོ་ཚད་སྤྱི་སུམ་སྟོང་ནས་ལྔ་སྟོང་བར་ཡོད་པའི་ཨེར་རི་བོའི་ལ་དང་། ཁྲོ་ལ་སོགས་ལ་ཆེན་པོ་བཅུ་བཞི་རྒྱུག་དགོས་པ་དང་། ཛ་རླབས་དྲག་དུ་འཕྱུར་བའི་འབྲི་ཆུ་དང་རྒྱ་མོ་དངུལ་ཆུ་སོགས་ཆུ་ཆེན་པོ་བཅུ་ལྷག་ཙམ་རྒལ་དགོས་པ། ལི་དབར་བཅུ་ཕྲག་ཁ་ཤས་ཡོད་པའི་གཡང་གཟར་ཅན་གྱི་བྲག་རི་དང་། གློག་རོང་། རྒྱུག་འགྲོའི་བྱེ་སྟོང་། འཁྱག་ཀླུང་བཅས་འགྲིམ་དགོས་པ་ལ་སོགས་པའི་ས་གཤིས་ཀྱི་གནས་ཚུལ་ཁྱད་པར་ཅན་དང་རྙོག་འཛིང་ཆེ་བ་ཞིག་ཡིན་ཞིང་།

མཚོ་བོད་གཞུང་ལམ་ལ་ཆ་བཞག་ན་མཚོ་སྔོན་ཞིང་ཆེན་ཁོངས་ཟི་ལིང་གྲོང་ཁྱེར་ནས་བོད་ཀྱི་ལྷ་ས་གྲོང་ཁྱེར་བར་ལི་དབར་བརྒྱ་ཕྲག་ཁ་ཤས་ཡོད་པའི་བྱེ་ཐང་འགྲིམ་དགོས་པ་དང་། རྒྱ་མཚོའི་ངོས་ལས་མཐོ་ཚད་སྤྱི་བཞི་སྟོང་ལྔ་སྟོང་ཡོད་པའི་ཁུ་ནུ་ལ་དང་ཐང་མགོ་ལ་སོགས་ལ་ཆེན་པོ་རྒྱུག་དགོས་པ། ཆུ་དམར་དང་འབྲི་ཆུ་སོགས་ཆུ་བོ་ཆེན་པོ་ཁ་ཤས་རྒལ་དགོས། དབྱར་གྱི་དུས་སུའང་ཁ་བ་འབབ་པ་དང་། དགུན་གྱི་དུས་སུ་རི་བོ་ཁ་བས་བསྒྲུམས་ཏེ་སྡོད་ཀྱི་ཡོད་པ་བཅས་ཀྱི་ས་ཆ་ཞིག་རེད། དེར་བརྟེན་སྐབས་དེར་དགྲ་བོས་ཆེག་ཐག་བཅད་ནས་འཛམ་གླིང་གི་ཡང་སྙིང་དུ་གཞུང་ལམ་བཟོ་ཐུབ་ཀྱི་མ་རེད། གལ་སྲིད་བཟོ་ཐུབ་པའི་དབང་དུ་བཏང་ནའང་རླངས་འཁོར་ཡུན་རིང་པོ་ཤར་གཏོང་ཐུབ་ཀྱི་མ་རེད་ཅེས་ཤོད་ཀྱི་ཡོད་པ་རེད། འོན་ཀྱང་མའོ་ཙེ་ཧྲང་གི

དགོངས་པས་དྲག་ཆས་སྲས་པའི་མི་དམངས་ཀྱི་དམག་དཔུང་དང་ལས་བཟོ་རྣམས་ཀྱིས་རང་གྲུབ་བཙན་ས་མང་པོ་གཏོར་བ་དང༌། ཁ་བ་བུ་ཡུག་དང་གྲང་ངར་ལས་རྣམ་པར་རྒྱལ་བ། ལ་མཐོན་པོ་བརྒྱབ་པ་དང་ཆུ་ཆེན་པོ་བརྒལ་བ། བོད་ཀྱི་ལོག་སྤྱོད་ཀྱི་ཞིང་བྲན་བདག་པོའི་གྲལ་རིམ་གྱིས་བཀག་འགོག་དང་གཏོར་བཤིག་རྣམ་པ་སྣ་ཚོགས་བྱས་པ་རྣམས་ཙ་གཏོར་དུ་བཏང་བ་བཅས་ལ་བརྟེན་ནས་གཞུང་ལམ་གསར་བཟོ་བྱེད་རྒྱུ་དེ་ལེགས་འགྲུབ་བྱུང་བར་མ་ཟད། ལོ་བཅུ་ལྷག་གི་རིང་ལ་དཀའ་ངལ་ཏ་ཅང་ཆེ་བའི་གནས་ཚུལ་འོག་སྐྱངས་འཁོར་འགག་མེད་ཤར་གཏོང་ཐུབ་པའི་འགན་ལེན་ཡང་བྱེད་ཐུབ་པ་བྱུང་བའི་དབང་གིས་རང་བྱུང་ཁམས་དབང་དུ་བསྡུ་བའི་སྟབས་ཆེན་གྱི་བྱས་རྗེས་ངོ་མཚར་ཅན་ཞིག་བཞག་པ་རེད། དེ་བཞིན་ཞིན་བོད་གཞུང་ལམ་གྱི་དཀའ་ཚེགས་ཀྱང་ཁྲིན་བོད་དང༌། མཚོ་བོད་གཞུང་ལམ་གཉིས་ལས་ཆུང་བ་མེད། དེ་ནི་ཞིན་ཅང་གི་ཐ་ལི་མུའུ་གསོང་སའི་ཡེ་ཁྲིང་ཞེས་པའི་ས་ཆ་ནས་བོད་ཀྱི་མངའ་རིས་ས་ཁུལ་ཁོངས་ཀྱི་སྤུ་ཧྲིང་བར་གྱི་ལམ་རྒྱུད་ཚང་མ་རྒྱ་མཚོའི་ངོས་ལས་མཐོ་ཚད་སྨི་བཞི་སྟོང་ལྔ་སྟོང་ཡོད་པའི་ས་མཐོའི་ཐོག་ཏུ་འཁྱིལ་ཡོད་སྐབས་མཁའ་ལྷུང་སྐྱབ་ལ་གནམ་གཤིས་ཀྱི་འགྱུར་ལྡོག་ངེས་པ་མེད་པ་ཞིག་ཡིན་མོད། འོན་ཀྱང་གཞུང་ལམ་དེའང་ལོ་གཅིག་ལྷག་ཙམ་གྱི་ནང་དུ་གསར་བཟོ་བྱས་ཏེ་སྐྱངས་འཁོར་ཤར་གཏོང་ཐུབ་པ་བྱུང་བ་རེད།

གཞུང་ལམ་གཙོ་བོ་དེ་དག་གི་ཐོག་ནས་སྐྱངས་འཁོར་ཤར་གཏོང་ཐུབ་པ་བྱུང་རྗེས་སྤྱིལ་ཐག་རིང་པོ་ཁ་ཤས་ཤིག་བཏང་བ་ལྟར་བོད་དེ་མེས་རྒྱལ་ནང་ཁུལ་དང་ཡུག་གཅིག་ཏུ་དམ་པོར་སྤྲེལ་ཞིང༌། དེས་རྒྱ་བོད་མི་རིགས་བར་གྱི་མཐུན་སྒྲིལ་ལ་ཤུགས་སྣོན་རྒྱག་རྒྱུ་དང༌། རྒྱལ་ཁབ་བརྟན་སྲུང་བྱེད་རྒྱུ། བོད་ས་ཁུལ་གྱི་ཆབ་སྲིད་དང༌། དཔལ་འབྱོར། རིག་གནས་ཀྱི་ལས་དོན་བཅས་གོང་འཕེལ་གཏོང་རྒྱུ། བོད་མི་དམངས་ཀྱི་འཚོ་བ་ལེགས་བཅོས་བྱེད་རྒྱུ་བཅས་ཀྱི་ཐད་ལ་ནུས་པ་ཏ་ཅང་ཆེན་པོ་ཐོན་ཡོད་པ་རེད། དེ་བཞིན་བོད་ཀྱི་ལས་བྱེད་པ་དང་ངལ་རྩོལ་མི་དམངས་འབོར་ཆེན་གཞུང་ལམ་དེ་དག་བརྒྱུད་ནས་མེས་རྒྱལ་ནང་ཁུལ་དུ་ཕྱིན་ཏེ་ལྟ་སྐོར་དང༌། མཚམས་འདྲི། སློབ་སྦྱོང་བཅས་བྱེད་ཀྱི་ཡོད་པ་དང༌། རྒྱ་རིགས་ལས་བྱེད་པ་དང་ལས་བཟོ་འབོར་ཆེན་གཞུང་ལམ་དེ་དག་བརྒྱུད་ནས་བོད་དུ་ཡོང་སྟེ་འཛུགས་སྐྲུན་གྱི་བྱ་བར་གཞུག་གི་ཡོད་པ་རེད། དེ་འབྲེལ་བོད་ཡིག་ཏུ་བསྒྱུར་པའི་མའོ་ཀྲུའུ་ཞིའི་གསུང་རྩོམ་ཡང་མེས་རྒྱལ་གྱི་རྒྱལ་ས་པེ་ཅིན་ནས་བོད་ཀྱི་ས་ཆ་ཁག་ལ་དུས་ཐོག་ཏུ་དབོར་ཡོང་བར་བརྟེན་བོད་རིགས་མི་དམངས་ཀྱིས་དགའ་བསུ་ཚད་མེད་བྱེད་ཀྱི་ཡོད་པ་རེད།

Translation

The "Golden Bridge" of Unity and Happiness

For the ten or more years since the peaceful liberation of Tibet, units of the People's Liberation Army, and (Chinese) cadre and workers who volunteered to go to Tibet in accordance with the appeal of Mao Zedong and the party, have been (lit., are) developing Tibet. With the powerful support of the Tibetan people and people of the various nationalities of the motherland, they have struggled (to overcome) innumerable difficulties and have constructed one after another (three) highways on the very roof of the world—the Sichuan-Tibet, the Qinghai-Tibet, and the Xinjiang-Tibet highways. A great achievement has been obtained concerning traveling and transportation and other types of work since now more than 90% of the counties in Tibet are directly accessible by car. These achievements reflect the brilliant victory of Mao Zedong's thoughts and the brilliant victory of the party's policies with regard to minority nationalities.

Previously, the road construction troops, the broad cadre and workers, and the Tibetan people showed revolutionary courage tolerating difficulties and bearing hardships. Showing heroic dignity taming great mountains and diverting large rivers, and disdaining difficulties and struggling against hardships that occurred one after another, they constructed the highways. For example, the Sichuan-Tibet highway which goes from Chengdu in Sichuan Province to Lhasa, passes through fourteen great mountain passes such as Mt. Er and Trola, whose altitudes range from 3,000 to 5,000 meters above sea level, crosses more than ten great rivers such as the turbulent Yangtse and Salween, and has unusual and troublesome geological features which had to be crossed such as rocky mountains with precipitous gorges 20-30 kilometers wide, canyons, shifting sand deserts and glaciers.

And as for the Qinghai-Tibet highway which goes from Xining in Qinghai Province to Lhasa, winds through hundreds of kilometers of deserts and crosses great mountain passes such as the Kunlun pass and the Tangkola pass whose altitudes are 4,000 to 5,000 meters above sea level. It also had to cross several great rivers such as the Chuma and theYangtse. It is a place where the mountains are enveloped by snow in winter and even in summer there is snowfall.

Because of this, at that time our enemies stated that highways cannot be built on the roof of the world and even if it were possible, it would not be in use for long. However, the people's army and cadre and workers, armed with Mao Zedong's thoughts overcame many natural barriers, withstood bitter cold and snow blizzards, crossed high mountains and great rivers, thoroughly eliminated the various obstruction and destructive activities of the Tibetan reactionary serf-owing class, and thus successfully completed the construction of the highways. Not only that, but despite great difficulties for over ten years, they have taken the responsibility of keeping the highways open so that vehicles could be driven without any obstacles. Their feat is an extraordinarily great achievement in the conquest of nature.

Similarly, the difficulties that confronted the construction of the Xinjiang-Tibet highway were no less than those of the Sichuan and Qinghai-Tibet highways. The Xinjiang highway, which goes from Yecheng in the Tarim Basin up to Purang in the Ngari region of Tibet, is on high terrain at altitudes of 4,000-5,000 meters above sea-level. Because of this, not only is the air thin but the weather is very changeable. Nevertheless, the road was completed within a year, and vehicles can travel without any hindrance.

Because vehicles can travel straight on those main road, Tibet has been merged firmly with the Motherland. That has had a strong effect on reforming the livelihood of the Tibetan people via strengthening the friendship of the Chinese and Tibetan peoples, adding to the security of the nation, and improving the political, economical and cultural affairs of Tibet. Similarly, large numbers of Tibetan cadre and laborers have been able to travel via these roads to the Motherland for tours, visits and study. And large numbers of Chinese cadres and workers have come to Tibet to participate in development projects. Related to that, the works of Mao Zedong that have been published in Tibetan are being regularly brought to various parts of Tibet from the capital Beijing, and the Tibetan people are enthusiastically welcoming these.

5. Reading number five

ཀྲུང་གོའི་མི་དམངས་བཅིངས་འགྲོལ་དམག་གི་རྩ་ཚིག

(1949 ལོའི་ཟླ་ 4 ཚེས་ 25 ལ་)

གོ་མིང་དང་ལོག་སྤྱོད་ཕྱོགས་ཁག་གིས་ཞི་བདེའི་ཁ་དན་ཁས་མ་བླངས་པར་མི་རིགས་ལ་ངོ་རྒོལ་དང་མི་དམངས་ལ་ངོ་རྒོལ་བྱེད་པའི་དམག་འཁྲུག་གི་ལངས་ཕྱོགས་ནག་ཉེས་ཅན་དེ་མཁྲིགས་བཟུང་བྱེད་གི་ཡོད་པ་རེད། རྒྱལ་ཡོངས་མི་དམངས་གིས་མི་དམངས་བཅིངས་འགྲོལ་དམག་གིས་གོ་མིང་དང་ལོག་སྤྱོད་ཕྱོགས་ཁག་མགྱོགས་པོ་རྩ་མེད་བཏང་རྒྱུའི་རེ་བ་བྱེད་གི་ཡོད་པ་རེད། ང་ཚོས་མི་དམངས་བཅིངས་འགྲོལ་དམག་ལ་དཔའ་མཛངས་རྟུལ་ཕོད་གིས་མདུན་ལ་སྐྱོད་དེ་འགོག་རྒོལ་བྱེད་ཕོད་མཁན་གོ་མིང་དང་གི་ལོག་སྤྱོད་དམག་དཔུང་ཚང་མ་རྩ་མེད་བཏང་ཐབས་དང་། རང་ཉིད་ལ་འགྱོད་བཤགས་མི་བྱེད་མཁན་དམག་འཁྲུག་གི་ཉེས་ཅན་ཚང་མ་འཛིན་བཟུང་། རྒྱལ་ཡོངས་མི་དམངས་བཅིངས་འགྲོལ། ཀྲུང་གོའི་མངའ་ཁོངས་དང་བདག་དབང་རང་བཙན་དང་ཆ་ཚང་ཡོད་པའི་སྲུང་སྐྱོབ། རྒྱལ་ཡོངས་མི་དམངས་གིས་གཅིག་སྒྱུར་དངོས་གནས་ཅིག་ཡོང་རེ་སྐོམ་པས་རྒྱ་འདོད་ལྟར་བྱེད་པ་དེ་དངོས་སུ་འགྲུབ་པ་བཅས་བྱེད་དགོས་ཟེ་བཀའ་ཕབ་ཡོད། མི་དམངས་བཅིངས་འགྲོལ་དམག་ག་པར་སླེབས་སར་ལས་རིགས་ཁག་གི་མི་དམངས་གིས་རོགས་རམ་ཡོང་བའི་རེ་བ་ཆེན་པོ་ཡོད། འདིར་སྡོམ་ཁྲིམས་བརྒྱད་ཁྱབ་བསྒྲགས་བྱས་པ་དེ་ར་ང་ཚོའི་མི་དམངས་ཡོངས་རྫོགས་དང་མཉམ་དུ་བརྩི་སྲུང་བྱེད་འདོད་ཡོད།

(དང་པོ་) མི་དམངས་ཡོངས་རྫོགས་གི་ལུས་སྲོག་དང་རྒྱུ་ནོར་སྲུང་སྐྱོང་བྱེད་རྒྱུ། གྲལ་རིམ་དང་། ཆོས་དད། ལས་ཀ་བཅས་ག་རེ་ཡིན་མིན་ལ་མ་བལྟོས་པའི་ལས་རིགས་ཁག་གི་མི་དམངས་ཚང་མས་སྒྲིག་ལམ་བརྩི་སྲུང་བྱེད་རྒྱུ་དང་མི་དམངས་བཅིངས་འགྲོལ་དམག་དང་མཉམ་ལས་བྱེད་རྒྱུའི་རེ་བ་ཡོད། མི་དམངས་བཅིངས་འགྲོལ་དམག་གིས་ཡང་ལས་རིགས་ཁག་གི་མི་དམངས་དང་མཉམ་ལས་བྱེད་གི་ཡིན། གསར་བརྗེར་ངོ་རྒོལ་པ་དང་། ཡང་ན་གདོར་བཤིག་པ་གཞན་དག་གིས་གོ་སྐབས་དང་བསྟུན་ནས་ཕུང་དཀྲུག་དང་། ཡང་ན་འཕྲོག་བཅོམ། ཡང་ན་གདོར་བཤིག་བྱས་ན་དེ་ར་ཉེས་ཆད་ནན་པོ་བཅད་ཐག་ཆོད་ཡིན།

(གཉིས་པ་) མི་རིགས་འབྱོར་ལྡན་གྲལ་རིམ་གི་བཟོ་ཚོང་ཞིང་ཕྱུགས་བཅས་གི་ལས་རིགས་སྲུང་སྐྱོང་བྱེད་རྒྱུ། སྒེར་གིས་བདག་གཉེར་བྱེད་པའི་བཟོ་གྲྭ་དང་། ཚོང་ཁང་། དངུལ་ཁང་། མཛོད་ཁང་། གྲུ་གཟིངས། གྲུ་ཁ། ཞིང་ར། ཕྱུགས་ར། སོགས་ཚང་མར་སྲུང་སྐྱོང་བྱས་ནས་གནོད་འཚེ་མི་ཡོང་བ་བྱེད་གི་ཡིན། ལས་རིགས་ཁག་གི་ལས་བཟོ་རྣམས་གིས་སྔར་རྒྱུན་ལྟར་ཐོན་སྐྱེད་བྱེད་པ་དང་། ལས་རིགས་ཁག་གི་ཚོང་ཁང་རྣམས་གིས་སྔར་རྒྱུན་ལྟར་ཚོང་ལས་བྱེད་པའི་རེ་བ་ཡོད།

(གསུམ་པ་) དཔོན་ངན་གི་མ་རྩ་གཞུང་བཞེས་བཏང་རྒྱུ། གོ་མིན་ཏང་ལོག་སྤྱོད་སྲིད་གཞུང་དང་དཔོན་ངན་ཆེ་གྲས་གིས་བདག་གཉེར་བྱེད་པའི་བཟོ་གྲྭ་དང་། ཚོང་ཁང་། དངུལ་ཁང་། མཛོད་ཁང་། གྲུ་གཟིངས། གྲུ་ཁ། ལྕགས་ལམ། ཡིག་སྐྱེལ། གློག་འཕྲིན། གློག་ཐག། ཁ་པར། རང་འབབ་གི་ཆུ། ཞིང་ར། ཕྱུགས་ར་སོགས་ཡིན་ཕྱིན་ཚང་མ་མི་དམངས་སྲིད་

གཞུང་གིས་རྩིས་ལེན་བྱེད་དགོས། དེ་ཚོའི་ཁོངས་ལ་མི་རིགས་འགྱུར་ལྡན་གྲལ་རིམ་གི་བཟོ་ཚོང་ཞིང་ཕྱུགས་བཅས་གི་ལས་རིགས་པ་སྒེར་གི་མ་རྐང་ཡོད་པ་རྣམས་རྩད་བཅད་ནས་ཁོངས་འཕེར་བྱུང་རྗེས་དེ་ཚོའི་དབང་ཆ་ཁས་ལེན་བྱེད་དགོས། མི་དམངས་སྲིད་གཞུང་གིས་དཔོན་ངན་མ་རྩའི་ཁེ་ལས་རྩིས་ལེན་མ་བྱས་གོང་ལ་དེ་ཚོའི་ནང་ལས་ཀ་བྱེད་མཁན་མི་སྣ་ཚོས་སྔར་རྒྱུན་ལྟར་ལས་ཀ་བྱེད་དགོས་པ་མ་ཟད། རྒྱུ་ནོར་དང་། འཕྲུལ་འཁོར། དཔེ་རིས་དང་རེའུ་མིག རྩིས་ཐོ། ཚགས་ཡིག་སོགས་ཡང་སྲུང་སྐྱོང་བྱེད་རྒྱུའི་འགན་འཁུར་དེ་ཞིབ་བཤེར་དང་རྩིས་ལེན་བྱེད་རྒྱུར་སྒྲུག་དགོས། དེ་ཚོ་སྲུང་སྐྱོང་བྱས་ནས་བྱས་རྗེས་བཞག་ཡོད་མཁན་རྣམས་ལ་བྱ་དགའ་སྤྲད་དགོས། ལས་ཀར་སྒྱིད་ལུག་དང་གཏོར་བཤིག་བྱེད་མཁན་རྣམས་ལ་ཉེས་ཆད་བཅད་དགོས། མི་དམངས་སྲིད་གཞུང་གིས་རྩིས་ལེན་བྱས་རྗེས་སུ་མཐུད་ནས་ཞབས་འདེགས་ཞུ་འདོད་ཡོད་མཁན་ཚོར་སོ་སོའི་ཡོན་ཚད་ལ་བལྟས་ནས་ལས་ཀ་སྤྲད་དེ་གནས་མེད་ཡུལ་གྱུར་ལ་མི་འགྲོ་བ་བྱེད་དགོས།

(བཞི་པ་) གཞུང་སྒེར་གི་སློབ་གྲྭ་དང་། སྨན་ཁང་། རིག་གནས་སློབ་གསོའི་ལས་ཁུངས། ལུས་རྩལ་བྱེད་ས། སྤྱི་ཕན་གི་ལས་དོན་གཞན་དག་བཅས་ཚང་མར་སྲུང་སྐྱོང་བྱེད་རྒྱུ། ལས་ཁུངས་དེ་ཚོའི་ནང་ལས་ཀ་བྱེད་མཁན་མི་སྣ་ཚང་མས་སྔར་རྒྱུན་ལྟར་ལས་ཀ་

བྱེད་རྒྱུའི་རེ་བ་ཡོད། མི་དམངས་བཅིངས་འགྲོལ་དམག་གིས་དེ་ཚོ་ལ་སྲུང་སྐྱོང་བྱས་ནས་གནོད་འཚེ་མི་ཡོང་བ་བྱེད་དགོས།

Translation

Proclamation of the Chinese People's Liberation Army

April 25, 1949

The Kuomintang reactionary clique has not accepted the peace offer and persists in taking a criminal military position which opposes the people and the nationalities. The people all over the country hope that the People's Liberation Army will speedily wipe out the Kuomintang reactionary group.We have ordered the People's Liberation Army to advance forward courageously to try to wipe out all the reactionary Kuomintang military forces who dare to resist, to arrest all the war criminals who do not repent their own crimes, to liberate people of the whole country, to protect Chinese territorial integrity, sovereignty, and independence, and to achieve true unification which, like a thirsty man wanting water, is the hope of people all over the country. We have high hopes that people in all walks of life will help the People's Liberation Army wherever it goes. Together with all our people we want to abide by the eight-point covenant that is proclaimed here [Note: This is actually an excerpt.].

1. Protect the lives and property of all the people. We hope people in all walks of life, regardless of class, religion, and occupation, will abide by the laws and will cooperate with people in all walks of life. We will severely punish counter-revolutionaries or other saboteurs who seize the opportunity to create disturbances, loot or sabotage.
2. Protect the industrial, commercial, agricultural, and livestock enterprises of the national bourgeoisie. We shall protect all privately owned factories, shops, banks, warehouses, ships, ferry landings, livestock farms, farms, etc., and see to it that no harm comes to them. We hope that office personnel and workers in all occupations will maintain production as usual and that shops in all trades will do business as usual.
3. The People's Government must take charge of all the shops, banks, warehouses, ships, ferry landing, railroads, postal services, telegraphs, electricity, telephones, water supplies, farms, livestock ranches, etc., which are owned and operated by the reactionary Kuomintang government and the big bureaucrats, and (must) confiscate bureaucratic capital. In these enterprises, the ownership of the private shares of the national bourgeoisie engaged in industry, commerce, agriculture or livestock will be investigated, and after verification, will be recognized. Before the People's Government takes charge of the bureaucrat-capitalist enterprises, the people who are working in them must not only work as usual but they must also take responsibility for protecting property, machinery, designs and charts, account books, records, etc., and must wait for the investigation and take-over. Those who are protecting these well must be rewarded. Those who are not diligent and sabotage them must be punished. Those who continue to want to render service after the People's Government takes over should be given jobs in accordance with their own qualifications so that they do not become destitute and homeless.
4. We hope to protect all government, private schools, hospitals, cultural-educational institutions, athletic fields, and other public welfare works, and to have all the people work in these enterprises continue to work as usual. The People's Liberation Army must protect them and see to it that no harm shall come to them.